NOTES

ON

THE HEBREW TEXT

OF THE

BOOKS OF KINGS

WITH AN INTRODUCTION AND APPENDIX

BY THE

REV. C. F. BURNEY, M.A.

FELLOW AND LECTURER IN HEBREW OF S. JOHN BAPTIST'S COLLEGE, OXFORD

Wipf & Stock
PUBLISHERS
Eugene, Oregon

FIRST PUBLISHED 1903

Wipf and Stock Publishers
199 W 8th Ave, Suite 3
Eugene, OR 97401

Notes on the Hebrew text of the Books of Kings
with an Introduction and Appendix
By Burney, C.F.
ISBN: 1-59244-820-8
Publication date 8/26/2004
Previously published by Cambridge, 1903

CONTENTS

Page

INTRODUCTION:—

§ 1. *Structure of Kings* ix

§ 2. *Characteristics of the Chief Ancient Versions of Kings* xx

§ 3. *The Synchronisms of the Compiler* xli

LIST OF ABBREVIATIONS xlv

NOTES ON 1 KINGS 1

NOTES ON 2 KINGS 260

APPENDIX:—

1. *Inscription of Mesha', king of Moab* 371
2. *The Siloam Inscription* 374
3. *Inscription of the Monolith of Shalmaneser II*, ll. 78–102 375
4. *Fragment of the Annals of Shalmaneser II* . . 376
   Descriptive Inscription from the Obelisk of Shalmaneser 377
5. *Narrative of Sennacherib's Third Campaign* (B.C. 701), *from the Taylor Cylinder*, Col. II. l. 34–Col. III. l. 41 377

ADDITIONS 380

INDEX 381

PLATES.

1. Bronze Stand from Larnaka . . . . *to face* p. 91
2. Bronze Stand from Enkomi . . . . *to face* p. 92

PREFACE

THE aim of the present work is to provide a critical and grammatical commentary upon the Hebrew text of Kings, after the model of Dr. Driver's *Notes on the Hebrew Text of the Books of Samuel.* In writing the Notes, the needs of beginners in the study of the Hebrew language have been prominent in my mind, and so I have endeavoured to deal with some fulness with questions of grammar, while at the same time making reference to the best authorities upon the subject. For the purposes of textual criticism it has seemed worth while to utilize as largely as might be the evidence of the Versions. Thus, as far as possible, all variants and additions of the Versions have been cited, where it may reasonably be supposed that these form original elements of the text from which the Version in question was made; upon the view that such readings are worthy of record, even where no definite verdict can be passed as to their value in relation to the Massoretic text. The structure of Kings, and the characteristics of the various sources of the work, have also been dealt with in brief. The Appendix contains the more important contemporary inscriptions which throw light upon the narrative of Kings.

In making use of the work of my predecessors in the same field, I trust that I have in every case made acknowledgement of my obligations. I feel, however, that special acknowledgement is due to Prof. B. Stade for the debt which these Notes owe to his valuable articles on the text of Kings which have appeared from time to time in the *Zeitschrift* of which he is the editor. Lest it should be thought that in places I have drawn too largely upon his arguments and results, it must be pleaded that in such cases my aim has been to place these results within the reach of English students, for whom too often, through ignorance of German, they are inaccessible.

It is a special pleasure to me to express my gratitude to Dr. Driver. To his teaching and example is due most of what may be of value in this book; and I have never been without his kindly encouragement and ready suggestion upon points of difficulty.

In conclusion, my thanks are due to Mr. J. C. Pembrey, M.A., Oriental Reader at the University Press, for the great pains which he has taken in revising and passing the sheets for the press.

C. F. B.

S. JOHN'S COLLEGE, OXFORD,
November, 1902.

INTRODUCTION

§ 1. *Structure of Kings.*

The fact that Kings, like the other historical books of the Old Testament, is based upon pre-existing written sources is universally recognized; and the evidence upon which this elementary proposition is based need not here be set forth [1]. That the main editor or compiler of these sources was a Deuteronomist, i. e. that his work was inspired by the religious revival which took place in the eighteenth year of Josiah (B.C. 621) under the influence of the newly discovered book of Deuteronomy, appears both from his religious standpoint and from his phraseology. This editor is therefore hereinafter cited under the symbol R^D (Deuteronomic Redactor).

To R^D is due the stereotyped form into which the introduction and conclusion of a reign is thrown, and which constitutes, as it were, the framework upon which the narrative as a whole is built. The regularity of the method of R^D in the construction of this framework is worthy of special notice. The form in which the account of a reign is introduced is as follows. *For kings of Judah*:—1. A synchronism of the year of accession with the corresponding reigning year of the contemporary king of Israel, probably calculated by R^D himself. This, commencing with Abijah, naturally ceases with Ḥezekiah, upon the fall of the kingdom of Israel. 2. Age of the king at accession. 3. Length of his reign. 4. Name of the queen-mother. This, together with 2, 3, is drawn from the *Annals* (ספר דברי הימים) which are so constantly cited by R^D. 5. A brief verdict upon the king's character, framed in accordance with the Deuteronomic standard. *For kings of Israel*:—1. A synchronism of the year of accession

[1] Cf. the writer's article in Hastings, *BD*. pp. 857 *f.*

with the corresponding reigning year of the contemporary king of Judah. 2. Length of the king's reign, drawn from the *Annals*. 3. A brief verdict as to his character, always unfavourable, and generally consisting of two parts: *a*. Statement of the general fact that he did evil in the sight of Yahwe; *b*. More special mention of his following the sins of Jeroboam[1]. The conclusion of the account of a reign takes the following form:—1. An indication of the principal source employed by R^D, containing further details as to the king in question. Usually we read[2]:—

<table>
<tr><td rowspan="3">ויתר דברי פ׳ וכל אשר עשה הלא הם (המה) כתובים על ספר</td><td>דברי שלמה</td></tr>
<tr><td>דברי הימים למלכי יהודה</td></tr>
<tr><td>דברי הימים למלכי ישראל</td></tr>
</table>

---

[1] The usual formula is as follows:—

<table>
<tr><td>He did not depart from</td><td rowspan="3">the sins of J.</td><td rowspan="4">which he caused Israel to sin.</td></tr>
<tr><td>He walked after (in)</td></tr>
<tr><td>He clave to</td></tr>
<tr><td colspan="2">He walked in the way of J. and in his sin (sins)</td></tr>
</table>

So I. 15. 26 (Nadab), *v.* 34 (Ba'asha), 16. 26 (Omri), II. 3. 3 (Jehoram), 10. 31, cf. *v.* 29 (Jehu), 13. 2 (Jehoaḥaz), *v.* 11 (Jehoash), 14. 24 (Jeroboam II), 15. 9 (Zechariah), *v.* 18 (Menaḥem), *v.* 24 (Pekaḥiah), *v.* 28 (Pekaḥ). In all these cases the antecedent of the relative אשר החטיא is not ירבעם, but חטאות יר׳; cf. II. 17. 21. I. 16. 30 (Aḥab), II. 17. 22 חטאות יר׳ without אשר החטיא וג׳; I. 22. 53 (Aḥaziah), II. 23. 15 אשר החטיא את ישראל, referring not to חטאות (omitted), but to ירבעם; 'J. who made Israel to sin.' In I. 16. 13 the sins of Ba'asha and Elah, and in II. 21. 11 of Manasseh (אשר החטיא את יהודה) are spoken of in the same terms.

[2] When further details, general or special, are mentioned as existing in the source, these usually stand immediately after וכל אשר עשה; e. g. I. 11. 41 וחכמתו. An exception is I. 15. 23 (Asa), where וכל גבורתו precedes.

Slight variations of the stereotyped form are:—

1. ויתר כל דברי וג׳ I. 15. 23 (Asa).

2. Total omission of וכל אשר עשה; without further details five times, viz. I. 14. 19 (Jeroboam), 16. 20 (Zimri), II. 14. 18 (Amaziah), 15. 11 (Zechariah), 15. 15 (Shallum); with further details, II. 20. 20 (Ḥezekiah).

Reading אשר עשה five times, viz. I. 16. 27 (Omri), II. 1. 18 (Aḥaziah of Israel), 14. 15 (Jehoash of Israel), 16. 19 (Aḥaz), 21. 25 (Amon); ואשר עשה I. 16. 5 (Ba'asha); וגבורתו אשר עשה twice, I. 16. 27 (Omri), 22. 46 (Jehoshaphat).

3. הנם in place of הלא הם five times, viz. I. 14. 19 (Jeroboam), II. 15. 11, 15, 26, 31 (Zechariah Shallum, Pekaḥiah, Pekaḥ).

2. Mention of the king's (*a*) death and (*b*) burial[1]:—

וישכב פ׳ עם אבתיו { וַיִּקָּבֵר / ויקברו אתו } (עם אבתיו) ב׳

3. Notice of the due succession of the king's son:—

וימלך פ׳ בנו תחתיו

The following table exhibits the regularity with which this system is carried out. When any fact above mentioned as belonging to the introduction is omitted in that position, but added subsequently in the narrative of the reign or in the summary, this is indicated by the sign + :—

Introduction.			*Conclusion.*	
		David	1 2 *a b*	I. 2. 10
I. 3. 3, 11. 4–6, 42		Solomon		
		Kings of Judah.		
14. 21, 22, 31	2 3 4 (5) + 4	Rehoboam	1 2 *a b* 3	14. 29, 31
15. 1–3	1 3 4 5	Abijah	1 2 *a b* 3	15. 7^a, 8
15. 9–11	1 3 4 5	Asa	1 2 *a b* 3	15. 23^a, 24
22. 41–44	1 2 3 4 5	Jehoshaphat	1 2 *a b* 3	22. 45, 50
II. 8. 16, 17	1 2 3 5	Jehoram	1 2 *a b* 3	II. 8. 23, 24
8. 25–27, 9. 29	1 2 3 4 5 + 1	Ahaziah	2 *b*	9. 28^b
11. 3	+ 3	Athaliah	. . .	. . .
12. 1–4	2 1 3 4 5	Jehoash	1 2 *b* 3	12. 20, 22
14. 1–4	1 2 3 4 5	Amaziah	1 2 *b* (*a*)	14. 18, 20^b (22^b)
15. 1–4	1 2 3 4 5	Azariah	1 2 *a b* 3	15. 6, 7
15. 32–35	1 2 3 4 5	Jotham	1 2 *a b* 3	15. 36, 38
16. 1–4	1 2 3 5	Ahaz	1 2 *a b* 3	16. 19, 20
18. 1–3	1 2 3 4 5	Hezekiah	1 2 *a* 3	20. 20, 21
21. 1, 2	2 3 4 5	Manasseh	1 2 *a b* 3	21. 17, 18
21. 19–22	2 3 4 5	Amon	1 2 *b* 3	21. 25, 26
22. 1, 2	2 3 4 5	Josiah	1 2 *b* (3)	23. 29, 30
23. 31, 32	2 3 4 5	Jehoahaz	. . .	. . .
23. 36, 37	2 3 4 5	Jehoiakim	1 2 *a* 3	24. 5, 6
24. 8, 9	2 3 4 5	Jehoiachin	. . .	. . .
24. 18, 19	2 3 4 5	Zedekiah	. . .	. . .

[1] Once with singular active verb used impersonally: וַיִּקְבֹּר אֹתוֹ 'And (one) buried him,' II. 21. 26 (Amon).

Introduction.		*Kings of Israel.*		*Conclusion.*
I. 13. 33*f.*, 14. 20a	+ 3 *b* 2	Jeroboam	1 2 *a* 3	I. 14. 19, 20
15. 25, 26	1 2 3 *a b*	Nadab	1	15. 31
15. 33, 34	1 2 3 *a b*	Ba'asha	1 2 *a b* 3	16. 5, 6
16. 8, 13	1 2 + 3	Elah	1	16. 14
16. 15a, 19	1 2 + 3 *a b*	Zimri	1	16. 20
16. 23, 25, 26	1 2 3 *a b*	Omri	1 2 *a b* 3	16. 27, 28
16. 29–31a	1 2 3 *a b*	Aḥab	1 2 *a* 3	22. 39, 40
22. 51, 52	1 2 3 *a b*	Aḥaziah	(3) 1	II. 1. 17, 18
II. 3. 1–3	1 2 3 *a b*	Jehoram	. . .	. . .
10. 29, 31, 36	+ 3 *b b* 2	Jehu	1 2 *a b* 3	10. 34, 35
13. 1, 2	1 2 3 *a b*	Jehoaḥaz	1 2 *a b* 3	13. 8, 9
13. 10, 11	1 2 3 *a b*	Jehoash	1 2 *a* (3) 2 *b* 1 2 *a b* 3	13. 12*f.*, 14. 15*f.*
14. 23, 24	1 2 3 *a b*	Jeroboam II	1 2 *a* 3	14. 28, 29
15. 8, 9	1 2 3 *a b*	Zechariah	1	15. 11
15. 13	1 2	Shallum	1	15. 15
15. 17, 18	1 2 3 *a b*	Menaḥem	1 2 *a* 3	15. 21, 22
15. 23, 24	1 2 3 *a b*	Pekaḥiah	1	15. 26
15. 27, 28	1 2 3 *a b*	Pekaḥ	1	15. 31
17. 1, 2	1 2 3 *a*	Hoshea	. . .	. . .

In the body of the narrative there are certain formulae which are employed for the introduction of a historical notice to indicate that it is more or less contemporaneous with the events of the narrative immediately preceding. The frequency with which these formulae occur, especially in the brief citation of facts from the *Annals*, renders the inference fair that they are due to the hand of R^D, and represent his method of piecing together the extracts derived from his sources. Of such formulae the most frequent is אז; but we also find the expressions בעת ההיא, בימיו, בימים ההם. Cf. *note*, p. 35.

Besides the construction of the framework of the book and the welding of the material, R^D is also responsible for a number of passages of varied length which point and enforce the religious purpose of his composition. These passages generally take the form of a commentary upon the causes which were operative in bringing about the developments of history, framed in accordance with the Deuteronomic model. Very frequently, also, R^D allows himself considerable latitude in the expansion and adaptation of the *speeches* contained in the narrative, in illustration of the same standpoint. In passages of this character the hand of R^D may readily be distinguished. They exhibit a constant recurrence of strongly marked phrases, to be found elsewhere for the most part only in Deuteronomy or in the books which exhibit the influence of Deuteronomy, and therefore presumably derived from that source. Other expressions stand alongside of these Deuteronomic expressions, and are of a piece with the thoughts to which they give voice; and these possess an individuality of their own, and are peculiar (or nearly so) to Kings.

The phrases characteristic of R^D receive comment in the *Notes* as they occur. For convenience of reference, however, a list is here given.

Deuteronomic phrases:—

1. שמר משמרת י׳, p. 14.
2. הלך בדרכי י׳, p. 14.
3. שמר חקתיו וג׳, p. 14.
4. למען תשכיל את כל אשר תעשה, p. 14.
5. למען יקים וג׳, p. 14; cf. I. 12. 15.
6. בכל לב (לבבו, לבבם) ובכל נפש (נפשו, נפשם), pp. 14, 125.
7. שמר הברית והחסד ל׳, pp. 30, 116.
8. כיום הזה, p. 30.
9. עמך אשר בחרת, p. 31.
10. הניח י׳ אלהי לי מסביב, p. 53.
11. בחר of Yahwe's *choosing* Jerusalem, p. 115.
12. י׳ אלהי ישראל אין כמוך . . . מתחת, p. 116.
13. אשר נתת (נתן, נתתי) לאבותם, p. 119.
14. באחד שעריו, p. 121.
15. כל הימים . . . האדמה, p. 122.
16. ידך החזקה וזרעך הנטויה, p. 122.
17. כל עמי הארץ, p. 122.
18. נתן לפני, p. 124.
19. השיב אל לב, p. 124.
20. ושבו אליך . . . ובכל נפשם, p. 125.

21. כי עמך ונחלתך . . . ממצרים, p. 125.
22. כור הברזל, p. 125.
23. נתן מנוחה לעמו, p. 126.
24. לא נפל דבר אחד, p. 126.
25. י׳ אלהינו (—ך, —כם), p. 126.
26. למען דעת וג׳, p. 127.
27. כי י׳ הוא האלהים אין עוד, p. 127.
28. לשום שמי שם, p. 130.
29. כל הימים used absolutely; 'for ever,' p. 130.
30. והלכתם . . . להם, p. 131.
31. למשל ולשנינה, p. 132.
32. דבק ב, p. 152.
33. הלך אחרי, p. 152.
34. עשה הרע בעיני י׳, p. 152.
35. עשה הישר בעיני י׳, p. 170.
36. מלא אחרי י׳, p. 153.
37. התאנף, p. 153.
38. והיה אם תשמע, p. 171.
39. השמיד מעל פני האדמה, p. 185.
40. הכעים, p. 186.
41. מעל האדמה הטובה הזאת, p. 187.
42. על כל גבעה גבהה וג׳, p. 192.
43. ככל התועבת . . . ישראל, p. 192.
44. הוריש, p. 192.
45. גלולים, p. 196.
46. כל נשמה, p. 200.
47. הבלים, p. 200.
48. לא אבה (ל)השחית, p. 295.
49. למחות את שם וג׳, p. 320.
50. ויקשו את ערפם, p. 332.
51. שמר לעשות, p. 353.

The following phrases, though not derived directly from Deuteronomy, belong to R^D in common with Jeremiah, whose writings exhibit strong Deuteronomic affinities:—

52. כי שמך נקרא על הבית הזה, p. 123.
53. אשלח מעל פני, p. 132.
54. כל עבר עליו וג׳, p. 133.
55. לא שב . . . מדרכו הרעה, p. 184.
56. הנני מביא רעה אל (על), p. 186.
57. עבדי (עבדיו) הנביאים, p. 330[1].

Phrases and modes of expression wholly or nearly peculiar to R^D are as follow:—

58. כאשר הלך דויד, and similar references, p. 31.
59. למען דוד אביך (עבדי), p. 153.
60. למען היות ניר וג׳, p. 170.
61. לא יכּרת לך וג׳, p. 15.
62. בנה בית לשם י׳, p. 28.
63. אשר כמוך וג׳, p. 31.
64. להיות שמי שם, p. 115.
65. לבב שלם עם י׳, p. 128.
66. הרע (לעשות) מכל אשר (היו) לפניו, p. 186.
67. משתין בקיר, p. 186.
68. עצור ועזוב, p. 186.
69. ובערתי אחרי, p. 187.
70. המת וג׳, p. 187.
71. התמכר לעשות הרע וג׳, p. 249.
72. לא סר מן, p. 268.
73. רק הבמות לא סרו וג׳, p. 27.

As Kings now stands, the earliest possible *terminus a quo* for the composition of the book is the date of the latest event related, viz. Jehoiachin's release from prison in the thirty-seventh year of his captivity, i.e. B.C. 561, some twenty-five years after the fall of Jerusalem. As, however, the writer states that the privileges granted by Evil-Merodach to Jehoiachin were continued 'all the days of his life' (II. 25. 30), the strong presumption is created that the words were not penned so early as B.C. 561, but some time later, viz.

[1] Cf. also the phrases noticed by Dri. *LOT.*[6] 203, in the later *chh.* of 2 Kings.

subsequently to Jehoiachin's death, whenever that may have occurred. Agreeable to such an exilic date as is implied by the last two chapters of 2 Kings are certain passages in the body of the work which seem to presuppose the captivity of Judah. These are I. 11. 39; II. 17. 19, 20; 23. 26, 27, and perhaps, though not so clearly, I. 9. 7–9; II. 20. 17, 18; 21. 10–15; 22. 15–20; cf. *notes ad loc.* To these we may add the reference in I. 5. 4 to Solomon's dominion as extending over all the kings 'beyond the River,' a statement which, as referring to the country west of the Euphrates, implies that the writer is living in Babylon on the east side of the river (cf. *note* on עבר הנהר, p. 49).

On the other hand, there are certain indications which show that the main editing of Kings by R^D must have taken place prior to the decay and fall of the Judaean monarchy. Chief among these is the use of the phrase 'unto this day' (עד היום הזה) in the statement that the condition of affairs which the writer is describing continues to exist up to the time of writing. If this phrase always or most frequently occurred in the course of lengthy narratives excerpted by R^D from his sources, there might be room for the theory that a statement which was true as it stood in the old pre-exilic narratives had, through oversight on the part of an exilic editor, been allowed to stand after, through changed conditions, it had lost its force, or rather had become untrue and misleading. But, as a matter of fact, the expression is employed in connexion with terse statements of facts derived from the *Annals*, and in such cases can be due to no other hand than that of R^D himself, who, in using the phrase, either formulates his own statement, or intelligently admits a statement which he is able to verify. The cases of the use of 'unto this day' which should be noticed as implying the continued existence of the kingdom of Judah are the following:—I. 8. 8 (the ends of the staves of the ark still to be seen projecting from the Adytum into the Holy Place); 9. 21 (the Canaanites still subjected by Israel to forced labour, as they had been under Solomon); 12. 19 (the division between the ten tribes and the house of David still in existence); II. 8. 22 (Edom still successful in shaking off the yoke of Judah); 16. 6 (the Edomites still hold Elath, from which the Judaeans were expelled by Rezin, king of Aram). For other occurrences of 'unto this day,' not necessarily presupposing a pre-exilic date, but illustrating the frequency of the formula as employed by R^D, cf. *note* on p. 107.

Again, it seems to be clear that, at the time when R^D is writing, the Davidic dynasty still possesses a monarch reigning at Jerusalem. David has, and is still to have, a *lamp* before Yahwe at Jerusalem continually; cf. No. 60 of the phrases of R^D above noticed. The expression 'before Yahwe at Jerusalem' (I. 11. 36) implies further that the Temple is still standing intact, a point which is also assumed in the dedication prayer of I. 8. 15–53, which owes its present form to R^D (cf. pp. 112 *ff.*). Throughout this prayer the leading petition is that supplication made *in* or *towards Yahwe's Temple built by Solomon* may meet with a favourable answer; cf. *vv.* 29, 30, 31 *f.*, 33, 35, 38, 42, 44, 48. We may notice also I. 9. 3, which likewise occurs in a section in which the hand of R^D is prominent:—'I have hallowed this house which thou hast built to put my name there for ever; and mine eyes and my heart shall be there perpetually.' Upon these grounds it may be concluded that the main editing of Kings (viz. that by R^D) must have taken place prior to the destruction of the Judaean kingdom, and that such sections of the book as imply an exilic standpoint are therefore of the nature of later redactional additions and interpolations.

For the work of R^D, influenced, as we have seen him to be, by the spirit and language of Deuteronomy, the *terminus a quo* is the discovery of Deuteronomy in the year B.C. 621, the *terminus ad quem* the destruction of Jerusalem B.C. 586. And since the writer's standpoint seems to indicate that he wrote before the glamour of Josiah's reformation had wholly or nearly faded during the latter days of the Judaean monarchy, the assumption is fair that he undertook and completed his book not later than B.C. 600[1].

[1] So Kue. *Ond.* § 26; Wellh. *C.* pp. 298 *ff.*, &c. König, on the contrary, holds that the editor of Kings compiled his work not earlier than B.C. 588, i.e. during the Exile (*Einleitung*, § 53. 3).

From the preceding examination and conclusion as to the date of the main redaction of Kings, it is clear that the pre-exilic book must have received certain additions at the hand of a later editor or editors before it attained the form in which we now possess it. The chief of these additions is the appendix, which carries the history down to the year B.C. 561. To this appendix belongs certainly II. 24. 10—25. 30, and, presumably, 23. 31—24. 9. The conclusion of the pre-exilic book has, however, probably been worked over by the second editor, and so adapted to receive his addition that it is now impossible exactly to discover its position. Any of the *vv.* 25, 28, 30 of *ch.* 23 might have formed a conclusion scarcely more abrupt than the present conclusion, *ch.* 25. 30. *Ch.* 23. 29^a, if not intentionally imitated in style in *ch.* 24. 1^a, must be by the same hand, i.e. presumably the hand of the second editor. But again, it is unlikely that R^D should have appended the usual summary of a reign in *v.* 28 without mentioning the manner of the king's death. The statement of *v.* 25^b seems at first sight to presuppose the writer's acquaintance with the characters of all the succeeding kings of Judah, but may be a later insertion, as *vv.* 26, 27 certainly are. On the whole, the most suitable ending to the pre-exilic book would be *vv.* 29, 30, 28 of *ch.* 23, in that order.

It is noticeable that, apart from the difference of standpoint involved in the destruction of the Judaean kingdom and the Exile, the mould of mind of the author of the appendix and of the passages above noticed (p. xvi) which presuppose the captivity of Judah is essentially the same as that of R^D. Thus it is reasonable to employ the symbol R^{D2} in referring to a later redactor of the same school of thought. It must not, however, be supposed that R^{D2} is in every case necessarily one and the same writer, since it is obvious that more than one Deuteronomist may have had a hand in the revision of Kings. In point of fact it can be argued with high probability that such was the case. For the Deuteronomic passage II. 17. 34^b–40 almost certainly refers to the Samaritans of *post-exilic* times (cf. *note ad loc.*); yet it may fairly be assumed that if the author of the appendix had written in post-exilic times he would have given some account of the restoration from exile.

Kings, as it stands in the Hebrew Bible, has, again, undergone still later revision than that of $R^{D\,2}$. This is clear from certain variations in form and order between the MT. and the recension of the text which is represented by the LXX. While in some cases the condition of the LXX text is greatly inferior to that of MT., yet, on the other hand, it is clear that in a number of sections LXX preserves a superior arrangement in order, or a simpler form, of narrative, which points to the fact that MT. has suffered dislocation and interpolation at the hands of a reviser or revisers of a date later than the separation of the two recensions. As instances of this we may notice I. 4. 20—5. 14; 5. 15—7 in the main, 8. 1–13, 11. 1–13 (cf. *notes ad loc.*), and the position of MT. I. 21 after 19, so that 22 succeeds 20 without a break in the narrative. It is noticeable in certain cases that the additions which are found in MT. are just those passages which are coloured by the influence of the Priestly Code (P) in the Hexateuch. Cf. *notes* on I. 6. 11–14; 8. 1–11. Supposing, therefore, for the sake of simplicity that the author of the interpolations and changes in order as seen in MT. was one and the same redactor, he may conveniently be represented by the symbol R^{P} (Priestly Redactor).

Thus the pedigree of our Books of Kings may be represented as follows:—

ORIGINAL SOURCES:—Book of the Acts of Solomon, Chronicles of the Kings of Judah, Chronicles of the Kings of Israel, &c. &c.

Pre-exilic Redactor
influenced by Deut. [R^{D}]

Exilic and post-exilic Editors
influenced by Deut. [$R^{D\,2}$]

Post-exilic Editor influenced by Priestly Code [R^{P}] MASSORETIC TEXT.	Hebrew original of LXX TEXT.

§ 2. *Characteristics of the Chief Ancient Versions of Kings.*

For the general characteristics of the Ancient Versions of the Old Testament, and a just estimate of their value for the purposes of textual criticism, the reader is referred to Dr. Driver's Excursus in the Introduction to his *Notes on the Hebrew Text of the Books of Samuel*, § 3, pp. xxxvi–lv. All that is here attempted is a brief account of the Versions of Kings, framed upon the lines laid down by Dr. Driver in dealing with Samuel in § 4 of the same Introduction.

1. The Septuagint.

A. Before a Version can be used to good purpose for the criticism of the MT., it is important to recognize the fact that *all* variations from this latter are not due either to paraphrase or to a different reading in the Hebrew original from which the translation was made. The texts of the Versions, like the MT., were liable to *corruption*, and we find as a matter of fact that corrupt readings do exist in LXX, to a greater or less extent in different books.

But this corruption of single words or sentences is not the only feature in the Greek text which appears to belong to the vicissitudes of transmission. We also not infrequently meet with *conflate* or *double renderings* which are apparently due to the addition of a second translation of a passage, made by some scribe in the margin of the MS., probably because he considered that the first rendering did not adequately represent the sense of the original. This second translation came later on to be incorporated by another scribe in the text itself.

(*a*) Instances of corruptions in the Greek text. These are far more numerous in Cod. B than in Luc.:—

I. 1. 9. אבן Ἀιθή for λίθου. Luc. Ἀ., Σ., Θ. read λίθον.

ib. אנשי ἀδρούς for ἄνδρας (read by Luc.).

1. 49. ויחרדו ויקמו καὶ ἐξανέστησαν. This represents the latter word. The translation of the former, καὶ ἐξέστησαν (*al. exempl.*), has fallen out owing to the resemblance between the two Greek words.

2. 6. לא תורד *σὺ κατάξεις* for *οὐ κατάξεις*. The opposite change, *οὐ* for *σύ*, perhaps occurs in *v.* 9 (supposing, with Luc., Vulg., the original to have been ואתה, not ועתה).

4. 10. The whole *v.* corrupt in Luc. (cf. *note ad loc.*).

4. 11. *ἀνὰ Δάν* for *'Αβινάδαβ*. *ἀνὰ φαθεί* for *Ναφάθ*.

4. 20 (MT. 5. 7). האלה *οὕτως* for *οὗτοι* (read by Luc.).

5. 4 (MT. 5. 18). פגע *ἁμάρτημα* probably for *ἀπάντημα* (read by Luc., Cod. A).

5. 5 (MT. 5. 19). לבנות *οἰκοδομήσω* for *οἰκοδομῆσαι* (read by Luc.).

5. 6 (MT. 5. 20). ידע *ἰδίως* for *εἰδώς* (Luc.).

7. 3 (MT. 7. 15). *τὸ αἰλάμ* for *τῷ αἰλάμ* (Luc.), apparently representing an original לאולם (cf. *note* on 7. 15).

ib. Luc. *καὶ οὗτος* for *καὶ οὕτως* (LXX), representing an original וְכֵן (cf. *note*).

7. 9 (MT. 7. 20). לעבר *τῷ πήχει* for *τῷ πάχει* (Luc.), i. e. לְעָבְיוֹ.

7. 10 (MT. 7. 23). שפתו *τείχους* for *χείλους* (Luc.).

7. 45 (MT. 7. 8). אשר ישב שם *ἐν οἴκῳ καθήσεται ἐκεῖ* for *ἐν ᾧ κ. ε.* (Luc.).

8. 16. להיות *μεῖναι* for *εἶναι* (Luc.). Initial *μ* by dittography from preceding *'Ιερουσαλήμ*.

8. 39. ונתת Luc. *καὶ δικαιώσεις* for *καὶ δώσεις* (LXX).

8. 59. ביומו *ἐν ἡμέρᾳ ἐνιαυτοῦ* for *ἐν ἡμ. αὐτοῦ* (Luc.).

9. 28. אופירה *εἰς Σωφηρά* for *εἰς 'Ωφηρά*. So 16. 28 *f.*

11. 36. ניר Luc. *θέλησις* for *θέσις* (LXX).

15. 27. ויכהו *ἐχάραξεν αὐτόν* perhaps for *ἐπάταξεν αὐτόν* (Cod. A). Luc. *ἐχαράκωσεν αὐτόν* appears to be an attempt to improve the first reading.

16. 15. גבתון *Γαβαών* for *Γαβαθών*, *v.* 17.

16. 16[b], 17 *ff.* עמרי *Ζαμβρεί* for *'Αμβρεί*.

16. 17. מגבתון *ἐν Γαβαθών* for *ἐκ Γ.* (Luc.).

18. 5. בהמה *σκηνῶν* for *κτηνῶν* (Cod. A. Cf. Luc.).

18. 10. והשביע *καὶ ἐνέπρησεν* according to Klo., for *καὶ ἐνέπλησεν*, i. e. וְהִשְׂבִּיעַ.

18. 32. תעלה *θάλασσαν* probably an alteration of the transliteration *θααλά* (Luc.). So *v.* 38.

18. 45. וירכב καὶ ἔκλαεν for καὶ ἐξέλαεν or ἔλαεν. Luc. has further altered LXX into καὶ ἔκλαιε.

19. 3. γῆν for τῆς (τήν Cod. A).

21. 14 *ff.* (MT. 20. 14 *ff.*). המדינות τῶν χορῶν for τῶν χωρῶν (Luc.).

21. 33 (MT. 20. 33). וימהרו καὶ ἐσπείσαντο for καὶ ἔσπευσαν (Luc.).

22. 13. פה אחד ἐν στόματι ἐπί for ἐν στ. ἑνί (Luc.).

22. 16. עד כמה פעמים πεντάκις for ποσάκις (Luc.).

22. 26. אל אמן πρὸς Σεμήρ for πρὸς Ἐμήρ.

II. 3. 21. ומעלה καὶ εἶπον Ὦ for καὶ ἐπάνω (Luc.), an alteration due to the preceding καὶ ἀνεβόησαν, i.e. וַיִּצָּעֲקוּ for וַיִּצְעֲקוּ.

5. 17. משא γομόρ for γόμος (Luc.).

6. 5. שאול κεκρυμμένον for κεχρημένον (Luc., 'A., Σ., Θ.).

10. 6. את גדלי וג' Luc. οὓς οἱ ἁδροί for οὗτοι ἁδροί of LXX, where את is taken as sign of accusative.

10. 26. מצבות στολήν for στήλην (Luc.).

11. 12. ויכו כף καὶ ἐκράτησαν τῇ χειρί for καὶ ἐκρότησαν τ. χ. (Luc.).

12. 1 (MT. 12. 2). מבאר שבע ἐκ γῆς Βηρσάβεε for ἐκ τῆς Β.

12. 8 (MT. 12. 9). בדק βδέλυγμα for βέδεκ (Luc.).

12. 15 (MT. 12. 16). הם αὐτῶν for αὐτοί (Luc.).

14. 7. בני מלח ἐν Ῥεμέλε for ἐν Γεμέλε (Luc. Γαιμέλεχ, Cod. A. Γαιμέλα).

14. 11. אשר ליהודה γῇ τοῦ Ἰούδα for τῇ τοῦ Ἰ.

15. 20. שם Luc. ἔτι for ἐκεῖ (LXX).

15. 25. בארמון ἐναντίον probably for ἐν ἄντρῳ. Cf. I. 16. 18 where אל ארמון is translated εἰς ἄντρον.

17. 6. וערי מדי Luc. ἐν ὁρίοις Μήδων, an alteration of καὶ Ὀρῆ Μ. (LXX). Cf. also 18. 11.

18. 20. אמרת Luc. σὺ καὶ πᾶς for Σὺ εἶπας (cf. *note ad loc.*).

19. 12. אשר שחתו οὐ διέφθειραν for οὓς δ. (Luc.).

22. 20. את המלך οἱ βασιλεῖς for τῷ βασιλεῖ (Luc.).

23. 5. והשבית καὶ κατέκαυσεν for καὶ κατέπαυσεν. So *v.* 11.

23. 6. לעפר Luc. ὡς χοῦν for εἰς χ. (LXX).

23. 36. מן רומה ἐκ Κρουμά for ἐκ Ῥουμά.

25. 17. שבכה ורמנים σακαχαρθαί for σαβὰχ καὶ ῥοαί (Cod. A).

(*b*) Instances of double renderings are more frequent in Luc. than in Cod. B :—

I. 1. 36. כן יאמר י׳ אלהי אדני המלך = Luc. *πιστώσαι ὁ θεὸς τοὺς λόγους τοῦ κυρίου μου τοῦ βασιλέως· οὕτως εἶπε κύριος ὁ θεός σου, κύριε μου βασιλεῦ.*

1. 40. מחללים בחללים ושמחים שמחה גדולה = Luc. *ἐχόρευον ἐν χοροῖς καὶ εὐφραινόμενοι εὐφροσύνῃ μεγάλῃ ηὔλουν ἐν αὐλοῖς καὶ ἔχαιρον χαρᾷ μεγάλῃ.*

1. 47. וגם באו עבדי = Luc. *καί γε ἦλθον οἱ δοῦλοι . . . καὶ εἰσεληλύθασι μόνοι* (לְבַדָּם for עבדי in second rendering).

2. 5. בחגרתו = Luc. *ἐν τῇ ζωῇ μου καὶ ἐπὶ τῇ ζώνῃ . . . μου.*

4. 6. ואחישר על הבית = *καὶ 'Αχεὶ ἦν οἰκονόμος, καὶ 'Ελιὰκ ὁ οἰκονόμος, καὶ 'Ελιὰβ υἱὸς Σὰφ ἐπὶ τῆς πατριᾶς*, apparently a triple rendering (cf. *note ad loc.*).

6. 15. עד קירות = *ἕως τῶν δοκῶν καὶ ἕως τῶν τοίχων. δοκῶν* = קוֹרוֹת.

6. 34 (MT. 7. 12b). *κυκλόθεν . . . καταπέτασμα* probably represents an original מִסָּבִיב (מֵסַב) read a second time as מָסָךְ (cf. *note ad loc.*).

7. 3 (MT. 7. 15). חוט = Luc. *περίμετρον . . . σπαρτίον.*

7. 6 (MT. 7. 18). *καὶ ἔργον κρεμαστόν, δύο στίχοι . . . ἔργον κρεμαστόν, στίχος ἐπὶ στίχον*, representing ומעשה ?שני טורים (cf. *note ad loc.*).

7. 9 (MT. 7. 20). *ἐπίθεμα τὸ μελάθρον* representing כתרת repeated from beginning in place of הבטן אשר. Luc. also repeats *ἐπ' ἀμφοτέρων τῶν στύλων.*

7. 22 (MT. 7. 36). וליות = *κατὰ πρόσωπον ἔσω*, read as לפנימה and doubly rendered.

7. 32 (MT. 7. 47). [אשר עשה] מרב מאד מאד = Luc. *οὗ ἐποίησεν ἄρδην . . . ἃ ἐποίησε ταῦτα ἐκ τοῦ πλήθους σφόδρα* (cf. *note ad loc.*).

8. 28. לפניך = *ἐνώπιόν σου πρὸς σέ.*

8. 60. הוא האלהים = *ὁ θεός, αὐτὸς θεός.*

8. 66. ויברכו את המלך = Luc. *καὶ εὐλόγησεν αὐτόν. καὶ εὐλόγησαν καὶ αὐτοὶ τὸν βασιλέα* (cf. *note ad loc.*).

11. 43. *εἰς τὴν γῆν Σαρειρά* for *εἰς τὴν Σ.* (Luc.), representing an original אל הצרדה (cf. *note ad loc.*).

15. 15. ויבא . . . בית י׳ = Luc. καὶ εἰσήνεγκεν Ἀσὰ εἰς τὸν οἶκον κυρίου . . . καὶ εἰσήνεγκεν εἰς τὸν οἶκ. κ.

16. 33. τοῦ ἐξολοθρευθῆναι . . . ἐκακοποίησεν apparently represents a doublet לְהַשְׁחִית הִשְׁחִית.

18. 38. ואת המים אשר בתעלה = Luc. καὶ τὸ ὕδωρ τὸ ἐπ' αὐτῶν, καὶ τὸ ὕδωρ τὸ ἐν τῇ θααλά.

18. 43ᵇ. שב שֶׁבַע פעמים. Cf. *note ad loc.*

18. 44. מים = Luc. ὕδωρ ἀπὸ θαλάσσης.

20. 4 (MT. 21. 4). ויבא אחאב אל ביתו סר וזעף = Luc. καὶ ἦλθεν Ἀ. πρὸς οἶκον αὐτοῦ συγκεχυμένος καὶ ἐκλελυμένος . . . καὶ ἐγένετο τὸ πνεῦμα Ἀ. τεταραγμένον.

20. 25 (MT. 21. 25). רק = πλὴν ματαίως, the word being repeated as ריק (רֵיקָם).

21. 1 (MT. 20. 1). ויעל ויצר על שמרון = καὶ ἀνέβη καὶ περιεκάθισεν ἐπὶ Σαμάρειαν . . . καὶ ἀνέβησαν καὶ περιεκάθισαν ἐπὶ Σ. (Luc. ἐπ' αὐτήν).

21. 16 (MT. 20. 16). מֶלֶךְ עזר אתו = Luc. (*v.* 15) καὶ ὁ βασιλεὺς Ἐζὲρ μετ' αὐτοῦ . . . (*v.* 16) βασιλεῖς οἱ συμβοηθοὶ μετ' αὐτοῦ.

22. 17. לא אדנים לאלה = οὐ Κύριος τούτοις θεός; לָאֵלֶּה read a second time as לֵאלֹהַּ.

22. 20. ויאמר זה בכה וזה אמר בכה = Luc. καὶ εἶπεν οὗτος οὕτως καὶ οὗτος οὕτως. καὶ εἶπεν Οὐ δυνήσει. καὶ εἶπεν Ἐν σοί (בְּךָ for בכה).

22. 35. ויצק דם המכה אל חיק הרכב = καὶ ἀπεχύννετο αἷμα ἐκ τῆς πληγῆς εἰς τὸν κόλπον τοῦ ἅρματος . . . καὶ ἐξεπορεύετο τὸ αἷμα τῆς τροπῆς ἕως τοῦ κόλπου τοῦ ἅρματος.

II. 1. 2 *ff.* אלהי עקרון = Luc. προσόχθισμα θεὸν Ἀκκαρών.

1. 4, 6. לכן = Luc. οὐχ οὕτως. διὰ τοῦτο.

3. 21. ויצעקו מכל חגר חגורה ומעלה = Luc. καὶ παρήγγειλαν παντὶ περιζωννυμένῳ παραζώνην καὶ παρατείνοντι, καὶ ἐβόησαν ἐκ παντὸς παραζωννυμένου παραζώνην καὶ ἐπ' ἄνω.

3. 23. החרב = Luc. ῥομφαίας· ἐρίσαντες γάρ.

4. 34. ויגהר עליו = Luc. καὶ συνέκαμψεν ἐπ' αὐτὸν καὶ ἰγαὰδ ἐπ' αὐτόν.

4. 35. ויגהר וג׳ apparently triply rendered in Luc. Cf. *note ad loc.*

6. 8. פלני אלמני = τόνδε τινὰ ἐλιμωνί (unless τόνδε τινά = פלני simply).

7. 2. השליש = Luc. ὁ τριστάτης ὁ ἀπεσταλμένος (? הַשָּׁלוּחַ).

7. 5. בנשף = Luc. *ἐν τῷ σκότει ἤδη διαυγάζοντος.* So *v.* 7, *ἐν τ. σκ. ἤδη διαφώσκοντος.*

7. 10. ויקראו אל שער העיר = Luc. *καὶ ἐβόησαν εἰς τὴν πύλην τῆς πόλεως καὶ ἐκάλεσαν τοὺς στρατηγοὺς τῆς πόλεως.*

8. 1. וגם בא אל הארץ שבע שנים = Luc. *καὶ παρέσται ἐπὶ τὴν γῆν ἑπτὰ ἔτη· καί γε ἦλθεν κ.τ.λ.* (בא rendered (1) as participle, (2) as perfect.)

9. 17. שפעת = Luc. *τὸν κονιορτὸν τοῦ ὄχλου.*

10. 29. לא סר יהוא מאחריהם = Luc. *οὐκ ἀπέστη ἀπ' αὐτῶν 'Ιού· ὀπίσω αὐτῶν ἐπορεύετο.*

11. 2. אחזיה = Luc. *'Οχοζίου τοῦ ἀδελφοῦ αὐτῆς* (אָחִיהָ).

11. 9. הכהן = Luc. *ὁ συνετὸς ἱερεύς* (firstly הֶחָכָם).

11. 14. והשרים = Luc. *καὶ οἱ ᾠδοὶ . . . καὶ οἱ στρατηγοί.*

11. 15. הוציאו אתה אל מבית לשדרת = Luc. *'Εξαγάγετε αὐτὴν ἔσωθεν τῶν σαδηρώθ, καὶ εἰσαγάγετε αὐτὴν ὀπίσωθεν οἴκου τῶν στρατηγῶν* (השרים for השדרת).

14. 10. הכבד = Luc. *ἡ βαρεῖα· ἐνδοξάσθητι.*

14. 14. התערבות = Luc. *τῶν συμμίξεων τῶν βδελυγμάτων* (הַתֹּעֲבוֹת).

14. 26. מרה מאד = Luc. *πικρὰν σφόδρα, δι' ὅτι ἐλεπτύνθη.*

16. 18. השבת = Luc. *τῆς καθέδρας τῶν σαββάτων.*

17. 5. בכל הארץ = Luc. *ἐπὶ πᾶσαν τὴν γῆν . . . καὶ εἰς πᾶσαν τὴν γῆν αὐτῆς.*

17. 32. Cf. *note ad loc.*

18. 17. בתעלת = Luc. *ἐν τῇ ἀναβάσει ἐν τῷ ὑδραγωγῷ.*

19. 3. ותוכחה = Luc. *καὶ ὀνειδισμοῦ καὶ ἐλεγμοῦ.*

19. 28. ושאננך = Luc. *καὶ τὸ στρῆνός σου καὶ τὰ ἐνθυμήματά σου.*

20. 13. נכתה = Luc. *τῆς ὑπάρξεως αὐτοῦ καὶ τοῦ νεχωθά.*

21. 6. הרבה = Luc. *ἐπλήθυνε, καὶ ἐπλήθυνε.*

21. 23. ויקשרו . . . עליו = Luc. *καὶ συνεστράφησαν . . . ἐπ' αὐτὸν καὶ ἐπεβούλευσαν αὐτῷ.*

23. 6. האשרה = Luc. *τὸ ἄλσος τῆς 'Ασηρώθ.*

23. 12. וירץ משם = Luc. *καὶ καθεῖλεν αὐτὰ ἐκεῖθεν καὶ ἐξήνεγκεν αὐτὰ καὶ συνέτριψε,* apparently a triple rendering.

23. 16. ויפן = Luc. *καὶ ἀπέστρεψεν . . . καὶ ἐξένευσε.*

B. There are also characteristics of the Version which appear to be due to the translator. The more important of these may now be noticed, with a few illustrations.

(1) Paraphrase.

(*a*) This usually takes place for the sake of making clear the sense of some Hebrew word or phrase which would be liable to be misunderstood in the Greek if literally translated :—

I. 2. 32. את דמו *τὸ αἷμα τῆς ἀδικίας αὐτοῦ.*

4. 20 (MT. 5. 7). כל הקרב *πάντα διαγγέλματα.*

4. 22 (MT. 5. 2). לחם *τὰ δέοντα.*

8. 56. לא נפל דבר *οὐ διεφώνησεν λόγος.*

9. 27. ידעי הים *ἐλαύνειν εἰδότας θάλασσαν.*

15. 4. ניר *κατάλειμμα.*

19. 18. נשק לו *προσεκύνησεν αὐτῷ.*

21. 12 (MT. 20. 12). שימו וישימו *Οἰκοδομήσατε χάρακα· καὶ ἔθεντο χάρακα.*

22. 34. לתמו *εὐστόχως.*

(*b*) At other times paraphrase appears to be used for no apparent reason, merely at the whim of the translator :—

I. 3. 17. ואלד עמה *καὶ ἐτέκομεν.*

5. 12 (MT. 5. 26). שניהם *ἀνὰ μέσον ἑαυτῶν.*

9. 5. מעל כסא ישראל *ἡγούμενος ἐν Ἰσραήλ.*

17. 13. אל תיראי *θάρσει.*

(*c*) Somewhat different are the cases in which phrases are arbitrarily altered by the translator, because it seemed to him that some better expression could be substituted :—

I. 2. 29. אצל המזבח *κατέχει τῶν κεράτων τοῦ θυσιαστηρίου.*

2. 38. ימים רבים *τρία ἔτη* (from *v.* 39).

9. 6. נתתי *ἔδωκεν Μωυσῆς.*

10. 5. לא היה בה עוד רוח *ἐξ ἑαυτῆς ἐγένετο.*

(*d*) Or again, paraphrase may take place when the expression used in the original was somewhat offensive in the eyes of the translator. Under this head comes, e. g., the removal of anthropomorphic expressions applied to God :—

I. 3. 10. בעיני אדני ἐνώπιον Κυρίου.

II. 2. 11. השמים ὡς εἰς τὸν οὐρανόν (of the translation of Elijah).

24. 3. על פי י׳ ἐπὶ τὸν θυμὸν Κυρίου.

(*e*) The last form of paraphrase to be noticed is the translation of a word or phrase by *guess*, the context being taken as a guide to the sense:—

I. 10. 11. אלמגים πελεκητά.

17. 21. ויתמדד καὶ ἐνεφύσησεν.

18. 21. על שתי הסעפים ἐπ' ἀμφοτέραις ταῖς ἰγνύαις, guided by the preceding פסחים.

21. 11 (MT. 20. 11). מפתח ὁ ὀρθός, guided by חֹגֵר rendered ὁ κυρτός from Talmudic חִגֵּר.

(2) In striking contrast to the paraphrastic tendency, we find renderings in which extreme literality appears to have been the aim of the translator.

(*a*) Thus at times attempts are made to represent in Greek the Hebrew constructions, or to preserve the fancied force of Hebrew words, and the result is a rendering which is often grotesque.

Examples of Hebraisms from I. 1. 2 are the following:—

1. 7. ויעזרו אחרי καὶ ἐβοήθουν ὀπίσω (contrast Luc. καὶ ἀντελαμβάνοντο αὐτοῦ).

1. 12. איעצך נא עצה συμβουλεύσω σοι δὴ συμβουλίαν.

1. 13. לכי . . . ואמרת εἴσελθε . . . καὶ ἐρεῖς.

1. 14. עודך מדברת . . . ואני אבוא ἔτι λαλούσης σου . . . καὶ ἐγὼ εἰσελεύσομαι.

1. 17. אתה נשבעת בי׳ אלהיך σὺ ὤμοσας ἐν τῷ θεῷ σου (but Luc. κατὰ τοῦ κ. τοῦ θ.).

1. 51. ויגד . . . לאמר ἀνηγγέλη . . . λέγοντες (but Luc. καὶ ἀπήγγειλαν . . . λέγοντες).

2. 2. אנכי הלך ἐγώ εἰμι πορεύομαι. Cf. II. 4. 13; 10. 9; 22. 20.

2. 37. והיה ביום צאתך ועברת καὶ ἔσται ἐν τῇ ἡμέρᾳ τῆς ἐξόδου σου καὶ διαβήσῃ (but Luc. ἐν τῇ ἡμ. τῆς ἐξ. σου ᾗ διαβήσῃ).

2. 42. ידע תדע כי מות תמות γινώσκων γνώσῃ ὅτι θανάτῳ ἀποθανῇ.

(*b*) Sometimes difficult words, instead of being guessed at, are interpreted very literally according to the sense of the root:—

I. 6. 20. סגור *συνκεκλεισμένῳ.*

7. 28. מסגרות *συνκλειστόν.*

16. 20. קשרו אשר קשר *τὰς συνάψεις αὐτοῦ ἃς συνῆψεν.*

II. 10. 19. בעקבה *ἐν πτερνισμῷ.*

12. 3. הורהו *ἐφώτισεν αὐτόν*, apparently connecting the Hebrew word with אור.

12. 21. ויקשרו קשר *καὶ ἔδησαν πάντα δεσμόν.*

14. 14. התערבות *τῶν συμμίξεων.*

14. 19. ויקשרו עליו קשר *καὶ συνεστράφησαν ἐπ' αὐτὸν σύστρεμμα.* Cf. 15. 8, 30.

(*c*) Another device in the case of a hard word was simply to transliterate it into Greek letters. Such transliterations are very characteristic of Kings, particularly of the second book:—

I. 4. 19. נְצִיב *νασέφ*, Luc. *Νασείβ.*

5. 11 (MT. 5. 25). מַכֹּלֶת *μαχείρ* (*al. exempl. μαχάλ*).

ib. כֹּר *κόρους.*

ib. כֹּר (correctly בַּת) *βαίθ.*

6. 7; *al.* (MT. 6. 3). אוּלָם *αἰλάμ.*

6. 10; *al.* (MT. 6. 5). דְּבִיר *δαβείρ.*

6. 22; *al.* (MT. 6. 23). כְּרוּבִים *χερουβείν.*

7. 14; *al.* (MT. 7. 27). מְכֹנוֹת *μεχωνώθ.*

11. 14. שָׂטָן *σατάν.*

14. 28. תָּא *θεέ*, Luc. *θεκουέ.*

18. 32, 38. תְּעָלָה Luc. *θααλά.*

19. 4. רֹתֶם *Ῥαθμέν*, Luc. *ῥαθαμείν.*

II. 2. 14. אַף־הוּא *ἀφφώ.*

3. 4. נֹקֵד *νωκήθ.*

4. 34. וַיִּגְהַר Luc. *καὶ ἰγαάδ.*

4. 39. אֹרֹת *ἀριώθ.*

4. 42. בְּצִקְלֹנוֹ Cod. A *βακελλέθ* (but cf. *note ad loc.*).

5. 19. כִּבְרַת *δεβραθά*, Luc. *χαβραθά.*

6. 8. פְּלֹנִי אַלְמֹנִי *ἐλιμωνί*, Luc. *φελμουνί.*

6. 25. קַב *κάβου.*
8. 8, 9. מִנְחָה *μαανά,* Luc. *μαναά.*
8. 15. מַכְבֵּר *χαββά.*
9. 13. גֶּרֶם *γαρέμ.*
10. 10. אֵפוֹא *ἀφφώ.*
10. 22. הַמֶּלְתָּחָה *τοῦ οἴκου μεσθαάλ.*
11. 4. לַכָּרִי וְלָרָצִים *τὸν Χορρεὶ καὶ τὸν Ῥασείν.*
11. 6. מַסָּח Luc. Μεσσαέ.
11. 8. שְׂדֵרוֹת *ἀηδώθ,* Luc. *σαδηρώθ.*
11. 12. הַנֵּזֶר *ἰέζερ.*
12. 6; *al.* בֶּדֶק *βέδεκ.*
12. 10. הַמִּזְבֵּחַ *ἰαμειβείν.* Cod. A *ἀμμασβή.*
14. 7. בְּגֵי־הַמֶּלַח *ἐν Ῥεμέλε,* Luc. *ἐν Γαιμελέχ.*
15. 5. הַחָפְשִׁית *ἀφφουσώθ.*
17. 6. עָרֵי *Ὀρή.* So 18. 11.
20. 12. מִנְחָה *μαναάν.*
20. 13. נְכֹתֹה *νεχωθά.*
22. 14. מִשְׁנֶה *μασενά.*
23. 4. שַׁדְמוֹת *σαλημώθ.*
23. 5. כְּמָרִים *χωμαρείμ.*
ib. מַזָּלוֹת *μαζουρώθ.*
23. 7. קְדֵשִׁים *καδησείμ,* Luc. *καδησείν.*
ib. בָּתִּים *χεττιείν* (cf. *note ad loc.*).
23. 10. תֹּפֶת *τάφεθ,* Luc. *Θαφφέθ.*
23. 11. פַּרְוָרִים *φαρουρείμ.*
23. 13. הַמַּשְׁחִית *τοῦ Μοσοάθ,* Luc. *Ἀμεσσώθ.*
23. 24. תְּרָפִים *θεραφείν.*
25. 5. עַרְבוֹת *ἀραβώθ.*
25. 12. גבים *ταβείν.*
25. 14. יָעִים *ἰαμείν.*
25. 17. כֹּתֶרֶת *χωθάρ.*
ib. שְׂבָכָה *γαβαχά.* Cod. A *σαβαχά.*

(3) Another characteristic is the insertion of additional words and sentences by the translator.

(*a*) Such additions are frequently made to fill out the sense, and to make the meaning more clear. Very frequently the subject of a verb is added when the reference seems to be ambiguous:—

I. 2. 22. ὁ ἀρχιστράτηγος ἑταῖρος[1].

2. 32. τὸ αἷμα αὐτῶν, added as obj. of לא ידע.

2. 35. εἰς ἱερέα πρῶτον.

3. 9. ἐν δικαιοσύνῃ, explaining the force of לשפט.

3. 15. κατὰ πρόσωπον τοῦ θυσιαστηρίου τοῦ[1].

3. 27. τῇ εἰπούσῃ Δότε αὐτῇ αὐτό, added to remove the seeming ambiguity of the king's command[1].

4. 21 (MT. 5. 8). ὁ βασιλεύς, subj. of אשר יהיה שם.

8. 53 (MT. 8. 12). ὑπὲρ τοῦ οἴκου ὡς συνετέλεσεν τοῦ οἰκοδομῆσαι αὐτόν[1].

15. 19. διάθου, before ברית[1].

18. 24. ὁ ἐλάλησας, after הדבר.

19. 19. ἐν βουσίν, after והוא חרש.

(*b*) Additions are also very frequently made for the sake of bringing one passage into strict conformity with another:—

I. 2. 26. τῆς διαθήκης, ארון הברית being the usual (Deuteronomic) phrase.

2. 29. καὶ θάψον αὐτόν, to agree with *v.* 31.

2. 37. καὶ ὥρκισεν αὐτὸν ὁ βασιλεὺς ἐν τῇ ἡμέρᾳ ἐκείνῃ, in agreement with *v.* 42.

9. 20. καὶ τοῦ Χαναναίου . . . καὶ τοῦ Γεργασαίου, added to make up the number of the *seven* heathen nations of Palestine.

12. 20. καὶ Βενιαμείν, to agree with *vv.* 21, 23.

21. 23. καὶ οὐ θεὸς κοιλάδος, to agree with *v.* 28.

The relationship of the recension of Lucian to that of Cod. B[2] cannot here be discussed; but it is clear that the author had access to sources which preserved unimpaired original readings of which

---

[1] Discussed in the *notes* on the text.

[2] The origin of the text of Codd. A and B in 3 Kings has been discussed at length by S. Silberstein in *ZATW.*, 1893–4.

we should otherwise have remained in ignorance[1]. Instances of such readings in the text of Kings will be found in the *notes*. Cf. I. 1. 28; 2. 5; 11. 8b; 13. 11; 18. 5. II. 3. 25; 5. 1; 7. 7; 10. 11; 12. 5; 15. 10; 17. 2, 7, 27; 18. 34; 24. 13; 25. 4.

2. The Targum.

The chief characteristics of this version may be noticed very briefly.

(*a*) A very marked tendency to do away with anthropomorphic or otherwise seemingly unworthy expressions used with reference to God:—

I. 1. 17. ביהוה אלהיך, Targ. במימרא דיהוה אלהך. So constantly.

3. 10. בעיני אדני, Targ. קדם יהוה.

8. 15. בפיו, Targ. במימריה.

8. 24. ותדבר בפיך, Targ. וגזרתא במימרך.

8. 29. להיות עיניך פתחת, Targ. למיהוי רעיא קדמך. So *v.* 52.

8. 33. ושבו אליך, Targ. ויתובון לפולחנך.

9. 6. מאחרי, Targ. מבתר פולחני.

9. 9. עזבו את יהוה, Targ. שבקו ית פולחנא דיהוה.

ib. אלהים אחרים, Targ. טעות עממיא, to avoid applying the name אלהים to false gods.

(*b*) A general tendency to paraphrase:—

I. 1. 33. גחון, Targ. שילוחא. So *vv.* 38, 45.

1. 38. והכרתי והפלתי, Targ. וקשתיא וקלעיא. So *v.* 44.

1. 42. איש חיל, Targ. גבר דחיל חטאין. So several times.

2. 7. קרבו אלי, Targ. סופיקו צורכיי.

2. 24. אשר עשה לי בית, Targ. דקיים לי מלכו.

3. 16. זנות, Targ. פונדקאן, πανδοκεύτριαι, a softening down of the original.

3. 18. אין זר, Targ. זכאין.

6. 4. חלוני שקפים אטמים, Targ. כוין פתיחן מלגיו וסתימן מלברא.

---

[1] Cf. Dri. *Sam.* p. lii. The value of Luc. for the emendation of the MT. of Kings has been noticed by I. Hooykaas, *Iets over de grieksche vertaling van het Oude Testament* (Rotterdam, 1888).

6. 10. ויאחז, Targ. וטליל.

7. 2. בית יער הלבנון, Targ. בית מקרת מלכיא.

8. 16. להיות שמי, Targ. לאשראה שכינתי.

8. 19. היצא מחלציך, Targ. דתוליד.

8. 27. האמנם, Targ. ארי מן סבר ומן דמי בקושטא.

8. 39. מכון שבתך, Targ. אתר בית שכינתך.

(*c*) A tendency to make explanatory insertions, without any equivalent in the original:—

I. 1. 24. מלכותא in the phrase כורסי מלכותא = כִּסֵּא. So constantly.

5. 13. ואיתנבי על מלכי בית דוד דעתידין למשלט בעלמא הדין ובעלמא דמשיחא; perhaps a haggadic explanation of וידבר על העצים . . . בקיר.

6. 6. למיהוי רישי שריתא ניחין על זיזיא.

8. 2. בירחא דעתיקיא קרן ליה ירחא קדמאה. MT. simply בירח האתנים.

8. 9. דעליהון כתיבין עשרה פיתגמי קימא. Cf. also *v.* 21.

8. 65. חנא . . . חנוכת ביתא. So MT. in 2 Chr. 7. 9.

As a whole this version represents a recension much nearer to MT. than that of any other ancient version.

3. The Peshitto.

This translation appears to have been made from a Hebrew text similar in many respects to that presupposed by LXX, though more nearly related to MT. than the LXX original[1]. Instances of the agreement in readings between Pesh., LXX, and Luc. will be found in the *notes*. Cf. I. 2. 26, 29; 6. 9; 7. 10, 15^b; 8. 37; 10. 8. II. 6. 2. As has been noticed by Dri. in the case of Samuel, the original of Pesh. seems to have been related to that of Luc.: cf. I. 1. 40; 4. 34; 18. 29. II. 2. 14; 10. 14; 14. 29; 19. 15. Affinities with the Vulg. may also be noticed: cf. I. 7. 7, 42;

[1] A conspectus of the variations between Pesh. and MT. in 1 Kings has been given by J. Berlinger, *Die Peschitta zum* 1. (3.) *Buch der Könige und ihr Verhältniss zu MT., LXX. und Trg.* (Berlin, 1897).

9. 18. Cases in which Pesh. agrees with LXX, Luc., Vulg. against MT. are frequent.

The general characteristics of the Version are those of a close and accurate, though not too servile, representation of the original. Paraphrase is occasionally employed—most frequently in the case of words or phrases which appeared to the translator to need elucidation, and here and there slight additions have been made to the text for the same reason. The following instances may be noticed.

(*a*) Paraphrase:—

I. 1. 36. כן יאמר ܗܟܢܐ ܢܥܒܕ 'So may (Yahwe) *do.*'

1. 50. ויחזק בקרנות המזבח ܘܐܚܕ ܓܘܣܐ ܒܩܪܢܬܐ ܕܡܕܒܚܐ 'and *took refuge at* the horns of the altar.'

2. 42. ביום צאתך והלכת אנה ואנה ܒܝܘܡܐ ܕܬܦܘܩ ܡܢ ܐܘܪܫܠܡ ܘܬܥܒܪ ܢܚܠܐ ܕܩܕܪܘܢ 'In the day that thou goest forth *from Jerusalem and crossest the brook Kidron.*'

3. 16. ותעמדנה לפניו אל המלך ܠܡܕܝܢ ܩܕܡ ܡܠܟܐ ܫܠܝܡܘܢ '*to plead their case before king Solomon.*'

3. 18. ויהי ביום השלישי ܘܡܢ ܒܬܪ ܬܠܬܐ ܝܘܡܝܢ 'and *after three days.*'

8. 26. אשר דברת ܕܝܡܝܬ 'which thou didst *swear.*'

12. 32*f.* בחמשה עשר יום לחדש ܒܡܠܝܐ 'on the *full moon.*'

14. 10. כאשר יבער הגלל ܐܝܟ ܕܡܬܩܛܦܝܢ ܥܢܒܐ ܕܟܪܡܐ ܟܕ ܫܠܡ ܩܛܦܐ '*as the grapes of a vineyard* are swept away *when the vintage is finished.*'

20. 33. ויעלהו ܘܐܘܬܒܗ ܥܡܗ 'and he *caused him to sit with him.*'

21. 11. הישבים בעירו ܕܝܬܒܝܢ ܒܡܕܝܢܬܐ ܥܡ ܢܒܘܬ 'who dwelt in *the* city *with Naboth.*'

II. 2. 10. הקשית לשאול ܐܘܪܒܬ ܠܡܫܐܠ 'thou hast made a *large* request.'

3. 7. כמוני כמוך ܣܠܩ ܐܢܐ ܐܝܟ ܕܐܢܬ '*I will go up* like thee.'

4. 42. מבעל שלשה ܡܢ ܡܕܝܢܬ ܓܢܒܪܐ 'from *the city of the mighty men.*'

5. 11. ואסף המצרע ܘܐܬܐܣܐ ܡܢ ܓܪܒܐ 'and *I should be healed of leprosy.*'

7. 2, 17, 19. השליש ܓܒܪܐ 'the *man.*'

9. 11. שיחו ܫܛܝܘܬܗ 'his *folly.*'

23. 11. וישבת ܘܩܛܠ 'and he *slew.*'

23. 29. על מלך אשור ܥܠ ܡܒܘܓ 'against *Mabbogh.*'

(*b*) Additions:—

I. 1. 10. ܒܪ ܝܗܘܝܕܥ 'son of Jehoiada,' after בניהו; ܕܕܘܝܕ 'of David,' after הגבורים.

1. 11. ܢܒܝܐ 'the prophet,' after נתן.

1. 21. ܒܫܠܡܐ 'in peace,' after עם אבתיו.

1. 39. ܘܢܬܢ ܢܒܝܐ 'and Nathan the prophet,' after צדוק הכהן.

8. 22. ܘܨܠܝ 'and prayed,' after ויפרש כפיו השמים.

11. 18. ܬܒ ܠܘܬܝ 'Dwell with me,' after אמר לו (cf. *note ad loc.*).

19. 1. ܢܒܝ̈ܐ ܕܒܥܠܐ ܘܕܚܡܢ̈ܐ 'the prophets of Ba'al and of the sanctuaries,' for simple הנביאים.

II. 4. 13. ܫܦܝܪ 'prosperously,' before בתוך וג׳.

6. 12. ܠܐ ܗܘܐ ܡܢ ܕܝܠܢ 'It is none of us,' for simple לוא.

10. 15. ܘܐܡܪ ܠܗ 'And he said to him,' before תנה את ידך.

11. 14. ܐܝܟ ܥܝܕܐ ܕܡܠܟ̈ܐ 'according to the custom of kings,' for simple כמשפט.

14. 27. ܒܪ ܝܗܘܐܚܙ 'son of Jehoaḥaz,' after בן יואש.

15. 29. ܘܠܐܒܠ ܡܚܘܠܐ ܘܠܟܠܗ ܒܝܬ ܡܥܟܐ 'and Abel-Meḥolah and all Beth-Ma'achah,' for ואת אבל בית מעכה.

18. 27. Insertion of negative: ܕܠܐ ܬܐܟܠܘܢ . . . ܘܠܐ ܬܫܬܘܢ for לאכל . . . ולשתות.

19. 35. ܘܚܙܘ 'and beheld,' after וישכימו בבקר.

In certain cases the renderings of Pesh. seem to exhibit connection with Targ.; cf. I. 1. 33, 38, 45 גחון, Pesh. ܫܝܠܘܚܐ, Targ. שילוחא; 1. 38 הכרתי והפלתי, Pesh. ܘܩܫ̈ܬܐ ܘܪܡܝܢ ܒܩܠܥ̈ܐ, Targ. וקשתיא וקלעיא; 2. 5 וישם . . . ברגליו, Pesh. ܘܣܡ ܐܢܘܢ ܐܝܟ ܕܒܩܪܒܐ ܘܐܫܕ ܕܡܗܘܢ ܒܫܠܡܐ ܕܒܚܨ̈ܘܗܝ ܘܕܫ ܒܡܣܐܢ̈ܘܗܝ ܕܒܪ̈ܓܠܘܗܝ, Targ. ודמי דתחשיב דמהון עלוהי כדם תבירי קרבא ויתיב להון בכמנת שלמא ואשד דמהון באיספניקי בבחרציה ודש בטלריתא

דברגלוהי; 5. 32 והגבלים, Pesh. ܘܐܓܒ̈ܘܠܐ, Targ. וארגובליא; 18. 21 אתם פסחים על שתי הסעפים, Pesh. ܦܠܓܝܢ ܐܢܬܘܢ ܒܬܪ̈ܬܝܢ ܦܠ̈ܓܝܟܘܢ. Targ. אתון פלינין לתרין פלגון; 22. 34 משך בקשת לתמו, Pesh. ܢܓܕ ܗܘܐ ܒܩܫܬܐ ܠܩܘܒܠܗ, Targ. נגד בקשתא לקיבליה. A few cases of agreement in rendering with Vulg. may also be noticed: I. 6. 1 ויבן, Pesh. ܫܪܝ ܠܡܒܢܝܘ, Vulg. *aedificari coepit*; 18. 45 ויהי עד כה ועד כה, Pesh. ܘܟܕ ܗܘ ܡܬܦܢܐ ܠܟܐ ܘܠܟܐ, Vulg. *cumque se verteret huc atque illuc*; 22. 48 ומלך וג׳, Pesh. ܘܡܠܟܐ ܠܝܬ ܒܐܕܘܡ ܕܩܐܡ, Vulg. *nec erat tunc rex constitutus in Edom*; II. 4. 35 ויזורר, Pesh. ܘܐܬܦܩܣ, Vulg. *et oscitavit*.

Cases of corruption in the text of Pesh. are not numerous, and are nearly confined to confusion or transposition of letters in proper names: I. 4. 10 שכה, Pesh. ܣܘܟܬ; 4. 12 יקמעם, Pesh. ܢܩܡܥܡ; 5. 4 תפסח, Pesh. ܬܦܣܚ; 22. 10 בגרן, Pesh. ܒܪܝܐ for ܒܐܕܪܐ; II. 2. 25 שב, Pesh. ܬܘܒ for ܬܒ; 4. 23 שלום, Pesh. ܫܠܡܘܬܐ for ܫܠܡ; 4. 28 תשלה, Pesh. ܬܠܬܠ; 9. 2 נמשי, Pesh. ܡܫܡܝ; 9. 27 יבלעם, Pesh. ܢܒܠܥܡ; 14. 7 יקתאל, Pesh. ܢܩܬܐܝܠ; 15. 16 *ff.* מנחם, Pesh. ܡܫܝܚܡ; 17. 31 נבחז, Pesh. ܡܚܠܣ; 18. 2 אבי, Pesh. ܐܦܝ; 21. 1 חפצי בה, Pesh. ܣܒܝܡܒܗ; 21. 18, 26 עזא, Pesh. ܥܠܐ. Cases of double renderings may be found in I. 20. 33 והאנשים ינחשו וימהרו ܘܓܒܪ̈ܐ ܢܚܫܐ ܗܘܘ ܟܕ ܗܘܘ ܓܒܪ̈ܐ ܢܚܫܘ ܘܐܬܡܗܪܘ; 22. 34 לתמו ܠܩܘܒܠܗ ܠܡܫܡܠܝܬ; II. 19. 4 ונשאת תפלה ܘܬܟܠܐ ܘܬܨܠܐ; 19. 28 יען התרגזך אלי ܥܠ ܕܐܬܥܫܢܬ ܘܐܬܪܘܪܒܬ ܥܠܝ.

4. The Latin Versions.

(*a*) The Old Latin Version[1] is known to us only in a fragmentary form. For Kings we possess the fragments collected by Sabatier (chiefly from the Fathers), and published in 1743 in his *Bibliorum Sacrorum Antiquae Versiones Latinae*, vol. i; extracts from the margin of a Gothic MS. (tenth century) at Leon in Spain[2],

[1] The question whether the Old Latin represents one version or several distinct translations is discussed by H. A. A. Kennedy in Hastings, *BD.* iii. p. 48.

[2] It should be noticed, however, that F. C. Burkitt (*The Old Latin and the Itala*, p. 9, in the Cambridge *Texts and Studies*, vol. iv) regards it as 'by no

published by Vercellone in 1864 in *Variae Lectiones Vulgatae Latinae editionis*, vol. ii; *Palimpsestus Vindobonensis*, published by J. Belsheim in 1885, containing I. 11. 41—12. 11; 13. 19–29; 14. 6–15; 15. 34—16. 28; 18. 23–29; II. 6. 6–15; 10. 5–13; 10. 24–30; 13. 14–22; 15. 32–38; 17. 1–6, 15–20; *Ein neues Fragment des Quedlinburger Itala-Codex*, published by A. Düning in 1888, containing I. 5. 9 (MT. 5. 23)—6. 11. To these may be added the quotations in Augustine's *Speculum* (i. e. the *Liber de diuinis scripturis siue Speculum*, which in the N. T. is quoted amongst O. L. MSS. as *m*)[1], not included by Sabatier in his work; and the edition of Lucifer by Hartel (*Corp. Script. Eccles.*, Vienna, 1886) may be used to advantage to check the quotations of Sabatier from this writer. The Version, as based upon the Greek text, possesses a secondary value for the purposes of textual criticism. The fragments of Kings which have survived, especially those from the margin of the Gothic MS., testify to a close connexion of the original Greek with the MSS. which were in later times employed by Lucian in the formation of his recension of the LXX. As might have been expected, the text of the Old Latin is not identical with Luc., many of the doublets and other glosses which are found in Luc. having presumably crept into the Greek text subsequently to the formation of the Latin translation; but, on the whole, the testimony of the Old Latin points to a high antiquity for the type of Greek text preserved by Luc. The following points of connexion between Old Latin and Luc. may be noticed:—

I. 1. 40. Goth. *et populus cantabat canticis et melodiis, et gaudebant gaudio magno; organizantes in organis, et iucundabantur in iucunditate magna; et resonabat omnis terra in voce eorum.*	Luc. *καὶ πᾶς ὁ λαὸς ἐχόρευον ἐν χοροῖς καὶ εὐφραινόμενοι εὐφροσύνῃ μεγάλῃ* **ηὔλουν ἐν αὐλοῖς καὶ ἔχαιρον χαρᾷ μεγάλῃ**, *καὶ ἤχησεν ἡ γῆ ἐν τῇ φωνῇ αὐτῶν.*

means certain that this interesting document does not represent readings extracted and translated from some Greek codex, so that it may have no connexion with the Old Latin properly so called.'

[1] Cf. edit. by F. Weihrich, Vienna, 1887 (*Corp. Script. Eccles.*).

2. 5. Goth. *et uindicavit sanguinem belli in pace; et dedit sanguinem innocentium in uita mea, et zona mea, quae erat circa lumbos meos,&c.*	Luc. *καὶ* **ἐξεδίκησεν** *αἷμα πολέμου ἐν* **εἰρήνῃ καὶ ἔδωκεν αἷμα ἀθῷον** (so Cod. A) *ἐν* **τῇ ζωῇ μου καὶ** *ἐπὶ τῇ ζώνῃ τῆς ὀσφύος μου κ.τ.λ.*
3. 18. Sab. *peperit etiam haec mulier filium.*	Luc. *ἔτεκε καὶ ἡ γυνὴ αὕτη* **υἱόν.**
3. 24. Goth. *Accipite mihi machaeram.*	Luc. *Λάβετέ* **μοι** *μάχαιραν.* So Cod. A.
8. 53. Goth. *Solem statuit in caelo Dominus, et dixit, &c.*	Luc. *Ἥλιον ἔστησεν ἐν οὐρανῷ Κύριος* **καὶ** *εἶπε κ.τ.λ.*
9. 8. Goth. *et domus haec altissima.*	Luc. *καὶ ὁ οἶκος οὗτος ὁ ὑψηλός.*
10. 11. Goth. *trabes multas valde non dolatas.*	Luc. *ξύλα πολλὰ σφόδρα* **ἀπελέκητα.**
10. 26. Goth. *Et erant Salomoni* XL *millia equarum in quadrigis foetantium.*	Luc. *καὶ ἦσαν τῷ Σολομῶντι* **τεσσαράκοντα** (so Cod. A[1]) *χιλιάδες ἵππων θηλειῶν εἰς ἅρματα* **τοῦ τίκτειν.**
10. 28. Goth. *et ex Thecua et ex Damasco erant negotiatores regis.*	Luc. *καὶ ἐκ Θεκουε* **καὶ ἐκ Δαμασκοῦ.** *καὶ οἱ ἔμποροι τοῦ βασιλέως, κ.τ.λ.*
13. 11. Goth. *et pseudo-propheta alius senior.* Sab. *et propheta alius.*	Luc. *καὶ προφήτης* **ἄλλος** *πρεσβύτης.*
14. 27. Goth. *ianuam domus Domini.*	Luc. *τὸν πυλῶνα οἴκου* **κυρίου.**
15. 19. Goth. *Testamentum esto inter me et inter te.*	Luc. *Διαθήκη* **ἔστω** *ἀνὰ μέσον ἐμοῦ καὶ ἀνὰ μέσον σοῦ.*
16. 24 *ff.* Vind. *Ambri.*	Luc. **Ἀμβρί.** Cod. B. *Ζαμβρεί.*
16. 29. Vind. *gasiba.*	Luc. **Γαζουβά.** Cod. B. **Γαβουζά** (עֲזוּבָה MT. 22. 42).
18. 21. Goth. *Usquequo claudicamini utrisque femoribus vestris?*	Luc. *Ἕως πότε ὑμεῖς χωλανεῖτε ἐπ' ἀμφοτέραις ταῖς ἰγνύαις* **ὑμῶν;**
18. 44. Goth. *Adducens aquam de mari.*	Luc. *ἀνάγουσα ὕδωρ* **ἀπὸ θαλάσσης.**
18. 45. Sab. *Et plorabat, et ibat Achab in Iezrael.*	Luc. *καὶ* **ἔκλαιε** (so Cod. A) *καὶ ἐπορεύετο Ἀχαὰβ εἰς Ἰεζραήλ.*
II. 1. 2. Goth. *Et ascendit Ochozias, &c.*	Luc. *καὶ* **ἀνέβη** *Ὀχοζίας κ.τ.λ.*
1. 7. Goth. *Qualis est hominis iustitia qui ascendit obviam vobis?*	Luc. **Τί** *τὸ* **δικαίωμα** *τοῦ ἀνδρὸς τοῦ ἀναβάντος εἰς συνάντησιν ὑμῖν;*
2. 14. Goth. *et transiit per siccum in eremum.*	Luc. *καὶ διῆλθε* **διὰ ξηρᾶς.**
2. 23. Goth. *et lapidabant eum.*	Luc. *καὶ* **ἐλίθαζον** *αὐτόν.*
3. 10. Goth. *vocavit Dominus hos tres reges tradere in manu Moab.*	Luc. *κέκληκε κύριος τοὺς τρεῖς βασιλεῖς* **τούτους παραδοῦναι** *ἡμᾶς εἰς χεῖρας* **Μωάβ.**
3. 20. Goth. *ecce aquae veniebant de via eremi Sur ex Edom.*	Luc. *ἰδοὺ ὕδατα ἤρχετο* **ἐξ** *ὁδοῦ* **τῆς ἐρήμου Σοὺδ ἐξ** *Ἐδώμ.*
4. 16. Goth. *Noli, domine, homo Dei, deridere ancillam tuam.*	Luc. **Μή,** *κύριε* **ἄνθρωπε τοῦ Θεοῦ** (so Cod. A), *μὴ* **ἐκγελάσῃ** *τὴν δούλην σου.*
4. 19. Goth. *Caput doleo.*	Luc. **Τὴν** *κεφαλήν μου* **ἀλγῶ.**

4. 28. Goth. *Si poposci filium a domino, non sic poposci sicut tu fecisti.*	Luc. Μὴ *ᾐτησάμην υἱὸν παρὰ τοῦ κυρίου μου* ; οὐχὶ σὺ πεποίηκας ;
4. 35. Goth. *et inspiravit in eum.*	Luc. καὶ ἐνέπνευσεν ἐπ' αὐτόν.
5. 19. Goth. *chabratha terra.*	Luc. χαβραθὰ τὴν γῆν.
5. 23. Goth. *Et dixit Naaman instantius: Accipe &c.*	Luc. *καὶ* εἶπε Νεε*μὰν* ἐπιεικῶς Λαβὲ κ.τ.λ.
6. 8. Goth. *In locum phalmunum obsessionem faciamus.*	Luc. Εἰς *τὸν τόπον* τὸν φελμουνὶ ποιήσωμεν ἔνεδρον.
9. 17. Goth. *pulverem populi Hieu.*	Luc. *τὸν κονιορτὸν* τοῦ ὄχλου Ἰού.
10. 6. Vind. *accipiat unusquisque nutritorum caput eius quae nutrivit ex filis regis.*	Luc. λαβέτω ἕκαστος *τὴν κεφαλὴν* τοῦ υἱοῦ *τοῦ κυρίου αὐτοῦ.*
10. 11. Goth. *omnes cognatos eius.* Vind. *proximos eius.*	Luc. *πάντας τοὺς* ἀγχιστεύοντας *αὐτοῦ.*
10. 29. Vind. *set a peccatis Hieroboam fili Nabat qui peccare fecit Israel non discessit Ieu rex set abit post uaccas peccati quae erant in Bethel et in Dan.* Goth. *non recessit Hieu, sequens observantiam uaccarum peccati.*	Luc. *πλὴν ἀπὸ ἁμαρτιῶν* Ἰεροβοὰμ *υἱοῦ* Ναβάτ, *ὃς ἐξήμαρτε τὸν* Ἰσραήλ, *οὐκ ἀπέστη ἀπ' αὐτῶν* Ἰού· ὀπίσω αὐτῶν ἐπορεύετο, *τῶν δαμάλεων* τῆς ἁμαρτίας *τῶν χρυσῶν τῶν ἐν* Βαιθὴλ *καὶ ἐν* Δάν.
10. 36. Goth. + *Et erat annus (secundus) Gotholiae cum regnare coepisset Hieu filius Namesse, &c.*	Luc. + ἐν ἔτει δευτέρῳ τῆς Γοθολίας βασιλεύει κύριος τὸν Ἰοὺ υἱὸν Ναμεσσί, κ.τ.λ. (cf. *note ad loc.*).
11. 12. Goth. *dedit super eum sanctificationem.*	Luc. *ἔδωκεν ἐπ' αὐτὸν* τὸ ἁγίασμα.
11. 14. Goth. *et scidit Gotholia vestimentum suum.*	Luc. *καὶ διέρρηξε* τὸ ἱματισμὸν αὐτῆς Γοθολία.
13. 15. Goth. *Accipe sagittam et bolidas.*	Luc. Λαβὲ *τόξον καὶ* βολίδας.
13. 17. Vind. *et sagitta salutis in Israel.*	Luc. *καὶ βέλος σωτηρίας ἐν* Ἰσραήλ.
16. 18. Goth. *mesech sabbathorum.*	Luc. *τὸν θεμέλιον τῆς καθέδρας* τῶν σαββάτων.
17. 2. Goth. *Et fecit malignum in conspectu Domini prae omnibus qui fuerunt ante eum.*	Luc. *καὶ ἐποίησε τὸ πονηρὸν ἐνώπιον κυρίου* παρὰ πάντας τοὺς γενομένους *ἔμπροσθεν αὐτοῦ.*
17. 4. Goth. *Et invenit rex Assyriorum in Osee cogitationem adversus eum, et misit nuntios Adramelec Aegyptium inhabitantem in Aegypto, et erat ferens munera regi Assyriorum ab anno in annum.* Vind. *et misit nuntios at Adramelec Ethiopem habitantem in Aegypto, et offerebat Osee munera regi Assyriorum ab anno in annum.*	Luc. *καὶ εὗρεν ὁ βασιλεὺς* Ἀσσυρίων *ἐν* Ὡσῆε ἐπιβουλήν, *δι' ὅτι ἀπέστειλεν ἀγγέλους πρὸς* Ἀδραμελὲχ τὸν Αἰθίοπα τὸν κατοικοῦντα ἐν Αἰγύπτῳ, καὶ ἦν Ὡσῆε φέρων δῶρα τῷ βασιλεῖ Ἀσσυρίων ἐνιαυτὸν κατ' ἐνιαυτόν.

17. 4. Vind. *et iniuriam fecit ei rex Assyriorum.*	Luc. καὶ ὕβρισε τὸν Ὡσῆε ὁ βασιλεὺς Ἀσσυρίων.
18. 34. Goth. + *Ubi sunt dii terrae Samariae?*	Luc. + καὶ ποῦ εἰσὶν οἱ θεοὶ τῆς χώρας Σαμαρείας;
19. 7. Goth. *auditionem malignam.*	Luc. ἀγγελίαν πονηράν.
23. 11. Lucifer + *in domo domus, quam aedificauerunt reges Israel excelso illi Babal et omni militiae caeli.*	Luc. + ἐν τῷ οἴκῳ ᾧ ᾠκοδόμησαν βασιλεῖς Ἰσραὴλ ὑψηλὸν τῷ Βάαλ καὶ πάσῃ τῇ στρατιᾷ τοῦ οὐρανοῦ.

(*b*) The general characteristics of the Vulgate of the Old Testament have been dealt with by Nowack, *Die Bedeutung des Hieronymus für die alttestamentliche Textkritik* (Göttingen, 1875). Cf. also H. J. White in Hastings, *BD.* iv. pp. 883 *f.* Jerome describes his method of translation in the introduction to his commentary on Ecclesiastes. He claims for his version a certain independence, as a direct translation from the original Hebrew; but states at the same time that he has kept fairly closely to the LXX where there is no great discrepancy between this version and the Hebrew, and confesses to having had before him and made use of the versions of Aquila, Symmachus, and Theodotion[1]. Instances from Kings of Jerome's employment of these later Greek versions may be noticed; and it will be seen that here, as in other books, the version of Symmachus seems to have been most frequently used as a model:—

I. 4. 13. לו חבל ארגב Σ. καὶ αὐτὸς εἶχε τὸ περίμετρον τοῦ Ἀργάβ, Vulg. *ipse praeerat in omni regione Argob.*

6. 8. בלולים Ἀ. (καὶ ἐν) κοχλίαις, Vulg. *per cochleam.*

9. 18. במדבר בארץ Ἀ., Σ. τὴν ἐν τῇ γῇ τῆς ἐρήμου, Vulg. *in terra solitudinis.*

10. 28. ומקוה Ἄλλος· καὶ ἐκ Κωά, Vulg. *et de Coa.*

---

[1] '. . ., hoc breuiter admonens, quod nullius auctoritatem secutus sum; sed de Hebraeo transferens, magis me Septuaginta interpretum consuetudini coaptaui: in his dumtaxat quae non multum ab Hebraicis discrepabant. Interdum Aquilae quoque et Symmachi et Theodotionis recordatus sum, ut nec nouitate nimia lectoris studium deterrerem, nec rursum contra conscientiam meam, fonte ueritatis omisso, opinionum riuulos consectarer.'

11. 36. למען היות ניר Σ. *ὑπὲρ τοῦ διαμένειν λύχνον*, Vulg. *ut remaneat lucerna.*

12. 7. ועניתם 'A., Σ. *καὶ εἴξεις αὐτοῖς*, Vulg. *et petitioni eorum cesseris.*

16. 3. מבעיר אחרי בעשא Σ. *τρυγήσω τὰ ὀπίσω* (Βαασά), Vulg. *demetam posteriora Baasa.*

20. 12. בסכות 'A. *ἐν συσκιασμοῖς*, Vulg. *in umbraculis.* Similarly in *v.* 16.

20. 38. באפר 'A. *ἐν σποδῷ*, Σ. *σποδῷ*, Vulg. *aspersione pulveris.*

20. 40. כן משפטך אתה חרצת Ἄλλος· *τοῦτο τὸ κρίμα ὃ σὺ ἔτεμες*, Vulg. *Hoc est iudicium tuum, quod ipse decreuisti.*

II. 3. 4. היה נקד Σ. *ἦν τρέφων βοσκήματα*, Vulg. *nutriebat pecora multa.*

4. 7. ושלמי את נשיכי Σ. *καὶ ἀπόδος τῷ δανειστῇ σου*, Vulg. *et redde creditori tuo.*

9. 11. ואת שיחו 'A., Σ. *καὶ τὴν ὁμιλίαν αὐτοῦ*, Vulg. *et quid locutus est.*

11. 10. השלטים Σ. *τὴν πανοπλίαν*, Vulg. *arma.*

12. 6. והם יחזקו את בדק הבית לכל אשר ימצא שם בדק Σ. *καὶ αὐτοὶ ἐπισκευασάτωσαν τὰ δέοντα τοῦ οἴκου, ὅπου ἂν εὑρεθῇ δεόμενον ἐπισκευῆς*, Vulg. *et instaurent sarta tecta domus, si quid necessarium viderint instauratione.*

23. 12. וירץ משם 'A. *καὶ ἐδρόμωσεν ἀπὸ ἐκεῖθεν*, Vulg. *et cucurrit inde.*

23. 24. הגללים 'A. *τὰ μορφώματα*, Vulg. *figuras idolorum.*

The Hebrew text employed by Jerome seems to have been very similar to, though not identical with, MT.[1] His version possesses the characteristics of a good translation, and aims at giving the sense of the original rather than at extreme literality of rendering. Phrases and sentences are sometimes filled out in order to make their meaning clearer; cf. I. 2. 40 וילך שמעי ויבא את עבדיו מגת *ivitque ad Achis in Geth ad requirendum servos suos, et adduxit eos de Gath;* 3. 5 שאל מה אתן לך *Postula quod vis ut dem tibi;* 3. 13

[1] Cf. Nowack, *op. cit.* p. 55.

כל ימיך *cunctis retro diebus;* 6. 27 וכנפיהם *alae autem alterae;* 8. 24. כיום הזה *ut haec dies probat.* Occasionally, though not often, the translator goes astray in his desire for lucidity; cf. I. 1. 41[b] ויאמר מדוע קול קריה הומה *sed et Ioab, audita voce tubae, ait; 'Quid sibi &c.';* 16. 7 ועל אשר הכה אתו *ob hanc causam occidit eum, hoc est, Iehu filium Hanani, prophetam.*

§ 3. *The Synchronisms of the Compiler.*

The table on the following page exhibits a scheme of the synchronisms of R^D, as they appear in MT., LXX, and Luc. The upward pointing arrow ↑ indicates a discrepancy with a preceding calculation, the downward pointing arrow ↓ a discrepancy with a calculation following; while the double-headed arrow ↕ points to disagreement both with the preceding and following.

Examination of the three columns makes the fact plain that Luc. exhibits a different scheme of synchronism to MT. from Omri of Israel (I. 16. 23) down to Jehoram of Israel (I. 1. 17). This scheme conflicts with the synchronisms which go before and follow after, and which belong to the system of MT.; but, so far as it goes, is self-consistent, and is the cause of the placing of the narrative of Jehoshaphat's reign (MT. I. 22. 41 *ff.*) before that of Aḥab at the close of I. 16 in both Luc. and LXX, and of the substitution of Ὀχοζίας for יהושפט in the narrative of II. 3 in Luc. On the other hand, LXX, which agrees partly with Luc. and partly with MT., is clearly a patchwork of the two schemes. Two traces of the scheme of Luc. have crept into MT.; viz. in I. 16. 23, where the synchronism according to MT. scheme should be the 27th or 28th year of Asa; and in II. 1. 17, where the Lucianic synchronism co-exists with that of MT. in II. 3. 1. The other inconsistencies of MT. are probably for the most part due to textual corruption. Thus in II. 13. 10 the reading of 39th for 37th brings about agreement both with the preceding and following synchronisms; in II. 15. 1 the substitution of 14th for 27th removes

			MT.		LXX.		Luc.	
	Kingdom.	*King.*	*Length of reign.*	*Synchronism.*	*Length of reign.*	*Synchronism.*	*Length of reign.*	*Synchronism.*
I. 14. 20	I	Jeroboam	22	—	↓22	—	↓22	—
I. 14. 21	J	Reḥoboam	17	—	17	—	17	—
I. 15. 1	J	Abijah	3	18th of Jeroboam	6	18th of Jeroboam	6	18th of Jeroboam
I. 15. 9	J	Asa	41	20th of Jeroboam	41	↑24th of Jeroboam	41	↑24th of Jeroboam
I. 15. 25	I	Nadab	2	2nd of Asa	2	2nd of Asa	2	2nd of Asa
I. 15. 33	I	Ba'asha	24	3rd of Asa	24	3rd of Asa	24	3rd of Asa
I. 16. 8	I	Elah	2	26th of Asa	2	↑20th of Asa (*v.* 6)	2	↑20th of Asa (*v.* 6)
I. 16. 15	I	Zimri	—	27th of Asa	7	wanting	—	22nd of Asa
I. 16. 23	I	Omri	12	↕31st of Asa	12	↑31st of Asa	12	↑31st of Asa
I. 16. 29	I	Aḥab	22	38th of Asa	22	2nd of Jehoshaphat	22	2nd of Jehoshaphat
I. 22. 41	J	Jehoshaphat	25	4th of Aḥab	25	↓11th of Omri (16. 28 *f.*)	25	11th of Omri (16. 28 *f.*)
					25	4th of Aḥab		
I. 22. 52	I	Aḥaziah	2	17th of Jehoshaphat	2	17th of Jehoshaphat	2	24th of Jehoshaphat
II. 1. 17	I	Jehoram		↑2nd of Jehoram J	12	18th of Jehoshaphat	12	↓2nd of Jehoram J
II. 3. 1	,,	,,	12	18th of Jehoshaphat	12	18th of Jehoshaphat	12	
II. 8. 16	J	Jehoram	8	5th of Jehoram I	↓40	5th of Jehoram I	8	↑5th of Jehoram I
II. 8. 25	J	Aḥaziah	1	12th of Jehoram I	1	12th of Jehoram I	1	11th of Jehoram I
II. 9. 29	,,	,,		11th of Jehoram I		11th of Jehoram I	1	11th of Jehoram I
II. 10. 35	I	Jehu	28	—	28	—	28	—

II. 11. 3	J	Athaliah	6	—	6	—	6	—
II. 12. 2	J	Jehoash	40	7th of Jehu	40	7th of Jehu	40	7th of Jehu
II. 13. 1	I	Jehoaḥaz	17	23rd of Jehoash J	17	23rd of Jehoash J	17	23rd of Jehoash J
II. 13. 10	I	Jehoash	16	↕37th of Jehoash J	16	↕37th of Jehoash J	16	↕37th of Jehoash J
II. 14. 1	J	Amaziah	29	2nd of Jehoash I	29	2nd of Jehoash I	29	2nd of Jehoash I
II. 14. 23	I	Jeroboam	41	15th of Amaziah	41	15th of Amaziah	41	15th of Amaziah
II. 15. 1	J	Azariah	52	↕27th of Jeroboam	52	↕27th of Jeroboam	52	↕27th of Jeroboam
II. 15. 8	I	Zechariah	½	38th of Azariah	½	38th of Azariah	½	38th of Azariah
II. 15. 13	I	Shallum	1/12	39th of Azariah	—	39th of Azariah	1/12	39th of Azariah
II. 15. 17	I	Menaḥem	10	39th of Azariah	10	39th of Azariah	10	39th of Azariah
II. 15. 23	I	Pekaḥiah	2	50th of Azariah	2	50th of Azariah	↓10	50th of Azariah
II. 15. 27	I	Pekaḥ	20	52nd of Azariah	20	52nd of Azariah	20	52nd of Azariah
II. 15. 32	J	Jotham	16	2nd of Pekaḥ	16	2nd of Pekaḥ	16	2nd of Pekaḥ
II. 16. 1	J	Aḥaz	16	17th of Pekaḥ	16	17th of Pekaḥ	16	17th of Pekaḥ
II. 17. 1	I	Hoshea	9	↑12th of Aḥaz	9	↑12th of Aḥaz	9	↑12th of Aḥaz
II. 18. 1	J	Ḥezekiah	29	3rd of Hoshea	29	3rd of Hoshea	29	3rd of Hoshea
II. 21. 1	J	Manasseh	55	—	55	—	55	—
II. 22. 1	J	Josiah	31	—	31	—	31	—
II. 23. 31	J	Jehoaḥaz	¼	—	¼	—	¼	—
II. 23. 36	J	Jehoiakim	11	—	11	—	11	—
II. 24. 8	J	Jehoiachin	¼	—	¼	—	¼	—
II. 24. 18	J	Zedekiah	11	—	11	—	11	—

the double inconsistency, if we make R^D assign 51 years to the reign of Jeroboam II in place of the 41 years of II. 14. 23. The 12th year of Aḥaz in II. 17. 1, which disagrees with preceding synchronisms, is in agreement with the ten years assigned to Pekaḥiah in Luc. II. 15. 23 in place of the two years of MT.; and thus may belong to a different scheme.

The inconsistencies of R^D's system of chronology, as compared with the chronology of the period as known to us from the Assyrian inscriptions, are conveniently stated in G. W. Wade's *Old Testament History*, pp. 319 *ff*.

LIST OF PRINCIPAL ABBREVIATIONS EMPLOYED.

'A. = Aquila's Greek Version, as cited in Field, *Origenis Hexaplorum quae supersunt*, and in F. C. Burkitt, *Fragments of the Books of Kings according to the translation of Aquila* (3 Kgs. 21 (20 MT.) 7–17; 4 Kgs. 23. 12–27), 1897.

AV. = Authorized Version.

Baed. = K. Baedeker, *Palestine and Syria*, 3rd edit., 1898.

Benz. = I. Benzinger, *Die Bücher der Könige*, 1899.

Ber. = E. Bertheau, *Die Bücher der Chronik*, 2e Aufl., 1873.

Bö. = F. Böttcher, *Neue exegetisch-kritische Aehrenlese zum A. T. 2e Abtheilung*, 1864.

Buhl, *Geogr.* = F. Buhl, *Geographie des alten Palästina*, 1896.

CIG. = *Corpus Inscriptionum Graecarum.*

CIS. = *Corpus Inscriptionum Semiticarum.*

Cod. A. = *Codex Alexandrinus* of the Septuagint.

COT. = E. Schrader, *The Cuneiform Inscriptions and the O. T.* (trans. from the 2nd German edit.), 1885.

D^2 = The Deuteronomic editor (in citations from Joshua and Judges).

DB.^{2} or *BD.*^{2} = *Dictionary of the Bible*, ed. by W. Smith, 2nd edit. of vol. i, 1893.

Dri. = S. R. Driver.

Authority = *Authority and Archaeology Sacred and Profane*, 1899.

Deut. = *A Critical and Exegetical Commentary on Deuteronomy* (Internat. Crit. Series), 1895.

LOT^6 = *An Introduction to the Literature of the O. T.*, 6th edit., 1897.

Sam. = *Notes on the Hebrew Text of the Books of Samuel*, 1890.

Tenses = *A Treatise on the Use of the Tenses in Hebrew*, 3rd edit., 1892.

E = The Elohistic document in the Hexateuch.

Encyc. Bibl. = *Encyclopaedia Biblica*, ed. by T. K. Cheyne and J. Sutherland Black, 1899 *ff*.

Ew. = H. Ewald, *History of Israel*, vols. iii and iv, 1871.

Ew. § = H. Ewald, *Syntax of the Hebrew Language of the O. T.* (trans. from the 8th German edit.), 1881.

Field = F. Field, *Origenis Hexaplorum quae supersunt; sive veterum interpretum Graecorum in totum V. T. fragmenta*, 1875.

Ges. or Ges. *Thes.* = W. Gesenius, *Thesaurus linguae Hebraeae*, 1829.

Ges.-Buhl = *W. Gesenius' Heb. und Aram. Handwörterbuch über das A. T.*, bearbeitet von F. Buhl, 13e Aufl., 1899.

G-K. = *Gesenius' Hebrew Grammar, as edited and enlarged by E. Kautzsch* (trans. from the 26th German edit. by A. E. Cowley, 1898).

Grä. = H. Grätz, *Geschichte der Israeliten*, 1875.

H = The code known as 'the Law of Holiness' in Leviticus.

Hastings, *BD.* = *Dictionary of the Bible*, ed. by J. Hastings, 1898–1902.

Heb. Lex. Oxf. = *A Heb. and Eng. Lexicon of the O. T., based on the Lexicon of Gesenius as translated by E. Robinson*, ed. by F. Brown, S. R. Driver, and C. A. Briggs, Oxford, 1892 *ff*.

Hoo. = I. Hooykaas, *Iets over de grieksche vertaling van het Oude Testament*, 1888.

J = The Jahvistic document in the Hexateuch.

JE = The work of the compiler of the documents J and E in the Hexateuch.

Jos. = *Flavii Iosephi Opera*, recognovit B. Niese, 1888.

Kamp. = A. Kamphausen, *Die Bücher der Könige*, in E. Kautzsch's *Die Heilige Schrift des A. T.*, 1894.

KAT.[3] = *Die Keilinschriften und das A. T.*, von E. Schrader, 3e Aufl. neu bearbeitet von H. Zimmern und H. Winckler, 1e Hälfte, 1902.

Kau. = E. Kautzsch, *Abriss der Geschichte des alttest. Schrifttums*, in *Die Heilige Schrift des A. T.*, 1894.

KB. = *Keilinschriftliche Bibliothek*, Bde 1, 2, 1889–1890.

Ke. = C. F. Keil, *Die Bücher der Könige*, 2e Aufl., 1876.
Kit. = R. Kittel, *Die Bücher der Könige*, 1900.
Kit. *Hist.* = R. Kittel, *A History of the Hebrews*, vol. ii, trans., 1896.
Klo. = A. Klostermann, *Die Bücher Samuelis und der Könige*, 1887.
Kö. = F. E. König.
Lehrg. = *Hist.-krit. Lehrgebäude der Heb. Sprache:* 1e Hälfte, 1881; 2e Hälfte, 1er Theil, 1895.
Syntax = *Hist.-compar. Syntax der Heb. Sprache*, 1897.
Kue. = A. Kuenen.
Ond. = *Hist.-krit. Onderzoek*, 2nd edit., 1887 (German trans., 1890).
Hex. = *The Origin and Composition of the Hexateuch* (trans. of part 1 of the preceding), 1886.
Luc. = Lucian's recension of the Septuagint as edited by P. Lagarde (*Librorum V. T. canonicorum pars prior*, 1883).
LXX = Cod. B of the Septuagint according to the text of H. B. Swete (*The O. T. in Greek according to the Septuagint*, vol. i, 1887).
Maspero = G. Maspero, *Histoire ancienne des peuples de l'Orient classique*, 3 vols., 1895–1899.
MT. = Massoretic Text (D. Ginsburg, 1894; Baer and Delitzsch, 1895).
Oort = *Textus Hebraici emendationes quibus in V. T. neerlandice vertendo usi sunt A. Kuenen, I. Hooykaas, W. H. Kosters, H. Oort*, edidit H. Oort, 1900.
P = The Priestly Code in the Hexateuch.
PEF. = *Palestine Exploration Fund.*
Mem. = *Memoirs.*
Qy. St. = *Quarterly Statement.*
Pesh. = Peshiṭto (ed. Lee).
R^D = The Deuteronomic Redactor of Kings (cf. pp. ix *ff.*).
R^{D2} = Later Deuteronomic Editors of Kings (cf. p. xviii).
R^P = The Priestly Redactor (or Redactors) of Kings (cf. p. xix).
Rob. *BR.* = E. Robinson, *Biblical Researches in Palestine and the adjacent Regions*, 3rd edit., 3 vols., 1867.

Rost = P. Rost, *Die Keilschrifttexte Tiglat-Pilesers III*, 1893.
R. Sm. = W. Robertson Smith.
OTJC[2] = *The Old Testament in the Jewish Church*, 2nd edit., 1892.
Rel. Sem.[2] = *The Religion of the Semites*, 2nd edit., 1894.
RV. = Revised Version.
Σ. = Symmachus' Greek Version, as cited in Field, *Origenis Hexaplorum quae supersunt.*
Sieg. u. Sta. = C. Siegfried und B. Stade, *Hebräisches Wörterbuch zum A. T.*, 1893.
Smith, *Hist. Geogr.* = G. A. Smith, *The Historical Geography of the Holy Land*, 1894.
Sta. = B. Stade, various articles on the text of Kings in *ZATW.*
Sta. § = B. Stade, *Lehrbuch der Hebräischen Grammatik*, 1er Theil, 1875.
Stanley, *SP.* = A. P. Stanley, *Sinai and Palestine in Connection with their History*, new edit., 1883.
Θ. = Theodotion's Greek version, as cited in Field, *Origenis Hexaplorum quae supersunt.*
Targ. = The Targum of Jonathan (ed. Lagarde).
Th. = O. Thenius, *Die Bücher der Könige*, 2e Aufl., 1873.
Vet. Lat. = The Old Latin Version.
Vulg. = The Vulgate.
Wellh. *C.* = J. Wellhausen, *Die Composition des Hexateuchs und der historischen Bücher des A. T.*, 1889.
ZA. = *Zeitschrift für Assyriologie.*
ZATW. = *Zeitschrift für die alttest. Wissenschaft.*

al. = *et aliter*, 'and elsewhere.'
וג׳ = וְגוֹמַר = '&c.'
פ׳ = פְּלֹנִי = 'such a one (unnamed).'
† indicates that all occurrences in O. T. of a particular word or phrase have been cited.

NOTES

ON

THE BOOKS OF KINGS

I. 1. 1–2. 46. *Close of the history of David. Establishment of Solomon as his successor*[1].

1. 1. בא בימים] A regular idiom. Lit. '*entered into days*,' just as we should say, *advanced in years*. So Gen. 18. 11; 24. 1; Josh. 13. 1; 23. 1, 2 †.

בַּבְּגָדִים] 'With *the* clothes,' which are immediately suggested to the reader by the previous ויכסהו. This use of the article with well-known objects is very common in Heb., and imparts a peculiar vividness to the narrative. Cf. *v.* 39 אֶת־קֶרֶן הַשֶּׁמֶן, בַּשּׁוֹפָר; *ch.* 17. 10 בַּכְּלִי 'in *the* vessel,' almost, 'in *your* vessel,' *v.* 12 בַּכַּד 'in *the* jar,' used in every household for the purpose specified; II. 8. 15; 1 Sam. 10. 25; 18. 10; *al.* Da. § 21[d].

ולא יחם לו] The imperfect expresses the habitual character of the king's condition: 'he *was not*,' or, '*used not to be* warm.' This usage is somewhat rare in prose: cf. *ch.* 8. 8 וְלֹא יֵרָאוּ הַחוּצָה; Gen. 2. 25 וְלֹא יִתְבֹּשָׁשׁוּ; 1 Sam. 1. 7[b] וְלֹא תֹאכַל; 2. 25[b] וְלֹא יִשְׁמְעוּ. Dri. *Tenses*, §§ 30, 42 β, 85 *Obs.*

2. אדני המלך] A ceremonious form of address which is almost constant. המלך אדני 2 Sam. 14. 15 † (cf. המ׳ אדניך 1 Sam. 26. 15 †). המלך alone is comparatively rare.

---

[1] This section forms the continuation of 2 Sam. *chh.* 9–20, and is probably by the same author. See Dri. *LOT.* 179, and especially Wellh. *C.* 260.

נערה בתולה] A common form of apposition, the second substantive defining more closely the meaning of the first. Cf. *ch.* 3. 16 נָשִׁים זֹנוֹת; *ch.* 7. 14 אִשָּׁה אַלְמָנָה; Deut. 22. 28; Gen. 21. 20 רֹבֶה קַשָּׁת; Isa. 23. 12 הַמְעֻשָּׁקָה בְּתוּלַת וגו׳; *al.* G-K. § 131, 2[a]; Ew. § 287[e] ([b]): Da. § 29[b].

ועמדה] 'And let her stand.' Imperf. with ו *consec.* the continuation of the cohortative יבקשו. Dri. *Tenses*, § 113, 2; Da. § 55[a]. The phrase עמד לפני is used idiomatically of those who were in constant attendance upon a superior: cf. *ch.* 10. 8; 12. 8 (‖ 2 Chr. 10. 6); Jer. 52. 12; Deut. 1. 38. Of the service of יהוה, *ch.* 17. 1; Ezek. 44. 15; Judg. 20. 28; *al.*

סכנת] 'Attendant,' 'care-taker'; in the masc. סֹכֵן Isa. 22. 15 as a title of Shebna the superintendent of the palace, and also, it seems, in a Phoenician inscription from Lebanon belonging probably to the eighth century B.C., of a guardian or governor of a city, סכן קרתחדשת עבד חרם מלך צדנם 'Soken of the New City, servant of Ḥiram, king of the Sidonians,' *CIS.* I. i. 5.

The word—unless Cheyne is right in connecting it (*Isaiah.* ii. 153) with the Assyrian *šaknu*, 'a high officer,' from *šakin*, 'to set up, place'—will be derived from סכן which in the Hiph'il means to *deal familiarly with;* Num. 22. 30 הַהַסְכֵּן הִסְכַּנְתִּי לַעֲשׂוֹת 'Did I ever deal familiarly to do?' i.e. 'was I ever wont to do?' Ps. 139. 3 כָּל־דְּרָכַי הִסְכַּנְתָּה 'With all my ways thou art familiar'; Job 22. 21 הַסְכֶּן־נָא עִמּוֹ 'Become familiar with him.'

Pesh. ܡܫܡܫܢܝܬܐ 'serving'; LXX, Vulg. more freely *θάλπουσα*, foveat; Targ. קריבא '*near* to him.'

בחיקך] So Pesh., Θ., 'Ο Ἑβραῖος (Syro-Hex. ܥ. ܠ. ܒܥܘܒܟ), Targ. (לותך); בחיקו LXX, Luc., Vulg. There is no reason for doubting the originality of MT. Such a change from 3rd to 2nd pers. is quite in accordance with Hebrew usage in cases in which a superior is addressed. Cf. 1 Sam. 25. 28 כִּי־מִלְחֲמוֹת יְהוָֹה אֲדֹנִי נִלְחָם וְרָעָה לֹא־תִמָּצֵא בְךָ מִיָּמֶיךָ; 22. 15; *al.*

3. השונמית] Vulg. *Sunamitidem*, Targ. דמן שונם, LXX, Luc. Σωμανῖτιν, Pesh. ܫܘܢܡܝܬܐ. The title השונמית is also applied (II. 4. 12, &c.) to Elisha's hostess at Shunem. הַשּׁוּלַמִּית, Song 7. 1,

is usually thought to be a variation; cf. rendering of Pesh., and modern name of the village.

שׁוּנֵם was one of the cities assigned to the tribe of Issachar, Josh. 19. 18; 1 Sam. 28. 4 it is mentioned as the place where the Philistines encamped, near to the Israelite encampment at גִּלְבֹּעַ, and also to עֵין דּוֹר *v.* 7; II. 4. 8†, a city visited by Elisha, not very far from Mt. Carmel, *v.* 25. The site appears to have been that of the modern *Solam*, a village on the south-west slope of the *Jebel Nebi Daḥi* (called 'little Hermon'), about five miles north of *Jebel Fuk'ua* (Mt. Gilboa), and three miles north of *Zer'in* (Jezreel). Cf. Rob. *BR.* ii. 324; Stanley, *SP.* 344; Baed. 243.

4. יפה] So LXX, Vulg., Targ.; יְפַת מַרְאֶה Luc., Pesh. Though יְפַת תֹּאַר, יְפַת מַרְאֶה are common expressions, yet יפה used absolutely is still more frequent. MT. may therefore be retained.

5. מתנשא] The participle expresses the *continuous* development of Adonijah's plans, Dri. *Tenses*, § 135, 1. A single event of brief duration, such as the open declaration of his claims, would have been represented by the perf., or by the imperf. with ו *consec.*

ויעש] 'He made,' i.e. '*instituted.*' For this use of עשה, cf. 2 Sam. 15. 1 וַיַּעַשׂ לוֹ אַבְשָׁלוֹם מֶרְכָּבָה וג׳.

רצים לפניו] The usual bodyguard of a king. Cf 1 Sam. 22. 17; *ch.* 14. 28; II. 11. 4; *al.*

6. ולא עצבו] 'Had not *grieved* him.' עצב means *to hurt*, either bodily, Eccl. 10. 9 מַסִּיעַ אֲבָנִים יֵעָצֵב בָּהֶם, or mentally, Isa. 54. 6 עֲצוּבַת רוּחַ; 2 Sam. 19. 3, such mental pain sometimes culminating in *anger*, as seems to be the case here and in 1 Sam. 20. 3, 34; Gen. 34. 7. LXX καὶ οὐκ ἀπεκώλυσεν αὐτόν seems to presuppose וְלֹא עֲצָרוֹ 'had not *held him back*'; cf. 18. 44. So Klo. Against this reading is the following עשית which, as used of a past event, is opposed to the notion of holding back *before* an action. The other Verss. give the sense 'reprove,' and seem to be guessing from the context; Luc. καὶ οὐκ ἐπετίμησεν αὐτῷ, Vulg. *nec corripuit eum*, Pesh. ܘܠܐ ܟܠܐ ܗܘ, Targ. ולא אכלימה.

מימיו] '*Out of* his days'; i.e. at any time during the whole course of his life. An idiomatic expression; cf. 1 Sam. 25. 28

וְרָעָה לֹא־תִמָּצֵא בְךָ מִיָּמֶיךָ; Job 38. 12† הֲמִיָּמֶיךָ צִוִּיתָ בֹּקֶר[1]. '*Ever*,' as used in English, will be found to fit each of these cases.

ואתו ילדה אחרי אבשלום] The object, as being the interesting member of the sentence, is brought to the beginning and receives a slight emphasis. This is not uncommon. Cf. 1 Sam. 15. 1 אתי שלח יהוה; 25. 43; *ch.* 14. 11; *al.* Dri. *Tenses*, § 208, 1.

ילדה] '*One* bore.' A semi-impersonal use of the verb; *sc.* הַיֹּלֶדֶת. RV., by accommodation to Eng. idiom, substitutes a pass.; '*He was born*.' Cf. *ch.* 14. 10 כַּאֲשֶׁר יְבַעֵר הַגָּלָל 'as *one* sweeps away dung,' or, 'as dung is swept away'; *ch.* 22. 38 וַיִּשְׁטֹף; *al.* The assumed cognate participle as subj. is sometimes actually expressed; Deut. 22. 8; Isa. 28. 4. Ew. § 294^b, Da. § 108, *Rem.* 1. Klo.'s emendation וְאִשְׁתּוֹ יָלְדָה אֲחוֹת אַבְשָׁלוֹם is quite unnecessary.

7. ויהיו דבריו עם יואב] 'And his words (i.e. *negotiations*) were with Joab.' The idiom is similar to 2 Sam. 3. 17 ודבר אבנר היה עם זקני ישראל; cf. Judg. 18. 7, 28 ודבר אין להם עם אדם.

ויעזרו אחרי אדניה] A pregnant construction; RV. 'and they following Adonijah helped him.' Cf. Deut. 12. 30 השמר לך פן תנקש אחריהם; 1 Sam. 7. 2 וַיִּנָּהוּ אחרי י׳ 'went mourning after'; Ruth 2. 3 ותלקט אחרי; *ch.* 14. 10 ובערתי אחרי; 16. 3 מבעיר אחרי; Jer. 50. 21 החרם אחרי; Lev. 26. 33 והריקתי אחריכם חרב; Ezek. 5. 2, 12; 12. 14; Deut. 1. 36, *al.* מִלֵּא אחרי.

8. שמעי ורעי] These persons are not mentioned elsewhere as holding positions of importance about the court of David or Solomon. Neither שמעי, one of the twelve officers who provided victuals for Solomon's household (*ch.* 4. 18), nor שמעי the Benjamite of Gera seems to have been of sufficient importance to satisfy the mention in this passage; and the name רעי occurs nowhere else. Hence, the text is probably corrupt. Among suggested emendations, the most worthy of notice is that of Klo. who follows Luc. καὶ Σαμαίας καὶ οἱ ἑταῖροι αὐτοῦ, i.e. ושמעיה וְרֵעָיו, so far as regards the

---

[1] Job 27. 6 לֹא־יֶחֱרַף לְבָבִי מִיָּמָי is similar if with RV. we supply an object '*me*' to יחרף; 'my heart shall never reproach me.' But more obviously the object is found in מימי; 'my heart shall not reproach *any one of* my days.'

second word, and emends the first ושלמה. This suggestion וּשְׁלֹמֹה וְרֵעָיו is to some extent supported by the enumeration in *v.* 10, and would imply that the other princes *did* side with Adonijah, as seems to have been the case from *v.* 19 ויקרא לכל בני המלך. Th.'s emendation וְחוּשַׁי רֵעֶה דָוִד, derived partly from Jos.'s explanation of ורעי as ὁ Δαυίδου φίλος, is plausible. LXX, Vulg., Pesh., Targ. agree with MT.

הגבורים] David's army of picked warriors; 2 Sam. 10. 7; 16. 6; 20. 7; 1 Chr. 19. 8; 28. 1; 29. 24; Song 4. 4. The names of the principal men among them are given in 2 Sam. 23. 8–39; ‖ 1 Chr. 11. 11–47.

אשר לדוד] This construction takes the place of the *stat. constr.* because הַגִּבּוֹרִים (with the article) was the regular title for the army mentioned, and is regarded almost as a proper name, Da. § 28, *Rem.* 5[3]. Such a method of avoiding the *stat. constr.* is especially frequent with proper names; Judg. 18. 28; 19. 14 הַגִּבְעָה אֲשֶׁר לְבִנְיָמִן; *ch.* 15. 27; 17. 9; *al.*

9. עם אבן הזחלת] An idiomatic use of עם; '*by*' or '*close to.*' Cf. Gen. 35. 4 האלה אשר עם שכם; Josh. 7. 2; Judg. 18. 3; 19. 11; 2 Sam. 20. 8; *al.*

הזחלת] 'The serpent'; so called from *crawling;* Deut. 32. 24 זֹחֲלֵי עָפָר; Mic. 7. 17†. This root corresponds to Ar. زحل *to withdraw, lag behind,* and is quite distinct from זחלתי Job 32. 6 = Ar. ذحل = Aram. ܕܚܠ *to fear.* Wellh. (*Reste Arab. Heidentums*, 2e Ausg. 146) compares הזחלת with the Ar. name of Saturn, *Zuḥal*, i.e. (Lane, *Lex.*, 1220) *he who withdraws*, the planet being so named because it is remote, and said to be in the Seventh Heaven.

עין רגל] Pesh. ܥܝܢ ܩܨܪܐ, Targ. עין קצרא, i.e. *spring of the fuller*, רגל being used of *treading* linen with the feet. Mentioned as one of the landmarks upon the boundary line between Judah, Josh. 15. 7, and Benjamin, Josh. 18. 16; during Absalom's rebellion the hiding-place of Jonathan and Ahimaaz whilst awaiting news from Jerusalem, 2 Sam. 17. 17†. The spring has with great probability been identified with the modern 'Fountain of the Virgin,' called '*Ain Umm ed-Deraj*, i.e. 'spring of the mother of steps,' the source which supplies the pool of Siloam. Opposite the fountain there is a rough flight of stone steps leading up the rock to the village of Siloam, and called by the fellaḥîn *Ez-Zehweileh*, i.e. זחלת. See *PEF. Qy. St.*, 1869–70, p. 253; *DB*². i. 943 *f.*

11. ויאמר נתן . . . לאמר] Luc. καὶ ἦλθε Ναθὰν πρὸς Βηρσάβεε μητέρα Σολομῶντος καὶ εἶπεν, i.e. וַיֵּלֶךְ נָתָן . . . וַיֹּאמַר. This is rather preferable to MT., as being less abrupt. So Klo.

12. איעצך . . . ומלטי] 'Let me counsel thee . . . and save thou,' equivalent to 'Let me counsel thee . . . *that thou mayest save.*' The Imperative with ו, ומלטי, stands in place of the usual cohortative with weak ו, expressing with greater force the *purpose* of the action described by the previous verb. Cf. Gen. 12. 2 . . . אעשך לגוי גדול וֶהְיֵה ברכה; 20. 7; 2 Sam. 21. 3; II. 5. 10; *al.* See Dri. *Tenses*, § 65; Ew. § 347ª; G-K. § 110, 2ᵇ; Da. § 65ᵈ.

13. כי] Like ὅτι *recitativum*, introducing the direct narration. Cf. *ch.* 11. 22 ויאמר לו פרעה כי מה אתה חסר עמי; 20. 5; 21. 6; II. 8. 13; Gen. 29. 32, 33; 1 Sam. 2. 16; 10. 19; *al.* Inverted commas are the equivalent in English. RV. rendering 'assuredly,' is not to be followed. Cases like Gen. 18. 20 זעקת סדם ועמרה כי רבה 'the cry on account of Sodom and Gomorrah is *verily* great'; Ps. 118. 10, 11, 12 בשם יהוה כי אמילם 'in the name of Yahweh I will *surely* cut them off,' where כי is joined closely to the verb, are quite different.

14. עודך מדברת . . . ואני אבוא] The two clauses are placed in parallelism, and thus their co-ordination in time is marked with as great vividness as is possible. Cf. *vv.* 22, 42; II. 6. 33 עודנו מדבר עמם והנה המלאך ירד אליו; Gen. 29. 9; *al.* Without עוד in the first clause, *ch.* 14. 17; II. 2. 23; 4. 5; *al.* Dri. *Tenses*, §§ 166–169; G-K. § 116, 5, *Rem.* 4; Da. § 141.

ומלאתי את דבריך] Lit. 'I will *fill up* thy words,' i.e. give them the confirmation of my testimony; so, 'I will *confirm* thy words.' Elsewhere, מלא דבר means to *fulfil a prediction* by subsequent actions; *ch.* 2. 27; 2 Chr. 26. 21.

15. מְשָׁרַת] A contraction or corruption of מְשָׁרֶתֶת.

18. ועתה אדני המלך וג׳] Read וְאַתָּה for ועתה with LXX, Luc., Vulg., Pesh., Targ., and some 200 Codd. So Th., Klo., Kamp.

The pronoun is necessary to mark and emphasize the change of subject in clause *b*, in contrast to the subject of clause *a*, אדניה.

20. ואתה אדני המלך] So LXX, Pesh.; but read וְעַתָּה for ואתה with Targ. and many Codd. So Th. ועתה is employed to summarize the conclusion of all that has gone before. Bathsheba draws together the threads of her speech, and explains why she has brought the state of affairs under the king's notice. This use of ועתה is very common. Cf. e.g. 1 Sam. 25. 26, 27; Gen. 3. 22; *ch.* 2. 9; 8. 25. Klo.'s violent emendation is quite unnecessary.

עיני . . . עליך] Expressing concentration of attention. Cf. 2 Chr. 20. 12 כי עליך עינינו; Jer. 22. 17 כי אין עיניך ולבך כי אם על בצעך.

22. עודנה וג׳] Cf. *v.* 14 *note.*

24. אתה אמרת וג׳] The interrogation is indicated by the tone in which the words are spoken. Cf. *ch.* 21. 7 אתה עתה תעשה מלוכה על ישראל; II. 5. 26; 9. 19; 1 Sam. 11. 12; 21. 16; 22. 7; Gen. 27. 24; *al.* G-K. § 150, 1; Da. § 121.

25. ולשרי הצבא] So LXX, Vulg., Pesh., Targ.; but Luc. *καὶ τὸν ἀρχιστράτηγον Ἰωάβ*, i.e. וּלְיוֹאָב שַׂר הַצָּבָא (as in *v.* 19; cf. *v.* 7; *ch.* 2. 22), is to be followed. So Hoo. Against MT. it is improbable (i) that Nathan should have omitted express mention of Joab, and (ii) that he should have made an assertion, ולשרי הצבא, which would at the moment seem to implicate Benaiah, who next to Joab was one of David's principal generals.

26. לי אני] For the re-enforcement of the suffix pronoun by the personal pronoun, cf. 1 Sam. 19. 23 עליו גם הוא; 25. 24 בי אני אדני העון; Hag. 1. 4 העת לכם אתם לשבת וג׳. G-K. § 135, 2c; Ew. § 311a, Da. § 1.

עבדך] Luc. *τὸν υἱόν σου*, i.e. בִּנְךָ. So Klo., Hoo., correctly. MT. seems to have been altered after *v.* 19. As Klo. notices, the title of submission, appropriate in the mouth of Bathsheba when speaking of her son, is out of place as coming from Nathan.

27. אם] Infrequent in single direct questions. When so employed it is usually equivalent to *num?* Judg. 5. 8 מָגֵן אִם־יֵרָאֶה וָרֹמַח; Am. 3. 6; Isa. 29. 16; Jer. 48. 27; Job 6. 12; 39. 13. In Gen. 38. 17 אִם־תִּתֵּן עֵרָבוֹן עַד שָׁלְחֶךָ it represents *An?* Da. § 112 *end.*

מֵאֵת] *From proximity with*, used to express *origin from;* a more idiomatic expression than the simple מן. מאת is very usual when יהוה is the source named. See instances cited on 2. 15.

נהיה] 'Has been brought about.' Cf. 12. 24; ‖ 2 Chr. 11. 4 כי מאתי נהיה הדבר הזה.

28. קראו לי] לי *Dativus commodi*. Cf. II. 4. 24 אַל־תַּעֲצָר־לִי לִרְכֹּב; 2 Sam. 18. 5 לְאַט־לִי; Judg. 16. 9.

ותבא לפני המלך ותעמד לפני המלך] So Targ. LXX, Vulg. presuppose ותבא לפני המלך ותעמד לפניו; Pesh. ותבא לפניו ותעמד לפני המלך; Luc. ותבא ותעמד לפני המלך. The unnaturalness of Pesh., לפניו preceding לפני המלך instead of *vice versâ*, and its disagreement with LXX, Vulg., point to the probability of all three being attempts to mend the tautology of MT. This repetition is no doubt due to a mistake of the scribe's eye, ותעמד being first omitted, and then added at the end with a repetition of the words which properly followed it. Thus we may, with Klo., Hoo., adopt the reading of Luc. Th. favours that of LXX, Vulg.

29. אשר פדה וג'] So exactly 2 Sam. 4. 9.

30. כי כאשר . . . כי כן] The first כי introduces the subject of the oath; cf. 2. 24; 18. 15; *al.;* the second כי resumes the first כי after the long intervening clause. Cf. 1 Sam. 14. 39 חי יהוה . . . כי אם ישנו ביונתן בני כי מות ימות; 25. 34; 2 Sam. 3. 9; Jer. 22. 24; Gen. 22. 16, 17.

33. הפרדה אשר לי] '*Mine own* mule'; more emphatic than פִּרְדָּתִי. Cf. 1 Sam. 25. 7 הרעים אשר לך '*thy* shepherds,' emphasized in view of the claim which follows; 2 Sam. 14. 31 את החלקה אשר לי '*my* field,' in contrast to the suffix of עבדיך. Da. § 28, *Rem.* 5[5]. Notice the difference between this class of examples of the construction אשר ל, and that noticed upon *v.* 8. While *here* the emphasis is upon the possessive pronoun, *there* it falls upon the strict definition of the substantive.

אל נחון] Some MSS. קרי אל, כתיב על. See *v.* 38.

נחון] Pesh. ܫܝܠܘܚܐ, Targ. שילוחא (here and in *vv.* 38, 45) identify with the pool of Shiloaḥ or Siloam; and this is favoured by 2 Chr. 33. 14, where it is stated that Manasseh built an outer wall to the city of David on the west side of *Giḥon in the ravine*, the נחל referred to being probably that of the קִדְרוֹן. The topography of מוצא מימי גיחון העליון is a much disputed subject. See *DB*². i. 1186.

35. נגיד] Lit. *one placed in the fore front*, so '*leader*.' The word in early Hebrew is characteristic of the more elevated style, and is frequent in Sam., Ki., especially in prophetical utterances. 1 Sam. 9. 16; 10. 1; 13. 14; 25. 30; 2 Sam. 5. 2; 6. 21; 7. 8; *ch.* 14. 7; 16. 2; II. 20. 5.

36. אמן כן יאמר י׳ וג׳] So Vulg., 'A., Σ., and substantially Targ. אמן כן תהי רעוא מן קדם יי. Pesh. ܐܡܝܢ ܘܗܟܢܐ ܢܥܒܕ ܡܪܝܐ ܐܠܗܟ; 2 Codd. Kennicott and 1 de Rossi כֵּן יַעֲשֶׂה. Cf. Jer. 28. 6. LXX Γένοιτο οὕτως· πιστώσαι ὁ Θεὸς τοῦ κυρίου μου τοῦ βασιλέως. Luc. Γένοιτο οὕτως· πιστώσαι ὁ Θεὸς τοὺς λόγους τοῦ κυρίου μου τοῦ βασιλέως· οὕτως εἶπε Κύριος ὁ Θεός σου, κύριέ μου βασιλεῦ. A double rendering. Pesh. ܢܥܒܕ is almost certainly a paraphrase of the somewhat harsh expression of MT. LXX, Luc. must have read יַאֲמֵן for יאמר, and then probably added the necessary object את דברי. Klo. follows this, emending אָמֵן כֵּן יַאֲמֵן יְהוָֹה אֱלֹהֶיךָ אֶת־דִּבְרֵי אֲדֹנִי הַמֶּלֶךְ; and so Hoo. But to say אמן '*true*,' i.e. '*may it come true*,' and then to continue כן יאמן וג׳, is mere tautology. There is no reason for the rejection of MT.

37. יְהִי] Read יהי Kt. with LXX, Vulg.

38. הכרתי והפלתי] David's bodyguard, doubtless composed of foreigners, mentioned only during his reign; *v.* 44; 2 Sam. 8. 18 (‖ 1 Chr. 18. 17); 15. 18; 20. 7, 23 (Q're). The names are *gentilic* in formation; G-K. § 86, 2, *Rem.* 5. In 1 Sam. 30 הכרתי are connected with the Philistines; cf. *v.* 14 with *v.* 16; and this is also the case with כְּרֵתִים which occurs Ezek. 25. 16; Zeph. 2. 5†. This latter is rendered Κρῆτες by LXX, and hence it is thought that כַּפְתּוֹר, from which the Philistines are said (Am. 9. 7; Deut. 2. 23; cf. Jer. 47. 4) to have emigrated, denotes Crete[1]. פלתי has been

---

[1] Sayce, following Ebers, formerly identified כפתור with the Egyptian *Kaft-ur* or 'greater Phoenicia,' i.e. the coast-land of the Delta (*The Higher Criticism*, 136), but has now abandoned this view (*Academy*, April 14, 1894, p. 314).

supposed, though without ground from analogy, to be a contraction of פלשתי. Th.'s objection to the view that the כרתי ופלתי were foreigners, on the score that David, who was so patriotic and devoted to the worship of the only God, would not have surrounded himself with a foreign bodyguard, will not hold good, in view of the important positions occupied by Uriah the Hittite 2 Sam. 11. 15, and by Ittai the Gittite 2 Sam. 18. 2.

על גחון] In *v.* 33 the better reading is אל גחון. There are many scattered instances of על used in place of אל after a verb of motion; *ch.* 20. 43 (21. 4 אל); 22. 6 (|| 2 Chr. 18. 5 אל); 1 Sam. 2. 11; 2 Sam. 15. 20; Mic. 4. 1 (|| Isa. 2. 2 אל); Isa. 22. 15 (אל . . . על); 66. 20 (56. 7 אל); Ezek. 1. 20 (*v.* 12 אל); 44. 13 (אל . . . על . . . אל); Jer. 1. 7; 31. 11 (אל . . . על); 36. 12; *al.*

40. מְחַלְּלִים בַּחֲלִלִים] So Vulg., and second rendering of Luc.; (Vet. Lat. second rendering *organizantes in organis;* Pesh. ܘܩܝܫܝܢ ܒܨܢܨܠܐ 'were striking sistra'). LXX, and first rendering of Luc. ἐχόρευον ἐν χοροῖς. So perhaps Targ. משבחין בחנגיא[1]. Vet. Lat. first rendering *cantabat canticis et melodiis*. Ew., following LXX, reads מְחֹלְלִים בִּחִילִים on the ground that it is unlikely that 'all the people' would be able to play flutes. But, as Th. remarks, the form חילים never occurs (always מְחֹלוֹת), and *round dances*, which would be denoted by חלל, would be unsuitable in a hasty procession. To this we may add the consideration that the stress seems to be laid upon the *noise* which was made; ותבקע הארץ בקולם. Klo.'s emendation הֹלְכִים בַּחֲלִלִים (cf. Isa. 30. 29) is unnecessary. A denom. חִלֵּל = 'to play the flute' may well be formed from חָלִיל.

ותבקע וג'] The sound of the shouting is compared to the deep rumbling produced by the splitting of the ground during an earthquake. In Num. 16. 31 the phrase וַתִּבָּקַע הָאֲדָמָה is used of an earthquake phenomenon. Th.'s objection to MT. is insufficient.

---

[1] But חנגא *may* have the meaning 'musical instrument'; *Pesachim* 111[b] תלו חנגא בגויה 'they hung a harp in the hollow of the tree'; Targ. Jerus. on Ex. 32. 19 וחנגין בידיהון דרש' 'and harp in the hands of the sinners'; Targ. Ps. 5. 1 לשבחא על חנגין = Heb. למנצח אל הנחילות. See Levy or Jastrow, s. v. *Studia Biblica*, ii. p. 34.

41. והם כלו וג׳] 'They *having finished* eating'; a circumstantial clause with the personal pronoun standing as subject. So very frequently; II. 5. 18 והוא נשען על ידי 'he leaning on my hand'; Gen. 15. 2; 18. 8; *al.* Dri. *Tenses*, § 160.

מדוע קול הקריה הומה] 'Wherefore is there the sound of the city in tumult?' So Vulg., excellently, *Quid sibi vult clamor civitatis tumultuantis?* הומה is properly an accus. of *state*, and forms a kind of secondary predicate. Cf. *ch.* 14. 6 קוֹל רַגְלֶיהָ בָּאָה בַפֶּתַח (באה of course referring to the suffix of רגליה); Song 5. 2 קול דודי דופק; Gen. 3. 8. See Dri. *Tenses*, § 161, *Obs.* 2.

For the use of the word המה, cf. Isa. 22. 2; Jer. 6. 23; Ps. 46. 7.

42. עודנו וג׳] Cf. *v.* 14 *note.*

איש חיל] Not 'a man of *valour*,' but 'a man of *worth*'; as also in the expression בן חיל *v.* 52. That חיל can have this meaning is shown by its application to a woman; Ruth 3. 11; Prov. 31. 10; cf. *v.* 29. Targ., here and in *v.* 52; *ch.* 2. 2 (see *note*); 2 Sam. 23. 20, seeks to reproduce this special sense by גבר דחיל חטאין 'a man who fears sin.'

43. אבל] With a slight adversative force, '*Nay but*,' in repudiation of Adonijah's suggestion that he is the bearer of good tidings. In late Heb. this adversative signification is strongly marked, '*howbeit*'; Dan. 10. 7, 21; Ezra 10. 13; 2 Chr. 1. 4; 19. 3; 33. 17. In classical Heb., though weaker, it is never really absent: Gen. 17. 19 אבל שרה אשתך ילדת לך בן '*Nay but* Sara thy wife shall bear thee a son,' in response to Abraham's wish that Ishmael might be his representative; 42. 21 אבל אשמים אנחנו על אחינו *however much we may try to repudiate it*, our guilt has found us out; 2 Sam. 14. 5 אבל אשה אלמנה אני the woman *anticipates any refusal* of the king to take up her cause by pleading that she is a widow; II. 4. 14† אבל בן אין לה Gehazi points out that the woman would like, *not* the offers of *v.* 13, *but* the bestowal of a son. Thus 'verily' or 'of a truth,' the translation of RV. in all these five passages except Gen. 17, is insufficient.

45. ותהם הקריה] 1 Sam. 4. 5 ותהם הארץ; Ruth 1. 19 ותהם כל העיר.

47. Luc. inserts καὶ εἰσεληλύθασι μόνοι after τὸν κύριον ἡμῶν τὸν

βασιλέα Δαυίδ. This seems to point to a Hebrew original in which וגם באו עבדי, at the beginning of the verse, had been by mistake written a second time after אדנינו המלך דוד, and then, making no sense in that position, had been altered into וגם באו לְבַדָּם. Klo. sees in *μόνοι* לְבַדָּם a variant of לברך.

אלהיך] Kt., Pesh.; אלהים Q're, LXX, Vulg., Luc., Targ. The latter should have the preference.

48. אשר נתן היום ישב וג׳] Insert מִזַּרְעִי after היום upon the authority of LXX, Luc. *ἐκ τοῦ σπέρματός μου.* So Th., Klo. The happiness of the event consisted not in the fact that David was to have a successor, which was only natural, but that this successor was to be one of his own family—his son. Pesh., Targ. insert ܒܪ, בר. They probably translated from a text in which, like MT., מזרעי had fallen out, and thus felt the necessity for some such insertion.

ועיני ראות] 'Mine eyes beholding it'; a circumstantial clause. The idiom occurs again Deut. 28. 32; 2 Sam. 24. 3; Jer. 20. 4.

50. קרנות המזבח] The four corners of the brazen altar, made of one piece with it (Ex. 27. 2 ועשית קרנתיו על ארבע פנתיו ממנו תהיין קרנתיו), and apparently projecting, for they could be grasped (here, and *v.* 51; 2. 28), and also broken off (cf. Amos 3. 14 ונגדעו קרנות המזבח).

51. ויגד לש׳ לאמר] See *note, ad fin.* on *ch.* 16. 16 וישמע וג׳.

כיום] Properly 'to-day' (כ having a temporal force, as e.g. in 1 Sam. 5. 10 ויהי כבוא ארון וג׳), so 'now,' and then acquiring the special sense '*first of all*': Gen. 25. 31 מכרה כיום את בכרתך לי; 1 Sam. 2. 16 קטר יקטירון כיום החלב.

אם ימית] 'That he will not slay.' The oath which is implied would take some such form as כה יעשה לו אלהים וכה יוסיף (cf. II. 6. 31; 1 Sam. 3. 17; 25. 22), and thus by the suppression of the apodosis אם 'if' of the protasis, gains the sense of an emphatic negative. This is very common; cf. *ch.* 2. 8; II. 2. 2; 3. 14; 1 Sam. 3. 14; *al.* Da. § 120; Ew. § 356[a].

52. לא יפל משערתו וג׳] 'There shall not fall *even a single hair of him* to the ground.' The fem. שערה is a *nomen unitatis;* cf. Judg. 20. 16 כָּל־זֶה קֹלֵעַ בָּאֶבֶן אֶל־הַשַּׂעֲרָה וְלֹא יַחֲטִא; G-K. § 122, 4[d]. משערתו

properly means '*starting from* one of his hairs'; cf. Deut. 15. 7 אֶבְיוֹן מֵאַחַד אַחֶיךָ 'a poor man, even (*starting from*) one of thy brethren.' This use of מן, called مِنْ ٱلزَّائِدَةُ (من *otiose*), is very frequent in Ar. when a negation, prohibition, or interrogation with هل precedes; Qor. 6. 38 مَا فَرَّطْنَا فِي ٱلْكِتَابِ مِنْ شَيْءٍ 'We have neglected nothing whatsoever (lit. *starting from* anything) in the Book'; 67. 3 مَا تَرَى فِي خَلْقِ ٱلرَّحْمَٰنِ مِنْ تَفَاوُتٍ 'Thou canst see *no sort of* diversity in God's creation'; *ibid.* هَلْ تَرَى مِنْ فُطُورٍ 'Seest thou *any* gap?' The other occurrences of the proverbial phrase are 1 Sam. 14. 45 אם יפל משערת ראשו ארצה; 2 Sam. 14. 11† אם יפל משערת בנך ארצה.

53. מעל המזבח] 'From *upon* the altar': cf. *ch.* 2. 34 ויעל. The verb עלה also occurs in the sense of *going up upon* an altar, *ch.* 12. 32, 33; II. 16. 12; 23. 9; 1 Sam. 2. 28; and conversely ירד is used of *descent from* the altar here and in Lev. 9. 22. In Ex. 20. 26 *steps* to the altar are expressly forbidden, and hence it has been thought that the ascent was by an *inclined plane*, leading up to a *ledge* (perhaps the כַּרְכֹּב of Ex. 27. 5) which ran round the altar. Solomon's altar, according to 2 Chr. 4. 1, was ten cubits high, and therefore must have been approached by an incline, or by steps; and the altar described by Ezekiel is pictured as having steps leading up to it (43. 17 וּמַעֲלֹתֵהוּ פְּנוֹת קָדִים). Jos. (*Wars*, v. 5, § 6) states that in Herod's Temple the ascent to the altar was by an inclined plane.

2. 1. ויקרבו וג׳] So Gen. 47. 29.

ויצו] צוה is used of a man's last commands; cf. especially 2 Sam. 17. 23 ויצו אל ביתו; II. 20. 1; ‖ Isa. 38. 1 צו לביתך; cf. also Gen. 50. 12, 16; Deut. 31. 23, 25. In New Heb. צַוָּאָה = *a will; Baba bathra* 147[a].

2. אנכי הלך וג׳] Cf. Josh. 23. 14.

וחזקת] RV. 'Be thou strong therefore.' The perf. with ו *consec.* is used as a mild imperative; cf. *v.* 6 ועשית; *ch.* 3. 9 ונתת; 8. 28; *al.* See Dri. *Tenses*, § 119 δ; G-K. § 112, 4[b].

והיית לאיש] Cf. 1 Sam. 4. 9 היו לאנשים. So LXX, Vulg., Pesh., and substantially Σ. (καὶ ἔσο ἀνδρεῖος). Luc. καὶ ἔσει εἰς ἄνδρα δυνάμεως,

Targ. ותהא לגבר דחיל חטאין (cf. *ch.* 1. 42, *note*), and several Codd. Vulg. *esto vir fortis* seem to presuppose והיית לאיש חיל. The regular phrase, however, is היה לבן חיל, cf. *ch.* 1. 52; 1 Sam. 18. 17; 2 Sam. 2. 7; *al.;* and Luc. accordingly in all these passages keeps υἱόν. This makes it probable that δυνάμεως here is only a paraphrastic addition.

3, 4. This passage, in its present form, is due to the pre-exilic Deuteronomic compiler (R^D)[1]. Notice especially the phrases ושמרת את משמרת י׳ Deut. 11. 1; י׳ אלהיך cf. *ch.* 8. 58 *note;* ללכת בדרכיו Deut. 8. 6; 10. 12; 11. 22; *al.;* לשמר חקתיו וג׳ Deut. constantly; למען תשכיל וג׳ Deut. 29. 8; למען יקים וג׳ Deut. 9. 5; בכל לבבך ובכל נפשך Deut. 4. 29; 6. 5; *al.*

3. תשכיל] 'Understand' (so as to *manage successfully*). For השכיל with accus., cf. Ps. 64. 10; 106. 7; Deut. 32. 29; and with the special *nuance* of our passage, Deut. 29. 8 למען תשכילו את כל אשר תעשון. In the application of the word to clause *b*, את כל אשר תפנה שם, there is a slight zeugma.

תפנה] The use of the word is illustrated by Prov. 17. 8 אל כל אשר יפנה ישכיל; 1 Sam. 14. 47 (emend יִוָּשֵׁעַ) בכל אשר יפנה ירשיע.

4. את דברו] The promise referred to is the substance of 2 Sam. 7. 12–16 (Nathan's prophecy).

ללכת לפני] The phrase הלך לפני י׳ is peculiar to Kings; *ch.* 3. 6 (as here, followed by באמת); 8. 23, 25 (‖ 2 Chr. 6. 14, 16); 9. 4 (‖ 2 Chr. 7. 17)†. Elsewhere the phrase is התהלך לפני י׳; II. 20. 3 ‖ Isa. 38. 3 (followed by באמת); 1 Sam. 2. 30; Gen. 17. 1; 24. 40; 48. 15; Ps. 56. 14; 116. 9†.

לאמר אם ישמרו . . . לאמר] The second לאמר introduces the express words of the promise after a brief summary of the conditions; '*Said he.*' Such cases of resumption after an intervening sentence are not uncommon in Heb.; cf. *ch.* 1. 30 כי כאשר . . . כי כן; 8. 30 ושמעת . . . ושמעת וסלחת; 8. 41, 42 ובא . . . ובא; 13. 11 ויספר[ו] . . . ויספרום; 1 Sam. 29. 10 השכם . . . והשכמתם; Lev. 17. 5 למען אשר יביאו . . . והביאֻם; *al.* The second לאמר is omitted by Cod. Kennicott 170, Th., Kamp., and not expressed by Luc., Vulg.

[1] See *Introduction.*

לא יכרת וג׳] Cf. *ch.* 8. 25 (|| 2 Chr. 6. 16); 9. 5 (|| 2 Chr. 7. 18); Jer. 33. 17. לך is dat. of reference, 'pertaining unto thee.'

מעל] Lit. 'from (sitting) upon,' so '*off*.' A regular idiom; cf. the phrases מֵעַל הַחֲמוֹר 1 Sam. 25. 23; מֵעַל הַגָּמָל Gen. 24. 64; מֵעַל הַמִּזְבֵּחַ *ch.* 1. 53; מֵעַל רֹאשִׁי Gen. 40. 17; מֵעַל הָאֲדָמָה Deut. 28. 21; *al.*

5. ויהרגם] '*How that* he slew them.' The ו is epexegetical of the somewhat vague preceding expression את אשר עשה וג׳. Other instances of the Imperf. with ו *consec.*, '*how that*' or '*in that*,' used to explain a preceding עשה, are *ch.* 18. 13 את אשר עשיתי... ואחבא; 1 Sam. 8. 8; Gen. 31. 26. See Dri. *Tenses*, § 76[a]; Da. § 47 *end.*

וישם דמי מלחמה בשלם] A very unnatural expression. (i) As it stands it can only mean, (*a*) 'He placed the blood of war upon peace,' or (*β*) taking וישם absolutely, 'He set (i.e. paraph. *shed*) the blood of war during time of peace.' But such an absolute use of שים, followed neither by ב or על of that upon which the object is placed, nor by a second accus. or by ל expressing the result of the action denoted by the verb, is extremely improbable. (ii) Why is the blood of Abner and Amasa called דמי מלחמה? This is inexplicable. Doubtless we ought, with Klo., Hoo., to emend וישם after Luc. καὶ ἐξεδίκησεν, Vet. Lat. *et vindicavit*, i.e. וַיִּקֹּם דמי מלחמה בשלם, the only change being the substitution of ק for ש. Joab's crime consisted in having *avenged* in time of peace, blood shed in war—the blood of Asahel justifiably shed by Abner in self-defence. Thus דמי מלחמה is fully explained, and forms an admirable antithesis to בשלם. For the use of נקם דמים cf. Deut. 32. 43 דם עבדיו יקום. LXX καὶ ἔταξεν seems to have had MT. reading; while Vulg. *et effudit*, Targ. ודמי דתחשיב דמהון עלוהי כדם חבירי קרבא, Pesh. ܘܣܡ ܐܢܘܢ ܐܝܟ ܕܒܩܪܒܐ are probably paraphrastic explanations of the same.

ויתן דמי מלחמה בחגרתו] Here we have the same difficulty as to the application of דמי מלחמה. The reading of Cod. A, Luc. αἷμα ἀθῷον is favoured by the fact that Luc. preserves the correct text just before. Accordingly, Bö. suggests דָּמִים לְחִנָּם; Th. דָּם נָקִי; Klo. דְּמֵי חִנָּם or דָּמִים לְחִנָּם. The last expression is the best; cf. *v.* 31

והסירת דמי חנם אשר שפך יואב. Doubtless, as Th. suggests, the corruption arose through the previous דמי מלחמה standing directly above דמי חנם in the MS. from which the copy was made. Targ. דמיהון, Pesh. ܕܡܝܗܘܢ presuppose דמיהם, which may well have arisen from דמי חנם.

6. ולא תוֹרֵד] The employment of the jussive form with לא is rare. Other instances are, Gen. 24. 8; 1 Sam. 14. 36; 2 Sam. 17. 12; Ezek. 48. 14; Gen. 4. 12; Deut. 13. 1; Joel 2. 2. See G-K. § 109, 1[b]; Dri. *Tenses*, § 174 *Obs.* For the expression הוריד שיבת פ׳ שאול(ה) cf. *v.* 9; Gen. 42. 38; 44. 29, 31.

7. והיו באכלי] 'Let them be *among*, &c.' Cf. Am. 1. 1 עמוס אשר היה בנקדים; Prov. 23. 20 אל תהי בסבאי יין.

כי כן קרבו אלי] 'For *so* did they draw near to me,' i.e. 'with such kindness as thou art to show to them'; Th. So LXX οὕτως. If we adopt this explanation, it is unnecessary to suppose, with Hitzig, that כי כן stands for כי על כן, as is suggested by Pesh. ܡܛܠ ܕ; cf. Targ. ארי, Vulg. *enim*. Luc. οὗτος is a corruption of οὕτως.

קרבו אלי] Klo., following Luc. οὗτος παρέστη ἐνώπιόν μου, emends קִדְּמוּ אֹתִי; cf. Deut. 23. 5 לא קדמו אתכם בלחם. This is an unnecessary change. LXX ἤγγισαν, Vulg. *occurrerunt* agree with MT.; Targ. סופיקו צורכיי, Pesh. ܩܕܡܘܢܝ ܒܠܚܡܐ paraphrase.

8. בן הימיני] '*The* Benjamite.' So Judg. 3. 15; 2 Sam. 16. 11; 19. 17†. Cf. בֵּית הַלַּחְמִי 1 Sam. 16. 18; בֵּית־הַשִּׁמְשִׁי 1 Sam. 6. 14; בֵּית הָאֱלִי *ch.* 16. 34; אֲבִי הָעֶזְרִי Judg. 6. 11. In 1 Chr. 27. 12 Kt. לבנימיני (i.e. לַבִּנְיָמִינִי, the origin being forgotten, and the word treated as a single one. Cf. הָאִיעֶזְרִי Num. 26. 30); Q're anomalously לַבֶּן יְמִינִי. Cf. Kö. *Syntax*, § 302[d].

נמרצת] Niph'al again in Mic. 2. 10; Job 6. 25; Hiph'il, Job 16. 3†. The word may be connected with Ar. مَرِضَ *to be sick*,—'a curse *made sick*,' and so '*a sore* or *severe curse*.' Cf. with similar use of a passive participle, מַכָּה נַחְלָה Jer. 14. 17.

9. ועתה] So Targ., Pesh. LXX omits. Luc., Vulg. וְאַתָּה; so Th., Klo., Kamp. MT. should be retained; see *note* on *ch.* 1. 20.

10, 11. This short mention of David's death and burial, and the statement of the length of his reign, is in its present form the work of R[D], whose method of introducing and summarizing the account of a reign is noticed at length in *Introd.*

10. עיר דוד] The ancient city of Jerusalem taken by David from the Jebusites[1], called מְצֻדַת צִיּוֹן 2 Sam. 5. 7; ‖ 1 Chr. 11. 5; צִיּוֹן *ch.* 8. 1. Zion is expressly named in 1 Macc. 4. 37 *f.;* 7. 33 as the hill upon which the Temple stood, and this is further borne out by such expressions as י׳ צבאות השכן בהר צ׳ Isa. 8. 18; צ׳ קדוש ישראל Isa. 60. 14; ציון הר קדשי Ps. 2. 6; הר ציון זה שכנת בו Ps. 74. 2; *al.* In 2 Chr. 33. 14 it is said of Manasseh that 'he built an outer wall to the city of David, on the west side of Giḥon in the ravine (*note* on *ch.* 1. 33), even to the entering in at the fish gate; and he compassed about the Ophel, &c.'

Thus it seems clear that the site of עיר דוד was upon the somewhat low south-east hill of Jerusalem (הָעֹפֶל), the Temple being on the north, and Solomon's palace upon the south, closely adjoining the Temple[2]. The tradition which places Zion upon the south-*west* hill appears to be no earlier than the fourth century A.D.; and the modern maps which so locate it are certainly incorrect. See Sta. *Ges.* i. 315 *f.; Encyc. Brit.* ed. 9, Art. *Jerusalem* (Pt. II); Baed. 21 *f.*

13. ויבא . . . אם שלמה] LXX, Luc. add καὶ προσεκύνησεν αὐτῇ, i.e. וַיִּשְׁתַּחוּ לָהּ; possibly genuine, and accepted by Klo. Th. is doubtful, remarking that it is quite as likely to have been inserted by a copyist from *v.* 19, on the consideration that Adonijah would not have acted with less deference than king Solomon.

---

[1] The name יְבוּס applied to the city, Judg. 19. 10, 11; 1 Chr. 11. 4, 5† (cf. Josh. 15. 8; 18. 16, 28 P), is probably no real archaism, but a literary derivative from the name of the ancient inhabitants. Cf. Moore (*Judges*, p. 413), who quotes Judg. 1. 7, 21; Josh. 15. 63 (JE), as showing that the city was called Jerusalem before the time of David, and concludes that 'the question has been set at rest by the Amarna tablets (about 1400 B.C., before the Israelite invasion) in which the name *Urusalim* repeatedly occurs, while there is no trace of a name corresponding to Jebus.'

[2] This agrees with the statement of Ezek. 43. 7[b], 8[a]; 'And the house of Israel shall no more defile my holy name, neither they nor their kings, . . . in their setting of their threshold by my threshold, and their doorpost beside my doorpost, and there was but the wall between me and them.'

השלום באך] So 1 Sam. 16. 4. Lit. 'Is thy coming peace?' the abstract substantive being used instead of an adjective. So very frequently with this word; Gen. 43. 27 הֲשָׁלוֹם אֲבִיכֶם; Judg. 6. 24 ויקרא לו יהוה שלום 'he called it, Yahwe is *peace*'; 1 Sam. 25. 6; 2 Sam. 17. 3; Isa. 60. 17; Mic. 5. 4; Ps. 120. 7; 147. 14; Prov. 3. 17; Job 5. 24; 21. 9†; cf. also Num. 25. 12 בריתי שלום 'my covenant—peace,' i.e. 'my peaceful covenant.' With other words; Ex. 17. 12 ויהי ידיו אמונה 'and his hands were *firmness*'; Ps. 110. 3 עמך נדבת 'thy people is *freewillingness*'; &c. See Dri. *Tenses*, § 189, 2.

14. דבר לי אליך] II. 9. 5; Judg. 3. 19, 20.

ותאמר] LXX, Luc., Pesh., Vulg., some Codd. add לו.

15. לי היתה המ׳] '*Mine* was the kingdom.' לי is greatly emphasized by position: cf. Job 15. 19 להם לבדם נתנה הארץ; Hag. 2. 8 לי הכסף ולי הזהב.

עלי שמו . . . פניהם] Expressing attention concentrated in expectancy; cf. the phrase עין על *ch.* 1. 20. In its other occurrences, Ezek. 29. 2; 35. 2† (a variation of שים פנים אל), the expression is used with a hostile *nuance*. שים פנים followed by an infin. with ל describes a purpose at the point of time at which it is about to be put into execution. II. 12. 18 וישם חזאל פניו לעלות על ירושלם; Jer. 42. 15, 17; 44. 12; Dan. 11. 17.

לִמְלֹךְ] Klo. compares II. 12. 18; but this is not quite parallel, the subject of the infin. לעלות being, as in the other passages above cited, the same as that of וישם, while the subject of לִמְלֹךְ is different from that of שמו. Two Codd. De Rossi and all Verss. presuppose the easier reading לְמֶלֶךְ.

מיהוה] The ordering of events in a manner opposed to human calculations is, as Klo. notices, specially spoken of as a divine interposition. Judg. 14. 4 ואביו ואמו לא ידעו כי מיהוה היא; cf. Prov. 16. 1. There is a similar use of מֵאֵת יהוה; *ch.* 12. 24; II. 6. 33; Josh. 11. 20; Ps. 118. 23; *al.*

16. אנכי שאל] The participle used of the immediate future as it merges into the present; the *futurum instans*. 'I am about to ask,' almost equivalent to the simple present 'I ask.' Cf. *v.* 20.

אל תשבי את פני] So Vulg., Pesh., Targ.; but LXX, Luc. *τὸ πρόσωπόν σου*, i.e. את פניך; and in *vv.* 17, 20 LXX reads *οὐκ ἀποστρέψει τὸ πρόσωπον αὐτοῦ ἀπὸ σοῦ* for לא ישיב את פניך, and *μὴ ἀποστρέψῃς τὸ πρόσωπόν σου* for אל תשב את פני. On the contrary, לא אשיב את פניך at the end of *v.* 20 is rendered *οὐκ ἀποστρέψω σε.* In all these cases, Luc., Targ., Vulg. (paraph. in *v.* 17, *neque enim negare tibi quidquam potest*), Pesh. (ܐܦܝ̈ for פניך in *v.* 17) agree in supporting the reading of MT.

The usage of the expression השיב פנים is as follows. It occurs, as in the LXX text of these passages, of *turning one's own face away from anything*, only in Ezek. 14. 6 שובו והשיבו מעל גלוליכם ומעל כל תועבתיכם השיבו פניכם; cf. Ezek. 18. 30 where there is probably an ellipse of פנים. השיב פנים ל *to turn one's own face towards*, Dan. 11. 18, 19. On the other hand, the expression is used as here in *vv.* 16, 17, 20 of MT., of turning away *the face of another* in *repulse*, in II. 18. 24; || Isa. 36. 9 ואיך תשיב את פני פחת אחד וג׳, and Ps. 132. 10; || 2 Chr. 6. 42 אל תשב פני משיחך. So also in the opposite expression of *the acceptance of an overture*, נשא פנים, it is always the face of *another person* which is raised.

Thus evidence is all in favour of the retention of MT. text in *vv.* 16, 17, 20.

18. טוב] A formula of assent; cf. 1 Sam. 20. 7; 2 Sam. 3. 13.

19. וישתחו לה] So Vulg., Pesh., Targ. LXX, Luc. *καὶ* (LXX *κατ-*) *εφίλησεν αὐτήν* presuppose וַיִּשַּׁק לָהּ or וַיִּשָּׁקֶהָ. Bö. prefers MT., supposing that LXX reading points to an alteration on the part of the Alexandrian Jews, who thought that such an act of obeisance was unworthy of king Solomon. Th. also points out that the ceremonial which follows—the placing of a throne for the queen-mother and her sitting at the king's right hand—is in favour of MT.

The importance of the position of the queen-mother הַגְּבִירָה is attested by *ch.* 15. 13; || 2 Chr. 15. 16 (cf. II. 10. 13; Jer. 13. 18; 29. 2), and by the frequent special mention of her name; *ch.* 14. 21, 31; 15. 2, 10; 22. 42; II. 8. 26; 12. 2; *al.* Thus, as far as can be judged, there would be nothing incongruous in the king's bowing to her.

Klo. adopts LXX reading, describing the action denoted by MT. as 'gegen alle Etiquette'; but as a matter of fact we know too little about the customs of ancient eastern monarchs to be able to dogmatize upon what might fittingly have taken place, and what not so.

20. אַל־תָּשֶׁב] Here the close connexion of אל to the jussive by means of *Maqqef* causes a retraction of the tone, just as in the case of the Imperf. with ו *consec.* Cf. 1 Sam. 9. 20 אַל־תָּשֶׂם; 2 Sam. 17. 16 אַל־תָּלֶן; *al.*

21. יֻתַּן את אבישג] The passive verb is impersonal, and the object of the action denoted by it follows in the accus.; 'Let there be giving as regards Abishag,' so, 'Let one give,' or, 'Let her be given.' So with the same verb Num. 32. 5 יֻתַּן את הארץ הזאת לעבדיך; cf. also *ch.* 18. 13 הלא הֻגַּד לאדני את אשר עשיתי; 2 Sam. 21. 11; Gen. 27. 42; *al.* See G-K. § 121, 1; Ew. 295[b]; Da. § 79.

22. ולמה] '*And* why?' 'why then?' The ו is very forcible, and here gives a sarcastic turn to the sentence. Cf. II. 7. 19 והנה י׳ עשה ארבות בשמים היהיה כדבר הזה '*Pray*, if Yahwe were to make windows in heaven, could this thing come to pass?' Other instances of the ו with למה are Num. 14. 3; 20. 4; Judg. 6. 13; 12. 3. See Dri. *Tenses*, § 119 γ, *n.* 1.

לָמָּה] With accent *Milra'* before the following את, instead of לָ֫מָּה. This accentuation is always adopted before words beginning with א, ע, or ה, for the sake of avoidance of *hiatus*. See Sta. § 372[a].

ולו ולאביתר ... צרויה] RV. 'Ask for him the kingdom ... *even for him, and for Abiathar* &c.' A somewhat dubious rendering. As the text stands ולו can scarcely be correct, and must be omitted as dittography from the first two letters of the following word.

All Verss., however, LXX, Luc., Vulg., Pesh., and probably Targ. (paraph. הלא בעיצא הוו הוא ואביתר), presuppose ולו אביתר הכהן ולו יואב וג׳ '*And on his side* are Abiathar the priest, and Joab &c.' As Th. says, it is natural that a second reason for asking the kingdom for Adonijah should be mentioned. So Bö. For this sense of לו, cf. Ex. 32. 26 מי ליהוה אלי; Josh. 5. 13 הלנו אתה אם לצרינו.

The addition of LXX, Luc., after Joab's name, ὁ ἀρχιστράτηγος ἑταῖρος, appears to be merely a gloss, ὁ ἀρχ. being Joab's usual title, and ἑταῖρος explaining the reference of לו, 'To him Joab . . . *is an ally*.'

Klo., starting from the addition of ἑταῖρος in LXX, Luc., and comparing the Targ. paraphrase הלא בעיצא הוו וג׳, supposes that a word has fallen out at the end of the sentence in MT., and accordingly would supply חֶבֶר; 'To him and to Abiathar . . . *there is an alliance*.' But against this it is to be noticed that the word which is constantly used in the historical books to denote a *conspiracy* or *alliance* is never חֶבֶר but always קֶשֶׁר (cf. II. 11. 14; 12. 21; *al.*), and again, it seems very doubtful whether Targ., if it had had חבר at the end of the sentence, would have represented it by בעיצא at the beginning.

23. כה יעשה וג׳] II. 6. 31; 1 Sam. 3. 17; 14. 44; 20. 13; 25. 22; 2 Sam. 3. 9, 35; 19. 14; Ruth 1. 17. In the mouths of heathen a *plural* verb is used; *ch.* 19. 2; 20. 10†.

כי] If the substance of the oath be a *negation*, it is usual to introduce it by אם '*if*'; *ch.* 20. 10 כה . . . יוספו אם ישפק עפר שמרון לשעלים וג׳ 'So may the gods do to me, and more also, *if* the dust of Samaria suffice for handfuls &c.'; II. 6. 31 כה . . . יוסף אם יעמד ראש אלישע בן שפט עליו היום; 1 Sam. 3. 17; 25. 22. In analogy with this we should expect אם לא if the substance be an *assertion;* and this occurs once; 2 Sam. 19. 14. It is usual, however, to break off after the oath, and introduce its subject by כי, the break in connexion being represented in English by a dash. So in our passage; 'God do so to me and more also—Adonijah hath spoken this word against his life'; *ch.* 19. 2 כה . . . יוספון כי כעת מחר אשים את נפשך כנפש אחד מהם 'So do the gods, &c.—to-morrow I will make &c.'; 1 Sam. 14. 44; 20. 13; 2 Sam. 3. 9; Ruth 1. 17.

כי is thus very frequently used to introduce an *assertion* after the oath חַי יהוה, *and with a suppression of* כה יעשה וג׳; cf. *v.* 24; *ch.* 1. 30; 18. 15; 1 Sam. 14. 39; 20. 3, 21; 25. 34; *al.* (about nineteen times in all). In such a case אם לא occurs only once,

Num. 14. 28, outside of Ezekiel where it is characteristic and uniformly takes the place of the usual construction with כי; 5. 11; 17. 16, 19; 20. 33; 33. 27; 34. 8; 35. 6† (this last a gloss according to Cornill)[1].

If the oath introduced by חי י׳ with a suppressed כה יעשה וג׳ have a *negative* substance, אם occurs constantly.

בנפשו] '*At the cost of* his life'; *Beth pretii*. Cf. 2 Sam. 23. 17 ההלכים בנפשתם 'who went *at peril of* their lives'; Prov. 7. 23; Lam. 5. 9. So *ch.* 16. 34; Josh. 6. 26 בבכרו . . . ובצעירו; 1 Chr. 12. 19 בראשינו; *al.*

24. עשה לי בית] Used idiomatically of Yahwe's assurance to Solomon of *a posterity*. So 2 Sam. 7. 11 והגיד לך י׳ כי בית יעשה לך י׳; cf. Exod. 1. 21. The more usual phrase is בנה בית; 1 Sam. 2. 35; 2 Sam. 7. 27; (|| 1 Chr. 17. 10, 25); *ch.* 11. 38.

25. וימת] LXX, Luc. presuppose the addition אֲדֹנִיָּהוּ בַּיּוֹם הַהוּא 'and A. died that same day.' So Th., and Klo. with om. of name.

26. ענתת] A city of Benjamin, Isa. 10. 30; assigned to the priests, Josh. 21. 18; 1 Chr. 6. 45; the home of Jeremiah, Jer. 1. 1. The modern name is *Anâta*, 2½ miles north-north-east of Jerusalem. This agrees with the statements of Jos. (*Ant.* x. 7, § 3), who places it at twenty stadia from the city, Eusebius (*Onom.*) three miles, Jerome (*ad Jerem.* cap. 1) three miles '*contra septentrionem Jerusalem*.' Rob. *BR.*, i. 437 *f.*; Baed. 118.

על שדיך] על used in place of אל; cf. 1. 38 *note*.

ארון] So all Verss. The occasion to which reference is made seems naturally to be that described in 2 Sam. 6. 12 *ff.* Th., Klo. emend אֵפוֹד, finding an allusion (as is the case in the following וכי התענית וג׳) to the days of David's outlawry, when Abiathar, fleeing from the slaughter of the priests at Nob, carried with him to David the *Ephod* which was used in obtaining the oracle of Yahwe; 1 Sam. 23. 6, 9. But neither אפוד (אדני) יהוה nor אפוד אלהים (Klo.) occurs elsewhere, and, if any correction of the text be deemed desirable, הָאֵפוֹד simply is alone in accordance with usage.

[1] With omission both of apodosis and of formal oath אם לא is by no means infrequent. Cf. *ch.* 20. 23 *note*.

אדני יהוה] אדני, not found in LXX, Luc., Pesh., is probably a mistaken repetition of ארון.

LXX, Luc. insert διαθήκης, i.e. ברית, after κιβωτόν. This is a gloss derived from the expression ארון ברית י׳ which is frequent elsewhere (see 3. 15 *note*). Other instances of this same insertion are Josh. 3. 13, 15 (twice); 4. 10, 11; 6. 12, 13; 1 Sam. 6. 3, 18; 7. 1 (twice); 2 Sam. 6. 10.

לפני דוד] 'In the presence of,' suggesting the idea of '*at the direction of* David.' So Num. 8. 22 לעבד את עבדתם באהל מועד לפני אהרן ולפני בניו; 1 Chr. 24. 6 ויכתבם . . . לפני המלך.

27. למלא וג׳] 1 Sam. 2. 27–36.

28. ואחרי אבשלום לא נטה] So LXX, Targ.; but Luc., Vulg., Pesh. presuppose וְאַחֲרֵי שְׁלֹמֹה, adopted by Jos. (*Ant.* viii. 1, § 4 φίλος γὰρ ἦν αὐτῷ ['Αδωνίᾳ] μᾶλλον ἢ τῷ βασιλεῖ Σολομῶνι), and also by Th., Ew., Grä.

This emendation makes the sentence a little diffuse, since its statement is already contained by implication in the previous words כי יואב נטה אחרי אדניה. On the other hand, a back reference to the position taken by Joab *in the other rebellion of David's reign* is very natural.

29. והנה] Without a specific suffix or pronoun following, the reference being unmistakable. Cf. Gen. 24. 30 ויבא אל האיש והנה עֹמֵד על הגמלים; 37. 15; 18. 9; 16. 14.

אצל המזבח] LXX, Luc., Pesh. אָחַז בְּקַרְנוֹת הַמִּזְבֵּחַ. Hence Th. thinks that בקרנות has fallen out of MT., and אחז then become corrupted into אצל. But the use of אצל is very natural here (used frequently in connexion with מזבח; Lev. 1. 16; 6. 3; 10. 12; *al.*), and forms an appropriate variation to the phrase used in *v.* 28. It is much more probable that the alteration of the above-mentioned Verss. is merely due to that desire for the strict uniformity of parallel passages which is so characteristic, e. g. of the LXX translators. *Ch.* 1. 51 appears to have suggested the change. So Klo.

וישלח שלמה] After שלמה LXX, Luc. add πρὸς 'Ιωὰβ λέγων, Τί γέγονέν σοι ὅτι πέφευγας εἰς (Luc. πέφευγες ἐπὶ) τὸ θυσιαστήριον; καὶ εἶπεν 'Ιωάβ Ὅτι ἐφοβήθην ἀπὸ προσώπου σου, καὶ ἔφυγον πρὸς (τὸν) Κύριον. καὶ ἀπέστειλεν ὁ Σαλωμών. This is translated by Th. אֶל־יוֹאָב לֵאמֹר מֶה הָיָה לְךָ כִּי נַסְתָּ אֶל־הַמִּזְבֵּחַ וַיֹּאמֶר יוֹאָב כִּי יָרֵאתִי מִפָּנֶיךָ וָאָנוּס אֶל־יְהוָה וַיִּשְׁלַח שְׁלֹמֹה, and adopted by him as genuine on the ground that a scribe's eye might very well have passed by mistake from the first וישלח שלמה to the second. So Bö., Klo. The words exhibit no attempt to justify the action of Solomon, nor does there seem to be any other reason for their addition by a later hand; a consideration which favours their genuineness.

פגע בו] LXX, Luc. add *καὶ θάψον αὐτόν*, through desire, as Th. remarks, for conformity with *v.* 31.

Klo. would emend וְהוֹצִיאֵהוּ for פגע בו. This is unsupported by any Vers., and though it may seem at first sight to be required by the words of *v.* 30 כה אמר המלך צא, yet this is not really the case. The king, in issuing the command פגע בו, supposed that Joab could be brought away from the altar and executed, but Benaiah, meeting with his refusal to leave the asylum, returned to the king for further instructions.

31. וקברתו] Added out of consideration for the dignity of his position. Cf. II. 9. 34, and contrast II. 9. 10; Jer. 22. 19; Isa. 14. 19; Ps. 79. 3, where the loss of burial is mentioned as a mark of deep dishonour.

וַהֲסִירֹתָ] It is very rare to find the tone not thrown forward with ו *consec.* in 1st and 2nd sing. of verbs ע״ו (or ע״ע). This and וַהֲצֵרֹתִי Jer. 10. 18; וַהֲשִׁיבוֹתִי Am. 1. 8, are probably all the cases which exist. Dri. *Tenses*, § 110, 5, *Obs.*

מעלי] 'From *upon* me'; the blood being regarded as resting upon the head of the guilty person; so *vv.* 33, 37; 2 Sam. 3. 29. Cf. Jon. 1. 14 אל תתן עלינו דם נקיא; 2 Sam. 16. 8; S. Matt. 27. 25.

32. והשיב י׳ . . . על ראשו] 1 Sam. 25. 39; Judg. 9. 57.

את דמו] LXX, Luc. *τὸ αἷμα τῆς ἀδικίας αὐτοῦ*, a paraphrase based upon the supposition that דמו refers, not to Joab's own blood, but to the blood unjustly shed by him.

33. מעם י׳] So *ch.* 12. 15; Ruth 2. 12; Ps. 121. 2; *al.* Cf. the analogous use of מאת י׳ *ch.* 1. 27 *note*.

34. ויעל] 'Went *up*'; in accordance with the expression מעל המזבח *ch.* 1. 53 *note.*

בביתו] So LXX, Vulg., Targ.; Th., Klo. Cf. 2 Chr. 33. 20 ויקברהו ביתו. Luc., Pesh. presuppose בְּקִבְרוֹ, and this is favoured by Kamp. who thinks it extremely unlikely that Joab should have had a *house* in the wilderness.

במדבר] Kamp. suggests בְּמִדְבַּר יְהוּדָה; Judg. 1. 16; Ps. 63. 1.

35. After על הצבא LXX, Luc. insert *καὶ ἡ βασιλεία κατορθοῦτο ἐν Ἰερουσαλήμ.* These words are those of *v.* 46[b] of MT. והממלכה נכונה ביד שלמה, בידשלמה being read as בירשלם.

The correct position of the sentence seems to be at the end of *v.* 35 from which in MT. it was separated by the insertion of the Shimei section. Solomon's establishment in the kingdom resulted from the death of his powerful adversaries Adonijah and Joab, and could not have been much enhanced by the death of Shimei some three years later. The fact that in LXX, Luc. these words precede the sentence which relates the elevation of Zadok to the high-priesthood, seems to suggest that this latter is an addition of a later editor, suggested by the detail which refers to Benaiah's succession to Joab.

36. לשמעי] Luc. adds *υἱὸν Γηρά*, i.e. בֶּן־גֵּרָא as in *v.* 8, adopted by Klo., and by Hoo. as coming appropriately at the beginning of the narrative.

37. ועברת] The Perf. with ו *consec.* used in continuation of an Infin. describing a hypothetical event. So in *v.* 42 ביום צאתך והלכת; 8. 33 בהנגף עמך . . . ושבו; *cf.* Dri. *Tenses*, §§ 117, 118; Da. § 55[c].

At the end of the verse LXX, Luc. add *καὶ ὥρκισεν αὐτὸν ὁ βασιλεὺς ἐν τῇ ἡμέρᾳ ἐκείνῃ*, i.e. וַיַּשְׁבִּיעֵהוּ הַמֶּלֶךְ בַּיּוֹם הַהוּא. Th., following Bö., regards these words as genuine, on the ground that if they had been an insertion from *v.* 42 (הלוא השבעתיך ביהוה), ביהוה would have been read and ביום ההוא would not have occurred. So Klo., who remarks that since violation of the oath of Yahwe was the ground of Shimei's execution, the swearing of the oath must be mentioned in the previous narrative. These reasons, however, are hardly consistent. Had the passage been genuine, it ought to have followed *v.* 38[a]; after Shimei has expressed his assent to the king's decision in general terms, the king then proceeds to take an oath of him. But if Shimei had *at first* taken the oath, he would not have then gone on to use the words of *v.* 38ª. The swearing of the oath of Yahwe may well be *implied* in the account of *vv.* 37, 38ª.

38. ימים רבים] LXX, Luc. τρία ἔτη derived from the beginning of the next verse. This is another instance of the harmonizing tendency of the LXX translator, tending to support the judgement expressed above on the LXX passage in *v.* 37.

39. שני עבדים לשמעי] The circumscription of the genitive is employed for greater indefiniteness. שְׁנֵי עַבְדֵי שׁ׳ might have meant '*the* two servants of Shimei.' Cf. *ch.* 5. 15 אֹהֵב היה חירם לדוד, not 'David's friend,' but 'a friend of David'; 1 Sam. 16. 18 בן לישי 'one of Jesse's sons.' Da. § 28, *Rem.* 5[1].

40. וילך שמעי] Luc. adds ἐξ Ἱερουσαλήμ. If genuine, the words call special attention to the fact that Shimei passed beyond the limits of his parole; though this seems to be clearly enough implied in the preceding וילך גתה. Klo. supposes Luc.'s reading to be an error for εἰς Ἱερ., and so adopts וילך שמעי ירושלימה. But in this case we should surely expect וַיָּשָׁב and not וילך.

41. וישב] LXX, Luc. καὶ ἀπέστρεψεν (Luc. ἐπέστρεψε) τοὺς δούλους αὐτοῦ, i.e. וַיָּשֶׁב אֶת־עֲבָדָיו; doubtless a mere gloss. Solomon was informed of Shimei's having left Jerusalem, and, as Klo. points out, it was of no importance to tell him whether on his return he was accompanied by his runaway slaves or not.

42. ואעד בך] 'I solemnly admonished thee,' lit. '*protested against*,' the ב following the verb pointing to the person *against* whom the admonition is directed. Cf. Gen. 43. 3 העד העִד בנו האיש; II. 17. 13; 1 Sam. 8. 9; *al.*

טוב הדבר שמעתי] 'Good is the matter; I have heard it,' i.e. I intend to obey it. So Klo., who compares השתחויתי in 2 Sam. 16. 4. טוב הדבר is thus used absolutely as a formula of assent in *v.* 38; *ch.* 18. 24; cf. Deut. 1. 14; 1 Sam. 9. 10 (דברך). This sense is given by Pesh. ܫܦܝܪ ܦܬܓܡܐ܃ ܗܘܝܬ ܫܡܥܬ, and apparently by Targ. תקין פיתגמא שמעית. Vulg., Luc. take שמעתי as a relative sentence; *quem audivi*; ὃ ἤκουσα; and this is the sense which is given by RV. Such an omission of the relative is, however, very rare in Heb. *prose*. LXX om. through oversight.

43. שבעת י׳] Ex. 22. 10; 2 Sam. 21. 7†. The meaning of the phrase is elucidated by 1 Sam. 20. 42 אשר נשבענו שנינו אנחנו בשם י׳.

44. והשיב] LXX, Luc., Vulg., Pesh. presuppose a past tense וַיָּשֶׁב 'he hath requited'; probably correctly. The fact that Shimei by his act of perjury had brought the death penalty upon himself was Yahwe's requital for his wickedness towards David. MT. may perhaps be a correction to accord with *v.* 32, where, however, the case is different; והשיב את דמו.

3. 1—11. 43. *History of the reign of Solomon.*

The kernel of the narrative is *chh.* 5. 15—7. 51, the description of Solomon's building operations, with its sequel, *ch.* 8. Around this are grouped (*chh.* 4. 1—5. 14; *chh.* 9, 10) a series of notices, for the most part brief, illustrative of the king's wisdom, magnificence, and prosperity.

Ch. 3 forms an introduction to the whole, detailing Solomon's request for wisdom, with a signal instance of its exercise: *ch.* 11, as a conclusion, gives a description of the circumstances which paved the way for the disruption of the kingdom.

3. 3–15. *The vision at Gibeon. Solomon's request for wisdom.*

Ch. 3. 4–15=2 Chr. 1. 3–13.

3. 1. There can be little doubt that this verse, together with *ch.* 9. 16, 17ª, originally formed part of the document embodied in the early part of *ch.* 5 (see *note* on *chh.* 4. 20—5. 14).

2, 3. The disapprobation of במה worship is based upon the law of Deuteronomy, which restricts sacrifice to the central sanctuary; see 12. 4–18, esp. *vv.* 13, 14. Similar notices are found in *ch.* 15. 14 (Asa); 22. 44 (Jehoshaphat); II. 12. 4 (Jehoash); 14. 4 (Amaziah); 15. 4 (Azariah); *v.* 35ª (Jotham). In every case the formula is nearly identical, and follows upon a general commendation of the king's conduct; ויעש [לעשות *ch.* 22. 43] הישר בעיני יהוה. Cf. also the condemnation of Rehoboam's worship, *ch.* 14.

22, 23 (but this may have been mixed with definite idolatry; cf. *v.* 24 וגם קדש היה בארץ), and the wholesale reprobation of the calf-worship of the Northern kingdom as summarized in II. 17. 7–23.

The old narrative treats במה worship as a matter of course; so here in *v.* 4, and in 1 Sam. 9. 12, 14; 7. 9, 17; 10. 8; *al.* Upon this subject, see R.Sm. *OTJC.*, Lect. viii; *DB*², Art. *Deuteronomy*, § 15; Dri. *Deut.* xlix. *ff.* Thus *vv.* 2, 3 both exhibit the influence of Deuteronomy. It is obvious, however, that they cannot be assigned to one author. In *v.* 3 the subject, as in *vv.* 1, 4, is Solomon, while in *v.* 2 *the people* are specified. Verse 3 simply places two facts side by side without any attempt at correlation;—Solomon loved Yahwe, only he sacrificed and burned incense on the high-places: *v.* 2 supplies an explanation;—This במה worship was a popular custom, due to the fact that the house of Yahwe was not yet built. Hence *v.* 3 is the work of R^{D}, and opens the account of Solomon's reign by introducing the narrative of the vision at Gibeon; *v.* 2 proceeds from an exilic or post-exilic editor who, with a view to explaining Solomon's conduct, inserted the phrase which he found to be frequent elsewhere רק העם מזבחים בבמות, together with the explanation which follows כי לא נבנה בית וג׳, and, in order to illustrate this latter, probably moved *v.* 1, which mentions the fact of the house of Yahwe being not yet built, from the position which it properly occupies in *ch.* 5 LXX (*note*). In LXX of this *ch.* *v.* 1 is wanting and *v.* 2 fragmentary.

2. לשם י׳] So *ch.* 5. 17, 19; 8. 17, 20, 44, 48. The original is 2 Sam. 7. 13 הוא יבנה בית לשמי quoted in *ch.* 5. 19; 8. 19.

3. ויאהב . . . ללכת] A distinctively D phrase. Deut. 10. 12; 11. 22; 19. 9; 30. 16. Cf. also 7. 9; 11. 1, 13; 13. 4; 30. 6, 20.

vv. 4–15. This section shows clear traces of the hand of R^{D}. In 2 Chr. 1. 3–13 the story appears in a shorter form, and apparently without the additions of the Compiler. That Chr., however, does not exhibit the narrative in its original simplicity is proved by the details of *vv.* 3–6 and *v.* 13 מלפני אהל מועד (cf. *ch.* 8. 4^{a} *note*); by the late words מדע *vv.* 10, 12; נכסים *v.* 12; and the unclassical expression נתון לך *v.* 12.

1 Kings 3.		2 Chr. 1.	
וילך המלך גבענה לזבח שם	4	Much expanded by the	3–6
כי היא הבמה הגדולה אלף		Chronicler.	
עלות יעלה שלמה על המזבח			
ההוא: בגבעון נראה	5	בלילה ההוא נראה אלהים	7
יהוה אל שלמה בחלום		לשלמה	
הלילה ויאמר אלהים שאל		ויאמר לו שאל	
מה אתן לך: ויאמר שלמה	6	מה אתן לך: ויאמר שלמה	8
אתה עשית עם עבדך דוד		לאלהים אתה עשית עם דויד	
אבי חסד גדול כאשר הלך		אבי חסד גדול	
לפניך באמת ובצדקה ובישרת			
לבב עמך ותשמר לו את			
החסד הגדול הזה ותתן לו		והמלכתני	
בן ישב על כסאו כיום הזה:		תחתיו:	
ועתה יהוה אלהי אתה	7	עתה יהוה אלהים יאמן	9
המלכת את עבדך תחת דוד		דברך עם דויד אבי כי אתה	
אבי ואנכי נער קטן לא אדע		המלכתני	
צאת ובא: ועבדך בתוך עמך	8		
אשר בחרת עם רב אשר לא		על עם רב כעפר	
ימנה ולא יספר מרב: ונתת	9	הארץ: עתה	10
לעבדך לב שמע לשפט את		חכמה ומדע תן לי ואצאה	
עמך להבין בין טוב לרע כי		לפני העם הזה ואבואה כי	
מי יוכל לשפט את עמך		מי ישפט את עמך	
הכבד הזה: וייטב הדבר	10	הזה הגדול:	
בעיני אדני כי שאל שלמה			
את הדבר הזה: ויאמר	11	ויאמר	11
אלהים אליו יען אשר שאלת		אלהים לשלמה יען אשר	
את הדבר הזה ולא שאלת		היתה זאת עם לבבך ולא	
לך ימים רבים ולא שאלת		שאלת עשר נכסים וכבוד	
לך עשר ולא שאלת נפש		ואת נפש שנאיך וגם	
איביך ושאלת לך הבין		ימים רבים לא שאלת	
לשמע משפט: הנה	12	ותשאל לך חכמה ומדע	

1 Kings 3.	2 Chr. 1.
עשיתי כדברך הנה	אשר תשפוט את עמי אשר
נתתי לך לב חכם ונבון	המלכתיך עליו׃ החכמה 12
אשר כמוך לא היה לפניך	והמדע נתון לך
ואחריך לא יקום כמוך׃	
13 וגם אשר לא שאלת נתתי	
לך גם עשר גם כבוד	ועשר ונכסים וכבוד אתן
אשר לא היה כמוך איש	לך אשר לא היה כן למלכים
14 במלכים כל ימיך׃ ואם	אשר לפניך ואחריך לא
תלך בדרכי לשמר חקי	יהיה כן׃
ומצותי כאשר הלך דויד	
אביך והארכתי את ימיך׃	
15 ויקץ שלמה והנה חלום	
ויבוא ירושלם ויעמד לפני	ויבא שלמה לבמה אשר 13
ארון ברית יהוה ויעל	בגבעון ירושלם מלפני
עלות ויעש שלמים ויעש	אהל מועד וימלך על
משתה לכל עבדיו׃	ישראל׃

The words overlined are the work of R^D; those marked by the dotted line may possibly be due to him. Probably the original form of the narrative was very near to that of Kings, with omission of the insertions of R^D.

The work of R^D may first be considered:—

6. הלך לפניך] See *note* on *ch.* 2. 4.

ובצדקה וג׳] Deut. 9. 5 בצדקתך וביֹשֶׁר לבבך, the only place where the two words are joined. ישרת *fem.* only here.

ותשמר לו את החסד] Deut. 7. 9, 12 ושמר י׳ אלהיך לך . . . ואת החסד. Cf. also *ch.* 8. 23; ‖ 2 Chr. 6. 14; Neh. 1. 5; 9. 32; Ps. 89. 29†.

ותתן לו וג׳] A reminiscence of *ch.* 1. 48^b.

כיום הזה] So again in *ch.* 8. 24, 61 (R^D). The phrase calls attention to the fulfilment of a promise or threat, and is frequent in Deut. and in books which show the influence of Deut. Deut. 2. 30; 4. 20, 38; 8. 18; 10. 15; 29. 27; Jer. 11. 5; 25. 18; 32. 20; 44. 6, 23; 1 Chr. 28. 7; 2 Chr. 6. 15; (|| 1 Ki. 8); Dan. 9. 7, 15. כְּהַיּוֹם הַזֶּה Deut. 6. 24; Jer. 44. 22; Ezr. 9. 7, 15; Neh. 9. 10. Elsewhere the phrase occurs only in Gen. 50. 20 (E); 1 Sam. 22. 8, 13†. Gen. 39. 11 is different.

8. עמך אשר בחרת] Deut. 7. 6 כי עם קדוש אתה לי׳ אלהיך בך בחר י׳ אלהיך להיות לו לעם סגלה; 14. 2; cf. 4. 37.

10. וייטב הדבר וג׳] Cf. Deut. 1. 23 וייטב בעיני הדבר; Gen. 41. 37 (JE); Josh. 22. 33 (P).

12. לב חכם ונבון] The two adjectives are so coupled in Deut. 1. 13; 4. 6.

אשר כמוך . . . כמוך] Cf. II. 23. 25 וכמהו לא היה לפניו מלך אשר שב אל י׳ בכל לבבו ובכל נפשו ובכל מאדו ככל תורת משה ואחריו לא קם כמהו, a passage clearly marked as belonging to R^D by the quotation from Deut. 6. 4. So also II. 18. 5.

14. אם תלך בדרכי לשמר חקי וג׳] See *ch.* 2. 3, 4 *note*.

כאשר הלך דויד] R^D constantly refers to David as the standard of piety; *vv.* 3, 6; *ch.* 9. 4; 11. 4, 6, 33, 38; 14. 8; 15. 3, 5, 11; II. 14. 3; 16. 2; 18. 3; 22. 2. Cf. *note* on *ch.* 11. 12.

והארכתי את ימיך] With י׳ as subject only in this passage. There are two more usual constructions:—(1) *Prolong one's own days*, as in Deut. 4. 26 לא תאריכֻן ימים עליה; (2) *Days grow long*, ימים being subject and האריך intransitive (*internal* Hiph.; G-K. § 53, 2); Ex. 20. 12 למען יארִכון ימיך.

15. If according to *v.* 4 '*the* great high-place' was at Gibeon, it is difficult to understand why Solomon should have returned to Jerusalem to offer sacrifice, except from the Deuteronomic standpoint. Hence the whole verse, at least in its present form, may be due to R^D.

ארון ברית י׳] Mainly a D expression. *Ch.* 6. 19; 8. 1, 6; Deut. 10. 8; 31. 9, 25, 26; Josh. 3. 3; 8. 33 (sections belonging to the Deuteronomic editor, marked as D^2; see Dri. *LOT.* 97); Jer. 3. 16; ארון הברית Josh. 3. 6 bis, 8; 6. 6† (all D^2).

Elsewhere ארון ברית י׳ occurs Num. 10. 33; 14. 44; Josh. 4. 7, 18; 6. 8 (all JE); 1 Sam. 4. 3, 4, 5 (LXX om. ברית), and several times in Chr. ארון הברית Josh. 4. 9 JE: ארון ברית האלהים 1 Sam. 4. 4 (LXX om. ברית); 2 Sam. 15. 24; 1 Chr. 16. 6; Judg. 20. 27†. In the curious expressions of Josh. 3. 11, 14, 17 (JE) ארון הברית אדון כל הארץ, הארון הברית, הארון ברית יהוה, הברית is doubtless an interpolation[1].

4. וילך] LXX, Luc. καὶ ἀνέστη καὶ ἐπορεύθη, i.e. וַיָּקָם וַיֵּלֶךְ, adopted by Klo. on the ground that it more appropriately introduces the festive occasion which, as the Chronicler, II. *ch.* 1, shows, was the inaugural action of the young king's reign.

המלך] LXX om.; Luc. Σολομῶν.

כי היא הבמה הגדולה] 'For it was *the* great high-place,' i.e. *the greatest* high-place; an idiomatic method of expressing the superlative degree. The article with the adjective implies that the subject is pre-eminently characterized by the quality described. Gen. 44. 12 בַּגָּדוֹל החל ובַקָּטֹן כלה 'he began with *the eldest* and finished with *the youngest*.' Da. § 34; G-K. § 133, 3.

יעלה] Probably frequentative; '*used to offer*.' אלף thus need not denote the number of victims slaughtered upon this single occasion, but may be a round number describing the many sacrifices which the king offered from time to time.

על המזבח ההוא: בגבעון נראה] LXX, Luc., Vulg., Pesh. presuppose עַל הַמִּזְבֵּחַ הַהוּא בְּגִבְעוֹן: וַיֵּרָא; a reading scarcely to be preferred, since the omission of the relative אשר before בגבעון is contrary to usage, and ההוא would in such a case be redundant. The reference of ההוא must be to הבמה הגדולה, which of course connotes the presence of an altar. Th. thinks that the Verss. read על המזבח הוא בגבעון which he renders 'upon the altar which is in Gibeon,' a strange use of הוא which can scarcely be paralleled even by Gen. 38. 21 איה הקדשה הוא בעינים.

---

[1] In *pre*-Deut. writings the phrases in use are אֲרוֹן יהוה, הָאָרוֹן in JE in the Hexateuch (only Josh.); אֲרוֹן אֱלֹהִים (הָאֱלֹהִים), אֲרוֹן יהוה, הָאָרוֹן in the old narratives of Sam. and Kings. The latest expression of all is אֲרוֹן הָעֵדוּת P.

Klo.'s suggestion על מזבח הנחשת אשר בגבעון (cf. 2 Chr. 1. 6) is quite unnecessary.

5. בחלום הלילה] Gen. 20. 3; 31. 24†. Cf. Job 33. 15 בחלום חזיון לילה.

מה] Used as relative without antecedent; 'ask *what* I shall give thee.' So exactly *ch.* 14. 3 הוא יגיד לך מה יהיה לנער 'he shall tell thee what shall happen to the child'; cf. Judg. 9. 48; Eccl. 11. 2. Correctly speaking מה is really the indefinite antecedent ('*anything*,' as in 2 Sam. 18. 22; *al.*), and the relative אשר is omitted. This can be seen from Num. 23. 3 וּדְבַר מַה־יַּרְאֵנִי, lit. 'and word of anything (which) he shall show me.' In the late Heb. of Ecclesiastes we find the relative expressed after מה, ·מַה־שֶּׁ; 1. 9; 3. 15; 6. 10; *al.* Ew. § 331[b].

6. עמך] The phrase הלך עם י׳ is very unusual. The only other occurrence appears to be Mic. 6. 8 והצנע לכת עם אלהיך. Cf. the expression התהלך את האלהים Gen. 5. 22, 24; 6. 9†. The common phrase is הלך לפני י׳ which occurs just before.

7. צאת ובא] An idiom expressing the discharge of duties pertaining to a particular position; 1 Sam. 18. 16; Deut. 31. 2.

8. אשר לא ימנה וג׳] *ch.* 8. 5 (‖ 2 Chr. 5. 6). Cf. Gen. 16. 10; 32. 13. For the *nuance* of the Imperf. '*cannot* be numbered,' cf. Dri. *Tenses*, § 37[a].

9. לב שמע] Not merely a heart *attentive* to the directions of Yahwe, but expressing further the result of such attention—'an *understanding* heart.' For this sense of שמע, cf. *v.* 11 לשמע משפט; Gen. 41. 15 תשמע חלום לפתר אתו. More commonly it is employed with a negative to express the non-understanding of a foreign tongue; Gen. 11. 7; Deut. 28. 49; *al.*

בין טוב לרע] Lev. 27. 33; 2 Sam. 19. 36†.

לשפט את עמך הכבד הזה] Pesh. ܠܡܕܢܘ ܠܥܡܟ ܥܡܐ ܗܢܐ ܪܒܐ suggests לשפט את עמך העם הכבד הזה, while Vulg. *judicare populum istum, populum tuum hunc multum*, perhaps points to the same reading with a transposition of עמך and העם in translation. MT. is, however, confirmed by 2 Chr. 1. 10 את עמך הזה הגדול.

11. שאלת לך] 'Hast asked for *thyself*.' So only in ‖ 2 Chr.

I. 11; II. 4. 3; 1 Sam. 12. 17, 19; Isa. 7. 11. This *Dativus commodi* is employed far more frequently in the sense, 'ask for some one else'; most commonly in the phrase שאל לפ׳ לשלום; 1 Sam. 17. 22; Gen. 43. 27; *al.*

ושאלת] '*But* hast asked.' The ו connects two *contrasted* ideas, and, by aid of the tautology ולא שאלת, ושאלת, gains a rather strong adversative sense, '*but*.' Somewhat similar, but not so marked, are *ch.* 2. 26 איש מות אתה וביום הזה לא אמיתך 'worthy of death art thou, *but* to-day I will not kill thee'; *ch.* 11. 33, 34 (ולא אקח); *al.* This use of ו is common in Prov.; cf. *ch.* 10 throughout.

The ו *simplex* places the idea in strict co-ordination with the preceding, thus preserving the assonance which would have been destroyed by וַתִּשְׁאַל.

הבין] So Isa. 56. 11 לא ידעו הבין; Ps. 32. 9.

12. עשיתי...נתתי] Perfects of certitude used here, as frequently, in a divine promise; Gen. 15. 18; Josh. 6. 2; Judg. 1. 2; *al.* The action determined upon by the will of the speaker is regarded as already accomplished. Dri. *Tenses*, § 13; Da. § 41.

לא היה] 'Shall not have been,' future perfect; or more strictly, '*was not* (*ever*),' upon any occasion that can be specified.

13. אשר לא היה . . . כל ימיך] 'So that there shall not have been any like thee among kings [all thy days].' Here כל ימיך makes no sense, and the sentence is quite complete without it. Vulg. attempts to explain, *cunctis retro diebus*, but doubtless LXX, Luc. are right in their omission of the phrase. It arose probably from an erroneous repetition of כָּמוֹךָ.

15. ויבוא] LXX *καὶ ἀνέστη καὶ παραγίνεται εἰς*, Luc. *καὶ ἀνέστη καὶ εἰσῆλθεν*, i. e. וַיָּקָם ויבא; possibly genuine.

לפני ארון] LXX, Luc. *κατὰ πρόσωπον τοῦ θυσιαστηρίου τοῦ κατὰ πρόσωπον (τῆς) κιβωτοῦ*, i. e. לִפְנֵי הַמִּזְבֵּחַ אֲשֶׁר לפני ארון וג׳. Th., Klo. think that this represents the original text, and that the recurrence of לפני occasioned the omission in MT. More probably the additional words are an insertion of the translator who wished to remove the impression that Solomon passed into the immediate presence of the Ark.

3. 16–28. *A notable example of Solomon's exercise of wisdom.*

16. אז תבאנה] The use of אז to introduce a fresh detail or narrative is very frequent in Kings. The other instances are *ch.* 8. 1, 12; 9. 11b, 24b; 11. 7; 16. 21; 22. 50; II. 8. 22b; 12. 18; 14. 8; 15. 16; 16. 5†. Doubtless this was one of the methods by which R^D pieced together his various sources, and was employed when he wished to show that an event was more or less contemporaneous with the preceding narrative. When greater definiteness seemed desirable, he employed the phrases בימים ההם II. 10. 32; בימיו *ch.* 16. 34; בעת ההיא *ch.* 14. 1 (see *note* on each passage).

תבאנה] The use of the Imperf. after אז introducing a past event is very usual. So in nine of the cases enumerated above, and also Ex. 15. 1; Num. 21. 17; *al.* The event is pictured as *growing out of* the previous circumstances indicated by אז; a form of idea which has become stereotyped in the ordinary construction of the Imperf. with ו *consec.* See Dri. *Tenses*, §§ 67, 68. Probably in Kings R^D sometimes substituted אז with Imperf. for an Imperf. with ו *consec.* standing in his source; cf. *ch.* 8. 1 where we actually meet with a shortened form of the Imperf., אָז יַקְהֵל. When, as in *ch.* 8. 12; 9. 24b; *al.*, the *Perfect* is employed with אז, the mere occurrence of the *fact* seems to be dwelt upon, without special stress upon its time relationship. G-K. § 107, 1, *Rem.* 1.

17. בי] Properly '*supplication*,' and then '*oh*' or '*pray*.' The word seems to be from √בי״י, Ar. بَيَّ 'to supplicate.' Others derive from בעה = Aram. בְּעָא 'to ask,' and make the word a contraction of בְּעִי; like בֵּל for בְּעֶל, רוּת for רְעוּת. Cf. Targ. rendering בבעו, Pesh. ܒܒܥܘ ܐܢܐ ܡܪܝ, here and elsewhere.

עמה] '*With* her,' i.e. 'in her company'; Lev. 25. 39 כי ימוך אחיך עמך 'if thy brother be waxen poor *near* thee'; Ex. 22. 24; Gen. 31. 38. When used of proximity to several persons '*among*' is a fair equivalent; Judg. 18. 25 אל תשמע קולך עמנו 'make not thy voice to be heard among us.' This use of עם with *persons* is closely similar to that with *places* noticed on *ch.* 1. 9.

18. ללדתי] ל with back reference to the point of departure, '*after* my deliverance.' Cf. Gen. 7. 10 ויהי לשבעת הימים 'and it came to pass *after* seven days'; 2 Sam. 13. 23.

זולתי] Not 'except,' as usually (*ch.* 12. 20; Deut. 1. 36; *al.*), but, with a looser connexion with what precedes, '*but only.*' So Deut. 4. 12† תמונה אינכם ראים זולתי קול. Cf. the occasional *nuance* of εἰ μή, ἐὰν μή in N.T.; Gal. 2. 16 εἰδότες δὲ ὅτι οὐ δικαιοῦται ἄνθρωπος ἐξ ἔργων νόμου, ἐὰν μὴ διὰ πίστεως Ἰησοῦ Χριστοῦ. S. Luke 4. 25–27.

19. אשר] '*Because*'; *ch.* 8. 33 אשר יחטאו לך; 15. 5; Gen. 30. 18; 31. 49; *al.* More precise are עַל אֲשֶׁר 2 Sam. 12. 6; מִפְּנֵי אֲשֶׁר Ex. 19. 18; כַּאֲשֶׁר 1 Sam. 28. 18; מֵאֲשֶׁר &c.

21. ואתבונן אל] 'I looked carefully *at.*' So Isa. 14. 16† אליך יתבוננו.

22. אמרת] The participle lends pictorial effect; '*was saying.*'

23. זאת אמרת] LXX, Luc. σὺ λέγεις, i.e. אַתְּ אָמַרְתְּ; scarcely so good as MT., where the participle nearly represents the true English present; 'this one *says*,' 2 Sam. 18. 27. Dri. *Tenses*, § 135, 2 *end.*

זאת . . . חאת] '*This one . . . and the other*'; *ch.* 22. 20 ויאמר זה בכה וזה אמר בכה 'and one said on this wise and another on that.' Da. § 5.

25. גזרו] 'Cut *in twain.*' So with the substantive, Ps. 136. 13 לגזר ים סוף לגזרים 'into *two* parts'; Gen. 15. 17.

At end of verse Luc. adds καὶ τὸ τεθνηκὸς ὁμοίως διέλετε, καὶ δότε ἀμφοτέραις. So Jos. This appears to be a translator's addition, derived, as Klo. notices, from the law in Ex. 21. 35.

26. נכמרו] So Gen. 43. 30; Hos. 11. 8 (with נִחוּמַי as subject). The ground idea is 'to be *hot*'; cf. Lam. 5. 10 עורנו כתנור נכמרו.

רחמיה] Here, as elsewhere, constantly in the plural, representing the seat of compassion or affection.

על בנה] '*Over* her son,' applied appropriately to the infant, but in Gen. 43 אל '*towards*,' with reference to grown men.

הַיָּלוּד] So *v.* 27; 1 Chr. 14. 4 הַיְלוּדִים; but elsewhere only in the expression ילוד אשה three times in Job. In Syr. ܝܠܘܕܐ is a common form.

27. תנו לה את הילוד החי] Since the woman who spoke last was the one who desired the division of the child, we must suppose that the king, in uttering the words תנו לה, made a gesture to indicate that he referred to the other woman. Luc. (so LXX, omitting τὸ ζῶν, τῇ γυναικί) removes the ambiguity by reading Δότε τὸ παιδίον τὸ ζῶν τῇ γυναικὶ τῇ εἰπούσῃ Δότε αὐτῇ αὐτό; a mere exegetical paraphrase. Th., following Bö., supposes that the original may have been תְּנוּ אֹתוֹ לָאֹמֶרֶת תְּנוּ לָהּ אֶת־הַיָּלוּד הַחַי, and that thus אתו לאמרת תנו may have fallen out by homoioteleuton. But if the LXX translator had had these words before him, why should he have transposed אתו and הילוד החי?

28. חכמת אלהים] Wisdom *sent by* or *proceeding from* God. Cf. חִתַּת א׳ Gen. 35. 5; פַּחַד א׳ 2 Chr. 20. 29.

חכמה is here used in the special sense of *shrewdness* and *keen insight into human nature*. Cf. the bearing of the term *wise* as applied to the woman of Tekoa 2 Sam. 14. 2 *ff.*; and the woman of Abel-Meholah 2 Sam. 20. 16. Upon the later development of the term as seen in the '*Ḥokhma* literature' of the Old Testament, cf. Dri. *LOT.*, pp. 368 *ff.*

4. 1—5. 14. *Solomon's officers of state. His prosperity and wisdom.*

Ch. 5. 1[a] = 2 Chr. 9. 26. *Ch.* 5. 6 = 2 Chr. 9. 25[a].

4. 2. השרים אשר לו] The circumlocution has the effect of retaining the greater definiteness which would have been sacrificed if שָׂרָיו had been written. Cf. *note* on *ch.* 1. 8, and Da. § 28, *Rem.* 5[2].

עזריהו בן צדוק הכהן] הכהן must refer to עזריהו and not to צדוק, just as elsewhere in the list, the title of the office refers to the man first specified, and not to his father. Hence Vulg., *filius Sadoc sacerdotis*, interprets wrongly. LXX, Luc. omit הכהן, as also כהן in *v.* 5, apparently under the impression that its usage is not to be reconciled with *v.* 4 צדוק ואביתר כהנים. Pesh., Targ. follow MT. The Chronicler, I. 5. 36, mentions an Azariah as הוא אשר כִּהֵן בבית אשר בנה שלמה בירושלם, a statement apparently misplaced from *v.* 35 (see Bertheau, *ad loc.*), where it will refer to our Azariah who is mentioned as son of Ahimaaz son of Zadok. Probably Azariah succeeded to Zadok, and exercised the office of high-priest at the consecration of the new Temple at Jerusalem, and during far the longer portion of Solomon's reign. We know that the statement of *v.* 4^b^, as regards Abiathar, only holds good for a very short period during this reign (*ch.* 2. 26 *f.*), and very possibly this is also true of Zadok, whose son Ahimaaz was a man of some experience at the time of Absalom's rebellion (2 Sam. 15. 35, 36), and who therefore must have been well advanced in years at the time of Solomon's accession.

3. אליחרף] The only occurrence of this name. LXX Ἐλιάφ, Luc. Ἐλιάβ seem to substitute the more ordinary אֱלִיאָב.

שישא] LXX Σαβά, Luc. Σαφάτ. In 1 Chr. 18. 16 the same man is called שַׁוְשָׁא, LXX Ἰησοῦς, Luc. Σουσά.

In 2 Sam. 8. 17 apparently the same person appears as שְׂרָיָה, LXX Ἀσά, Luc. Σαραίας; 2 Sam. 20. 25 Kt. שיא, Q're שְׁוָא, LXX Ἰησοῦς, Luc. Σουσά.

Hence—(i) The form שריה has only weak attestation. It is supported by Luc. once, by LXX never[1].

(ii) The form Ἰησοῦς occurring twice in LXX cannot be original, since it is most improbable that so ordinary a name as יהושוע should have suffered corruption. On the other hand, it is very likely that Σουσά has become corrupted into the well-known Ἰησοῦς.

(iii) The form שושא is supported—

(*a*) By שישא in 1 Ki. 4. 3, the interchange of י and ו being of constant occurrence.

(*β*) By Σουσά twice in Luc.

---

[1] It is true that this is the form adopted in three places by Pesh., and in two by Vulg.; but in the case of proper names we cannot attach much importance to the testimony of Vulg., Pesh., Targ., since either the lists in the Heb. texts used by these translators appeared in a later form resembling that of MT., or else some sort of arbitrary uniformity with MT. has been produced by later hands. In the cases to which allusion is here made, correction for the sake of uniformity with 2 Sam. 8. 17 appears to have taken place.

(γ) In some degree by Ἰησοῦς twice in LXX, and, as regards the second שׁ, by Ἀσά in a third passage.

Hence שַׁוְשָׁא has by far the best attestation, and may be adopted.

4. ובניהו . . . הצבא] LXX om. through oversight.

וצדוק ואביתר כהנים] No part of the register in its original form as an official state document. This naturally headed the list with the name of the high-priest of the time, עזריהו בן צדוק. The insertion was made by R^D or by some one still earlier who wished, as a matter of historical interest, to notice that Zadȯk and Abiathar were priests at the commencement of the reign.

5. עזריהו] LXX Ὀρνειά, Luc. Ὀρνιά seem to presuppose אֲדֹנִיָּהוּ with corruption of ר into ד. This officer is apparently not elsewhere mentioned under either name.

זבוד] Only here. Luc. Ζαχούρ, i.e. probably זַכּוּר, a name of frequent occurrence. Pesh. ܙܟܘܪ in part supports this reading.

כהן] A peculiar use of the term to denote some high official whose functions we cannot precisely determine. Cf. 2 Sam. 8. 18 ובני דוד כהנים היו, paraphrased by the Chronicler, I. 18. 17 הראשנים ליד המלך. Dri. (*Sam., ad loc.*) argues from the uniform use of כהן in Heb. that the office, if possibly semi-secular and at times extended to non-priestly men of good family, must have belonged in the first place to the priestly class.

רֵעֶה המלך] This anomalous punctuation of the *st. constr.* is found again in 2 Sam. 15. 37 רֵעֶה דָוִד, and, according to Norzi, in 16. 16 in the best MSS. Klo. omits, as an exegetical gloss to explain the difficult כהן; but all Verss. reproduce the word.

6. ואחישר על הבית] This is the only important official named, *vv.* 2–7, whose father is not mentioned[1]. Hence there is probably some corruption of text.

LXX seem to have a triple, and Luc. a double rendering.

LXX	καὶ Ἀχεὶ ἦν οἰκονόμος	i.e.	ואחי [שׂר] על הבית
	καὶ Ἐλιὰκ ὁ οἰκονόμος	,,	ואליאך [שׂר] על הבית
	καὶ Ἐλιὰβ υἱὸς Σὰφ ἐπὶ τῆς πατριᾶς	,,	ואליאב בן שׁף על ?

[1] Verse 4^b is no exception: see *note*.

Luc. καὶ 'Αχιὴλ οἰκονόμος i.e. ואחיאל [שר] על הבית
καὶ 'Ελιὰβ υἱὸς 'Ιωὰβ „ ואליאב בן יואב על?
ἐπὶ τῆς στρατιᾶς

The name אֱלִיאָב which occurs in three renderings (ך is a mistake for ב in אליאך) appears to be the genuine form. Probably also the two letters שר, which appear to occur in LXX 1, 2, Luc. 1, and in LXX 3 under the form Σάφ, are a remnant of the father's name. Hence we may conjecture

וֶאֱלִיאָב בֶּן־שָׁרָ[יָה] עַל־הַבָּיִת

Th. supposes that LXX 3 (Luc. 2) are a translation of some words which have fallen out of MT., and hence after ואחישר על הבית he would restore וֶאֱלִיאָב בֶּן־שָׁפָט עַל־הַמִּשְׁמַעַת, supposing that LXX πατριᾶς read מִשְׁפָּחָה for משמעת. So Ew.

על הבית] Prefect of the palace, discharging the king's domestic affairs. This office existed subsequently both in the Northern (*ch.* 16. 9; 18. 3; II. 10. 5) and Southern (II. 18. 18; *al.*) kingdoms, and was a position of the highest dignity, being held by Jotham the heir to the throne of Judah after his father Azariah had been smitten with leprosy II. 15. 5; cf. also the exalted language used of Eliakim upon his promotion Isa. 22. 21, 22. The palace prefect was also called סֹכֵן Isa. 22. 15; see *note* on *ch.* 1. 2.

אדנירם] So LXX, Luc. This form of the name, which occurs also in *ch.* 5. 28, is doubtless correct. The form אֲדֹרָם (2 Sam. 20. 24; *ch.* 12. 18; ‖ 2 Chr. 10. 18 הֲדֹרָם) is either a contraction or a corruption.

המס] The forced labour exacted by Solomon for his building operations, according to *ch.* 9. 15–22 only from the Canaanite nations, but according to *ch.* 5. 27 from all Israel. That the latter statement is correct is proved by the unpopularity of Adoniram, who was stoned by men of the ten tribes; *ch.* 12. 18. The מס is mentioned as existing at the end of David's reign, 2 Sam. 20. 24, and is also spoken of as enforced upon the Canaanites at the conquest of the land; Jos. 17. 13 (JE); Judg. 1. 28; *al.*

7. יהיה על] 'It was *incumbent upon*': Ezek. 45. 17 ועל הנשיא

יהיה העולות וג׳; without היה Ezra 10. 4, 12; 2 Sam. 18. 11; *al.* The Imperf. expresses the *periodical* nature of the duty.

על אחד] Read עַל־הָאֶחָד with Q're; LXX, Luc. ἐπὶ τὸν ἕνα. The article is necessary to express the idea of distribution.

8. בן חור] Correct. LXX, Luc. Βαιώρ, a corruption. All twelve officers are mentioned either by their patronymic only, or by their particular name with the addition of the patronymic, which is in no case omitted.

9. בן דקר] LXX υἱὸς Ῥῆχας, Luc. υἱὸς Ῥῆχαβ. The name occurs nowhere else, unless בִּדְקַר II. 9. 25 represents a contraction of it. Luc.'s בֶּן־רֵכָב is at least as probable.

מקץ] Not elsewhere mentioned. LXX Μακεμάς, i.e. apparently מִכְמָשׂ (cf. 1 Sam. 13. 2, 5; 14. 31 Μαχεμάς), cannot be right, since it is clear that the place must have lain, with the others belonging to the same officer, in or about the district originally assigned to Dan, and in the west borders of Judah. Luc. Μαγχάς, and other Verss. support MT.

שעלבים] Judg. 1. 35†. שַׁעַלַבִּין Josh. 19. 42†. One of David's heroes is described in 2 Sam. 23. 32 as הַשַּׁעַלְבֹנִי.

בית שמש] The modern *'Ain Shems,* a village about four miles west-south-west of Jerusalem. Rob. *BR.* ii. 223 *f.*

ואלן בית חנן] LXX καὶ Ἐλὼμ ἕως Βηθλαμάν, Luc. καὶ Αἰλὼν ἕως Βαιθναάμ, read as the names of *two* places, doubtless correctly. In Josh. 19. 43 אילון is mentioned as a town of Dan, and בית חנן appears to have been discovered under the modern name *Beit-Ḥanûn,* a short distance east-north-east of Gaza. Rob. *BR.* ii. 35; Baed. 154. We may, therefore, read וְאֵלוֹן עַד בֵּית־חָנָן; cf. *v.* 12 עד אבל מחולה. So Klo., Kamp.

10. בן חסד . . . חפר] LXX υἱὸς Ἕσωθ, Βηρναμαλουσαμηνχὰ καὶ Ῥησφαραχείν. This, when transliterated, upon the whole supports MT.

MT. בן חסד בארבת לו סכה וכל ארץ חפר
LXX בן חסד בארנם לו ס[מ]נח ו ריץ פרח

The place ארבות is not mentioned elsewhere, but may possibly be the same as אֲרָב Josh. 15. 52, a city near Hebron. The נם of

LXX may easily be a corruption of בת of MT., and ארנם certainly does not point to any known place of a different name. Since יַרְמוּת (probably the modern *Yarmûk*) is mentioned with סכה in Josh. 15. 35, it has been thought, with some plausibility, that this place lies concealed under ארבות. So Th.

The correctness of סכה, which has been identified with *Shuweikeh* close to *Beit Nettîf*, is not to be doubted. Rob. *BR*. ii. 16, 21; Baed. 161. LXX reads נ for כ, ח for ה, and inserts מ, perhaps a corruption of ס erroneously repeated. LXX, פרח is merely a transposition of חפר, which latter seems to be correct, Josh. 12. 17.

Luc. Μαχεὶ υἱὸς Ἐχωβὴρ Βηθναμαλουζὰ καὶ Ἀμηχὰ καὶ τῆς Φαραχινανα-δάβ is clearly a further corruption of LXX through an attempt to resolve it into sense. Εσωθ Βηρ- has become Εχωβηρ, then Βηρ- is repeated under the form Βηθ-, -σαμηνχα is divided into -ζα (και) Αμηχα, Ρησ- becomes της, and finally -φαραχειν with the אבינדב of the next *verse* appears as Φαραχιναναδάβ.

11. בן א׳ כל נפת דאר] 'Ben-Abinadab—all the high country of Dor'; correct. For נפת דאר, cf. Josh. 12. 23 נָפַת דּוֹר; 11. 2 נָפוֹת דּוֹר.

The meaning of the root נוף is illustrated by Ps. 48. 3 יְפֵה נוֹף 'beautiful *in elevation*,' of Mount Zion.

LXX ἀνὰ Δάν is a corruption of Ἀβιναδάβ, and ἀνὰ Φαθεί of Ναφάθ. The words ἀνὴρ Ταβληθεί represent דאר טפת read as נאר טבלת. Probably נאר was at first attached to נפת by the translator, the whole being transliterated Ναφαθανηρ, which afterwards came to be divided.

טָפַת] With the old f. termination. So with other personal names, both f.:—בָּשְׂמַת *v.* 15; Gen. 26. 34; מַחֲלַת Gen. 28. 9; 2 Chr. 11. 18; or, more strangely, m.:—גְּנֻבַת *ch.* 11. 20; גִּינַת *ch.* 16. 21; בְּכוֹרַת 1 Sam. 9. 1; גָּלְיַת 1 Sam. 17. 4 *ff.*; אֲחֻזַּת Gen. 26. 26. It is noticeable that most of these names are non-Israelitish: אחזת, גלית Philistine; גנבת probably Edomite or a Semiticized Egyptian name like אָסְנַת Gen. 41. 45; מחלת Ishmaelite; and טפת, בשמת, if daughters of Solomon's foreign wives, probably Canaanite; בשמת Gen. 26. 34 being specified as Hittite. עֲנָת, mentioned Judg. 3. 31; 5. 6 as the parent of שַׁמְגַּר, is the name of the Canaanite goddess, traces of whose cult appears in the localities בֵּית־עֲנָת Judg. 1. 33; בֵּית־עֲנוֹת Josh. 15. 59; עֲנָתוֹת Jer. 1. 1; *al.*

Similarly, we find a number of place-names with this termination, these being clearly Canaanite in origin:—מֵפָעַת (perhaps a segholate termination) Josh. 13. 18; מַעֲרָת Josh. 15. 59; בָּצְקַת Josh. 15. 39; II. 22. 1; הַמִּכְמְתָת Josh. 16. 6; גִּבְעַת (? text obscure) Josh. 18. 28; הַדָּבְרַת Josh. 19. 12; דָּבְרַת Josh. 21. 28; קַטָּת Josh. 19. 15; חֶלְקַת Josh. 19. 25; חֶלְקָת Josh. 21. 31; שִׁיחוֹר לִבְנָת Josh. 19. 26; חַמַּת, רַקַּת Josh. 19. 35; בַּעֲלָת Josh. 19. 44; *ch.* 9. 18; צְפַת Judg. 1. 17; טַבָּת Judg. 7. 22; צָרְפַת Ob. 20; *ch.* 17. 9, 10; and perhaps נָיוֹת 1 Sam. 19. 18 (on vocalization, cf. Dri. *ad loc.*)[1]. Outside Palestine we have אֵילַת Deut. 2. 8; *al.;* and מחרת in Moab, Mesha, *l.* 14.

Comparing the inscriptions of neighbouring countries, it may be noticed that both Phoenician and Aramaic afford many examples of f. proper names in *-ath*, this being the regular f. termination in Phoen. as in Moabitic: Phoen. (*CIS.*) כבדת *Kabdath*, 372, *al.;* ארשת *'Arishath*, 307, *al.;* עלשת *'Elishath*, 481, *al.*, &c.;—Aram. Nabathean (Euting, *Nabatäische Inschriften*) בנית *Bunayyath*, 13; גזיאת *Guzai'ath*, 15; הינת *Hînath*, 26, &c.; while Aramaic alone yields instances of m. names with this termination;—Nabathean (Euting) חרתת *Ḥaritath* (Aretas); בגרת *Bagrath*, 8; מרת *Murrath*, 18; חמלת *Ḥamlath*, 7; מנעת *Mun'ath*, 6, 19; עבידת *'Obaidath*, 23, 24; עמירת *'Amirath*, 19;—Palmyrene (De Vogüé, *Syrie Centrale*) אדינת *'Odainath*, 21, *al.;*—Babylon (*CIS.*) אמדת *'Ummadath*, 66;—Assyria, ארתדת *'Artadath*, 100. Phoenician, on the other hand, only exhibits m. names in *-ath* compounded with the f. name of the goddess מלכת *Milkath*, just as Aramaic abounds in m. compounds of the f. אלת *'Allath*.

12. תענך ומגדו] Mentioned together as the scene of the great battle of Deborah and Barak with the Canaanites; Judg. 5. 19. תענך now appears as *Ta'annûk*, not far to the south-west of *Zer'în*, i.e. יזרעאל. מגדו is conjectured by Rob. to be the modern *Lejjûn*,

[1] No attempt has been made to include or classify proper names in Chr.

the Legio of Jos. and Eusebius, said by them to be three or four Roman miles from Taanach. This place lies north-west of *Ta'annûk*, and due west of *Zer'în*. *BR.* ii. 316, 328; Baed. 227; Smith, *Hist. Geogr.* 386 *f.*

בית שאן] Also בֵּית שְׁאָן 1 Sam. 31. 10, 12; or בֵּית־שַׁן 2 Sam. 21. 12; the Scythopolis of later times, and now, by a rather strange contraction, *Beisân* to the west of the other cities, and near the Jordan. Baed. 222; Smith, *Hist. Geogr.* 357 *ff.*

צרתנה] *Ch.* 7. 46 mentioned with סֻכּוֹת (see *note*); Josh. 3. 16 said to be near אָדָם, i.e. probably the modern ford of *ed-Dâmieh* close to *Qarn Ṣarṭabeh*, with which, however, צרתן cannot be identified (Van de Velde, &c.) without violence to philology. 2 Chr. 4. 17 reads צְרֵדָתָה for צָרְתָן of *ch.* 7. 46; צְרֵדָה being mentioned, *ch.* 11. 26, as the home of Jeroboam in the hill-country of Ephraim. The identification of the two places seems, however, to be doubtful.

עד מעבר] 'As far as *the other side of*'; not as RV. marg. 'as far as *over against*,' i.e. *on this side of*. The former is the universal sense of the phrase used from the point of view of the speaker or writer. Thus בְּעֵבֶר הַיַּרְדֵּן, מֵעֵבֶר לַיַּרְדֵּן can denote either the country to the east of Jordan, Num. 22. 1; Deut. 1. 1; Josh. 17. 5; or that to the west of Jordan, Deut. 3. 20, 25; 11. 30; Josh. 5. 1; 9. 1; 12. 7; according to the position or point of view of the user of the phrase. In Num. 32. 19 the double מעבר does not violate the rule, but is employed by way of *contrast*, the first being spoken from the actual position of the speaker east of Jordan, and the second from the new point of view pictured by the calling up before the mind of the country west of Jordan. So in Josh. 22. 7, the phrase is used with reference to the position of the *other* half-tribe on the east. See Dri. *Deut.* xlii. *f.*

יקמעם] A place of this name is mentioned, 1 Chr. 6. 53†, as a Levitical city in the hill-country of Ephraim. In Josh. 21. 22 (|| 1 Chr.) the name is given as קִבְצַיִם, identified by Col. Conder (*Handbook*, 417) with *Tel el-Kabûs* near Bethel. This locality is much too far south of the cities previously named to suit the present mention, and, besides this, the הר אפרים has already been assigned (*v.* 8) to בן חור. This יקמעם therefore cannot be the יקמעם of 1 Chr., unless Conder's identification is wrong, and the city lay quite in the north of the הר אפרים. Rob. *BR.* iii. 115 follows AV. in regarding the name as a corruption of יָקְנְעָם, Josh. 21. 34, *al.*, which he finds as *Tell Qaimûn*, south-east of Carmel. Baed. 228.

13. ברמת גלעד] Cf. *note* on *ch.* 22. 3.

After the first לו, LXX, Luc. omit לו . . . חות by homoioteleuton.

חות] 'the tent-villages'; Ar. حَوَى *collect together*, حِوَآءٌ *a group of tents near together.*

חות יאיר . . . בגלעד] So Num. 32. 40, 41; Judg. 10. 4, rightly. Deut. 3. 14; Josh. 13. 30 (D^2) locate the villages in Bashan. See Dri. *Deut.*, *ad loc.*, who explains the origin of the mistake.

חבל ארגב] Targ. פלך טרכונא 'the region of Trachonitis,' i. e. the modern *El-Leja*, a district to the south of Damascus, forming a great lava-bed of about 350 square miles in extent. This identification seems, however, to be improbable. See Dri. on Deut. 3. 4, 5; and in *DB. Edinb. s.v.* Argob.

ערים גדלות וג'] 'Great cities . . . walls and bars of bronze'; or, as we should say, '*with* walls, &c.' The extension חומה וג', in loose apposition to ערים גדלות, serves in part to describe the cities, in part to characterize their greatness. Cf. Deut. 3. 5; 2 Chr. 8. 5. Dri. *Tenses*, § 188, 1.

14. מחנימה] LXX Μααναιέιον, Luc. ἐν Μαχειλάμ, perhaps read מַחֲנַיִם; but, as Klo. says, the ה *loc.* can be justified by supposing the implication of some such expression as '*appointed* to M.'

15. לאשה] LXX, Luc. om. through oversight.

16. באשר] LXX, Luc. om.; but allusion to this district follows naturally after נפתלי in previous verse.

ובְעָלוֹת] No such place as עָלוֹת is mentioned elsewhere, and בַּעֲלֹת of *ch.* 9. 18 is apparently the same as the בעלת of Josh. 19. 44 mentioned among the cities assigned to Dan, and so unsuitable, since this district has already been dealt with in *v.* 9. LXX ἐν τῇ Μααλά, Cod. A καὶ ἐν Μααλώτ. This suggests וּמַעֲלוֹת or וּבְמַעֲלוֹת, and accordingly Th. thinks that the country round about Accho and Achzib may have been known as 'the steps' or 'ascents,' even if the original reading of the Heb. text was not מַעֲלֵה צוֹר; cf. Josh. 10. 10 מעלה בית חורן. Against this, we have no trace elsewhere of the use of the term in this district. Luc. ἐν τῇ Γαλαάδ seems to be merely an alteration of LXX. Gilead is dealt with in *vv.* 13, 19. Klo. suggests וּזְבֻלוּן, and since this tribe would naturally be mentioned in connexion with אשר, נפתלי, and יששכר, the emendation is probably correct.

19. בארץ גלעד] LXX, Luc. ἐν τῇ γῇ Γάδ. Probably a mistake. The land of Gad is rather too precise, part of the kingdoms of Sihon and Og having been assigned to Reuben and the half-tribe of Manasseh; Josh. 13. 21, 30 *f.* On the other hand, from the wider term ארץ גלעד we conclude that Geber ben-Uri had supervision of all the country east of Jordan not assigned in *v.* 13.

ונציב אחד אשר בארץ] RV. 'and he was the only officer which was in the land.' This is usually interpreted thus: As the district was a very large one, more than one officer might have been expected to superintend it; but as a matter of fact this was not the case, probably because the country was rugged and thinly populated. But this translation, together with its explanation, would at least require וְהוּא הַנְּצִיב הָאֶחָד אֲשֶׁר בָּאָרֶץ הַהִיא, and there are no signs of the text ever having existed in this form. LXX καὶ νασὲφ εἷς ἐν γῇ Ἰούδα, Luc. Νασεὶβ ἐν τῇ γῇ Ἰούδα make the reference to be to yet one more officer who has supervision over Judah, thus restoring the number *twelve* which these Verss. would otherwise have lost through the corrupt rendering in *v.* 11[a]. But it is strange that this officer should be thus vaguely mentioned without record of his name, nor does Luc. appear to be correct in viewing נציב as a proper name; and besides this, having adopted the obviously original בן אבינדב of *v.* 11[a], we have now *thirteen* officers in contradiction to the statement of *v.* 7.

Klo. ingeniously suggests וְנָצִיב אֶחָד עַל כָּל־הַנִּצָּבִים אֲשֶׁר בָּאָרֶץ '*and one officer was over all the officers who were in the land,*' the allusion being to עזריהו בן נתן who is mentioned in *v.* 5 as על הנצבים. Such a second passing notice of this official at the end of the list would be most appropriate. The emendation is to some extent supported by Vulg., *super omnia quae erant in illa terra*, and may be worthily adopted[1].

Verse 20—*chapter* 5. 14.

This section appears in LXX, Luc. in a form somewhat different to MT. 4. 20; 5. 1, 5, 6, and part of *v.* 4 (מתפסח . . . הנהר) do not appear, but are to be found in the addition at the end of *ch.* 2. 46. At the close of *v.* 19 of *ch.* 4 the text continues with *ch.* 5 in the following order: *vv.* 7, 8, 2–4, 9–14, after which follow *ch.* 3. 1; *ch.* 9. 16, 17ᵃ. Thus the commencement of *v.* 7 וכלכלו הנצבים האלה וג׳ hinges directly on to the section *ch.* 4. 7–19 which enumerates the נצבים and their respective districts. This explains הָאֵלֶּה of *ch.* 5. 7, which is otherwise anomalous. There can be no question that the text of the section, as preserved by LXX, is complete in itself, and bears the stamp of originality rather than the somewhat confused account of MT. The disturbing factors in MT. appear to have been 4. 20; 5. 1, 5[2]. These, which contain no very precise information, were added probably not from a written source but from oral tradition, by an exilic or post-exilic[3] scribe, who desired reference to the happy times under Solomon's golden age. The insertion led to the dislocation of *vv.* 7, 8, causing them to be placed after *vv.* 2, 3, 4. Probably the same hand excerpted the notice about Pharaoh's daughter and her dowry from its true position after *v.* 14, dividing it and placing part at the beginning of *ch.* 3 (for the reason given on 3. 2, 3 *note ad fin.*) and part as a sequel to the mention of גזר in *ch.* 9. 15.

20. כחול וג׳] A common simile for a very large multitude; so exactly 2 Sam. 17. 11; cf. 1 Sam. 13. 5; Josh. 11. 4; Judg. 7. 12.

5. 1. היה מושל] The participle with the substantive verb em-

---

[1] Cf. Jos. (*Ant.* viii. 2, § 3) ἐπὶ δὲ τούτων εἷς πάλιν ἄρχων ἀποδέδεικτο.

[2] Verse 6 belongs properly to *ch.* 10 where it occurs in LXX, Luc. in connexion with *v.* 26.

[3] Necessarily so; for exilic hands had already been at work upon *ch.* 5. 4 (*note*) in the part which is common both to LXX and MT.

phasizing the idea of *duration—'was ruling'*; so *v.* 24 'was giving,' continuously for some long period; *ch.* 12. 6; *al.* Dri. *Tenses*, § 135, 5.

מן הנהר וג׳] The ideal limits of Israel's dominion; cf. Gen. 15. 18; Ex. 23. 31; Deut. 1. 7; 11. 24; Josh. 1. 4. הנהר '*the river*' always denotes נְהַר פְּרָת, the Euphrates; hence Vulg. *a flumine terrae Ph.*, Pesh. ܡܢ ܢܗܪܐ ܕܐܪܥܐ ܕܦܠܫܬܝܐ, which make ארץ פ׳ an accus. of place, are quite wrong. ארץ פ׳ is an accus. of *motion towards*, 'to the land of the Ph.'; cf. Gen. 45. 25 ויבאו ארץ כנען. Da. § 69[b]. 2 Chr. 9. 26 reads ועד ארץ פ׳.

ועד גבול מ׳] '*Even to* the boundary of Egypt.' The גבול מצרים seems to be the *Wady el-Arîsh*, which bounded the southern extremity of Philistia, and is mentioned elsewhere as the southern boundary of Palestine; *ch.* 8. 65; Num. 34. 5; Josh. 15. 4, 47; Isa. 27. 12.

מגשים...ועבדים] 'They brought &c.'; impersonal. Cf. Gen. 39. 22 את כל אשר עשים שם הוא היה עשה 'whatsoever was done (*lit.* they did) there, he was the doer of it.' This use of the participle with the indefinite subject unexpressed is somewhat uncommon. Cf. Dri. *Tenses*, § 135, 6.

מנחה] '*Tribute*'; so II. 17. 3; Judg. 3. 15, 17; 2 Sam. 8. 2, 6. Elsewhere the word has the more general sense of *a present* brought voluntarily to gain favour in the eyes of the recipient; II. 8. 8; 20. 12; Gen. 32. 14. As a sacrificial term the word in P denotes *the meal-offering*. Cf. further, *ch.* 18. 29 *note*.

3. רעי] 'Pasture'; a ἅπαξ λεγ. The common word is מִרְעֶה. According to the vocalization of בָּקָר *st. abs.*, רְעִי stands in apposition, defining the class under which these cattle fall; '*meadow-fed cattle.*' Dri. *Tenses*, § 188, 1.

ויחמור] LXX, Luc. om.

ברברים אבוסים] ב׳ is a ἅπαξ λεγ. The root אבס is seen again in Prov. 15. 17, שור אבוס 'a stalled ox,' the substantives אֵבוּס 'stall,' Isa. 1. 3; Prov. 14. 4; Job 39. 9; and מַאֲבוּס 'granary,' Jer. 50. 26†. All Verss. give the sense of fatted or selected *fowls*, without specifying the kind; Kimḥi *capons*, Ges. *geese* (from ברר,

to be pure or white), Th. *guinea-fowls* (an onomatop. from the cry of these birds).

4. עבר הנהר] '*The other side of* the river'; referring to Solomon's dominions to the west of the Euphrates. The phrase, as in Ezra 4. 10, 11, 16, 17, 20; 5. 3, 6; 6. 6, 8, 13; 7. 21, 25; 8. 36; Neh. 2. 7, 9; 3. 7, implies an *exilic* standpoint. The passage, therefore, is an insertion later than the redaction of the book by the pre-exilic R^D; but not so late as the dislocation caused by the insertion of 4. 20; &c. See *note ad loc.* On the other hand, the phrase as used in *ch.* 14. 15 (R^D); Josh. 24. 2, 3, 14, 15; 2 Sam. 10. 16; || 1 Chr. 19. 16†; cf. Isa. 7. 20 (בְּעֶבְרֵי נָהָר) denotes the country *east* of Euphrates, from a *western* standpoint.

מתפסח . . . הנהר] The omission in LXX, Luc., though perhaps marking the words as an insertion later than the main part of the *v.*, and by the same hand as 4. 20; &c., may, on the other hand, be merely due to homoioteleuton, the scribe's eye passing from the first עבר הנהר to the second.

מכל עבריו] 'Upon all *sides* of him.' So Jer. 49. 32 מכל עבריו אביא את אידם; cf. Ex. 32. 15 לֻחֹת כְּתֻבִים משני עבריהם. The text of Van der Hooght reads עבדיו, a scriptural error unconfirmed by any Cod. or Vers.

5. תחת גפנו וג'] An idiom expressive of pastoral prosperity; Mic. 4. 4†; cf. Zech. 3. 10; II. 18. 31.

מדן ועד באר שבע] The standing phrase to express all the territory of Israel between the north and south limits; Judg. 20. 1; 1 Sam. 3. 20; 2 Sam. 3. 10; 17. 11; 24. 2, 15†. מבאר שבע ועד דן occurs in 1 Chr. 21. 2; 2 Chr. 30. 5†.

6. ארבעים אלף] So Vulg., Pesh., Targ.; and Luc. in 10. 26. LXX in 10. 26 τέσσαρες χιλιάδες, and so 2 Chr. 9. 25 ארבעת אלפים. The smaller number is adopted by Ew., Th., and others, and is perhaps more likely to be correct.

ארות] אֻרְיוֹת || 2 Chr. 9. 25; אֻרָוֹת לכל בהמה ובהמה 2 Chr. 32. 28†. 'Stalls'; Ar. إِرْيٌ and آرِيّ; Aram. ܐܘܪܝܐ, corresponding e.g. to אֵבוּס Isa. 1. 3; and to φάτνη S. Luke 2. 7.

7. יְעַדְּרוּ] 'Omitted'; Pi'el only here. Elsewhere Niph'al, 'be

missing,' six times. In Ar. غَذَرَ is used of a sheep lagging behind the rest of the flock.

8. והשערים...שם] 'And the barley, &c., they used to bring unto the place to which it might pertain.' The subject of יהיה is השערים והתבן, naturally thought of collectively. Each officer had in his month to supply the different עָרֵי הָרֶכֶב, to which allusion is made in *ch.* 10. 26. So Klo., RV. *marg.* 2; &c. LXX, Luc., Vulg. supply הַמֶּלֶךְ as subject of יהיה, and this is followed by RV. *marg.* 1. It seems clear, however, that the word supplied is merely a wrong explanatory gloss on the part of the translator. The business of the נצבים can scarcely have been to follow the king from place to place with fodder for the limited number of horses which he might have with him.

For the *nuance* of the imperf. יהיה cf. Dri. *Tenses*, § 38 β.

רכש] RV. 'swift steeds.' From the contrast to סוסים the word seems to denote some special kind of horse, whether used for riding, Est. 8. 10, 14, or for chariots, Mic. 1. 13†. In Pesh. ܪܶܟܫܳܐ is the constant equivalent of סוס when used as a collective sing., or in the pl.

9. רחב לב] 'Breadth of heart.' לב is here used as the seat of the intellect; cf. Job 12. 3 גם לי לבב כמוכם לא נפל אנכי מכם, and 24; Jer. 4. 9; the expression חֲסַר לֵב 'devoid of intelligence,' peculiar to Prov., where it occurs eleven times, 7. 7; *al.* (חֲסַר תְּבוּנוֹת once as a variation 28. 16); and the common phrase חֲכַם־לֵב Ex. 31. 6; *al.*

With our phrase cf. Ps. 119. 32 דרך מצותיך ארוץ כי תרחיב לבי.

כחול וג'] Here the figure is suggested not, as in *ch.* 4. 20, by the innumerable grains, but by the vastness of the level expanse.

10. בני קדם] In Gen. 29. 1 this expression is used of Mesopotamia, but elsewhere, Judg. 6. 3, 33; 7. 12 (coupled with מדין ועמלק); Isa. 11. 14; Jer. 49. 28 (|| קֵדָר); Ezek. 25. 4, 10 (טירותיהם 'their *tents*,' mentioned *v.* 4); Job 1. 3†, the phrase denotes the Arabian tribes to the east of Israel, and spreading as far as the Euphrates. So also, while הררי קדם Num. 23. 7 (|| אֲרָם) are the mountains of Mesopotamia, ארץ קדם Gen. 25. 6 is the land into which Abraham sent the בְּנֵי הַפִּילַגְשִׁים previously enumerated as *Arab*

tribes, and הר הקדם Gen. 10. 30 seems to be the Arabian hill-country called *en-Nejd* stretching eastward from *Ḥaḍramaut.* Thus Solomon's wisdom seems to be compared, not with the wisdom of the Chaldeans, who were chiefly known as astrologers, but with that of the Arabs, whose country, as Ke. points out, is the fatherland of proverbial wisdom. Agreeable to this is the mention, *ch.* 10, of the visit of the queen of Sheba in south-west Arabia, who came to test Solomon's wisdom with hard enigmas. So Ke., Ew., Th.

חכמת מצרים] The wisdom of the חַרְטֻמִּים, men of the priestly class who employed themselves in the study of hieroglyphics, astronomy, and magic; Gen. 41. 8; Ex. 8. 3, 14; *al.* Ebers, *Aegypten,* p. 344 *f.* Cf. also Isa. 19. 11; Acts 7. 22.

11. איתן האזרחי וג׳] The four (דָּרַע for דרדע; but Codd., Luc., Pesh., Targ. agree with Kings) are mentioned with זמרי 1 Chr. 2. 6 as sons of זֶרַח the son of Judah by Tamar, Gen. 38. 30. So Targ. interprets האזרחי as בר זרח. In 1 Chr. 15. 17, 19 a Heman and an Ethan appear with Asaph as appointed by the Levites to be precentors in the temple, the three representing the families of Kohath (1 Chr. 6. 18), Merari (1 Chr. 6. 29), and Gershom (6. 24–28) respectively. In 1 Chr. 25. 1 הימן and יְדוּתוּן (cf. 1 Chr. 16. 41, 42; 2 Chr. 5. 12; 35. 15; apparently the same as איתן) are mentioned as הַנִּבְּאִים בְּכִנֹּרוֹת וג׳, and in *v.* 5 הימן is called חֹזֵה המלך בדברי האלהים. Ps. 88 is ascribed in the title to הימן האזרחי, Ps. 89 to איתן האזרחי, Pss. 39, 62, 77 to ידותון. Hence the chronicler distinguishes Ethan and Heman, the sages of the tribe of Judah, from Ethan and Heman the musicians, who were Levites; and further, his statement that they were sons of Zeraḥ need not conflict with that of Kings, 'sons of Maḥol,' since Zeraḥ, as is suggested by the title האזרחי, may have been the remoter ancestor, Maḥol the immediate father. On the other hand, the author of the Psalm titles, in naming his men Ezraḥites, seems to be introducing a confusion between the Levites and the Judaeans.

שמו] 'His name,' i.e. his *fame;* cf. the phrases עָשָׂה שֵׁם לְ 2 Sam. 7. 9; *al.;* הָיָה לְשֵׁם Isa. 55. 13; אַנְשֵׁי הַשֵּׁם Gen. 6. 4; cf. Num. 16. 2; בְּנֵי בְלִי שֵׁם Job 30. 8.

12. שירו] שיר is never elsewhere used as a collective. Hence Klo. reads וַיִּהְיוּ שִׁירָיו, supposing that the scribe's eye was caught by the similar ויהי שמו in the previous line.

חמשה ואלף] LXX, Luc., several Codd. Vulg. presuppose חֲמִשָּׁה אֲלָפִים. This latter, as a *round* number, seems preferable.

13. העצים] As a general rule the sing. collective denotes growing trees, the pl. pieces of wood, logs, or timber, as e.g. in *v.* 22; *ch.* 15. 22. When in classical Hebrew the pl. is used of living trees, there seems to be some emphasis, however slight, upon the *different varieties.* So here, Judg. 9. 8 *ff.* (Jotham's parable), and perhaps Isa. 7. 2[1].

Elsewhere the pl. use appears to be late or poetical; Isa. 44. 14; Ezek. eight times; Joel 1. 12, 19; Song of Sol. 2. 3; 4. 14; Ps. 96. 12; ‖ 1 Chr. 16. 33; Ps. 104. 16†.

14. מאת כל מלכי וג׳] '*Deputed by* all the kings, &c.'; so exactly 2 Sam. 15. 3 ושמע אין לך מאת המלך RV. 'there is no man deputed of the king to hear thee.' Ew. makes מאת וג׳ a closer definition of מכל העמים 'specially *some from among* all kings, &c.' For this sense it would be more natural to read מן simply without את[2], and even so the expression would be rather strange.

Luc. inserts καὶ ἐλάμβανε δῶρα before מאת, and similarly Pesh. ܘܡܩܒܠ ܗܘܐ ܩܘܪܒܢܐ, i.e. וַיִּקַּח מִנְחָה adopted by Klo., Hoo., and very probably correct. The reception of rich presents would be one mark of the prosperity of an ideal eastern monarch; cf. e.g. Ps. 72. 10.

5. 15—7. 51. *Solomon's building operations; chiefly, the construction of the Temple and its furniture.*

Chh. 5. 15—7. 51 supply the basis of 2 Chr. 1. 18—5. 1.

15. חירם] The name is contracted from אֲחִירָם 'brother of the

[1] Josh. 10. 26, 27 ויתלם על חמשה עצים וג׳ is probably no exception. The meaning seems to be 'five *gibbets,*' and, in addition, the numeral influences the use of the pl.

[2] מאת '*from proximity with*' (see *Heb. Lex.*, Oxf., p. 86) is too closely specific of locality to be used in such a sense as this.

lofty One,' a form which occurs as a Heb. name, Num. 26. 38. The same contraction in Phoenician is seen in the names חמלכת *Ḥimilcat*, for אחמלכת 'brother of Milcat'; חתמלכת *Ḥothmilcat*, for אחתמלכת 'sister of Milcat.' So in Heb. חִיאֵל for אֲחִיאֵל *ch.* 16. 34. The form חוּרָם occurs in 2 Chr. 2. 2, 10, 11; *al.*: cf. the variants אֲבִיגַיִל 1 Sam. 25. 3, *al.*, אֲבוּגַיִל Kt. *v.* 18; חֲמִיטַל Kt., חֲמוּטַל Q're II. 23. 31, 24. 18; פְּנִיאֵל Gen. 32. 31, פְּנוּאֵל *v.* 32; אֲבִירָם *ch.* 16. 34, Assyr. *Abu-ra-mu*, *COT.* ii. 479.

אל שלמה . . . למלך] LXX (Luc. τοῦ) χρίσαι τὸν Σ. merely represents a corruption of MT., which latter is supported by other Verss.

אתו] Emphatic by position: 'they had anointed *him*'; perhaps with reference to the events of *ch.* 1.

תחת אביהו] LXX, Luc. ἀντὶ Δαυεὶδ τοῦ πατρὸς αὐτοῦ, correct, as being more circumstantial. The immediate mention of the name דוד in the next sentence favours its inclusion here also.

אהב . . . לדוד] Cf. *ch.* 2. 39 *note.*

כל הימים] 'All the days,' with the implication 'all *his* days.' So very frequently in preference to the use of the suffix כָּל־יָמָיו, כָּל־יְמֵי, &c.; *ch.* 12. 7; 14. 30; II. 13. 3; Gen. 43. 9; 44. 32; 2 Sam. 13. 37[b]; *al.* In 1 Sam. 1. 28 we have the expanded phrase כל הימים אשר היה. Upon the phrase כל הימים used absolutely (Deuteronomic) in the sense 'continually,' cf. *ch.* 9. 3 *note.*

16–19. These verses have, in their present form, been amplified by R[D] upon the lines of 2 Sam. 7. On *v.* 17 לבנות בית לשם י׳ cf. *ch.* 3. 2 *note*: *v.* 19 הוא יבנה הבית לשמי 2 Sam. 7. 13; *v.* 18 ועתה הניח י׳ אלהי לי מסביב 2 Sam. 7. 1, 11; cf. Deut. 12. 10; 25. 19; Josh. 21. 42; 23. 1 (D[2]), and also Deut. 3. 20; Josh. 1. 13, 15; 22. 4 (both D[2]).

17. אלהיו] LXX, Luc. τοῦ θεός μου, an error.

המלחמה אשר סבבהו וג׳] The speaker, in using המלחמה *the state of warfare*, has implicit in his mind הָאֹיְבִים *the enemies*, who were its cause, and so immediately passes into the pl. סְבָבֻהוּ, and is able to continue עד תת י׳ אֹתָם. Cf. Judg. 5. 7 חדלו פרזון (*government* for *governors*). This manner of thought is illustrated by the less extreme case Isa. 25. 3 קִרְיַת גוים עריצים ייראוך (where the thought of the sing. קרית is lost in the idea of the גוים who inhabit it), and by the common use of a sing. collective for a pl. Cf. Ew. § 317[b]; Da. § 17.

LXX, Vulg., Pesh. render המלחמה by a pl. '*wars*'; Luc. τῶν πολεμίων, Targ. עבדי קרבא paraphrase 'enemies.' From this latter Klo. would emend אַנְשֵׁי מִלְחָמָה; but this is unnecessary, and also out of accord with Heb. idiom, the phrase always denoting members of Israel's[1] standing army, never their foes. The expression איש מלחמות תעי 2 Sam. 8. 10 (|| 1 Chr. 18. 10) is different.

תחת כפות רגלו] Cf. Mal. 3. 21.

18. שטן] Illustrated by *ch.* 11. 14, 23, 25; 1 Sam. 29. 4.

פגע רע] 'Evil chance'; Eccl. 9. 11 † עת ופגע יקרה את כלם 'time and *chance* encounters all of them.' פֶּגַע is something which *meets* one; cf. the use of the verb, 1 Sam. 10. 5 ופגעת חבל נבאים; Am. 5. 19; *al.*

19. אמר לבנות] 'I *purpose to* build.' So Ex. 2. 14 הלהרגני אתה אמר; 1 Sam. 30. 6; 2 Sam. 21. 16; Ezr. 20. 8; Ps. 106. 23. Similarly in the sense '*promise to*,' *ch.* 8. 12 אמר לשכן; II. 8. 19.

With the meaning '*command to*' the phrase occurs 2 Sam. 1. 18; 2. 26; and very frequently in late Heb., 1 Chr. 13. 4; 15. 16; Est. 1. 10; Dan. 1. 3, 18; 2. 2; *al.*; and in the Aramaic of Dan. 2. 12, 46; 3. 13, 19; 5. 2.

20. צוה ויכרתו] 'Command and let them hew,' i.e. 'command *that they hew*'; the voluntative with weak ו expressing regularly the *purpose* of the previous act. Dri. *Tenses*, § 62.

ארזים] LXX, Luc. ξύλα, i.e. עֵצִים, probably a correction in view of the fact that (*v.* 22) Ḥiram supplied Solomon not merely with עצי ארזים but also with עצי ברושים. Cedar wood, as the most important necessity, may very well be specially mentioned.

21. יהוה] Luc. κύριος ὁ θεὸς τοῦ Ἰσραήλ. So || 2 Chr. 2. 11; Klo., Hoo. As Klo. remarks, the expression יהוה אלהי ישראל is more

---

[1] Joel 4. 9 is the only passage where the phrase is used of foreign armies; and here too the אנשי המ' are spoken of, not as Israel's foes, but from the point of view of the גוים themselves.

appropriate in the mouth of Ḥiram than יהוה only. Vulg. *Dominus Deus* preserves part of the original text.

22. אעשה את כל חפצך] So *v.* 23; and of doing one's own pleasure, Isa. 46. 10; 48. 14; 58. 13†.

23. דברות] ἅπαξ λεγ. LXX, Luc. σχεδίας, Pesh. ܡܫܘܛܐ, Targ. תורגסין; '*rafts*' or '*floats*.' This meaning agrees with the following ונפצתים 'I will break them up'; cf. Ps. 2. 9; Jer. 48. 12. Vulg. *in ratibus* is a guess from the context.

In ‖ 2 Chr. 2. 15 רַפְסֹדוֹת, a ἅπαξ λεγ. of doubtful derivation, is used.

24. ויהי חירום נתן] Cf. *v.* 1 *note*.

25. ושלמה נתן וג׳] The subject is intentionally emphasized so as to throw the sentence into antithesis with *v.* 24 ויהי חירום נתן. Cf. *ch.* 10. 10, 13 ותתן למלך . . . והמלך שלמה נתן; 12. 29 וישם את האחד בבית אל ואת האחד נתן בדן; 18. 42 ויעלה אחאב . . . ואליהו עלה; 22. 20b ויאמר זה בכה וזה אמר בכה; Gen. 4. 2, 3, 4; 36. 4. See Dri. *Tenses*, § 160, *Obs.*, who calls this variation in order, 'the Hebrew equivalent to μὲν . . . δὲ of the Greeks.'

מַכֹּלֶת] For מַאֲכֹלֶת Isa. 9. 4, 18†, with assimilation of the weak cons. א. Sta. § 112, 1, *Rem.* 2 quotes as parallels בְּסַאסְּאָה for בְּסַאְסְאָה Isa. 27. 8; אֶדַּדֶּה for אתדאדה from דאה (or a redup. of the syll. דא) Isa. 38. 15; שִׁשֵּׁאתִיךָ for שִׁאֲשֵׁאתִיךָ Ezek. 39. 2. More frequent is the dropping of the quiescent א with a lengthening of the preceding vowel; so מָסֹרֶת for מאסֹרֶת Ezek. 20. 37; אָזִין for אַאֲזִין Job 32. 11; *al.* G-K. § 24, 3; § 68, 2, *Rem.* 1; Sta. 112, 1.

עשרים כר שמן] The כר was a dry measure, and the quantity specified is much too small. We must follow LXX, Luc. (and Pesh. for the numeral), and read עֶשְׂרִים אֶלֶף בַּת שֶׁמֶן; cf. 2 Chr. 2. 9. So Jos., Th., Klo., Kamp.

שמן כתית] '*Beaten* oil,' obtained by the pounding of the olives in a mortar. This is specified for the lamp of the Tabernacle, Ex. 27. 20; Lev. 24. 2; and to form part of the מנחת בקר and מנחת ערב, Ex. 29. 40; Num. 28. 5†.

שנה בשנה] So Lev. 25. 53; Deut. 15. 20; *al.* 'Year by year,' properly, 'year *for* year,' the meaning being that what was done in one year exactly corresponded to that which was done in others.

Cf. *ch.* 10. 25 דְּבַר שָׁנָה בְשָׁנָה. *Heb. Lex.*, Oxf., p. 90[a], compares יוֹם בְּיוֹם in very late Heb., Neh. 8. 18; 1 Chr. 12. 23; *al.;* כְּיוֹם בְּיוֹם 1 Sam. 18. 10†; כְּפַעַם בְּפַעַם Num. 24. 1; Judg. 16. 20; *al.;* חֹדֶשׁ בְּחֹדֶשׁ 1 Chr. 27. 1†.

26. כאשר דבר לו] Cf. *ch.* 8. 20 כאשר דבר י׳; *v.* 56 ככל אשר דבר; *v.* 53. The idea and phrase are those of D; cf. Deut. 1. 21; 6. 3; 9. 3; *al.;* Dri. *Deut.* lxxxi, who cites from D fifteen occurrences of כאשר דבר י׳ (לְ), besides instances from the compiler of Judg., Josh. Thus the whole of *v.* 26[a] must be assigned to R[D]; and this is confirmed by the fact that the back-reference seems to be not so much to the original narrative of the vision at Gibeon, where Solomon's request is not for חכמה precisely but for לב שמע לשפט את עמך להבין וג׳ (*ch.* 3. 9; cf. *v.* 11), as to R[D]'s own addition (*v.* 12) which states Yahwe's definite promise of a לב חכם ונבון.

27. ויעל] 'Brought up' or '*raised*' a forced levy. So *ch.* 9. 15 המס אשר העלה; cf. *v.* 21 ויעלם ... למס עֹבֵד.

28. וישלחם ... חליפות] 'He sent them *in* relays.' ח׳ is an accus. of manner or condition, a usage very common in Heb., whether the accus. be a substantive, adjective, or participle. Such an accus. may determine either the *object*, as here; *ch.* 20. 18 תפשום חיים 'take them alive' (*as* living ones); or the *subject;* II. 5. 2 וארם יצאו גדודים 'and Aram went forth *in* bands'; 18. 37 קרועי בגדים. Da. § 70; Dri. *Tenses*, § 161, 2, 3. Instances of this accus. of state referring to a *genitive* are noticed *ch.* 1. 41.

חליפות] For the meaning cf. Job 10. 17 חליפות וצבא 'a host in *detachments* or *relays*.' Similar is Job 14. 14 כל ימי צבאי איחל עד בוא חליפתי 'all the days of my warfare would I wait, until *my relief* should come,' the figure being that of a soldier at his post.

בביתו] We should expect אִישׁ בְּבֵיתוֹ as in Ezek. 8. 12; *al.* Hence we must suppose either that איש has fallen out, or, with Th., that it is implicit in בביתו. Klo.'s בְּבֵיתָם, which he restores from the free rendering of LXX, Luc. ἐν τοῖς οἴκοις αὐτῶν, is an impossibility in good Heb. style.

29. נשא סַבָּל] Lit. 'bearing as porters,' or 'bearers, porters,' סַבָּל being in apposition to נשא. LXX, Luc., Vulg., Pesh. read

נֹשֵׂא סַבָּל 'bearing *burdens*.' 2 Chr. 2. 1, 17, based upon this verse, omits נשא and reads אִישׁ סַבָּל, סַבָּל.

The relationship of this 70,000 + 80,000 to the 30,000 of *vv.* 27, 28, is obscure. According to 2 Chr. 2. 16, 17 the former consisted of 'the strangers that were in the land of Israel.' Probably *vv.* 29–32 are from a different source to *vv.* 27, 28. So Ew., Sta.; the latter noticing that הלבנון of *v.* 28 is in *v.* 29 called ההר.

30. שלשת אלפים ושלש מאות] LXX τρεῖς χιλιάδες καὶ ἑξακόσιοι, in agreement with 2 Chr. 2. 1, 17, and probably genuine. So Th., Klo. Th.'s attempt to divide the 3,600 into the 70,000 + 80,000 = 150,000 of *v.* 29, + 30,000 of *v.* 28 = 180,000, thus assigning fifty workmen to each overseer, seems to be unlawful; since it places the 30,000 Israelites upon the same footing as the 150,000 strangers, and, in supposing that the overseers had charge of the work of the former, is neither consonant with the statement of 2 Chr. 2, nor with the view that *v.* 28, *vv.* 29 *ff.* are portions of different documents.

Luc. for the second number gives ἑπτακόσιοι, *Cod.* A πεντακόσιοι.

31. ויצו המלך] LXX om., probably owing to the transposition noticed below. Luc. καὶ ἐνετείλατο ὁ βασιλεὺς τοῖς ἄρχουσιν, i.e. לַנִּצָּבִים, scarcely improves MT., and is probably merely an exegetical addition.

In LXX, Luc. *vv.* 31, 32ª are placed after *v.* 32ᵇ, *ch.* 6. 1. Sta. points out that this gives a bad succession, because the command to prepare the stone in the fourth year follows the statement in 5. 17 (LXX) that the hewing of stones and timber had been going on for three years. He also notices that in *vv.* 31, 32ª, 32ᵇ MT. הסיע, פסל, הכין naturally follow one another in appropriate order.

32. וְהַגִּבְלִים] Difficult. As the word stands it has been taken in two senses—

(i) '*The stone-squarers*.' So apparently Targ. וארגובליא, Pesh. ܘܐܪܓܘܒܠܐ[1], and hence AV. However, the word is not used else-

[1] The derivation is doubtful. Levy thinks the word a transposition from the Gk. ἐργολάβος, while Jensen, *ZA.* vii. 218, explains by the Assyr. *bargulu*.

where in Heb. with such a meaning, and if it be adopted we must suppose that the ו is employed for closer specification, '*namely*,' which is improbable.

(ii) '*The Gebalites.*' So Vulg. *Giblii*, RV., Ges., Ke., Ew., Kamp. The ו must then mean '*and especially*,' the men of Gebal being particularly singled out from among the servants of Ḥiram. But, as Th. remarks, no one has as yet succeeded in explaining why they should receive such special notice.

Hence it seems probable that we have here a corruption, and that we must look for some *verb* following upon the preceding ויפסלו. So LXX *καὶ ἔβαλαν αὐτούς*, Luc. *καὶ ἐνέβαλον αὐτούς*. Th. restores וַיְגַבְּלֻם '*and they bordered them with grooved edges*,' and so substantially Klo. וְהִגְבִּילוּם. Th.'s emendation is favoured by *Sieg. u. Sta.; Heb. Lex.*, Oxf., and may be adopted.

לבנות הבית] LXX omits and reads instead *τρία ἔτη*. Luc. *τρισὶν ἔτεσιν εἰς τὴν οἰκοδομὴν τοῦ οἴκου*. This addition is favoured by Th., who thinks that without it *v.* 32^{b} is pointless, and supposes that three years' preparation of stone and timber preceded the commencement of the building, *ch.* 6. 1, in order that the work might go on without interruption. On the other hand, Sta., Klo. regard the words as a false inference from 6. 1. The former points out that even supposing that a very short time elapsed between the commencement of Solomon's reign and his intercourse with Ḥiram, yet, notwithstanding, a longer time than three years is needed for the hewing of the timber in Lebanon and its conveyance to Jerusalem. Sta. thinks also that the long duration of the work of building is not to be understood, if at the commencement stone and timber were already prepared. On these grounds MT. seems to be preferable.

6. 1. As has been noticed above, LXX inserts this verse before *vv.* 31, 32^{a} of *ch.* 5. In its place we now have *ch.* 6. *vv.* 37, 38^{a} which give the dates of laying the foundation of the Temple and of its completion. Wellh. (*C.* 267) remarks that these latter verses in MT. break the continuity between 6. 36 and 7. 1–12, while in the position which they occupy in LXX they completely supersede *v.* 1 MT. which holds the 'very unfortunate position' above mentioned. Hence he concludes that *v.* 1 is the work of a later editor who relegated *vv.* 37, 38ª to their present place in MT. to make room for his addition, and that LXX represents the original text[1]. This will account for the position of *v.* 1 in LXX, the late addition having been first written in the margin of a MS., and afterwards incorporated in the text as best it could be. As a mark of the different authorship of *v.* 1 Wellh. notices that it uses חדש where *vv.* 37, 38ª have ירח; בחדש זו הוא החדש השני standing in place of בירח זו הוא החדש השני.

Another consideration favours the lateness of this verse. The number 480 appears to be not strictly historical, but to be a *round* number obtained, as recognized by Bertheau and Nöldeke, from 40 × 12, forty years being regarded as the approximate length of a generation[2], and frequently occurring in Judges in descriptions of the duration of periods of peace or oppression[3]. Attempts have been made so to arrange previous chronological notices that they may together correspond to this given period[4]; but no scheme has been entirely successful.

Now it is at least conceivable that the author of our verse may have been influenced by that fondness for the construction of artificial periods of similar length exhibited by the chrono-

---

[1] Sta. agrees with Wellh. that *v.* 1 is a late insertion, but refuses to regard the position of *vv.* 37, 38ª in LXX as original, on the ground that a notice as to the completion of the building is out of place at the commencement, the expressions לכל דבריו ולכל משפטו pointing backward to a previous description. This argument scarcely seems to carry conviction.

[2] So in S. Matt. 1. 17 ἀπὸ τῆς μετοικεσίας Βαβυλῶνος ἕως τοῦ Χριστοῦ γενεαὶ δεκατέσσαρες, 40 × 14 = 560, approximates very fairly to the real length of the period—586 years.

[3] So of the peace enjoyed after the victories of Othniel (3. 11), Deborah (5. 31), Gideon (8. 28), Ehud (3. 30) eighty years, i.e. 40 × 2; and of the Philistine oppression (13. 1). Samson's judgeship (16. 31) twenty years, is half a generation. Cf. the periods assigned for Eli's judgeship (1 Sam. 4. 18), and for the reigns of David (2 Sam. 5. 4) and Solomon (1 Ki. 11. 42).

[4] Cf. Wellh. *Prolegomena*, 230 *f.* Jos. states the number of years to have been 492.

logist in S. Matt. I. 17, and may thus have purposely approximated the length of the little-known period from the Exodus to the building of the Temple to the chronology of some subsequent period for the knowledge of which he possessed available sources.

If then we start from the commencement of Solomon's Temple, and add together the years of the reigns of the kings of Judah as given by R[D], we obtain the following result:—

Solomon (40 – 3 years before the commencement of the Temple)	37	I. 11. 42.
Rehoboam	17	14. 21.
Abijam	3	15. 2.
Asa	41	15. 10.
Jehoshaphat	25	22. 42.
Jehoram	8	II. 8. 17.
Ahaziah	1	8. 26.
Athaliah	6	11. 3.
Jehoash	40	12. 2.
Amaziah	29	14. 2.
Azariah	52	15. 2.
Jotham	16	15. 33.
Ahaz	16	16. 2.
Hezekiah	29	18. 2.
Manasseh	55	21. 1.
Amon	2	21. 19.
Josiah	31	22. 1.
Jehoahaz	—	23. 31.
Jehoiakim	11	23. 36.
Jehoiachin	—	24. 8.
Zedekiah	11	24. 18.
Total	430	

To this 430 add the fifty years of the Babylonian exile, and we have from the commencement of the Temple down to the return from Babylon a second period of 480 years[1] which may be fairly considered as having determined the duration assigned to the former period. Thus *v.* 1 appears to be the work of a *post*-exilic editor, the same no doubt as will later on come into prominence through the insertions made by him under the influence of the Priestly Code[2].

The reading of LXX, *ἐν τῷ τεσσαρακοστῷ καὶ τετρακοσιοστῷ ἔτει*, is a mistake, but cannot be explained with Th., following Winer, ii. 327, *note* 2, as arising from a confusion of פ = 80 with מ = 40. In ancient Hebrew writing the method of expressing numeration, in cases where the number was not fully written in words, was most probably a system of strokes and similar signs, such as we find in Phoenician inscriptions. We have not the slightest evidence to prove that the comparatively late system of expressing numbers by means of letters was ever adopted in Hebrew MSS. of OT.

Luc. agrees with LXX as to the position assigned to *vv.* 37, 38ᵃ in place of *v.* 1, but continues *καὶ ᾠκοδόμησεν αὐτὸν ἐν ἑπτὰ ἔτεσιν, καὶ ᾠκοδόμει τὸν οἶκον τῷ κυρίῳ*, i. e. *vv.* 38ᵇ, 1ᵇ. This has obviously been added to Luc. by a later hand, both sentences in MT. belonging to the author of *v.* 1ᵃ.

2. ששים אמה ארכו] So Vulg., Pesh., Targ., and 2 Chr. 3. 3 (MT. and all Verss.). LXX, Luc. *τεσσαράκοντα μῆκος αὐτοῦ*, the translator apparently fancying erroneously that the reference is to the היכל or Holy Place, exclusive of the דביר, and so altering the text from *v.* 17.

ועשרים] Read ועשרים אמה with LXX, Luc., Vulg., Pesh.

שלשים אמה קומתו] So Vulg., Pesh., Targ.; but LXX, Luc. *καὶ πέντε καὶ εἴκοσι ἐν πήχει τὸ ὕψος αὐτοῦ*. In 2 Chr. 3. 3, and in the description of the dimensions of Ezekiel's Temple (41. 2), there is no record of the height.

3. על פני רחב] 'Upon the face of the breadth,' i. e. *corresponding to it;* but על פני הבית means simply '*before* the house.'

---

[1] This has been already noticed by Sta., *Ges.* i. 88 *ff.;* Kau., *Abriss,* 172.

[2] And therefore elsewhere cited as Rᴾ.

עשר באמה רחבו] LXX omits through oversight.

After *v.* 3, LXX, Luc. insert *v.* 14 *καὶ ᾠκοδόμησεν τὸν οἶκον καὶ συνετέλεσεν αὐτόν*. In spite of what Klo. says to the contrary, it seems to be clearly inconsistent to mention the completion of the house before the details as to its roofing, side-chambers, &c. LXX order is therefore to be rejected.

4. חַלּוֹנֵי שְׁקֻפִים אֲטֻמִים] שקפים (only again in 7. 4[1]) probably means '*frames*,' the reference being to the beams or stones which were fitted together to form the outline of the window. רְבֻעִים שָׁקֶף (7. 5†) doubtless signifies 'square *in framework*'; שקף denoting the beams or stones which formed the sides and lintel of the doorway; מַשְׁקוֹף (Ex. 12. 7, 22, 23†) is the lintel or portal; and the Talmudic שְׁקוֹף has the same meaning 'lintel.' Ar. سَقَّفَ means *to roof a building with a vaulted roof*, سَقْفٌ *an arched or vaulted roof*, the original signification probably being that assigned by Ges., to bend down, incline[2], then, to place upon, especially applied to beams, and so, to joist or construct with beams. אטם is again applied to windows Ezek. 40. 16; 41. 16, 26; and is used in the expression אֹטֵם אָזְנוֹ 'stopping his ear,' Prov. 21. 13; Isa. 33. 15: Ar. أَطَمَ I. *to cover, hide, be contracted*, IV. *to close* (*a door*): Syr. ܐܛܝܡ *compressed, contracted*, then, *thick, solid*, and even *hard, stubborn* (of a disposition and of anger).

Thus our phrase may be rendered either (i) '*Windows with frames closed in*,' possibly by gratings (this being implied merely and *not* stated), or more probably (ii) '*Windows with narrowed frames*,' i.e. wide on the inner side of the thick wall, and gradually sloping so as to form a mere slit on the outer side, like the windows of ancient western fortresses. So probably Vulg. *fenestras obliquas*, and certainly Pesh. ܟܘܐ ܡܣܬܟܝܢܬܐ ܘܐܛܝܡܬܐ 'windows oblique and narrowed' (cf. Ezek. 40. 16 ܘܟܘܐ ܕܡܣܬܟܝܢ ܡܢ ܠܓܘ ܘܩܛܝܢܝܢ ܠܒܪ 'windows oblique within and small without'); Targ. כוין פתיחן מלגיו

---

[1] שקופים is restored by Cornill in Ezek. 41. 16 חלוני שקופים אטומות.

[2] In Ar. the term أَسْقَفُ is used of the *flexible* neck of the ostrich. Lane, *Lex.* 1383.

מלברא וסתימן 'windows opened within and closed without'[1]; Jesu bar-Ali who explains that ܟܘ̈ܐ ܐܛܝ̈ܡܬܐ are ܟܘ̈ܐ ܕܠܐ ܬܪ̈ܝܨܢ ܒܪ̈ܝܢ. ܐܠܐ ܡܥܩܡܢ ܚܕ ܓܒ ܠܣܘܟܠܐ. 'windows which are not cut through straightly (i. e. squarely), but narrowed upon one side obliquely'; Kamp.; and Cornill on Ezekiel, so far as regards אטמים,—'schräg einfallende Fenster.'

The Greek Verss. generally connect שקפים with השקיף 'to look or lean out of a window':—LXX θυρίδας παρακυπτομένας κρυπτάς, *al. exempl.* διακυπτομένας κρυπτάς, and so Θ.; Σ. θυρίδας καὶ ἐκθέτας ἐπισκέποντας; 'Α. ἀποβλέπουσας βεβυσμένας; Luc. θυρίδας δεδικτυωμένας κρυπτάς. Perhaps LXX, Θ., 'Α. mean 'with prospects obstructed,' whether by grating or otherwise. So Vet. Lat. *prospicientes absconsas*. Luc. δεδικτ. is probably a corruption of διακυπτ. in view of the explanation noticed below.

RV., Ke., Th., Ew., Sta., Kamp. (and Cornill in Ezek. 41. 16) give to שקפים the sense of *lattices*, *gratings*, or *transverse beams*; but this seems to rest upon pure conjecture; and, besides bearing no resemblance to the meaning of other Hebrew words from the same root, is unsuitable to the use of the same word by the same writer in 7. 4 (see *note*). The rendering of אטמים by RV., Ke., Th., Sta. '*fixed*,' '*festgemachte*,' appears to be an accommodation to the meaning given to שקפים, and fails of justification.

5. ויבן] LXX ἔδωκεν, i. e. וַיִּתֵּן; possible (cf. נתן, *v.* 6), but not superior to MT. Luc. καὶ ἐποίησεν, i. e. וַיַּעַשׂ, is influenced by the recurrence of this word in *vv.* 4, 5[b].

יצוע]. The meaning seems to be something spread upon or applied to the wall of a house, so '*side-buildings*' or '*wings*.' So approximately Pesh. ܣܚܪ̈ܬܐ lit. 'surroundings,' Targ. זיזא probably 'projecting buildings.' The word denotes the whole wing, not the single stories: see *notes* on the other occurrences *vv.* 6, 10†. Hence LXX, Luc. μέλαθρα, Vulg. *tabulata*, whence RV. 'stories,' are not quite correct.

---

[1] These Verss., however, appear to derive their rendering 'open (oblique), closed (narrowed)' from the whole phrase שקפים אטמים; and so apparently RV. marg.

Q're יָצִיעַ probably aims at distinction from יָצוּעַ 'bed,' Gen. 49. 4; *al.*

סביב את קירות הבית] LXX, Luc. om. As Sta. points out, the words appear to be merely a gloss upon סביב להיכל ולדביר. So Kamp. The strange accentuation, which places the zaqef in each case upon סביב, cannot be correct.

ויעש צלעות סביב] LXX om., but merely through oversight. The words are found in Luc. and the other Verss., and are, as Sta. remarks, indispensable. צלע, properly a *rib*, is thought to be used distinctively of a *side*-chamber here and in the description of Ezekiel's Temple, but seems to be employed of chambers more generally in 7. 3. Cf. *note* on 7. 2 *ad fin.*

6. היצוע התחתנה] יצוע (the *whole* wing, *v.* 5) is here unsuitable, and is also a masc. word. LXX, Luc. ἡ πλευρά, Targ. מחיצתא point to הַצֵּלָע as the original reading, doubtless correctly. Cf. *v.* 8 הצלע התיכנה. So Th., Sta.; and Klo. doubtfully.

מגרעות] 'Rebatements'; ἅπαξ λεγ. The meaning is clear from the context, and from the common sense of גרע 'take away' or 'diminish.' So perhaps LXX, Luc. διάστημα. Pesh., Targ., guessing from context, ܡܦܩ̈ܐ, נפקתא 'ledges'; Vulg. *trabes*.

לבלתי אחז בקירות הבית] 'That (the beams) should not have hold in the walls of the house.' The absence of the subject, not previously mentioned, is very harsh; and we may reasonably suppose that הַקּוֹרוֹת has fallen out before בקירות, owing to the similarity of the two words. Cf. the confusion of these words in *v.* 15. Targ. rightly supplies a subject רישי שריתא 'the ends of the beams.'

7. This verse intrudes itself very awkwardly into the midst of the account of the construction of the side-chambers, and, if forming a part of the original description, must at any rate be out of place. Kamp. assigns the notice to R^D, and Sta., following Ew., regards it as a gloss from the margin, and so presumably by a later hand,—perhaps the post-exilic author of *v.* 1, &c. The tradition of the building of the Temple without the use of tools and of previously prepared material is doubtless

derived from or connected with the command of Ex. 20. 25 (J); Deut. 27. 5, 6 (cf. especially the phrase אבנים שלמות) with regard to an altar of stone, and so *can* have been written by the pre-exilic R^D^, as is suggested by the occurrence of the verse in the same position in LXX, Luc.

On the other hand, the notice is not in the spirit of R^D^—whose insertions, as a rule, subserve a definitely *religious* purpose—and rather answers to the desire for curious details characteristic of a later (post-exilic) age; while the awkward position of the verse is strange to the really skilful handling by R^D^ of his materials, and more nearly resembles the work of the later editor who has complicated the descriptions of *chh.* 6, 7 throughout.

We may therefore assign the insertion to the post-exilic editor (R^P^), and suppose that in LXX the verse was added by a copyist from a Hebrew MS.

אבן שלמה מסע] 'Stone rough-hewn *in* (*as regards*) quarrying.' מסע, in loose apposition (Dri. *Tenses*, § 188, 1; Da. § 29c), defines the sense in which the stone could be described as שלמה.

שלמה] 'Whole,' as hewn from the quarry, without any further preparation by sawing or otherwise. The term, as employed of the stones of an altar, Deut. 27. 6; Josh. 8. 31, probably denotes stones in their natural condition. מַסָּע, in this sense a ἅπαξ λεγ., is the 'action of removal,' from Hiph'il הִסִּיעַ 'pluck up,' used of moving stones from the quarry in 5. 31. The whole expression אבן וג׳ is an accus. of material; and with an active verb בָּנָה את הבית אבן וג׳ would have formed the second or remoter accus., as in Deut. 27. 6; 7. 15. Dri. *Tenses*, § 195. Cf. Ew. § 284c; Da. § 80.

כל כלי] For כל at the close of a category *asyndetos* summarizing all possibilities of the class cf. *ch.* 8. 37 כל נגע כל מחלה.

נשמע] The verb agreeing, not with the whole list, but with the nearest subs. כל כלי in sing. Cf. Deut. 8. 13 כסף וזהב ירבה לך; Hos. 4. 11 זנות ויין ותירוש יקח לב; Da. § 114a.

8. התיכנה] LXX, Luc. τῆς ὑποκάτωθεν, Targ. ארעיתא presuppose הַתַּחְתֹּנָה, which is doubtless correct. So Th., Ew., Sta., Klo., Kamp., Benz., Kit.

לולים] A ἅπαξ λεγ., the meaning of which is not quite clear. RV. 'winding stairs' is derived from LXX, Luc. ἑλικτὴ (εἱλικτὴ) ἀνάβασις, 'A. (καὶ ἐν) κοχλίαις, Vulg. *cochlea,* Targ. מסבתא; so Ke., Th., Ew., Klo., Kamp. Pesh., however, renders ܒܡܫܩܦܐ 'through *a trap-door,*' and Sta. thinks that this is nearly correct. In Rabb. Hebrew[1] לול can mean a falling shaft covered by a trap-door; *Middoth* 4, 5 לולין היו פתוחין בעליה לבית קדש הקדשים שבהן היו משלשלין את האומנין בתיבות כדי שלא יזונו עיניהן מבית קדשי הקדשים 'There were *lûlîn* in the loft opening into the Holy of Holies through which they used to let down the workmen in boxes that they might not feast their eyes within the most Holy Place.' We also have the word used to denote a hollow room covered above; *Pesachim* 34ᵃ, 77ᵃ, *al.;* and afterwards it comes to mean a hen-roost; *Shabbath* 102ᵇ, 122ᵇ, *al.* Hence Sta. understands by לולים hollow chambers covered above with trap-doors, through which one might ascend by means of a ladder or steps like those of hen-roosts.

Adopting this explanation we may render '*trap-door covered ascents.*'

9. This verse is obviously out of place, breaking the connexion between *vv.* 8 and 10; and, accordingly, with Sta. it shares the fate of *v.* 7 as being a late gloss. Against this it should be noticed (i) that the verse contains the only allusion to the roofing of the house, a detail not likely to be omitted; and (ii) that mention of the completion of the house ought fitly to come into a description of the building, and may reasonably do so immediately after the details as to the construction of the house proper, and before those which concern its inward embellishments[2]. Thus we may regard the verse as original, excepting the words גבים ושדרת not found in LXX, Luc., and place it after *v.* 10, from which position it has been transposed by a very early error of transcription[3].

[1] Cf. Levy, *s. v.*

[2] Verse 15 immediately continues with a description of את קירות הבית מביתה.

[3] This conclusion is confirmed by the repetition (*v.* 14) of 9ᵃ by the author of the interpolation *vv.* 11–14. See *note.*

Thus the sequence in description—walls, porch, windows, wings, roofing—is perfect, the last detail aptly rounding off the account of the outside building of the house.

גבים ושדרת בארזים] A rather strange expression. If we adopt RV. 'beams and planks of cedar,' we must suppose that the ב is a variety of the ב *essentiae*; '*consisting of* cedar.' LXX, Luc. καὶ ἐκοιλοστάθμησεν τὸν οἶκον ἐν κέδροις, Pesh. ܘܐܣܛܦܗ ܠܒܝܬܐ ܒܩܝܣܐ ܕܐܪܙܐ seem to have read simply ויספן את הבית בארזים, which was probably the original form of the sentence. The words גבים ושדרת are then a later gloss added to explain more precisely the use to which the cedar beams were put.

גבים ושדרת] גבים elsewhere means 'pits' or 'cisterns'; II. 3. 16; *al.*; while שדרות in its other occurrences, II. 11. 8, 15; || 2 Chr. 23. 14†, denotes 'ranks' of men. Ew., taking גבים to mean lit. 'cavities,' explains that the roof consisted 'of an ornamental ceiling in squares, with small pieces of cedar wood as dividing beams.' This agrees with LXX insertion ※ φατνώμασιν καὶ διατάξεσιν ◄ κέδροις, 'panels and cedar boards in rows[1],' Vulg. *laquearibus*, 'with panelled roofs.' Adopting this explanation we may render, '*panels and parallel beams*.' Targ. explains וטליל ית ביתא בהנתוכין ועילא מינהון סידרא דריכפת רישי שרית ארזיא 'And he roofed the house with rafters, and above them were a series of cedar boards joined together.' Lagarde (*Armenische Studien*, § 499; *Mittheil.* i. 211) for גבים reads גְּבָּרִים, which he connects with Persian گنبد, Armen. γμβεθ, 'vaulted roofs.'

10. Somewhat obscure. MT. is adopted by Ke., Th., Kamp., Klo.; the last explaining:—'He built it (each story) evenly against the wall of the whole house, until it was five cubits high, and then the connexion with the house and the roof of the side-chambers was formed by the cedar beams and planks, which rested upon the rebatements of the house.' Of course this process is conceived to have taken place three times, so that the three stories when

[1] But not, as stated by Ew., with LXX ἐκοιλοστάθμησεν, 'made with vaulted roof,' which, as above noticed, is a translation of ויספן merely. Cf. Hag. 1. 4 בְּבָתֵּיכֶם סְפוּנִים, ἐν οἴκοις ὑμῶν κοιλοστάθμοις.

built and roofed must have had a height of fifteen cubits. Against this it should be noticed that יצוע in *v.* 5 denotes not a single story (called הַצֵּלָע *v.* 8), but the whole wing consisting of three stories; hence Sta. is probably correct in reading חָמֵשׁ עֶשְׂרֵה אַמָּה for חמש אמות of MT. So Kit.

The subject of ויאחז, rightly divined by RV., Ke., Sta., Klo., Benz., is היצוע; 'It rested on the house with beams of cedar.' Sta. compares לבלתי אחז of *v.* 6. On the contrary, Verss., RV. marg., Th., Kamp., Kit. make the subject to be the same as that of ויבן; Vulg. *operuit domum*, Targ. וטליל ית ביתא 'he roofed the house,' giving a wrong sense to ויאחז. LXX καὶ συνέσχεν τὸν σύνδεσμον (Luc. τοὺς συνδέσμους) appear to have read ויאחז את היצוע. This reading is favoured by Ew., but is probably merely a mistranslation, due to the mistake in the subject of ויאחז noticed above.

11–14. Omitted by LXX, Luc. Verses 11–13 are assigned by Kue., Wellh., Kamp., Benz., Kit. to R^D; but this is certainly incorrect. The section, it is true, contains some D phrases, such as could and did pass from D into P; but other expressions belong solely to P or to H, and thus mark the verses as the work of R^P. This conclusion is rendered certain by the LXX omission. Verse 14 is by the same hand as *vv.* 11–13; *v.* 9^a being repeated in order to round off the interpolation and attach it to the preceding narrative.

The following are marks of authorship which require notice:—

12. אם תלך בחקתי] This phrase, which never occurs in Deut., is found twice in Jer. 44. 10, 23. On the other hand, it is distinctively characteristic of H, occurring Lev. 26. 3 (cf. 18. 4), and constantly in Ezekiel, whose connexion with P, and especially with H, is well ascertained[1]; 5. 6, 7; 11. 20; 18. 9, 17; 20. 13, 16, 19, 21†. Cf. the phrase הָלַךְ בְּחֻקּוֹת הַגּוֹיִם Lev. 18. 3; 20. 23 (H).

ואת משפטי תעשה] The exact phrase (with יהוה as spokesman; מִשְׁפָּטַי) belongs to H; Lev. 18. 4; Ezek. 5. 7; 11. 12; 18. 17; 20. 24; 1 Chr. 28. 7. In *ch.* 11. 33 לעשות הישר בעיני

[1] Cf. Dri. *LOT.*, pp. 45 *ff.*

וחקתי ומשפטי כדוד אביו, the passage belongs to R^D, but the words וח׳ ומ׳ are an insertion by R^P, as is shown by their omission in LXX, Luc.

Even with הַמִּשְׁפָּטִים, מִשְׁפָּטָיו the phrase is not specially characteristic of Deut.[1]; 26. 16; 33. 21 (Blessing of Moses in Appendix). Elsewhere, Neh. 10. 30.

Similar H phrases are (שָׁמַר) מִשְׁפָּטִים אֲשֶׁר יַעֲשֶׂה אֹתָם הָאָדָם וָחַי בָּהֶם Lev. 18. 5; Ezek. 20. 11, 13, 21†; יִשְׁמֹר מִשְׁפָּטִים וְעָשָׂה אֹתָם Lev. 19. 37; 20. 22; 25. 18; Ezek. 11. 20; 20. 19; 36. 27.

ושמרת את כל מצותי] The phrase appears first in Ex. 20. 6 (E); Deut. 5. 10 לְשֹׁמְרֵי מִצְוֹתַי, and is then very frequent in Deut.; passing on to R^D in Kings, I. 2. 3; 9. 6; 11. 34; *al.*; and to P, which shows several occurrences.

ללכת בהם] So exactly only in Lev. 18. 4 (H) את משפטי תעשו ואת חקתי תשמרו ללכת בהם. D's phrase is ללכת בדרכי י׳; cf. *ch.* 2. 3.

והקמתי את דברי אתך] The expression הקים דבר with יהוה as subj. is found once in Deut. 9. 5, and twice in R^D, *ch.* 2. 4; 12. 15; || 2 Chr. 10. 15; but is also more general; 1 Sam. 1. 23; Jer. 33. 14; Dan. 9. 12; cf. Isa. 44. 26.

אשר דברתי אל דוד] Referring, like R^D in 2. 4, to Nathan's prophecy, 2 Sam. 7. 12–16.

13. ושכנתי בתוך בני ישראל] Very distinctive of P; Ex. 25. 8; 29. 45; Num. 5. 3; 35. 34; Ezek. 43. 9. No occurrences in D.

With the whole verse cf. Lev. 26. 11, 12 (H) ונתתי משכני בתוככם ולא תגעל נפשי אתכם: והתהלכתי בתוככם והייתי לכם לאלהים ואתם תהיו לי לעם:.

12. הבית . . . בנה] A *casus pendens*, 'As for this house,' &c., imperfectly reinforced, after the long protasis, by ושכנתי בתוך בני ישראל (*v.* 13), where we should strictly expect בְּתוֹכוֹ. Cf. Dri. *Tenses*, § 197, *Obs.* 2. Thus we need not, with Kamp., Benz.,

[1] D's usual phrases are שמר משפטים לעשות 'observe judgements to do them'; 5. 1; 7. 11; 11. 32; 12. 1; 2 Ki. 17. 37; Ezek. 20. 21 (cf. 18. 9): לִמֵּד משפטים לעשות 'teach (some one else) judgements to do them'; 4. 1, 5, 14; 6. 1.

suppose that before הבית some words have fallen out, such as עֵינַי יִהְיוּ פְּתוּחוֹת אֶל־ 'mine eyes shall be open toward,' as in *ch.* 8. 29.

15. מביתה] Omitted by LXX, Luc.; but scarcely to be dispensed with.

קִירוֹת הַסִּפֻּן] Read קוֹרוֹת הַסִּפֻּן 'the *rafters* of the ceiling,' with the former part of the doublet in LXX, Luc. ἕως τῶν δοκῶν, Vulg. *laquearia*, Pesh. ܡܛܠܠܘܗܝ. So Bö., Th., Sta., Klo., Kamp., Benz., Kit.

צפה עץ מבית] Rejected by Sta. as a summary of the contents of the verse which has come into the text from the margin, and by Klo., Benz., Kit. as a later gloss added to guard the expression ויבן . . . בְּ against misunderstanding. The words, however, appear in all Verss., and may very well form with the previous מקרקע וג׳ a circumstantial clause; 'And he built the walls of the house within with boards of cedar, *overlaying* with wood within from the floor of the house to the rafters of the ceiling.' Cf. Dri. *Tenses*, § 163, who quotes *ch.* 7. 51 ויבא . . . את הכלים נתן וג׳ 'and he brought in the vessels . . ., *placing* them,' &c.

16. ויבן וג׳] 'And he built off the twenty cubits from the innermost part of the house with boards of cedar.' ירכתי means 'the furthest extremity,' and may be applied to the most secret recesses of a house or cave employed as a place of hiding, Am. 6. 10; 1 Sam. 24. 4; or as women's apartments, Ps. 128. 3; or again in the phrase ירכתי ארץ, to the most inaccessible limits of the earth, Jer. 31. 7; *al.;* cf. ירכתי צפון Ezek. 38. 6; *al.;* ירכתי בור Ezek. 32. 23. מן of מירכתי denotes the point of departure in measurement, as e.g. 1 Sam. 20. 37 ממך והלאה 'on beyond thee.'

הקירות] Read הַקּוֹרוֹת with LXX, Luc. ἕως τῶν δοκῶν, Vulg. *superiora*, Pesh. ܡܛܠܠܘܗܝ. So the authorities cited for the same emendation in *v.* 15.

16ᵇ. ויבן] וַיַּעַשׂ is the reading of 1 Cod., LXX, Luc., Θ., Vulg. So Th.

לו] *Dativus commodi*, as in 1. 28; lit. 'he built for himself'; so Kamp. 'baute er sich's.' Th., RV. 'he even built (them) for it,' i.e. for the house, are incorrect.

לִדְבִר] 'For an adytum.' The word דביר, which only occurs

in this section of Kings, *chs.* 6-8, in the parallel account in 2 Chr. 3-5, and in Ps. 28. 2 [1], is connected with Ar. دَبَرَ *to be behind*, whence دُبْر, دُبُر *hindmost* or *back part*, and so doubtless denotes the *back* or *innermost* room of the Temple. 'A., Σ. χρηματιστηρίον, Vulg. *oraculi*, whence AV., RV. 'oracle,' connect דביר incorrectly with דִּבֶּר 'to speak.'

לקדש הקדשים] So *ch.* 7. 50; 8. 6. The phrase occurs four times in P of the innermost sanctuary, Ex. 26. 33, 34; Num. 4. 4, 19; in Num. 18. 9, 10 it refers to the offerings of the b'nê Israel כל מנחתם וג'; קדשי הקדשים Lev. 21. 22 is the portion of the sons of Aaron; קדש קדשים, seventeen times in P, is applied to the brazen altar, the altar of incense, the twelve cakes of shew-bread, and the portions of various sacrifices which fell to the priests.

These are all occurrences of the phrase in P. Elsewhere it is found only in late books influenced by P; Ezek., Chr., Ezra, Neh., Dan.; and in the three passages noticed in Kings. Thus the phrase in Kings is clearly a gloss made by a post-exilic interpolator under the influence of P, to explain the possibly obsolete term דביר in 6. 16; 8. 6; and בית הפנימי in 7. 50.

The inclusion of the phrase in LXX, Luc. in each passage suggests that it is not due to the post-exilic editor R^P, whose glosses and changes are usually absent from the Greek Vers., or obviously inserted later from the margin, but to earlier post-exilic interpolators upon a smaller scale [2].

17-20[a]. וארבעים . . . . קומתו] The passage as it stands is remarkably involved, and appears to exhibit a double stratum of glosses. LXX reads καὶ τεσσαράκοντα πηχῶν ἦν ὁ ναὸς κατὰ πρόσωπον τοῦ δαβεὶρ ἐν μέσῳ τοῦ οἴκου ἔσωθεν, δοῦναι ἐκεῖ τὴν κιβωτὸν διαθήκης Κυρίου. εἴκοσι πήχεις μῆκος, καὶ εἴκοσι πήχεις πλάτος, καὶ εἴκοσι πήχεις τὸ ὕψος αὐτοῦ, i.e. וְאַרְבָּעִים בָּאַמָּה הָיָה הַבַּיִת לִפְנֵי (*v.* 17) הַדְּבִיר בְּתוֹךְ הַבַּיִת מִפְּנִימָה לָתֵת שָׁם אֶת־אֲרוֹן בְּרִית יְהוָה׃ (*v.* 19)

[1] The word should probably be restored in II. 10. 25; see *note*.

[2] These seem to have been mere *scribes* or copyists, not to be dignified by the title 'editor,' working under the influence of P, and thus their small insertions may be cited as belonging to SS^P.

עֶשְׂרִים אַמָּה אֹרֶךְ וְעֶשְׂרִים אַמָּה רֹחַב וְעֶשְׂרִים אַמָּה קוֹמָתוֹ (*v.* 20). So substantially Luc.

Here we notice the omission of הוא ההיכל, also lacking in Vulg., explanatory of הבית in *v.* 17; and the entire absence of *v.* 18, which contains details of the wood-carving of the house. These are clearly insertions made by R^P. By their removal the monstrous לִפְנָי at the close of *v.* 17, together with ולפני הדביר at the commencement of *v.* 20, is explained as arising out of the original לפני הדביר at the close of *v.* 17, through the confusion incident upon the introduction of *v.* 18.

But the account, even as simplified by LXX, cannot stand in its original form. The mention (*v.* 19) of the situation of the דביר is superfluous after *v.* 16, and the expression את ארון ברית יהוה belongs to D; see *note* on 3. 15. Thus *v.* 19 is also an insertion, though of earlier date than those first noticed, and possibly even due to R^D. The description originally ran as follows: (*v.* 17) וְאַרְבָּעִים בָּאַמָּה הָיָה הַבַּיִת לִפְנֵי הַדְּבִיר׃ (*v.* 20) וְהַדְּבִיר עֶשְׂרִים אַמָּה אֹרֶךְ וְעֶשְׂרִים אַמָּה רֹחַב וְעֶשְׂרִים אַמָּה קוֹמָתוֹ׃ 'And forty cubits was the house before the adytum. And the adytum was twenty cubits long, and twenty cubits broad, and twenty cubits high.' So Sta., except for the retention of הוא ההיכל (*v.* 17), against LXX, Luc., Vulg.

18. אל הבית] The preposition אל is not used in a loose way for על, RV. '*on* the house,' i.e. on its walls; but rather expresses presence *in* or *at* the building as pictured from a distance; '*in* the house.' Cf. II. 10. 14 וישחטום אל בור בית עקד 'They slew them *at* the pit of Beth-'Eqed'; Ezek. 31. 7 ושרשו אל מים רבים 'its root was *by* many waters'; 47. 7 הנה אל שפת הנחל עץ רב 'behold, *at* the edge of the ravine there were many trees.'

מקלעת] 'Carving'; only again *vv.* 29, 32; *ch.* 7. 31; while the verb קלע *vv.* 29, 32, 35† is also peculiar to this one interpolator.

פקעים] 'Gourds'; 7. 24†. פַּקֻּעֹת II. 4. 39† means wild gourds gathered from a גֶּפֶן שָׂדֶה. According to Tristram, *DB.*² 1244, the *Colocynthis agri* is denoted.

פטורי צצים] 'Open flowers'; *vv.* 29, 32, 35†.

19. לתתן] This anomalous form of the infin. constr. occurs once again, *ch.* 17. 14 Kt., where Q're is תֵּת. König's view (*Lehrg.* I. i. p. 305) that the double occurrence precludes the theory of textual corruption, and that the final ן is a parasitical addition due to the fact that vulgarly the recollection of the connexion of תֵּת with נתן was totally obliterated, is very forced and unnatural.

20. ויצפהו זהב סגור] Sta. argues at length against the originality of all passages which speak of the use of gold plating in Solomon's Temple, making in brief the following points:—

(i) If for the manufacture of brazen vessels a Syrian workman had to be imported (7. 13 *ff.*), it is highly improbable that sufficiently skilful workers in gold were to be found among the men of Israel.

(ii) Later notices in Kings which mention the treasures of the Temple make no allusion to the gold-plating. Thus, 14. 26, Shishak carries off only the אוצרות בית יהוה such as would presumably be stored in the side-chambers, and the golden shields of Solomon; II. 14. 14, Joash king of Israel makes booty of the gold and silver vessels found בית יהוה ובאוצרות בית המלך; II. 16. 17, Ahaz in his need uses merely the great *bronze* vessels found in the Temple; II. 18. 16, Hezekiah overlays the doors of the היכל יהוה with gold-plating, but afterwards cuts it off and sends it to the king of Assyria.

(iii) Verses 21 *f.*, 30 stand in wrong position; *v.* 21, so far as it refers to the gold-plating of the house, is wanting in LXX; and *vv.* 22, 30 are otherwise rendered suspicious by their contents.

(iv) Ezekiel, in his description of the future Temple, knows of no such gold-plating.

Thus in this connexion *vv.* 20b (in part, ויצפהו זהב סגור), 21 (all but לפני הדביר), 22, 28, 30, 32b are omitted by Sta.

These arguments, though weighty, are not entirely convincing. צפה may denote not necessarily a heavy gold-plating as in II. 18. 16, but a thin gilding with *liquid* gold[1], such as called for no very

[1] In Prov. 26. 23 כֶּסֶף סִיגִים מְצֻפֶּה עַל־חָרֶשׂ one thinks of a potsherd silvered over, not coated with *plates* of silver.

special skill in preparation and application to the wood, and also need not imply so prodigious a supply of the metal, nor have been calculated to attract the cupidity of a foreign foe bent upon hastily pillaging the treasures of the Temple. Again, the fact that certain notices are absent from LXX rather favours than otherwise the originality of the remainder. Quite probably the narrative has here, as elsewhere, been subject to later glosses; but the total denial to the original account of all references to the employment of gold in Solomon's Temple must be deemed extremely precarious.

זהב סגור] Apparently '*choice*' or '*precious* gold' (cf. the alternative זהב טוב of 2 Chr. 3. 8); though how the word gains this sense is quite uncertain. A subs. סְגוֹר occurs Job 28. 15.

ויצף מזבח ארז] But if the altar was merely overlaid with cedar boards, what was its inner material? As Sta. remarks, an altar if of stone or earth could scarcely be covered outside with boards. LXX, Luc. καὶ ἐποίησεν θυσιαστήριον, i. e. וַיַּעַשׂ מִזְבֵּחַ, is doubtless correct as regards the verb, but the mention of the material אֶרֶז is indispensable, and must have fallen out through oversight. So Bö., Th., Sta., Klo., Kamp., Benz., Kit.

21. LXX, Luc. have only the last four words of this verse which they refer to the altar. This seems to be correct. The remainder of the verse is a gloss inserted later, and breaking the connexion. The whole sentence ought to run וַיַּעַשׂ מִזְבֵּחַ אֶרֶז לִפְנֵי הַדְּבִיר וַיְצַפֵּהוּ זָהָב.

וַיְעַבֵּר בְּרַתִּיקוֹת זָהָב] This can only mean 'he drew golden chains across,' lit. '*he made a crossing with*,' &c.; but this is very harsh.

In 2 Chr. 3. 14 mention is made of הַפָּרֹכֶת the *veil*; and, in accordance with Th.'s suggestion, it is at least conceivable that in our passage R[P] may have written, or intended to write, וַיְעַבֵּר אֶת־הַפָּרֹכֶת וגו׳ 'and he drew the veil across with chains of gold.' עבר Pi'el is only so used in this passage. The sing. רַתּוֹק occurs in Ezek. 7. 23 (but disappears under Cornill's emendation), and a pl. רַתֻּקוֹת Isa. 40. 19†. Klo. makes the very conjectural emendation וְאַרְבַּע קַרְנֹתָיו זָהָב 'and its four horns were of gold,' referring to the altar.

22[b]. וכל המזבח וג׳] But we have already been informed about the overlaying of the altar with gold in the previous verse. This passage, omitted by LXX, Luc., is doubtless a gloss, and owes its existence to the gloss in the previous *v.* 21 ויצף . . . ברתיקות זהב which, by breaking the connexion, destroyed the original statement with reference to the gold-plating of the altar, and so caused the necessity for an additional clause to that effect.

23. עצי שמן] So Vulg., Targ. LXX omits. Luc. ἐκ ξύλων κυπαρισσίνων, Pesh. ܕܩܝܣܐ ܕܫܡܝܫܐ. MT. correct.

קומתו] As the verse stands the reference of the suffix is obscure. RV. 'each' is an unsatisfactory escape from the difficulty, and no real translation. LXX, Luc. μέγεθος ἐσταθμωμένον, for which Th. suggests קוֹמָה מְתֻכֶּנֶת; but Sta. points out that this cannot mean 'upright stature,' since תִּכֵּן only signifies 'to adjust.' ἐσταθ. appears to be merely a translator's flourish. Sta. most cleverly removes all difficulty by placing *v.* 26 between *v.* 23[a] and *v.* 23[b]. This is doubtless correct. The suffix of קומתו is satisfied by reference to הכרוב השני in *v.* 26[b], and the account of the measurements of the כרובים closes very appropriately with the summary *v.* 25[b] מדה אחת וקצב אחד לשני הכרבים.

All Verss. follow the wrong order of MT.

27. ויתן את הכרובים] LXX, Luc. καὶ ἀμφότερα χερουβείν, i. e. וּשְׁנֵי הַכְּרוּבִים. So Klo., who notices that the fact that the כרובים were brought into the דביר has already been stated in *v.* 23[a] ויעש בדביר וג׳. Th., Sta. adopt שני as more precise, but retain ויתן את of MT. This latter, as introducing the statement that when so placed their wings touched the wall on either side, can scarcely be considered redundant.

ויפרשו] One MS. ויפרש; so Pesh. ܘܦܪܣ. Possible, but not preferable to MT.

את כנפי הכרבים] LXX, Luc. τὰς πτέρυγας αὐτῶν, i. e. אֶת־כַּנְפֵיהֶם, doubtless correct. So Bö., Th., Sta., Klo., Kamp., Benz., Kit.

ותגע וג׳] LXX seems to convey the idea that *each* כרוב had four wings:—*καὶ ἥπτετο πτέρυξ μία τοῦ τοίχου, καὶ πτέρυξ ἥπτετο τοῦ τοίχου τοῦ δευτέρου· καὶ αἱ πτέρυγες αὐτοῦ αἱ ἐν μέσῳ τοῦ οἴκου ἥπτοντο πτέρυξ πτέρυγος.* This is very inferior to the plain statement of MT. supported by Luc. and the other Verss.

29, 30. These verses, though both appearing in LXX, Luc., appear to form no part of the original account. Verse 29 is obviously by the same hand as *v.* 18, assigned to R^P, and *v.* 30 is redundant after *v.* 22[a], and also out of place.

29. מֵסַב] Probably to be emended מְסָבִיב with Klo.

מלפנים ולחיצון] The reference of 'within and without' is rather ambiguous, a remark which also applies to the similar words in *v.* 30. Klo.'s emendation, לַפְּנִימִי וְלַחִיצוֹן 'both of the inner and of the outer house,' is probably correct; cf. Ezek. 41. 17. The expression הַבַּיִת הַפְּנִימִי is used of the דביר *v.* 27; *ch.* 7. 50.

31. ואת פתח] LXX, Luc., Pesh., Targ. seem to presuppose וּלְפֶתַח; and so Klo. This *may* be original, but is quite as likely to be a paraphrase of the somewhat difficult MT. The latter, as Sta. notices, is quite possible, and may be paralleled; cf. Ex. 26. 1 וְאֶת־הַמִּשְׁכָּן תַּעֲשֶׂה עֶשֶׂר יְרִיעֹת; Dri. *Tenses*, § 195, 1. Th., in retaining MT., cites Ew. § 284[a] for the usage.

Vulg. *et in ingressu oraculi*, takes את פתח הדביר to be an accus. of place as in *ch.* 7. 40 בית יהוה *in templo domini*.

האיל] Of doubtful meaning. Neither Sta. 'door-opening,' nor RV., &c. 'lintel,' seems to be correct; for according to either of these renderings the breadth of the איל ought to be commensurate with that of the doorway, whereas in Ezek. 41. 3 the former is said to be two cubits (broad), the latter six cubits; cf. Ezek. 40. 9—the porch eight cubits, the איל two cubits. Again, the איל is spoken of as something standing in equal proportions upon either side of an entrance or porch; Ezek. 40. 48[a] וַיָּמָד אֵל אֻלָם חָמֵשׁ אַמּוֹת מִפֹּה וְחָמֵשׁ אַמּוֹת מִפֹּה (on 48[b] see Cornill's emendation); cf. 41. 1. Thus the explanation of Bö. (*Proben alttest. Schriftklärung*. 302 *ff.*), *pilasters* or projections in a wall upon either side of an entrance, appears to be near to the truth. So Pesh. ܦܪ̈ܣܛܕܘܗܝ 'its παραστάδες[1],' Cornill 'Wandpfeiler,' Kit. 'Einfassung,' and apparently RV. marg. 'posts.' Somewhat similar is the suggestion '*crepidines*,' of Ges., who quotes the passages where the word occurs, and the ancient interpretations.

חֲמִשִּׁית] So Baer. Less accurate texts חֲמִשִׁית. Upon the analogy of 7. 5 וְהַמְּזוּזוֹת רְבֻעִים שֶׁקֶף, and the necessary and obvious emendation at the close of *v.* 33 מְזוּזוֹת רְבֻעוֹת, חמשית ought to mean '*a pentagonal*' . So Vulg. *postesque angulorum quinque*, Bö., Th., Sta., Kamp., Benz., Kit. Pesh. ܡܚܡܫܝܢ suggests the possibility of an original חֲמִשּׁוֹת exactly analogous to רְבֻעִים of 7. 5. The explanation '*a fifth part*' of the entire wall, adopted by Ges., Ke., Klo., is alien to the context, the breadth of the wall not having been mentioned since *v.* 20.

האיל מזוזות חמשית] It is impossible to regard האיל מזוזות as a case of apposition, 'the pilasters *were* doorposts,' &c., because איל is not identical with מזוזות. Hence it is best to adopt Sta.'s emendation הָאַיִל וְהַמְּזוּזוֹת ח׳, rendering 'the pilasters and doorposts were (i.e. formed) a pentagonal.' It is, however, conceivable that the text may have originally read האיל חמשית, and that מזוזות is a gloss from the margin as an (incorrect) explanation of the difficult איל.

32, 35. By the same hand as *vv.* 18, 29.

32. ושתי דלתות וג׳] A *casus pendens;* 'as for the two doors,' &c.

וְקָלַע] The perf. with weak ו here and in *v.* 35, if part of the original text, would be 'an isolated irregularity' (Dri. *Tenses*, § 133, 2), but the construction marks the style of the post-exilic interpolator. Klo. וַיְקַלַּע; but this, if possible in *v.* 32, is scarcely so in *v.* 35.

וַיָּרֶד] From רדד; 'and he *spread out* the gold upon the cherubim,' &c. The word is that which is used in Targ. Onk. as an equivalent of רִקַּע; Ex. 39. 3; Num. 17. 4; and its use thus forms another

[1] Unless this represent προστάς, 'vestibule.' The other Verss. give no help; Targ. אילהי 'but' misunderstands; LXX, Luc., Vulg. omit.

post-exilic indication. Luc. *καὶ κατέβαινεν*, i.e. וַיֵּרֶד; Pesh. ܘܐܚܦܝ, i.e. וַיְּרַב; Targ. ונסיך, apparently וַיָּרֶק or וַיֹּרֶד; Vulg. *et operuit*, a guess. Klo.'s reading וַיֵּרֶד is unnecessary.

33. מאת רבעית] LXX *στοαὶ* (Luc. *στοὰς*) *τετραπλῶς*, i.e. מְזוּזוֹת רְבֻעוֹת 'doorposts standing foursquare,' is doubtless correct. Cf. *ch.* 7. 5. So Th., Sta., Kamp., Benz., Kit. The verse, all but the last two words, is with *v.* 32 omitted by LXX through homoioteleuton with the end of *v.* 31.

34ᵇ. קלעים] All Verss. rightly presuppose צלעים as in *v.* 34ᵃ. So Th., Sta., Klo., Kamp.

גלילים] 'Revolving,' or 'turning on hinges,' so '*folding*.' Thus only here. In Ezek. 41. 24 the doors are called שְׁתַּיִם מוּסַבּוֹת דְּלָתוֹת.

35. וצפה] Cf. *v.* 32 *note* on וקלע.

מְיֻשָּׁר עַל־הַמְּחֻקֶּה] 'Applied evenly to the carving.' ישר Pu'al only here; Pi'el 'make straight or even,' of a way, &c.

36. החצר הפנימית] Surrounding the Temple, and *innermost* as contrasted with the חצר האחרת 7. 8, containing the King's palace, both courts lying inside the חצר הגדולה which enclosed the whole group of buildings. See *note* on 7. 12ᵇ, and plan in Sta. *Ges.* i. 314.

At the end of this verse LXX, Luc. continue with the words *κυκλόθεν, καὶ ᾠκοδόμησε κ.τ.λ.* This seems to represent MT. *ch.* 7. 12ᵇ, where it receives discussion.

7. 1–12ᵃ appear in LXX, Luc. at the close of the *ch.*, being apparently so placed by some scribe who thought it better to give the account of the Temple furniture in immediate sequence to that of the Temple itself, and not separated by the description of Solomon's other buildings. This is shown to be a late dislocation by the fact that *v.* 12ᵇ has been accidentally left behind in making the alteration, and now follows immediately after the close of *ch.* 6, instead of after *v.* 12ᵃ to which it clearly belongs. MT., which describes all the buildings first and then the furniture of the Temple, is correct.

2. ארבעה] LXX, Luc. *τριῶν*. Hence Sta. adopts שלשה as in agreement with the statement in *v.* 3 ארבעים וחמשה חמשה עשר הטור.

This, he contends, must refer to the עמודים, and not to the צלעות (Th.) a fem. noun; Ezek. 41. 8. So Kamp., Benz., Kit.

Sta. takes the following view of the construction of the house:—'It was a house of which the back and sides upon the ground-floor were formed of walls, while the front of the bottom story was formed by the fifteen pillars of the first row. The pillars of the second and third rows stood within the building, exactly corresponding to the pillars of the first row. The second story was formed by a number of chambers lying in three rows or flights' (*ZATW.* 1883, p. 150). A further description, together with excellent plans of the building, may be seen in *Ges.* i. 318 *ff.* It may be doubted, however, whether Sta. is correct in his arrangement of the chambers which he assigns to one single story above the pillars. The expressions of *vv.* 4, 5 שקפים שלשה טורים... שלש פעמים seem to suggest *three stories* of chambers (so Kit.), and this is agreeable to the height of the building, thirty cubits, even supposing these stories to have been higher than those of the Temple wings (6. 6)—perhaps six cubits each, with the pillars below the first floor of some twelve cubits in height. The house seems to have obtained its name from the fact that the pillars, open to view from the outside, gave to the spectator the idea of a forest of trees. The rooms, if in three stories, may have run right through the breadth of the building, having a window or windows at either end, i.e. at the front and back of the house. This explains *v.* 4 ומחזה אל מחזה שלש פעמים 'and window was over against window three times.' The doors, on the other hand, opening from one room into another, ran lengthways down the centre of the building. Thus each room had two doors opposite to one another and communicating directly with the rooms on either side. This seems to satisfy the expression ומול פתח אל פתח שלש פעמים 'and door was over against door three times,' which we shall adopt in *v.* 5 at the suggestion of LXX, Luc.

We have no information as to staircase or number of chambers. The kind of rooms above described are not strictly the same as those described in 6. 5 *ff.*, supposing the term צלעות to really denote '*side*-chambers.' But the use of צלע '*a rib*,' to describe a chamber is very obscure, and we can scarcely say for certain what sort of room could be so called, and what not. צלעות may perhaps refer to the main beams[1], which, resting on the pillars and running from wall to wall, formed the basis of the partitions between the different chambers, and were, so to speak, the ribs of the building.

כרתות] 'Beams,' as *cut* or *sawn* into the required dimensions. LXX, Luc. ὠμίαι, i. e. כְּתֵפוֹת 'shoulder-pieces' at the top of the pillars, forming a support for the beams. Cf. the use of the word in *v.* 30. This is adopted by Klo., Benz., Kit., but is scarcely superior to MT.

3. After על העמודים LXX, Luc. insert καὶ ἀριθμὸς τῶν στύλων, i. e. וּמִסְפַּר הָעַמּוּדִים. By this addition the verse is relieved, and the precise reference of the number made perfectly clear.

4. שקפים] Explained by Th., Sta., Klo., Kamp., Benz. as the main beams supporting the floors and ceilings of the chambers; a meaning possibly agreeable to the Ar. سَقْفٌ quoted on 6. 4. It should be noticed, however, that *v.* 4[b] ומחזה אל מחזה וג׳ seems obviously to refer back to the preceding statement, as though מחזה and שקפים were closely connected in meaning. Hence it seems preferable to assign to שקפים, here as in 6. 4, the meaning '*window-frames*.' So RV. 'prospects.' Kit. 'Fenster (?).'

5. והמזוזות] Read וְהַמֶּחֱזוֹת with LXX, Luc. καὶ αἱ χῶραι. So Th., Sta., Klo., Kamp., Benz., Kit.

רבעים שקף] Cf. 6. 4 *note*.

ומול מחזה אל מחזה שלש פעמים] LXX καὶ ἀπὸ τοῦ θυρώματος (Luc. ἀπὸ θύρας) ἐπὶ θύραν τρισσῶς, i. e. וּמִפֶּתַח אֶל־פֶּתַח שָׁלֹשׁ פְּעָמִים, probably standing for וּמוּל פֶּתַח אֶל־פֶּתַח וג׳, which may be adopted. Sta. reads פתח אל פתח, regarding מול as a gloss arising from a marginal note פתח מול פתח.

6. שלשים] LXX πεντήκοντα. But Luc., Vulg., Pesh., Targ. support MT.

---

[1] Cf. the use of the term to denote the *beams* or *boards* which went to form the inner walls of the house, and the partition-wall of the adytum; *ch.* 6. 15, 16[a].

After רחבו and before ואולם LXX inserts ἐζυγωμένα, Luc. ἐζυγωμένη. This appears to be a mere gloss by which it was sought to explain the relationship between the second אולם and the אולם העמודים. Or possibly the word may form a doublet of רחבו, the letters being transposed and read as some part of חבר, perhaps מְחֻבָּר.

עב] The meaning is very obscure, and can only be guessed. LXX, Luc. render lit. πάχος, Vulg. *epistylia*, 'cross-beams,' Pesh. ܦܪܘܢ 'entrance hall,' Targ. סקופתא 'threshold.' The word occurs again Ezek. 41. 25 וְעָב עֵץ אֶל־פְּנֵי הָאוּלָם מֵהַחוּץ. Here Cornill hazards 'Vordach,' and this is perhaps what is intended by Vulg. in Kings—the front part of the roof of the porch, possibly forming a kind of projecting *cornice*. *Sieg. u. Sta.* also suggests 'Vordach, Schutzdach.' Th., Sta., Klo., Kamp. doubtfully follow the suggestion of Targ., and suppose the word to mean an entrance with steps.

7. אשר ישפט שם] 'Where he *should* or *might* judge'; Dri. *Tenses*, § 39 β.

וְסָפֻן] The usual construction would be אלם משפט עשה סָפֻן בארז 'he made the porch covered,' &c.; cf. Dri. *Tenses*, § 161. 2. It is rare for the participle to be preceded by וְ when thus introducing a subordinate idea as a secondary predicate. See instances under *Obs.* 1 of Dri. § cited.

עד הקרקע] Vulg. *usque ad summitatem*, Pesh. ܘܥܕܡܐ ܠܡܛܠܠܬܗ read עַד־הַקּוֹרוֹת, which is to be adopted. So Ew., Th., Sta., Kamp., Benz.; and Klo. doubtfully. Kit. retains MT. The second half of the verse has fallen out in LXX, Luc.; but, according to Field, *Hex.*, the Complutensian reads ἀπὸ ἐδάφους ἕως ὑπερῴου.

8. אשר ישב שם] The same *nuance* as in *v.* 7 ישפט.

חצר האחרת] Also called חֲצַר אֻלָם הַבַּיִת; see *notes* on *v.* 12[b]; *ch.* 6. 36.

It is unusual in classical Hebrew (though customary in post-biblical Hebrew) to omit the article with a subs. when its adj. is so defined according to rule. Cf. חָצֵר הַגְּדוֹלָה *v.* 12. Dri. (*Tenses*, § 209. 1) collects instances of the usage which 'appears to have arisen in connexion with familiar words, which were felt to be sufficiently definite in themselves without the addition of the article.'

מבית לאולם] LXX renders curiously *ἐξ ἐλισσομένης τούτοις*, Luc. *ἐξελισσομένη τούτοις*, apparently a misreading לְאֻלָּה . . . מ, the former word being some Pu'al or Hoph'al participle. MT. correct.

יעשה] The tense is quite anomalous, and cannot be explained, the perfect alone being suitable to describe a single fact in so prosaic a connexion[1]. It is at least possible that some scribe, intending to copy וּבַיִת עָשָׂה, wrote by mistake וביתו עשה through confusion with וביתו at the beginning of the verse, and that this וביתועשה was subsequently interpreted as ובית יעשה. The omission of יעשה in LXX suggests as a second hypothesis that the word may be a later gloss carelessly inserted.

9. כמדות] 'According to measurements,' i.e. of regular dimensions, and not of various sizes. So *v.* 11.

מְגֹרָרוֹת] 'Sawn'; only here. A *dĕnom.* from מְגֵרָה which is derived from גרר 'drag.' Both subs. מגרה and *denom.* verb in Qal and Niph'al occur in post-biblical Hebrew.

מַסַּד] 'Foundation'; a *ἅπαξ λεγ.* from יסד, the י being assimilated according to the small class of contracted verbs פ״י; G-K. § 71. Other contracted forms from this root are מוּסָּד Isa. 28. 16; לְיסּוֹד 2 Chr. 31. 7.

עד הטפחות] RV. 'unto the coping'; so LXX, Luc. *ἕως τῶν γείσων* (with a Schol. *στεφανωμάτων ἢ ἄκρων*), and approximately Σ. (*ἕως*) *τῶν ἀπαρτισμάτων*, Vulg. *usque ad summitatem parietum*, Pesh. ܘܥܕܡܐ ܠܟܠܠ; Th., Klo., *Sieg. u. Sta.* Sta., Kamp., Kit. follow Ges. in rendering *mutules* or projecting stones (Kragsteine) upon which the ends of the beams rested. The word, which occurs only here in this sense, elsewhere means a 'handbreadth'; *v.* 26; *al.* So Targ. בפושכיא, 'A. (*ἕως*) *τῶν παλαιστωμάτων*.

The first וּמִחוּץ, which is indispensable, has fallen out in LXX,

---

[1] Kö., however (*Lehrg.* I. ii. § 368 *k*), classes the use with *ch.* 20. 33[a] ינחשו as an *Inchoative*.

Luc. through oversight. The second וּמִחוּץ is very difficult. As Sta. remarks, it forms no contrast to החצר הגדולה. Sta.'s emendation ומבית יהוה is, however, not quite correct. We ought rather to read וּמֵחֲצַ[ר בֵּית יְהוָֹה], a correction which accords with *v.* 12, and accounts for the letters* ומחצ in MT.

10. ומיסד] LXX, Luc. τὴν τεθεμελιωμένην, Pesh. ܘܡܫܬܐܣܐ, apply this specially to the great court. It seems better to regard it as having a vague general application to כל אלה at the beginning of *v.* 9; all the buildings. Sta. 'und fundamentirt (war alles).' So Th., Kamp., Benz.

12ᵇ. ולחצר . . . הבית] As has before been noticed, LXX, Luc. at the close of *ch.* 6. 36 contain the words κυκλόθεν· καὶ ᾠκοδόμησε τὸ καταπέτασμα τῆς αὐλῆς τοῦ αἰλὰμ τοῦ οἴκου τοῦ κατὰ πρόσωπον τοῦ ναοῦ, i.e. probably מִסָּבִיב וַיִּבֶן מָסָךְ לַחֲצַר אֻלָם הַבַּיִת אֲשֶׁר עַל־פְּנֵי הַהֵיכָל. This seems to represent MT. *ch.* 7. 12ᵇ ולחצר בית יהוה הפנימית ולאלם הבית. מסך certainly cannot be original, the phrase ויבן מסך being absurd. The word is probably therefore a corruption of מִסָּבִיב repeated from the preceding, and καὶ ᾠκοδόμησε is clearly a gloss formed through repetition of ויבן 6. 36ᵃ, to explain the connexion of καταπέτασμα with the previous sentence. The first מִסָּבִיב is genuine, and should be restored before לַחֲצַר in place of the ו of MT. LXX is also correct in reading וְלַחֲצַר אֻלָם הַבַּיִת (this referring to חצר האחרת of *v.* 8), but has omitted לחצר בית יהוה הפנימית through the homoioteleuton לחצר. Possibly, as Sta. thinks, הפנימית is a gloss from 6. 36, and redundant after בית יהוה. Finally, the sentence אשר על פני ההיכל appears to be a gloss derived from 6. 3, והאולם על פני היכל הבית, through a wrong identification of the אולם here mentioned.

We may therefore read *v.* 12ᵇ מִסָּבִיב לַחֲצַר בֵּית־יְהוָֹה (הַפְּנִימִית) וְלַחֲצַר אֻלָם הַבַּיִת 'round about the (inner) court of the House of Yahwe, and the court of the porch of the palace.'

13, 14. In 2 Chr. 2. 12, 13 the workman is called חוּרָם אָבִי, and he is בֶּן־אִשָּׁה מִן־בְּנוֹת דָּן. According to Giesebrecht (*ZATW.* i. 239 *ff.*) the text of Chr. is the more original, the name חורם אבי (misunderstood as by LXX in Chr.) having undergone correction in Kings, and אלמנה being an insertion to suggest that this builder of Solomon's Temple was purely Israelitish, and not half Phoenician.

15–22. This very mutilated and obscure account may be compared with the summary in *vv.* 41, 42; ‖ 2 Chr. 4. 12, 13, and with the description in II. 25. 17, of which a better and fuller form exists in Jer. 52. 21–23.

15ª. ויצר] LXX, Luc. *καὶ ἐχώνευσε*, i.e. וַיִּצֹּק; probably correct. So Th., Sta., Klo., Kamp., Benz., Kit.

את שני העמודים נחשת] LXX omits by oversight. Luc. reads all but נחשת, which is scarcely necessary after the precise statement of *v.* 14 לעשות כל מלאכה בנחשת, and so *may* be a gloss, but on comparison with *vv.* 16, 27, 30, 38 is more likely to be original[1], נחשת being an accus. of material. At this point Luc. adds *τῷ αἰλὰμ τοῦ οἴκου*, and so also LXX with *τό* by mistake for *τῷ*, i.e. לְאוּלָם הַבַּיִת. This is accepted by Sta. on the ground that the expression שני העמודים '*the* two pillars,' requires some such specification of their destined position to justify the use of the article. So Th., Klo., Kamp., Kit.

15ᵇ. שמנה . . . השני] LXX *ὀκτὼ καὶ δέκα πήχεις ὕψος τοῦ στύλου· καὶ περίμετρον τέσσαρες καὶ δέκα πήχεις ἐκύκλου αὐτόν, τὸ πάχος τοῦ στύλου· τεσσάρων δακτύλων τὰ κοιλώματα· καὶ οὕτως στύλος ὁ δεύτερος*, i.e. שְׁמֹנֶה עֶשְׂרֵה אַמָּה קוֹמַת הָעַמּוּד וְחוּט שְׁתֵּים־עֶשְׂרֵה אַמָּה יָסֹב אֹתוֹ עֳבִי הָעַמּוּד אַרְבַּע אֶצְבָּעוֹת נָבוּב וְכֵן הָעַמּוּד הַשֵּׁנִי 'eighteen cubits was the height of the (one) pillar, and a thread of twelve cubits compassed it about; the thickness of the pillar was four fingers; it was hollow: and the second pillar was similar.' This description corresponds accurately with that which is given in Jer. 52. 21, and is doubtless correct, except that הָאֶחָד is to be retained with MT. after the first העמוד. LXX text is confirmed substantially by Luc., and in part by Pesh. ܘܪܘܡܗ ܕܥܡܘܕܐ ܚܕ ܬܡܢܥܣܪܐ ܐܡܝܢ. ܘܚܘܛܐ ܕܬܪܬܥܣܪܐ ܐܡܝܢ ܚܕܪ ܠܗ. ܘܗܟܢܐ ܠܥܡܘܕܐ ܐܚܪܢܐ 'the height of the one pillar was eighteen cubits, and a thread of twelve cubits compassed

[1] On the other hand, *v.* 23 omits נחשת in MT. and Verss.

it about; and the second pillar was similar.' So Ew., Th.[1], Sta., Klo., Kamp., Benz.[1], Kit.[1]

יסב] '*Could* or *might* encompass'; so *v.* 23 יסב, *v.* 26 יכיל '*could* contain' (or in this instance perhaps '*contained*,' as a customary state). Dri. *Tenses*, § 37 β. Da. (§ 44, *Rem.* 2) is scarcely correct when he renders 'encompassed' or 'ran round,' 'in describing the course of an ornamentation,' as if this חוט or the קו of *v.* 23 were *part of the ornamentation*, and not rather an imaginary line of measurement.

נבוב, adopted in the emendation, occurs, besides the passage cited in Jer., Ex. 27. 8; 38. 7 נְבוּב לֻחֹת 'hollow, with boarded sides,' of the altar of burnt offering, and figuratively Job 11. 12† 'a *hollow*' or '*empty-headed* man.'

16. כתרות] 'Chapiters'; only used in the description of these pillars, here and in II. 25, 2 Chr., Jer. Connected with the root כתר 'surround,' Pi'el, Judg. 20. 43; Ps. 22. 13, from which comes the late word כֶּתֶר 'diadem,' three times in Est.†, and in new Hebrew.

מצק נחשת] 'A casting of brass,' so 'of cast or molten brass.' מוצק as in *vv.* 23, 33, 37; cf. Job 38. 38 'a congealed mass.' נחשת has fallen out of LXX, but is found in Luc. and the other Verss., and, as in the previous verse, is to be retained. LXX is also wrong in its omission of החמש . . . השנית.

17. שבכים . . . שרשרות] LXX, Luc. καὶ ἐποίησε δύο δίκτυα, i.e. וַיַּעַשׂ שְׁתֵּי שְׂבָכִים, are correct, the words מעשה . . . שרשרות being certainly a gloss. שבכים (הַשְּׂבָכוֹת, הַשְּׂבָכָה) occurs in all the other descriptions, but the expressions מעשה שבכה, גדלים, שרשרות are not so found[2]. LXX is followed by Th., Sta., Kamp., Benz., Kit.; and Klo. as regards the addition of ויעש שתי.

שבכים] With pl. ־ים only here; elsewhere שְׂבָכוֹת from sing. שְׂבָכָה. The word is derived from Ar. شَبَكَ *interweave*, whence شَبَكَة

[1] Th. presupposes הַנְּבוּבִים instead of נָבוּב, but otherwise agrees with the text as given above. Benz. וְעָבְיוֹ, Kit. וְעָבְיוֹ (omitting הָעַמּוּד).

[2] The statement in 2 Chr. 3. 16 is doubtless derived from the gloss in our passage.

net (for catching fish, birds, &c.), and in biblical Hebrew, outside the description of these pillars, it occurs only in II. 1. 2 of the *lattice* of a window, and in Job 18. 8, where the parallel word is הָרֶשֶׁת 'the net[1].' Thus the meaning in this description is clearly '*network*' or '*trellis*.'

גְּדִלִים] 'Festoons'; Deut. 22. 12 of the *fringes* of a garment. Ar. جَدِيلٌ *a bridle of plaited thongs*. Syr. ܓܕܠ very commonly means *to plait* or *interweave*; e.g. S. Matt. 27. 29, of plaiting the crown of thorns.

שרשרות] 'Chains'; 2 Chr. 3. 5, 16; so in Ex. 28. 14; 39. 15†, of the ornaments or fastenings of the breastplate. שַׁרְשֹׁת Ex. 28. 22 is a corruption of the same. The word is a Pilpel (intensive) form from שרר 'twist.'

לכתרת אשר על ראש העמודים] LXX περικαλύψαι τὸ ἐπίθεμα τῶν στύλων, Luc. ἐπικαλύψαι τὰ ἐπιθέματα τῶν στύλων, i.e. לְכַסּוֹת אֶת־כֹּתְרֹת (כֹּתֶרֶת) הָעַמּוּדִים. In *v.* 18 we meet with a sentence which is very like a combination of these readings of MT. and LXX, viz. לְכַסּוֹת אֶת־הַכֹּתָרֹת אֲשֶׁר עַל־רֹאשׁ הָרִמֹּנִים. Here הָרִמֹּנִים is quite incomprehensible, and we may follow Pesh. ܕܥܡ̈ܘܕܐ and emend העמודים agreeably to *v.* 41[b]. This sentence of *v.* 18 is not to be found in LXX, Luc., and thus Th., Sta. are doubtless correct in supposing that, after having fallen out of *v.* 17 in MT., it was first written in again on the margin, and then inserted in the text in a wrong position, viz. in *v.* 18. So Kamp., Benz., Kit.

שבעה . . . ושבעה] LXX, Luc. δίκτυον . . . καὶ δίκτυον, i. e. שְׂבָכָה . . . וּשְׂבָכָה; doubtless correct. So Bö., Th., Sta., Klo., Kamp., Benz., Kit.

Thus *v.* 17, as restored, will run:—וַיַּעַשׂ שְׁתֵּי שְׂבָכִים לְכַסּוֹת אֶת־הַכֹּתָרוֹת אֲשֶׁר עַל־רֹאשׁ הָעַמּוּדִים שְׂבָכָה לַכֹּתֶרֶת הָאֶחָת וּשְׂבָכָה לַכֹּתֶרֶת הַשֵּׁנִית׃ 'And he made two trellises to cover the chapiters which were upon the top of the pillars; a trellis for the one chapiter, and a trellis for the second chapiter.'

---

[1] The root סבך, which ought properly to be שׂבך, occurs Nah. 1. 10; Job 8. 17 with the meaning 'intertwine.' Hence come סְבָךְ, סֹבֶךְ 'thicket.'

18. העמודים] Obviously incorrect. At this stage of the description the statement 'he made the pillars' is out of place. Two MSS. read הָרִמֹּנִים 'the pomegranates,' and this is to be adopted with Bö., Th., Sta., Klo., Kamp., Benz., Kit. Vulg., Pesh., Targ. follow MT.; LXX, Luc. *καὶ ἔργον κρεμαστόν*, i. e. ? . . . וּמַעֲשֵׂה[1] a misreading of ויעש הרמנים.

ושני טורים סביב על השבכה] LXX, Luc. *δύο στίχοι ῥοῶν χαλκῶν δεδικτυωμένοι*, i. e. [הָאֶחָת] וּשְׁנֵי טוּרֵי רִמֹּנִים נְחֹשֶׁת עַל־הַשְּׂבָכָה. *δεδικτ.* is thought by Klo. to be a corruption of *δικτύῳ ἑνί*, which is possible (cf. *v.* 42 *τῷ δικτύῳ τῷ ἑνί*), but not really necessary. LXX reading is correct, and is adopted by Sta., Kamp. So Th., with addition of סביב.

LXX, Luc. continue with *ἔργον κρεμαστόν, στίχος ἐπὶ στίχον.* This appears to be merely a doublet of the previous *καὶ ἔργον κρεμαστόν, δύο στίχοι.*

The sentence לכסות וג׳ having been adopted into its proper position in *v.* 17, *v.* 18 now ends abruptly with וכן עשה לכתרת השנית, no special reference being previously made to הכתרת האחת. Th. therefore inserts, before the closing sentence, *v.* 20ᵇ in the form in which it appears in Pesh. ܘܪܘܡܢܐ ܡܐܬܝܢ ܬܪܝܢ ܣܕܪܝܢ ܚܕܪ ܚܕܪ ܥܠ ܟܘܬܪܬܐ ܚܕܐ, i. e. וְהָרִמֹּנִים מָאתַיִם שְׁנֵי טוּרִים סָבִיב עַל־הַכֹּתֶרֶת הָאֶחָת, MT. being improved by the addition of שני, and the emendation האחת for השנית. This is satisfactory; and it is worthy of notice that Pesh. continues this sentence with ܘܗܟܢܐ ܠܟܘܬܪܬܐ ܐܚܪܬܐ, precisely the same words with which it is finished off when placed in *v.* 18. The transposition is adopted by Sta., Benz. with omission of the words שני טורים on the ground that they have already occurred in the earlier part of the verse—a scarcely justifiable belief in the writer's extreme precision in avoiding even the smallest repetition. Kamp., Kit. also follow Th., reading טורים as in MT. for שני טורים; and Klo., while taking *v.* 20ᵇ into *v.* 18,

---

[1] This can scarcely represent ומעשה שבכה, since שבכים is correctly rendered *δίκτυα* in the preceding verse; nor can it well translate ומעשה שרשרות, this being elsewhere suitably rendered *ἔργον πλοκῆς*, Ex. 28. 14; *ἔργον ἁλυσιδωτοῦ*, *v.* 22; *ἔργον ἐμπλοκίου*, 39. 15; and *χαλαστά*, 2 Chr. 3. 5, 16.

expands and alters the whole verse thus formed to a quite unnecessary extent.

Thus the probably original form of *v.* 18 is:—וַיַּעַשׂ אֶת־הָרִמֹּנִים וּשְׁנֵי טוּרֵי רִמֹּנִים נְחֹשֶׁת עַל־הַשְּׂבָכָה הָאֶחָת וְהָרִמֹּנִים מָאתַיִם שְׁנֵי טוּרִים סָבִיב עַל־הַכֹּתֶרֶת הָאֶחָת וְכֵן עָשָׂה לַכֹּתֶרֶת הַשֵּׁנִית׃ 'And he made the pomegranates; and two rows of pomegranates in brass were upon the one trellis, and the pomegranates were two hundred[1], two rows round about upon the one chapiter; and so did he to the second chapiter.'

19, 20[a], 22. The *vv.* 19, 20 appear in LXX, Luc. *after v.* 21, while *v.* 22 is altogether missing. Now *v.* 21, which relates the erection and naming of the pillars, ought obviously to come at the close of the description; and this consideration, together with the state of LXX text, goes, as Sta. has seen, to point to the probability of *vv.* 19, 20[a], 22 being merely a gloss.

This is still further borne out if we compare the contents of these verses with the description of the chapiters given in the original text. In *vv.* 16–18 all that we gather with regard to the chapiters relates to their size, and to the trellises and pomegranates with which they were ornamented. The description of their appearance seems to come naturally to an end with the sentence וכן עשה לכתרת השנית at the close of *v.* 18, and then *v.* 21, containing the account of their erection in their destined position, might fitly be expected to follow as the conclusion of the reference. But instead of this we have fresh details with regard to the מַעֲשֵׂה שׁוּשַׁן, i. e. apparently the lily-like form of the chapiters, and the chapiters properly so called seem to be distinguished from a part of the pillar immediately beneath them which is known as הַבֶּטֶן. Now it is reasonable to suppose that in a consistent description the account of the *actual form and appearance* of the chapiters would *precede* rather than follow the reference to such

[1] In view of the precise statement of the number of the pomegranates as 100 in Jer. 52. 23, it may be questioned whether we ought not in this passage also to read מֵאָה for מאתים.

appendages as the pomegranates and trellises. But, assuming for the moment that the additional details are genuine, let us turn to *vv.* 41, 42, where a summary of Hiram's work at the pillars is given. Here we have mention of the עַמֻּדִים themselves, the גֻּלֹּת הַכֹּתָרוֹת which surmounted them, the שְׂבָכוֹת, and the רִמֹּנִים; but there is not the slightest reference to any מַעֲשֵׂה שׁוּשַׁן of the chapiters, nor to a part called הַבֶּטֶן connected with them. Hence we may confidently regard *vv.* 19, 20[a], 22 as a gloss added to the text by a later hand. The interpolator's idea of the form of the chapiters appears to have resembled the accompanying illustration. Judging from the ex-

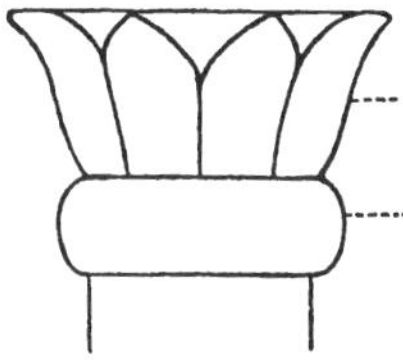

.... מַעֲשֵׂה שׁוּשַׁן *vv.* 19, 22.
.... גֻּלַּת הַכֹּתֶרֶת *v.* 42,
or הַבֶּטֶן *v.* 20 'nach der Profilansicht.'

pression גֻּלֹּת הַכֹּתָרוֹת in *v.* 42, he supposed the existence of a bowl-shaped portion of the pillar underneath the actual chapiter, which looked at, as Th. says, 'nach der Profilansicht,' might be described as הַבֶּטֶן. This led him to add the account of the shape of the actual chapiters, which he describes as מַעֲשֵׂה שׁוּשַׁן. The original narrator, however, in speaking of גֻּלֹּת הַכֹּתָרוֹת, appears to mean the actual chapiters, which from their rounded form might be thus described.

19. באולם] So Vulg., Pesh., Targ. Probably correct, and an awkward intimation of the position occupied by the pillars 'in the porch.' Cf. the notice which we derive from Luc. in *v.* 15 לאולם הבית, and *v.* 21. LXX, Luc. κατὰ τὸ αἰλάμ, i.e. כָּאוּלָם, seems to be an easy correction of this, and scarcely increases the lucidity of the expression.

20. מלעמת] 'In connexion with': cf. Ex. 25. 27 לְעֻמַּת הַמִּסְגֶּרֶת תִּהְיֶיןָ הַטַּבָּעֹת; 28. 27; *al.* לְעֻמַּת in the Hexateuch is peculiar to P. With מן only in this passage. LXX τῶν πλευρῶν points to a misreading לְצַלְעֹת. For the other peculiarities of this verse in LXX cf. *notes* on corruptions and doublets in *Introduction*.

לְעֻבַּר] 'Over against' or 'at the side of'; RV. 'beside.' Cf. the use of עבר illustrated 5. 4 *note*.

23. מוצק] LXX om. through oversight. Luc. χυτήν.

שלשים] LXX τρεῖς (Luc. τριῶν) καὶ τριάκοντα through a mistaken repetition of שלשים as שלש. The measure given is the circumference answering to the diameter עשר באמה משפתו עד שפתו.

קוה] Q're קָו is the usual word. Kt. קָוֶה only occurs elsewhere Jer. 31. 38; Zech. 1. 16, with Q're קָו in each place. וְקָו שְׁלֹשִׁים בָּאַמָּה is a case of apposition; 'a line—thirty cubits.' So Ex. 27. 16 מָסָךְ עֶשְׂרִים אַמָּה; Dri. *Tenses*, § 192. 1.

יסב] See *v.* 15 *note*.

24. עשר באמה] This can only be translated as it is by Vulg., Pesh., Targ. 'for ten cubits.' The rendering of RV. marg. 'ten (sc. פקעים) in a cubit,' besides supposing, as Sta. remarks, the mistake of עשר for עשרה, is quite contrary to the universal usage of the expression. We find the same words occurring in ‖ 2 Chr. 4. 3, and the most obvious explanation is to suppose that an early scribe, perhaps R^D himself, through lapse of memory confused the circumference of the sea with its diameter, when all the while he was intending to write שְׁלֹשִׁים בָּאַמָּה. Sta. omits.

מקפים את הים סביב] Omitted by LXX, but contained in Luc., Vulg., Pesh., Targ. Sta. regards the sentence as a gloss on the ground that the author never elsewhere uses the word הקיף, and has already said סביב סבבים אתו. So Kamp., Benz., Kit.

שני טורים . . . ביצקתו] LXX, Luc. om., probably through oversight. Th., Sta., Klo., Kamp., Benz., Kit. retain as original.

26. This verse in LXX, Luc. precedes *v.* 25, an emended order which is certainly to be adopted. It is only natural that the remaining details with regard to the sea—its thickness, the formation of its brim, and its interior capacity—should precede the account of the oxen upon which it was placed. So Sta., Kamp., Benz., Kit.

אלפים בת יכיל] Not found in LXX, Luc.; but the similar reference to the contents of the lavers in *v.* 38, ארבעים בת יכיל, speaks for the genuineness of the notice in this case also. On the tense יכיל, cf. *v.* 15 *note* on יסב.

Fig. 1.

BRONZE STAND FROM LARNAKA.

27–37. This difficult section, which was formerly regarded as involved in almost hopeless obscurity, has received considerable elucidation through recent discoveries in Cyprus. Two bronze stands of late Mycenaean workmanship[1] have been unearthed, the one from Larnaka and the other from Enkomi. The light which these bronzes were capable of throwing upon the ten מכונות of Solomon's Temple was first noticed by A. S. Murray with reference to the stand from Enkomi: *Journal of Royal Inst. of Brit. Architects*, 1899, vii. pp. 20 *ff.* The subject was worked out at length by A. Furtwängler in an article in the *Sitzungsberichte der philos.-philol. und der histor. Classe der kgl. bayer. Akademie der Wissenschaften zu München*, 1899, Bd. 2, Heft 3. This was followed by a detailed examination by Stade of the section in Kings in the light of the new discoveries (*ZATW.* 1901, pp. 145 *ff.*), in which he largely modified his earlier views upon the subject, as expressed in the article on Solomon's buildings (*ZATW.* 1883), and illustrated by a figure in his *Ges.* i. p. 341. Figures of the Cyprus bronzes are here given[2]. That from Larnaka measures 39 cm. in height, 23 cm. in width of side, 12 cm. in diameter of wheels; that from Enkomi is 16 cm. in height, and about 13 cm. in width.

It is clear that we have two divergent accounts of the מכונות combined in *vv.* 27–37. This was first noticed by Klo., who distinguished *vv.* 34–36 as belonging to a second account. His view was accepted in the main by Benz. Furtwängler regards *vv.* 32–36 as the remains of an ancient doublet; while Sta. supposes that the two accounts have been not simply placed side by side, but to a large extent interwoven. Sta. notices the following double descriptions:—1. Decoration of the מכונה

[1] Furtwängler places the date of the Necropolis at Enkomi *cir.* B.C. 1200–1000. Cf. *Antike Gemmen*, Bd. iii. 440.

[2] The upper figure in Plate 1 I have been kindly allowed by Dr. Furtwängler to reproduce from his article; the under figure I owe to Mr. J. L. Myres, of Christ Church, Oxford, who obtained the photograph for me through the British Commissioner at Cyprus. The two reproductions in Plate 2 are from photographs taken by the University Press.

with figures in *v.* 29 and *v.* 36. The two verses exhibit discrepancies (*a*) in description of the figures—*v.* 29 mentions lions, oxen, and cherubim, *v.* 36 cherubim, lions, and palm trees; (*b*) in naming the part of the מכונה so decorated—*v.* 29 מסגרות and שלבים, *v.* 36 לחית. 2. The Wheels. These are described briefly in *v.* 30[a], and in detail in *vv.* 32, 33. 3. The כתפות of the corner pillars in *v.* 30 and *v.* 34. Obviously the indefinite וארבע כתפות of *v.* 34 belongs to an account in which the parts so named have not been previously mentioned. 4. The part at the top of the מכונה which held the laver. This is called פיהו in *v.* 31, while in *v.* 35 the name has fallen out. 5. The double statement that the ידות of the wheels were of one part with the מכונה; *v.* 32 and *v.* 35.

While, however, it is certain that *vv.* 34–36 cannot, from their contents, belong to the preceding account, this is not necessarily the case with *vv.* 33, 34, since there is nothing in the contents of these verses to prevent us from regarding them as a description of the wheels in detail, after their brief mention in *v.* 30[a].

27. LXX, Luc. give the length of the bases as five cubits, the breadth as four cubits, and the height as six cubits. Sta. remarks that from this difference between length and breadth the inference might be drawn that the lavers standing upon the מכונות were not round but elliptical; but that this is opposed to *v.* 28, where the 'four cubits' can only be taken as the diameter of a round laver. The מכונות of Figs. 1 and 2 are square, and have round cylinders to hold the lavers. Thus the measurements of MT., four × four, are to be accepted. It seems not improbable that the six cubits of LXX, Luc. represent the *total height* of the מכונה three cubits + the אופנים 1½ cubits (*v.* 32) + the פה 1½ cubits (*v.* 31).

28. מסגרת] The question as to whether this word means 'borders' (RV.) or 'panels' (RV. marg.) is not at all elucidated by the Verss. LXX, Luc. *συγκλειστόν* translate according to the sense of the root, and perhaps vocalize מְסֻגֶּרֶת; Vulg. *interrasile* + *sculpturae* appears to be merely guessing; Pesh., Targ. ܓܕܢܦܐ, גדנפין is the word used by Pesh. to translate מגרעות in *ch.* 6. 6, with the meaning 'ledges.' The only other connexion in which מסגרת

PL. 2

BRONZE STAND FROM ENKOMI

in a similar sense occurs, viz. as a part of the table of shewbread, Ex. 25. 25, 27; 37. 12, 14, is greatly in favour of the meaning 'border' (i.e. what we now call the *frame* of the table), whether immediately below the top of the table, as in our modern tables, or connecting the ends of the legs; cf. especially מִסְגֶּרֶת טֹפַח 'a border of a handbreadth,' scarcely 'a panel of a handbreadth.'

שלבים] Only in this description of the bases. The Puʿal participle of a verb שלב occurs Ex. 26. 17; 36. 22† שְׁתֵּי יָדוֹת לַקֶּרֶשׁ הָאֶחָד מְשֻׁלָּבֹת אִשָּׁה אֶל־אֲחֹתָהּ 'there shall be two tenons to each board, *morticed* one to another.' In Talmudic שליבה denotes *the rung of a ladder*; so *Maccoth* 7[b] היה עולה בסלם ונשמטה שליבה מתחתיו 'he was mounting a ladder when a rung gave way beneath him.' Hence we may understand by שלבים the corner uprights of the מכונה, and possibly also uprights at regular intervals between the corners (cf. Fig. 2). The מסגרות then ran horizontally בין השלבים, forming a connexion or framework to the corner uprights. Cf. the four horizontal bars in Fig. 2. Perhaps the best rendering of שלבים is '*supports*.' Vulg., Pesh. seem to approximate to the right meaning with their renderings *juncturas*, ܣܘܟ̈ܠܐ 'connexions'; Targ. שליביא, LXX, Luc. ἐξεχομένων.

מסגרות להם ומסגרת בין השלבים] Are the second מִסְגְּרֹת different from the first? i.e. ought we to render ומסגרת 'and *also* border-frames'? or, if the two are identical, why do we not read וְהַמִּסְגְּרֹת 'and *the* border-frames,' already mentioned? Again, why הַשְׁלַבִּים '*the* supports,' when these have *not* been previously mentioned? Klo., observing these difficulties, emends מִסְגְּרֹת לָהֶם וּשְׁלַבִּים לָהֶם וְהַמִּסְגְּרֹת בֵּין הַשְּׁלַבִּים 'they had border-frames and supports, and the border-frames were between the supports.' It is preferable to suppose that the first מסגרות has been written by mistake for שלבים which would naturally be first mentioned; שְׁלַבִּים לָהֶם וּמִסְגְּרֹת בֵּין הַשְּׁלַבִּים '*they had supports, and there were border-frames between the supports.*'

29. אריות וג׳] Cf. the winged figures of Fig. 1, and the lions (?) of Fig. 2.

ועל השלבים כן] 'And upon the supports *likewise*.' The rendering of Furtwängler, 'And upon the supports *there was a pedestal*,' is unsuitable, because this part of the מכונה is described below in *v.* 31 not as a כֵּן but as a פֶּה.

ממעל] Follow LXX, Luc. וּמִמַּעַל '*and* above and below &c.'

ליות] Doubtless a corruption of וְלַכְּרוּבִים, which is desiderated after לאריות ולבקר. The corruption is due to the influence of *v.* 30 end.

מעשה מורד] LXX, Luc. appear to explain rightly ἔργον καταβάσεως, 'step-work,' or, as we should say, '*bevelled work*'; i.e. probably the edges of the מסגרת were bevelled in the form of steps:—

or a section viewed from the end would have appeared thus:—

The ornamental borders in Fig. 1, above and below the winged figures, have something of this character.

30. סרני] A ἅπαξ λεγ.; but in Syr. ܣܪܢܐ 'axle' is common. Probably the axles were similar in form to those of Fig. 1.

וארבעה פעמתיו וג'] RV. 'and the four feet thereof had undersetters.' If כְּתֵפֹת (lit. 'shoulders') could mean 'undersetters,' we might identify them with the diagonal stays which strengthen the legs in Figs. 1 and 2. But these stays would scarcely be described as 'shoulder-pieces,' and in fact they seem to be denoted by a more suitable term ידות in *v.* 32. Moreover, they could scarcely be described as מִתַּחַת לַכִּיֹּר, i.e. immediately under the laver. The position of these כְּתֵפֹת should rather be that of the four birds (doves?), at the four upper corners of the מכונה in Fig. 1, which might aptly be described as '*shoulder-pieces*.' So Hommel, Furtwängler, Sta. But then ארבעה פעמתיו (rather אַרְבַּע פַּעֲמֹתֶיהָ, with reference to the מכונה), 'its four feet,' can scarcely be correct; for we cannot, with Sta., force the interpretation and suppose that 'the corner pillars with reference to their lower ends could very well be described as the פעמות of the מכונה.' When we are speaking of the shoulder-pieces we are thinking of the *upper* ends of the corner pillars, and besides, these corner pillars or supports have already been described as שלבים. In the second account, *v.* 34, four כְּתֵפוֹת are said to have been אֶל אַרְבַּע פִּנּוֹת הַמְּכֹנָה 'at the four *corners* of the base.' A more suitable term to describe the position of the shoulder-pieces could not be selected, and we may follow Kamp. in emending וְאַרְבַּע פִּנּוֹתֶיהָ '*and its four corners had shoulder-pieces.*' LXX, Luc. μέρη αὐτῶν appears to be an alteration of the difficult פעמתיו into פֵּאֹתָן; cf. Ex. 25. 26, where עַל אַרְבַּע הַפֵּאֹת is rendered ἐπὶ τὰ τέσσαρα μέρη.

מעבר איש ליות] ליות (לְוִיֹּת) appears to denote 'wreaths' or 'spiral work,' such as forms the principal ornamentation in Fig. 2, and appears round the cylinder in Fig. 1. מעבר איש is properly '*beyond* or *at the side of each.*' Cf. the phrase מכל עבריו '*at* all *sides* of him,' *ch.* 5. 4 *note.* We may render '*with spirals at the side of each.*' The spirals may have run between the shoulder-pieces along the top edges of the מכונה.

31. ופיהו] Read וּפִיהָ '*and its mouth,*' the suffix referring to the מכונה. The פה is clearly the mouth or opening of the cylinder, seen in Figs. 1 and 2, to contain the laver. So Furtwängler, Sta.

מבית לכתרת] R. V. 'within the chapiter.' But כֹּתֶרֶת, elsewhere always the *crown* or *chapiter* of a column, scarcely seems a suitable term to describe the part of the מכונה which contained the פה; and the fact that the word is defined by the article rather indicates that it refers to something already mentioned. We may therefore follow Ew.'s emendation (adopted by Klo., Sta., and others), and read מִבֵּית לַכְּתֵפֹת '*within the shoulder-pieces,*' just described.

ומעלה באמה] A number must have fallen out before באמה, and this was probably אֶחָד (Kamp., Sta.). But ומעלה, which qualifies the statement as to the height, ought naturally to follow after it. We may therefore read אֶחָד בָּאַמָּה וָמַעְלָה '*was one cubit and upwards.*' The statement which comes later in the verse, אמה וחצי האמה, is merely a repetition of the same fact in more exact terms, and ought probably, therefore (with Sta.), to be regarded as a marginal gloss.

מעשה כן] '*After the structure* (*form*) *of a pedestal.*' כן is used of the pedestal of the כִּיּוֹר in Ex. 30. 28; 31. 9; *al.*

ומסגרתיהם וג׳] If this sentence is in place, the statement ought naturally to refer to the פֶּה. But then we should expect וּמִסְגְּרֹתָיו, i.e., in contrast to the round opening itself, '*its borders were foursquare, not round*,' thus forming a pedestal which corresponded in shape to the square מכונה beneath. If this be the meaning of the passage, the pedestal differed from those in Figs. 1 and 2, which are round outside as well as inside. Sta. considers the statement to be out of place, and, reading מִסְגְּרֹתֵיהֶן, refers it to the border-frames of the מכונה proper.

32. וידות האופנים במכונה] '*And the stays of the wheels were in the base*'; i.e. of one casting with it. ידות seems to denote the diagonal stays, which are seen under the מכונות in Figs. 1 and 2.

33. גביהם] 'Their felloes'; i.e. the rounded portion of the wheel, from גבב 'to be curved.' So, in this sense, Ezek. 1. 18†.

וחשקיהם וחשריהם] Both ἅπαξ λεγγ. Ges. connects the former word with חשק 'cleave to' or 'join,' so חֲשׁוּקִים 'those which join' sc. the felloe to the nave, i. e. the *spokes*; but his derivation of the latter word from Ar. حشر *congregavit*, so חִשּׁוּר 'place in which the spokes *come together*,' i. e. the *box* or *nave*, seems more than doubtful, since, apart from the dubious meaning, a wrong interchange of consonants is implied.

34. מן המכנה כתפיה] '*Of one casting with* the base were its shoulder-pieces.' The same meaning is to be attached to ממנה in *v.* 35. Cf. Ex. 27. 2. Sta. regards *v.* 34^b as a gloss, mainly on the ground of the masc. pl. form כתפיה in place of כתפותיה.

35. ובראש המכונה וג׳] The subject of the sentence has fallen out. In accordance with *v.* 31 it should be פֶּה, or some similar term.

חצי האמה] אמה וחצי האמה must have been read, if this account originally agreed with that of *v.* 31.

ידתיה ומסגרתיה] The ידות on the top of the מכנה cannot be identified; the מסגרות are probably those described in *v.* 31^b.

36. ויפתח] 'He carved.' The subject is Ḥiram.

הלחת] 'The panels' are peculiar to this second account. Judging by the reference to the figures carved upon them, we may suppose that they answer to the מסגרות of *vv.* 28, 29.

ידתיה ועל ומסגרתיה] To be rejected as an erroneous dittography from the preceding verse. ועל was probably added later as an attempt to give sense to the words as they stand. So Kamp., Sta.

ותמרת] Palm trees take the place of the oxen of *v.* 29. Cf. the palms (?) in Fig. 1 between the winged figures.

כמער וג׳] Read מעבר איש ליות סביב, in accordance with *v.* 30.

37. קצב אחד] LXX, Luc. omit.

לְכֻלָּהְנָה] The suffix occurs once again, בְּתוֹכְהֶנָה Ezek. 16. 53, also in pause. Cf. G-K. § 91 *f*; Sta. § 352 *b*. Klo. emends לְכֹל הֵנָּה.

39ª. LXX καὶ ἔθετο τὰς πέντε μεχωνὼθ ἀπὸ τῆς ὠμίας τοῦ οἴκου ἐξ ἀριστερῶν omits הבית מימין וחמש על כתף through homoioteleuton. Luc. further omits πέντε, thus making it appear that *all* the bases were placed on the left; but this is clearly an emendation of LXX text.

40. הכירות] LXX, Luc. τοὺς λέβητας, Vulg. *lebetes*, i.e. הַסִּירוֹת 'the pots.' Pesh. ܟܩܐ̈ ܘܩܕܪ̈ܐ, i.e. הכירות והסירות. הסירות is doubtless correct. It occurs ‖ 2 Chr. 4. 11; in the summary *v.* 45 (‖ 2 Chr. 4. 16); and in II. 25. 14; Jer. 52. 18, where the allusion is apparently to the same vessels. So Th., Sta., Klo., Kamp., Benz., Kit.

סיר is usually a cooking pot in which flesh (Ex. 16. 3) or broth (II. 4. 38 *ff.*) is boiled; but as a sacrificial implement it is mentioned in connexion with the brazen altar; Ex. 27. 3 וְעָשִׂיתָ סִּירֹתָיו לְדַשְּׁנוֹ 'and thou shalt make its pots *to take away its ashes*.'

היעים] 'The shovels'; included (Ex. 27. 3; 38. 3; Num. 4. 14) among the כְּלֵי הַמִּזְבֵּחַ, and employed for transferring the ashes into the סירות; cf. Kimḥi's explanation:—שהיו מסירים בהם הדשן כתרגומו במגרפיתא שהיה גורף בהם הדשן מהמזבח. A verb יעה occurs Isa. 28. 17† ויעה ברד מחסה כזב, probably 'and hail shall *sweep away* the refuge of lies'; Ar. وَعَى I. 'collect into one place.'

המזרקות] 'The bowls,' which were used for *tossing* or dashing the blood *in a volume* against the altar. Cf. the use of the verb זרק in e.g. Ex. 24. 6 וחצי הדם זרק על המזבח. The action denoted is constantly distinct from that expressed by הִזָּה 'sprinkle with the fingers'; Lev. 4. 6; *al.* מזרק is always sacrificial, except in Am. 6. 6 השתים במזרקי יין 'who drink in (i.e. *out of*) bowls of wine.'

בית יהוה] Accus. of place as in Gen. 18. 1, 10; *al.* Da. § 69.

41. גלת הכתרת] Cf. *note* on *vv.* 19, 20ª, 22.

42. שני טורים רמנים] 'Two rows—pomegranates'; cf. Dri. *Tenses*, § 194. It would be more natural to read either שְׁנֵי טוּרֵי רִמֹּנִים as in *v.* 18ª above emended, or else רִמֹּנִים שְׁנֵי טוּרִים 'pomegranates *in* two rows,' שני ט׳ being then an accus. of manner: Da. § 70.

על פני העמודים] Certainly wrong. LXX, Luc. are probably correct in reading עַל־שְׁנֵי הָעַמּוּדִים. So Th., Sta., Klo. Vulg., Pesh. presuppose על ראש העמודים as in *v.* 41. So Kamp., Benz., Kit.

45. האהל] Q're הָאֵלֶּה certainly correct. Thus Targ. translates האלין, and then, apparently with reference to Kt., adds the gloss כעובד מני משכנא דעבד משה 'according to the structure of the vessels of the Tabernacle which Moses made.' LXX, Luc., Vulg. omit the word. Pesh. ܕܡܫܟܢܐ, probably a paraphrase of Kt. הָאֹהֶל. Sta., in adopting Q're, points out that the וְ before את כל הכלים האלה must (as in Vulg.) be omitted, since otherwise האלה is unnecessary.

After the sentence אשר עשה חירם למלך ש׳ בית י׳, LXX, Luc. add *καὶ οἱ στύλοι τεσσαράκοντα καὶ ὀκτὼ τοῦ οἴκου τοῦ βασιλέως καὶ τοῦ οἴκου Κυρίου· πάντα τὰ ἔργα τοῦ βασιλέως ἐποίησεν Χειράμ* . . . , i.e. וְהָעַמּוּדִים אַרְבָּעִים וּשְׁמֹנָה לְבֵית הַמֶּלֶךְ וּלְבֵית יְהוָה אֶת־כָּל־מְלֶאכֶת הַמֶּלֶךְ עָשָׂה חִירָם. It is to be noticed that *vv.* 41–45ª sum up the work of Ḥiram, which is described in detail in *vv.* 15–40; *vv.* 41, 42 corresponding to *vv.* 15–22, *v.* 43 to *vv.* 27–39, *v.* 44 to *vv.* 23–26, and *v.* 45ª to *v.* 40. If, however, the LXX addition be regarded as genuine, we have here a matter of great importance mentioned for the first time in the summary without previous detailed description of any kind. And not only so, but a work so considerable as the casting of these forty-eight pillars is mentioned last of all, even subsequently to the notice of the making of articles so comparatively unimportant as the brazen pots, &c. We may therefore regard the passage as a gloss, of uncertain source. So Sta.; but Bö., Th., Benz., and to some extent Klo., adopt as genuine.

נחשת ממרט] '*Burnished* brass.' The verb מרט is used again in the participle Pu'al מֹרָטָה for מְמֹרָטָה Ezek. 21. 15, 16, and Qal passive מְרוּטָה Ezek. 21. 14, 33, of a *burnished* sword; and in Isa. 18. 2, 7 מוֹרָט (for מְמֹרָט) describes the *polished* appearance of the skin of the Ethiopians. Elsewhere the word is used of plucking out hair, and this is the first meaning in Ar. and Syr. The Verss. merely guess at the sense of ממרט. Targ. נחש טב, Vulg. *de aurichalco*, Pesh. ܢܚܫܐ ܕܩܘܪܢܬܝܐ, LXX χαλκᾶ ἄρδην[1], Luc. simply χαλκᾶ ἦν.

46–50. This section as it stands can scarcely exhibit its original form.

(i) וינח . . . מאד] *v.* 47 is very obscure and awkward. It can only mean, 'And Solomon *left* all the vessels because of their very great number.' This we have to interpret, 'He *left them unweighed*,' a forced and unparalleled explanation.

(ii) It is unnatural to say that the brass could not be weighed because the vessels were so *numerous*. We have just had a description of the great vessels, &c., which were made by Ḥiram, the sea, the bases and lavers, and the two pillars, the casting of which must have taken an enormous quantity of brass; and in comparison with this the brass used for the pots, shovels, &c., however numerous they may have been, must have been comparatively trivial in quantity. Hence, the reason why the brass went unweighed was not *the number* of the vessels, most of which were small, but the *great quantity* of brass which was used, chiefly for the comparatively few large vessels.

(iii) After the very lengthy description of the brazen vessels made by Ḥiram, it is surely strange that so short a summary (*vv.* 48–50) of the golden vessels, &c., should be given, without any account of their appearance or mention of their maker. We are justified in regarding an allusion of such brevity, in the midst of a document which seems to aim at peculiar minuteness in description, as the work of a later hand who desiderated some reference to the *golden* vessels of the Temple[2].

[1] This is simply a paraphrase derived from the context, and cannot represent בִּמְאֹד of Th.; still less Klo.'s נְחֹשֶׁת חֵרֶם or מָחֳרָם, supposed to mean 'consecrated (?) brass,' according to the (free) rendering of Mal. 3. 24 פֶּן־אָבוֹא וְהִכֵּיתִי אֶת־הָאָרֶץ חֵרֶם, μὴ ἔλθω καὶ πατάξω τὴν γῆν ἄρδην.

[2] These verses are omitted by Sta., together with *v.* 47.

Turning to the Verss., we find that LXX, Luc. presuppose a considerably divergent text. In both *v.* 47 precedes *v.* 46, and *vv.* 47, 48ᵃ exhibit striking variation from MT.

LXX, *v.* 47, *οὐκ ἦν σταθμὸς τοῦ χαλκοῦ οὗ ἐποίησεν πάντα τὰ ἔργα ταῦτα ἐκ πλήθους σφόδρα· οὐκ ἦν τέρμα τῶν σταθμῶν τοῦ χαλκοῦ.*

v. 46. As in MT., omitting המלך.

v. 48ᵃ. *καὶ ἔλαβεν ὁ βασιλεὺς Σαλωμὼν τὰ σκεύη ἃ ἐποίησεν ἐν οἴκῳ.*

vv. 48ᵇ–50. Substantially as in MT.

This may be re-translated:—

v. 47. אֵין מִשְׁקָל לַנְּחֹשֶׁת אֲשֶׁר עָשָׂה אֶת־כָּל־הַכֵּלִים [?] הָאֵלֶּה מֵרֹב מְאֹד מְאֹד לֹא נֶחְקַר מִשְׁקַל הַנְּחֹשֶׁת׃

v. 46. As in MT., omitting המלך.

v. 48ᵃ. וַיִּקַּח הַמֶּלֶךְ שְׁלֹמֹה אֶת־הַכֵּלִים אֲשֶׁר עָשָׂה בֵּית [יְהוָה].

Luc. is slightly different:—

v. 47. *οὐκ ἦν σταθμὸς τοῦ χαλκοῦ οὗ ἐποίησεν ἄρδην· πάντα τὰ σκεύη ἃ ἐποίησε, ταῦτα ἐκ τοῦ πλήθους σφόδρα· οὐκ ἦν τέρμα τῷ σταθμῷ τοῦ χαλκοῦ.*

v. 46. As in MT., omitting המלך.

v. 48ᵃ. *καὶ ἔδωκε Σολομῶν ὁ βασιλεὺς τὰ σκεύη ἃ ἐποίησεν ἐν τῷ οἴκῳ κυρίου.*

vv. 48ᵇ–50. Substantially as in MT.

Translate:—

v. 47. אֵין מִשְׁקָל לַנְּחֹשֶׁת אֲשֶׁר עָשָׂה בִּמְאֹד [?] כָּל־הַכֵּלִים הָאֵלֶּה אֲשֶׁר עָשָׂה מֵרֹב מְאֹד מְאֹד לֹא נֶחְקַר מִשְׁקַל הַנְּחֹשֶׁת׃

v. 46. As in MT., omitting המלך.

v. 48ᵃ. וַיַּנַּח הַמֶּלֶךְ שְׁלֹמֹה אֶת־הַכֵּלִים אֲשֶׁר עָשָׂה בֵּית יְהוָה.

In *v.* 47 Luc.'s rendering can scarcely be original. The repetition of אשר עשה, and the construction of כל הכלים in apposition to לנחשת, are very awkward. On the other hand, LXX text is here very clear and good, completely disposing of difficulty (i) by the substitution of אין משקל וג׳ for וינח שלמה, and of (ii) by the reference of מרב מאד מאד back to אין משקל לנחשת instead of to את כל הכלים. Luc.'s text of this verse probably arose through the insertion of *ἄρδην* as a doublet of מרב מאד מאד, this breaking the sentence and causing the repetition of *ἃ ἐποίησε*.

By the transposition of *v.* 47 and *v.* 46 we gain a better sequence, the great quantity of brass being naturally mentioned before the locality in which the vessels, &c., were cast.

In *v.* 48a Luc. is to be preferred to LXX. The וינח שלמה of the commencement of *v.* 47 MT. is here referred to its proper place, and its position in MT. is perhaps explained by the transposition of *vv.* 46 and 47. The writer, having wrongly written *v.* 46 first, was proceeding to write *v.* 48 which properly followed it, when he noticed that he had omitted *v.* 47, and so added it then and there. Thus the first two words of *v.* 48 came to be placed at the beginning of *v.* 47.

According to Luc., *v.* 48a describes the destination of the golden vessels; it ought, however, properly to refer to the brazen vessels, and to conclude the account of them. This should naturally lead the way to *v.* 51, the conclusion of the whole notice. The alteration of *v.* 48a in MT. ויעש for וינח, and in LXX καὶ ἔλαβεν for καὶ ἔδωκε, is most probably due to the gloss *vv.* 48b–50 which mentions the golden vessels.

Upon these grounds the following may plausibly be considered the original text of these *vv.* 46–51:—

v. 47. אֵין מִשְׁקָל לַנְּחֹשֶׁת אֲשֶׁר עָשָׂה אֶת־כָּל־הַכֵּלִים הָאֵלֶּה מֵרֹב מְאֹד מְאֹד לֹא נֶחְקַר מִשְׁקַל הַנְּחֹשֶׁת׃

v. 46. As in MT., omitting המלך.

v. 48. וַיַּנַּח [הַמֶּלֶךְ] שְׁלֹמֹה אֶת־הַכֵּלִים אֲשֶׁר עָשָׂה בֵּית יְהוָֹה׃

v. 51. As in MT.

v. 47. 'There was no weight to the brass wherewith he made all these vessels, because it was exceeding much; the weight of the brass was not found out. *v.* 46. In the plain of Jordan did he cast them, in the clay ground between Succoth and Zarethan. *v.* 48. And [King] Solomon placed the vessels in the house of Yahwe.

v. 51. 'Thus all the work that king Solomon wrought in the house of Yahwe was finished. And Solomon brought in the things which David his father had dedicated, even the silver and the gold and the vessels, placing them in the treasuries of the house of Yahwe.'

46. ככר הירדן] 'The *circle* of the Jordan'; ‖ 2 Chr. 4. 17; Gen. 13. 10, 11†; called also הַכִּכָּר '*the* circle,' Gen. 13. 12; 19. 17; Deut. 34. 3; 2 Sam. 18. 23; *al.* The term, a Pilpel form (כִּרְכָּר) from כרר 'move in a circle,' is used of the depressed region which forms the lower stage of the Jordan valley by which the river flows into the Dead Sea; but may in the earliest times have been exclusively applied to the fertile region occupied by the circle of cities forming the עָרֵי הַכִּכָּר; Gen. 13. 12; 19. 29. See Stanley, *SP.* 284.

במעבה האדמה] RV. 'In the *clay* ground'; so Vulg. *in terra argillosa.* מעבה, root עבה 'to be thick, dense' (*ch.* 12. 10), only occurs here, ‖ 2 Chr. 4. 17 having בַּעֲבִי הָאֲדָמָה. Moore (on Judg. 7. 22) emends במעברת [ה]אדמה 'at the crossing (ford) of Adamah,' regarding Adamah as identical with אָדָם of Josh. 3. 16 (*ed-Damieh*) which is there said to be near צרתן.

סכות] The identification of Rob. (*BR.*, iii. 309 *ff.*) with *Sâkût* (*'Ain es-Sâqâṭ*) on the west bank of Jordan some nine miles south of Beisan, though suiting the connexion with צרתן which is mentioned (*ch.* 4. 12) together with בית שאן, is improbable as being philologically unsound. Moore, in accordance with his emendation above noticed, thinks סכות to be the place named in Genesis and Joshua *east* of Jordan. This, according to the Talmud (*Shebiith* ix. 2, *Gemara*), was in later times called דרעלה Dar'ala, i.e. probably 'the present *Tell Deir 'Alla*, a high mound in the Jordan valley, about one mile north of the Jabbok.' G. A. Smith, *Historical Geography*, 585; Buhl, *Geogr.* 259 *f.*

51^b^. נתן] The perf. *asyndetos* as a circumstantial clause; 'he placed,' &c., so '*placing*,' &c. Cf. *ch.* 13. 18 כחש לו; Dri. *Tenses*, § 163.

13–51. Wellh. comments upon the absence of any allusion to the making of the *brazen altar* in this description of the Temple furniture, assuming that, in accordance with the mention of an altar in *ch.* 8. 64; II. 16. 14, 15, such a reference must have originally existed, and has therefore been purposely removed by the post-exilic editor, upon the supposition that the brazen altar of Moses mentioned by P was, like the Ark, still in existence. Now, as we have seen, the glosses of R^P are for the most part either absent in LXX, Luc., or can at any rate be easily detected and separated from the original text into which they have come from the margin; and the method of treating the LXX text as representing upon the whole a recension untouched by R^P has, through the results, justified itself as reasonable. Thus, if mention of the casting of the brazen altar had existed in the original description, some trace of it would certainly have remained in LXX; but this is not the case. And not only so, but there are no other traces of the rejection by R^P of the statements of the original[1], such a proceeding being quite contrary to his method, which was to interpolate without excision.

Again, as will be seen, the section *ch.* 8. 1–11 has been largely interpolated by R^P, and in *v.* 4 there is mention of the carrying up to the Temple of the ארון יהוה ואת אהל מועד ואת כל כלי הקדש אשר באהל. If, therefore, this editor had only just previously excised from *ch.* 7 the mention of the making of the brazen altar for the reason above noticed, he would surely have expressly named it in *ch.* 8. 4 among the furniture of the אהל מועד which was taken up to the Temple.

Thus we may confidently conclude that mention of the brazen altar was, for whatever reasons, *not* contained in the original recension of 7. 13–51. The allusion in 2 Chr. 4. 1 ויעש מזבח נחשת עשרים אמה ארכו ועשרים אמה רחבו ועשר אמות קומתו is marked as a late addition by the absence of all detail in the description.

[1] The addition of LXX, Luc. in *v.* 45, with reference to the forty-eight pillars, is to be regarded as a gloss, for reasons above given.

8. *Dedication of Solomon's Temple.*

Ch. 8=2 Chr. 5. 2—7. 10.

8. 1. [אז יקהל שלמה וג׳] LXX prefaces these words with the sentence καὶ ἐγένετο ὡς συνετέλεσεν Σαλωμὼν τοῦ οἰκοδομῆσαι τὸν οἶκον Κυρίου καὶ τὸν οἶκον ἑαυτοῦ μετὰ εἴκοσι ἔτη. So Luc., with the variation ἐν τῷ συντελέσαι Σολομῶντα. This is regarded by Bö., Th. as part of the original text. But more probably the words are an addition of the translator, who objected to the use of אז without 'any definite point of attachment in the preceding narrative.' This peculiar use of the particle is, however, characteristic of R^D (see collected instances in 3. 16 *note;* and cf. Dri. *LOT.* 192), and it is very noticeable that in no single case does אז occur as introduction to the apodosis of a sentence, after the protasis has contained a definite notice of the point of departure. In such a case the usual construction would certainly be וַיְהִי . . . ו׳ (cf. 9. 1, 2), and there is no reason why this should have been relinquished in favour of וַיְהִי . . . אָז. The form of the gloss was determined by 9. 1, and the time-notice μετὰ εἴκοσι ἔτη derived from the addition of שבע שנים 6. 38, and שלש עשרה שנה 7. 1.

1–11. This section has clearly received considerable interpolation by post-exilic hands under the influence of P. In LXX *vv.* 1–5 appear in a considerably shorter form, which reads smoothly and without trace of abridgement:—τότε ἐξεκκλησίασεν ὁ βασιλεὺς Σαλωμὼν πάντας τοὺς πρεσβυτέρους Ἰσραὴλ ἐν Σειὼν τοῦ ἐνεγκεῖν τὴν κιβωτὸν διαθήκης Κυρίου ἐκ πόλεως Δαυείδ, αὕτη ἐστὶν Σειών, (2) ἐν μηνὶ Ἀθαμείν. (3) καὶ ἦραν οἱ ἱερεῖς τὴν κιβωτὸν (4) καὶ τὸ σκήνωμα τοῦ μαρτυρίου καὶ τὰ σκεύη τὰ ἅγια τὰ ἐν τῷ σκηνώματι τοῦ μαρτυρίου· (5) καὶ ὁ βασιλεὺς καὶ πᾶς Ἰσραὴλ ἔμπροσθεν τῆς κιβωτοῦ θύοντες πρόβατα, βόας, ἀναρίθμητα. So substantially Luc. Here we notice the following omissions:—

1. [ואת כל ראשי המטות נשיאי האבות לבני ישראל אל המלך שלמה] Here ראשי . . . האבות belongs distinctively to P. Cf. ראשי המטות || 2 Chr. 5. 2; Num. 30. 2†. ראשי אבות המטות Num. 32. 28; Josh. 14. 1†. ראשי האבות למטות Josh. 19. 51†. ראשי אבות [האבות] Ex. 6. 25; Num. 31. 26; 36. 1; Josh.

21. 1, and very frequently in Chr., Ezra, Neh. (34 times)†. [האבות ,אֲבֹתָם] ראשי בית אבות Ex. 6. 14; Num. 7. 2, and four times in Chr.† נשיא in the Hexateuch occurs but once outside P, Ex. 22. 27 (J); in P 82 times, Ezek. 37 times, Chr. six times†.

ירושלם] Probably original. The reading of LXX, Luc. seems to be a scriptural error due to the occurrence of ציון at the end of the verse.

2. ויקהלו אל המלך שלמה כל איש ישראל] An addition rendered almost necessary to introduce the date after the weighting of the previous verse with the long insertion above noticed. Niph. נקהל occurs most often in P, Lev. 8. 4; Num. 16. 3; 17. 7; 20. 2; Josh. 18. 1; 22. 12, and in books influenced by P (Ezek. 38. 7; Chr., Ezra, seven times); though not unknown in earlier writings, Ex. 32. 1 (JE), Judg. 20. 1; 2 Sam. 20. 14; Jer. 26. 9†. Notice the phrase המלך שלמה here and in the additions of *vv.* 1, 5 contrasted with שלמה *vv.* 1, 12, or המלך *v.* 5, of the original narrative.

בחג הוא החדש השביעי] The reference בֶּחָג being drawn from *v.* 65 ויעש שלמה בעת ההיא את החג, the editor plausibly assumes from the mention of its duration שבעת ימים[1] that this was *the* Feast, i.e. the Feast of Tabernacles, and so adds the statement הוא החדש השביעי as in Lev. 23. 34 (H). In Dt. 16. 13 the date is more vaguely defined as בְּאָסְפְּךָ מִגָּרְנְךָ וּמִיִּקְבֶךָ.

3. ויבאו כל זקני ישראל] A resumption from *v.* 1ª, due to the number of additions intervening.

4. ויעלו את ארון .יהוה] In *vv.* 3, 5, 7 (twice), 9 simply הָאָרוֹן.

ויעלו אתם הכהנים והלוים] The distinction drawn between priests and Levites implies the standpoint of P. Cf. Dri. *Deut.* 219:—'The term Levite, it must always be remembered, has in Deuteronomy a different meaning from "Levite" in P. In P it denotes the members of the tribe,

[1] On the rejection of ושבעת ימים ארבעה עשר יום, cf. *note ad loc.*

exclusive of the priests, the descendants of Aaron; in Deuteronomy it denotes *all* members of the tribe, without distinction. The "Levites" of P are inferior members of the tribe, who are assigned various subordinate duties in connexion with the Tabernacle (Num. 3–4; 18. 1–7), but are peremptorily forbidden to intrude upon the office of priest. In Deuteronomy this sharp distinction between priests and the common Levites is not recognized; it is implied (18. 1ª) that *all* members of the tribe are qualified to exercise priestly functions; 18. 1ᵇ, 2ᵇ assign to the whole tribe the altar-dues reserved in Num. 18. 20 for the priests alone; and 18. 6–8, relating to the "Levite" coming from the country to reside at the central sanctuary, describes his services there in terms which elsewhere, when used in ritual connexion, denote regular priestly duties.'

In contrast to this distinction of *v.* 4ᵇ, cf. *vv.* 3, 6, 10, 11 where הַכֹּהֲנִים alone are mentioned; and *ch.* 12. 31 where *all* Levites seem to be regarded as fit to exercise priestly functions:—ויעש כהנים מקצות העם אשר לא היו מבני לוי.

5. שלמה] Inserted for the sake of accordance with the title used in *vv.* 1ᵇ, 2.

עדת] The phrase עֲדַת יִשְׂרָאֵל is of constant occurrence in P, outside which it never occurs but here and in ‖ 2 Chr. 5. 6.

הנועדים עליו אתו] יעד means to *appoint* or *define* a place or time, and Niph'al נועד has the sense *set oneself at the appointed place.* This latter occurs very constantly in a ceremonial connexion, and so used is characteristic of P; ‖ 2 Chr. 5. 6; הנועדים עלי [על י׳] Num. 14. 35; 16. 11; 27. 3; ונועדו אליך Num. 10. 3, 4; and, with י׳ as subject, ונועדתי (אועד)ל Ex. 25. 22; 29. 42, 43; 30. 6, 36; Num. 17. 19. Cf. the phrase אֹהֶל מוֹעֵד (see below) 'the tent of *meeting*,' i.e. of Yahwe and His people in the person of their representative. Elsewhere Niph'al נועד is only used without ceremonial connotation; Josh. 11. 5 (JE); Am. 3. 3; Ps. 48. 5; Job 2. 11; Neh. 6. 2, 10†.

ולא ימנו מרב] LXX, Luc. ἀναρίθμητα for the whole אשר לא יספרו ולא ימנו מרב appears at first sight to omit the last three words. But a comparison of *ch.* 3. 8, where the same phrase is rendered by LXX ὃς οὐκ ἀριθμηθήσεται, suggests that the translator's single word is intended to satisfy the whole expression in the Hebrew.

Further omissions of LXX in this section (*vv.* 1–11) are:—

6. ברית יהוה] Omitted by LXX only, but contained in Luc. The phrase is properly Deuteronomic (cf. 3. 14 *note*).

8. ויהיו שם עד היום הזה] Quite different in character from the other omissions. The phrase implies a *pre-exilic* standpoint, and is thus original, and has been removed by the LXX translator (or by a later copyist) because in his time its purport had ceased to be true. עד היום הזה occurs again 9. 13, 21; 10. 12; 12. 19; II. 2. 22; 8. 22; 10. 27 (עד היום); 14. 7; 16. 6; 17. 23, 34, 41. The phrase is in most cases the addition of R^D, and thus has important bearing upon the date of compilation of Kings. See *Introduction*.

10, 11. בית יהוה] LXX omits יהוה and reads הַבַּיִת. Luc. in both cases τὸν οἶκον Κυρίου.

Thus it is clear that the omissions in LXX (*vv.* 1–5) are later additions to the text from the hand of R^P. But beyond these additions, in the text which is common to LXX and MT. there are a few phrases which exhibit unmistakeably the influence of P. These must be prior to the separation of the recensions represented by MT. and LXX, and therefore prior also to R^P; and are to be assigned to late exilic or early post-exilic scribes influenced by P, mentioned above (*ch.* 6. 16) under the symbol SS^P. The phrases in question are as follow:—

4ª. אהל מועד] This phrase occurs a few times in JE; Ex. 33. 7; Num. 11. 16; 12. 4; Deut. 31. 14; but is chiefly characteristic of P, in which it occurs some 132 times. Outside the Hexateuch, it is found only in 1 Sam. 2. 22; *ch.* 8. 4ª; and in Chr. In 1 Sam. the last member of the verse, containing the expression, is wanting in LXX, and seems to be of the character of an interpolation. So Wellh., Kamp., Budde. Probably also in our passage אהל מועד (the tent of Moses) has been substituted for an original הָאֹהֶל (the tent of David; *ch.* 1. 39). LXX, Luc. τοῦ μαρτυρίου after באהל in this verse is probably added for the sake of uniformity with the previous אהל מועד.

6. אל קדש הקדשים] Cf. *ch.* 6. 16 *note.*

8, 10. מן הקדש] הקדש is 'the holy place,' i.e. the outer room of the Temple, called הַהֵיכָל in 6. 17, 33; 7. 21. The term is obviously used in relation to the name given to the inner room קדש הקדשים, as is the case in Ex. 26. 33 והבדילה הפרכת לכם בין הקדש ובין קדש הקדשים.

8. ולא יראו החוצה] Probably added by the same hand as מן הק׳, to guard against the supposition that the staves were exposed to the public gaze.

Thus the original form of the section *vv.* 1–11, as it left the hand of R^D^, was probably as follows:—

1 אז יקהל שלמה את כל זקני ישראל ירושלם להעלות את ארון ברית
2, 3 יהוה מעיר דוד היא ציון: בירח האתנים: וישאו הכהנים את הארון:
4, 5 ואת האהל ואת כל כלי הקדש אשר באהל: והמלך וכל ישראל לפני
6 הארון מזבחים צאן ובקר אשר לא יספרו ולא ימנו מרב: ויביאו
הכהנים את ארון ברית יהוה אל מקומו אל דביר הבית אל תחת
7 כנפי הכרובים: כי הכרובים פרשים כנפים אל מקום הארון ויסכו
8 הכרבים על הארון ועל בדיו מלמעלה: ויארכו הבדים ויראו ראשי
9 הבדים על פני הדביר ויהיו שם עד היום הזה: אין בארון רק שני
לחות האבנים אשר הניח שם משה בחרב אשר כרת יהוה עם בני ישראל
10 בצאתם מארץ מצרים: ויהי בצאת הכהנים והענן מלא את הבית:
11 ולא יכלו הכהנים לעמד לשרת מפני הענן כי מלא כבוד יהוה
את הבית:

The words overlined are the work of R^D^; those marked by the dotted line may perhaps be due to him.

1, 6. ארון ברית יהוה] Cf. 3. 15 *note.* Probably הארון stood in the original narrative, as in *vv.* 3, 5, 7, 9.

8. ויהיו שם וג׳] Discussed above.

9. אשר כרת י׳ עם בני ישראל] The idea of the covenant between Yahwe and Israel appears first in JE; Ex. 19. 5; 24. 7, 8; 34. 10, 27; but is brought into special prominence through the emphasis laid upon it in Deuteronomy; cf. 5. 2 *f.* יהוה אלהינו כרת עמנו ברית בחרב; 4. 23; *al.* The supposition that this sentence is the work of R^D explains its imperfect connexion with the preceding, the only antecedent to אשר כרת being שני לחות האבנים. Doubtless R^D was thinking of the idea of the covenant (הברית) implied by these לחות, and so made his insertion in its existing form. So vague a relationship of relative to antecedent would scarcely be possible if the whole verse were by one hand. LXX, Luc. insert after לחות האבנים, πλάκες τῆς διαθήκης, i.e. לֻחוֹת הַבְּרִית, an addition which brings the sentence into close accord with Deut. 9. 9 לקחת לוחת האבנים לוחת הברית אשר כרת יהוה עמכם. Probably this is a gloss inserted to smooth away the roughness in connexion. The explanation of אשר כרת י׳ '*where* Yahwe made,' &c., with an ellipse of ברית as in 1 Sam. 20. 16; 22. 8, is possible but scarcely necessary.

Possibly בצאתם מארץ מצרים may also belong to R^D, in continuation of the preceding. If, however, it belong to the first narrative, it probably originally ran בצאת בני ישראל וג׳.

12. אז אמר. See *ch.* 3. 16 *note.*

אמר לשכן] 'Hath *promised to* dwell'; RV. 'Hath said that He will dwell'; 1 Chr. 27. 23 אמר י׳ להרבות את ישראל; 2 Chr. 21. 7; Est. 4. 7. With ל of the person to whom the promise is made, II. 8. 19. Cf. *ch.* 5. 19 *note.*

בערפל] ערפל is frequently mentioned as the sign of Yahwe's theophany:—‖ 2 Chr. 6. 1; Ex. 20. 21; Dt. 4. 11; 5. 19; 2 Sam. 22. 10; ‖ Ps. 18. 10; Ps. 97. 2; Job 22. 13. The word is connected seven times with עָנָן, twice with חֹשֶׁךְ, once with צַלְמוּת, and once with עָבִים. ערפל had the appearance of the dark lowering storm-cloud, as is clear from 2 Sam. 22. 10 *ff.* and Ex. 20. 21; cf. 19. 16.

13. בית זבל] Possibly 'a house of *elevation*,' or '*lofty* house.' For the meaning of זְבוּל 'elevation' or 'height,' Schrader (*COT.* i. 175) quotes Assyr. *bît zabal* = בית זבל; Cheyne (*Isa.* ii. 172 *f.*) cites M. Stanislas Guyard as stating that Assyr. possesses the root *zabâlu* = *nasû* (נשא) in the sense of 'bearing,' and hence (but by *inference* merely) of 'elevating.' This interpretation suits all the Biblical occurrences of זבול as well as, or better than, the old unphilological explanation 'habitation'; ‖ 2 Chr. 6. 2; Isa. 63. 15; Hab. 3. 11; Ps. 49. 15 (Cheyne מִזְּבֻל)†. The verb occurs once, Gen. 30. 20 הפעם יזבלני אישי 'This time will my husband *extol* me.' In New Heb. זבול = 'temple'; *Berachoth* ix. 13b אותן שפשטו ידיהן בזבול 'those (heathen) who stretched out their hands against the temple.'

מכון לשבתך] So Ex. 15. 17 מכון לשבתך פעלת יהוה. מְכוֹן שִׁבְתְּךָ *vv.* 39, 43, 49, cf. Ps. 33. 14. מכון gives prominence to the idea of the *fixed security* of Yahwe's dwelling-place. So מְכוֹן כִּסְאֶךָ Ps. 89. 15; מְכוֹן כִּסְאוֹ Ps. 97. 2; מְכוֹנִי Isa. 18. 4.

עולמים] Used adverbially, 'for ever,' in place of the more prosaic לְעוֹלָם. So only ‖ 1 Chr. 6. 2; Ps. 61. 5 אגורה באהלך עולמים.

The two *vv.* 12, 13 occur in LXX *after* the section *vv.* 14–53, and exhibit considerable divergence from MT. Τότε ἐλάλησεν Σαλωμὼν ὑπὲρ τοῦ οἴκου ὡς συνετέλεσεν τοῦ οἰκοδομῆσαι αὐτόν

> Ἥλιον ἐγνώρισεν ἐν οὐρανῷ Κύριος·
> εἶπεν τοῦ κατοικεῖν ἐκ γνόφου.
> Οἰκοδόμησον οἶκόν μου, οἶκον ἐκπρεπῆ σαυτῷ,
> τοῦ κατοικεῖν ἐπὶ καινότητος.

οὐκ ἰδοὺ αὕτη γέγραπται ἐν βιβλίῳ τῆς ᾠδῆς; So Luc. with the variations ἔστησεν for ἐγνώρισεν, καὶ εἶπε for εἶπεν, ἐν γνόφῳ for ἐκ γνόφου, εὐπρεπῆ for ἐκπρεπῆ, ἐπὶ βιβλίου for ἐν βιβλίῳ. Here the words ὑπὲρ . . . αὐτόν are clearly a gloss, due to the fact that when the section *vv.* 14–53 is made to precede *v.* 12 the reference of Solomon's words in this latter verse is not immediately obvious. The remainder, however, as is shown by Wellh. (*C.* 271), presupposes, after the easy correction of a few translator's errors, a text substantially superior to MT. ἐγνώρισεν perhaps represents הֵבִין[1] an error for הֵכִין which Luc. renders rightly ἔστησεν, σαυτῷ לוֹ for לִי, ἐπὶ καινότητος עֲלוּמִים for עוֹלָמִים, τῆς ᾠδῆς הַשִּׁיר for הַיָּשָׁר. We thus may retranslate :—

אָז אָמַר שְׁלֹמֹה
שֶׁמֶשׁ הֵכִין בַּשָּׁמַיִם יְהוָֹה
אָמַר לִשְׁכֹּן בָּעֲרָפֶל׃
בְּנֵה בֵיתִי בֵּית נָוֶה לִי
לָשֶׁבֶת עוֹלָמִים
הֲלֹא הִיא כְתוּבָה עַל־סֵפֶר הַיָּשָׁר׃

'Then said Solomon,
The sun hath Yahwe set in the heavens,
But hath promised to dwell in thick darkness;
—Build my house, a house of habitation for me,
That I may dwell therein for ever.
Is it not written in the Book of the Upright[2]?'

Here in *v.* 12, in place of the single clause of MT., we have two antithetically parallel distichs, setting in pointed contrast the sun brightly shining in the sky above and the thick black cloud which fills and overhangs the House of Yahwe. The substance of Yahwe's command and promise is appropriately introduced in *v.* 13[a b], while *v.* 13[c], as in Josh. 10. 13 (Joshua at the battle of Beth-ḥoron), 2 Sam. 1. 18 (David's lament over Saul and Jonathan), bears the stamp of genuineness and ensures the antiquity of the short extract. Klo. follows LXX in *v.* 12, supposing that ἐγνώρισεν translates יוֹדֵעַ, a mistaken reading of יִוָּדַע—'The sun *is manifest* in the heavens.' In *v.* 13[a b], however, he abides by MT.[3], with

---

[1] But הֵבִין is never elsewhere in LXX rendered by γνωρίζω.

[2] So Kamp. Wellh. reads עֲרָפֶל for בָּעֲרָפֶל, בְּסֵפֶר for עַל־סֵפֶר, but in both cases Luc. indicates the more accurate reading.

[3] But more probably the expressions זְבֻל, מָכוֹן exhibit traces of a later phase of thought as to Yahwe's dwelling-place. See above as to usage and occurrence of these phrases.

the small alteration וַאֲנִי בָנִיתִי for בנה בניתי from ‖ 2 Chr. 6. 2, while *v.* 13[c] LXX is bracketed as doubtful. Jos.'s somewhat lengthy reproduction of Solomon's words (*Ant.* viii. 4, § 2) depends upon a combination of Kings and Chronicles freely wrought up and expanded. Thus καὶ ἐξ ὧν σαυτῷ εἰργάσω γεγονότα τὸν οὐρανὸν οἴδαμεν κ.τ.λ. represents Ἥλιον ἐγνώρισεν ἐν οὐρανῷ Κύριος of 1 Kings, while Τοῦτον δέ σοι κατεσκεύασα τὸν ναὸν ἐπώνυμον is drawn from καὶ ἐγὼ οἰκοδόμηκα οἶκον τῷ ὀνόματί σου, 2 Chr. 6. 2.

Vulg. agrees closely with MT. Pesh. ܡܪܝܐ ܐܢܬ ܐܡܪܬ ܠܡܫܪܐ ܒܥܪܦܠܐ 'Lord, *thou hast* promised to dwell in thick darkness,' is probably an arbitrary alteration from 3rd to 2nd pers. in view of the use of the 2nd pers. in the following verse. Targ. יהוה אתרעי לאשראה שכינתיה בירושלם 'Yahwe hath been pleased to establish his *Shechinah* in Jerusalem' is obviously a paraphrase in the translator's usual style. Nevertheless, Th., finding difficulty in the use of ערפל '*black* darkness' to describe the appearance of the כבוד י׳ or שכינה, by inference a *bright* cloud, obtains by combination of Pesh. and Targ. the emendation יְהוָה אַתָּה אָמַרְתָּ לִשְׁכֹּן בִּירוּשָׁלָםִ 'Yahwe, thou hast promised to dwell in Jerusalem,' a somewhat prosaic statement which is partially anticipated by Bö.'s suggestion יְהוָה הָאֹמֵר לִשְׁכֹּן בְּיִשְׂרָאֵל.

14–66. This long section, containing Solomon's address to the people (*vv.* 14–21), the dedication prayer (*vv.* 22–53), the blessing (*vv.* 54–61), and the short account of the festival (*vv.* 62–66), presents throughout clear indications that it owes its present form to the hand of R[D]. The final portion (*vv.* 62–66) may perhaps exhibit an older narrative into which Deuteronomic additions have been incorporated, but the remainder, and especially the central prayer of dedication, has been so thoroughly amplified by the editor that it is impossible to discover any older kernel upon which he may have based his work. The choice of subjects in the successive divisions of the prayer seems for the most part to have been suggested by the catalogue of curses contained in Deut. 28. 15–68.

	1 Kings 8.		Deut. 28.
31	את אשר יחטא איש לרעהו וג׳		
33	בהנגף עמך ישראל לפני אויב	25	יתנך י׳ נגף לפני איביך
35	בהעצר שמים ולא יהיה מטר	23, 24	והיו שמיך אשר על ראשך נחשת וג׳
37	דבר כי יהיה	21	ידבק י׳ בך את הדבר וג׳
	שדפון ירקון	22	יככה י׳ . . . בשדפון ובירקון
	ארבה חסיל	38	ומעט תאסף כי יחסלנו הארבה. Cf. also *vv.* 39, 42.
	כי יצר לו איבו וג׳	52	והצר לך בכל שעריך. Cf. *vv.* 49 *ff.*
	כל נגע כל מחלה		*vv.* 22, 27, 35, 59–61.
41	וגם אל הנכרי		
44	כי יצא עמך למלחמה		
46	אשר יחטאו לך . . . ונתתם לפני אויב ושבום וג׳		*vv.* 36, 37, 64–68.

Deuteronomic phraseology is noticed below verse by verse.

It is more difficult to decide whether the section has suffered interpolation at the hands of later Redactors.

(i) The division of the prayer *vv.* 46–49, which brings forward the possibility of a general captivity of Israel in punishment for sins, is considered by Wellh. (*C.* 270), Sta. (*Ges.* i. 74), Kamp., Benz., Kit. to be marked by its contents as not earlier than the Exile, and therefore later than R^{D}[1].

Against this view may justly be cited the vagueness of the terms of *v.* 46 ושבום שביהם אל ארץ האויב רחוקה או קרובה, and the fact that the writer (*v.* 48) appears to regard the Temple as still standing during the period of the Exile, . . . והתפללו אליך דרך ארצם והבית אשר בנית לשמך. But the chief argument for the pre-exilic date of the passage is to be derived from comparison of Deut. 28, which, as we have seen above, forms to some extent the model of the dedication prayer. This *ch.* 28 is regarded by all critics as

[1] Wellh., Sta. seem to regard these verses as determining the exilic date of the whole section *vv.* 14–66. Kamp. assigns *vv.* 44–53 to D^2; Benz., Kit. *vv.* 44–51.

being, if not an integral portion of D (*chs.* 5–26)[1], at least closely akin to D in standpoint and date, and thus certainly pre-exilic; yet notwithstanding, *vv.* 36, 37, 64–68 threaten a captivity of the nation in language decidedly more definite than that of the passage of the prayer which has been called in question. We may therefore be content to regard these verses as containing nothing necessarily opposed to the supposition of a pre-exilic authorship, and so, as of one piece with the whole, *vv.* 22–53[2].

(ii) Sta. (*Ges.* ii. 248 *note*) regards אל השמים *v.* 30, and the local accusative השמים *vv.* 32, 34, 36, 39, 43, 45, 49 as later insertions made upon the view that Yahwe's habitation was not the Temple, as is suggested by the old narrative, *vv.* 11–13, but the heavens, out of which he exercised a supervision over the Temple. Accordingly, portions of *vv.* 22, 54 ויפרש כפיו השמים; וכפיו פרשות השמים, and *v.* 27 which questions the possibility of God's dwelling upon the earth, are also assigned to the same hand.

This opinion of Sta. is decidedly favoured by syntactical considerations. The local accusative השמים '*in* heaven,' following upon ואתה תשמע, *v.* 32 *al.*, can scarcely be paralleled. Th. compares חצר האחרת *ch.* 7. 8. Da. § 69, *Rem.* 1 places it among words subordinated in the accusative more freely 'in elevated speech and poetry[3].' ופנית, again, at the commencement of *v.* 28 hinges very imperfectly on to the end of *v.* 27, and much more readily follows upon *v.* 26.

If this view be adopted, אל מקום שבתך *v.* 30 will refer originally not to the heavens but to the Temple, agreeably to the idea not only of the old narrative, but of the framer of the prayer (R^D); cf. *v.* 38 ופרש כפיו אל הבית הזה, where *the House* seems to be regarded as Yahwe's abode; *vv.* 35, 42, *al.* So also מכון שבתך *vv.* 39, 43, 49, where, upon the removal of השמים, מִמְּכוֹן שבתך must be restored.

---

[1] Kue. *Hex.* § 7, 21; Dri. *Deuteronomy*, 303 *f.*

[2] Cf. Kue. *Ond.* § 26, 5.

[3] || 2 Chr. 6. 21, 23, 25, 30, 33, 35, 39 reads מן השמים, but in *v.* 27 השמים as in Kings.

The view that heaven, not the Temple, is Yahwe's proper abode, belongs to exilic times, and doubtless owed its origin to the destruction of the first Temple. Cf. Isa. 66. 1 כה אמר י׳ השמים כסאי והארץ הדם רגלי אי זה בית אשר תבנו לי. On the other hand, according to Ezekiel the newly constructed Temple and city are to be specially dignified by Yahwe's Presence, though doubtless according to a more heightened and spiritual conception; 48. 35 ושם העיר מיום יהוה שמה.

15. י׳ אלהי ישראל] A phrase very characteristic of R^D. Cf. *vv.* 17, 20, 23, 25, (26 om. י׳); 11. 9, 31; 14. 7, 13; 15. 30; 16. 13, 26, 33; 22. 54; II. 10. 31; 14. 25; 21. 12; 22. 15, 18. Elsewhere in Kings the phrase is found only in I. 1. 30, 48; II. 9. 6; 19. 15, 20, and in I. 17. 1, 14 where the text is doubtful (see *note*).

After אלהי ישראל LXX, Luc. insert σήμερον, i.e. הַיּוֹם. This is natural, and probably original; cf. *ch.* 5. 21 ויאמר ברוך יהוה היום.

אשר דבר . . . מלא] So *v.* 24; Jer. 44. 25. The special reference of אשר דבר וג׳ is to 2 Sam. 7. 5 *ff.*: cf. *v.* 16^a with 2 Sam. 7. 6^a; *v.* 16^b with 2 Sam. 7. 8–11; *v.* 19 with 2 Sam. 7. 13^a.

16. לא בחרתי בעיר וג׳] Cf. Deut. 12. 5, 11, 18, 21, 26; *al.* So in *vv.* 44, 48; 11. 13, 32, 36; 14. 21; II. 21. 7; 23. 27; all R^D or R^D2.

להיות שמי שם] So *v.* 29; II. 23. 27. Cf. לָשׂוּם שמי שם *ch.* 9. 3 *note.*

17. ויהי עם לבב] 'It was *at* the heart' (*apud cor*, lit. *with* the heart). This idiomatic use of עם is of fair frequency; *v.* 18; ‖ 2 Chr. 6. 7, 8; *ch.* 10. 2; ‖ 2 Chr. 9. 1; 1 Chr. 22. 6; 28. 2; 2 Chr. 1. 11; 24. 4; 29. 10; Deut. 8. 5; 15. 9; Josh. 14. 7†.

לשם י׳] *Ch.* 3. 2 *note.*

19. היצא מחלציך] Only ‖ 2 Chr. 6. 9; Gen. 35. 11 ומלכים מחלציך יצאו.

20. ויקם י׳ את דברו] 2 Sam. 7. 25.

כאשר דבר י׳] *Ch.* 5. 26 *note.* LXX om. יהוה.

21. ברית י׳ אשר כרת וג׳] *Ver.* 9 *note.* Luc. διαθήκη Θεοῦ, but ברית אלהים seems only to occur Lev. 2. 13; 2 Chr. 34. 32; Ps. 78. 10; Prov. 2. 17, and in the very rare expression ארון ברית אלהים upon which see *ch.* 3. 15 *note.* כרת LXX, Luc. διέθετο Κύριος.

23. אין כמוך . . . מתחת] Deut. 4. 39 יהוה הוא האלהים בשמים ממעל ועל הארץ מתחת אין עוד; Josh. 2. 11b (D²).

שמר הברית והחסד] Deut. 7. 9; Neh. 1. 5; 9. 32; Dan. 9. 4. Cf. Deut. 7. 12; Ps. 89. 29.

לעבדיך וג׳] Owing to the influence of the following verse this has become altered in LXX into *τῷ δούλῳ σου τῷ πορευομένῳ ἐνώπιόν σου ἐν ὅλῃ τῇ καρδίᾳ αὐτοῦ*, while in Luc. we have further the paraphrase *τῷ πατρί μου* for *τῷ δούλῳ σου*. Doubtless MT. is correct. The verse enunciates Yahwe's character as shown in His dealings with His servants *in general*.

ההלכים לפניך] *Ch.* 2. 4 *note*.

בכל לבם] *Ch.* 2. 3, 4 *note*.

24. אשר שמרת . . . לו] LXX *ἃ ἐφύλαξας τῷ δούλῳ σου Δαυεὶδ τῷ πατρί μου*, making אשר refer not to יהוה of the previous verse, but to הברית והחסד, and omitting the then redundant את אשר דברת לו. This interpretation depends upon the reading of עַבְדְּךָ for עֲבָדֶיךָ in the previous verse, since אֲשֶׁר שָׁמַרְתָּ לְעַבְדְּךָ, שֹׁמֵר . . . לְעַבְדְּךָ are simply tautologous if יהוה be regarded as the antecedent of אשר.

כיום הזה] *Ch.* 3. 6 *note*.

25. לא יכרת וג׳] *Ch.* 2. 4 *note*.

רק אם ישמרו וג׳] *Ch.* 2. 4 *note*.

כאשר הלכת לפני] *Ch.* 3. 14 *note*.

26. יֵאָמֶן נא דבריך] As in Gen. 42. 20 וְיֵאָמְנוּ דִבְרֵיכֶם; 2 Chr. 1. 9.

דְּבָרֶיךָ] LXX, Luc., Pesh. confirm Q're דברך.

27. הַאֻמְנָם] Elsewhere only ‖ 2 Chr. 6. 18; Num. 22. 37 (JE); Ps. 58. 2; הַאַף אֻמְנָם Gen. 18. 13 (J).

אֻמְנָם serves to point the question very forcibly, '*Is it indeed the case that.*' On the other hand, the form אָמְנָם, which occurs nine times, seems, with the single possible exception Job 19. 5, to be reserved for *non*-interrogative asseverations.

יֵשֵׁב] '*Can* God dwell.' So לא יכלכלוך '*cannot* contain Thee;' Dri. *Tenses*, § 37. *a*.

על הארץ] ‖ 2 Chr. 6. 18 אֶת־הָאָדָם עַל־הָאָרֶץ. So LXX, Luc. here add *μετὰ ἀνθρώπων*, Targ. בגו בני אינשא. This is probably genuine, and is adopted as such by Th., Klo., Benz.

השמים ושמי השמים] Deut. 10. 14; 2 Chr. 2. 5. שמים ושמי השמים || 2 Chr. 6. 18. שמי השמים Ps. 148. 4.

אַף כי] Lit. *Indeed* (or strictly, *adding*) *that* this house (cannot contain Thee); so, with reference to the preceding sentence, '*how much less* this house.' Cf. 2 Chr. 32. 15; Prov. 17. 7; Job 4. 19 (without כי); 9. 14; 15. 16; 25. 6, where, as here, the preceding sentence states a negation. When preceded by a positive statement אַף כי naturally gains the sense '*how much more*'; so Deut. 31. 27; 2 Sam. 16. 11; Prov. 11. 31; *al.*

28. ופנית] '*So* turn Thou'; so ושמעת *v.* 30. Cf. *note* on וחזקת *ch.* 2. 2.

אל תפלת עבדך ואל תחנתו] LXX, Luc. ἐπὶ τὴν δέησίν μου appear to have passed, through oversight, from תפלת to תחנתו, and then not unnaturally to have read י the suffix of 1st pers. instead of ו.

אלהי] LXX, Luc. ὁ Θεὸς Ἰσραήλ. The more personal reference of MT. agrees better with the preceding עבדך. Possibly LXX Ἰσραήλ arose from a mistaken repetition of the last letter of אלהי and the first of לשמע, יל being regarded as a contraction of ישראל.

ואל התפלה] LXX omits. The words are, however, found in Luc. and the other Verss., and are demanded by the following מתפלל which cannot refer merely to הָרִנָּה.

29. להיות עינֶך פתֻחֹת] || 2 Chr. 6. 20; *v.* 52; 2 Chr. 6. 40; 7. 15; Neh. 1. 6.

לילה ויום] So Vulg., Targ.; but LXX, Luc., Pesh., || 2 Chr. 6. 20 יומם ולילה, probably an arbitrary alteration to the more usual order. At the close of the verse LXX, Luc. add ἡμέρας καὶ νυκτός.

30. אל מקום שבתך אל השמים] '*At* Thy dwelling-place, even *at* heaven.' Cf. *ch.* 6. 18 *note.*

30b. ושמעת] LXX, Luc. καὶ ποιήσεις, i.e. וְעָשִׂיתָ. This, though adopted by Klo., appears to be merely a correction of the translator, who took offence at the repetition of the verb שמע, and so made the alteration in order to produce an outward harmony with *vv.* 32, 43. But these two cases are different from our passage. It is only appropriate that ועשית should be used of punishing the wicked and vindicating the righteous (*v.* 32), or of bringing about the request of the stranger (*v.* 43), but here, where the question is simply of *forgiveness* which would not need to be manifested in any outward action, ועשית would be less apposite. On the other hand, ושמעת, as a resumption from the commencement of the verse after the lengthy intervening sentence, is quite in accordance with Hebrew usage. Cf. *ch.* 2. 4 *note.*

31. את אשר יחטא] Rather difficult. את אשר seems to be used in the same way as אשר alone, which occurs here and there in the sense *'in case'* or *when;* cf. *v.* 33 אשר יחטאו לך; Lev. 4. 22 אשר נשיא יחטא ועשה וג׳; Deut. 11. 27; 18. 22; Josh. 4. 21; Isa. 31. 4. Just possibly את אשר was intended in the first instance for a kind of *accusativus pendens* which should have owed subordination to ואתה תשמע *v.* 32, 'That which &c. . . . do thou hear,' but owing to the length of the intervening sentence the connexion was imperfectly effected. LXX, Luc. ὅσα ἂν ἁμάρτῃ, Vulg. *Si peccaverit,* Pesh. ܐܢ ܢܣܟܠ paraphrase slightly to overcome the difficulty; Targ. ית דיחוב literal. || 2 Chr. 6. 22 אם יחטא. So Lev. 4. 3, 13, 27 compared with *v.* 22 above cited.

לרעהו] 'Against,' or strictly, *'with reference to* his neighbour.' So most commonly; Gen. 20. 6; 40. 1; 1 Sam. 7. 6; *al.*

ונשא בו אלה] The phrase only here and || 2 Chr. 6. 22. נשא 'take up,' i. e. עֲלֵי־פֶה Ps. 50. 16, or עַל־שְׂפָתָיִם Ps. 16. 4.

ובא אלה] Scarcely correct. If the sense intended were 'and the oath come,' we should expect וּבָאָה הָאָלָה. LXX, Luc. καὶ ἐξαγορεύσῃ, Pesh. ܘܢܐܡܐ, Targ. ויומיניה all presuppose וְאָלָה, and Vulg. *et venerit propter juramentum* seems to be a slightly paraphrastic rendering of the same text. Thus, with Klo., Kamp., Benz., we may emend וּבָא וְאָלָה 'and he come and swear,' in preference to the suggestion of Bö., followed by Th., וּבָא אָלֹה 'and he come swearing,' and the alternative of Kamp., adopted by Kit., וּבָא בְאָלָה 'and he enter into an oath' (cf. Neh. 10. 30).

32. ועשית] 'And shalt do.' An absolute use of עשה, the implied object being 'that which is meet to be done,' as is shown by the following ושפטת וג׳. Such a pregnant use of this verb with יהוה as subject is not infrequent in lofty or poetic style; Ps. 119. 126

עת לעשות לי׳; 22. 32; 37. 5; 52. 11; Isa. 44. 23; 64. 3; Jer. 14. 7; Ezek. 20. 9, 14, 22; Dan. 9. 19. With another subject cf. 1 Sam. 26. 25; Isa. 10. 13; Dan. 8. 12, 24; 11. 28, 30, 32; 2 Chr. 31. 21.

להרשיע] '*In respect of* condemning,' or, '*so as to* condemn.' ל of reference explains the action described by ושפטת.

לתת דרכו בראשו] ‖ 2 Chr. 6. 23. Elsewhere only in Ezek. 9. 10; 11. 21; 16. 43; 22. 31†. Cf. 17. 19, and the kindred phrase והשיב י׳ את רעתך בראשך *ch.* 2. 44.

33. בהנגף . . . לפני אויב] Luc. *καὶ ἐν τῷ πταῖσαι τὸν λαόν σου Ἰσραὴλ ἐνώπιόν σου καὶ πεσεῖν ἐνώπιον ἐχθρῶν αὐτῶν*, i. e. בְּהִנָּגֵף עַמְּךָ יִשְׂרָאֵל לְפָנֶיךָ וְנָפְלוּ לִפְנֵי אוֹיֵב. Very probably correct, the scribe's eye passing from לפניך to לפני. The idea that Yahwe smites Israel by the hand of a foreign nation is found in 1 Sam. 4. 3 למה נגפנו י׳ היום לפני פלשתים; cf. Judg. 20. 35. So Deut. 28. 25 יתנך י׳ נִגָּף לפני איביך.

אשר יחטאו לך] 'In case they shall sin against thee'; scarcely as RV. here and in *v.* 35, 'because *they have sinned* against thee.' Cf. *v.* 31 *note.*

ושבו אליך והודו] LXX, Luc. agree with ‖ 2 Chr. 6. 24 in omitting אליך, the meaning then being, 'and shall once more confess'; cf. *v.* 47 ושבו והתחננו. But the phrase שוב אל י׳ is very frequent; cf. *v.* 48; Deut. 30. 10; Hos. 5. 4; 7. 10; 14. 3; 1 Sam. 7. 3; Isa. 44. 22; *al.;* and ought not here to be rejected. A kindred phrase is שוב עד־י׳; Deut. 4. 30; 30. 2; Hos. 14. 2; *al.*

והתחננו אליך] Here also אליך is omitted by LXX, Luc. General usage favours MT.; *v.* 47 (LXX, Luc. *δεηθῶσίν σου*); Deut. 3. 23; Job 8. 5; Ps. 30. 9; 142. 2; Gen. 42. 21; II. 1. 13. ‖ 2 Chr. 6. 24 לפניך; cf. *v.* 59; *ch.* 9. 3. התחנן is elsewhere followed by לְ, but appears to be never used absolutely.

34. עמך] So Luc., Vulg., Targ.; but LXX *τοῦ δούλου σου,* i. e. עַבְדְּךָ, Pesh. ܕܥܒܕܟ ܘܕܥܡܟ either a doublet or in conformity with *v.* 36. MT., which is agreeable to the phrase in *v.* 33, is to be retained.

אשר נתת לאבותם] So *vv.* 40, 48; cf. *ch.* 14. 15; II. 21. 8 (R^D); Deut. 26. 15 and the common phrase of Deut. אשר יהוה אלהינו

(לך) נָתַן לנו, referring to the land or to portions of it; Deut. 1. 20, 25; 2. 29; 3. 20; 4. 40; 5. 16; *al.*

35. יָשׁוּבוּן] The form of the 3rd and 2nd pers. pl. of the imperf. with the so-called *Nûn paragogicum* is not uncommon in Hebrew. Cf. this same verb, Isa. 35. 10; 51. 11; Jer. 44. 28; *al.*; תְּמֻתוּן Gen. 3. 3, 4; יְקוּמוּן Deut. 33. 11; 2 Sam. 22. 39; *al.* This form is usual in Aram. and in class. Ar.; יִקְטְלוּן, ܢܶܩܛܠܽܘܢ *neqtᵉlûn*, يَقْتُلُونَ *yaqtulûna*. See Wright, *Compar. Sem. Gramm.* pp. 184, 145, for the origin of the termination. In Hebrew the form is rather an affected than a real archaism, and is most common in elevated poetical style, or in pause as being heavier and more impressive.

כִּי תַעֲנֵם] According to vocalization the only possible rendering is 'when thou shalt answer them,' Pesh. ܡܳܐ ܕܬܥܢܐ ܐܢܘܢ, Targ. ארי תקביל צלותהון; but this is unsuitable. Hence it is better to follow LXX, Luc. ὅταν ταπεινώσῃς αὐτούς, Vulg. *propter afflictionem suam*, and to vocalize כִּי תְעַנֵּם 'when thou shalt humble them.' So Th., Kamp., Benz., Kit. Klo.'s emendation כִּי תַכְנִעֵם, after 2 Chr. 7. 14, is unnecessary.

36. אשר ילכו בה] 'In which they *are to* walk' or '*should* walk.' For this *nuance* of the imperf. cf. Ex. 10. 26 לא נדע מה נעבד את י׳ עד באנו שמה 'We do not know how we *are to* serve Yahwe until we come thither.' Dri. *Tenses*, § 39 *a*.

נתתה ... לנחלה] 'Gavest ... *for an inheritance*'; so ‖ 2 Chr. 6. 27; Deut. 29. 7; Josh. 11. 23 (D²); 14. 13 (E recast by D²); Ps. 136. 21; Num. 18. 21, 24 (P; in these verses the reference is to *tithe*, not to *the land*)†. So היה לנחלה Josh. 14. 9, 14 (E recast by D²); 24. 32 (E); Ezek. 36. 12; 44. 28†. The usual phrase of Deuteronomy is נתן נחלה; Deut. 4. 21; 15. 4; 19. 10; 20. 16; 21. 23; 24. 4; 25. 19; 26. 1; Ps. 135. 12†. נתן בנחלה occurs Num. 36. 2 (P)†; חלק בנחלה Num. 26. 53 (P); Josh. 13. 7 (D²); נפל בנחלה (הפיל) Josh. 13. 6; 23. 4 (D²); Num. 34. 2 (P); Judg. 18. 1; Ezek. 45. 1; 47. 14, 22†.

37. רעב כי יהיה] This order—subject, conjunction, verb—serving to give slight emphasis to the subject, is common in P; Lev. 1. 2;

2. 1; 4. 2; 5. 1, 4, 15, 21; 7. 21; *al.;* Num. 5. 12; cf. Ezek. 3. 19; 14. 9, 13; 18. 5, 18, 21; 33. 6. So Isa. 28. 18; Mic. 5. 4; Ps. 62. 11.

חסיל] A kind of locust; ‖ 2 Chr. 6. 28; Ps. 78. 46; Joel 1. 4; 2. 25; Isa. 33. 4†. This and the other words used to denote the locust, חָגָב, גֵּבִים, גָּזָם, יֶלֶק, and the ordinary אַרְבֶּה, cannot with any degree of certainty be distinguished as describing different species or stages of growth. A verb חסל occurs once; יַחְסְלֶנּוּ הָאַרְבֶּה 'the locusts *shall consume* it,' Deut. 28. 38. In Aram. חסל means 'bring to an end'; so Targ., Jer. וחסיל כספא = Heb. וַיִּתֹּם הכסף; but most frequently, as in Syr., has gained the more special secondary sense 'wean.' LXX, Luc., connecting ארבה חסיל as one expression, render ἐρυσίβη 'red blight.'

בארץ שעריו] So ‖ 2 Chr. 6. 28. The expression is very forced and unnatural, even if it can be regarded as giving any sense at all. LXX, Luc. ἐν μιᾷ τῶν πόλεων αὐτοῦ, Pesh. ܒܚܕܐ ܡܢ ܡܕܝܢܬܗܘܢ furnish the correct text, בְּאַחַד שְׁעָרָיו '*in any of* his gates,' a regular phrase of D; Deut. 15. 7; 16. 5; 17. 2; 23. 17; cf. 18. 6†. So Klo., Kamp., Benz., Kit., Oort. Th. emends בְּאַחַת עָרָיו; but this is not the usual phrase, nor is it postulated by the renderings of LXX, Luc., Pesh. which very commonly represent שערים by πόλεις, ܡܕܝܢܬܐ; cf. Deut. 12. 17, 18, 21; 15. 7; 17. 2; *al.*

כל נגע וג׳] Cf. כל כלי וג׳ *ch.* 6. 7 *note.*

38. כל תפלה וג׳] The construction is somewhat involved, since כל תפלה כל תחנה can scarcely be regarded as part of the category formed by the plagues mentioned in *v.* 37. Thus *v.* 37 must be regarded as breaking off with an aposiopesis, and the apodosis ואתה תשמע וג׳ as answering to the protasis formed by the second and different category כל תפלה וג׳; 'Whatsoever prayer, &c., there be, *or*, If there be any prayer, &c. . . . , then hear thou,' &c.

לכל עמך ישראל] LXX, Luc. omit correctly. The words are a gloss upon לכל האדם, to explain that this refers to Israel in contrast to הנכרי of *v.* 41. So Klo., Kamp., Benz., Kit.

ידעון] So *v.* 43. Cf. *v.* 35 *note.*

נגע לבבו] A rather obscure expression. The idea seems to be that each man will recognize in the case of his *particular* plague, be it famine, pestilence, or some other above enumerated, that it is sent by God as a punishment for his sin. So ‖ 2 Chr. 6. 29 נגעו ומכאבו. Klo., however, interprets נגע, not as 'plague,' but as 'Berührung,' '*the touching* of his heart';—'Because God will through the misfortune awaken the humiliating consciousness of sin.' So apparently LXX, Luc. ἁφὴν καρδίας αὐτοῦ. Cf. 1 Sam. 10. 26.

39. ונתת לאיש ככל דרכיו] ‖ 2 Chr. 6. 30; Jer. 17. 10; 32. 19; Ezek. 7. 9.

40. כל הימים . . . האדמה] ‖ 2 Chr. 6. 31; Deut. 4. 10; 12. 1; 31. 13†. Cf. *note* on כל הימים *ch.* 9. 3.

אשר נתת וג׳] *Note* on *v.* 34.

41. אל הנכרי] Dependent upon אתה תשמע, *v.* 43, as is noticed by Th. So apparently LXX, Luc. καὶ τῷ ἀλλοτρίῳ . . . καὶ σὺ εἰσακούσῃ.

Vulg. *et alienigena*, Targ. מן בר עממין seem to take the expression as a kind of *casus pendens*, 'as for the stranger,' a use of אל scarcely to be justified. Pesh. ܥܠ ܢܘܟܪܝܐ seems to mean 'on behalf of the stranger,' and supposes the ellipse of some such expression as ܒܥܝܢܐ 'I pray.'

LXX, Luc. in ‖ 2 Chr. 6. 32 read πᾶς ἀλλότριος, and Klo. accordingly emends כָּל־הַנָּכְרִי 'jeder Fremdling.'

ובא וג׳] Deut. 29. 21 הנכרי אשר יבא מארץ רחוקה.

41, 42. ובא . . . הנטויה] These fifteen words have fallen out in LXX, Luc. through homoioteleuton. For the second ובא reinforcing the first after the intervening words cf. *ch.* 2. 4 *note*.

42. את ידך החזקה וזרעך הנטויה] The two phrases occur in combination ‖ 2 Chr. 6. 32; Deut. 4. 34; 5. 15; 7. 19; 11. 2; 26. 8; Jer. 21. 5 (different order); 32. 21 (אֶזְרוֹעַ); Ezek. 20. 33, 34; Ps. 136. 12†. יד חזקה alone, Deut. 3. 24; 6. 21; 7. 8; 9. 26; 34. 12; Ex. 3. 19; 6. 1; 32. 11 (all JE); 13. 9 (E); Num. 20. 20 (JE; referring to Edom); Neh. 1. 10; Dan. 9. 15†. Cf. Josh. 4. 24 (D^2). זרוע נטויה alone, Deut. 9. 29; II. 17. 36; Jer. 27. 5; 32. 17; Ex. 6. 6 (P)†.

43. כל עמי הארץ] ‖ 2 Chr. 6. 33; *vv.* 53, 60; Deut. 28. 10; Josh.

4. 24 (D²); Ezek. 31. 12; Zeph. 3. 20 are the only occurrences of the exact phrase. LXX, Luc. omit הארץ.

לְיִרְאָה] ‖ 2 Chr. 6. 33. A common phrase in Deut.; 4. 10; 5. 26; 6. 24; 8. 6; 10. 12; 14. 23; 17. 19; 28. 58; 31. 13; Jer. 32. 39; Neh. 1. 11; Ps. 86. 11†.

כי שמך נקרא על הבית הזה] 'That thy name is called over this house,' i. e. in token of *ownership*. The phrase is most clearly elucidated by 2 Sam. 12. 27, 28, where Joab, having taken Rabbath-Ammon, sends to David that he may come and complete the capture, פן אלכד אני את העיר ונקרא שמי עליה 'lest *I* take the city, and my name be called over it,' as having the credit of its conquest.

The phrase occurs besides:—as here, of the Temple ‖ 2 Chr. 6. 33; Jer. 7. 10, 11, 14, 30; 32. 34; 34. 15; of the chosen people Deut. 28. 10; Jer. 14. 9; Isa. 63. 19; 2 Chr. 7. 14; of Jerusalem Jer. 25. 29; of Jerusalem and the chosen people Dan. 9. 18, 19; of Jeremiah Jer. 15. 16; of the nations Am. 9. 12†.

44. אל יהוה] So Targ. קדם יהוה. The other Verss. are different; LXX, Luc. *ἐν ὀνόματι Κυρίου*, Vulg. *te*, Pesh. ܩܕܡܝܟ ܡܪܝܐ; ‖ 2 Chr. 6. 34 (MT. and Verss.) אֵלֶיךָ. Probably אֵלֶיךָ is original, and the MT. reading due to this having been read אל יה׳. LXX seems to have had the reading of MT., and to have paraphrased in order to explain the transition from the second to the third person.

דרך העיר] '*In the direction of* the city.' So *v.* 48; ‖ 2 Chr. 6. 34, 38; *ch.* 18. 43 הבט דרך ים 'look *toward* the sea,' Ezek. 8. 5; 41. 12; *al.*

העיר אשר בחרת בה] *Note* on *v.* 16.

והבית וג׳] *Ch.* 3. 2 *note.*

45. ועשית משפטם] 'And wilt execute their right.' The exact phrase (עשה משפט פ׳, with יהוה as subject) occurs only besides in *v.* 49; ‖ 2 Chr. 6. 35, 39; *v.* 59; Deut. 10. 18; Mic. 7. 9; Ps. 9. 5†.

46. כי אין וג׳] Cf. Eccl. 7. 20 כי אדם אין צדיק בארץ אשר יעשה טוב ולא יחטא.

ואנפת בם] LXX rather curiously *καὶ ἐπάξεις αὐτούς*, Luc. *καὶ ἐὰν ἐπαγάγῃς ἐπ' αὐτούς*. This latter may perhaps be explained by supposing an ellipse of *ὀργήν*. Cf. Ps. 7. 12, where זֹעֵם is rendered ὀργὴν ἐπάγων, Isa. 26. 21 ἐπάγει τὴν ὀργήν for לפקד עון. Similarly LXX may be a corruption of ἐπάξεις αὐτοῖς, the alteration being due to some one who supposed the sense intended by the Greek to be '*lead them away* and deliver them up,' &c. In LXX of ‖ 2 Chr. 6. 36 there is a further alteration—καὶ πατάξεις αὐτούς. Luc., however, renders καὶ ἐὰν θυμωθῇς ἐπ' αὐτούς.

ונתתם לפני אויב] 'And thou *set them before* the foe,' i. e. deliver them over to his power and disposal. The other occurrences of the phrase in this sense are ‖ 2 Chr. 6. 36; Deut. 1. 8, 21; 2. 31, 33, 36; 7. 2, 23; 23. 15; 28. 7, 25; 31. 5; Josh. 10. 12; 11. 6 (both D[2]); Judg. 11. 9; Isa. 41. 2†.

47. והשיבו אל לבם] 'And shall bring back to their heart,' or as we should say, 'their mind.' So RV. 'shall bethink themselves.' ‖ 2 Chr. 6. 37; Deut. 4. 39; 30. 1; Isa. 44. 19; 46. 8 (עַל־לֵב); Lam. 3. 21†. The verse is a reminiscence of Deut. 30. 1 *ff.*

בארץ שביהם] LXX ἐν γῇ μετοικίας αὐτῶν, Luc. ἐν τῇ γῇ τῆς μετοικεσίας αὐτῶν agree with ‖ 2 Chr. 6. 37 in reading בְּאֶרֶץ שִׁבְיָם, which is probably correct. Cf. Jer. 30. 10; 46. 27.

חטאנו וג'] Cf. Ps. 106. 6; Dan. 9. 15, both reminiscences of this passage.

חטאנו וְהעוינו] Weak ו co-ordinating two synonymous ideas. Cf. Isa. 1. 2 בָּנִים גִּדַּלְתִּי וְרוֹמַמְתִּי; 1 Sam. 12. 2; Deut. 2. 30; *al.*; Dri. *Tenses*, §§ 131, 132. חטא, like ἁμαρτάνειν, means literally to *miss the mark*; so Job 5. 24 ופקדת נוך ולא תחטא 'And thou shalt visit thy pasture and shalt miss nothing'; and in Hiph'il, Judg. 20. 16. עוה = Ar. عَوَى *bend*; so Hiph. העוה *make crooked* (with obj. דַּרְכָּם Jer. 3. 21), i. e. *act perversely*. רשע, a more general word, *act wickedly*, perhaps has its origin in the notion of *raising a tumult*; Job 34. 29 והוא ישקט ומי ירשע; cf. Job 3. 17. רשענו *asyndetos* after the two previous verbs connected by ו is a little harsh, and, following the suggestion of Ps. 106. 6, it seems preferable to reject the ו before העוינו, and to read חטאנו העוינו רשענו. So LXX, Vulg., Targ. Pesh., on the other hand, inserts ܘ before the last verb, ܚܛܝܢ ܘܥܘܝܢ ܘܐܪܫܥܢ. Luc., omitting והעוינו, Ἡμάρτομεν, ἠνομήσαμεν. ‖ 2 Chr. 6. 37 חטאנו העוינו ורשענו.

48. ושבו אליך . . . ובכל נפשם] Deut. 30. 10; II. 23. 25; cf. Jer. 3. 10. On שוב אל י׳ cf. *v.* 33 *note;* on בכל לבבם וג׳ cf. *ch.* 2. 3, 4 *note.*

אשר שבו אתם] LXX, Luc. οὗ μετήγαγες αὐτούς possibly read אשר שְׁבִיתָם, but more probably render somewhat freely, as is the case with Vulg. *ad quam captivi ducti fuerint.*

דרך ארצם] *Note* on *v.* 44.

אשר נתתה] *Note* on *v.* 34.

העיר אשר בחרת] *Note* on *v.* 16.

והבית וג׳] *Note* on *ch.* 3. 2.

49. את תפלתם . . . משפטם] LXX, Luc. omit. The words are very probably a gloss from *v.* 45. In this former verse the phrase ועשית משפטם, of vindicating Israel's *right* against the encroachments of their foes, is highly appropriate; but in *v.* 49, where the captivity is regarded as a just penalty for sins committed, the force of the expression is scarcely so immediately apparent, the idea of *a right* and of *concession granted through forgiveness* (וסלחת *v.* 50) being somewhat incompatible.

50. לעמך . . . לך 1] LXX, Luc. omit. The following words ולכל פשעיהם down to the close of *v.* 51 are not found in ‖ 2 Chr. 6. 39.

ונתתם לרחמים] Neh. 1. 11; Ps. 106. 46; the latter being probably a reminiscence of our passage: cf. *v.* 47 *note* on חטאנו וג׳.

51. כי עמך ונחלתך . . . ממצרים] Deut. 9. 26, 29. In application to the chosen people עם and נַחֲלָה appear as parallel terms;—Deut. 32. 9; Isa. 47. 6; Joel 2. 17; 4. 2; Ps. 28. 9; 78. 62, 71; 94. 5, 14; 106. 4, 5, 40. Cf. Mic. 7. 14.

כור הברזל] Deut. 4. 20; Jer. 11. 4†. The meaning of the phrase may be illustrated by Isa. 48. 10, בחרתיך בכור עני 'I have tested thee in the furnace of affliction.'

52. להיות וג׳] *Note* on *v.* 29. ‖ 2 Chr. 6. 40 עתה אלהי יהיו נא עיניך פתחות ואזניך קשבות לתפלת המקום הזה. Similarly LXX, Luc. in our passage insert καὶ τὰ ὦτά σου, i.e. וְאָזְנֶיךָ, after עיניך. This is probably a gloss due to the idea of the unsuitability of *eyes only* being open to a supplication. The words of 2 Chr. are probably no older than the Chronicler, if we may judge by the use of קַשֻּׁב

which appears to be a late form; 2 Chr. 7. 15; Ps. 130. 2†; קַשֻּׁבֹת Neh. 1. 6, 11†.

בכל קראם אליך] Deut. 4. 7† בְּכָל־קָרְאֵנוּ אֵלָיו. For the constr. cf. Gen. 30. 41 בְּכָל־יַחֵם הַצֹּאן; 1 Chr. 23. 31 לְכֹל הַעֲלוֹת עֹלוֹת.

53. כי אתה הבדלתם וג׳] Cf. Lev. 20. 24, 26 (H) אני יהוה אלהיכם אשר הבדלתי אתכם מן העמים; ואבדיל אתכם מן העמים להיות לי.

לנחלה] Cf. Deut. 4. 20 להיות לו לעם נחלה. Israel is styled Yahwe's נחלה also in II. 21. 14 (R^{D2}); Jer. 12. 7, 8, 9; Mic. 7. 18; Isa. 19. 25: see further the cases given on *v.* 51. חֶבֶל נחלתו Deut. 32. 9; שֵׁבֶט נחלתו Jer. 10. 16; 51. 19; Ps. 74. 2 (ש׳ נחלתך); Isa. 63. 17 (שִׁבְטֵי נחלתך). The *land* of Israel is named the נחלה of Yahwe in Jer. 2. 7; 16. 18; 50. 11; Ps. 68. 10; 79. 1; cf. 2 Sam. 20. 19; 21. 3; Ex. 15. 17 (הר נחלתך; E).

מכל עמי הארץ] *Note* on *v.* 43.

כאשר דברת] *Ch.* 5. 26 *note.*

ביד משה] 'By the *hand* of Moses,' i. e. by *his agency*. The idiom is very frequent of a word of Yahwe delivered through the agency of a prophet;—*ch.* 12. 15; 14. 18; 15. 29; 16. 7, 12, 34; 17. 16; II. 9. 36; 10. 10; 14. 25; 17. 13, 23; 21. 10; 24. 2; 1 Sam. 28. 15, 17; *al.*

54. וכפיו וג׳] 'With his hands spread forth &c.'; a circumstantial clause, giving further detail as to Solomon's attitude whilst kneeling. Cf. *v.* 22.

55. קול גדול] Accus. of closer specification, defining the *manner* of the action described by ויברך. Cf. Ps. 3. 5 קולי אל י׳ אקרא; 142. 2. Ew. § 279[d].

56. אשר נתן מנוחה לעמו] Cf. Deut. 12. 9 לא באתם עד עתה אל המנוחה; Ps. 95. 11 אם יבאון אל מנוחתי.

ככל אשר דבר] *Ch.* 5. 26 *note.*

לא נפל דבר אחד] So Josh. 21. 43; 23. 14 (both D^2); cf. II. 10. 10. The use of the Hiph'il is similar: '*suffer to fall*' (though not of *Yahwe's* words) 1 Sam. 3. 19; Est. 6. 10.

57. יהוה אלהינו] So *vv.* 59, 61, 65; II. 18. 22; 19. 19; י׳ אלהיך *ch.* 1. 17; 2. 3 (R^D); 10. 9; 13. 6, 21; 17. 12; 18. 10; י׳ אלהיכם II. 17. 39; 23. 21 (both R^D). The phrases י׳ אלהיך, י׳ אלהינו (most

frequent), י׳ אלהיכם are very characteristic of Deuteronomy, occurring more than three hundred times. In D² of Joshua there are four occurrences of י׳ אלהיך, twenty-seven occurrences of י׳ אלהיכם. Elsewhere in Hexateuch:—J, E, JE י׳ אלהינו nine times, viz. Ex. 3. 18; 5. 3; 8. 22, 23; 10. 25, 26; Josh. 18. 6; 24. 17, 24; י׳ אלהיך twelve times, viz. Gen. 27. 20; Ex. 15. 26 (D?); 20. 2, 5, 7, 10, 12; 23. 19; 32. 4, 8; 34. 24, 26; י׳ אלהיכם six times, viz. Ex. 8. 24; 10. 8, 16, 17; 23. 25; Josh. 4. 5: P י׳ אלהינו three times, viz. Ex. 8. 6; Josh. 22. 19, 29; י׳ אלהיכם seven times, viz. Num. 10. 9, and in the phrase אני י׳ אלהיכם Ex. 6. 7; 16. 12; Lev. 11. 44; Num. 10. 10; 15. 41 (twice): H י׳ אלהיכם twice, viz. Lev. 23. 28, 40; אני י׳ אלהיכם twenty-one times, viz. Lev. 18. 2, 4, 30; 19. 2, 3, 4, 10, 25, 31, 34, 36; 20. 7, 24; 23. 22, 43; 24. 22; 25. 17, 38, 55; 26. 1, 13. In other books the phrases occur here and there, but not 120 times in all. Cf. Dri. *Deut.* lxxix.

58. להטות לבבנו אליו] Cf. Josh. 24. 23ᵇ (perhaps added to E by D²).

ללכת בכל דרכיו ולשמר וג׳] *Ch.* 2. 3, 4 *note*.

ומשפטיו] LXX, Luc. omit, probably through oversight. With MT. cf. Deut. 26. 17; 30. 16, where precisely the same enumeration is made.

59. ויהיו דברי . . . קרבים] Contrast Ps. 22. 2 רחוק מישועתי דברי שאגתי.

ומשפט עמו] So Luc., Vulg., Pesh., Targ. LXX omits through oversight.

דבר יום ביומו] Lit. 'matter of a day in its day'; so RV. 'as every day shall require.' The idiom is not infrequent, being used e. g. of the daily allowance of Jehoiachin at the court of the king of Babylon, II. 25. 30 (‖ Jer. 52. 34); and of that of Daniel and his friends, Dan. 1. 5; of the manna gathered by the people, Ex. 16. 4; or again of the daily burden imposed by the Egyptian task-masters, Ex. 5. 13, 19.

60. למען דעת וג׳] Cf. Josh. 4. 24 (D²). On כל עמי הארץ cf. *v.* 43 *note*.

כי י׳ הוא האלהים אין עוד] Deut. 4. 35, 39. Cf. also the exclamation of the populace upon the issue of the trial between Elijah and the false prophets, *ch.* 18. 39.

61. והיה לבבכם שלם וג׳] Cf. *ch.* 11. 4; 15. 3, 14 (all R[D]). LXX, Luc., Vulg. suggest לְבָבֵנוּ for לבבכם; probably an alteration suggested by the following אלהינו.

י׳ אלהינו] *Note* on *v.* 57.

ללכת וג׳] *Ch.* 2. 3, 4 *note.*

כיום הזה] *Ch.* 3. 6 *note.*

62. לפני יהוה] Luc. ἐνώπιον Κυρίου τοῦ Θεοῦ, perhaps under the influence of י׳ אלהינו *v.* 57.

63. וצאן . . . אלף] LXX omits.

64. את חלבי השלמים] 'The fat *or* choice portions of the peace-offerings.' So Lev. 6. 5; 2 Chr. 29. 35; cf. Gen. 4. 4 מבכרות צאנו ומחלבהן 'of the firstlings of his flock and of their *fat pieces*.' The slight variations of LXX, Luc. in the enumeration of the sacrifices are due to error in transmission of the Greek text.

65. בעת ההיא] The phrase is that of R[D]. Cf. *ch.* 14. 1 *note*. In Deuteronomy בעת הַהִוא is of frequent occurrence in the retrospects, when events more or less contemporaneous are co-ordinated by the writer; 1. 9, 16, 18; 2. 34; 3. 4, 8, 12, 18, 21, 23; 4. 14; 5. 5; 9. 20; 10. 1, 8. Possibly also ביום ההוא *v.* 64[a] may mark the hand of R[D], though this phrase is not so characteristic. In *ch.* 13. 3; 16. 16; 22. 35; II. 3. 6 the expression is quite as likely to be part of the old narrative. On בימים ההם R[D] cf. II. 10. 32.

הֶחָג] '*The* Feast'; i. e. probably the Feast of Tabernacles as the most important festival of the year; cf. Neh. 8. 14; *v.* 2 *note.*

מלבוא חמת וג׳] The whole kingdom from extreme north to extreme south. Jeroboam II is said to have restored the kingdom of Israel מלבוא חמת עד ים הערבה II. 14. 25; cf. Am. 6. 14. לבוא lit. '*at the entry of*'; לבוא חמת Num. 13. 21; 34. 8; Josh. 13. 5; Judg. 3. 3; 1 Chr. 13. 5; Ezek. 47. 20; 48. 1; לבוא מִדְבָּרָה 1 Chr. 5. 9; לבוא מצרים 2 Chr. 26. 8; לבוא צְדָדָה Ezek. 47. 15. On נחל מצרים, the *Wady el-Arîsh*, cf. *ch.* 5. 1 *note.*

י׳ אלהינו] *Note* on *v.* 57. After this LXX, Luc. have the words ἐν τῷ οἴκῳ ᾧ ᾠκοδόμησεν, ἐσθίων καὶ πίνων καὶ εὐφραινόμενος (Luc. adds *καὶ αἰνῶν*) *ἐνώπιον κυρίου θεοῦ ἡμῶν*, i.e. according to Klo. בַּבַּיִת אֲשֶׁר בָּנָה אֹכֵל וְשֹׁתֶה וְשָׂמֵחַ וּמְהַלֵּל לִפְנֵי י׳ אֱלֹהֵינוּ; so substantially Th., Benz., Oort. These words have the ring of genuineness, and may easily have been omitted in MT. through homoioteleuton.

שבעת . . . יום] LXX has here simply *ἑπτὰ ἡμέρας*, i.e. שִׁבְעַת יָמִים, the remaining words ושבעת . . . יום being omitted. The manner in which the next verse continues, ביום השמיני וג׳, LXX, Luc. *καὶ ἐν τῇ ἡμέρᾳ κ.τ.λ.*, establishes the genuineness of the shorter שבעת ימים, and points to the conclusion that the remainder of the sentence is an insertion in accordance with 2 Chr. 7. 9, probably due to R[P]. So Th., Klo., Kamp., Benz., Kit., Oort.

66. ביום] LXX, Luc., Pesh., Vulg. correctly presuppose וּבַיּוֹם. The omission of the ו was made when the gloss was added at the end of the previous verse.

ויברכו את המלך] LXX *καὶ εὐλόγησεν αὐτόν*, 'and they blessed him,' i.e. *the king*, as in MT. The plural verb with הָעָם as subj. is rendered in LXX by sing., as e.g. in *ch.* 1. 39, 40; 12. 30; *al.* Luc., however, taking *καὶ εὐλόγησεν αὐτόν* in the sense 'and he blessed *it*,' i.e. *the people*, makes the addition *καὶ εὐλόγησαν καὶ αὐτοὶ τὸν βασιλέα*, and thus exhibits a double rendering.

שמחים וטובי לב] So Est. 5. 9. טובי לב has the meaning *cheerful* or *merry*; Prov. 15. 15 טוב לב משתה תמיד 'the merry-hearted has a continual feast.' Cf. Judg. 16. 25 Q're ויהי כְּטוֹב לבם; Eccl. 9. 7 שתה בלב טוב יינך; and the verbal phrase יטב לב פ׳ 'one's heart is cheerful,' *ch.* 21. 7; Judg. 18. 20; 19. 6, 9; Ruth 3. 7. טוּב לבב (לב) 'cheerfulness of heart,' Deut. 28. 47; Isa. 65. 14.

9. 1–9. *Solomon's Second Vision.*

Ch. 9. 1–9 = 2 Chr. 7. 12–22.

1–9. This account is coloured throughout by the spirit of Deuteronomy, and, owing to the terms in which it speaks of the exile of Israel and the destruction of the Temple (*vv.* 7–9; cf. emendation in *v.* 8), is regarded by Kue., Wellh., Sta., Kamp., Benz., Kit. as the work of R[D2] in exilic times.

Such a conclusion, however, is by no means inevitable. The

expression of *v.* 3 לשום שמי שם עד עולם וג׳ goes quite as far to prove a pre-exilic position, as do the words of *vv.* 6–9 to argue a post-exilic point of view; nor are the terms of these latter verses so definite as to forbid the opinion that they were penned by R^D in the reign of Josiah; cf. *note* on *ch.* 8. 46–49 under *vv.* 14–66 *note.* If *vv.* 7–9 *do* imply an exilic standpoint, *vv.* 6–9 (and not the whole section) will belong to R^D2, *vv.* 1–5 to R^D.

1. את כל חשק ש׳ אשר חפץ וג׳] 'All the pleasure of Solomon which he wished to do.' The substantive חֵשֶׁק only occurs again Isa. 21. 4 נֶשֶׁף חִשְׁקִי 'the twilight of my pleasure,' and in *v.* 19, || 2 Chr. 8. 6, with the cognate verb, את חֵשֶׁק ש׳ אשר חָשַׁק לבנות וג׳. Pesh., Targ., which render in *v.* 1 ܘܟܠܗ ܨܒܝܢܗ ܕܫܠܝܡܘܢ ܕܨܒܐ ܠܡܥܒܕ, וית כל רעות שלמה דאיתרעי למעבד, and similarly in *v.* 19, appear therefore in the former verse, as in the latter, to have read חָשַׁק for חָפֵץ, probably correctly. LXX, Luc. καὶ πᾶσαν τὴν πραγματείαν Σ. ὅσα ἠθέλησεν ποιῆσαι; Vulg. paraphrastically, *et omne quod optaverat et voluerat facere.*

3. את תפלתך ואת תחנתך וג׳] The expressions of R^D in *ch.* 8; cf. *vv.* 33, 38, 54; *al.* LXX τῆς φωνῆς τῆς προσευχῆς σου κ.τ.λ., i.e. אֶת־קול תפלתך וג׳; but Luc., Vulg., Pesh., Targ. as MT.

After התחננתה לפני LXX, Luc. add (Luc. ἰδοὺ) πεποίηκα (LXX σοι) κατὰ πᾶσαν τὴν προσευχήν σου, i.e. הִנֵּה עָשִׂיתִי כְּכָל־תְּפִלָּתְךָ; so Th., Klo., Oort. The words are probably genuine; cf. *ch.* 3. 12 הנה עשיתי כדבריך.

הקדשתי] '*I have hallowed,*' referring to the previous manifestation of Yahwe's glory in the house, *ch.* 8. 10; or else a perfect of certitude referring to time really future, as in English we might say 'I hallow.' For this latter explanation cf. Dri. *Tenses*, § 13.

לשום שמי שם] So *ch.* 11. 36; 14. 21; II. 21. 4, 7 (referring to I. 9. 3) all R^D. Cf. להיות שמי שם *ch.* 8. 16 *note.* In Deuteronomy the ordinary phrase is לְשַׁכֵּן שמו שם 'to cause his name to dwell there'; 12. 11; 14. 23; 16. 2, 6, 11; 26. 2. לשום שמו שם only in 12. 5, 21; 14. 24.

והיו עיני ולבי שם] In response to *ch.* 8. 29, 52.

כל הימים] 'All the days,' i.e. 'continually,' as a parallel to

עד עולם. So *ch.* 11. 36, 39; II. 8. 19; 17. 37 (all R^D). The phrase is very characteristic of Deut., occurring 4. 40; 5. 26; 6. 24; 11. 1; 14. 23; 18. 5; 19. 9; 28. 29, 33; cf. also Josh. 4. 24 (D^2); 1 Sam. 2. 32, 35 (Deut. redactor); Jer. 31. 35; 32. 39; 33. 18; 35. 19. Thus the expression *used absolutely* appears to be purely Deuteronomic. In Deut. 4. 10; 12. 1; 31. 13; *ch.* 8. 40 it is defined and to some extent limited by the added words אשר אתם (הם) חיים על האדמה. Upon כל הימים used in a strictly limited sense of the lifetime of an individual (non-Deut.) cf. *ch.* 5. 15 *note.*

4. אם תלך לפני] *Ch.* 2. 4 *note.*

כאשר הלך דוד] *Ch.* 3. 14 *note.*

בתם לבב] Gen. 20. 5, 6 (E); Ps. 78. 72; 101. 2†.

צויתיך] LXX, Luc. ἐνετειλάμην αὐτῷ, referring the clause to David. Probably a later correction.

חקי] LXX, Luc., Vulg., Pesh., ‖ 2 Chr. 7. 17 read וְחֻקַּי correctly. So Th., Klo., Kamp., Benz., Kit.

חקי ומשפטי תשמר] *Ch.* 2. 3, 4 *note.*

5. כסא ממלכתך] Deut. 17. 18; 2 Sam. 7. 13 (Deut. redactor); 2 Chr. 23. 20†; cf. Hag. 2. 22. Elsewhere כסא הַמְּלוּכָה (once; *ch.* 1. 46), כסא מַלְכוּת, כסא הַמְּלָכִים (מְלָכִים).

כאשר דברתי על דוד] 'As I spake *concerning* David.' So *ch.* 2. 4 אשר דבר עלי. Several Codd., however, read אל דוד '*unto* David,' and this is also suggested by LXX, Luc., Vulg., Pesh., Targ.

לא יכרת וג׳] *Ch.* 2. 4 *note.*

6. אם שוב תשבון . . . מאחרי] Cf. Num. 14. 43; 32. 15 (both JE); Josh. 22. 16, 18, 23, 29 (P?); 1 Sam. 15. 11; Jer. 3. 19.

ולא תשמרו מצותי וג׳] *Ch.* 2. 3, 4 *note.*

אשר נתתי לפניכם] Cf. Jer. 9. 12; 26. 4 (referring to תורתי); 44. 10 (בתורתי ובחקתַי).

והלכתם . . . להם] So exactly ‖ 2 Chr. 7. 19; Josh. 23. 16 (D^2); cf. Deut. 11. 16; 17. 3. The phrase עבד אלהים אחרים occurs also Deut. 7. 4; 13. 7, 14; 28. 36, 64; Jer. 16. 13; Judg. 10. 13 (Deut. compiler); Josh. 24. 2, 16 (E); 1 Sam. 8. 8; 26. 19; cf. Jer. 44. 3. אלהים אחרים with עבד, not preceding as governing verb, but closely following with suffix in reference, is found *v.* 9 (‖ 2 Chr. 7. 22);

II. 17. 35; Deut. 8. 19; 13. 3; 28. 14; 30. 17; 31. 20; Jer. 11. 10; 13. 10; 16. 11; 22. 9; 25. 6; 35. 15; Judg. 2. 19 (Deut. compiler). אלהים אחרים without עבד:—*ch.* 11. 4, 10; 14. 9; II. 17. 7, 37, 38; 22. 17 (|| 2 Chr. 34. 25) all R[D]; II. 5. 17; Deut. 5. 7; 6. 14; 11. 28; 18. 20; 31. 18; Jer. 1. 16; 7. 6, 9, 18; 19. 4, 13; 32. 29; 44. 5, 8, 15; Judg. 2. 12, 17 (Deut. compiler); Ex. 20. 3 (E); 23. 13 (J); Hos. 3. 1; 2 Chr. 28. 25†.

7. אשר נתתי להם] Cf. *note* on *ch.* 8. 34.

אשלח מעל פני] Cf. Jer. 15. 1 שַׁלַּח מֵעַל־פָּנַי וְיֵצֵאוּ (reference to הָעָם הַזֶּה).

למשל ולשנינה] So || 2 Chr. 7. 20; Deut. 28. 37; Jer. 24. 9, these being all the occurrences of שנינה. משל thus used denotes a *proverb* or *byword* used in mockery, שנינה a *pointed*, *witty*, or *spiteful saying*, the speech and its object being in both cases identified. משל alone in this sense Ps. 44. 15; 69. 12; Ezek. 14. 8 (לִמְשָׁלִים).

8. והבית הזה יהיה עליון] This can only mean 'And this house shall be most high,' and we cannot, with RV., force the language and render 'And though this house be so high.' || 2 Chr. 7. 21 והבית הזה אשר היה עליון is an obvious correction. LXX supports MT. καὶ ὁ οἶκος οὗτος ἔσται ὁ ὑψηλός, and this in Luc., for the sake of gaining some sort of sense, has been altered into καὶ ὁ οἶκος οὗτος ὁ ὑψηλός, ἔσται κ.τ.λ.

Pesh., however, in reading ܚܪܒ '*desolate*' in place of עליון, suggests an original והבית הזה יהיה עִיִּים 'And this house shall be *ruinous heaps*.' This, as giving excellent sense and supposing merely a small corruption in the MT., may reasonably be regarded as the true text: cf. Mic. 3. 12 וירושלם עיין תהיה (עיין for assonance with ציון), || Jer. 26. 18 (עיים); Ps. 79. 1 (לעיים). Targ. וביתא הדין דהוה עילי יהי חריב appears to embody a double rendering; but Th., Klo., Kamp. suppose that it represents the original text:— וְהַבַּיִת הַזֶּה אֲשֶׁר הָיָה עֶלְיוֹן יִהְיֶה לְעִיִּין. Such a text, however, would imply that the Chronicler copied אשר היה עליון from Kings before textual corruption set in; and in this case, why did he not also transcribe יהיה לעיין which must have existed in his MS. of Kings? Or are we to suppose that he *did* copy these words, and that subsequently through coincidence this reference to עיין disappeared both from Kings and Chronicles?

Vulg. *Et domus haec erit in exemplum* is a paraphrase of which it is impossible to determine the precise original.

כל עבר עליו וג׳] Cf. Jer. 18. 16 (reference to the land of Israel); 19. 8 (Jerusalem); 49. 17 (Edom); 50. 13 (Babylon); Zeph. 2. 15 (Nineveh). Similar also is Lam. 2. 15.

ואמרו וג׳] For this question put by the heathen from outside, together with its answer in *v.* 9, cf. Deut. 29. 23–27; Jer. 22. 8 *f.*

9. ויחזיקו באלהים אחרים] The phrase occurs only here and in ‖ 2 Chr. 7. 22. Deut. above quoted has וילכו ויעבדו אלהים אחרים וישתחוו להם; Jer. וישתחוו לאלהים אחרים ויעבדום.

9. 10—10. 29. *Further details of Solomon's magnificence and wisdom.*

Chh. 9. 10—10. 29=2 Chr. 8. 1—9. 24, 27, 28. 2 Chr. 1. 14–17.

Mainly a series of short notices drawn from the same sources as *chh.* 4—5. 14. The originals appear to have been cut up and pieced together with no great skill; but whether the arrangement throughout is due to R^D, or later hands have employed themselves in altering the sequence of the account, it is impossible to determine. In LXX, Luc. the arrangement is somewhat different, but scarcely superior, to that of MT.; *v.* 24^a (אָז for אך; add בַּיָּמִים הָהֵם after לה), *vv.* 10–14 (om. ויהי מקצה *v.* 10^a), *vv.* 26–28 (*v.* 26^a being connected on to *v.* 14 by addition of the words ὑπὲρ οὗ after καὶ ναῦν—a later device), *ch.* 10. 1–22; *ch.* 9. 15, 17^b–22; *ch.* 10. 23–25; *v.* 26 combined with *ch.* 5. 6; *ch.* 5. 1^a; *ch.* 10. 27–29.

One single original document appears to be represented by *ch.* 9. 10, 17, 18, 19, 15, 20, 21, 22, 23, and these verses may very well have originally taken this order, the completion of Solomon's building operations being first narrated, and then followed by an account of the forced levy raised to carry out these works. After *v.* 23 there probably followed in the original a list of the *names* of the שרי הנצבים. The statement of *v.* 24^b, connected by R^D to *v.* 24^a by אז (*ch.* 3. 16 *note*), is probably from the same document.

Next to the account of the king's building activity—his most important work, there would naturally follow mention of his achievement next in importance—the provision of an efficient shipping for the increase of his wealth from external sources. This succeeds in *ch.* 9. 26–28; *ch.* 10. 11. But reference to the ships naturally leads up to mention of the imports introduced by their means, as we see in *ch.* 9. 28; *ch.* 10. 11, and the use to which these rare and valuable materials were put. Thus there follows *ch.* 10. 12, 14–22. The general subject of imports suggests allusion to a specially important item—horses from Egypt (or Muṣri), apparently first introduced into the kingdom of Solomon in any considerable numbers:—*ch.* 10. 26 (with *ch.* 5. 6; see *note* on 4. 20—5. 14), 28, 29.

Thus the disturbing factors introduced into this main account are seen to be *ch.* 9. 11–13, 14, 16, 24ᵃ, 25; *ch.* 10. 1–10, 13, 23–25, 27. Notice in *ch.* 9. 11, 16, 24 the awkward pluperfects pointed by the order—subj., verb, obj., חירם מלך צר נשא את ש׳, פרעה מלך מצרים עלה וג׳, אך בת פרעה עלתה וג׳, and marking the passages as mere *excerpts* from sources which in describing a regular sequence of events must have read וַיִּנַּשֵּׂא חירם, וַיַּעַל פרעה, וַתַּעַל בת פרעה. In *v.* 11ᵇ אז יתן וג׳ cannot represent the apodosis of *v.* 10, since אז used in this connexion in place of ו *consec.* would be quite without analogy (cf. *ch.* 8. 1 *note*). Moreover, even if *v.* 11ᵇ *could* form the apodosis, the parenthesis *v.* 11ᵃ would come in with very great awkwardness. Verse 16 has already been discussed (*note* on 4. 20—5. 14), and together with *ch.* 3. 1 has been seen to fall into its proper position after *v.* 14 of *ch.* 5. From the same source would seem to be derived *v.* 24ᵃ, while *v.* 25, though clearly alien to its immediate context, cannot definitely be assigned to any special source. *Ch.* 10. 1–10, 13 is an ancient narrative introduced at this point to illustrate Solomon's wealth and wisdom, much in the same way as *ch.* 3. 16–28 serves to depict his discernment in judgement; and the two stories may very possibly be derived from the same source. Finally, *vv.* 23–25, 27 of *ch.* 10, couched in vague and generalizing statement, are probably relatively late in origin, and are here introduced to give the finishing touch to the picture of Solomon's prosperity.

11. נִשָּׂא] For נִשֵּׂא 2 Sam. 5. 12. On the confusion of verbs ל״א and ל״ה cf. *note* on *ch.* 17. 14.

אז יתן וג׳] On the use of אז as employed by R[D] cf. *ch.* 3. 16 *note*. In place of this notice we find in the parallel account 2 Chr. 8. 1, 2 the statement that Ḥiram gave Solomon certain cities, and that Solomon built these and settled Israelite inhabitants in them; an explanation of the transaction probably grounded upon objection to the idea that Solomon parted with any portion of his territory. Jos. (*Ant.* viii. 5, § 3) states that when Ḥiram had inspected the cities and found them displeasing, he sent word to Solomon that he did not need them.

ארץ הגליל] 'Land of *the circuit*' or '*district*,' the title applied to a region in Naphtali on the north border of the kingdom of Israel, and adjoining Ḥiram's dominions. Cf. Josh. 20. 7; 21. 32; 1 Chr. 6. 61, where קֶדֶשׁ is mentioned as belonging to this district. In Isa. 8. 23 the phrase גְּלִיל הַגּוֹיִם 'district of the nations' is applied to the land of Zebulon and Naphtali, and would seem to imply that the population was for the most part non-Israelitish. הַגְּלִילָה Ezek. 47. 8†; גְּלִילוֹת Josh. 13. 2 (ג׳ הפלשתים); 18. 17; 22. 10, 11 (ג׳ הירדן); Joel 4. 4†, are used more generally as geographical terms.

13. ארץ כבול] The name is obviously regarded as employed to express Ḥiram's dissatisfaction with the cities. Thus Ew.'s explanation is probably correct, that the name is connected with כ + בַּל '*like nothing*,' so 'good for nothing,' 'worthless.' This does not embody a true etymology, but is intended for a witty play of words suggested by similarity of sound; cf. Gen. 11. 9 בָּבֶל connected with בלל as if for בַּלְבֶּל; Mic. 1. 10–15 בְּגַת אַל־תַּגִּידוּ play upon גת — נגד, בְּבֵית לְעַפְרָה עָפָר הִתְפַּלָּשְׁתִּי, לָרֶכֶשׁ — לָכִישׁ, אַכְזִיב — אַכְזָב, מָרֵשָׁה — הַיֹּרֵשׁ; *al.* Jos. (*Ant.* viii. 5, § 3) explains μεθερμηνευόμενον γὰρ τὸ Χαβαλὼν κατὰ Φοινίκων γλῶτταν, 'οὐκ ἀρέσκον' σημαίνει, a statement which seems to have no further foundation than the inference to be drawn from *v.* 12[b]. LXX, Luc. in interpreting Ὅριον, must have read גְּבוּל. Talm., *Shabbath*, 54[b],

gives the fanciful derivation שהיו בה בני אדם שמכובלין בכסף ובזהב '(A land) in which men dwelt who were *bound* with silver and gold (fetters).' No modern interpretation commends itself.

כבול is mentioned, Josh. 19. 37, as one of the towns assigned to Asher; and Jos. (*Vit.* 42–44) speaks of Χαβωλώ in the district of Ptolemais forty stadia west of Jotaparta. The town is identified by Rob. (*BR.* iii. 88) with the modern *Kabûl.* Thus it may be supposed that the name of one of the twenty cities was given by Ḥiram to the whole district.

עד היום הזה] Cf. *ch.* 8. 8 *note.*

15. המס אשר העלה] *Ch.* 5. 27 *note.*

המלוא] Part of the fortifications of the city of David, existing in the old Jebusite city (2 Sam. 5. 9; ‖ 1 Chr. 11. 8), and mentioned, as here, in connexion with the walling up of the breaches of the city (*ch.* 11. 27), and the repair of the wall and towers by Hezekiah (2 Chr. 32. 5). Joash is said to have been murdered at בֵּית מִלֹּא (II. 12. 21), but it is not clear whether this was at Jerusalem; and in Judg. 9. 6, 20 a בית מלוא is mentioned in connexion with the city of Shechem.

The word is usually connected with the root מלא *be filled,* and interpreted as meaning *something which fills or banks up* (a Pi'el form causat. of Qal), and thus *an earthwork.* So Targ. renders מיליתא, this word being elsewhere used to translate Hebrew סֹלְלָה; 2 Sam. 20. 15 וישפכו סללה אל העיר=וצברו מיליתא על קרתא; II. 19. 32; Jer. 32. 24; *al.* Cf. also Talm. מוליא 'filled-up ground *or* mound,' *Baba bathra,* 54[a] שקיל מוליא ושדי בנוציא 'If one takes *earth from the mound* and throws it on the low ground.' This derivation cannot, however, be regarded as certain. The word may, as Moore (*Judg.* 9. 6) suggests, be Canaanite in origin; and it seems reasonable to suppose that the Millo was not a simple earthwork, but rather a massive fortress or tower built into that part of the city wall where such a protection was specially needed. So LXX, Luc. render ἡ ἄκρα. מגדל שכם, Judg. 9. 46, may thus perhaps be identical with בית מלוא of 9. 6, 20.

חצר] A chief city of North Canaan belonging to King Jabin, and captured and burnt by Joshua (Josh. 11. 1, 10; *al.*). The city was not far from the waters of Merom, the modern lake of *Hûleh* (Josh. 11. 5), and was afterwards assigned to the tribe of Naphtali (Josh. 19. 36). In Judg. 4 a second Jabin king of Ḥazor is mentioned as oppressing Israel, and as conquered by Deborah and Barak. The site is not well ascertained. Buhl (*Geogr.* 236) finds the name preserved in the modern name of the valley *Merj-el-Ḥaḍîre*, S.S.W. of *Ḳedes* (קֶדֶשׁ Josh. 19. 37), on the N. side of the *Wadi 'Auba* which runs into the lake of *Hûleh*. Cf. also Baed. 297.

מגדו] *Ch.* 4. 12 *note.*

גזר] A town on the border of Ephraim assigned by Joshua as a Levitical city (Josh. 16. 3; 21. 21). Horam king of Gezer came to the assistance of Lachish against Joshua, but was defeated and his army utterly destroyed by the Israelites (Josh. 10. 33). The city of Gezer, however, held out against the invader, and seems to have remained in the hands of its Canaanite (and Perizzite, LXX) inhabitants until the days of Solomon (Josh. 16. 10). The site of Gezer has been discovered by M. Clermont-Ganneau in the modern *Tell-Jezer* about eighteen miles W.N.W. of Jerusalem. On this and on the inscription תחמגזר, i.e. probably 'the boundary of Gezer,' which confirms the authenticity of the site, cf. *PEF.* 1873, 78*f.*; 1875, 74*f.*; Hastings, *BD. s.v.*; Smith, *Hist. Geogr.* 215*ff.*

16. שִׁלֻּחִים] 'A dowry' given when the wife is 'sent away' from the home of her parents; cf. Mic. 1. 14, and the use of the verb שִׁלַּח Gen. 24. 59.

17. בית חרן תחתון] Also בית חורון הַתַּחְתּוֹן ‖ 2 Chr. 8. 5; so called in distinction from (עליון) בית חורון הָעֶלְיוֹן 1 Chr. 7. 24; *al.* בית חורן without closer specification also occurs: Josh. 10. 10, 11; 18. 14; *al.* In Josh. 10. 10, 11, LXX reads Ὡρωνείν i.e. חֹרֹנַיִם 'the two Ḥorons'; so 2 Sam. 13. 34 ἐκ τῆς ὁδοῦ τῆς Ὡρωνήν stands in place of the corrupt מדרך אחריו, and is adopted by Wellh., Dri., Budde. Elsewhere (Isa. 15. 5; *al.*) חרנים is a Moabite city. The two Beth-ḥorons were upon the boundary line of Ephraim (Josh. 16. 3, 5), and the pass running between them was the scene of Joshua's pursuit of

the five Amorite kings who made a combined attack upon Gibeon (Josh. 10. 10, 11). In modern times they have been with certainty identified, the lower with *Beit 'Ûr et-taḥta*, the upper with *Beit 'Ûr el-fôqa*, the former being about one mile north-west of the latter, which is some three or four miles north-west of Gibeon,—*el-Jîb*. See Rob. *BR*. iii. 250 *f.*, *PEF. Mem.* iii. 86.

18. בעלת] ‖ 2 Chr. 8. 6. Mentioned Josh. 19. 44† as a city assigned to Dan. The conjectural site is *Bel'aîn* about two and a-half miles north of *Beit 'Ûr et-taḥta*. *PEF. Mem.* ii. 296.

תַּ֫מֹר] Q're תַּדְמֹר, i.e. Palmyra the modern *Tudmur*, is supported by all Verss.[1], and by ‖ 2 Chr. 8. 4 (so all Verss.). The other towns, however, mentioned *vv.* 17, 18 are all in South Palestine, and in Ezek. 47. 19; 48. 28 we have a תָּמָר cited as being in the extreme south of the land—פְּאַת נֶגֶב תֵּימָנָה. Thus in spite of ‖ 2 Chr., which connects Solomon's building of Tadmor with a successful campaign against Ḥamath-zobah, Kt. in our passage seems to deserve the preference. So Bö., Th., Kamp., Benz., Kit.; Smith, *Hist. Geogr.* 270 *note* 2, 580 *note* 2.

במדבר בארץ] 'In the wilderness in the land'; a vague and pointless statement. בארץ cannot be intended to distinguish the city from another of the same name outside the land, for in such a case a closer definition of the locality would be expected. Vulg. *in terra solitudinis*, Pesh. ܒܐܪܥܐ ܕܡܕܒܪܐ suggest בְּאֶרֶץ הַמִּדְבָּר 'in the desert country.' The phrase בארץ מדבר occurs only in the poetical passage Deut. 32. 10 and in Prov. 21. 19, but might reasonably be used in plain prose. Targ. follows MT., while LXX, Luc. (*ch.* 10. 23) omit. Very probably בארץ is the corruption of some place-name. So Bö. בְּמִדְבַּר פָּארָן; plausible, but rather far towards the south. Kit. בַּמִּדְבָּר בְּאֶרֶץ יְהוּדָה. Perles (*Analekten zur Textkritik des A.T.*, 22), following Eichhorn, regards בארץ as a contraction of בָּאֲרָם צוֹבָה 'באר' צ, upon the view that Q're תדמר is correct, and comparing 2 Chr. 8. 3, 4.

19. ואת חשק וג'] Cf. *v.* 1 *note.*

---

[1] LXX Ἰεθερμάθ, i.e. את תרמר, ד being misread ר. The passage in LXX occurs *ch.* 10. 23.

20, 21. כל העם . . . בניהם] This form of *casus pendens*, where a substantive is reinforced by the pronominal suffix of a following substantive, is idiomatic and frequent. 1 Sam. 2. 10 יהוה יֵחַתּוּ מְרִיבָו; Gen. 17. 15 שרי אשתך . . . את שְׁמָהּ; 34. 8 שכם . . . נפשו. Cf. other instances in Dri. *Tenses*, § 197, 2.

21. בניהם אשר נתרו . . . ויעלם] The predicate introduced by ו *consecutive* after the preceding *accusativus pendens* בניהם; a rather uncommon construction. Cf. *ch.* 12. 17 ובני ישראל הישבים בערי יהודה וימלך עליהם רחבעם; *ch.* 15. 13 וגם את מעכה אמו ויסרה מגבירה; II. 16. 14; Dri. *Tenses*, § 127 *a*.

מַס־עֹבֵד] 'A forced levy of bondmen.' עבד is sing. collective. So Gen. 49. 15; Josh. 16. 10†.

עד היום הזה] Cf. *ch.* 8. 8 *note*.

22. ומבני ישראל וג׳] But cf. the statement of *ch.* 5. 27, and see *ch.* 4. 6 *note*.

שלישיו] A word of unknown meaning and derivation. LXX which here omits (*Cod.* A, Luc. τρισσοί) elsewhere usually renders τριστάτης, a term to which Origen on Ex. 14. 7 gives as one explanation among others the meaning, *one of three warriors in a chariot;* Εἰς τὰς χρείας τῶν πολέμων ἅρματα ἐποίουν μεγάλα, ὡς καὶ τρεῖς χωρεῖν· ἵν᾽ ὁ μὲν εἷς ἡνιοχῇ, οἱ δὲ δύο πολεμῶσιν. So Greg. Nyss.; cf. the more precise rendering of LXX in Ex. 15. 4 ἀναβάτας τριστάτας. This explanation, which appears to depend upon the context of Ex. 14. 7, has been adopted by some moderns, but is purely conjectural, and is rightly opposed by Dillmann, who points out that the ancient chariot as figured on the monuments has usually but two occupants—the driver and the fighting man, and that only kings and the highest officers would have had in addition a third man as shield-bearer. It may be added that in accordance with Ex. 14. 7 וְשָׁלִשִׁם עַל־כֻּלּוֹ *third man* could not describe a spare man acting as armour-bearer, but would denote the most important occupant of the chariot, viz. the combatant. This meaning, however, is opposed to the use of the word of an officer immediately attendant upon a king, whether in a chariot (II. 9. 25) or elsewhere (II. 7. 2, 17, 19; 15. 25).

Derivation thus failing, the most that can be said is that, judging from the context of our passage (׳ש next to שרי רכבו) II. 9. 25; 10. 25 (שלישים coupled with רצים 'foot-runners' as though in contra-distinction); Ex. 14. 7, שלישים may have been a class of warriors usually connected with chariots; but it is with wisdom that AV., RV. 'captains' agree with Vulg. *duces*, Pesh. ܓܢܒܪܘܗܝ, Targ. גיברוהי in rendering by a very general term.

23. חמשים וחמש מאות] LXX (section following *ch.* 2. 35) gives the number as *τρεῖς χιλιάδες καὶ ἑξακόσιοι*, Luc. *τρεῖς χιλιάδες καὶ ἑπτακόσιοι*—probably an arbitrary alteration of the translator with the view of bringing the number into correspondence with that of *ch.* 5. 30 with which our verse is closely parallel in wording. The other Verss. support MT. 550.

Possibly after the completion of the Temple and Palace the number of the שרי הנצבים may have been greatly diminished, and in any case it is easier to believe that the exact parallelism of the Greek translator is a change for the sake of conformity, than that *vice versâ* the alteration was made in MT. for no apparent reason. || 2 Chr. 8. 10 gives the number as חמשים ומאתים, a variation explained by Kennicott as a misreading רנ for דנ; but such a method of notation in early OT. MSS. is highly improbable. Cf. *ch.* 6. 1 *note*.

24. אך] Very difficult. Th. explains '*As soon as* . . . then he built, &c.' אך has here a restrictive sense *only* or *scarcely*, and the meaning *as soon as* is determined by the following אז which marks the point of time immediately following that denoted by אך עלתה. But the case is scarcely parallel to the only two examples which can be compared, Gen. 27. 30 אך יצא יצא יעקב . . . ועשו אחיו בא, and Judg. 7. 19 אך הקם הקימו את השמרים ויתקעו בשופרות, for in both these passages great stress is laid upon the very immediate sequence in time of the two events described, and to suppose the existence of a similar stress in our passage would be absurd. Moreover, the back reference of אז to אך is opposed to the characteristic usage of this former particle in Kings—its employment with merely vague reference to the period which is being described, and without

distinct attachment to any definite point of time (*ch.* 3. 16 *note*). And further, the change of subject implied in בנה, without mention of the new subject שלמה, is very strange. Thus some slight corruption of the text may reasonably be supposed.

Vulg., Pesh., Targ. seem to agree with MT., except for the addition of שלמה after בנה in Vulg., Pesh.—probably a translator's addition made for the sake of lucidity. LXX, Luc. offer two renderings—the first in the insertion following *ch.* 2. 35, the second in immediate sequence to *ch.* 9. 9. The former translation exactly follows MT., except for reading οὕτως, i.e. probably כֵּן, in place of אַךְ. The latter rendering is somewhat different:—Τότε ἀνήγαγεν Σαλωμὼν τὴν θυγατέρα Φαραὼ ἐκ πόλεως Δαυεὶδ εἰς οἶκον αὐτοῦ ὃν ᾠκοδόμησεν αὐτῷ ἐν ταῖς ἡμέραις ἐκείναις. This agrees closely with the MT. of ‖ 2 Chr. 8. 11; and supposing the LXX translator to have inserted τότε upon his own responsibility or through a misreading אָז for וְאֵת, and also to have read בֵּיתֹה, לֹה for בֵּיתָהּ, לָהּ, we may believe the original text of our passage to have been וְאֶת־בַּת פַּרְעֹה הֶעֱלָה שְׁלֹמֹה מֵעִיר דָּוִד אֶל־בֵּיתָהּ אֲשֶׁר בָּנָה לָהּ בַּיָּמִים הָהֵם. This emendation removes all difficulties above noticed. The אך of MT. will thus be a scribe's error for ואת due to the occurrence of the same two letters in במלאכה the word immediately preceding; and further, it is possible that פרעהעלה may have been copied by mistake for פרעההעלה, and that later on a second scribe, perceiving that עלה must thus refer to בת פרעה, may have altered it into the feminine עלתה.

25. והעלה] 'Used to offer;' frequentative.

והקטיר אתו אשר לפני י׳] Scarcely original. The curious אִתּוֹ cannot be used in place of עָלָיו and refer to the altar (Pesh., Targ., Ges.), nor can we believe (Ew., Th.) that it refers to Solomon;—'He would offer incense *by himself*' (without the intervention of another)[1]. LXX, Luc. (after *ch.* 2. 35) altogether omit the words אתו אשר, and seem simply to have read והקטיר לפני יהוה. So Oort.

[1] Th. cites Gen. 39. 6; Isa. 44. 24 for this use of אִתּוֹ, and regards אשר as a mistaken insertion.

Klo. ingeniously suggests והקטיר אֶת־אִשּׁוֹ לפני י׳ 'and would burn *his fire-offering* before Yahwe'—a very plausible emendation.

ושלם את הבית] RV. 'So he finished the house,' and so all Verss.;—LXX, Luc. καὶ συνετέλεσεν τὸν οἶκον, Vulg. *perfectumque est templum*, Pesh. ܘܫܠܡܗ ܠܒܝܬܐ, Targ. ושלם ית ביתא. It is impossible, however, to explain why the perfect with ו *consecutive* should be thus used, as though the fact narrated were in due sequence to the preceding frequentatives והעלה . . . והקטיר; and moreover such a statement is out of place in this connexion, where events are being recorded which must have taken place only *after* the completion and consecration of the building. Hence Ew. renders 'and he would *take leave of* (*say farewell to*) the house'; Th. 'and he would *completely furnish* the house,' i. e. provide upon each occasion of his visits that all the requirements of the Temple and its services should be fully met. Neither of these translations can be justified by analogy; and it seems not improbable that the letters ושלם are a mistaken repetition of ושלמים in the earlier part of the verse, and את הבית a later addition to form a complete sentence intended to convey the meaning given by the Verss.

26. אשר את אלות] 'Which is *near* Eloth'; an idiomatic use of the preposition in definition of locality. Cf. II. 9. 27 במעלה גור אשר את יבלעם; Judg. 3. 19; 4. 11; Ezek. 43. 8. For the similar use of עִם see *ch.* 1. 9 *note*.

28. ארבע מאות ועשרים] LXX ἑκατὸν εἴκοσι is unsupported by Luc. and the other Verss., all of which agree with MT.

10. 1. לשם יהוה] 'Through the name of Yahwe'; lit. '*at* the name.' The meaning is that the fame of Yahwe's name led to the diffusion of a report concerning the wise and prosperous king who enjoyed His favour and protection; and this is in full accordance with the prominence which the queen in this story assigns to Yahwe as the chooser and supporter of Solomon (*v.* 9). The phrase לשם י׳ occurs elsewhere Josh. 9. 9; Isa. 60. 9; Jer. 3. 17†, and the *nuance* of the preposition is closely similar to that in the expression לקול '*at* the sound of'; Jer. 10. 13 לקול תתו המון מים בשמים; 11. 16; 51. 16; Ezek. 27. 28; Hab. 3. 16; Ps. 42. 8; Job 21. 12. Cf. also

Ps. 18. 45 לשמע אזן ישמעו לי '*At* the hearing of the ear they shall obey me'; Job 42. 5.

There is thus no need to have recourse to the emendation of Klo., Kamp., Benz., Kit., וְאֶת־שֵׁמַע הַבַּיִת אֲשֶׁר בָּנָה לְשֵׁם יהוה 'and the report of the house which he had built to the name of Yahwe.' LXX, Luc. καὶ τὸ ὄνομα Κυρίου, Pesh. ܘܫܡܗ ܕܡܪܝܐ are probably merely loose renderings, and do not presuppose וְשֵׁם, in place of which, as Th. points out, we should rightly expect וְאֶת־שֵׁם.

חידות] RV. '*hard questions*' is perhaps the best rendering; cf. Prov. 1. 6 דברי חכמים וחידתם. The word here denotes something less trivial than the mere *riddle* of Samson, Judg. 14. 12 *ff.*, but, on the other hand, has not advanced to the later sense of a perplexing question of ethics or morals, Ps. 49. 5; 78. 2.

2. עם לבבה] *Ch.* 8. 17 *note.*

5. מושב עבדיו ומעמד משרתיו] 'The *sitting* of his servants and the *attendance* of his ministers.' For מעמד in this sense cf. the phrase עמד לפני used of *service; ch.* 1. 2 *note.* This explanation alone suits the context. The whole of *v.* 5 down to ומשקיו refers to Solomon's magnificent *display at his banquets.* עבדיו are his courtiers and משרתיו his waiters, and naturally in this connexion מלבשיהם their gorgeous robes call for special notice. On the other hand, Th.'s explanation of מושב, מעמד as substantives of *place,* denoting the *dwellings* or *quarters* of Solomon's servants, is quite alien to the context. It is impossible to think that the mere *dwellings* of the king's servants should be singled out either for their magnificence or number as exciting the queen's admiration, while no special mention is made of the impression left upon her by the sight of the Palace, the Temple, and the Lebanon house. The mention also of the garments and the cup-bearers is upon this interpretation deprived of significance.

There is no difficulty in assigning to these substantives with מ preformative a signification other than that of *place.* The Arabic nouns of this form (*nomina vasis*) are used of *place* or *time,* and e.g. مَجْلِسٌ '*the place where,* or *time when, several persons sit, room, assembly, party*' (Wright, i. 221) may aptly be quoted in this special connexion. So in Hebrew we may cf. e.g. מִשְׁפָּט, מוֹצָא, where, as with מושב, מעמד, the idea of *time* or *place of action* seems to have passed further into definition of the *action* itself.

ומשקיו] Pesh. adds ܘܡܠܒܘܫܝܗܘܢ i.e. a repetition of the previous ומלבשיהם; an unnecessary redundancy.

ועלתו אשר יעלה בית יהוה] 'And his burnt-offering which he used to offer at the house of Yahwe.' Here it is still the large scale of the king's *doings*, rather than his buildings, which forms the writer's theme. So all Verss. both here and in ‖ 2 Chr. 9. 4, RV. marg., Th., Klo., Kamp., Kit. ‖ 2 Chr. reads עֲלִיָּתוֹ, doubtless intending to convey the sense 'the ascent by which he used to go up to the house of Yahwe'; and this rendering is adopted by RV., Ke., Ew.

לא היה בה עוד רוח] 'There was no more *spirit* in her'; i.e. Solomon's display of wisdom and magnificence deprived her of all *courage* to attempt further to compete with him. The *nuance* of רוח is like that in the English expression 'a woman of *spirit*,' and may be partly paralleled by the use of the term in *ch.* 21. 5; Gen. 45. 27 and the phrases עֲצוּבַת רוּחַ Isa. 54. 6, דַּכְּאֵי רוּחַ Ps. 34. 19. The common explanation following LXX, Luc. καὶ ἐξ ἑαυτῆς ἐγένετο, 'she was beside herself (with *astonishment*),' misses the precise meaning.

6. אמת היה הדבר] '*Truth* was the saying.' The abstract substantive used in place of an adjective; cf. *ch.* 2. 13 *note*, and Dri. *Tenses*, § 189, 2. The *order* of words is highly emphatic; *Tenses*, § 208.

7. לא הגד לי החצי] LXX οὐκ εἰσὶν (Luc. ἔστι κατὰ) τὸ ἥμισυ καθὼς ἀπήγγειλάν μοι, merely a somewhat paraphrastic rendering of the same text. In place of החצי ‖ 2 Chr. 9. 6 has חֲצִי מַרְבִּית חָכְמָתֶךָ.

הוספת וג׳] LXX, Luc. προστέθεικας ἀγαθὰ πρὸς (LXX αὐτὰ ἐπὶ) πᾶσαν τὴν ἀκοὴν ἣν ἤκουσα ἐν τῇ γῇ μου, i.e. הוֹסַפְתָּ טוֹב אֶל־כָּל־הַשְּׁמוּעָה אֲשֶׁר שָׁמַעְתִּי בְּאַרְצִי. Probably correct.

חכמה seems to be the addition of a later precisionist, and is really covered by טוב which includes everything which makes for *prosperity*. The repetition of בארצי (from *v.* 6) is not out of place.

LXX πρὸς αὐτὰ ἐπὶ πᾶσαν κ.τ.λ. probably arises from repetition of אל read first as אֲלֵיהֶם. ‖ 2 Chr. יספת אל השמועה אשר שמעתי.

8. אנשיך] LXX, Luc., Pesh. presuppose נָשֶׁיךָ 'thy *wives*'; so in ‖ 2 Chr. 9. 7 Luc. (Pesh. omits). Adopted by Bö., Klo., Kamp., Benz., Kit., Oort. correctly. אנשיך by the side of עבדיך is redundant, and, as Klo. suggests, may be a later alteration in view of the facts of *ch.* 11. 1–3.

9. לעלם] LXX στῆσαι εἰς τὸν αἰῶνα, Luc. τοῦ στῆσαι αὐτὸν εἰς τὸν αἰῶνα agree with ‖ 2 Chr. 9. 8 לְהַעֲמִידוֹ לְעוֹלָם. This addition, which is almost indispensable, may be adopted. Klo.'s emendation מִכָּל־הָעַמִּים is not to be preferred.

11. עצי אלמגים] So *v.* 12†. עצי אלגומים 2 Chr. 2. 7; 9. 10, 11†. The tree is usually thought to be the red sandal-wood (*Pterocarpus santalinus*) which is very heavy, fine grained, and of a brilliant red colour, and is said still to be highly esteemed in the east for the construction of lyres and other musical instruments. The meaning and derivation of the word are, however, quite uncertain: Hastings, *BD.* i. 63; Tristram, 332[1]. LXX ξύλα πελεκητά (Luc. ἀπελέκητα), Vulg. *ligna thyina*, Pesh. ܡܬܩܠܐ ܕܩܘܣܛܐ (explained by lexx. as a scented and variegated wood, sandal-wood), Targ. אעי אלמוגיא.

12. מסעד] 'A support' or 'supports,' i.e. upon the easiest interpretation, *pilasters* or *light buttresses*; so LXX, Luc. ὑποστηρίγματα, Vulg. *fulcra*. The substantive only occurs here, and ‖ 2 Chr. 9. 11 reads מְסִלּוֹת, perhaps 'terraces' or 'verandahs,' an explanation which Th. seeks to fit also to מסעד. This rendering, however, like that of Pesh. ܠܬܪܨܝܬܐ 'ornamentation,' Ke., Ew. 'balusters' or 'balustrade,' Bö., Klo. 'furniture,' depends merely upon conjecture.

לא בא כן וג׳] 'There came not *thus* (i.e. in such quantity and of such excellence) almug trees,' and so, by accommodation to Eng. idiom, 'there came not *such* almug trees.' Cf. Ex. 10. 14 לפניו לא היה כן ארבה כמוהו 'before them there were no such locusts as they.'

---

[1] The latest discussion is that by Cheyne (*Expository Times*, July, 1898, pp. 470 *ff.*), who cites Assyr. *êlammâku*, a tree used by Sennacherib in building his palaces.

After אלמגים in *v.* 12[b] LXX, Luc. add ἐπὶ τῆς γῆς, i.e. עַל־הָאָרֶץ, perhaps correctly. Cf. ‖ 2 Chr. 9. 11 ולא נראו כהם לפנים בארץ יהודה.

עד היום הזה] *Ch.* 8. 8 *note.*

13. והמלך שלמה נתן] Upon the emphatic position of the subject, in antithesis to *v.* 10[a 1], cf. *ch.* 5. 25 *note.*

כיד המלך] 'According to the king's *hand*,' i.e. his '*bounty*.' So Est. 1. 7; 2. 18†. ‖ 2 Chr. 9. 12 reads מלבד אשר הֵבִיאָה אל המלך for which Ber. emends מלבד אשר הֵבִיא לָהּ המלך.

15. לבד מאנשי התרים] Very difficult. Supposing אנשי התרים to denote 'men of the merchants' (though תור *spy out*, *investigate* has nowhere else the sense of *trading*, and the phrase אנשי הת׳ is peculiar), we still seek allusion, not to the traders themselves, but to the *revenue* which they produced. Thus RV., going further than MT. warrants, renders 'Beside *that which* the chapmen *brought*'; LXX, Luc. χωρὶς τῶν φόρων τῶν ὑποτεταγμένων, Targ. בר מאגר אומניא suggest ? ... לְבַד מֵעֹנֶשׁ 'beside the *duties* &c.[2]'; cf. II. 23. 33 where עֹנֶשׁ is rendered φόρον by Luc.; 2 Chr. 36. 3 וַיַּעֲנֹשׁ LXX, Luc. καὶ ἀπέβαλεν φόρον. So Bö. לְבַד מֵעַנְשֵׁי הַתָּרִים, Th. לְבַד מֵעָנְשֵׁי הָרְדוּיִם; but הרדוים 'the subject people' is not to be paralleled. The best and easiest emendation, though independent of any Vers., is that suggested by Kamp. for the whole half-verse לְבַד מֵאֲשֶׁר בָּא מִסַּחַר הָרֹכְלִים 'beside that which came from the traffic of the merchants.'

כל מלכי הערב] RV. 'all the kings of *the mingled people*.' LXX, Luc. πάντων τῶν βασιλέων τοῦ (Luc. τῶν ἐν τῷ) πέραν, i.e. כל מלכי הָעֵבֶר; Vulg. *omnes reges Arabiae;* Pesh. ܘܟܠܗܘܢ ܡܠܟܐ ܕܥܪܒܝܐ, so ‖ 2 Chr. 9. 14 וְכָל־מַלְכֵי עֲרָב; Targ. וכל מלכי סומכוותא 'and all the kings of the allied peoples.' These מַלְכֵי הָעֶרֶב are mentioned Jer. 25. 24 as הַשֹּׁכְנִים בַּמִּדְבָּר, and in connexion with כָּל־מַלְכֵי עֲרָב 'all the kings of Arabia.' In Jer. 25. 20 כָּל־הָעֶרֶב are cited together with כָּל־מַלְכֵי אֶרֶץ הָעוּץ, and in Ezek. 30. 5 כּוּשׁ וּפוּט וְלוּד וְכָל־הָעֶרֶב וְכוּב.

---

[1] Verse 12 must have originally followed immediately upon *v.* 10; cf. *note* on *ch.* 9. 10—*ch.* 10. 29.

[2] Perhaps Vulg. is a paraphrase of the same: Excepto eo, quod afferebant viri, *qui super vectigalia erant.*

In Jer. 50. 37 they appear as the mercenaries of the king of Babylon. Hence it may be inferred that these were kings or sheiks of the mixed nomad tribes of SE. Arabia who came more or less under Solomon's power and so were subject to tribute.

In Ex. 12. 38 עֵרֶב רַב 'a great mixed multitude' is mentioned as coming up out of Egypt with Israel, and in Neh. 13. 3 כָּל־עֵרֶב 'all the mixed multitude' is separated from the returned exiles by Nehemiah; but the connexion of these with הָעֶרֶב is not clear.

ופחות הארץ] פחות 'viceroys' or 'governors.' The view that these are identical with the נצבים of *ch.* 4. 7–19 (Th.; Ber. on || 2 Chr. 9. 14) is opposed by the close connexion with the *foreign* מלכי הערב. More probably the reference is to petty *vassal-princes* who were allowed to retain a nominal suzerainty at the price of an annual tribute: cf. the inscription (l. 12) in which Panammu is termed פחי ואחי יאדי 'viceroy and neighbour-king of Ya'di,' appointed by 'his lord the king of Asshur' (Lidzbarski, *Nordsemit. Epigr.* 443). Elsewhere in OT. the title is used of military commanders under the Aramaean Hadadezer *ch.* 20. 24 *note*, and the Assyrian Sennacherib II. 18. 24 *note*, || Isa. 36. 9, of governors under the Babylonian king, Jer. 51. 23, 57, the king of Media, Jer. 51. 28, and the Assyrian (and Chaldean) Ezek. 23. 6, 12, 23; but with far the greatest frequency of governors of provinces appointed by the Persian monarchs, e.g. of Zerubbabel, Hag. 1. 1, 14; 2. 2, 21; Nehemiah, Neh. 5. 14, 18; 12. 26; the governors generally 'beyond the River,' Neh. 2. 7, 9, &c.

Many critics, regarding פחה as a Persian word connected with Sanskrit *paksha* or *pakkha*, *friend* or *ally*, are obliged therefore to consider the occurrences in Kings as late interpolations (cf. especially Giesebrecht, *ZATW.* i. 233). Against this Schrader argues with force, citing the use of the term in Assyr. *paḥat*, pl. *paḥâti*, *viceroy*, and abstract *piḥat*, *satrapy* in the Khorsabad inscription of the time of Sargon (B.C. 722–705), two centuries before the Persian era, and maintaining the purely Semitic character of the word: *COT.* i. 175 *f.*

The feminine termination of פֶּחָה pl. פַּחוֹת is perhaps to be explained as used with a term denoting *office*, as in Ar. خَلِيفَةٌ 'viceroy,' خَالِقَةٌ 'creator,' *al.;* cf. G-K. § 122 *r*[1].

16. מאתים צנה זהב שחוט] 'Two hundred targets—beaten gold,' זהב standing in explanatory apposition to צנה, and defining the *class* to which it belongs. So in *v.* 17 ושלש מאות מגנים זהב שחוט, שלשת מנים זהב. Cf. Dri. *Tenses*, §§ 186–188.

זהב שחוט] Only in this connexion; *v.* 17 ||2 Chr. 9. 15, 16†[2]. '*Beaten* gold,' RV., Bö., Ke., Th., Ber., Klo., Kamp., שחט meaning *strike* or *beat down*. So LXX, Luc. χρυσᾶ ἐλατά. The other Verss. give the sense '*fine* or *pure* gold';—Vulg. *de auro purissimo*, Pesh. ܕܕܗܒܐ ܡܫܒܚܐ, Targ. דדהבא טבא. The explanation '*alloyed* gold,' Ges., Winer, obtained from Ar. شَحَطَ *dilute wine with water*, cannot be maintained.

יעלה על] Lit. '*went up upon*,' describing the laying of the gold plating upon the (wooden) framework or foundation. The Imperf. describes the *norm* which *characterized* each shield of the class.

18. זהב מופז] Probably, as RV., *al.* '*finest* or *purest* gold.' So LXX, Luc. χρυσίῳ δοκίμῳ, Targ. דהבא טבא, ||2 Chr. 9. 17 זהב טהור. The verb occurs only here, but the substantive פָּז nine times. Identification with Ar. فَضَّ *break*, *separate*, on the view that this may be used of separating the gold from the ore (Ges.), seems to be precarious. Pesh., Arab. presuppose זהב מֵאוֹפִיר 'gold from Ophir'; so Pesh., Targ. in Jer. 10. 9 זהב מֵאוּפָז, and many moderns in Dan. 10. 5 כתם אוּפָז. Vulg. *auro fulvo nimis*.

21. משקה] 'Drink'; so Lev. 11. 34.

סגור] *Ch.* 6. 20 *note*.

אין כסף לא נחשב] Scarcely, as the accents suggest, and as rendered by LXX, Luc., Vulg. 'There was no silver, it was not accounted of'; but rather a negation strengthened by duplication of the negative, 'silver was *not* accounted of *at all*.' Such a duplication is found in Zeph. 2. 2 בטרם לא יבוא עליכם 'before there

[1] The meaning and use of the term קֹהֶלֶת is too uncertain to permit of its being cited as a parallel.

[2] In Jer. 9. 7 Kt. חֵץ שׁוֹחֵט 'a *destroying* arrow' is to be preferred; see Graf, *ad loc.*

come upon you,' and in the phrase הַמִּבְּלִי אֵין, II. 1. 3, 6, 16 המבלי אין אלהים בישראל; Ex. 14. 11. Cf. Ew. § 323. Pesh. ܘܡܟܣܦܐ ܠܐ ܗܘܐ ܡܬܚܫܒ omits one negative, thus agreeing with ‖ 2 Chr. 9. 20 which is without לא.

22. אני תרשיש] 'A fleet of Tarshish'; i.e. a fleet consisting of ships such as were used by the Phoenicians for communication with their distant colony at Tartessus in Spain. ‖ 2 Chr. 9. 21 makes Tarshish the destination of the ships, כי אניות למלך הלכות תרשיש עם עבדי חורם (so 2 Chr. 20. 36, 37), but that this is incorrect is shown by mention of the cargo of the ships—products of the *East*, and by the reference in *ch.* 22. 49 to Jehoshaphat's fleet or ship (see *note ad loc.*) of Tarshish which was stationed at Ezion Geber on the Aelanitic gulf in order to go to Ophir. Cf. *ch.* 9. 26–28 where the allusion is doubtless to one and the same fleet of Solomon[1].

שנהבים] Cod. A[2], Vulg., Targ., and in ‖ 2 Chr. 9. 21, LXX, Luc. render '*elephants' teeth*'; Pesh. in both places ܦܝ̈ܠܐ 'elephants'; Vulg. in Chr. *ebur*. Elsewhere 'ivory' is always שֵׁן alone, or with the generic art. הַשֵּׁן; and it is generally thought that some foreign word meaning 'elephants' is here represented by הַבִּים. So Ges., Ber. regard the word as a contraction of הָאִבִּים, and compare Sanskrit *ibha* = 'elephant.' Or הבים is thought to be a corruption of הַפִּיל, *pîl* being the Persian name for the elephant which has thence passed into Ar. and Aram. Assyr. *šin-ni pi-ri* denotes 'teeth of elephants.' In Ezek. 27. 15 there is mention of קרנות שן וְהָבְנִים 'horns of ivory and *ebony*' (הָבְנִים = Egypt. *heben*, Gk. ἔβενος, Lat. *hebenum*), and Bö., Th., following Rödiger and reading in our passage שֵׁן הַבִּים as two words, explain '*ivory* (*and*) *ebony*,' regarding הבים as a contraction or corruption of הבנים.

קופים] Pesh., Targ. transliterate; Cod. A, and in 2 Chr. LXX, Luc. πιθήκων, Vulg. *simias*. The word is doubtless foreign, and the rendering '*apes*' is generally adopted, upon comparison of

---

[1] Sayce (*Expository Times*, Jan. 1902, p. 179) argues for identification of תרשיש with Tarsus in Cilicia.

[2] The rendering of LXX, Luc. λίθων τορευτῶν καὶ πελεκητῶν (Luc. ἀπελεκήτων), for the whole שנהבים וקפים ותכיים, is obscure.

Sanskrit and Malabar *kapi*, from whence comes the Greek κῆβος, κεῖβος, κῆπος, a species of long-tailed monkey.

תכיים] Cod. A ταώνων, Vulg. *pavos*, Pesh. ܛܘܣܐ, Targ. טווסין, i. e. '*peacocks*'; ‖ 2 Chr. Luc. τεχείμ, LXX omits. Another foreign word. The Tamil or Malabar name for the peacock is *tógai* or *thógai*, and תכי may represent this, with interchange of the back-palatals *g*, *k*. So most moderns.

23. מלכי הארץ] LXX omits הארץ. With MT. cf. *ch.* 5. 14.

24. וכל הארץ] LXX, Luc., Pesh. presuppose וכל מלכי הארץ; so ‖ 2 Chr. 9. 23 probably rightly.

25. כלי כסף] LXX, Luc. omit, perhaps in view of *v.* 21[b].

נשק] Elsewhere (eight times) the word always denotes '*arms*' or '*armour*,' and this is the meaning here given by Vulg., Pesh., Targ. So RV., Bö., Th., Klo., Kamp., Kit. The mention of armour follows not inappropriately after שלמות 'raiment.' LXX, Luc. render στακτήν, 'oil of myrrh or cinnamon,' and this is favoured by Ew., Ber. who compare Ar. نَشِقَ 'breathe in an odour through the nostrils.' For this, however, regular interchange of consonants would require נשׂק. Possibly LXX was influenced in its rendering by the following בשמים ἡδύσματα.

26. ויהי לו . . . רכב] In place of this statement LXX reads καὶ ἦσαν τῷ Σαλωμὼν τέσσαρες χιλιάδες θήλειαι ἵπποι εἰς ἅρματα, Luc. καὶ ἦσαν τῷ Σολομῶντι τεσσαράκοντα χιλιάδες ἵππων θηλειῶν εἰς ἅρματα τοῦ τίκτειν, i. e. *ch.* 5. 6[a] with mistaken rendering of the rare word ארות. The following words of *ch.* 10. 26 and *ch.* 5. 6[b] are identical; ושנים עשר אלף פרשים. 2 Chr. 9. 25[a] = *ch.* 5. 6; 2 Chr. 1. 14[a] = *ch.* 10. 36[a]; 2 Chr. 9. 25[b] = 2 Chr. 1. 14[b] = *ch.* 10. 26[b]. Thus (as is testified by the partial combination of the two Kings' passages in LXX, Luc., and 2 Chr. 9. 25) the original account, which was properly incorporated in *ch.* 10 (see *note* on *ch.* 9. 10–*ch.* 10. 29), probably ran as follows:—וַיֶּאֱסֹף שְׁלֹמֹה רֶכֶב וּפָרָשִׁים וַיְהִי לִשְׁלֹמֹה אַרְבַּעַת אֲלָפִים אֻרְוֹת סוּסִים לְמֶרְכָּבוֹ וַיְהִי־לוֹ אֶלֶף וְאַרְבַּע־מֵאוֹת רֶכֶב וּשְׁנֵים עָשָׂר אֶלֶף פָּרָשִׁים וַיַּנְחֵם בְּעָרֵי הָרֶכֶב וְעִם הַמֶּלֶךְ בִּירוּשָׁלָםִ׃. Here the smaller number 4,000 is adopted in accordance with LXX and ‖ 2 Chr. 9. 25. The mention of the number of chariots is not found in LXX, Luc.,

but is agreeable to the reference to the ערי הרכב which follows. וַיַּנִּיחֵם of ‖ 2 Chr. in place of וַיַּנְחֵם has the support of all Verss.

27. את הכסף] Before these words LXX, Luc. insert *τὸ χρυσίον καί*—a later and unwarranted insertion.

בשפלה] Always (except Josh. 11. 16 שְׁפֵלָתֹה with suff.) with def. art. '*the* Lowland,' i.e. the tract of low hills or 'downs' lying between the maritime plain of Philistia and the mountain-country of Judah, and separated from the latter 'by a series of valleys, both wide and narrow, which run all the way from Ajalon to Beer-sheba.' Cf. Smith, *Geogr.* ch. x.

28. ומוצא וג׳] It may be regarded as certain that a place-name underlies the obscure מקוה. So LXX, Luc. ἐκ Θεκουε, for which Field cites a variant ἐκ Κωά. Eusebius (*Onom.*) Κώδ, πλησίον Αἰγύπτου is rendered by Jerome *Coa, quae est juxta Aegyptum*, and so Vulg. translates מקוה *de Coa*. Lenormant (*Les origines de l'histoire*, iii. 9) was the first to make identification with *Kuë*, i.e. the plain of Cilicia. The same discovery was independently arrived at by Winckler (*Alttest. Untersuchungen*, 168 *ff.*; cf. *Altoriental. Forschungen*, i. 28) together with its complement, viz. that מצרים does not in our passage denote Egypt, but the North Syrian land of *Muṣri*, south of the Taurus, which often figures in Assyrian inscriptions. The horse, which was unknown in Egypt before B.C. 1700–1500, can scarcely ever have been bred in sufficient numbers for wholesale exportation, while the pastures of N. Syria and Cilicia must have been eminently suited for breeding upon a large scale. With this agrees the statement of Ezek. 27. 14 that Israel derived horses, chargers, and mules not from Egypt but from *Togarmah*, i.e. N. Syria and Asia Minor. We may therefore render: 'And Solomon's import of horses was from Muṣri (perhaps מִמִּצְרִי or מִמֹּצָר) and from Kuë (וּמִקְוֵה); the king's traders received them from Kuë at a price.' So Hommel (*Gesch. Babyl.* 610), Benz., Kit. On Muṣri see further, II. 7. 6. König (*Fünf neue arab. Landschaftsnamen im A. T.* 25) agrees as to Kuë, but thinks that the fact that Solomon supplied horses for the Hittites and Aramaeans is inexplicable if they were obtained

from North Syria, but natural if they came from Egypt. It must be noticed also that Deut. 17. 16 connects the supply of horses with Egypt. Cf. Isa. 31. 1.

|| 2 Chr. 9. 28 ומוציאים סוסים ממצרים לשלמה ומכל הארצות. 2 Chr. 1. 16 as in Kings, but with מקוא (i.e. perhaps מִקּוֹא) for מקוה.

29. בשש מאות . . . בחמשים ומאה] LXX, Luc. ἀντὶ ἑκατὸν . . . ἀντὶ πεντήκοντα. In || 2 Chr. 1. 17 LXX, Luc. agree with MT.

לכל מלכי החתים] Cf. II. 7. 6 *note*.

בידם יצאו] LXX, Luc. κατὰ θάλασσαν ἐξεπορεύοντο, i.e. בַּיָּם יֵצֵאוּ, inferior to M. T.

11. 1–13. *Solomon's foreign wives, and his idolatry.*

This section in its present form is coloured by the hand of R^D. His phrases are as follow:—

2. אשר אמר וג'] The reference is to Deut. 7. 1–4; Ex. 34. 12–16 (J). Cf. Josh. 23. 7 (D^2).
בהם דבק] The same phrase is used with reference to the חטאות ירבעם II. 3. 3 (R^D). With reference to Yahwe it occurs in Deut. 4. 4 (adj. הַדְּבֵקִים); 10. 20; 11. 22; 13. 5; 30. 20; Josh. 22. 5; 23. 8 (both D^2); II. 18. 6 (R^D).

4. אלהים אחרים] Cf. *ch.* 9. 6 *note*.
ולא היה לבבו שלם וג'] Cf. *ch.* 8. 61 *note*.
כלבב דויד אביו] Cf. *ch.* 3. 14 *note* on כאשר הלך דויד.

5. וילך ש' אחרי] So, of following a false god, *v.* 10; *ch.* 21. 26; II. 17. 15 (all R^D); *ch.* 18. 18, 21; Deut. 4. 3; 6. 14; 8. 19; 11. 28; 13. 3; 28. 14; Judg. 2. 12, 19 (Deut. compiler); Jer. 2. 5, 23; 7. 9; 11. 10; 13. 10; 16. 11; 25. 6; 35. 15; Ezek. 20. 16; cf. Hos. 2. 7, 15†. Of following Yahwe *ch.* 14. 8 (R^D); 18. 21; Deut. 13. 5; 2 Chr. 34. 31; Hos. 11. 10†.

6. ויעש ש' הרע בעיני י'] So *ch.* 14. 22; 15. 26, 34; 16. 19, 25, 30; 21. 20, 25; 22. 53; II. 3. 2; 8. 18, 27; 13. 2, 11; 14. 24; 15. 9, 18, 24, 28; 17. 2, 17; 21. 2, 6, 15, 16, 20; 23. 32, 37; 24. 9, 19 (all R^D or R^{D2}); 2 Chr. 21. 6; 22. 4; 29. 6; 33. 2, 6, 22; 36. 5, 9, 12; Num. 32. 13 (JE); Deut. 4. 25; 9. 18; 17. 2; 31. 29; Judg. 2. 11; 3. 7, 12; 4. 1; 6. 1; 10. 6; 13. 1 (all Deut. compiler); 1 Sam. 15. 19; Jer. 52. 2†. Cf. 2 Sam. 12. 9; Isa. 65. 12; 66. 4; Jer. 32. 30; Ps. 51. 6.

ולא מלא אחרי י׳] Deut. 1. 36; Josh. 14. 8, 9, 14 (JE recast by D[2]); Num. 32. 11, 12 (JE)†.

9. ויתאנף] II. 17. 18 (R^D); Deut. 1. 37; 4. 21; 9. 8, 20†.
י׳ אלהי ישראל] Cf. *ch.* 8. 15 *note.*

11. ולא שמרת . . . חקתי] Cf. *ch.* 2. 3 *note.*

12. למען דוד אביך] Cf. *v.* 13 למען דוד עבדי; so *vv.* 32, 34; 15. 4; II. 8. 19; 19. 34; 20. 6 (all R^D)†.

13. למען ירושלם אשר בחרתי] Cf. *ch.* 8. 16 *note.*

The view that the latter portion of this section is not earlier than the exile (R^{D2}; so Kue. *vv.* 9–13, Kamp., Benz., Kit. *vv.* 9, 10) is based upon the words of *v.* 9 הנראה אליו פעמים, and presupposes that the narrative of the second vision, *ch.* 9. 1–9, comes from the hand of R^{D2}; but upon this opinion see *note ad loc.* On the other hand, the fact that *vv.* 11–13 speak of a division of the kingdom but make no mention of an exile, favours their pre-exilic authorship.

1–8. LXX, Luc. arrange differently. After the first four words of *v.* 1 והמלך ש׳ אהב נשים there follows *v.* 3^a; then the remainder of *v.* 1 in the form וַיִּקַּח נשים נכריות וג׳, and with the addition Σύρας אֲרָמִיּוֹת after עמוניות, καὶ Ἀμορραίας וַאֱמֹרִיּוֹת after חתית, and omission of צדנית; *v.* 2; *v.* $4^{a\alpha}$ ויהי לעת זקנת ש׳ followed by *v.* 4^b ולא היה לבבו וג׳; *vv.* 3^b, $4^{a\beta}$ represented by וַיַּטּוּ נָשָׁיו הַנָּכְרִיּוֹת אֶת־לְבָבוֹ אַחֲרֵי אֱלֹהֵיהֶן; *v.* 7 with εἰδώλῳ, i.e. אֱלֹהֵי, for שקץ in both cases and omitting בהר אשר על פני ירושלם, followed by *v.* 5^a in the form וּלְעַשְׁתֹּרֶת תּוֹעֲבַת צִדֹנִים; *v.* 8 where for מקטירות וג׳, LXX ἐθυμίων καὶ ἔθυον κ.τ.λ., Luc. reads ἐθυμία καὶ ἔθυε κ.τ.λ., i.e. מַקְטִיר וּמְזַבֵּחַ וג׳; *v.* 6.

This arrangement is, in the main, correct. The general allusion to Solomon's love of women leads on to the fact that many of his wives belonged to the neighbouring nations with whom intercourse was strictly forbidden, and that these wives turned away his heart after their strange gods. After mention in some detail of the concessions which the king made to their religious rites, the writer sums up by saying that Solomon did evil in the sight of Yahwe, and did not walk after Yahwe like David his father. This forms a natural and appropriate transition to *v.* 9 ויתאנף וג׳.

The following points call for special notice:—

The mention of the number of wives and concubines *v.* 3^a^ is no part of the original account, but is an addition from the margin which has come into MT. and LXX in a different position, and thus to some extent accounts for their variation in arrangement.

The words ויקח נשים of *v.* 1 have been omitted in MT. through homoioteleuton.

ואת בת פרעה '*and* the daughter of Pharaoh,' i.e. '*and also*,' or, as RV. marg., '*beside*.' Pharaoh's daughter is introduced not as a crowning instance, but rather as *not* falling under the count which is brought against Solomon, since she was not מן הגוים אשר אמר וג׳, i.e. the neighbouring nations whose territory fell within Solomon's dominions. Probably, however, the words are a later interpolation suggested by the mention of foreign wives and referring back to *ch.* 3. 1.

In the category of foreign wives *v.* 1^b^, LXX Σύρας ארמית is merely a doublet of אדמית. Καὶ Ἀμορραίας ואמֹריות *may* be original, since there is no special reason for its insertion unless it be a third representation of אדמית. צדנית is omitted through oversight. *Vv.* 3^b^, 4^aβ^ are a repetition of the same fact accounted for by the insertion at this point in MT. of *v.* 3^a^ from the margin.

LXX is correct in making the apodosis of the sentence ולא היה וג׳ after the time-determination ויהי לעת וג׳, and in then continuing with ויטו. The reading אלהיהן (from *v.* 2^a^) is, however, inferior to אלהים אחרים of MT.

בהר אשר על פני ירושלם *v.* 7 is a detail added by a later hand. LXX in reading אלהי for שקץ in this verse is more original, but the opposite change in *v.* 5, תּוֹעֲבַת (שקוץ) for אלהי, is probably a later alteration; cf. *note* on *v.* 33.

In *v.* 8^b^ Luc. supplies the original text. *Solomon himself* burnt incense and offered sacrifice to the strange gods, but this fact has been toned down by some later hand into the statement of MT. Syntax, however, has suffered in the process (we should expect at least הַמקטירות והַמזבחות). On the other hand, the original מקטיר וג׳,

determining the subject of עשה, is perfectly regular in construction; cf. e.g. Jer. 2. 26, 27; 17. 25.

Accordingly, the original narrative of R^D probably ran as follows:—

וְהַמֶּלֶךְ שְׁלֹמֹה אָהֵב נָשִׁים וַיִּקַּח נָשִׁים נָכְרִיּוֹת רַבּוֹת מֹאֲבִיּוֹת עַמֹּנִיּוֹת אֲדֹמִיֹּת צִדֹנִיֹּת חִתִּיֹּת [וַאֲמֹרִיּוֹת]. מִן־הַגּוֹיִם אֲשֶׁר אָמַר י׳ אֶל־בְּנֵי יִשְׂרָאֵל לֹא־תָבֹאוּ בָהֶם וְהֵם לֹא־יָבֹאוּ בָכֶם אָכֵן יַטּוּ אֶת־לְבַבְכֶם אַחֲרֵי אֱלֹהֵיהֶם בָּהֶם דָּבַק שְׁלֹמֹה לְאַהֲבָה. וַיְהִי לְעֵת זִקְנַת שְׁלֹמֹה וְלֹא־הָיָה לְבָבוֹ שָׁלֵם עִם־י׳ אֱלֹהָיו כִּלְבַב דָּוִד אָבִיו וַיַּטּוּ נָשָׁיו אֶת־לְבָבוֹ אַחֲרֵי אֱלֹהִים אֲחֵרִים. אָז יִבְנֶה שְׁלֹמֹה בָּמָה לִכְמוֹשׁ אֱלֹהֵי מוֹאָב וּלְמִלְכֹּם אֱלֹהֵי בְנֵי עַמּוֹן וּלְעַשְׁתֹּרֶת אֱלֹהֵי צִדֹנִים. וְכֵן עָשָׂה לְכָל־נָשָׁיו מַקְטִיר וּמְזַבֵּחַ לֵאלֹהֵיהֶן. וַיַּעַשׂ שְׁלֹמֹה הָרַע בְּעֵינֵי י׳ וְלֹא מִלֵּא אַחֲרֵי י׳ כְּדָוִד אָבִיו.

'Now King Solomon was a lover of women; and he took many strange wives, Moabites, Ammonites, Edomites, Zidonians, Hittites [and Amorites]; of the nations whereof Yahwe said unto the children of Israel, Ye shall not go among them, neither shall they come among you; for surely they will turn away your heart after their gods: Solomon clave unto these in love. And it came to pass, when Solomon was old, that his heart was not perfect with Yahwe his God like the heart of David his father; but his wives turned away his heart after other gods. Then did Solomon build a high place for Chemosh the god of Moab, and for Milcom the god of the children of Ammon, and for Ashtoreth the goddess of the Zidonians. And so did he for all his wives, burning incense and offering sacrifice to their gods. And Solomon did that which was evil in the sight of Yahwe, and went not fully after Yahwe, as did David his father.'

1. צִדֹנִיֹּת] From masc. sing. צִדוֹנִי Ezek. 32. 30; Judg. 3. 3, pl. צִדוֹנִים *v.* 5; *al.*, would naturally be formed fem. sing. צִדוֹנִית, pl. צִדוֹנִיּוֹת; and doubtless this last was the original pronunciation in our passage. For the Massoretic punctuation cf. Q're in Neh. 13. 23 אַשְׁדֳּדִיּוֹת עַמֳּנִיּוֹת, where Kt. is אַשְׁדּוֹדִיּוֹת עַמּוֹנִיּוֹת.

2. אכן] A strong asseveration, '*Surely.*' LXX, Luc. μή, Pesh. ܕܠܡܐ, Targ. דילמא suggest פֶּן־ (so Klo.), but this rendering is

merely an accommodation to the context, and weakens the force of the statement.

לאהבה] ל of reference defining the manner of the verb דבק. אהבה is the substantive, not the Infinitive construct.

3. ויהי לו נשים] The verb coming at the beginning of the sentence takes the 3rd masc. sing. as the simplest form, although really predicate to the pl. fem. subj. נשים. This constr. is not infrequent; cf. Gen. 1. 14 יְהִי מְאֹרֹת, but following the subj. once named וְהָיוּ וגו׳. So in *v.* 3[b] ויטו נשיו masc. pl. predicate precedes fem. pl. subj. Cf. Ew. § 316[a]; Da. § 113[b].

5. עשתרת אלהי צדנים] So *v.* 33. For this application of the term אלהים to a *goddess* cf. Phoen. לאלי עשתרת '*deo suo Astartae*' *CIS.* I. i. 4; Baethgen, *Semit. Relig.* p. 71.

7. אז יבנה] Cf. *ch.* 3. 16 *note.*

9. הַנִּרְאָה] Intended by the punctuators to represent a 3rd sing. *perfect* Niph. with the article used with relatival force; cf. Isa. 56. 3 הַנִּלְוָה. This construction of art. with perf. is well known in late Hebrew; e.g. 1 Chr. 26. 28 הַהִקְדִּישׁ; 29. 17 הַנִּמְצְאוּ; *al.;* but it is very noticeable that in classical Hebrew the only occurrences depend *upon the vocalization or accentuation*, and if this be altered we obtain the common construction of the participle with the article. So here הַנִּרְאֶה (as in Gen. 12. 7; 35. 1), Isa. 56. 3 הַנִּלְוֶה; and with forms of ע״ו verbs accented as 3rd fem. perf., Gen. 18. 21; 46. 27 הַבָּאָה, Isa. 51. 10 הַשָּׂמָה, *al.*, where change of accentuation gives הַבָּאָה, הַשָּׂמָה, 3rd fem. participle with article. We never meet with pl. forms הַנִּרְאוּ, הַבָּאוּ, where the constr. depends *upon the consonants*, except in the single instance Josh. 10. 24 הֶהָלְכוּא which may well be a corruption of הַהֹלְכִים. Hence it is reasonable to think that this construction of perf. with art. was unknown to early Hebrew, and that all supposed occurrences rest merely upon a theory of the punctuators.

The solitary instance of the article used as relative with a *preposition*, הֶעָלֶיהָ 'that which was on it,' 1 Sam. 9. 24, is probably a textual error. See Da. § 22 *Rem.* 4; Ew. § 331[b], 1; and especially Dri. *Sam.* I. 9. 24.

10. וצוה] The use of the perfect with waw *simplex* is an irregularity which cannot here be justified. In view of the vocalization of הַנִּרְאָה the participle in the previous verse as a perfect (see *note*), it seems possible that here also a change to the perfect may have been effected later, and that we should restore וּמְצַוֶּה in continuation of הַנִּרְאָה. So Klo.

ולא שמר] LXX καὶ φυλάξασθαι ποιῆσαι, Luc. καὶ φυλάξαι καὶ ποιῆσαι, i.e. וְלִשְׁמֹר לַעֲשׂוֹת—correct; cf. II. 17. 37; 21. 8. MT. is an easy alteration under the influence of ולא שמרת *v.* 11.

צוה] LXX, Luc., Vulg., Pesh. appear to presuppose צִוָּהוּ 'had commanded *him*,' but the addition of the suffix pronoun is not really necessary, and may be regarded as a natural translator's addition.

LXX, Luc. add to the end of the verse οὐδ' (Luc. οὐκ) ἦν ἡ καρδία αὐτοῦ τελεία μετὰ Κυρίου κατὰ τὴν καρδίαν Δαυεὶδ τοῦ πατρὸς αὐτοῦ, a gloss from *v.* 4.

11. עמך] '*With* thee,' i.e. 'in thy *thought*,' or, more fully, as referring to an action carried into effect, 'to be taken into reckoning in estimating thy *character*.' Cf. Job 10. 13 ידעתי כי זאת עמך parallel to ואלה צפנת בלבך; 23. 14; 27. 11; cf. Num. 14. 24.

בריתי וחקתי] LXX, Luc. τὰς ἐντολάς μου καὶ τὰ προστάγματά μου, i.e. מִצְוֹתַי וְחֻקֹּתַי; Cod. A. τὰ προστάγματά μου καὶ τὰς ἐντολάς μου, Pesh. ܦܘܩܕܢܝ ܘܢܡܘܣܝ ܘܩܝܡܝ, i.e., supposing ܦܘܩܕܢܝ to be an error for ܩܝܡܝ, בריתי וחקתי ומצותי. These variations in order seem to indicate that מצותי is a later addition made first upon the margin as being a word often coupled with חקתי.

12. אקרענה] LXX, Luc. λήμψομαι αὐτήν, i.e. אֶקָּחֶנָּה; so *v.* 13 אקרע LXX, Luc. λάβω, Vulg. *auferam*, i.e. אֶקַּח. This reading, as agreeing better with the phrase מיד בנך *v.* 12 (*v.* 11 קרע אקרע . . . מעליך), and according with *vv.* 34, 35, is to be adopted.

11. 14-25. *Solomon's adversaries; Hadad the Edomite and Rezon the Syrian.*

14-22. The narrative in its present form seems to be somewhat confused. Hadad, though but 'a little lad' at the time of his flight into Egypt, at once finds favour with Pharaoh, and receives from him a house, an allowance, and land. He then, in spite of his extreme youth, marries the sister of Pharaoh's queen Tahpenes, and his son Genubath is brought up in the palace together with Pharaoh's sons. The form אדר *v.* 17, as a variation of הדד, creates further suspicion as to the integrity of the narrative.

Winckler (*Alttest. Untersuchungen*, 1 *ff.*) believes that two accounts have here been interwoven, and attempts the task of unravelling the skein by the aid of a discriminating use of LXX. Winckler's two narratives run as follows:—

14 ויקם יהוה שטן לשלמה
את הדד האדמי מזרע
15 a^α, b^β המלוכה באדום. ויהי
בהכרית דוד את אדום
17 b ויך כל זכר באדום והדד
נער קטן. [ויקחהו אחד]
17 a^β מעבדי אביו [ויביאהו
מצרימה אל פרעה.]
19 וימצא הדד חן בעיני פרעה
מאד ויתנהו לתחפנים
20 a^β אשתו הגבירה ותגדלהו
20 b^β בתוך בית פרעה בתוך
21 בני פרעה. וישמע הדד
במצרים כי שכב דוד עם
אבתיו ויאמר אל פרעה
שלחני ואלך אל ארצי.
22 ויאמר לו פרעה כי מה
אתה חסר עמי והנך
מבקש ללכת אל ארצך
ויאמר לו כי שלח תשלחני
וישב הדד אל ארצו.

15 a^β ויהי בעלות יואב שר
הצבא לקבר את החללים
16 a כי ששת חדשים ישב שם
יואב וכל ישראל [ויכו
את כל אדום עַד־כַּלֵּה.]
17 a^α ויברח אדד הוא ואנשים
17 a^γ אדמיים אתו לבוא מצרים.
18 ויקמו ממדין ויבאו פארן
ויקחו אנשים עמם מפארן
ויבאו מצרים אל פרעה
ויתן לו בית ולחם אמר
19 b לו וארץ נתן לו. ויתן
לו אשה את אנות אחות
20 a^α תחפנים. ותלד לו את
20 b^α גנבת בנו ויהי גנבת בית
פרעה.

'And Yahwe raised up an adversary unto Solomon, Hadad the Edomite, of the royal seed in Edom. And it came to pass, when David cut off Edom, and smote every male in Edom, that Hadad was a little lad. [And one] of his father's servants [took him, and brought him into Egypt unto Pharaoh]. And Hadad found great favour in the sight of Pharaoh, and he gave him to Tahpenes his chief wife, and she brought him up in Pharaoh's house among the sons of Pharaoh. And Hadad heard in Egypt that David slept with his fathers, and he said to Pharaoh, Let me depart, that I may go to my own country. And Pharaoh said to him, What hast thou lacked with me, that, behold, thou seekest to go to thine own country? And he said to him, Let me in any wise depart. So Hadad returned to his own land.'

'And it came to pass, when Joab the captain of the host was gone up to bury the slain, that he remained there six months, even Joab and all Israel, [and they smote all Edom until they had utterly destroyed them]. And Adad fled, he and certain Edomites with him, to go into Egypt. And they arose out of Midian, and came to Paran; and they took men with them out of Paran, and they came to Egypt, unto Pharaoh. And he gave him a house, and appointed him victuals, and gave him land. And he gave him to wife Anoth the sister of Tahpenes. And she bare him Genubath his son; and Genubath lived in the house of Pharaoh.'

In the first narrative the *Edomite* Hadad is carried into Egypt by his father's servant, and brought up by Pharaoh's queen. The second account seems to make Adad a *Midianite* prince, who flees with his adherents into Egypt, taking with him certain Edomites[1]

[1] אנשים ארמיים. Had Adad and his followers been Edomites, such a specification would here have been unnecessary.

from Paran, and is well received by Pharaoh, who gives him for wife Anoth the sister of his queen. A son, Genubath, is born to him, but of his fate we are not informed. Winckler conjectures that just as the two accounts exhibit similarity in their commencement with David's campaign against Edom and in the allied names Hadad, Adad, so the conclusion of the second may have resembled that of the first in relating the journeying of Genubath from Egypt into Midian the land of his father, and his there establishing himself as an adversary to Solomon.

In the two accounts the following portions of MT. are rejected as glosses:—

(i.) *v.* $20^{a\beta}$ תחפנים, *v.* 21^{a} וכי מת יואב שר הצבא (introduced in accordance with *v.* 15 by the welder of the two narratives), *v.* 21^{b} הדד.

(ii.) *v.* 18^{b} מלך מצרים.

The sentences enclosed in square brackets are supplied by conjecture.

Words overlined are emendations dependent upon LXX, as follow:—

v. 14. מלך הוא] LXX *τῆς βασιλείας* = הַמְּלוּכָה. So Klo., Benz.

v. 15. בהיות] LXX *ἐν τῷ ἐξολοθρεύειν* = בְּהַכְרִית. So Klo., Kamp. Pesh. ܒܡܚܐ = בְּהַכּוֹת adopted by Bö., Th., Benz., Oort.

v. 20^{a}. ותגמלהו] LXX *καὶ ἐξέθρεψεν αὐτόν* = וַתְּגַדְּלֵהוּ. So Klo., Benz.

v. 22 end] LXX adds *καὶ ἀνέστρεψεν Ἀδὲρ εἰς τὴν γῆν αὐτοῦ* = וַיָּשָׁב הֲדַד אֶל־אַרְצוֹ.

v. 19^{b}. ויתן לו וג׳] Here ויתנהו לתחפנים is restored by conjecture in (i.). The name אנות in (ii.) is derived from LXX, Luc. *ch.* 12. 24^{e} *καὶ Σουσακεὶμ ἔδωκεν τῷ Ἰεροβοὰμ τὴν Ἀνὼ ἀδελφὴν Θεκεμείνας τὴν πρεσβυτέραν* (Luc. adds *ἀδελφὴν*) *τῆς γυναικὸς αὐτοῦ εἰς γυναῖκα·* (Luc. *καὶ*) *αὕτη ἦν μεγάλη ἐν μέσῳ τῶν θυγατέρων τοῦ βασιλέως, καὶ ἔτεκεν τῷ Ἰεροβοὰμ τὸν Ἀβιὰ υἱὸν αὐτοῦ,* a statement which occurs in the midst of the account of Jeroboam. Winckler considers the question whether this passage (obviously correspondent to MT.

ch. 11. 19[b], 20[a 1]) belongs properly to the Hadad or to the Jeroboam narrative, and concludes that the recurrence of the name Ἀνώ in *ch.* 12. 24 [g, k, l] (=MT. *ch.* 14. 2, 8, 9) makes for the latter view, but may be due to interpolation in accordance with *ch.* 12. 24[e]; while, on the other hand, the obviously incorrect position [2] of the account in LXX, and the supposition that Pharaoh would more reasonably have given his queen's sister as wife to a Midianite *prince* than to an Israelite *rebel*, are conclusively in favour of the former.

14. שטן] Cf. *ch.* 5. 18 *note.*

16. עד הִכרית] Cf. II. 3. 25 *note* on עד הִשאיר.

18. ולחם אמר לו] '*Assigned* or *appointed* him an allowance.' So exactly 2 Chr. 29. 24 כי לכל ישראל אמר המלך העולה והחטאת 'because for all Israel had the king appointed the burnt-offering and the sin-offering.' The same construction is common in Ar., where, however, the object is always connected with ب, which is said to strengthen the government of the verb, acting as an emphatic representation of the accusative; e.g. أَمَرَ لَهُ بِدِرْهَمٍ 'He assigned him a *dirhem* (piece of money).' Pesh., mistaking this *nuance* of אמר, connects ולחם closely with the previous ויתן לו בית, and supplies after אמר לו the words which Pharaoh is supposed to have spoken:—ܘܝܗܒ ܠܗ ܒܝܬܐ ܘܠܚܡܐ. ܘܐܡܪ ܠܗ. ܬܒ ܠܘܬܝ 'and he gave him a house and an allowance, and said to him, Dwell with me!'

19. הגבירה] Here 'the *queen*.' In *ch.* 15. 13; ‖ 2 Chr. 15. 16 גבירה is used of the *queen-mother*. The other occurrences of the word are II. 10. 13; Jer. 13. 18; 29. 2†, where it is not clear whether the reference is to the queen or to the queen-mother. גבירה properly denotes the '*chief lady*' of the harem, and Bö. is

---

[1] *αὕτη ἦν μεγάλη κ.τ.λ.* answers to *v.* 20[a] read as וַתִּגְדַּל הִיא בְּתוֹךְ בְּנוֹת הַמֶּלֶךְ וַתֵּלֶד וג׳.

[2] Jeroboam hears of Solomon's death, and asks leave to return to Ephraim (*v.* 34 or 24[d]); but Pharaoh, instead of granting his request, marries him to Anoth, by whom he has a son (*vv.* 35–37 or 24[d, e]). After this Jeroboam makes a fresh effort to depart, and, in spite of the delay, returns in time to be created king of Israel at the rebellion upon Reḥoboam's accession.

probably correct in assuming that this position would be usually occupied by the queen-mother, but, in the event of her death or removal, by the chief wife or queen. Cf. also Benz. There is no reason for thinking, with Klo., Kamp., Kit., that גבירה must always mean 'queen-mother,' and therefore emending הַבְּכִירָה after LXX, Luc. *ch.* 12. 24[e] τὴν πρεσβυτέραν. In *ch.* 11. 19, LXX τῆς μείζω, Luc. τὴν μείζω, i. e. הַגְּדוֹלָה, is also inferior to MT.

20. גנבת] On the form of the name cf. *note* on טפת *ch.* 4. 11.

21. כי שכב וג׳] So Gen. 47. 30; 2 Sam. 7. 12. Elsewhere (23 times in Kings and 10 times in ‖ 2 Chr.) the phrase forms part of the formula of R[D] in concluding his notice of a reign.

22. כי מה אתה וג׳] Not as RV. '*But* what hast thou lacked,' &c. כי, as in the second half of the verse כי שלח תשלחני, simply introduces the direct oration. See *ch.* 1. 13 *note.*

לא] Read Q're לוֹ. לא cannot mean 'nothing,' RV., and '*Nay* but,' &c., is inappropriate as an answer to the question.

23–25. LXX, Luc. omit *vv.* 23–25[aα] (down to שלמה), and then, in place of the impossible MT., continue αὕτη ἡ κακία ἣν ἐποίησεν Ἀδέρ· καὶ ἐβαρυθύμησεν (Luc. ἐβαρύνθη ἐπὶ) Ἰσραήλ, καὶ ἐβασίλευσεν ἐν τῇ (Luc. γῇ) Ἐδώμ, i. e. זֹאת הָרָעָה אֲשֶׁר עָשָׂה הֲדַד וַיָּקָץ בְּיִשְׂרָאֵל וַיִּמְלֹךְ עַל־אֱדוֹם 'This is the evil which Hadad did; and he abhorred Israel, and reigned over Edom[1].' This is correct both in reading and position, referring as it does the latter part of *v.* 25 to Hadad, and adding the necessary summary as to his relationship to Solomon. So Klo., Benz., Kit., Oort. The definiteness of the statement זאת הרעה suggests that in the original narrative some explicit account of Hadad's aggressions must have intervened after *v.* 22.

The short reference to Rezon, thus omitted by LXX, Luc., has been inserted between *vv.* 14[a] and 14[b], but clearly by a later hand. So placed, it breaks the connexion of the Hadad story, and necessitates the resumption καὶ Ἀδὲρ ὁ Ἰδουμαῖος 14[b], repeated

[1] Vulg. agrees with LXX in reading *et hoc est malum Adad*, but with MT. in the position of the notice concerning Rezon, and in reading אֲרָם for אֱדוֹם.

from 14[a]. The notice is ancient and genuine[1], but its original position cannot now be accurately determined.

23. רזון] See note on חֶזְיוֹן *ch.* 15. 18.

24. גדוד] Generally a *marauding band;* II. 5. 2; 6. 23; 13. 20, 21; 24. 2; 1 Sam. 30. 8, 15, 23; *al.* So, of the *foray* made by such a band, 2 Sam. 3. 22. The word is perhaps used of more regular detachments of an army 2 Sam. 4. 2; but this use seems generally to be late—1 Chr. 7. 4; 2 Chr. 25. 9, 10, 13; 26. 11.

בהרג דוד אתם] LXX, Luc. omit. The statement is probably a gloss from the margin, referring to *v.* 23[b]. So Klo., Winckler (*Alttest. Untersuchungen*, p. 60), Benz. In place of אתם read אֲרָם with Klo., Benz.

25. ויקץ] So, of racial hostility, Ex. 1. 12; Num. 22. 3, followed in both places by מִפְּנֵי, expressing dislike.

11. 26—14. 20. *History of Jeroboam.*

Ch. 11. 26–43 properly belongs to the section of 1 Kings, *chh.* 3. 1—11. 43, which deals with the reign of Solomon. See summary at head of *ch.* 3. Since, however, the history of Jeroboam commences with *v.* 26, it is convenient at this point to consider the structure of the narrative. The arrangement of events in LXX, Luc. presents a striking variation from that of MT., as may be best seen by a parallel summary of the two accounts.

MT.	LXX.
11. 26. Jeroboam, an Ephraimite of Zeredah, son of a widow, comes into prominence in connexion with Solomon's building operations at Jerusalem.	
11. 29. He is marked out as future king of the ten tribes by the prophet Aḥijah.	
11. 40. Solomon seeks to kill Jeroboam, who takes flight into Egypt, where he stays until the death of Solomon.	
11. 41. Death and burial of Solomon.	

[1] A notice so straightforward and unembellished can scarcely be thought (Kit. *Hist. Heb.* ii. 53) merely to have grown up out of the *lapsus calami* אֲרָם for אֱדֹם.

<table>
<tr><th>MT.</th><th>LXX.</th></tr>
<tr><td></td><td>11. 43. Jeroboam returns so soon as he hears of Solomon's death, and settles in Zeredah.
Repeated notice of Solomon's death.
Reḥoboam succeeds him.</td></tr>
<tr><td colspan="2">12. 1. Reḥoboam goes to Shechem to be crowned by all Israel.</td></tr>
<tr><td>12. 2. Jeroboam returns from Egypt upon the news of Reḥoboam's accession.</td><td></td></tr>
<tr><td>12. 3. The people of Israel summon him, and he and all Israel come and lay their grievances before Reḥoboam.</td><td>12. 3. The people (without Jeroboam) come and lay their grievances before Reḥoboam.</td></tr>
<tr><td colspan="2">12. 5. Reḥoboam, after asking a delay of three days, decides to answer the people harshly and to add to their burdens.</td></tr>
<tr><td>12. 12. Jeroboam and all the people come to Reḥoboam upon the third day to receive his answer.</td><td>12. 12. All Israel (without Jeroboam) come to Reḥoboam upon the third day to receive his answer.</td></tr>
<tr><td colspan="2">12. 13. Reḥoboam's answer results in the revolt of all Israel except the tribe of Judah</td></tr>
<tr><td></td><td>and Benjamin.</td></tr>
<tr><td colspan="2">12. 20. All Israel, when they hear of Jeroboam's return, send for him and make him their king.</td></tr>
<tr><td colspan="2">12. 21. Reḥoboam goes to Jerusalem, and assembles all Judah and Benjamin to fight against Jeroboam, but is restrained by the word of God through the prophet Shemaiah.</td></tr>
<tr><td></td><td>12. 24a. Repeated notice of Solomon's death and of Reḥoboam's accession. His age at accession, length of his reign, and his mother's name. Verdict as to his character.
12. 24b. Repeated introduction to Jeroboam;—an Ephraimite, son of a harlot. Solomon advances him.</td></tr>
</table>

MT.	LXX.
	12. 24[b]. Notice of Solomon's building operations, and of his chariots.
	12. 24[c]. Solomon seeks to kill Jeroboam, who flees into Egypt, where he remains until the death of Solomon.
	12. 24[d]. Jeroboam hears of Solomon's death, and asks leave of Pharaoh to return to his own country. Pharaoh, instead of granting the request, gives him his daughter Anoth as wife. She bears him Abijah.
	12. 24[f]. Jeroboam renews his request to return to Ephraim, and leaving Egypt arrives at Zeredah, where he gathers all the tribes of Ephraim, and builds a fort.
	12. 24[g]. Jeroboam's son falls sick at Zeredah. He sends his wife to inquire as to the issue of the sickness. Aḥijah prophecies the death of the child and the utter extirpation of Jeroboam's posterity (but without assigning any cause).
	12. 24[n]. Jeroboam goes to Shechem, and gathers the tribes of Israel against the arrival of Reḥoboam.
	12. 24[o]. Shemaiah the prophet marks out Jeroboam as future king of the ten tribes.
	12. 24[p]. The people lay their grievances before Reḥoboam, who, after asking a delay of three days, decides to answer the people roughly and to add to their burdens.
	12. 24[t]. Revolt of all Israel except the tribes of Judah and Benjamin.
	12. 24[x]. Reḥoboam assembles all Judah and Benjamin to fight against Jeroboam, but is restrained by the

MT.	LXX.
	word of Yahwe through the prophet Shemaiah.

12. 25. Jeroboam builds Shechem and Penuel.

12. 26. His calf-worship at Bethel and Dan a measure to prevent the return of Israel to the house of David.

13. 1. The narrative concerning the prophet who came from Judah to rebuke Jeroboam.

13. 33. In spite of this Jeroboam maintains his worship, and thus seals the doom of his house.

14. 1. Jeroboam's son falls sick at Tirzah. He causes his wife to disguise herself, and sends her to inquire of Aḥijah as to the issue of the sickness. She is at once recognized by Aḥijah, who prophecies the death of the child and the utter extirpation of Jeroboam's posterity, because of 'the sins of Jeroboam,' i. e. his idolatrous calf-worship.

14. 19. Death of Jeroboam; record of the length of his reign, and mention of his successor.

Here the following points are to be noticed:

1. The superiority of LXX to MT. in 11. 43—12. 24. Jeroboam would naturally return from Egypt upon the news of the death of Solomon (LXX), and would scarcely delay until he had received information of Reḥoboam's accession (MT.; read in 12. 2^b וַיָּשָׁב יָרָבְעָם מִמִּצְרָיִם with ‖ 2 Chr. 10. 2). This point, however, cannot be pressed, since MT. may not be intended to represent the logical order of events. The variations in *vv.* 3^a, 12^a are more important. From *v.* 20 in both MT. and LXX it is certainly to be gathered that Jeroboam had taken no part in the previous negotiations, but that news of his return first reached the people when they were looking around for a new leader after their rejection of the house

of David. This agrees with the previous narrative in LXX, but conflicts with the statements of MT. in *vv.* 3^a, 12^a. LXX is therefore to be preferred.

2. The inconsistency of LXX 12. 24^{a-z} with LXX 11. 43—12. 24, and its inferiority to MT.

(*a*) The section is inconsistent with the previous section in LXX. Many of its notices are mere duplications of what has been previously recorded in 11. 43—12. 24. Thus the notice of Solomon's death and Reḥoboam's accession, 12. 24^a, repeats 11. 41, 43; the introduction to Jeroboam, 12. 24^b, is superfluous after 11. 26; Solomon's attempt to kill Jeroboam is a repetition of 11. 40, and comes in very awkwardly without any narrative preceding to explain the king's action; 12. 24° is merely a variation of the story of 11. 29 *ff.*, and cannot exist side by side with it; 12. 24^{p-z} answers to 12. 3–24, while the whole account in its second form is inconsistent with the first account, in representing Jeroboam as having gathered the tribes to Shechem to meet Reḥoboam 12. 24^n, and so presumably as present during the negotiations, and taking part in them.

(*b*) The section is inferior to the narrative of MT. On LXX 12. 24^{d-f} as compared with MT. 11. 19^b *ff.* see *note* on *ch.* 11. 14–22. The relative value of the two forms of the story of the sickness of Jeroboam's son admits of some difference of opinion. See, for LXX, Winckler, *Alttest. Untersuchungen*, 12 *ff.*; for MT. Kit. *Hist.* ii. 206 *f.* The variation between the two narratives is clearly too considerable to admit of the supposition that the one was derived from the other; and it seems necessary to suppose that each was drawn independently from some earlier source. Thus regarded, LXX may represent the more original form of the story, since it is easier to believe that *vv.* 7–9, 14–16 MT.[1] are a later addition than that in LXX they were purposely cut out in order to place the story at the commencement of Jeroboam's career (Kit.). It is

[1] The work of R^D. His hand, however, is also to be traced in *v.* 10, which appears in LXX. See *notes ad loc.*

certain, however, that *from the point of view of* R^D the story in MT. occupies the right position, and, as intended to exemplify God's visitation upon Jeroboam on account of the idolatry of his calf-worship, aptly closes the history of his life, and is followed, *vv.* 19, 20, by the short notice as to his death. In LXX all reference to the death of Jeroboam is lacking, a point which further argues the inferiority of the section.

The inference to be drawn from the foregoing points is that the history of Jeroboam, as it left the hand of R^D, is represented, as nearly as can be determined, by MT., LXX 11. 26–42; LXX 11. 43—12. 24; MT. 12. 25—14. 20. LXX 12. 24^{a-z}, as both inconsistent with the previous section in LXX and inferior to MT., must be considered to be a history of Jeroboam which came independently into the hands of some copyist of the LXX, and was inserted after *ch.* 12. 24 at the expense of the omission of the original text.

The origin of the section LXX 12. 24^{a-z} is not clear. It may have been, and probably was, drawn in part from our Book of Kings (the recension of R^D). But, as has been noticed above, the story 12. 24^{g-n} appears to come from some independent source; and 12. 24^{a-f}, composed, like the LXX insertions in *ch.* 2 after *vv.* 35, 46, of fragments which in the main can be paralleled in MT., contains a few independent statements. Thus *v.* 24^b καὶ ᾠκοδόμησεν Σαλωμὼν (Luc. Ἰεροβοὰμ τῷ Σολομῶντι) τὴν Σαρειρὰ τὴν ἐν ὄρει Ἐφράιμ, καὶ ἦσαν αὐτῷ ἅρματα τριακόσια ἵππων, and καὶ ἦν ἐπαιρόμενος ἐπὶ τὴν βασιλείαν, *v.* 24^f καὶ ἐξῆλθεν Ἰεροβοὰμ ἐξ Αἰγύπτου, καὶ ἦλθεν εἰς γῆν Σαρειρὰ τὴν ἐν ὄρει Ἐφράιμ· καὶ ᾠκοδόμησεν Ἰεροβοὰμ ἐκεῖ χάρακα. Further, the narrative of *vv.* 24^{d-f}, though ultimately identical with MT. 11. 19 *ff.* (see *note*), must certainly have been derived from some other source than Kings.

The view of Kue. (*Ond.* § 26. 10) is that we have in this section a version of the history of Jeroboam undertaken in his interest, and thus representing him as marrying the daughter of Pharaoh, and purposely omitting a large portion of Aḥijah's prophecy against him. But, as Kit. points out, the fact that his mother is represented as a harlot, and the revolt laid at his door, is entirely alien to such a purpose[1].

11. 26–43. *Jeroboam's early career.*

11. 26. הצרדה] Only here in MT. LXX, Luc. Σαρειρά, here and in *v.* 43; 12. 24^b, f, k, l, n. In 11. 43; 12. 24^b Σαρειρά is said to be ἐν τῷ ὄρει Ἐφράιμ, perhaps an inference from *v.* 26. The view that צרדה is the same as צרתן (*ch.* 4. 12 *note*; 7. 46, where ‖ 2 Chr. 4. 17 has צְרֵדָתָה) is by no means certain.

In Judg. 7. 22 צְרֵרָתָה (with ה *loc.*) mentioned as the scene of the flight of the Midianites, is usually thought to be miswritten for צְרֵדָתָה, but nothing definite as to locality can be gathered from this passage, which seems to embody a confusion of sources (see Moore, *ad loc.*). Conder suggests as the site of צרדה *Ṣurda*, a small village four kilometres north-west of Bethel; *Memoirs*, ii. 295.

ושם אמו צרועה] LXX, Luc. omit, probably owing to the translator's eye passing from הצרדה to צרועה.

וירם] The ו *consec.* is here employed to introduce the predicate with some little emphasis after the words intervening between it and the subject: 'And Jeroboam, &c., *he* lifted up &c.' Cf. Gen. 30. 30 כי מעט אשר היה לך לפני ויפרץ לרב; 1 Sam. 14. 19; Dri. *Tenses*, § 127 *a*. These words are omitted in LXX, Luc. through confusion with *v.* 27^a.

27. וזה הדבר אשר] 'And this is the reason why &c.' So Josh. 5. 4 וזה הדבר אשר מל יהושע וג׳.

המלוא] *Ch.* 9. 15 *note.*

עיר דוד] *Ch.* 2. 10 *note.*

28. גבור חיל] 'A mighty man of *skill*,' i.e. 'a man of great ability.' So 1 Chr. 9. 13; cf. 1 Chr. 26. 8. So in Ruth 2. 1 (and perhaps 1 Sam. 9. 1) the phrase is used not in the special sense of great valour in battle, but of marked moral or material *worth.* Cf. *note* on חיל *ch.* 1. 42.

---

[1] Ranke takes the view that LXX 12. 24^a-z is of superior historical value to the previous section in LXX, and to MT.; see *Weltgeschichte*, iii. 2, pp. 4–12.

29. וימצא אתו . . . בדרך] LXX, Luc. add καὶ ἀπέστησεν αὐτὸν ἐκ τῆς ὁδοῦ, i.e. וַיְסִירֵהוּ מִן־הַדָּרֶךְ. The words, which are necessary in view of the following statement ושניהם לבדם בשדה, have fallen out of MT. through homoioteleuton. The motive of the action, to insure privacy, may be compared with 1 Sam. 9. 27, where Samuel causes Saul's servant to pass on before, and with II. 9. 2, where the young prophet is directed to take Jehu into חדר בחדר.

השילני] Cf. *ch.* 14. 1 *note.*

והוא] LXX, Luc., Pesh. וַאֲחִיָּה, probably original. In any case the reference is to Aḥijah (Th., Klo.) and not to Jeroboam (Ew.), the garment being assumed for the special purpose described in *v.* 30; cf. Jer. 13. 1 *ff.;* Isa. 20. 2.

ושניהם לבדם בשדה] LXX omits לבדם; Luc. reads ἐν τῇ ὁδῷ for בשדה. MT. correct.

31–39. Aḥijah's speech has taken its present form at the hands of R^D. Notice the following phrases:—

31. י׳ אלהי צבאות] Cf. *ch.* 8. 15 *note.*

32. למען דוד עבדי] So *v.* 34; cf. *v.* 12 *note.*

ירושלם העיר אשר בחרתי] So *v.* 36; cf. *ch.* 8. 16 *note.*

33. ולא הלכו בדרכי] So *v.* 38; cf. *ch.* 2. 3 *note.*

לעשות הישר בעיני] So *v.* 38; 14. 8; 15. 5, 11; 22. 43 (‖ 2 Chr. 20. 32); II. 10. 30; 12. 3 (‖ 2 Chr. 24. 2); 14. 3 (‖ 2 Chr. 25. 2); 15. 3, 34 (‖ 2 Chr. 26. 4; 27. 2); 16. 2 (‖ 2 Chr. 28. 1); 18. 3 (‖ 2 Chr. 29. 2); 22. 2 (‖ 2 Chr. 34. 2). Deut. 12. 25; 13. 19; 21. 9; and, with addition of הטוב, 6. 18; 12. 28. Elsewhere only Ex. 15. 26 (JE or D?); Jer. 34. 15. For the contrary phrase of R^D עשה הָרַע בעיני י׳ cf. *v.* 6 *note.*

כדוד אביו] Cf. *ch.* 3. 14 *note* on כאשר הלך דוד.

34. אשר בחרתי אתו] Cf. Deut. 17. 15 שום תשים עליך מלך אשר יבחר י׳ אלהיך בו.

36. למען היות ניר לדויד עבדי] So 15. 4; II. 8. 19 (‖ 2 Chr. 21. 7); cf. Ps. 132. 17. The figure of the unquenched lamp represents a lasting posterity; cf. Prov. 13. 9; Job 18. 6.

כל הימים] So *v.* 39; cf. *ch.* 9. 3 *note.*

לשום שמי שם] Cf. *ch.* 9. 3 *note.*

38. והיה אם תשמע] So Deut. 28. 1, 15; with pl. 11. 13; cf. 15. 5; 11. 28. In the same way (obedience the condition of a promise) כי תשמע Deut. 13. 19; 28. 2, 13; 30. 10; אשר תשמעו 11. 27.

לשמר וג׳] Cf. *ch.* 2. 3 *note.*

כאשר עשה דוד] Cf. *ch.* 3. 14 *note.*

ובניתי לך וג׳] Cf. the promise in 2 Sam. 7. 11, 16, 27 Nathan's prophecy referred to elsewhere by R^D;—*ch.* 2. 4; 5. 16–19. For the phrase cf. 1 Sam. 2. 35 and (עשה for בנה) 25. 28.

Not improbably the speech has received some few later additions. In *v.* 33 וחקתי ומשפטי is wanting in LXX, and the use of these terms after לעשות rather than לשמר being characteristic of P or H (see *ch.* 6. 12 *note*), the two words may reasonably be suspected as an insertion due to R^P. LXX also omits אשר שמר מצותי וחקתי at the end of *v.* 34, and though the phrase is Deuteronomic, yet the repeated אשר has something of the awkward ring of an insertion, and the words may be due to the same interpolator. The omission of the close of the speech by LXX ונתתי לך את ישראל: ואענה את זרע דוד למען זאת אך לא כל הימים, taken in connexion with the reference of *v.* 39—the affliction of the seed of David, but not for ever—suggests that this also may be an addition of exilic or post-exilic times; though, as Kue. points out, the statement of *v.* 39 *need* not imply an exilic standpoint: cf. 2 Sam. 7. 14b. The use of the imperf. with weak ו, ואענה, for the perf. with ו *consec.*, seems to be another mark of the late hand: cf. *ch.* 6. 32 *note* on וְקָלַע.

32. והשבט האחד] LXX, Luc. καὶ δύο σκῆπτρα, an alteration in view of *v.* 30b; *ch.* 12. 23. So *v.* 36. Cf. the addition καὶ Βενιαμείν in *ch.* 12. 20. The inconsistency in MT. between the '12 pieces' of *v.* 30 and the 10 + 1 of *vv.* 31, 32 perhaps points to a modification of the original narrative only partially effected.

33. יען אשר עזבוני] LXX, Luc., Vulg., Pesh. presuppose the sing. verb throughout the verse; עֲזָבַנִי וַיִּשְׁתַּחוּ . . . וְלֹא הָלַךְ. This, as agreeing with the sing. שלמה of *vv.* 31, 32, and the sing. מִיָּדוֹ of *v.* 34, is to be adopted.

לעשתרת אלהי צדנין וג׳] LXX, Luc. τῇ Ἀστάρτῃ βδελύγματι Σιδωνίων καὶ τῷ Χαμὼς καὶ ἐν τοῖς εἰδώλοις (Luc. εἰδώλῳ) Μωὰβ καὶ τῷ βασιλεῖ αὐτῶν (Luc. τῷ Μελχὸμ) προσοχθίσματι υἱῶν Ἀμμών, i. e. לעשתרת תּוֹעֲבַת צדנין ולכמוש אלהי מואב ולמלכם שִׁקּוּץ בני עמון[1]. MT., in reading אלהי in each case, is more original. The expressions תועבת, שקוץ represent alterations to avoid applying the term אלהים to heathen gods, in accordance with the feeling of a later time. Cf. the variations in *vv.* 5, 7 MT. and LXX.

צדנין] The plural termination ִין—, used in Aramaic and upon the Moabite stone, occurs in Hebrew some twenty-five times, chiefly in late Books. In earlier Books the form, if not dialectical (so perhaps Judg. 5. 10), is due to error in transcription under the influence of Aramaic. For the occurrences cf. G-K. § 87 *e;* Sta. § 323[a].

34. נשיא אשתנו] LXX, Luc. ἀντιτασσόμενος ἀντιτάξομαι αὐτῷ appear to have read נָשֹׂא אֶשָּׂאֶנּוּ, or better נָשֹׂא אֶשָּׂא לוֹ, interpreting נשא incorrectly in a reflexive sense 'lift myself up against'; cf. LXX rendering of Hos. 1. 6 כִּי נָשֹׂא אֶשָּׂא לָהֶם. Given the text of LXX, we might render 'for I will surely *forgive* him during his life-time &c.'; but this is inferior to MT.

37. ומלכת . . . נפשך] So exactly 2 Sam. 3. 21. Cf. Deut. 14. 26; 1 Sam. 2. 16. אִוָּה Pi'el and subs. אַוָּה are used almost exclusively in connexion with נֶפֶשׁ.

40. שישק] LXX Σουσακίμ, Luc. Σουσακείμ. Identified with Sheshonk I, first king of the twenty-second dynasty of Manetho. Cf. *ch.* 14. 25 *f. note.*

41 *ff.* ויתר וג׳] For this summarizing formula of R[D] see *Introd.*

וחכמתו] LXX, Luc. וְכָל־חָכְמָתוֹ, adopted by Th. upon the ground that *ch.* 5. 9–14 merely gives a summary account of this wisdom.

על ספר דברי ש׳] Luc. ἐν βιβλίῳ λόγων ἡμερῶν Σ., Vulg. *in libro verborum dierum S.*, i. e. על ספר דברי הימים לש׳, probably a correction in accordance with the phrase used in the records of the

[1] In LXX προσόχθισμα usually = תועבה, but never = שקץ; βδέλυγμα often = שֶׁקֶץ, שִׁקּוּץ, but more than twice as frequently = תועבה. In Deut. 7. 26 we get the two words in juxtaposition, שַׁקֵּץ תְּשַׁקְּצֶנּוּ וְתַעֵב תְּתַעֲבֶנּוּ, προσοχθίσματι προσοχθιεῖς καὶ βδελύγματι βδελύξῃ.

kings of Israel and Judah. 2 Chr. 9. 29 ושאר דברי ש׳ הראשנים והאחרונים הלא הם כתובים על דברי נתן הנביא ועל נבואת אחיה השילוני ובחזות יֶעְדּוֹ החזה על ירבעם בן נבט.

43. The notice with reference to the return of Jeroboam from Egypt, inserted correctly (see *note* on 11. 26—14. 20) by LXX, Luc. between *v.* 43^a and *v.* 43^b, must have run in the original:— וַיְהִי כִּשְׁמֹעַ יָרָבְעָם בֶּן־נְבָט וְהוּא עוֹדֶנּוּ בְמִצְרַיִם אֲשֶׁר בָּרַח מִפְּנֵי שְׁלֹמֹה וַיֵּשֶׁב בְּמִצְרַיִם וַיָּשָׁב וַיֵּלֶךְ אֶל־עִירוֹ אֶל־הַצְּרֵדָה אֲשֶׁר בְּהַר אֶפְרַיִם וַיִּשְׁכַּב הַמֶּלֶךְ שְׁלֹמֹה עִם־אֲבֹתָיו. LXX κατευθύνειν, Luc. more correctly καὶ κατευθύνει represents וַיָּשָׁב read as וַיְּשַׁר; cf. 1 Sam. 6. 12 וַיִּשַּׁרְנָה καὶ κατεύθυναν. In LXX τὴν γῆν Σαρειρά the word γῆν appears to be a corrupt repetition of τήν: cf. LXX *ch.* 12. 24^f, where LXX γῆν = Luc. τήν.

12. 1–24. *Reḥoboam's accession and the defection of the ten tribes.*

Ch. 12. 1–24 = 2 Chr. 10. 1—11. 4.

In this narrative *vv.* 15, 17, 21–24 appear to be additions of a later hand. *v.* 15, with its reference to the prediction of Aḥijah, probably presupposes *ch.* 11. 31 *ff.* in its present form, and must in this case be due to R^D. *vv.* 21–24, standing in close connexion with *v.* 15 (cf. *v.* 15 כי היתה סבה מעם י׳; *v.* 24 כי מאתי נהיה הדבר הזה), give a Judaic turn to the originally impartial narrative of *vv.* 1–20, and are scarcely consistent with the statement of *ch.* 14. 30 ומלחמה היתה בין רחבעם ובין ירבעם כל הימים, a genuine excerpt from the ancient annals. Notice further that, while *v.* 20 speaks only of the tribe of Judah, *vv.* 21, 23 are careful to make reference also to the tribe of Benjamin. *v.* 17, which stands in an awkward position, and is absent from LXX, is probably a later gloss, though not by the same hand as *vv.* 15, 21–24, since it makes no reference to Benjamin.

1. שכם] The Roman *Flavia Neapolis* and modern *Nâbulus*, lying under the north-east base of Mount Gerizim. See Rob. *BR.* ii. 275, 287 *ff.*; Baed. 252 *ff.*

2. וישב וג׳] Vulg., ∥ 2 Chr. 10. 2 וַיָּשָׁב יָרָבְעָם מִמִּצְרָיִם, correctly. Cf. *note* on *ch.* 11. 43 LXX.

3. See, on LXX, Luc., *note* on *chh.* 11. 26—14. 20. Pesh. omits קהל.

4. עלנו] על as a figure of *hard bondage* is very frequent, though always elsewhere of that imposed by a foreign nation:—Gen. 27. 40 (Israel's subjection of Edom); Lev. 26. 13; Hos. 11. 4; Jer. 2. 20 (Egypt); Isa. 9. 3; 10. 27; 14. 25 (Assyria); Jer. 27. 8, 11, 12; 28. 2, 4, 11, 14; 30. 8; Isa. 47. 6; Ezek. 34. 27 (Babylon); Deut. 28. 48 (general); of the moral restraints of religion Jer. 5. 5, cf. Lam. 3. 27; of the bonds of sin (late) Lam. 1. 14.

5. עֹד] LXX, Luc., Vulg., Pesh., Targ. presuppose עַד 'Depart *until* three days (sc. have elapsed),' i. e. 'until the third day.' This is doubtless correct. עֹד of MT. would rather suggest that a *previous* postponement had taken place.

העם] LXX, Luc. omit. Pesh. ܟܠܗ ܥܡܐ, i. e. כָּל־הָעָם.

6. וַיִּוָּעַץ] So with *pathaḥ* always in this form (11 times). According to König, *Lehrg.* I. i. 419, the emphatic pronunciation of the צ is better served by the broader '*Pathaḥ gadol* in place of *Pathaḥ qaton*' (=*Seghol*).

7. דברים טובים] 'Favourable words'; Zech. 1. 13.

כל הימים] Cf. *ch.* 5. 15 *note.*

8. אשר העמדים לפניו] 'Who were those who stood before him'; but this is harsh unless we read אשר הֵם העמדים וג׳. || 2 Chr. 10. 8, omitting אשר, gives the simple sense 'who stood before him,' and is doubtless correct.

10. ואתה] LXX, Luc. καὶ σὺ νῦν, i. e. ואתה עתה in conformity with *v.* 4.

קָטָנִּי] From *st. abs.* קֹטֶן. For vocalization cf. קָבָלּוֹ Ezek. 26. 9. Doubtless the original and correct form was קָטְנִי, like אָהֳלִי, פָּעֳלוֹ, with half-open syllable, and a later stage of pronunciation first raised the *ḥatef qameç* to the position of a full short vowel, and then proceeded in consequence to place it in a closed syllable by doubling the ל. So || 2 Chr. 10. 10 קָטָנִּי.

קטני, only here and in || 2 Chr., = 'my littleness,' so, no doubt rightly, 'my little finger,' Vulg., Pesh. LXX, Luc. ἡ μικρότης μου. Targ. paraphrases חלשותי 'my weakness.'

11. עקרבים] Explained by Pesh. ܡܪܓܢܐ, Targ. מרגנין, i.e. μάραγναι, 'scourges,' probably so named from being loaded with metal or

stones to produce keener *sting*. For the use of the article in בַּשּׁוטים, בָּעקרבים cf. *note* on בַּבגדים *ch.* 1. 1.

12. ויבו] Read Q're וַיָּבוֹא. The sing. verb agrees, as is frequently the case, with the nearest member of the compound subject. Cf. Da. § 114b. On this verse in LXX, Luc. cf. *note* on *chh.* 11. 26—14. 20.

13. ויען וג׳] 'And the king returned the people *a harsh response*.' For קָשָׁה '*something harsh*' cf. || 2 Chr. 10. 13; 1 Sam. 20. 10; *ch.* 14. 6; Ps. 60. 5; plur. קָשׁוֹת Gen. 42. 7, 30†.

15. סבה] A ἅπαξ λεγ.; something *turning* or bringing about, 'fate' or 'providence.' So LXX, Luc. μεταστροφή, Pesh. ܡܥܝܢܘܬܐ 'instigation'; Targ. פלונתא, passive, 'fated lot,' so || 2 Chr. 10. 15 נְסִבָּה ἅπαξ λεγ. The verb appears to be used with a similar sense in 1 Sam. 22. 22 אנכי סַבֹּתִי בכל נפש בית אביך 'I have brought about (sc. death) upon every member of thy father's house.' This, however, with ellipse of the direct object מָוֶת, is extremely harsh, and Th., Wellh., Dri., Budde emend חַבְתִּי '*I am guilty* in respect of &c.' In late Rabbinic Hebrew סִבָּה='cause.'

ביד אחיה] Cf. *ch.* 8. 53 *note*.

16. כל ישראל] Luc. πᾶς ὁ λαός, Vulg. *populus*.

לאמר וג׳] The words of Sheba son of Bichri are nearly identical; 2 Sam. 20. 1.

מה לנו חלק] 'There is *not* a portion to us'; practically equivalent to אֵין לנו חלק 2 Sam. 20. 1, but מה, originally interrogative=*num?* gives more emphatic point to the negation. This use of מה, though very usual in Arabic, is rare in Hebrew; Cant. 8. 4 מה תעירו ומה תעררו את האהבה answers to 2. 7; 3. 5 אם תעירו וג׳; cf. also Job 31. 1 ומה אתבונן על בתולה 'and how shall I gaze &c.'='and I will *not* gaze'; 9. 2; 16. 6; Prov. 20. 24. Ew. § 325b.

לְאֹהָלֶיךָ] With full long vowel in the antepenult upon which there dwells a *countertone*, thus facilitating the due pronunciation of the two weak letters אה. So אֹהָלָיו, אֹהָלִים. Cf. Sta. § 109.

ראה ביתך] The point of the taunt appears to be in the suffix of ביתך 'look to *thy* house' (so Th.), emphasizing the old division (2 Sam. 2. 4, 8–11) and jealous hostility (2 Sam. 2. 16; 19. 42–44) existing between the tribe of Judah and the northern tribes. For the nuance of ראה 'look after' cf. Gen. 39. 23. LXX, Luc. βόσκε τὸν οἶκόν σου, i. e. רְעֵה ביתך.

17. ובני ישראל] Luc. καὶ οἱ υἱοὶ Ἰούδα καὶ οἱ υἱοὶ Ἰσραήλ. The additional words represent a marginal correction afterwards inserted in the text.

ובני ישראל . . . וימלך עליהם] Cf. *ch.* 9. 21 *note.*

18. After וישלח המלך ר׳ Pesh. adds ܠܘܬ ܟܠܗ ܐܝܣܪܐܝܠ, i. e. אֶל־כָּל־יִשְׂרָאֵל.

אדרם] Luc., Pesh. read אֲדֹנִירָם; cf. *ch.* 4. 6 *note.*

המס] Cf. *ch.* 4. 6 *note.*

וירגמו . . . בו אבן] So with ב of person stoned ‖ 2 Chr. 10. 18; Lev. 24. 16†. Elsewhere once with עַל of person Ezek. 23. 47, but most generally with accusative Lev. 24. 14; *al.* (11 times). With ב of instrument בָּאבן, בָּאבנים Lev. 20. 2; Num. 14. 10; *al.*

19. עד היום הזה] Cf. *ch.* 8. 8 *note.*

20. שבט יהודה] LXX, Luc. add καὶ Βενιαμείν, for conformity with *v.* 23. Cf. *ch.* 11. 32, 36.

21. מאה ושמנים אלף] LXX, Luc. ἑκατὸν καὶ εἴκοσι χιλιάδες (-δας Luc.).

24. כי מאתי וג׳] Cf. *ch.* 1. 27.

12. 26–33. *Jeroboam's institution of the calf-worship.*

Judging by the stress which R^D constantly lays upon Jeroboam's cult as the cause of all subsequent deflexion of Israel from the pure worship of Yahwe (cf. *Introduction*), it is probable that this narrative has obtained its present *casting* at his hands, though there is no reason hence to infer that any detail of *fact* is underived from the older source. Kue. (*Ond.* § 25. 4) observes justly, 'Jeroboam's measures with reference to the worship must already have been related in older narratives, but it is only natural that the redactor, when dealing with a matter which so specially excited his interest, should not fail to set before us his own construction and his own verdict.' *vv.* 32, 33 serve to introduce the story of *ch.* 13. No special phrases of R^D are to be noticed.

28. רב לכם מעלות] Not, as RV. text, 'It is *too much for you* to go up' (this would be רַב מִכֶּם; cf. *ch.* 19. 7), but, as marg., 'Ye have gone up *long enough*.' The מן before עלות is logically redundant, as in Ezek. 44. 6 רַב־לָכֶם מִכָּל־תּוֹעֲבוֹתֵיכֶם 'Enough of all your abominations,' and the normal construction is that of Deut. 1. 6 רַב־לָכֶם שֶׁבֶת וג׳; 2. 3. Cf. the similar use of מן after הֲנָקֵל; Ezek. 8. 17 הֲנָקֵל לְבֵית יְהוּדָה מֵעֲשׂוֹת וג׳; but *ch.* 16. 31 הֲנָקֵל לֶכְתּוֹ.

הנה אלהיך וג׳] Cf. Ex. 32. 4, 8 (E).

29. וישם את האחד . . . ואת האחד נתן] For contrasted order of words cf. *ch.* 5. 25 *note*.

בית אל] The modern *Beitîn*, a short distance to the north of Michmash (*Mukhmâs*) of Benjamin, and so upon the southern frontier of Jeroboam's kingdom. For the substitution of Ar. *-în* for Heb. אֵל cf. *Zer'în*=יזרעאל. See Rob. *BR.* i. 448 *ff.*; Baed. 249.

30. לחטאת] Luc. adds τῷ Ἰσραήλ, לישראל, which, as more definite and agreeing with the frequent phrase of R^D אשר החטיא את ישראל, may be deemed correct.

וילכו וג׳] Obviously incomplete in making mention only of the worship at Dan. We should probably restore כִּי יֵלְכוּ הָעָם לִפְנֵי הָאֶחָד אֶל־בֵּית־אֵל וְלִפְנֵי הָאֶחָד עַד־דָּן 'for the people used to go before the one to Bethel and before the other unto Dan.' The words supplied may be thought to have fallen out through homoioteleuton, and in וילכו for כי ילכו we have a case of the confusion between כ and ו seen elsewhere in *ch.* 22. 37 וימת, LXX ὅτι τέθνηκεν, i.e. כִּי מֵת; Isa. 39. 1 וישמע for כי שמע; Jer. 37. 16 כי בא for ויבא; 1 Sam. 2. 21 כי פקד for ויפקד. Luc., which adds καὶ πρὸ προσώπου τῆς ἄλλης εἰς Βαιθήλ *after* the reference to Dan, probably exhibits a later restoration of the text, since, if this be regarded as the original order, it is not clear why the words should have fallen out. Vulg. *ibat enim populus ad adorandum vitulum usque in Dan* paraphrases in order to overcome the difficulty of the single האחד. LXX, Pesh., Targ. as MT.

31. ויעש את בית במות] Read, with Luc., ויעש ירבעם בית במות

'And Jeroboam made houses of high places,' i.e. temples erected upon the high places. בית is collective, as in II. 17. 29, 32 בְּבֵית הַבָּמוֹת of the temples of the various cults at Samaria. *Ch.* 13. 32; II. 23. 19, plur. בָּתֵּי הַבָּמוֹת. The use of את before the indefinite בית במות is anomalous; the case being different to *ch.* 16. 18 וישרף עליו את בית מלך 'and he burnt the king's house over him,' where בית מלך, like מקדש מלך, בית ממלכה Am. 7. 13, is really definite; cf. Da. § 22, *Rem.* 3; Ew. § 277^c^. Cases like 1 Sam. 24. 6 (cf. LXX); 2 Sam. 5. 24[1] (cf. || 1 Chr. 14. 15); 18. 18, where את appears to be used before an indefinite object, are probably textual errors.

מקצות העם] '*From among the whole of* the people'; lit. 'from the end of.' So *ch.* 13. 33; II. 17. 32; Gen. 19. 4 כל העם מִקָּצֶה 'all the people, *one and all*'; Jer. 51. 31 נלכדה עירו מִקָּצֶה 'his city is taken *throughout*'; Isa. 56. 11 כלם לדרכם פנו איש לבצעו מִקָּצֵהוּ 'all of them have turned to their own way, each to his gain, *one and all*'; Ezek. 25. 9 מעריו מִקָּצֵהוּ 'from his cities *in every quarter*'; 33. 2 איש אחד מִקְצֵיהֶם 'one man *from among the whole of them*.' The phrase may be illustrated e.g. by Num. 22. 41 וירא משם קְצֵה העם 'and he saw thence *the uttermost part of* the people,' and so, by implied inclusion, *the whole of them*.

32. בחמשה עשר יום] Pesh. ܒܟܣܐ here and in *v.* 33, i.e. 'upon the full moon'; cf. Heb. בַּכֶּסֶה Ps. 81. 4.

כֶּחָג] 'Like *the* feast,' i.e. the feast of Tabernacles; cf. *ch.* 8. 2, 65. This, however, was on the fifteenth day of the *seventh* month, Lev. 23. 34; hence the statement of *v.* $33^{a\beta}$.

ויעל על המזבח] Cf. *ch.* 1. 53 *note*.

כן עשה . . . אשר עשה] There can be little doubt that this latter portion of *v.* 32, together with the first three words of *v.* 33 ויעל על המזבח repeated from the previous verse, represents a very early gloss inserted on account of the omission in *v.* 30. After the loss of the words to be supplied in this latter verse, לפני האחד אל ביתאל ו, it is clear that the reference to the institution of the priests and the

[1] Da.'s explanation of את קול צעדה as 'a *known* kind of divine rustling' is inadequate; § 72, *Rem.* 4.

festival, *vv.* 31, 32$^{a\,\alpha}$, might be taken to refer only to the sanctuary at Dan, and so give rise to this explanatory insertion. Notice the awkwardness of כן עשה *asyndetos*, and והעמיד perf. with weak ו.

33. ויעל . . . השמיני] Pesh. omits.

אשר בדא מִלִּבֹּד] 'Which he had invented out of his own heart.' בדא occurs only once beside in OT.; Neh. 6. 8 מִלִּבְּךָ אַתָּה בוֹדָאם 'out of thine own heart art thou inventing them' (for בוֹדְאָם). In Rabbinic Hebrew and Aramaic the verb has the same meaning, always with a bad *nuance*. Q're מִלִּבּוֹ, with the sense 'at his own initiative,' is correct; cf. Num. 16. 28; 24. 13; Ezek. 13. 2, 17.

13. 1–32. *The prophecy against the altar at Bethel.*

The style of the language shows traces of decadence:—cf. וְנָתַן perf. with weak ו *v.* 3, צוה אתי, דבר אלי apparently first written as דָּבָר אֵלַי, צִוֵּיתִי *vv.* 9, 17, לנביא אשר השיבו *v.* 23 (but cf. *note ad loc.*), and perhaps מחת *v.* 7—and this fact, together with the anachronism בערי שמרון *v.* 32 (cf. II. 17. 24, 26; 23. 19), and the non-mention of the names of the principal actors, marks the narrative as being of comparatively late origin. It may be thought to have been a story previously current in the form of oral tradition, and to have assumed a literary form very shortly after the event predicted—the destruction of the altar at Bethel—had come about. Notice the precision of the statement יאשיהו שמו *v.* 2. The style is about contemporary with that of the annals of Josiah's reformation, II. 23. 1–15, 19–24, where the perf. with weak ו is used with some frequency:—*vv.* 4, 5, 8, 10, 12, 14, 15. It is, however, by no means to be hence inferred that the story is of the character of a *vaticinium post eventum*. Such a view presupposes that it, together with the notice of II. 23. 16–18, was inserted into Kings subsequently to the redaction of R^D (Wellh. *C.* 280; Kue. *Ond.* § 25. 4); whereas on the contrary *ch.* 12. 26 *ff.* appears to have been carefully edited by R^D so as to lead up to the story, and the resumption of the main narrative in *ch.* 13. 33, 34, forming the link to *ch.* 14. 1–20, constructs of the history a harmonious whole. If the story be merely a very late Judaean fiction, the point of the details as to the disobedience and punishment of the *Judaean* prophet seems to be quite inexplicable.

1. בדבר י׳] So *vv.* 2, 5, 9, 17, 18, 32. Elsewhere in this sense *ch.* 20. 35; 1 Sam. 3. 21; 2 Chr. 30. 12†. בִּדְבָרֵי י׳ 2 Chr. 29. 15†.

עמד על המזבח] Cf. *ch.* 1. 53 *note.*

2. כה אמר] Pesh. prefixes ܫܡܥܘ ܦܬܓܡܗ ܕܡܪܝܐ 'Hear the word of the Lord.'

ישרפו] Impers. 'shall they burn,' so 'shall be burnt.' LXX, Luc., Vulg., Pesh. presuppose יִשָּׂרֵף.

3. מופת] 'A wonder' or 'miracle,' as a proof of the divine commission; so Ex. 4. 21; 7. 9; 2 Chr. 32. 24, 31; cf. Deut. 13. 2, 3.

6. חל נא את פני י׳] 'Entreat the favour of Yahwe'; lit. '*Make sweet the face* &c.' Ar. حَلَا, حَلِيَ, Aram. חֲלִי, ܚܠܐ = *to be sweet* or *pleasant.*

כבראשנה] Judg. 20. 32; Isa. 1. 26; Jer. 33. 7, 11†. More loosely כְּבָרִאשֹׁנָה Deut. 9. 18; Dan. 11. 29†.

7. וּסְעָדָה] So וּצְעָקִי Jer. 22. 20, וּסְאָה II. 7. 18. Elsewhere we find *ḥatef-pathaḥ* with a sibilant after the *ū*-sound:—וּשֲׁבַע *ch.* 14. 21, וּשֲׁלַח II. 9. 17, וּשֲׁמָע II. 19. 16ᵃ, וּזֲהַב Gen. 2. 12, וּשֲׁקָה 27. 26, וּשֲׂדֵה Lev. 25. 34, וּשֲׁבֵה Judg. 5. 12, Dan. 9. 18. According to G-K. (§ 10 *g*) the *ḥatef-qameç* in the former cases arises under the influence both of the preceding *ū and* the following guttural; but probably König (*Lehrg.* I. i. 262) is correct in regarding the slightly fuller sound of this half-vowel as due to the more emphatic sibilants ס, צ.

מתת] Ezek. 46. 5. 11; Prov. 25. 14; Eccl. 3. 13; 5. 18†. A bye-form of the more usual מַתָּנָה, contracted from מַתֶּנֶת.

8. אם תתן וג׳] Cf. the words of Balaam, Num. 22. 18; 24. 13 (JE). On the form of the conditional sentence, expressing the merest (hyperbolical) possibility, cf. Dri. *Tenses*, § 143.

9. כי כן צוה אתי] 'For so one commanded me,' the implied subject being the voice of Yahwe, or, as in *v.* 18, the divine messenger. For other instances of this semi-impersonal construction, employed where the intervention of divine agency (or agencies) is implied,

cf. Zech. 9. 12 מגיד; and in plur. Job 7. 3 מִנּוּ־לִי; Ezek. 32. 25 נתנו. So in Aramaic Dan. 4. 22 טרדין; 4. 28 אמרין; *al.* It seems, however, to be not improbable that צוה אתי represents the alteration of an original צֻוֵּיתִי 'I was commanded.' Cf. Wellh. *C.* 280; Klo., Kamp., Benz., Kit. See on דבר לי *v.* 17.

11. נביא אחד זקן] '*A certain* old prophet.' For this use of אחד, mainly characteristic of northern Palestinian narrative and of the later style, cf. instances cited p. 209. The usage is common in Rabbinic Hebrew. Luc. προφήτης ἄλλος, i. e. נביא אַחֵר; 'and *another* prophet, an old man, was dwelling in Bethel.' אחר, where the name of neither prophet is mentioned, is most apposite, and may well be original.

ויבא בנו וג׳] LXX, Luc., Vulg., Pesh. presuppose וַיָּבֹאוּ בָנָיו וַיְסַפְּרוּ rightly, in accordance with plur. ויספרום *v.* 11ᵇ, אלהם *v.* 12.

היום] '*That* day.' So only here. The writer seems to lapse into the point of view of the sons, to whom it was היום '*to-day.*' Luc. ἐν τῇ ἡμέρᾳ ἐκείνῃ suggests the more usual בַּיּוֹם ההוּא, but is more likely to be an alteration of LXX ἐν τῇ ἡμέρᾳ.

ויספרום וג׳] Resuming the previous ויספרו; cf. *ch.* 2. 4 *note.* LXX, Luc. strangely καὶ ἐπέστρεψαν τὸ πρόσωπον τοῦ πατρὸς αὐτῶν, apparently reading through corruption ויסרפנם לאביהם, i. e. וַיָּסִירוּ פָּנִים לַאֲבִיהֶם; ἐπέστρεψαν an alteration of ἀπέστρεψαν.

12. וידבר אלהם אביהם] LXX, Luc. add λέγων; so Klo. לֵאמֹר. But the word is similarly absent in MT., and supplied by LXX, Luc. in *vv.* 17, 22.

אי זה הדרך] 'Where is the way?' so 'Which way?' So II. 3. 8; 2 Chr. 18. 23; Job 38. 19, 24, always, as here, with omission of relative אשר before the following verb. On the enclitic זה, strongly pointing the question, cf. *note* on למה זה *ch.* 14. 6.

וַיִּרְאוּ וג׳] 'Now his sons *had seen* &c.' LXX, Luc., Vulg., Pesh. are greatly superior in presupposing וַיַּרְאוּ 'and his sons *showed* (him).' So Benz., Kit. וַיַּרְאֻהוּ, Klo., Kamp. וַיֹּרֻהוּ; cf. Ex. 15. 25.

14. האלה] '*The* terebinth,' which the writer's vivid imagination pictures as the tree under which the prophet was sitting. So *ch.* 18. 4 ויחביאם . . . בַּמערה 'and hid them in *the cave,*' marked

as having thus afforded an asylum; 2 Sam. 17. 17 והלכה השפחה 'and *a wench* used to go &c.,' pictured by the writer as '*the* wench' simply as being the agent thus employed; 1 Sam. 9. 9 כה אמר האיש 'thus spake *the man*,' who, as a matter of fact, did so speak; but according to English idiom, 'thus spake *a man*'; 2 Sam. 15. 13; Gen. 14. 13; *al.* This method of thought may be most clearly understood in such a case as 1 Sam. 17. 34 ובא הארי 'and if *a lion* came,' where the speaker has had *active experience* of the coming of the lions which he thus recalls to his mind. Cf. Da. § 21 ϵ. This use of the article is a very idiomatic extension of the usage noticed in *ch.* 1. 1.

16. ולבוא אתך] LXX, Luc. omit. Pesh. ܘܠܡܥܠ ܠܒܝܬܟ, i. e. ולבוא בֵיתֶךָ 'and to enter thy house,' is preferable to MT.

ולא אשתה אתך] LXX, Luc., Vulg., Pesh. omit אתך, but Pesh. supplies the word after the previous ולא אכל.

17. כי דָבָר אלי] LXX, Luc., Pesh., Targ. suggest כי דֻבַּר אלי 'for *it was said* unto me.' So Wellh., Klo., Kamp., Benz., Kit. Cf. *note* on *v.* 9.

18. מלאך] As in *ch.* 19. 5; Zech. 1. 9, 14; *al.* מלאך יהוה *ch.* 19. 7; II. 1. 3, 15; Gen. 16. 7; 22. 11; Ex. 3. 2; *al.*

כחש לו] The perfect thus used *asyndetos* forms a circumstantial clause,—'*lying unto him*'; cf. *ch.* 7. 51 נתן; 18. 6 אחאב הלך וג׳ 'Ahab going one way &c.' Dri. *Tenses*, § 163.

19. וַיָּשָׁב אִתּוֹ] LXX, Luc. καὶ ἐπέστρεψεν αὐτόν, i. e. וַיָּשֶׁב אתו.

20. ויהי הם ישבים . . . ויהי וג׳] 'And it came to pass—they were sitting at the table—and there came &c.'; so, 'And it came to pass, *as they were sitting* at the table, that there came &c.' The circumstantial clause הם ישבים אל השלחן, elevated to so striking a position *in advance of* the principal sentence, lays great stress upon the moment of time at which the event described by the latter took place. Cf. II. 2. 11 ויהי המה הלכים הלוך ודבר והנה רכב אש וג׳ 'And it came to pass, *while they were going on and talking as they went*, that behold a chariot of fire &c.'; II. 8. 5. Cf. Dri. *Tenses*, § 165, who terms the participle thus used *the participle absolute.*

אל השלחן] '*At* the table'; cf. *ch.* 6. 18 *note* for this use of אל.

In Neh. 5. 17 we have עַל־שֻׁלְחָנִי, lit. '*above* or *over* my table'; 1 Sam. 20. 34 Jonathan gets up מעם השלחן '*from proximity with* the table.' When the idea of *eating* at the table is prominent, it is natural and accurate to use עַל '*upon*'; so 2 Sam. 9. 7, 10, 13, cf. Ezek. 39. 20. In *ch.* 2. 7; 18. 19; 2 Sam. 19. 29, however, we have the simple *st. constr.* employed;—אֹכְלֵי שֻׁלְחָן.

21. יען כי] So *ch.* 21. 29; Num. 11. 20; Isa. 3. 16; 7. 5; 8. 6; 29. 13. The more usual expression is יַעַן אֲשֶׁר; *ch.* 3. 11; 8. 18; *al.* יַעַן appears to be originally a substantive = '*response*,' contracted from יַעֲנֶה from verb ענה. So with מַעַן in the phrase לְמַעַן 'on account of,' 'in order (that).' Cf. עֵקֶב 'recompense' used in the sense 'in return for,' 'because'; Deut. 7. 12; *al.*

מרית פי י׳] So *v.* 26; 1 Sam. 12. 15; Num. 20. 24; 27. 14; Lam. 1. 18†; and with Hiph'îl Deut. 1. 26, 43; 9. 23; Josh. 1. 18; 1 Sam. 12. 14†.

22. לא תבא וג׳] Illustrated by the dying injunction of Jacob, Gen. 47. 30, and of Joseph, 50. 25.

23. שתותו] LXX, Luc., Pesh. add מַיִם in accordance with *vv.* 8, 16, 18, 19.

לנביא אשר השיבו] Very awkward. The sentence would most obviously mean 'for the prophet who had brought him back' (cf. *vv.* 20, 26), but in accordance with the context can only be rendered 'for the prophet whom he had brought back,' the suffix of השיבו referring back to the antecedent נביא, as in Aram.; cf. Duval, *Gramm. Syr.* § 399 *b.* LXX, Luc., in place of these words and the וילך of *v.* 24ᵃ, read καὶ ἐπέστρεψεν καὶ ἀπῆλθεν, i.e. וַיָּשָׁב וַיֵּלֶךְ: '*and he once more departed*'; probably the original text. Pesh. ܠܢܒܝܐ ܕܐܠܗܐ܂ ܘܗܦܟ ܘܐܙܠ, i.e. לְנְבִיא אֱלֹהִים וַיָּשָׁב וַיֵּלֶךְ, suggests that MT. arose from the incorporation into the text of the words לנביא אלהים, a marginal note explanatory of the previous לו.

24. ותהי . . . משלכת] Cf. *ch.* 5. 1 *note* on היה משל.

26ᵇ, 27. LXX omits.

26. כדבר וג׳] The phrase כדבר י׳ אשר דבר occurs frequently in Kings to call attention to the fulfilment of a prophecy. So *ch.* 22. 38. Most often mention of the prophetic agent is added in the form

בְּיַד פ׳;—*ch.* 14. 18; 15. 29; 16. 12, 34; 17. 16; II. 14. 25; 24. 2. Cf. also II. 10. 17; 4. 44; 7. 16; 9. 26; 1. 17; 23. 16; 2. 22.

28ª. וחמור והאריה] Emend וְהַחֲמוֹר והאריה. Klo. וַחֲמוֹרוֹ וג׳.

28ᵇ. את הנבלה] LXX τὸ σῶμα τοῦ ἀνθρώπου τοῦ θεοῦ, to harmonize with *v.* 29.

29. אל החמור] אל for על; cf. *ch.* 16. 13; 18. 46; II. 5. 11; 9. 3, 12; Josh. 5. 14; 1 Sam. 13. 13; *al.* For the converse change, after a verb of motion, cf. *ch.* 1. 38 *note.*

וישיבהו . . . לקברו] LXX, Luc. run more smoothly and naturally:—καὶ ἐπέστρεψεν αὐτὸν (Luc. αὐτὸ) εἰς τὴν πόλιν ὁ προφήτης, τοῦ θάψαι αὐτόν, i. e. וַיְשִׁיבֵהוּ הַנָּבִיא אֶל־הָעִיר לְקָבְרוֹ. LXX, however, is incorrect in omitting וינח את נבלתו of *v.* 30 and joining בְּקִבְרוֹ on to לקברו of *v.* 29.

30. ויספדו] Luc., Pesh. presuppose sing. וַיִּסְפֹּד.

הוי אחי] Cf. Jer. 22. 18.

31. אחרי קברו אתו] LXX, Luc. μετὰ τὸ κόψασθαι αὐτόν, Vulg. *cumque planxissent eum*, presuppose אחרי סָפְדוֹ עָלָיו.

במותי וקברתם אתי] 'When I die, then bury me.' For the ו *consec.* with perf. after the very terse time determination cf. Ezek. 24. 24 בבואה וידעתם 'When it (the sign) come to pass, ye shall know &c.' Dri. *Tenses*, § 123 β, Da. § 56.

32. בתי הבמות] Cf. *ch.* 12. 31 *note.*

בערי שמרון] Cf. *note* on *vv.* 1–32.

13. 33, 34. *A brief resumption by* Rᴰ *of the main thread of the history from the end of chapter* 12.

33. אחר הדבר הזה] 'After this *event.*' The phrase occurs only here, the more usual (and less precise) expression being אחר הדברים האלה *ch.* 17. 17; 21. 1; Gen. 15. 1; 22. 1; 40. 1; Ezr. 7. 1; Est. 2. 1; 3. 1†; אחרי הדברים האלה Gen. 22. 20; 48. 1; Josh. 24. 29; 2 Chr. 32. 1†.

לא שב . . . מדרכו הרעה] Jer. 18. 11; 25. 5; 26. 3; 35. 15; 36. 3, 7; Jon. 3. 8, 10; Ezek. 13. 22 (מדרכו הָרָע)†; and with pl.

II. 17. 13 (R^D); 2 Chr. 7. 14; Zech. 1. 4†. Cf. Jer. 23. 22; Ezek. 3. 19; 33. 11.

מקצות העם] Cf. *ch.* 12. 31 *note.*

ימלא את ידו] 'He used to fill his hand,' i.e. 'he would *install him*' as priest. The expression seems to be derived from the ceremony of filling the hands of the person to be consecrated with the choice portions of the sacrifice for a waive-offering Ex. 29. 22–25; Lev. 8. 25–28, these being called מִלֻּאִים Lev. 8. 28. The phrase is used of the consecration of the priest at Micah's sanctuary Judg. 17. 5, 12, but is elsewhere characteristic of P and of later Books.

ויהי כהני במות] Impossible. LXX, Luc., Vulg., Pesh. וַיְהִי כֹּהֵן לַבָּמוֹת 'and he became priest to the high-places'; so Kamp. Klo. prefers to follow Targ. and emend וְהָיוּ כֹּהֲנֵי בָמוֹת.

34. לחטאת וג׳] Read, with LXX, Luc., Pesh. לְחַטָּאת לְבֵית יר׳. Cf. *ch.* 12. 30ª.

להשמיד מעל פני האדמה] So Deut. 6. 15; Am. 9. 8†; cf. Josh. 23. 15 (D^2). השמיד, pass. נשמד is very frequent in Deut. (27 times); cf. Dri. *Deut.* 1. 27.

14. 1–18. *The sickness and death of Jeroboam's son Abijah.*

Upon the LXX Version of this narrative in its relationship to MT. see *note* on *chh.* 11. 26—14. 20. The story exhibits very clear traces of the hand of R^D in Aḥijah's prophecy *vv.* 7–16, with which should be compared the prophecies of Jehu son of Ḥanani against Ba'asha *ch.* 16. 1–4, of Elijah against Aḥab *ch.* 21. 20–24, and of the young prophet against the house of Aḥab II. 9. 6–10. The following phrases are to be noticed:—

7. י׳ אלהי ישראל] So *v.* 13. Cf. *ch.* 8. 15 *note.*

יען וג׳] So exactly *ch.* 16. 2ª.

8. ולא היית כעבדי דוד] Cf. *ch.* 3. 14 *note* on כאשר הלך דוד.

אשר שמר מצותי] Cf. *ch.* 2. 3 *note.*

הלך אחרי] Cf. *ch.* 11. 5 *note.*

בכל לבבו] Cf. *ch.* 2. 4 *note.*

לעשות וג׳] Cf. *ch.* 11. 33 *note.*

9. ותרע . . . לפניך] Cf. *ch.* 16. 25, 30, 33; II. 17. 2; II. 21. 11. As used of Jeroboam the expression מכל אשר היו לפניך is somewhat mechanical.

אלהים אחרים] Cf. *ch.* 9. 6 *note.*

להכעיסני] Not, as RV., 'to provoke me to anger,' but, 'to *vex* me' by treatment wholly undeserved. So subs. כַּעַס='*vexation*' or '*chagrin*,' the rendering 'grief' being too general, and 'anger' incorrect; cf. Ps. 10. 14; 1 Sam. 1. 16; Job 6. 2. The verb (Hiph'îl) is very characteristic of R^D:—*v.* 15; 15. 30; 16. 2, 7, 13, 26, 33; 21. 22; 22. 54; II. 17. 11, 17; 21. 6 (‖ 2 Chr. 33. 6), 15; 22. 17 (‖ 2 Chr. 34. 25); 23. 19, 26; cf. 2 Chr. 28. 25; Deut. 4. 25; 9. 18; 31. 29; 32. 16; Jer. 7. 18, 19; 8. 19; 11. 17; 25. 6, 7; 32. 29, 30, 32; 44. 3, 8. Elsewhere, with יהוה as obj., only six times. Pi'el, Deut. 32. 21.

10. הנני מביא רעה אל] Cf. *ch.* 21. 21; II. 22. 16 (‖ 2 Chr. 34. 24 על; cf. *v.* 20 ‖ 2 Chr. 34. 28) both R^D; Jer. 6. 19; 11. 11 (cf. *v.* 23); cf. 19. 15; 35. 17. With על II. 21. 12 R^D; Jer. 19. 3; 45. 5; cf. Jer. 17. 18; 23. 12; 36. 31; 49. 37; 51. 64.

משתין בקיר] *Ch.* 16. 11; 21. 21; II. 9. 8 R^D. Only besides 1 Sam. 25. 22, 34†.

עצור ועזוב] *Ch.* 21. 21; II. 9. 8; 14. 26 (all R^D); Deut. 32. 36†. The phrase means '*restrained and let loose*' (עזב as in Ex. 23. 5 'release'; Job 10. 1), i.e. '*all*,' every one being supposed to fall under one of the two categories. Cf. the expressions of Deut. 29. 18 הרוה את הצמאה; Isa. 2. 9 וישח אדם וישפל איש 'mean man . . . great man'; Ps. 49. 3; Job 12. 16; Eccl. 9. 2; and for examples from Ar. cf. *Thes.* 1008, 1362. The precise application of the phrase is obscure. The most plausible explanation is that of Ew. *Antiquities*, 170, '*kept in* (by legal defilement) *and at large.*' For this sense of עצור cf. Jer. 36. 5 אני עצור לא אוכל לבוא בית י׳; 1 Sam. 21. 8 נעצר לפני י׳. So R. Sm. *Rel. Sem.*[2] 456;

Dri. *Deut.* 32. 36. Other suggestions are:—'*bond and free,*' Ges.; cf. עצר II. 17. 4; Jer. 33. 1; *al.*: '*married and celibate,*' De Dieu, Ke.; Ar. عَزِيبٌ '*azîb* = 'celibate,' أَعْصَرُ '*a'ṣaru*, explained wrongly (cf. Roediger, *Thes.* Append. 104) as 'paterfamilias': '*under and over age,*' Th., Kamp., following Schmidt, 'puer, qui domi adhuc *detinetur*, et qui *emancipatus* est.' For the alliteration of the phrase Dri. (*loc. cit.*) cites נִין וָנֶכֶד Isa. 14. 22; Gen. 21. 23; Job 18. 19; עֵר וְעֹנֶה Mal. 2. 12; שֹׁד וָשֶׁבֶר Isa. 59. 7; 60. 18; Jer. 48. 3; Ecclus. 40. 9; שָׁמִיר וָשַׁיִת Isa. 5. 6; *al.* (7 times). Add נָע וָנָד Gen. 4. 12, 14; הֶגֶה וָהִי Ezek. 2. 10; צָנִיף וְצִיץ Ecclus. 40. 4; חַרְחֻר וָחֹרֶב Deut. 28. 22; Ecclus. 40. 9[1]; דֶּבֶר וָדָם Ezek. 5. 17; cf. 38. 22.

ובערתי אחרי] Cf. *ch.* 21. 21†; מבעיר אחרי *ch.* 16. 3†; both R^D.

11. המת וג׳] *Ch.* 16. 4; 21. 24† R^D; cf. II. 9. 10, 36; *ch.* 21. 19, 23; 22. 38.

15. מעל האדמה הטובה הזאת] So exactly Josh. 23. 13, 15 (D²) †. The usual phrase in Deut. of the land of Canaan is הארץ הטובה; cf. Dri. *Deut.* lxxxi.

אשר נתן לאבותיהם] Cf. *ch.* 8. 34 *note.*

16. בגלל חטאות וג׳] Cf. *ch.* 15. 30. Reference to the sins of Jeroboam in these terms is very constant in R^D. See *Introd.*

1. בעת ההיא] A phrase employed by R^D in synchronizing events narrated in different sources; II. 16. 6; 18. 16; 20. 12; 24. 10. Cf. *ch.* 8. 65; 11. 29; II. 8. 22. For similar expressions thus used cf. *note* on אז *ch.* 3. 16.

2. והשתנית] *Hithpa'el* only here: 'and thou shalt *change thyself,*' i. e. 'change thy clothes,' 'disguise thyself.' So in Syr. ܐܫܬܢܝ for ܐܬܫܢܝ Ethpe'el of ܫܢܐ, here and in *ch.* 22. 30; 1 Sam. 10. 6; *al.*

ולא ידעו] Impers., 'that (men) may not know,' so RV. 'that thou be not known.'

---

[1] The vocalization חֹרֶב 'drought,' in preference to חֶרֶב, is adopted by most moderns. Cf. Dri. *Deuteronomy, ad loc.*

אתי] Kt. אַתִּי as in II. 4. 16, 23; 8. 1; Judg. 17. 2; Jer. 4. 30; Ezek. 36. 13†; Q're always אַתְּ. אַתִּי is the more ancient form of the pron. 2nd pers. fem. sing., and appears to be a dialectical survival. Cf. Ar. أَنْتِ, Eth. አንቲ: *anti;* Assyr. *atti-e;* Syr. ܐܢܬܝ *att,* where ܝ, though written, is not pronounced.

שִׁלֹה] Also written שִׁלוֹ, שִׁילוֹ; probably originally שִׁלוֹן, and so גִּלֹה Josh. 15. 51; 2 Sam. 15. 12 originally גִּלוֹן, as forming adjectives שִׁילֹנִי *ch.* 11. 29; *al.;* גִּלוֹנִי 2 Sam. 15. 12; 23. 34. Wright, however (*Compar. Gramm.* 138 *f.*), suggests the possibility of an original *Shailâ'u, Gailâ'u* with termination like Ar. ـَاءُ. The site of Shiloh is described in Judg. 21. 19 as 'N. of Beth-el, E. of the highway which goes up from Beth-el to Shechem, S. of Lebonah,' and this accurately corresponds to the modern *Seilûn;* cf. Rob. *BR.* ii. 268 *ff.;* Baed. 250.

הוא דבר עלי למלך] 'He spoke of me *as* (lit. *for*) king,' i.e. predicted that I should be king; a use of ל common in such phrases as נתן ל, שים ל, עשה ל, פקד ל, but somewhat strange after דבר. Cod. A τοῦ βασιλεῦσαι, Vulg. *quod regnaturus essem*, Pesh. ܐܡܠܟ, Targ. למהוי מלכא suggest לִמְלֹךְ '*that I should reign,*' probably correctly. So Th., Klo., Kamp., Benz., Kit.

3. נקדים] Only elsewhere Josh. 9. 5, 12, where the word denotes dry fragments of old bread. Here probably some kind of *cakes* or dry *biscuits;* so LXX, Luc. κολλύρια, Vulg. *crustulam*, Pesh. ܟܣܢܐ, Targ. כיסנין (cf. Levy *s. v.*).

5. ויהוה אמר] 'Now Yahwe *had* said'; pluperfect. The writer, wishing to narrate an event *anterior* to that described in the previous verse ותבוא וג׳, cuts the thread of continuous narrative formed by the succession of imperfects with ו *consec.* by interposing the subject between the conjunction and the verb, and thus starts afresh from a new standpoint. Cf. *ch.* 22. 31 ומלך ארם צוה '*had* commanded,' prior to the commencement of the battle; II. 7. 17; 9. 16ᵇ; Gen. 31. 34; *al.;* Dri. § 76 γ *Obs.*

לדרש דבר] 'To seek an oracle.'† Cf. II. 1. 16 לדרש בדברו. The more usual phrase is לדרש את יהוה 'To seek, or inquire of Yahwe'; *ch.* 22. 8; II. 22. 18; Gen. 25. 22; *al.*

כָּזֹה וְכָזֶה] So Judg. 18. 4; 2 Sam. 11. 25. On זֹה cf. II. 6. 19 *note.*

ויהי כבאה וג׳] Read, with Cod. A, Vulg. וַיְהִי כבאה וג׳ 'And it came to pass that, as she came in, she was dissembling herself.' The sentence belongs to the narrator's description, and not, as the MT. vocalization is intended to indicate, to the words of Yahwe. מתנכרה lit. 'making herself strange' here and in *v.* 6; elsewhere in this sense only in Gen. 42. 7, of Joseph's conduct to his brethren.

6. את קול רגליה באה] 'The sound of her feet as she came in.' The participle באה agrees with the suffix of רגליה. So, if vocalization be correct, Ps. 69. 4 כָּלוּ עֵינַי מְיַחֵל וג׳ 'mine eyes consume as I wait &c.' Cf. *note* on *ch.* 1. 41.

למה זה] 'Why, now?' or, with emphasis, '*Why?*' The enclitic זה, with something of adverbial force, gives point and colour to the query. So often:—Gen. 18. 13; 25. 22; *al.* Cf. מַה־זֶּה *ch.* 21. 5; *al.;* מִי־זֶה 1 Sam. 17. 55, 56; *al.;* אֵי־זֶה *ch.* 13. 12 *note;* with ה interr. הַאַתָּה זֶה *ch.* 18. 7 *note;* הִנֵּה־זֶה *ch.* 19. 5 *note;* עַתָּה־זֶה *ch.* 17. 24; II. 5. 22. In Ar. ذَا is used in the same way:—لِمَاذَا, مَاذَا, مَنْ ذَا; cf. Fleischer, *Kleinere Schriften*, i. 355 *f.*

ואנכי שלוח אליך קשה] 'Seeing that I am sent unto thee with something harsh.' קשה is direct accusative after שלוח,—'given in commission something harsh,' and with an active verb would form the remoter accusative,—שְׁלָחַנִי קָשָׁה 'he has commissioned me (with) something harsh.' For this use of שלח with double accusative cf. Ex. 4. 28 כל דברי י׳ אשר שְׁלָחוֹ; so with צִוָּה, 1 Sam. 21. 3 המלך צוני דבר; Ex. 34. 32; *al.* For קשה cf. *ch.* 12. 13 *note.*

7. נגיד] Cf. *ch.* 1. 35 *note.*

9. ואתי השלכת וג׳] So Ezek. 23. 35; Neh. 9. 26. Of Yahwe's remission of sins, Isa. 38. 17†. Cf. Ps. 50. 17.

10. עצור וג׳] See *note* on *vv.* 1 *ff.*

כאשר יבער הגלל] Cf. *ch.* 1. 6 *note.*

12. בבאה] If not an error for בְּבֹא, an isolated instance of the feminine termination with infin. constr. of a verb ע״ו. The explanation of Ew. § 309[c], that the termination is suff. 3 fem. sing. (with omission of *Mappiq* from ה as in II. 8. 6; *al.*), and refers by anticipation to הָעִירָה, is very unnatural.

13. דבר טוב] 'Something good.'

14. זה היום] '*To-day!*' or 'this very day!' If the text be correct (cf. *note* following), זה is used δεικτικῶς, and adds point to היום which in English can scarcely be brought out but by emphasis in pronunciation. Occurrences of the pronoun thus preceding the subs. to which it is in apposition are rare and in most cases poetical. Cf., however, II. 6. 33 זֹאת הָרָעָה; Isa. 23. 13 זֶה הָעָם; Josh. 9. 12 זֶה לַחְמֵנוּ.

ומה גם עתה] Most obscure, and probably corrupt. The only possible rendering seems to be 'But what? (*sc.* do I say?' מה used *asyndetos* as in Prov. 31. 2), so with emphasis '*Nay*, even *now!*' The words thus form a climax to זה היום, as though this expression did not sufficiently depict the instant imminence of the destruction of Jeroboam's house.

15. אשריהם] 'Their Asherim.' The אֲשֵׁרָה was made of wood Judg. 6. 26, probably in most cases of a whole tree-trunk, Deut. 16. 21 (אֲשֵׁרָה כָּל־עֵץ in appos. 'an Ashera—any kind of tree'), and was planted (נטע Deut. *l.c.*) or set on end (העמיד 2 Chr. 33. 19) in the ground. When destroyed it is said to be cut down (כרת Judg. 6. 25; II. 18. 4; 23. 14), chopped down (גדע Deut. 7. 5; 2 Chr. 14. 2; 31. 1), plucked up (נתש Mic. 5. 13), pulled down (נתץ 2 Chr. 34. 7), or burnt (Deut. 12. 3; II. 23. 15)[1]. Thus אשרה is thought to designate a pole set up as a symbol or substitute for the sacred tree venerated by the ancient Semites as the abode of the deity. This pole appears to have usually stood beside the altar at the Bāmōth of the Canaanites, and to have been adopted from them by the Israelites in their perverted worship of Yahwe, or definitely extraneous worship; cf. Deut. 16. 21; Judg. 6. 25 *ff*. See R. Sm. *Rel. Sem.*[2] 187 *ff*.[2]

---

[1] שבר והדק 'broke in pieces and beat small,' 2 Chr. 34. 4, probably applies chiefly to the graven and molten images, and only by zeugma to the (wooden) Asherim. LXX, Luc., making a different division of the verse, read καὶ (Luc. ἐξ)έκοψε τὰ ἄλση, i.e. וַיְגַדַּע הָאֲשֵׁרִים.

[2] F. B. Jevons, *Introduction to History of Religion*, pp. 134 *f.*, collects instances of the use of symbolic poles among non-Semitic races:—'This *ashera* appears again amongst people which differ as widely as possible from one another in race and place and time: it is presupposed by the ξόανα of the

It is a moot question whether the name Ashera is also used to designate a particular Canaanite *goddess*. Mention is made of an *image* of the Ashera placed by Manasseh in the Temple, II. 21. 7, cf. *ch.* 15. 13 *note;* II. 23. 7 perhaps speaks of the making of 'shrines' for the Ashera (cf. *note ad loc.*); and the Ba'al and the Ashera are coupled together as the objects of idolatrous worship, *ch.* 18. 19 (but see *note*); II. 23. 4; cf. Judg. 3. 7. In the Tell-el-Amarna inscriptions we find a name *Abd-Aš̮ratu* = 'servant of Ashera' (cf. Schrader, *ZA.* iii. 363 *f.; KAT.*[3] i. 276), and the name occurs twice with doubtful significance in Phoenician inscriptions. Cf. Dri. *Deut.* pp. 201 *ff.*

Verss.:—LXX always ἄλσος, pl. ἄλση, except 2 Chr. 15. 16 τῇ Ἀστάρτῃ (so Luc.); 24. 18 ταῖς Ἀστάρταις (Luc. τῇ Ἀστάρτῃ); Isa. 17. 8; 27. 9 τὰ δένδρα; Luc. in II. 23. 4 τῇ Ἀσηρώθ. Vulg. always *lucus*, except Judg. 6. 25, 26, 30 *nemus*, 3. 7 *Astaroth*. Pesh. 19 times ܕܚܠܬܐ, pl. ܕܚ̈ܠܬܐ 'object of reverence'; Judg. 3. 7; 6. 25, 26, 28, 30 ܐܣܛܪܬܐ, pl. ܐܣܛܪ̈ܬܐ 'Astarte'; Deut. 16. 21; Mic. 5. 13 ܐܝ̈ܠܢܐ 'trees'; Deut. 7. 5; 12. 4 ܢܣ̈ܟܬܐ 'molten images' (?); 2 Chr. 15. 6; 24. 18 ܨܠܡܐ, pl. ܨܠ̈ܡܐ 'image'; 2 Chr. 34. 3; Isa. 17. 8 ܦܬܟܪ̈ܐ 'idols'; 2 Chr. 14. 2 ܐܢܕܪܝ̈ܛܐ ἀνδριάντας; 2 Chr. 17. 6 ܥܠ̈ܘܬܐ 'high-places'; 1 Chr. 31. 1; 33. 3; 34. 3 ܢܨ̈ܒܐ 'nemora' (?) Targ. transliterates.

מכעיסים] The participle determines the subject, forming the secondary predicate; 'because they have made &c., *vexing* Yahwe.' Cf. Dri. *Tenses*, § 161, 2.

16. ויתן] 'Shall *give up*.' Cf. the phrase נתן לפני אויב *ch.* 8. 46 *note.*

17. היא באה וג׳] Cf. *ch.* 1. 14 *note.*

Greeks; it is found among the Ainos; the gods of the Brazilian tribes were represented by poles stuck upright in the ground, at the foot of which offerings were laid; the Hurd Islanders "in their houses had several stocks or small pillars of wood, four or five feet high, as the representatives of household gods, and on these they poured oil [which takes the place of fat or blood], and laid before them offerings of cocoa-nuts and fish"; the Kureks at irregular times slaughter a reindeer or a dog, put its head on a pole facing east, and mentioning no name, say, "This for thee: grant me a blessing."'

14. 19, 20. *Summary of Jeroboam's reign.*

R[D]. Cf. *Introduction.*

19. דברי הימים] 'Acts of the days,' i. e. 'daily record of events,' and so 'annals.'

14. 21–31. *Reḥoboam, king of Judah.*

Ch. 14. 26–28, 31 = 2 Chr. 12. 9–11, 16.

Beside the introductory and summarizing formulae *vv.* 21, 22[a], 29–31 (see *Introd.*), the hand of R[D] is to be noticed in *vv.* 22–24 :—

21. בירושלם העיר וג׳] Cf. *ch.* 8. 16 *note.*

22. ויקנאו אתו] 'And they moved him to jealousy'; cf. Deut. 32. 21 המה קנאוני בלא אל. Cf. the phrase of the decalogue אֵל קַנָּא 'a jealous God,' Ex. 20. 5 (E); ‖ Deut. 5. 9, so Deut. 4. 24; 6. 15†. אֵל־קַנּוֹא Josh. 24. 19 (E); Nah. 1. 2†.

23. על כל . . . רענן] So exactly II. 17. 10 (R[D]); Jer. 2. 20; cf. II. 16. 4 (R[D], ‖ 2 Chr. 28. 4); Deut. 12. 2; Ezek. 6. 13; Jer. 3. 6, 13; 17. 2; Isa. 57. 5.

24. ככל התועבת . . . ישראל] So II. 16. 3 (‖ 2 Chr. 28. 3); 21. 2 (‖ 2 Chr. 33. 2) both R[D]. הוריש with יהוה as subj., used of driving out the nations of Canaan, occurs in JE Ex. 34. 24; Num. 32. 21; Josh. 3. 10, but elsewhere appears to belong entirely to D and to passages influenced by D :—Deut. 4. 38; 9. 4, 5; 11. 23; 18. 12; Josh. 13. 6; 23. 5, 9, 13; Judg. 2. 21, 23; *ch.* 21. 26; II. 17. 8; Ps. 44. 3†. ככל תועבת הג׳ cf. Deut. 18. 9; 2 Chr. 36. 14.

22. ויעש יהודה וג׳] LXX, Luc. *καὶ ἐποίησε Ῥοβοὰμ . . . καὶ παρεζήλωσεν αὐτὸν κ.τ.λ.* is inconsistent with the context which lapses into the pl. (LXX *οἱ πατέρες αὐτῶν*, *v.* 23, LXX, Luc. *καὶ ᾠκοδόμησαν*) as in MT. Luc. *οἱ πατέρες αὐτοῦ* (David and Solomon) is scarcely possible in view of the manner in which R[D] treats David as his standard of piety (*ch.* 3. 14 *note*).

23. במות] Cf. *ch.* 3. 2, 3 *note.*

מצבות] 'Pillars.' מַצֵּבָה is 'something set up,' i. e. a stone pillar or obelisk, doubtless representing the sacred stone which in primitive times was thought to be the abode of the deity. Cf. R. Sm. *Rel.*

Sem.[2] 203 *ff.* Thus Jacob sets up a rough stone as a Maççēba to mark the scene of a Theophany, and anoints it with oil, calling it the house of God, Gen. 28. 18, 22; 31. 13 (E); and Maççēbōth are raised by him and by Moses to indicate that Yahwe is witness or party to a covenant or agreement, Gen. 31. 44, 45, 51 *ff.* (E); Ex. 24. 3, 4 (JE); cf. also Isa. 19. 19, 20. The Maççēba played a prominent part in the worship of the Canaanites, standing, like the Ashēra, beside the altar at the Bāma. Its destruction is strictly enjoined in the Book of the Covenant, Ex. 23. 24, and in Deut. 7. 5; 12. 3, this latter code also forbidding its use for the worship of Yahwe, 16. 22. Jehu destroyed the Maççēbōth at the Temple of the Canaanite Ba'al, II. 10. 26*f.*, while Maççēbōth of all kinds were demolished with the destruction of the Bāmōth at the reformations under Hezekiah and Josiah. Cf. further, for the use of the term in Phoenician to denote a commemorative obelisk, Dri. *Deut.* p. 204.

אשרים] Cf. *v.* 15 *note.*

רענן] Prob. 'spreading,' i.e. with branches hanging down and affording shelter for such worship. Cf. Verss.:—LXX, Luc. *συσκίου*, Vulg. *frondosam*, Pesh. ܥܒܝܐ 'thick,' Targ. עבוף 'shady.' Etym. doubtful.

24. קדש] 'Temple prostitutes.' The word is here collective as in *ch.* 22. 47, and includes persons of both sexes, קְדֵשִׁים and קְדֵשׁוֹת, who were 'set apart' for the immoral rites of the Canaanites, carried on within the precincts of their sanctuaries. A law against the introduction of these practices into Israel is found in Deut. 23. 18. Asa, *ch.* 15. 12, and Jehoshaphat, *ch.* 22. 47, effected a banishment of קדשים from Judah, and Josiah destroyed the houses of the קדשים which, during Manasseh's reign, had been established even at the Temple of Yahwe, II. 23. 7.

LXX, Luc. *σύνδεσμος* erroneously read קֶשֶׁר for קדש.

25. עלה שושק] Cf. *ch.* 11. 40 *note.* This invasion of Palestine by Sheshonk is recorded in an inscription upon the walls of the temple of Amon at Karnak. From the list of cities subjugated it appears that the expedition was directed not only against Judah

but also against the N. kingdom. The name of Jerusalem cannot be identified in the list. Cf. Dri. *Authority*, 87 *f.*; Sta. *Ges.* i. 353 *f.*

26. After ואת אצרות בית המלך LXX, Luc. have the insertion *καὶ τὰ δόρατα τὰ χρυσᾶ ἃ ἔλαβεν Δαυεὶδ ἐκ χειρὸς τῶν παίδων Ἀδραάζαρ βασιλέως Σουβὰ καὶ εἰσήνεγκεν αὐτὰ εἰς Ἰερουσαλήμ.* The reference is to 2 Sam. 8. 7, where also LXX, Luc. contain an addition stating that Shishak made booty of these shields in his expedition against Jerusalem recorded in our passage. Th., noticing that LXX in Samuel renders שִׁלְטֵי by *χλιδῶνας*, while in Kings addition the word used is *δόρατα*, infers thence that while Samuel addition is certainly a gloss (so Wellh.), Kings addition must be based upon an authentic text. Possibly, however, both additions are later cross-references derived from some independent source. If original, the sentence of LXX in our passage represents וְאֶת־שִׁלְטֵי הַזָּהָב אֲשֶׁר לָקַח דָּוִד מִיַּד עַבְדֵי הֲדַדְעֶזֶר מֶלֶךְ צוֹבָה וַיְבִיאֵם יְרוּשָׁלֵם.

ואת הכל לקח] LXX, Luc. omit ו, rightly. In Pesh. the whole is wanting.

27. והפקיד] We should expect וַיַּפְקֵד in continuation of ויעש, since the shields appear to have been given permanently into the charge of the שרי הרצים. Possibly, however, והפקיד is intended as a frequentative, like ישאום, והשיבום *v.* 28 which are used of the recurrent occasions upon which the רצים carried the shields.

על יד] 'Upon the hand,' i.e. '*into the possession* or *care of*.' So with נתן Gen. 42. 37, תנה אתו על ידי, 'Give him *into my care*.' Cf. the phrase הִגִּיר עַל־יְדֵי־חֶרֶב, 'deliver *into the power of* the sword,' Jer. 18. 21; Ezek. 35. 5; Ps. 63. 11.

שרי הרצים] Cf. *ch.* 1. 5 *note*.

28. מדי] Lit. 'out of the sufficiency of,' and so, 'as often as.' Followed thus by Infin. ‖ 2 Chr. 12. 11; 1 Sam. 1. 7; 18. 30; II. 4. 8; Isa. 28. 19; Jer. 31. 19†.

תא] Prob. 'guard room'; Vulg. *armamentarium*. The word is only elsewhere used in Ezek. 40. 7 *ff.*, where it denotes the small guard chambers at the gates of the outer court of Ezekiel's Temple.

30. ומלחמה וג׳] Cf. *note* on *ch.* 12. 1–24. For this summary statement by R[D] of warfare recorded with some detail in the

Annals cf. *ch.* 15. 6, 16, 32, and *v.* 19, *ch.* 22. 46; II. 13. 12; 14. 15, 28.

כל הימים] Cf. *ch.* 5. 15 *note.*

31. The mention of the name of the queen-mother, repeated from *v.* 21, occurs only here in the summary of a reign, and is rightly omitted by LXX, Luc., Pesh., || 2 Chr.

אבים] So *ch.* 15. 1, 7 (twice), 8†. In every case, Luc. Ἀβιά, Pesh. ܐܒܝܐ presuppose אֲבִיָּה as in MT. 1 Chr. 3. 10; 2 Chr. 12. 16; 13. 1, 2, 3, 4, 15, 17, 19, 22, 23; LXX Ἀβιού, אֲבִיָּהוּ as in MT. 2 Chr. 13. 20, 21. We may therefore conclude that this latter name, either in its longer or shorter form, stood originally in the text of Kings, and was altered by a later hand into אבים, perhaps for the sake of making a distinction from אביה of *ch.* 14. 1.

15. 1–8. *Abijah, king of Judah.*

The whole account is framed by R^D. For *vv.* 1–3, 7, 8 cf. *Introd.*; *v.* 4 ניר cf. *ch.* 11. 36; *v.* 5 אשר עשה וג׳ cf. *ch.* 11. 33, and generally for reference to David *ch.* 3. 14.

1. אבים] Luc. adds υἱὸς Ῥοβοάμ, LXX υἱὸς Ἱεροβοάμ.

2. ושם אמו מעכה בת אבישלום] Precisely the same statement is made concerning Asa the *son* of Abijah *v.* 10; cf. *v.* 13. Hence Ew., Ke., Ber. suggest that the mother of Abijah continued to hold the position of גבירה or 'chief lady' during the reign of her *grandson* Asa. More probably there has occurred a very early confusion between the mothers of the two kings which cannot now be elucidated. Kit. (*Ges.*) supposes that both were named Maʿacha, and that the addition בת אבישלום in *v.* 10 is an erroneous insertion from *v.* 2. LXX, Luc. *v.* 2 Μααχά, θυγάτηρ Ἀβεσσαλώμ, *v.* 10 Ἀνά, θυγάτηρ Ἀβεσσαλώμ, so *v.* 10 Ἀνά; probably an alteration made to remove the difficulty, the repetition of the name Ἀβεσσαλώμ being against the originality of the reading. 2 Chr. 11. 20–22, which gives the name of Abijah's mother as מַעֲכָה and names her other sons, appears to be derived from an ancient source. In 2 Chr. 13. 2 she is called מִיכָיָהוּ, and so Vulg. *Michaia*, Jos. *Ant.* viii. 11, § 3 Μαχαία;

but LXX, Luc., Pesh. presuppose מעכה rightly, מיכיהו being elsewhere a male name. So Ew., Ber., Kamp., Kit., *Sieg. u. Sta.*

אבישלום] 2 Chr. 11. 20 אַבְשָׁלוֹם. Doubtless the son of David is here meant, and Jos. (*Ant.* viii. 10, § 1) is probably correct in saying that Ma'acha was really his *granddaughter*, her mother being Tamar the daughter of Absalom (2 Sam. 14. 27):—ἤγετο ὕστερον (Ῥοβόαμος) καὶ τὴν ἐκ τῆς Ἀψαλώμου θυγατρὸς Θαμάρης Μαχάνην ὄνομα καὶ αὐτὴν οὖσαν συγγενῆ. Thus Ma'acha bore the same name as her great-grandmother 2 Sam. 3. 3. The statement of 2 Chr. 13. 2 that she was the daughter of אוּרִיאֵל מִן־גִּבְעָה[1] perhaps implies (Ke., Ber.) that this Uriel married Tamar, Absalom's daughter.

4[a]. בירושלם] LXX, Luc. omit.

4[b]. בנו] LXX, Luc. τὰ τέκνα αὐτοῦ rightly presuppose בָּנָיו. So Klo., Kamp.

5. רק בדבר וג'] LXX omits. The words may perhaps be a qualification inserted by a later hand.

6. ומלחמה וג'] LXX, Luc. omit. The words are an erroneous insertion from *ch.* 14. 30. Pesh. reads ܐܒܝܐ ܒܪ ܪܚܒܥܡ 'Abijah son of R.' for רחבעם, and omits the similar statement in *v.* 7.

15. 9–24. *Asa, king of Judah.*

Ch. 15. 13–22 = 2 Chr. 15. 16—16. 6.

R[D]—introduction and summary; *v.* 14 (cf. *ch.* 3. 2, 3); casting of *v.* 12 (cf. *note* on הגללים below) and of *v.* 16 (cf. *ch.* 14. 30) from information derived from the Annals. From this source all further particulars of the reign are drawn.

12. הקדשים] LXX suitably renders τὰς τελετάς, for which Luc. by corruption reads τὰς στήλας. Cf. *note* on *ch.* 14. 24.

הגללים] 'The *idol-blocks*'; a term of opprobrium. Probably lit. 'logs' or 'rolling things,' from גלל 'to roll'; so Ges., &c. Ew. (*Die Lehre der Bibel von Gott*, ii. 264) prefers to render '*doll-images*,' as rolled or wrapped up in clothes, dressed up. Smend's proposal to connect the word with גֵּל, גָּלָל 'dung' (Ezek. 6. 4), as is done

[1] Luc. Ἀβεσσαλώμ is clearly a correction in accordance with 11. 20.

by the Rabbinic interpreters, is improbable. The word occurs elsewhere in Kings, *ch.* 21. 26; II. 17. 12; 21. 11, 21; 23. 24 (all R^D); and besides, Deut. 29. 16; Lev. 26. 30 (H), and thirty-nine times in Ezekiel †.

13. ויסרה] The ו *consec.* introduces the predicate after the *accus. pendens*, as in *ch.* 9. 21 (cf. *note*).

מגבירה] Cf. *ch.* 11. 19 *note.*

מפלצת לאשרה] 'A horrible thing for an ashera' (or 'for Ashera,' supposing the word here to denote a Canaanite goddess; cf. *note* on *ch.* 14. 15).

מפלצת only occurs again in ‖ 2 Chr. 15. 16, and its meaning, 'an object causing *shuddering* or *horror*,' must be determined from the use of the verb יִתְפַּלָּצוּן prob. 'tremble,' Job 9. 6†, and the substantive פַּלָּצוּת 'trembling' or 'horror,' Isa. 21. 4; Ezek. 7. 18; Ps. 55. 6; Job 21. 6†. The nature of this 'horrible thing' is not clear. It must have been some kind of idol or idolatrous symbol, and Vulg., Kings *in sacris Priapi*, *v.* 13^b *simulacrum turpissimum* [1], Chr. *simulacrum Priapi*, finds reference to a *phallus* cult. This explanation is adopted by Ew., Th., Ber., Kit.; Ew., citing the somewhat obscure תִּפְלַצְתְּךָ, perhaps 'Oh, thy *wantonness!*' Jer. 49. 16. LXX, Luc., Pesh. misunderstand, and Targ. offers no elucidation.

15. וקדשו] Read וְקָדָשָׁיו with ‖ 2 Chr. 15. 18 and LXX, Luc., Pesh., Targ. 'And he brought the votive gifts of his father and his own votive gifts into the house of Yahwe—silver and gold and vessels.'

17. הרמה] *Er-Râm*, two hours north of Jerusalem, and a short distance to the west of Geba (*Jeba'*). Rob. *BR.* i. 576; Smith, *Hist. Geogr.* 251.

לבלתי תת יצא ובא] Cf. Josh. 6. 1.

18. בן הדד] Three Aramaean kings of this name are generally

---

[1] The rendering *ne esset princeps in sacris Priapi, et in luco eius quem consecraverat* seems to presuppose a wrong rearrangement of words in some such form as מהיות גבירה למפלצת ולאשרה אשר עשהה; *v.* 13^b, *subvertitque specum eius, et confregit simulacrum turpissimum*, is probably merely a paraphrastic expansion of ויכרת מפלצתה.

supposed to be mentioned in these books; cf. *ch.* 20. 1 *ff.;* II. 13. 24. Winckler, however, regards the Ben-hadad of this passage as one with the Ben-hadad of *ch.* 20; an identification which postulates a reign of not much more than forty years in length. Cf. *Alttest. Untersuchungen*, pp. 60 *ff.* הֲדַד, the Aram. weather-god, is the same as רִמּוֹן (II. 5. 18 *note*); cf. the compound name הֲדַדְרִמּוֹן Zech. 12. 11; Baethgen, *Semit. Relig.* pp. 67 *f.*

חזיון] LXX Ἀζείν, Luc., Cod. A Ἀζαήλ. Ew., Th., Klo., &c. plausibly suggest the identification of חזיון with רזון of *ch.* 11. 23, whose name appears in LXX (11. 14) as Ἐσρώμ, Luc. Ἐσρών, Pesh. ܚܶܙܝܽܘܢ. Klo. regards חֶזְיוֹן as the original form of the name.

19. ברית וג׳] '*There is* a covenant between me and thee, &c.' LXX δίδου διαθήκην κ.τ.λ. is self-condemned.

20. עיון] Mentioned again in connexion with אבל בית מעכה and other cities of the north, as taken by Tiglath-Pileser in the reign of Pekah (II. 15. 29). Rob. suggests as the site of עיון the modern مرج عيون 'the plain of *'Ayûn*,' a fertile basin lying to the north of the plain of the *Hûleh*, and south-west of the ancient Dan. To the south of *Merj 'Ayûn* lies *Âbil*, probably the site of אבל בית מעכה. *BR.* ii. 438; iii. 372 *f.*

ואת כל כנרות] Th. is right in noticing that the reference, thus phrased, is to a *district*, and not to a city. So, as here in plural, Josh. 11. 2, and singular כִּנֶּרֶת Deut. 3. 17. In Josh. 19. 35 the allusion seems to be to a *city* כִּנֶּרֶת in the land of Naphtali, while in Num. 34. 11; Josh. 13. 27 we find mention of the *Sea of Cinnereth* יָם כִּנֶּרֶת, Josh. 12. 3 יָם כִּנֲּרוֹת. Targ., except Josh. 19. 35 where it preserves כנרת, renders גניסר, גינסר, this being the name adopted in later times; cf. 1 Macc. 11. 67 Γεννησάρ, S. Matt. 14. 34; S. Mark 6. 53; S. Luke 5. 1 Γεννησαρέτ. The region of Gennesaret is described by Josephus (*BJ.* iii. 10, § 8) as being of marvellous beauty and fertility, and accordingly is generally identified with the level plain *El-Ghuwêr* on the north-west shore of the lake of Galilee; Sta. *SP.* 374 *f.;* Rob. *BR.* iii. 348 *f.;* Smith, *Hist. Geogr.* 443. A city כִּנֶּרֶת may have lain in this district, but its site is unknown.

על כל ארץ נפתלי] RV., Kamp. '*with* all the land of Naphtali,' taking על in the sense '*in addition to*,' as in Gen. 32. 12 אם על בנים; Ex. 35. 22; Job 38. 32. But such a use of the preposition is here very unnatural, and LXX, Luc. *ἕως*, i. e. עַד '*even unto* the whole land of Naphtali,' preserve a superior reading.

‖ 2 Chr. 16. 4ᵇ reads, in place of *v.* 20ᵇ, וְאֵת כָּל־מִסְכְּנוֹת עָרֵי נַפְתָּלִי.

21. וַיֵּשֶׁב] LXX, Luc., Vulg. וַיָּשָׁב, incorrectly.

22. השמיע] 'Summoned.' In this special sense only again in Jer. 50. 29; 51. 27; Pi'el 1 Sam. 15. 4; 23. 8†.

אין נקי] 'Without exemption'; lit. 'none was exempted,' a circumstantial clause; Dri. *Tenses*, § 164. For נקי '*free*' *from obligation*, cf. Num. 32. 22 והייתם נקיים מיהוה ומישראל.

גבע] Now called *Jeba'*; south of *Mukhmâs* (Michmash) from which it is separated by the steep ravine called the *Wady es-Suweinet*, the scene of Jonathan's adventure 1 Sam. 14. 1 *ff.* Rob. *BR.* i. 440.

הַמִּצְפָּה] Also called הַמִּצְפֶּה Josh. 18. 26. No modern equivalent of the name has been discovered, but *Nebi Samwîl*, about five miles NNW. of Jerusalem, and visible therefrom, is plausibly regarded by Rob. (*BR.* i. 459 *f.*) and others as the site of the ancient city. Mizpah was well known in connexion with Samuel, 1 Sam. 7. 5 *ff.*, 16; 10. 17, and is described in 1 Macc. 3. 46 as being *κατέναντι Ἰερουσαλήμ*.

23. חלה את רגליו] 'He was diseased in his feet.' The accusative, as in Greek, specifies the part affected; cf. Gen. 3. 15 הוא ישופך ראש; Deut. 33. 11; *al.* Da. § 71; Ew. § 281, c. 3. Luc. after the words לעת זקנתו adds *ἐποίησεν Ἀσὰ τὸ πονηρόν, καί*—a gloss inserted to assign a cause for his disease, and perhaps with reference to the events described in 2 Chr. 16. 7–12.

15. 25–32. *Nadab, king of Israel.*

R^D *vv.* 25, 26, 29ᵇ–32.

27. לבית יששכר] '*Belonging to* the house of Issachar.' In place of ישׂשכר LXX reads Βελαάν, Luc. Βεδδαμά.

ויכהו בעשא] LXX *ἐχάραξεν αὐτόν*, Luc. *ἐχαράκωσεν αὐτόν*.

גבתון] Pesh. ܓܬ 'Gath,' an easy substitution of a well known for a less known place. So *ch.* 16. 15, 17.

28. לאסא מלך יהודה] LXX τοῦ Ἀσὰ υἱοῦ Ἀβιού.

תחתיו] Luc. Βαασὰ ἐπὶ τὸν Ἰσραήλ. LXX omits.

29. כל נשמה] 'Anything breathing'; lit. 'any breath.' So Deut. 20. 16; Josh. 10. 40; 11. 11, 14 (D^2); Ps. 150. 6†.

עד הִשמדו] Cf. II. 3. 25 *note* on עד הִשׁאיר.

כדבר י׳ אשר דבר] Reference to *ch.* 14. 14. Cf. *ch.* 13. 26 *note.*

ביד עבדו] Cf. *ch.* 8. 53 *note.*

30. בכעסו אשר הכעים] Cf. *ch.* 14. 9 *note.*

י׳ אלהי ישראל] Cf. *ch.* 8. 15 *note.*

32. A repetition of *v.* 16, rightly omitted by LXX, Luc.

15. 33—16. 7. *Baʿasha, king of Israel.*

The whole is framed by R^D.

16. 1–4. Cf. phraseology of Aḥijah's speech *ch.* 14. 7–16 *notes.*

2. נגיד] Cf. *ch.* 1. 35 *note.*

בחטאתם] Read בְּהַבְלֵיהֶם 'with their vain things,' as in *vv.* 13, 26 (cf. Deut. 32. 21), with LXX, Luc. ἐν τοῖς ματαίοις αὐτῶν, and probably Pesh. ܒܥܒܕ̈ܐ ܕܐܝ̈ܕܝܗܘܢ 'with the work of their hands.' So Klo.

7. ועל כל הרעה . . . ועל אשר הכה אתו] '*Both* because of all the evil, &c., *and* because he smote him.' The repeated ו, '*both* . . . *and*,' is, however, rare (poetical); Job 34. 29; Ps. 76. 7; except in the rather different class of instances cited *v.* 11. אתו refers to Jeroboam as personifying his house, and Vulg. is incorrect in paraphrasing *ob hanc causam occidit eum, hoc est, Iehu filium Hanani, prophetam.*

16. 8–14. *Elah, king of Israel.*

Framed throughout by R^D, with short notices from the Annals *vv.* 9, $10^{aa, b}$, 11^a.

9. שתה שכור] So *ch.* 20. 16. 'Drinking to excess'; lit. 'drinking, drunk,' the two words being in apposition, and the second making closer definition of the first. Cf. *ch.* 1. 2 *note* on נערה בתולה.

ארצא] LXX Ὠσά, Luc. Ἀσά.

אשר על הבית] Cf. *ch.* 4. 6 *note.* Targ. strangely explains ארצא as the name of an *idol;*—בית ארצא טעותא די בביתא בתרצה.

11[a], 12[a]. LXX, Luc. omit, through homoioteleuton, את כל בית בעשא.

11. משתין בקיר] Cf. *ch.* 14. 10 *note.*

וגאליו ורעהו] '*Neither* kinsmen *nor* friends.' The repeated ו, '*neither* . . . *nor*,' or without preceding negative, '*both* . . . *and*,' is used idiomatically in connecting an exhaustive category on to a previous more general statement, of which it is epexegetical. So Num. 9. 14 חֻקָּה אַחַת יִהְיֶה לָכֶם וְלַגֵּר וּלְאֶזְרַח הָאָרֶץ; Gen. 34. 28 אֶת־צֹאנָם וגו׳ וְאֵת אֲשֶׁר־בָּעִיר וְאֶת־אֲשֶׁר בַּשָּׂדֶה לָקָחוּ; Josh. 9. 23; Jer. 13. 14; 21. 6; Neh. 12. 28. גֹּאֵל is one to whom pertain the duties of a kinsman—in this case, the prosecution of a blood-feud; cf. the phrase גֹּאֵל הַדָּם '*the blood-avenger*,' 2 Sam. 14. 11; Deut. 19. 6, 12, and in P Num. 35. 19, 21, 24, 25, 27; Josh. 20. 3, 5 (om. LXX), 9. For ורעהו sing. used collectively cf. Da. § 17.

12. כדבר וג׳] Cf. *ch.* 15. 29.

ביד יהוא] LXX καὶ πρὸς Εἰού as in *v.* 1; MT. אל י׳, where, however, LXX reads ἐν χειρί E.

13. אל כל חטאות] אל for על; cf. *ch.* 13. 29 *note.* The sins of Ba'asha and his son are here spoken of in the terms usually applied by R[D] to the sins of Jeroboam. See *Introduction.*

להכעים] Cf. *ch.* 14. 9 *note.*

י׳ אלהי ישראל] Cf. *ch.* 8. 15 *note.*

16. 15–20. *Zimri, king of Israel.*

R[D], *vv.* 15[a], 19, 20, frames a brief narrative drawn from the Annals.

15. והעם חנים] LXX, Luc. καὶ ἡ παρεμβολὴ Ἰσραήλ, if not a direct paraphrase, probably arose from omission of ע, which gave the reading וְהַמַּחֲנִם or וְהַמַּחֲנֶה, to which the translator added the explanatory Ἰσραήλ. העם is used here, as in *ch.* 20. 15; 1 Sam. 14. 26; 30. 21; 2 Sam. 15. 17, of an *army* or *military detachment:* cf. Vulg. *porro exercitus obsidebat.*

16. וישמע העם החנים לאמר] The use of לאמר with a subj.

different from that of the preceding clause is idiomatic after the verb שמע. Cf. II. 19. 9; ‖ Isa. 37. 9; Deut. 13. 13; 1 Sam. 13. 4; 2 Sam. 19. 3. The new subj. is really the *implied obj.* of the preceding וישמע, e.g. אֶת־הַשֵּׁמַע 'the report,' or אֶת־דִּבְרֵי פ׳ 'someone's words.' This is apparent from Gen. 31. 1 וישמע את דברי בני לבן לאמר; 1 Sam. 24. 10 למה תשמע את דברי אדם לאמר; and, after a verb other than שמע, II. 5. 6 וַיָּבֵא הספר אל מלך ישראל לאמר; so perhaps 2 Sam. 13. 33; Jer. 7. 4.

More peculiar and not to be classed are the cases in which the subj. of לאמר is quite indefinite, and lies in a loose sense of the connexion with the preceding clause;—2 Sam. 7. 26 ויגדל שמך עד עולם לאמר י׳ צבאות אלהים על ישראל; Deut. 30. 12, 13 לא בשמים הוא לאמר מי יעלה וג׳; Ex. 5. 19.

Quite a distinct class, however, is formed by cases in which a *passive* verb is employed in the clause preceding לאמר, and the substitution of an active gives the subj. of לאמר;—וַיֻּגַּד לאמר *ch.* 1. 51; II. 6. 13; 8. 7; Gen. 22. 20; 38. 13, 24; Josh. 10. 17; 1 Sam. 15. 12; 19. 19; 2 Sam. 6. 12; Isa. 7. 2†; Ex. 5. 14 וַיֻּכּוּ שטרי בני ישראל . . . לאמר; 1 Sam. 9. 24 כי למועד שָׁמוּר לך לאמר; Isa. 29. 12 וְנִתַּן הספר . . . לאמר (cf. *v.* 11 אשר יִתְּנוּ אתו . . . לאמר).

וימלכו כל ישראל] Luc. καὶ ἐβασίλευσαν ὁ λαός, LXX καὶ ἐβασίλευσαν ἐν Ἰσραήλ. MT. is favoured by *v.* 17ᵃ.

18. ארמון בית המלך] 'the *keep* of the king's palace'; cf. II. 15. 25.

וישרף] Pesh. ܘܐܘܩܕܘ, i. e. וישרפו 'they (the besiegers) burnt &c.'

את בית מלך] Cf. *note* on *ch.* 12. 31.

16. 21, 22. *Civil war between the parties of rival aspirants to the throne of Israel, Tibni and Omri.*

The short notice comes from the Annals.

21. אז יחלק] Cf. *ch.* 3. 16 *note.*

העם ישראל] 'The people Israel'; a case of apposition exactly like הַמֶּלֶךְ דָּוִד; הָהָר שֹׁמְרוֹן *v.* 24. So Josh. 8. 33†; cf. Judg. 20. 22 העם איש ישראל.

לחצי] LXX, Luc. omit, and Klo., Kamp., Kit. regard as an erroneous dittography of the final letter of ישראל and the following חצי.

נינת] On form of name cf. *note* on טפת *ch.* 4. 11.

והחצי] 'And *the* half,' i. e. '*the other* half,' in sharply defined opposition to the previously mentioned חצי העם. LXX καὶ τὸ ἥμισυ τοῦ λαοῦ γίνεται ὀπίσω Ζαμβρεί (Luc. Ἀμβρί, τοῦ βασιλεῦσαι αὐτόν) is probably due to desire for uniformity with the preceding clause.

22. ויחזק . . . את העם] חזק thus followed by accusative only here; '*were strong as regards* the people,' so *prevailed over* them. Cf. the similar (but poetic) use of accus. in יְכָלְתִּיו 'I have prevailed over him,' Ps. 13. 5. The construction is, however, somewhat harsh in prose, and the connexion almost demands (Kamp.) the emendation עַל־הָעָם or מֵהָעָם. LXX for *v.* 22[a] καὶ ἡττήθη ὁ λαὸς ὁ ὢν ὀπίσω Θαμνεὶ υἱοῦ Γωνάθ, a reading probably due in the first place to omission of ויחזק . . . אחרי עמרי through homoioteleuton with *v.* 21 end.

וימת תבני] LXX, Luc. add καὶ Ἰωρὰμ ὁ ἀδελφὸς αὐτοῦ ἐν τῷ καιρῷ ἐκείνῳ, and then, after וימלך עמרי, μετὰ Θαμνεί (Luc. τὸν Θαβεννεί); i. e. *v.* 22[b] וַיָּמָת תִּבְנִי וְיוֹרָם אָחִיו בָּעֵת הַהִיא וַיִּמְלֹךְ עָמְרִי אַחֲרֵי תִבְנִי 'And Tibni died and his brother Joram at that time, and Omri reigned after Tibni.' The genuineness of this text is favoured by the fact that the additional words supply a detail unessential to the narrative, and thus not to be explained as a later invention. So Th., Kamp., Benz., Kit., Maspero.

16. 23–28. *Omri, king of Israel.*

The work of R^D, with short details from the Annals, *vv.* 23[b], 24.

23. בשנת שלשים ואחת שנה] But Zimri, who reigned but seven days, is said, *v.* 15, to have come to the throne in the twenty-seventh year of Asa. It might therefore be supposed that the civil war, *vv.* 21, 22, lasted some three or four years; but this is precluded by the synchronism in the case of Aḥab's accession, *v.* 29 'the thirty-eighth year of Asa,' which harmonizes with *v.* 15, supposing the interregnum to have been merely a matter of a few days or months—as might be inferred from the absence of special detail—and the length of Omri's reign to be correctly stated as twelve years. It must therefore be concluded that in the synchronism

for Omri's accession thirty-first is an error for twenty-seventh or twenty-eighth.

עמרי] Mentioned in Mesha's inscription, ll. 4 *f.*, as king of Israel who 'afflicted Moab for many days' (*Append.* 1). In the Cuneiform inscriptions Jehu is called 'son of Omri' (*Append.* 4), and the northern kingdom named *mât Ḫu-um-ri-i*, 'Omri-land,' or *mât Bît-Ḫu-um-ri-a*, 'Beth-Omri-land.' Cf. *COT.* i. 179 *f.*

24. שמרון] Sta. (*ZATW.* v. 165 *ff.*) argues very plausibly for an original vocalization שַׁמְרוֹן or שַׁמְרַיִן, upon the following grounds:—

1. The form of the name from which שמרון is said to be derived. First stating that שֹׁמְרוֹן cannot come from שֶׁמֶר but only from שֹׁמֵר, he goes on to prove the genuineness of the form שֶׁמֶר as against שֹׁמֵר, and its actual existence, together with the kindred שִׁמְרָת 1 Chr. 8. 21, שִׁמְרוֹן Gen. 46. 13; Num. 26. 24; 1 Chr. 7. 1, as a *clan* name[1]. שִׁמְרוֹן Josh. 19. 15; 11. 1 is also the name of a *city*, and this transference of a clan-name to a city has its analogy in חֶבְרוֹן (חֶבֶר clan name 1 Chr. 8. 17), אַיָּלוֹן, שַׁעַלְבִים[2], &c.

2. Ancient evidence for vocalization of שמרון.

(*a*) Cuneiform inscriptions. Three forms of the name occur: *Ša-mir-i-na, Ša-mí-ri-na, Ša-mí-ur-na.* These presuppose שַׁמְרוֹן or שַׁמְרַן or שַׁמְרָן.

(*b*) LXX Σαμάρεια. ει may represent Hebrew *ai* or *ê* or *î*. So שַׁמְרַיִן or שַׁמְרֵין or שַׁמְרִין.

(*c*) Aramaic forms ܫܡܪܝܢ, שָׁמְרַיִן (Ezra 4. 10, 17).

---

[1] That שֶׁמֶר is preferable to שֹׁמֵר in the two cases where the latter form occurs in MT. appears from the following facts. שׁוֹמֵר is found 1 Chr. 7. 32 as a proper name, probably of a clan, but in *v.* 34 the name appears as שֶׁמֶר (שָׁמֶר in pause). Further, one of the murderers of Joash, II. 12. 22, is named יְהוֹזָבָד בֶּן־שֹׁמֵר; but that this vocalization does not rest upon ancient tradition is clear from 2 Chr. 24. 26, where the same man is said to be son of שִׁמְרִית, a form presupposing שֶׁמֶר and not שֹׁמֵר. And moreover, while LXX in II. 12. 22 reads Σωμήρ, Luc. has the form Σεμμήρ, as in *ch.* 16. 24, LXX, Luc. Σεμήρ, Σεμμήρ, Σαμήρ.

[2] From names of animals used as clan totems.

(*d*) Testimony of LXX in *ch.* 16. 24. To mark derivation from Σεμήρ, Σαμήρ, שמרון is represented, not as usually by Σαμάρεια, but by Σεμερών, Σαεμερών, of which Σομορών (Luc., Cod. A) is a correction in accordance with MT.

Supposing therefore שַׁמְרוֹן, שַׁמְרַיִן to be the original form, the termination ַיִן is illustrated by דֹּתַיִן Gen. 37. 17 (Δωθαείμ), and answers to the more usual ַיִם which appears in the place-names רָמָתַיִם, מַחֲנַיִם. שַׁמְרַיִן may stand together with שַׁמְרוֹן, just as we find the two names עֶגְלַיִם (עֵין) and עֶגְלוֹן.

The reason why the name should have been altered in later times into שֹׁמְרוֹן Sta. is not prepared to explain. He suggests the possibility of an erroneous explanation of the Aramaic form with *å*, but admits that this merely postpones the question, since one must next inquire how the Aramaic form with *Qameç* is to be explained. That the form שֹׁמְרוֹן is, however, very young, appears from the LXX rendering in *ch.* 16. 24.

If, as seems to be the case, שֶׁמֶר was a clan-name, the hill upon which Omri built his city was probably already named Samaria, and bore this name as being the possession and residence of the clan שֶׁמֶר. But that this fact need not invalidate the statement that Omri bought the hill from a *man* named שֶׁמֶר may be argued from the many occurrences of clan-names used as personal names. Thus שִׁמְעִי, David's foe, bears a clan-name Num. 3. 21; *al.*, and the same is the case with חֶבֶר the Kenite; Saul's son 'Esh-ba'al has the name of the Benjamite clan אַשְׁבֵּל Gen. 46. 21; *al.*; אֵלָה, the name of Ba'asha's son, and also of the father of Hosea, is found as a clan-name Gen. 36. 41; גָּד the tribal-name is borne by a prophet in David's time; &c.

25. וירע וג׳] Cf. *ch.* 14. 9 *note.*

26. להכעים וג׳] Cf. *v.* 13.

28. At the close of Omri's reign LXX, Luc. insert the account of Jehoshaphat's reign = MT. *ch.* 22. 41–51 with certain variations, in accordance with the different system of synchronism which appears in Luc. See *Introduction.*

16. 29–34. **22.** 39, 40. *Aḥab, king of Israel.*

R^D embodies short notices from the Annals (substance of *v.* 31^b, *v.* 32, *v.* 34 to דלתיה).

29. אחאב] Mentioned once on the monolith of Shalmaneser II as *A-ḫa-ab-bu mâtu Sir-'-la-ai*, 'Aḥab of Israel'; cf. *Append.* 3, and *ch.* 20. 34 *note.*

30^b. מכל וג׳] LXX, Luc. prefix (Luc. καὶ) ἐπονηρεύσατο, i. e. וַיָּרַע, probably correctly. Cf. *v.* 25; *ch.* 14. 9 *note.*

31. ויהי הנקל וג׳] 'And it came to pass—was it a light thing his walking in the sins of Jeroboam?—and (that) he took &c.': so RV. 'And it came to pass, as if it had been a light thing &c., that he took &c.' For similar use of interrogative with נָקֵל, expressing surprise at the lengths to which any one can go in sinning, cf. Ezek. 8. 17 הֲנָקֵל לְבֵית יְהוּדָה מֵעֲשׂוֹת אֶת־הַתּוֹעֵבוֹת אֲשֶׁר עָשׂוּ־פֹה כִּי־מָלְאוּ וג׳ וְהִנָּם שֹׁלְחִים אֶת־הַזְּמוֹרָה אֶל־אַפָּם 'Is it a light thing to the house of Judah that they do all the abominations which they do here, for behold &c., that, lo, they are holding the branch to their nose?' i. e. they overleap moral offences, and indulge in definite idolatry (sun-worship).

אֶתְבַּעַל] The name is similarly vocalized by LXX Ἰεθεβάαλ, Luc. Ἰεθβάαλ, and would thus bear the meaning *with Ba'al*, i. e. under his protection. Jos., however, writes Ἰθώβαλος (*Ant.* viii. 13, § 1), i. e. אִתּוֹבַעַל *Ba'al is with him*, and this form is preferred by Th., Sta. According to Jos. (*C. Ap.* i. 18) Ittoba'al, who lived some fifty years after Ḥiram, was a priest of Astarte, who came to the throne by the murder of the usurper Phelles.

33. האשרה] Cf. *ch.* 14. 15 *note.*

לעשות וג׳] LXX, Luc. τοῦ ποιῆσαι παροργίσματα τοῦ παροργίσαι (Luc. adds καὶ ποιῆσαι) τὴν ψυχὴν αὐτοῦ (LXX τοῦ) ἐξολοθρευθῆναι (Luc. ἀνθ' ὧν) ἐκακοποίησεν ὑπὲρ πάντας κ.τ.λ., i. e. apparently לַעֲשׂוֹת כְּעָסִים לְהַכְעִים [וְ]אֶת־נַפְשׁוֹ לְהַשְׁחִית וַיָּרַע מִכֹּל וג׳. Scarcely superior to MT. Elsewhere כעסים II. 23. 26, כעס *ch.* 15. 30; 21. 22 form the direct obj. of הכעים; and omission of את י׳ אלהי ישראל (R^D; cf. *ch.* 8. 15 *note*) is unfavourable.

34. Luc. omits.

בימיו] A phrase of R^D used in synchronizing an event with the preceding narrative. So II. 8. 20; 23. 29; 24. 1; and 15. 19 (emend after LXX). For similar phrases thus employed cf. *ch.* 3. 16 *note* on אז.

חיאל] LXX Ἀχειήλ, i.e. אֲחִיאֵל. Cf. *note* on חירם *ch.* 5. 15.

בית האלי] Cf. *note* on בן הימיני *ch.* 2. 8.

באבירם . . . ובשגיב] ב = '*at the cost of*'; ב *pretii*. Cf. *note* on בנפשו *ch.* 2. 23. The statement suggests the possibility that the builder *sacrificed* his sons, perhaps by enclosing them alive in the foundation and wall, in order by this costly blood-offering to secure the prosperity of his city. Or, the tradition may have been that, through failure to perform such a rite, his eldest and youngest born were claimed by the offended deity at the initiatory and final stages of the building. For instances from various sources of the wide-spread primitive custom of human sacrifice 'in order to furnish blood at the foundations of a house or of a public structure,' cf. H. C. Trumbull, *The Threshold Covenant*, pp. 46 *ff.*

כדבר וג'] Josh. 6. 26.

Narratives of the Northern Kingdom.

I. 17-19; 20; 21; 22. 1-38. II. 1. 2-17$^{a\alpha}$; 2. 1-18, 19-22, 23-25; 3. 4-27; 4. 1-7, 8-37, 38-41, 42-44; 5; 6. 1-7, 8-23, 24-33; 7; 8. 1-6, 7-15; 9. 1—10. 28; 13. 14-19, 20, 21; (14. 8-14).

This great group consists of narratives dealing with the affairs of the kingdom of Israel. The stories are in most cases of some length, their high descriptive power and sympathetic feeling indicating that they have their origin in the kingdom to which they relate; and this conclusion is substantiated by such touches as I. 19. 3 באר שבע אשר ליהודה; II. 14. 11 בבית שמש אשר ליהודה. No blame is anywhere attached to the calf-worship of Bethel and Dan, the efforts of Elijah and his successor being wholly directed to the rooting out of the foreign cult of the Tyrian Ba'al.

Certain peculiarities of diction probably belong to the dialect of North Palestine. The following may be noticed:—

Suff. 2 f. sing. ־ֵכִי, pl. ־ֵיכִי:—Kt. II. 4. 2 לְכִי, 3 שְׁכֵנָיְכִי, 7 נִשְׁיֵכִי, בָּנַיְכִי. Elsewhere, sing. Cant. 2. 3; Ps. 103. 3, 4; Jer. 11. 15 (text corrupt), pl. Ps. 103. 3, 4, 5; 116. 7. Cf. Syr. suff. 2 f. sing. ܟܝ, pl. ܟܝܢ.

Pers. pron. 2 f. sing. Kt. אַתִּי:—II. 4. 16, 23; 8. 1. Elsewhere *ch.* 14. 2 (cf. *note*); Judg. 17. 2; Jer. 4. 30; Ezek. 36. 13†. Cf. Syr. ܐܢܬܝ. So probably Kt. הָלַכְתִּי II. 4. 23 stands for הָלַכְתְּ אַתִּי, as in Syr. ܩܛܠܬܝ for ܩܛܠܬ ܐܢܬܝ; Duval, *Gramm. Syr.* pp. 174 *f.*

Demonstr. pron. f. הֹו II. 6. 19. Cf. Aram. דָּא.

Infin. constr. verb ל״ה with suff. בְּהִשְׁתַּחֲוָיָתִי II. 5. 18, perhaps presupposing form without suff. הִשְׁתַּחֲוָיָה with termination as in Aram. Cf. Dalman, *Gramm. Jud.-Pal. Aram.* pp. 289 *f.*

Rel. ־שֶׁ in מִשֶּׁלָּנוּ II. 6. 11. So Judg. 5. 7 (North Palestine); 6. 17; 7. 12; 8. 26 (prob. Ephraimitic), and uniformly in Cant. (exc. title 1. 1). Elsewhere only in exilic or post-exilic writings[1]. In Phoenician rel. is אש with prosthetic א.

---

[1] The particle שֶׁל 'of' is thought by some to occur upon a haematite weight from Samaria, bearing an inscription upon either side which was at first read as רבע של רבע נצג 'the fourth part of the fourth part of a *néçegh* (?),' and dated *cir.* 8th century B.C. Careful examination of the original weight convinces the writer that Prof. Robertson Smith (*Academy*, Nov. 18, 1893, pp. 443 *ff.*) is correct in his view (based upon a close study of the original) that the much worn רבע של upon the one side is of earlier date than the clearly cut רבע נצג upon the other, this fact being especially marked in the different workmanship of the two inscriptions. To add one point to others already noticed by the Professor—in the older inscription the ע (which in the old character usually takes the shape of a circle) is formed by four straight cuts, which give the letter nearly the appearance of a quadrilateral. In the newer inscription, upon the other hand, attempt has been made to render the rounded form of the letter, at the cost of more than one slip of the graving tool.

It is also extremely doubtful whether the first letter of the supposed של is really a ש. If, however, this be the true reading, and Prof. Smith be correct in regarding של as an abbreviation of שָׁלֵם, the word is most simply to be regarded as an adjective in agreement with רבע, and the inscription denotes

Preservation of ה of art. after prep. בּ:—II. 7. 12 בְּהַשָּׂדֶה.

Kt. אֵיכָה = *where?* II. 6. 13. Elsewhere only Cant. 1. 7 *bis*. Cf. Aram. אֵיכָא, ܐܝܟܐ.

עַד־אֲלֵיהֶם, עַד־הֵם II. 9. 18, 20.

Constr. with suff. pron. anticipating obj. (akin to Syr.):— I. 19. 21 בִּשְּׁלָם הַבָּשָׂר; 21. 13 וַיְעִדֻהוּ . . . אֶת־נָבוֹת.

Indefinite use of אחד *a certain*:—I. 19. 4, 5; 20. 13, 35; 22. 9 (cf. *v*. 8); II. 4. 1; 7. 8; 8. 6: add I. 21. 1, LXX, Luc. Elsewhere I. 13. 11 (perhaps for אַחֵר); II. 12. 10; Judg. 9. 53; 13. 2; 1 Sam. 1. 1; 7. 9, 12; 2 Sam. 18. 10, and late Ezek. 1. 15; 8. 7, 8; 9. 2; 17. 7; 33. 2; Zech. 5. 7; Dan. 8. 13, 3; 10. 5[1].

To these may be added a few roots which betray the influence of Aram.:—שָׂפַק I. 20. 10; מְדִינוֹת 20. 14, 15, 17, 19 (elsewhere only very late); חֹרִים 21. 8, 11; הִשְׁלָה II. 4. 28. There is also a fair number of ἅπαξ λεγγ., some of which take the place of ordinary words and thus may be dialectical; e.g. שִׁנֵּס *gird*, I. 18. 46 (for חגר, אזר), אֲכִילָה *food*, 19. 8 (for אֹכֶל, אָכְלָה, מַאֲכָל); but of others nothing can be affirmed.

The narratives are clearly not all by one author.

(i) Some are histories of Elijah and Elisha, or of movements which they instituted in the direction of religious reform. (ii) In others the fate of the kingdom is regarded from a political standpoint, and this as determined mainly by the action of the *king*; though here also prophets play an important part as advisers and announcers of the oracle of Yahwe. Thus both classes have a religious colouring or motive, and may equally be regarded as

---

'*a full* (i.e. *complete* or *accurate*; cf. Deut. 25. 15, Prov. 11. 1) *quarter*.' In this case the difficult נצנ of the obverse may be a Niph'al participle נִצָּב '*set*' or '*appointed*'; so רבע נצב '*a standard quarter*.'

Prof. Smith's article, together with other correspondence upon the subject of the inscription, is collected in *PEF. Ay. St.*, July, 1894, pp. 220–231; October, 1894, pp. 284–287.

[1] אחד II. 25. 19 appears to have a certain force; '*One* Eunuch and five men, &c.' Cf. 1 Sam. 6. 7.

the work of men of prophetic training, perhaps members of the guilds which we see coming into prominence in some of the Elisha stories.

(i) To the former class belong I. 17–19; 21; II. 1. 2–17a α; 2. 1–18, 19–22, 23–25; 4. 1–7, 8–37, 38–41, 42–44; 5; 6. 1–7; 8. 1–6, 7–15; 9. 1—10. 28; 13. 14–19, 20, 21.

Of these, I. 17–19 forms a continuous narrative. From the abruptness of *v.* 1, no reason being assigned for Elijah's threat, and no point of connexion existing for מִזֶּה *v.* 3, it may be inferred that the commencement of the story has been omitted or abbreviated by R^D, and the specification אליהו התשבי מתשבי גלעד thus represents his summary introduction. The sequel also, in strict accordance with 19. 15, 16, is lacking, only one part of Yahwe's commission being fulfilled, *vv.* 19–21.

I. 21 is clearly out of place in MT., breaking the connexion between *ch.* 20 and its sequel *ch.* 22, and LXX, Luc. are no doubt correct in placing this narrative immediately after *ch.* 19. The dislocation may have been due to the desire to bring the prophecy of Aḥab's death (21. 19) nearer to the account of its occurrence (22. 35 *ff.*), and perhaps in a minor degree to the description of the king's mood as סר וזעף in 20. 43 as in 21. 4.

Most critics (Wellh., Dri., Kamp., Benz., Kit.; but Kue. is uncertain: *Ond.* § 25. 7) assign I. 21 to the same author as I. 17–19. Thus Wellh. cites as points of contact the central position occupied by Elijah, his eagle-like swoop upon Aḥab at the right moment, and the formulae ויהי אחר הדברים האלה 21. 1 (but cf. *note ad loc.*) as 17. 17, ויהי דבר י׳ אל א׳ 21. 17 as ודבר י׳ היה אל א׳ 18. 1.

On the other hand, it may be maintained that Elijah is not really the central figure as in I. 17–19. He does not appear upon the scene until *v.* 17, and then takes scarcely a more conspicuous position than Micaiah in 22. 8 *ff.* The king and his action form the centre of interest both at the beginning and end of the narrative. Further, Kue. notices the absence of any reference in 21 to 17–19 and *vice versâ*, the murder of Naboth forming the single crime of Aḥab and Jezebel in the one story, while in the other the sole pivot is the struggle between Yahwe and Ba'al. This, however, is a point of slight moment, and no definite conclusion can be reached as to the relative authorship of the two sections.

Of far greater interest and importance is the question of the connexion of I. 21 with its natural sequel II. 9. 1—10. 28. Critics generally argue or assume that the latter section is by a different author to the former, and most (Wellh., Dri., Kamp., Kit.) assign II. 9 *f.* to the writer of I. 20. 22; II. 3. 4–27, &c. (see below). The argument against identity of authorship of I. 21 and II. 9 *f.*, as stated by Wellh., is based upon supposed discrepancy in detail. While in I. 21 it is the *vineyard* of Naboth which is mentioned, and this is described as אצל היכל אחאב (*v.* 1), II. 9. 21–26 alludes to the חלקת נבות, i. e. his *portion* or *estate*, which lay outside the city. Again, I. 21. 13 records only the death of Naboth, while II. 9. 26 speaks also of the blood of his sons as calling for vengeance.

On the other hand, the following considerations clearly make for the unity of the two narratives:—

II. 9. 21ᵇ, the meeting of Joram ben-Aḥab with Jehu actually upon the estate of Naboth, is a touch of high dramatic power which demands that the writer should not only have *known* the story of Naboth (proved by *vv.* 25, 26), but should actually have written it down himself as an introduction to the sequel II. 9 *f.*

Thus a presumption is created in favour of *our* Naboth narrative being the story thus written.

The parallels between the prediction I. 21. 19, 23 and the fulfilment II. 9. 25, 26, 36 cannot be insisted upon, because I. 21. 19 *ff.* has been largely amplified by R^D (see *notes ad loc.*), and it is not now possible certainly to determine the original kernel of Elijah's prediction. It should, however, be noticed that the usual method of R^D is to expand rather than to excise, and, if this plan has here prevailed, the original speech must be contained in *vv.* 19, 20, 23ᵇ. The disagreement in points of fact between I. 21 and II. 9 proves upon examination to be non-existent. Aḥab's dispute with Naboth arose in the first instance about a vineyard adjoining the palace, but this was only a portion of Naboth's estate (חלקה), the whole of which would lapse to the king supposing that the family of Naboth became extinct. And I. 21. 15, where Jezebel tells Aḥab to go down and take possession of the vineyard, clearly implies the extirpation of the whole family: in the statement כי אין נבות חי כי מת the name נבות means Naboth *and his sons*, just as much as in *v.* 19 דמך גם אתה means the blood of Aḥab *and his son* (cf. *v.* 29[b]).

Most decisive, however, is the question of the supposed unity of II. 9. 1—10. 28 with I. 20. 22; II. 3. 4–27; 6. 8—7. 20. If this be granted, the diverse authorship of I. 21 and II. 9 *f.* seems necessarily to follow, since I. 21 can scarcely be regarded as of one piece with I. 20. 22. The place where the dogs lick the blood of Aḥab, 22. 38, is discordant with the prediction of 21. 19, and in general the interest of the writer of 20. 22—mainly, if not wholly, political—and his sympathetic feeling for the king of Israel, preclude the supposition that he is also the author of the Naboth story.

Wellh. cites the following coincidences in phraseology of II. 9 *f.* with I. 20. 22, &c.:—חדר בחדר II. 9. 2; I. 20. 30; 22. 25; חכה *tarry*, II. 9. 3; 7. 9; רכב הסוס 9. 18; 7. 14; הפך ידיו II. 9. 23; I. 22. 34; חפש חי II. 10. 14; 7. 12; I. 20. 18; חרא II. 10. 27; 6. 25. The importance of this collection is, however, open to doubt, since it contains no striking phrase, but such only as might be expected to occur in narratives nearly contemporaneous, and having, in the main, the same subjects in common.

On the other hand, a point of phraseology, apparently hitherto overlooked, sharply separates between II. 9 *f.* and I. 20. 22, &c., and seems absolutely to preclude the theory of a common authorship. This is the title which is ordinarily applied to the *king* in the course of the narrative.

I. 20. 22; II. 3. 4–27; 6. 8—7. 20 are, as might be expected, bound together by the use of a common title. In all the writer's phrase is מלך ישראל, and the proper name of the king, if it occurs at all, is in nearly every case reserved for the necessary specification at the commencement of a section. The facts are as follow:—

I. 20 אחאב מלך ישראל *vv.* 2, 13; מלך ישראל eleven times, viz. *vv.* 4, 7, 11, 21, 22, 28, 31, 32, 40, 41, 43; המלך *vv.* 38, 39 *bis*; אחאב simply *v.* 14.

I. 22 מלך ישראל seventeen times, viz. *vv.* 2, 3, 4, 5, 6, 8, 9, 10, 18, 26, 29, 30 *bis*, 31, 32, 33, 34; המלך *vv.* 15 *bis*, 16, 35, 37[b].

II. 3. 4–27 מלך ישראל eight times, viz. *vv.* 4, 5, 9, 10, 11, 12, 13 *bis*; אחאב simply *v.* 5 (probably from another source); המלך יהורם *v.* 6.

II. 6. 8—7. 20 מלך ישראל seven times, viz. 6. 8, 9, 10, 11, 12, 21, 26; המלך ten times, viz. 6. 28, 30; 7. 2, 6, 12, 14, 15, 17 *bis*, 18.

On the other hand, in II. 9 the king of Israel is called יורם or יהורם simply nine times, viz. *vv.* 14 *bis*, 16 *bis*, 17, 21, 22, 23, 24; once יהורם המלך *v.* 15; and once יהורם מלך ישראל in direct distinction from אחזיהו מלך יהודה *v.* 21; never מלך ישראל simply. The double occurrence of יורם simply in *v.* 16 is specially to be noticed, since, on account of the proximity of אחזיהו מלך יהודה, the specification מלך ישראל might have been expected.

Similarly, in I. 21 אחאב simply is usual; nine times (omitting the prophecy *vv.* 21–26), viz. *vv.* 2, 3, 4, 8, 15, 16, 20, 27, 29. אחאב מלך שמרון *v.* 1; אחאב מלך ישראל *v.* 18.

Now though this agreement in form of reference to the king cannot be pressed to prove *identity* of authorship for I. 21 and II. 9, any more than the fact that I. 17–19 always speaks of אחאב simply can be used to connect this section with I. 21, because different writers may easily have employed the same so obvious citation of the proper name; yet the fact of disagreement in form of reference between I. 21 and I. 20. 22, &c., ought to be emphasized as demonstrating *diversity* of authorship.

It is true that in I. 20. 22, &c., the general use of מלך ישראל may be explained as prompted to a large extent by contrast to מלך ארם; but this does not sufficiently account for the almost total omission of the king's proper name, which would certainly have occurred far more frequently had the author of II. 9 been the writer of these narratives. Contrast especially I. 22, II. 3. 4–27, where (excepting 3. 6) the names of Aḥab and Joram are never mentioned in spite of the close connexion with יהושפט מלך יהודה, with II. 9, where in connexion with אחזיהו מלך יהודה the usual form of citation is יורם, יהורם simply. And, again, notice the use of המלך simply five times in I. 22, ten times in II. 6. 8—7. 20, where the desire for distinction from מלך ארם cannot have been in the writer's mind, and the occasion might have been suitable for the use of the king's proper name.

By this point, therefore, the diverse authorship of I. 20. 22, &c., and II. 9 seems to be proved, and this dissociation adds weight to the arguments which have above been put forward in favour of the unity of II. 9. 1—10. 27 with I. 21.

II. 1. 2–$17^{a\alpha}$ is from a different source to the preceding Elijah narratives. This fact is marked by the form of the name אֵלִיָּה *vv.* 3, 4, 8, 12, peculiar to this section, and generally by the inferior literary merit of the composition. The story is probably much later than I. 17–19, I. 21 and sequel.

II. 2. 1–18, Elijah's translation, links itself closely on to some of the longer Elisha narratives which follow, as their introduction; but also might have formed a suitable close to the Elijah history, of which we possess a fragment in I. 17–19, if this can be thought to have gone on to embody also a history of Elisha. The following coincidences between the narratives are worthy of notice, and suggest that I. 17–19; II. 2. 1–18; 4. 1–37, to which we may add II. 5, may be the work of one author. In the case of II. 8. 7–15; 13. 14–19 the evidence is too slight to build upon.

Elijah.	*Elisha.*
I. 17. 8–24. Miraculous provision for the widow of Zarephath during famine, and the raising of her son from death.	II. 4. 1–7. Miraculous provision for the wife of one of the sons of the prophets. II. 4. 8–37. Raising to life of the son of the Shunammite woman.
I. 18. 26. וְאֵין קוֹל וְאֵין עֹנֶה; 29. וְאֵין קוֹל וְאֵין עֹנֶה וְאֵין קָשֶׁב.	II. 4. 31. וְאֵין קוֹל וְאֵין קָשֶׁב.

Elijah.	*Elisha.*
I. 18. 42. וַיִּגְהַר אַרְצָה.	II. 4. 34, 35. וַיִּגְהַר עָלָיו.
I. 19. 13, 19. Mention of Elijah's אַדֶּרֶת.	II. 2. 8, 13, 14. *ib.*
II. 2. 2, 4, 6. חַי י׳ וְחֵי־נַפְשְׁךָ אִם־אֶעֶזְבֶךָּ.	II. 4. 30. *ib.*
II. 2. 7. וַיַּעַמְדוּ מִנֶּגֶד; 15 .. וַיִּרְאֻהוּ מִנֶּגֶד.	II. 4. 25. וַיְהִי כִּרְאוֹת אִישׁ הָאֱלֹהִים אֹתָהּ מִנֶּגֶד.
II. 2. 17. וַיִּפְצְרוּ־בוֹ עַד־בֹּשׁ.	II. 8. 11. וַיָּשֶׂם עַד־בֹּשׁ.
II. 2. 12. אָבִי אָבִי רֶכֶב יִשְׂרָאֵל וּפָרָשָׁיו.	II. 13. 14. *ib.*

The short Elisha stories are probably popular tales handed down orally at first, and not put into writing till some considerable time after the longer narratives.

(ii) The second class includes I. 20; 22. 1–38; II. 3. 4–27; 6. 8–23, 24–33; 7; (14. 8–14). All these, with the exception of 14. 8–14, deal in the same style with the same subject—Israel's relations with Aram, and may not improbably flow from one hand. Notice especially the close bond of connexion between I. 22. 4, 7 and II. 3. 7, 11.

II. 14. 8–14, which stands apart from the other narratives, is marked as probably North Palestinian in origin by its tone, and especially by the reference *v.* 11 בבית שמש אשר ליהודה. Cf. I. 19. 3.

17. *Elijah the prophet predicts three years of famine. He is supported at the brook Kerîth by ravens, and afterwards at Zarephath by a widow, whose means of subsistence he miraculously maintains. He raises the widow's son from death.*

17. 1. התשבי] So *ch.* 21. 17, 28; II. 9. 36; 1. 3, 8. On the place Tishbe see below.

מִתֹּשָׁבֵי גלעד] R.V. 'Of the sojourners of Gilead.' תּוֹשָׁב occurs thirteen times elsewhere—eleven times in the Pentateuch exclusively in P and H, and in 1 Chr. 29. 15; Ps. 39. 13. The word may thus, but for this occurrence in Kings, be judged to be late. תושב is found eight times ‖ גֵּר, viz. Gen. 23. 4; Lev. 25. 23, 35, 47 *bis;* Num. 35. 15; 1 Chr. 29. 15; Ps. 39. 13; ‖ שָׂכִיר four times, viz. Ex. 12. 45; Lev. 22. 10; 25. 6, 40; while the participle הַגָּרִים refers to התושבים Lev. 25. 45. Thus תושב has much the same meaning as גר—a foreigner dwelling in the midst of Israel, and, if it can be in any way distinguished from this latter, seems to denote residence of a more fortuitous or transitory character; cf. Gen. 23. 4; Ps. 39. 13; 1 Chr. 29. 15. Elijah is thus said to have been a foreigner who had been sojourning, probably for a short time merely, in the region east of Jordan—a statement which ill accords with his zeal in extirpating the foreign Ba'al cult, and confirming the worship of Yahwe in the kingdom of Israel.

It should be noticed further that the *scriptio defectiva* of the *Ḥolem* in תִּשָׁבֵי is not found elsewhere among the thirteen other occurrences of the word, and is unusual in the case of *ō* arising out of the diphthong *aw*.

The difficulty thus apparent is met by the rendering of LXX ἐκ Θεσβῶν τῆς Γαλαάδ, Luc. ὁ ἐκ Θεσσεβῶν τῆς Γαλαάδ, i.e. מִתִּשְׁבֵּי (מִתִּשְׁבֵּה) גִּלְעָד '*of Tishbe in Gilead.*' Thus the gentilic הַתִּשְׁבִּי is further elucidated, and the native city or village of the prophet is named, as might have been expected; cf. *ch.* 19. 16; II. 14. 25; *al.* So Jos. (*Ant.* viii. 13, § 2) ἐκ πόλεως Θεσεβώνης τῆς Γαλαδίτιδος χώρας, and among moderns Ew., Th., Wellh., Kamp., Benz., Kit., *Sta. u. Sieg.*, &c. Klo., who reads 'aus Thisbe Gileads' in his text, suggests in the notes that LXX ὁ προφήτης (Θεσβίτης) ὁ ἐκ Θ.[1] stands for הַנָּבִי שֶׁמִּתשבי, and that this is a corruption of הַיָּבֵשִׁי מִיָּבֵשׁ גִּלְעָד 'the Jabeshite of Jabesh Gilead.' This, however, must presuppose that הַתִּשְׁבִּי is a corruption in all its six occurrences.

A place named Tishbe in Naphtali is mentioned Tobit 1. 2:— ὃς ᾐχμαλωτεύθη ἐν ἡμέραις Ἐνεμεσσάρου τοῦ βασιλέως Ἀσσυρίων ἐκ Θίσβης (Cod. A Θίβης), ἥ ἐστιν ἐκ δεξιῶν Κυδιὼς τῆς Νεφθαλεὶμ ἐν τῇ

[1] According to Field, in some texts ὁ προφήτης stands alone without Θεσβίτης. His note is:—'Sic Ald., Codd. III, XI, 44, 55, 64, 71, alii (inter quos 247), Syro-hex. (cum ܬܫܒܝܐ .ܘ in marg.), Arm. 1.'

Γαλειλαίᾳ ὑπεράνω Ἀσήρ. Thus the statement 'Tishbe *of Gilead*' may be intended to make distinction from this other place of the same name.

Van Kasteren (*Zeitschr. d. deutsch. Pal. Vereins XIII*, 207 *ff.*) identifies תשבה with *El-istib* upon the *Jebel Ajlûn*, some ten miles north of the Jabbok, and supports the metathesis (*st* for *ts*) by comparison of Ar. *Tell semak* = Sycaminos. To the south-east of *Istib* lie the ruins of a quadrangular chapel now bearing the name of *Mār Elyās*, and near to this is an insignificant grave which is said to be the grave of the prophet.

חי י׳ וג׳] Cf. *ch.* 18. 15; II. 3. 14; 5. 16.

י׳ אלהי ישראל] LXX Κύριος ὁ Θεὸς τῶν δυνάμεων, ὁ Θεὸς Ἰσραήλ. Luc. omits. In *v.* 14 LXX, Luc. Κύριος. Elijah's expression elsewhere *ch.* 18. 15; 19. 10, 14 is י׳ אלהי צבאות, and this, taken in connexion with the fact that י׳ אלהי ישראל is most generally a redactional phrase (cf. *ch.* 8. 15 *note*), favours the reading in *v.* 1 י׳ אלהי צבאות, and in *v.* 14 יהוה merely.

אשר עמדתי לפניו] 'Before whom I stand,' i.e. *whose servant I am*, the phrase being employed in the idiomatic sense noticed *ch.* 1. 2 *note*. The perfect is here used of an action commencing at some point of time indefinitely anterior, and continuing into the present.

אם יהיה השנים האלה וג׳] According to Jos. (*Ant.* viii. 13, § 2) this drought is mentioned by Menander the historian among the events of the reign of Ittoba'al of Tyre, and its duration is stated as one full year:—μέμνηται δὲ τῆς ἀνομβρίας ταύτης καὶ Μένανδρος ἐν ταῖς Ἰθωβάλου τῶν Τυρίων βασιλέως πράξεσι λέγων οὕτως· "ἀβροχία τ' ἐπ' αὐτοῦ ἐγένετο ἀπὸ τοῦ Ὑπερβερεταίου μηνὸς ἕως τοῦ ἐχομένου ἔτους Ὑπερβερεταίου, ἱκετείαν δ' αὐτοῦ ποιησαμένου κεραυνοὺς ἱκανοὺς βεβληκέναι, κ.τ.λ."

2. אליו] LXX, Luc. here and in *v.* 8 πρὸς Ἠλειού (Ἠλιάν), if not paraphrastic, seems to be an easy error אליהו (אל) for אליו. Cf. *v.* 11 where ויקרא אליה is rendered καὶ ἐβόησεν ὄπισω αὐτῆς Ἠλειού. For MT. cf. *ch.* 19. 9.

4. והיה וג׳] The substantive verb merely serves loosely to

introduce what follows. Dri. *Tenses*, § 121 *Obs.* 1, quotes also Ex. 4. 16; Ezek. 47. 10, 22.

6. מביאים] 'Were bringing.' The stress is on the continuity of their action during a period of some length.

לחם ובשר וג׳] LXX, Luc. ἄρτους τὸ πρωὶ καὶ κρέα τὸ δείλης, favoured by Klo., Kamp., Kit. upon the ground (Klo.) of a supposed reference to Ex. 16. 8, 12.

7. מקץ ימים] 'At the end of *some* days'; undefined. So Gen. 4. 3; 2 Sam. 14. 26†. Cf. Neh. 13. 6. The use of ימים *v.* 15 is similar.

9. צרפתה] The modern *Ṣarafand*, a large village near the sea, and some eight miles below Zidon. Cf. Rob. *BR.* 474 *ff.* So Jos. (*Ant.* viii. 13, § 2):—πόλιν οὐκ ἄπωθεν τῆς Σιδῶνος καὶ Τύρου, μεταξὺ γὰρ κεῖται.

וישבת שם] LXX, Luc. omit.

10. ויבא] LXX, Luc. omit.

בַּכְּלִי] 'In *the* vessel.' So בַּכַּד, בַּצַּפַּחַת *v.* 12. Cf. *note* on בבגדים *ch.* 1. 1.

11. לקחי] The first radical is thus preserved only again in imperat. 2 sing. masc. לְקַח Ex. 29. 1; Prov. 20. 16; Ezek. 37. 16†.

12. מעוג] 'A cake'; only again in the doubtful passage Ps. 35. 16. The more usual word is עֻגָּה *v.* 13; *al.*, possibly so named from its *rounded* or *twisted* shape, if we may suppose a connexion with Ar. عَوِجَ 'to be curved or distorted.' Pesh. ܠܐ ܐܝܬ ܠܝ ܡܕܡ, Targ. אם אית לי מידעם presuppose אם יש לי מְאוּמָה 'I have *nothing*,' a reading which, as Th. notices, agrees better than MT. with the following כי אם וג׳, and is therefore preferable. So Klo.

וְלִבְנִי] LXX, Luc. presuppose וּלְבָנַי 'and for my *children*'; and so *v.* 13 וּלְבָנַיִךְ for וְלִבְנֵךְ. So Th., upon the ground that the *pl.* agrees better with ביתה 'her *household*,' *v.* 15, and that MT. vocalization may be due to *vv.* 17 *ff.* These latter verses, however, certainly convey the impression that the boy was the widow's *only* son, and this perhaps gains confirmation from the parallel story of Elisha, II. 4. 8 *ff.*

14. תִּכְלָה] The final syllable anomalously vocalized after the

analogy of verbs ל״א; cf. יִקְרָה Dan. 10. 14[1]. For cases of the converse change—true ל״א vocalized as ל״ה, cf. נִשָּׂא *ch.* 9. 11; חֹטֶא Eccl. 8. 12; 9. 18; רִפֵּאתִי II. 2. 21; כָּלָאתִי Ps. 119. 101; G-K. § 75 *oo*; Sta. § 143 *ϵ*, *Rem.* 1 δ.

תתן] On Kt. cf. *ch.* 6. 19 *note.*

15. ותאכל הִוא־וָהִיא] Q're, which is postulated by the fem. verb, has the support of LXX, Luc., Pesh., Targ.

16. לא חסר] The predicate agrees with שמן, the principal number of the compound subj., and not with צפחת as in *v.* 14. Naturally it is the oil and not the cruse which is thought of as not failing. Cf. קשת גברים חתים 1 Sam. 2. 4; עיני גבהות אדם שפל Isa. 2. 11. Ew. § 317[c]; Da. § 116, *Rem.* 2.

17. בעלת הבית] 'The mistress of the house.' Similarly בעל הבית Ex. 22. 7 (E); Judg. 19. 22, 23. Klo.'s ingenious suggestion to emend בַּעֲלִית הַבַּיִת 'in the upper chamber of the house,' regarding this as a gloss from *v.* 19, is in fact refuted by the statement of that verse, ויעלהו.

נשמה] Luc. πνοὴ ζωῆς suggests נִשְׁמַת חַיִּים as in Gen. 2. 7. For MT., supported by LXX, Vulg., Pesh., Targ., cf. Dan. 10. 17.

18. מה לי ולך] 'What have I and thou (in common)?' i.e. 'What concern hast thou with my affairs?' The phrase occurs again in II. 3. 13; Judg. 11. 12; 2 Chr. 35. 21; מה לי ולכם 2 Sam. 16. 10; 19. 23, and in each case deprecates outside interference. This is further illustrated by NT.; S. Matt. 8. 29 Τί ἡμῖν καὶ σοί, υἱὲ τοῦ Θεοῦ; ἦλθες ὧδε πρὸ καιροῦ βασανίσαι ἡμᾶς; S. Jo. 2. 4 Τί ἐμοὶ καὶ σοί, γύναι; οὔπω ἥκει ἡ ὥρα μου. Cf. also S. Matt. 27. 19 μηδὲν σοι καὶ τῷ δικαίῳ ἐκείνῳ. By באת אלי וג׳ the woman seems to mean that the man of God, by living in her house, has directed God's attention to her, and that some secret sin, perhaps unknown to her and which might otherwise have escaped detection, has been the cause of her son's death.

19. מטתו] LXX, Luc., Pesh. seem to have read הַמִּטָּה.

[1] Here, however, the vocalization may have been determined by יִקְרָא of Gen. 49. 1, which seems to have suggested the words of Daniel. Cf. Bevan, *ad loc.*

20. מתגורר] *Hithpô'lel* only here, Hos. 7. 14 being probably corrupt. *Heb. Lex. Oxf.* cf. Ar. x. استجار 'seek hospitality with.'

21. ויתמדד] 'And he stretched himself out'; the only occurrence of the reflex *Hithpô'el.* Cf. the similar action of Elisha, II. 4. 34, and of S. Paul with Eutychus, καταβὰς δὲ ὁ Παῦλος ἐπέπεσεν αὐτῷ, Acts 20. 10. LXX, Luc. make the guess καὶ ἐνεφύσησεν.

על קרבו] על in place of אל; cf. *ch.* 1. 33 *note.*

22. ויחי . . . וישמע] LXX καὶ ἐγένετο οὕτως (Luc. adds καὶ ἐπεστράφη ἡ ψυχὴ τοῦ παιδαρίου εἰς αὐτόν), καὶ ἀνεβόησεν τὸ παιδάριον. Here, no doubt, the words of MT. have fallen out through the homoioteleuton על קרבו, while, as Klo. suggests, ויחי was read as ויהי, and possibly the first few words of *v.* 23 gave rise to וַיִּקְרָא הַיֶּלֶד. The additional words of Luc. represent a later attempt to restore the true text.

24. עתה זה] So II. 5. 22†. Cf. *ch.* 14. 6 *note.*

18. *Elijah's meeting with Aḥab in the third year of the famine. After the contest between Yahwe and Ba'al, and the destruction of Ba'al's prophets, the rain is sent by Yahwe.*

18. 1. ויהי ימים רבים וג'] 'And there were many days, and the word &c.,' i.e. 'And when many days had elapsed, the word &c.' For the sing. verb preceding the pl. subj., cf. *ch.* 11. 3 *note.* Elsewhere the phrase וַיְהִי מִיָּמִים occurs, Josh. 23. 1; Judg. 11. 4; 15. 1†, and so, according to Th., 3 Codd. in our passage; but the rendering of the Verss. is ambiguous as to the original text, and cannot be cited (Th., Klo.) in support of the alteration.

4. ויחביאם . . . וכלכלם] '*Hid them* (once for all) *and used to feed them* (at stated intervals).'

חמשים איש] LXX κατὰ (Luc. ἀνὰ) πεντήκοντα, Vulg. *quinquagenos et quinquagenos*, Pesh. ܚܡܫܝܢ ܚܡܫܝܢ, Targ. חמשין חמשין גברא presuppose the distrib. חֲמִשִּׁים חֲמִשִּׁים 'by fifty,' which is doubtless correct. Cf. *v.* 13.

בַּמְּעָרָה] Cf. *ch.* 13. 14 *note.*

5. לך בארץ] LXX Δεῦρο καὶ διέλθωμεν ἐπὶ τὴν γῆν (Luc. ἐν τῇ γῇ) presupposes לֵךְ וְנַעֲבֹר בָּאָרֶץ, agreeably to the following נמצא, and to *v.* 6 לעבר בה. So Th., Klo., Kamp., Benz., Kit.

ולוא נכרית מן בהמה] Impossible. Even a forced translation can merely give the sense that Aḥab feared to lose *some* only of the beasts, while the context clearly demands expression of the apprehension lest the whole should perish. The true text is given by Luc. καὶ οὐκ ἐξολοθρευθήσεται ἀφ' ἡμῶν κτήνη, i. e. וְלֹא תִכָּרֵת מִמֶּנּוּ בְּהֵמָה '*that cattle be not cut off from us.*' So Wellh.

6. הארץ] LXX, Luc., Pesh. suggest הַדֶּרֶךְ; inferior to MT.

לבדו] LXX, Luc. omit in reference to Aḥab.

7. ויכרהו] LXX, Luc. καὶ ἔσπευσεν, i. e. וַיְמַהֵר, preferred by Th., Klo. MT., however, agrees well with the fact that Obadiah had not before seen Elijah (cf. his question in this verse, and his statements as to himself *vv.* 12^{b}, 13), and must therefore have recognized him from popular description of his appearance.

האתה זה] The enclitic זה gives point and vivacity to the interrogation. So *v.* 17; 2 Sam. 2. 20, and in an indirect question Gen. 27. 21†. With omission of ה, אַתָּה זֶה Gen. 27. 24†. Cf. *note* on למה זה *ch.* 14. 6.

8. אני] Luc. omits.

10. ואמרו אין והשביע] 'And when they said, He is not (here), he would take an oath of &c.' LXX, Luc. render והשביע by καὶ ἐνέπρησεν, rightly recognized by Klo. as a corruption of καὶ ἐνέπλησεν, i. e. והשׂביע.

כי לא ימצאכה] 'That he *could* not find thee.' Dri. *Tenses*, § 37 β.

11. הנה אליהו] LXX omits.

12. ישאך על אשר וג'] Unless על be merely used in place of אל (*ch.* 1. 38 *note*), the constr. is pregnant: 'carry thee off (up) and set thee down *upon*.' Cf. II. 2. 16 פֶּן־נְשָׂאוֹ רוּחַ י' וַיַּשְׁלִכֵהוּ בְּאַחַד הֶהָרִים וג'.

13. הלא הגד וג'] For impers. passive governing the accus., cf. *ch.* 2. 21 *note*.

את אשר עשיתי . . . ואחבא] 'That which I did . . . *how* I hid &c.' Cf. *ch.* 2. 5 *note*.

15. חי וג'] Cf. *ch.* 17. 1 *note*.

כי היום וג'] כי introducing the substance of the oath. *Ch.* 2. 23 *note*.

16. וילך אחאב] LXX, Luc. καὶ ἐξέδραμεν Ἀχαὰβ καὶ ἐπορεύθη, i.e. וַיָּרָץ וילך א'. Th. notices that such haste is wholly conformable to the statement of *v.* 10.

18. הבעלים] 'The Ba'als.' Some contempt is conveyed by the use of the plural as contrasted with the one Yahwe. Cf. 1 Sam. 7. 4 'And the children of Israel put away the Ba'als and the Astartes, and served *Yahwe alone*.' The plural הבעלים has reference to the various local forms under which the Canaanite Ba'al was worshipped; cf. בַּעַל פְּעוֹר, בַּעַל בְּרִית, בַּעַל זְבוּב, and the place-names (local sanctuaries) בַּעַל שָׁלִשָׁה, בַּעַל גָּד, בַּעַל חֶרְמוֹן, *al.* For instances from *CIS.* of Phoenician titles of special Ba'als, cf. Dri. *Sam.*, pp. 49 *f.*

19. הבעל] LXX, Luc. τῆς αἰσχύνης, and so *v.* 25; i.e. הַבֹּשֶׁת '*the shameful thing*' substituted by a later hand, as in Hos. 9. 10 הֵמָּה בָּאוּ בַעַל־פְּעוֹר וַיִּנָּזְרוּ לַבֹּשֶׁת; Jer. 3. 24; 11. 13. Cf. also the same alteration in the proper names יְרֻבֶּשֶׁת 2 Sam. 11. 21 for יְרֻבַּעַל Judg. 6. 32; אִישׁ־בֹּשֶׁת 2 Sam. 2. 8[1] for אֶשְׁבַּעַל 1 Chr. 8. 33; מְפִיבֹשֶׁת 2 Sam. 4. 4 for מְרִיב בַּעַל 1 Chr. 8. 34; 9. 40ª or מְרִי־בַעַל 1 Chr. 9. 40ᵇ. In these latter cases בעל appears to have been used as a title of Yahwe, an ancient practice which was afterwards discouraged by the prophets (cf. Hos. 2. 18), and finally disappeared. Cf. Dri. *Sam.*, p. 95.

ונביאי האשרה ארבע מאות] Wellh. (so Sta., Kamp., Benz., Kit.), calling attention to the absence of את before נביאי and to the omission of any mention in *vv.* 22, 40[2], regards these words as a gloss, upon the ground that אשרה was not confused with the *goddess* עַשְׁתֹּרֶת until much later times. Cf. *ch.* 14. 15 *note*. Pesh. gives the number as 450.

20. בכל בני ישראל] LXX, Luc. are preferable in omission of בני; εἰς πάντα Ἰσραήλ.

את הנביאים] LXX, Luc. πάντας τοὺς προφήτας. Pesh. ܘܟܢܫ ܠܗܘܢ ܠܓܒܪ̈ܐ 'and gathered the men' may perhaps point to a reading וַיִּקְבְּצֵם, with suffix of indefinite reference.

---

[1] Εἰσβάαλ is the reading of Cod. 93 Holmes and οἱ λοιποί, i.e. Ἀ., Σ., Θ.

[2] LXX, Luc. make the addition in *v.* 22 καὶ οἱ προφῆται τοῦ ἄλσους (Luc. τῶν ἀλσῶν) τετρακόσιοι.

21. עד מתי וג׳] ‘How long are ye limping upon the two different opinions?’ The attempt to combine two religions so incompatible as Yahwe-worship and Baʿal-worship is compared to the laboured gait of a man walking upon legs of different length. סעפים appears to mean *divisions*, as rendered by Pesh. ܦܠܓܘܬܐ, Targ. פולגוון, Vulg. *partes*[1]; cf. סָעִיף ‘cleft’ or ‘fissure’ of a rock, Judg. 15. 8, 11; Isa. 2. 21; 57. 5; ‘branch’ Isa. 17. 6; 27. 10†. שְׂעִפִּים ‘thoughts’ (as dividing or distracting the mind, Ges.) Job 4. 13; 20. 2† may be the same word. LXX, Luc. render by ταῖς ἰγνύαις, and this is followed by Ew., Th., Benz., who explain סעפים as ‘knee-cavities (Kniekehlen), the place where the bone is *divided*,’ and regard the saying as a proverb of Elijah’s time.

22. אל העם] Pesh. omits. Targ. לכל עמא.

23. ויתנו] ‘*So* let them give.’ The ו is, however, not expressed in the Verss., excepting Targ.

24. בשם יהוה] LXX, Luc., Pesh. presuppose additional אֱלֹהֵי, probably an easy gloss in antithesis to the preceding אלהיכם.

הוא האלהים] ‘He is *the* God,’ i.e. *the true* God. Cf. *v.* 39.

טוב הדבר] LXX, Luc. add אֲשֶׁר דִּבַּרְתָּ; but for MT. cf. *ch.* 2. 38, 42.

25ᵇ. וקראו . . . תשימו] Pesh. omits.

26. הבעל עננו] The repetition of LXX, Luc. Ἐπάκουσον ἡμῶν, ὁ Βάαλ, ἐπάκουσον ἡμῶν is probably an imitation of *v.* 37.

ויפסחו על המזבח] ‘And they limped around the altar.’ ויפסחו, the intensive of the word used in *v.* 21, describes with some scorn the *pantomimic dance* (Ke., Th.) of the priests. LXX, Luc. καὶ διέτρεχον, Vulg. *transiliebantque*, Pesh. ܘܐܬܟܬܫܘ ‘exerted themselves,’ Targ. ומשתטן ‘leapt madly.’ Klo.’s suggestion וַיְפַזְּזוּ ‘and they danced’ (2 Sam. 6. 16) is unnecessary. Baethgen (*Semit. Relig.* 25) compares a Greek inscription from the neighbourhood of Berytus (*CIG.* 4536) Εἵλαθί μοι, Βαλμαρκώς, κοίρανε κώμων. Here Βαλμαρκώς must represent בַּעַל מַרְקֵד ‘Baʿal of the dance,’ or מַרְקִד ‘causing to dance,’ i.e. ‘worshipped in the dance.’

[1] Σ. ἀμφιβόλως, perhaps a corruption of ἀμφιβόλοις, ‘doubtful (opinions).’

אשר עשה] LXX, Luc., Vulg., Pesh. presuppose אֲשֶׁר עָשׂוּ 'which they had made,' correctly.

27. וַיְהַתֵּל] Usually regarded as imperf. Pi'el, and a secondary form from הֵתֵל Hiph'il of חלל. Cf. Sta. § 145 ε; *Heb. Lex. Oxf.* G-K. § 67 *y*; Kö. *Lehrg.* I. i, p. 352, explain as imperf. Hiph. of חלל with doubling of first radical (Aramaïzing form) as in יִסֹּב, and without elision of ה as in the forms תְּהָתֵלּוּ Job 13. 9, יְהָתֵלּוּ Jer. 9. 4. Sta., in adopting the former view, considers that these latter forms ought properly to be vocalized יְהַתְּלוּ, תְּ׳.

אליהו] LXX, Luc. add the gloss ὁ Θεσβείτης. Cf. *ch.* 17. 1 *note*. So Luc. *v.* 29.

כי שיח וג׳] 'Surely meditation, or surely going aside occupies him, or surely a journey occupies him!' שיח '*meditation*,' as producing a condition of abstraction (Pesh. ܪܢܝܐ), is preferable here to '*conversation*' (LXX, Luc., Vulg., Targ.). שיג (for סיג from סוג 'turn back'; cf. נָשׁוֹג 2 Sam. 1. 22 for נָסוֹג) is usually explained, after Jarchi, as an euphemism. But omission of וכי שיג לו in LXX, Luc., suggests that these words may be an erroneous repetition of the former. So Klo. The meaning of וכי דרך לו is brought out by paraphrase of LXX, Luc. καὶ ἅμα μή ποτε χρηματίζει αὐτός, 'perhaps he has business to transact!'

ויקץ] The *nuance* is '*must* (or *should*) be awakened.'

28. כמשפטם] LXX omits; but Luc. κατὰ τὸν ἐθισμὸν αὐτῶν.

29. In place of MT., LXX reads καὶ ἐπροφήτευσαν ἕως οὗ παρῆλθεν τὸ δειλινόν, καὶ ἐγένετο ὡς ὁ καιρὸς τοῦ ἀναβῆναι τὴν θυσίαν, καὶ ἐλάλησεν Ἠλειοὺ πρὸς τοὺς προφήτας τῶν προσοχθισμάτων λέγων Μετάστητε ἀπὸ τοῦ νῦν, καὶ ἐγὼ ποιήσω τὸ ὁλοκαύτωμά μου· καὶ μετέστησαν καὶ ἀπῆλθον. This is not, with Th., to be regarded as genuine, but is marked as a gloss which has usurped the place of the true text by the use of τὸ δειλινόν for הצהרים compared with *vv.* 26, 27 μεσημβρία, and τοὺς προφήτας τῶν προσοχθισμάτων as against οἱ προφῆται τοῦ Βάαλ *vv.* 22, 40, or revised τῆς αἰσχύνης *vv.* 19, 25. In Luc. this text has undergone revision, the reading of MT. being partially combined:— καὶ οὐκ ἦν φωνή inserted after θυσίαν. A similar glossing is to be seen in *v.* 36, LXX, Luc.

עד לעלות המנחה] '*Up to* (the time of) the offering of the oblation'; but *v.* 36 בעלות '*at* the offering.' עד ל (exc. Josh. 13. 5 = Judg. 3. 3 עד לבוא) is elsewhere very late, being confined to Chr., Ezra, Neh. The occurrences are cited Dri. *LOT.*, p. 506. In the earlier language עד alone is usual, as in Gen. 32. 25 עד עלות השחר; 19. 22; Judg. 6. 18; *al.* The phrase כעלות המנחה '*about* (the time of) the offering, &c.,' is also found in II. 3. 20, of the early morning, and not, as here, of the afternoon. The reference can scarcely be to anything else than the morning and evening offering *at the Temple at Jerusalem;* nor need this, as coming from a writer of the northern kingdom, cause difficulty, in view of the statement of *v.* 31[a]; see *note.*

מנחה in P always denotes a *meal-offering*, and this, according to the regulations of Ex. 29. 38–42; Num. 28. 3–8, was the regular accompaniment of the lamb which was to be offered morning and evening. But our passage clearly refers to the offering *generally*, of whatever it consisted at that time, and not to such a special portion of it as the term denotes in P. From 1 Sam. 26. 19 יָרַח מִנְחָה 'let him *smell* an offering,' smell i.e. the sweet smoke from the burning (cf. Gen. 8. 21), Gen. 4. 4; 1 Sam. 2. 17 (cf. *vv.* 15, 16), it appears that מנחה in early times could denote even an animal sacrifice, and was thus a general term for an *offering*, like קָרְבָּן in P. The use of the word with the meaning *present* (*ch.* 5. 1 *note*) is closely allied. Cf. Wellh. *Prolegomena*, pp. 61 *f.* Upon the difficult passage II. 16. 15 cf. *note ad loc.*

30[b]. וירפא וג'] 'And he *repaired* &c.': a use of רפא *heal* peculiar to this passage. In LXX, Luc. these words do not stand in this position, but appear between 32[a] and 32[b], 32[a] being somewhat abbreviated; *καὶ ᾠκοδόμησεν τοὺς λίθους* (LXX *ἐν ὀνόματι Κυρίου*), *καὶ ἰάσατο τὸ θυσιαστήριον* (Luc. *κυρίου*) *τὸ κατεσκαμμένον, κ.τ.λ.* This is a superficial rearrangement made because the altar could not be said to be repaired until the stones had been built up. But in MT., *v.* 30[b] states summarily what is re-stated in detail in *vv.* 31, 32, according to the diffuse but picturesque style of the writer. Gen. 27. 23, followed by the details of *vv.* 24–29, is similar.

מזבח י׳ ההרוס] Thus the spot selected on Carmel by Elijah was the site of a בָּמָה or local sanctuary which had been destroyed at the idolatrous reaction which had been brought about by Jezebel. Cf. *ch.* 19. 10 את מזבחתיך הרסו. These passages show incidentally the wide diffusion of such high-places for the (unmixed) worship of Yahwe throughout the northern kingdom. Cf. *ch.* 19. 18.

Th. cites Tac. *Hist.* ii. 78 [1]; Suet. *Vespas.* 5 [2] as stating that down to Vespasian's time an altar existed on Carmel without temple or statues.

31ᵃ. שתים עשרה אבנים וג׳] Cf. the setting up by Joshua at the crossing of the Jordan of two cairns, each consisting of twelve stones, one for each tribe, Josh. 4. 1 *ff.* (JE); and the erection of the twelve Maççēboth for the twelve tribes at the ratification of the 'Book of the Covenant,' Ex. 24. 1 *ff.* (JE).

This notice goes to show that the absence of any polemic on the part of Elijah against the calf-worship of the kingdom of Israel does not imply his tacit approval, but rather that while (so far as we know) tolerating it in face of the far more serious deflection caused by the introduction of the Phoenician Ba'al worship, he had in view as an ideal the ultimate union of the two kingdoms in the pure worship of Yahwe. Cf. *v.* 29 *note; ch.* 22. 7 *note.*

כמספר וג׳] LXX, Luc. *κατ' ἀριθμὸν* (Luc. *τῶν δώδεκα*) *φυλῶν* 'Ισραήλ, *ὡς ἐλάλησεν Κύριος πρὸς αὐτὸν κ.τ.λ.* The substitution of 'Ισραήλ for יעקב, however, makes the statement of 31ᵇ superfluous.

31ᵇ. אשר היה וג׳] The *precise words*, ישראל יהיה שמך, occur in Gen. 35. 10 (P), and this has caused Kue. and others to regard this half-verse as an addition under the influence of P. Kamp. goes further, taking the whole of *vv.* 31, 32ᵃ as a later gloss, and finding in them a contradiction to *v.* 30ᵇ (the mere *repair* of the altar; but see *note*); and it is most probable that, if the narrative

---

[1] 'Est Iudaeam inter Suriamque Carmelus, ita vocant montem deumque, nec simulacrum deo aut templum—sic tradidere maiores—ara tantum et reverentia.'

[2] 'Apud Iudaeam Carmeli dei oraculum consulentem ita confirmavere sortes, ut quidquid cogitaret volveretque animo, quamlibet magnum, id esse proventurum pollicerentur.'

has received *any* addition, this is the correct view. But the *fact* recorded in *v.* 31^b appears also in Gen. 32. 28, 29 (J), and too much stress must not be laid upon such a very easy coincidence with the words of P.

32. תעלה] 'A channel.' Cf. II. 18. 17; 20. 20, where the word means a 'conduit' or 'aqueduct.'

כבית] '(Of) about the capacity of.'

33. After *v.* 33^a, LXX, Luc. add ἐπὶ τὸ θυσιαστήριον ὃ ἐποίησεν, and at the close of the verse, καὶ ἐστοίβασεν ἐπὶ τὸ θυσιαστήριον.

34. שלשו] 'Do it a third time.' Elsewhere this denom. Pi'el means *Do on the third day* 1 Sam. 20. 19; *Divide into three parts* Deut. 19. 3†.

35. מלא] LXX ἔπλησαν, under the influence of the plural verbs in the preceding verse.

36. After אברהם יצחק וישראל LXX, Luc. add the gloss ἐπάκουσόν μου, Κύριε, ἐπάκουσόν μου σήμερον ἐν πυρί, and then continue καὶ γνώτωσαν πᾶς ὁ λαὸς οὗτος (cf. *v.* 37) in place of היום יודע.

37^a. Luc. omits.

37^b. את לבם] LXX, Luc. τὴν καρδίαν τοῦ λαοῦ τούτου.

38. אש יהוה] LXX, Luc. πῦρ παρὰ Κυρίου, Targ. אשתא מן קדם י׳ suggest אֵשׁ מֵאֵת־י׳, and this is adopted by Th., Klo., Kamp., on the supposition that מאת has been lost through proximity to the similar אש. After י׳ LXX, Luc. add ἐκ τοῦ οὐρανοῦ, as in Gen. 19. 24 גפרית ואש מאת י׳ מן השמים.

ואת האבנים וג׳] The different order of LXX, Luc., ואת האבנים ואת העפר following בתעלה, is certainly wrong, since לחכה must refer to את המים.

40. להם] LXX, Luc. πρὸς τὸν λαόν.

41. קול המון הגשם] 'There is a sound of *the roar* of rain.' המון means the loud rushing noise of a heavy downpour, as heard by Elijah's 'prophetically sharpened ear' (Klo.). So Pesh. ܙܘܥܐ, Targ. איתרגושת. Cf. Jer. 10. 13; 51. 16 לקול תתו המון מים בשמים.

42. ויעלה אחאב . . . ואליהו עלה] On the contrasted order cf. *ch.* 5. 25 *note*.

ויגהר] 'And he crouched.' The meaning, here and in the only

other occurrence II. 4. 34, 35, must be determined by the context. So Verss. in both passages.

43[b]. שב שׁבע פעמים] LXX Καὶ σὺ ἐπίστρεψον ἑπτάκι, καὶ ἀπόστρεψον ἑπτάκι. καὶ ἀπέστρεψεν τὸ παιδάριον ἑπτάκι. Luc. Ἐπίστρεψον καὶ ἐπίβλεψον ἑπτάκις. καὶ ἐπέστρεψε τὸ παιδάριον ἑπτάκις. Here the first sentence of LXX appears to contain a doublet, while in Luc. the text has been worked over, and the verb of the second member altered into ἐπίβλεψον, in accordance with *v.* 43[a]. The emphatic καὶ σύ of LXX has the appearance of originality, and supposing (with Klo.) אַתָּה to be a corruption of עַתָּה, we may restore:— וְעַתָּה שֻׁב שֶׁבַע פְּעָמִים וַיָּשָׁב הַנַּעַר שֶׁבַע פְּעָמִים '"Now return seven times." And the lad returned seven times.'

44. עלה מים] LXX, Luc. ἀνάγουσα ὕδωρ a mistaken reading מַעֲלָה מַיִם.

45. עד כה ועד כה] 'In a very short while.' The repetition expresses both the brevity of the interval and its indeterminateness. Vulg. explains differently *Cumque se verteret huc atque illuc*, and so Pesh. ܘܥܕܡܐ ܗܘ ܡܬܦܢܐ ܠܟܐ ܘܠܟܐ. Similarly Targ. paraphrases עד דמזדרז 'while he was harnessing.'

46. ויד י׳ היתה אל] So Ezek. 33. 22; but עַל instead of אל is usual:—II. 3. 15; Ezek. 1. 3; 3. 22; 37. 1; 40. 1. The phrase describes the powerful access of prophetic inspiration. Cf. also Ezek. 8. 1 ותפל עלי שם יד אדני י׳ 'And the hand of the Lord Yahwe fell upon me there'; Ezek. 3. 14 ויד י׳ עלי חזקה 'And the hand of Yahwe was strong upon me'; Isa. 8. 11 כה אמר י׳ אלי בחזקת היד 'Thus said Yahwe unto me with strength of hand.'

וישנס] The word is otherwise quite unknown. All Verss. give the meaning 'gird.'

19. *Jezebel seeks to take vengeance upon Elijah for the death of her prophets. Elijah flees into the wilderness of Judah, and then journeys on to Ḥoreb, where he receives Yahwe's further commission for the extirpation of Ba'al worship from Israel.*

19. 1. לאיזבל] LXX adds τῇ γυναικὶ αὐτοῦ, i.e. אִשְׁתּוֹ, which may have fallen out before the following את.

ואת כל אשר הרג] 'And all the details of his slaying'; lit. 'and all that he had slain.' This, however, is extremely forced, and, since כל is omitted by all Verss. except Targ., it may be supposed to be an erroneous insertion from the first half of the verse. So Th., Klo., Kamp., Benz., Kit.

כל הנביאים] LXX, Luc. omit כל.

2. LXX, Luc. preface Jezebel's speech with the words Εἰ σὺ εἶ Ἠλειοὺ (Luc. Ἠλιὰς) καὶ ἐγὼ (Luc. adds εἰμι) Ἰεζάβελ, i.e. אִם אַתָּה אֵלִיָּהוּ וַאֲנִי אִיזֶבֶל '*As surely as you are Elijah and I am Jezebel.*' The force and character of the words speak for their genuineness. So Th.

כה יעשון] Add לִי with all Verss. On the phrase cf. *ch.* 2. 23 *note*.

אַחַד מהם] With *st. const.* before the preposition, as in *ch.* 22. 13; 1 Sam. 9. 3; *al.* (Da. § 35, *Rem.* 2). Against the view that this shorter form אַחַד can ever represent *st. absol.* in 'the flow of speech' (Ew. § 267^b), as appears from the vocalization of the Massoretes in four instances, cf. Dri. on 2 Sam. 17. 22.

3. וַיַּרְא] Read וַיִּרָא '*And he was afraid*,' with all Verss. except Targ. So Th., Klo., Kamp., Benz., Kit.

וילך אל נפשו] 'And he went *for* his life'; lit. *on account of*. So II. 7. 7†. With על, Gen. 19. 17 המלט על נפשך.

4. רתם אחת] 'A broom.' This shrub, which bears in Ar. the same name رَتَمٌ, is the *Retama roetam* of modern botanists, the *Genista roetam* of older authors. It occurs with great frequency near Sinai and Petra, abundantly round the Dead Sea and in the ravines leading down to the Jordan valley, and occasionally in the wilderness of Judaea. The flower, a delicate white or purplish-pink blossom, appears in February in advance of the tiny foliage, and the shrub reaches a height of ten to twelve feet, affording a grateful shade. Tristram, pp. 359 *f.*; cf. Stanley, *Sin. Pal.*, p. 80. On the use of אחד cf. p. 209.

וישאל את נפשו למות] 'And he asked that his soul might die.' So exactly Jon. 4. 8. Ew. § 336^b calls the constr. 'a species of the Latin accusative with the infinitive.'

כי לא טוב וג׳] Rightly explained by Th.:—'As human I must one day die, and now it is death that I desire.'

5. תחת רתם אחד] LXX ἐκεῖ ὑπὸ φυτόν, Luc. ὑπὸ τὸ φυτὸν ἐκεῖ. Here the variation in order, and the fact that רתם אחת in the previous verse is simply transliterated, LXX Ῥαθμέν, Luc. ῥαθαμείν, suggest that the original text read ἐκεῖ alone, and that the remaining words are a later insertion after MT. In MT. the indefinite רתם אחד is strange after the shrub has been already mentioned, and the words have the character of a gloss taken directly from *v.* 4 to explain שָׁם of the original text. We may therefore restore וישכב ויישן שָׁם 'And he lay and slept *there*.'

הנה זה] Isa. 21. 9; Song of Sol. 2. 8, 9†. Cf. *ch.* 14. 6 *note.*

מלאך] LXX, Luc. τις, but in *v.* 7 ἄγγελος.

6. מראשתיו] The word means 'the places *or* parts near his head,' and, used as an adverbial accusative, should be rendered '*At his head.*' So 1 Sam. 19. 13; 26. 7; *al.*

עגת רצפים] 'A cake of (i. e. baked on) hot stones.' Ar. رَضْفٌ means a stone heated in the fire, to be dropped into milk for the purpose of making it boil. רִצְפָּה Isa. 6. 6 denotes a glowing ember.

8b *ff.*] The writer appears to know, and to be influenced by, the narrative of JE relating to Moses at Ḥoreb. Thus, with the forty days' fast cf. Ex. 34. 28; with the Theophany cf. Ex. 33. 18—34. 8, and especially *v.* 11 והנה י׳ עבר with Ex. 34. 6 ויעבר י׳ על פניו. The name חֹרֵב in the Hexateuch is peculiar to E, Ex. 3. 1; 17. 6; 33. 6, and to Deut., while the expression הר האלהים, always with reference to Ḥoreb, occurs elsewhere only in Ex. 3. 1; 18. 5; 24. 13 (E); 4. 27 (JE).

Perhaps, however, he was dependent, not upon the written source, but upon oral tradition. Contrast the מְעָרָה of Elijah with the נִקְרַת הַצּוּר in which Moses was placed, Ex. 33. 22. Our writer's tradition may have spoken of this latter as a מערה, and המערה *v.* 9, unless merely an example of the use of the definite article noticed *ch.* 13. 14, may mean '*the* cave' thus rendered famous in former times.

הר האלהים] LXX, Luc. omit אלהים.

9. מה לך פה] 'What hast thou here?' (to concern thee), so 'What doest thou here?' Cf. Judg. 18. 3; Isa. 22. 16; 52. 5†.

10. עזבו בריתך] LXX, Luc. ἐνκατέλιπόν σε, עֲזָבוּךָ, and so *v.* 14, where, however, in LXX τὴν διαθήκην σου has been added by a later hand.

11. והנה י׳ עֹבֵר] The participle picturesquely describes the Theophany as in course of occurrence, and is not, with LXX, Luc., to be rendered as a *fut. instans*, 'Behold Yahwe *shall* pass by,' as if the words formed part of the preceding speech.

רוח גדולה וחזק] The second adjective, as more remote from its subject, lapses into the masculine, and is then followed by masculine participles. So Jer. 20. 9 כְּאֵשׁ בֹּעֶרֶת עָצֻר בְּעַצְמֹתָי; cf. Ezek. 2. 9 יָד שְׁלוּחָה אֵלָי וְהִנֵּה־בוֹ וגו׳. 1 Sam. 15. 9, quoted by G-K. § 132 *d;* Da. § 32, *Rem.* 4, is certainly corrupt; cf. Dri. *ad loc.*

12. קול דממה דקה] 'The sound of *a light whisper.*' LXX, Luc. φωνὴ αὔρας λεπτῆς, and so Vulg. *sibilus aurae tenuis*, have excellently grasped the sense both of substantive and adjective. דממה is a gentle breeze Ps. 107. 29, or a murmur which can be compared with such a breeze Job 4. 16†. דקה *thin*, *fine*, and *small*, is only here used of a *sound*, but cf. the similar application of λεπτός. RV. marg. 'a sound of gentle *stillness*' is unsatisfactory, *stillness* being incompatible both with קול and דקה, and with כשמע of the following verse.

At the close of the verse, Cod. A adds the weak gloss κἀκεῖ Κύριος.

13. וילט] Hiph. only here. Qal particip. pass. 1 Sam. 21. 10; Isa. 25. 7. Cf. the similar action of Moses Ex. 3. 6 (E).

15. חזאל] Cf. *note* on II. 8. 15.

18. והשארתי וג׳] 'And I will spare in Israel seven thousand, even all the knees &c.'

וכל הפה וג׳] The kiss of homage offered to idols may be illustrated by Hos. 13. 2 זֹבְחֵי אָדָם עֲגָלִים יִשָּׁקוּן *kiss calves* of Bethel and Dan. Cf. Job 31. 27, which speaks of kissing the hand in worship of the heavenly bodies.

20. ויאמר אשקה וג׳] Cf. S. Luke 9. 61. LXX omits ולאמי by oversight.

אֶשֳּׁקָה] With ḥatef-qameç under the doubled sibilant. So with the emphatic letters ק, ט; אֲלַקֳּטָה Ruth 2. 2, 7; לְקֳחָה (for לקחה)

Gen. 2. 23; מְטֳּהָרוֹ Ps. 89. 45. Cf. G-K. § 10 *h;* Sta. § 104.

לך שוב וג׳] Elijah disclaims any special significance for his action, unless the call correspond with Elisha's own free impulse. The words לך שׁוּב do not merely grant Elisha's request, but give permission to return, if he will, to his ordinary pursuits.

21. בשלם הבשר] 'He boiled them, the (pieces of) flesh.' The pronom. suffix anticipates the object, as commonly in Syriac. Cf. also *ch.* 21. 13 וַיְעִדֻהוּ . . . אֶת־נָבוֹת; II. 16. 15 Kt. וַיְצַוֵּהוּ הַמֶּלֶךְ אָחָז אֶת־אוּרִיָּה הַכֹּהֵן. Cf. Da. § 29, *Rem.* 7, where a number of instances are cited from other books. LXX, Luc., however, omit הבשר, and it is thus possible that it may have come in as an explanatory gloss from the margin.

20. *Narrative of two campaigns of Ben-hadad II (Hadadezer) against Israel in successive years. In the first the Aramaeans besiege Samaria, and are beaten off by an unexpected sortie. In the second a pitched battle takes place at Aphek, the Aramaeans are defeated, and Ben-hadad falls into the hands of Ahab, who concludes a truce with him.*

1. בן הדד] The second Aramaean king of this name mentioned in Kings. Cf. *ch.* 15. 18 *note.* This Ben-hadad appears in the Cuneiform inscriptions under the name *Dad-'-id-ri, Dad-id-ri,* i. e. הֲדַדְעֶזֶר. Cf. further *v.* 34 *note; COT.* i. 190 *ff.*

ושלשים וג׳] Cf. the list of allied princes who are mentioned as taking the field with this Hadadezer at Qarqar against Shalmaneser II (*Append.* 3). Here, as in other cases (cited *COT. loc. cit.*), their total is given as twelve, perhaps a round number.

2. העירה] Luc., Pesh. omit.

3. הטובים] LXX omits.

5. כי שלחתי] כי introduces the direct oration: cf. *ch.* 1. 13 *note.*

ובניך] LXX, Luc. omit.

6. עיניך] LXX, Luc., Pesh., Vulg. presuppose עֵינֵיהֶם, correctly. The Aramaeans were to take whatever seemed worth taking *to them.* So Th., Klo., Kamp., Benz., Kit.

7. ולבני] So 'A. καὶ εἰς υἱούς μου. LXX καὶ περὶ τῶν υἱῶν μου καὶ περὶ τῶν θυγατέρων μου, Luc. καὶ περὶ τῶν τέκνων μου.

8. אל תשמע ולוא תאבה] 'Obey not, *nor* consent.' Continuation by לא with imperf. secures an even flow to the sentence, which would have been broken by reinforcement by the more energetic אל with jussive. So Am. 5. 5[a] וְאַל־תִּדְרְשׁוּ בֵּית־אֵל וְהַגִּלְגָּל לֹא תָבֹאוּ וּבְאֵר שֶׁבַע לֹא תַעֲבֹרוּ. Cf. Ew. § 350[a].

10. כה יעשון וג'] With pl. verb in the mouth of a polytheist, as in *ch.* 19. 2.

ישפק]. 'Shall suffice.' The only occurrence of the verb. Subs. סִפְקוֹ 'his sufficiency,' Job 20. 22 †. The root is common in Aram. in the same sense.

לשעלים] 'For *handfuls.*' Ezek. 13. 19; Isa. 40. 12 †. The boast implies that Samaria is unworthy of the prowess of a power like Aram, and at the same time promises its utter obliteration:—'So innumerable are my followers that they will be unable to secure even a handful each of the dust of the ruined city.' Jos. (*Ant.* viii. 14, § 2) explains strangely:—ἀπειλῶν ὑψηλότερον τῶν τειχῶν οἷς καταφρονεῖ χῶμα τούτοις ἐπεγείρειν αὐτοῦ τὴν στρατιὰν κατὰ δράκα λαμβάνουσαν.

ברגלי] 'At my feet,' i. e. *following me.* So II. 3. 9; 1 Sam. 25. 27; 2 Sam. 15. 16, 17; Judg. 4. 10; Ex. 11. 8 (J); Deut. 11. 6.

11. דברו] LXX, Luc. Ἱκανούσθω (Luc. ὑμῖν) must have read רַב; cf. *ch.* 19. 4; 12. 28.

אל יתהלל וג'] 'Let not him who is girding boast himself as he who is ungirding'; i. e. as Targ. rightly paraphrases לא ישתבח דמזדרז ונחת בקרבא כגברא דנצח וסליק מניה 'Let not him who is girding himself and going down into the battle boast himself as the man who has conquered and is coming up from it.' חגר refers to the buckling on of the sword; cf. 1 Sam. 17. 39; 25. 13; Judg. 18. 11; *al.* מפתח may be illustrated by Isa. 45. 1 וּמָתְנֵי מְלָכִים אֲפַתֵּחַ 'and the loins of kings will I ungird,' i. e. render them defenceless. LXX, Luc. μὴ καυχάσθω ὁ κυρτὸς ὡς ὁ ὀρθός interpret חגר from Rabb. Heb. חִגֵּר *lame,* and then guess at מפתח as expressing the antithesis.

12. שימו וישימו על העיר] Clearly an order for the renewal of the hostilities which had been suspended during the negotiations previously described. Render, '*Set yourselves in array, and they set themselves in array against the city.*' So Ges., Ke., Kit., *Sieg. u. Sta.*, RV. text. The expression covers every device which could be used to secure the downfall of the city[1], and it is therefore incorrect to postulate the ellipse of any *special object* after the verb, as is done by LXX, Luc. Οἰκοδομήσατε χάρακα, and similarly Klo., Benz. 'build battering rams,' Th., Kamp., RV. marg. 'place the engines': cf. Ezek. 4. 2; 21. 27. For שים used, as in our passage, to denote military mobilization *generally* (and so without expressed obj.) cf. Ezek. 23. 24 יָשִׂימוּ עָלַיִךְ סָבִיב; 1 Sam. 15. 2 שָׂם לוֹ בַּדֶּרֶךְ.

13. נביא אחד] Upon אחד cf. p. 209.

אחאב] LXX, Luc., Pesh. omit.

וידעת וג'] Cf. *v.* 28 with pl. verb וידעתם. The phrase is specially characteristic of Ezekiel (some sixty occurrences), and appears also six times in P[2]. Elsewhere it is found only in Ex. 10. 2 (JE); Isa. 49. 23, and + מוֹשִׁיעֵךְ 49. 26; 60. 16, + אֱלֹהֵיכֶם Joel 4. 17.

14. בנערי שרי המדינות] 'By the young men of the princes of the provinces.' These שרי המדינות ('Landvögte,' Ew., Th., Klo., Kamp., Kit.) were probably appointed to the prefecture of special districts, perhaps in the same way as the נִצָּבִים under Solomon *ch.* 4. 7 *ff.*[3], and bound, as a condition of their tenure, in times of emergency to provide the king with a certain number of warriors

---

[1] So Jos. (*Ant.* viii. 14, § 2) rightly expands the king's brief command:— *ὁ δ' εὐθέως τοῦτο προσέταξε καὶ περιχαρακοῦν τὴν πόλιν καὶ χώματα βάλλεσθαι καὶ μηδένα τρόπον ἀπολιπεῖν πολιορκίας.*

[2] In Ezek. the cases are:—וְיָדַעְתָּ 25. 7; 35. 4; וְיָדַעַתְּ 16. 62; 22. 16; וִידַעְתֶּם 6. 7, 13; 7. 4; 11. 10, 12; 12. 20; 13. 14; 14. 8; 15. 7; 20. 38, 42, 44; 25. 5; 35. 9; 36. 11; 37. 6, 13: 13. 9; 23. 49; 24. 24 (אֲדֹנָי י'); 7. 9 (+ מַכֶּה); וִידַעְתֶּן 13. 21, 23; וְיָדְעוּ 6. 10, 14; 7. 27; 12. 15, 16; 24. 27; 25. 11, 17; 26. 6; 28. 22, 23; 29. 6, 9, 21; 30. 8, 19, 25, 26; 32. 15; 33. 29; 34. 27; 35. 15; 36. 23, 38; 38. 23; 39. 6; 28. 24; 29. 16 (אֲדֹנָי י'); 28. 26; 34. 30; 39. 22, 28 (+ אֱלֹהֵיהֶם); 39. 7 (+ קָדוֹשׁ בְּיִשְׂרָאֵל). In P:—וִידַעְתֶּם Ex. 6. 7; 16. 12 (+ אֱלֹהֵיכֶם); וְיָדְעוּ 7. 5; 14. 4, 18; 29. 46 (+ אֱלֹהֵיהֶם).

[3] So Wellh. *Isr. u. Jud. Ges.* 66 *note.*

out of their own retinues. In contrast to these כל העם of *v.* 15 denotes the standing army; cf. *ch.* 16. 15 *note.* LXX in *v.* 14 Ἐν τοῖς παιδαρίοις τῶν ἀρχόντων τῶν χορῶν (Luc. χωρῶν), but *v.* 15 τοὺς ἄρχοντας, τὰ παιδάρια τῶν χ., and similarly *v.* 17 ἄρχοντες παιδάρια τῶν χ., *v.* 19 ἄρχοντα τὰ παιδάρια ἄρχοντα τῶν χ., as though נַעֲרֵי were a suspended *st. constr.* (cf. 1 Sam. 28. 7; Isa. 23. 12; *al.;* Da. § 28, *Rem.* 6) and the phrase meant 'the young men, the princes of the provinces,' i. e. 'the young princes &c.' Luc. in *v.* 19 renders as in *v.* 14, but *vv.* 15, 17 show signs of having first exhibited the same rendering as LXX and then undergone emendation:—τοὺς ἄρχοντας (οἱ ἄρχοντες) καὶ τὰ παιδάρια τῶν ἀρχόντων τῶν χωρῶν. Ἀ. *v.* 14 Ἐν παισὶν ἀρχόντων τῶν ἐπαρχιῶν, *v.* 15 τοὺς παῖδας ἀρχόντων τῶν ἐπ., *v.* 17 παῖδες ἀρχόντων . . ., *v.* 19 *deest.*

מי יאסר המלחמה] 'Who shall *join* battle?' i.e. make the first advance. So 2 Chr. 13. 3.

15. מאתים שנים ושלשים] LXX omits שנים.

כל בני ישראל] LXX, Luc. rightly presuppose כָּל־בְּנֵי חַיִל 'all the mighty men,' the phrase being explanatory of כל העם.

שבעת אלפים] LXX ἑξήκοντα, Luc. ἑξήκοντα χιλιάδας.

16. ויצאו בצהרים] LXX καὶ ἐξῆλθεν μεσημβρίας, Luc. καὶ ἐξῆλθεν ὁ βασιλεὺς μετ' αὐτῶν μεσημβρίας, an expansion explanatory of the sing. verb.

שתה שכור] *Ch.* 16. 9.

17. וישלח בן הדד] LXX, Luc. καὶ ἀποστέλλουσιν, the implied subj. being the outposts of the Aramaean host who observed the sortie, while the king was engaged at his carouse. The orig. text, if not וַיִּשְׁלְחוּ, was perhaps impers. וַיִּשְׁלַח 'and one sent,' rendered correctly by LXX, and with subj. erroneously supplied in MT.

20. ויכו איש אישו] 'And they smote each his man.' LXX, Luc. add καὶ ἐδευτέρωσεν ἕκαστος τὸν παρ' αὐτοῦ, and so Ew. restores וַיִּשְׁנוּ אִישׁ אִישׁוֹ 'and they repeated &c.,' the whole passage meaning 'and they slew each his man *repeatedly.*' The repetition of איש אישו is, however, extremely awkward, and the addition is certainly a later gloss. Had the original writer wished to lay stress upon the fact that each man slew more than one of the

opposing Aramaeans he would have added simply וַיִּשְׁנוּ or else הַכֵּה וְשָׁנֹה. But the point of the narrative is that *the first onslaught* was such that it immediately put the enemy to flight.

20b. וימלט וג׳] The sense of the last three words is obscure. The best rendering is that of RV. text, 'And Ben-hadad king of Aram escaped *on a horse with* (lit. *and*) *horsemen.*' פרשים must be thought to be loosely connected on to סוס by the ו as forming a concomitant factor to the king's escape. Cf. Cod. A ἐφ' ἵππων σου ἱππεῦσίν τισιν, Vulg. *in equo cum equitibus suis.* But the text would be greatly improved by the addition of עִמּוֹ after פרשים, as is suggested by Targ. על סוסון ועמיה תרין פרשין 'upon horses, two horsemen being with him.' Klo. emends עַל־סוּס הוּא וּפָרָשָׁיו.

21. ויך] LXX, Luc. καὶ ἔλαβεν, i. e. וַיִּקַּח. The king and his reserve availed themselves of the horses and chariots which had been abandoned by the Aramaeans in their panic, and were thus (Th.) able to effect the 'great slaughter' which the main body of the army, following the fugitives on foot, might have failed to accomplish. MT. describes a senseless waste of energy.

את הסוס] LXX πάντας τοὺς ἵππους.

וְהִכָּה] Apparently an irregular abandonment of the constr. of imperf. with ו *consec.* in favour of ו *simplex* with perf. Possibly, however, the vocalization is at fault, and the writer intended to use the infin. abs. וְהַכֵּה; cf. *ch.* 9. 25; Judg. 7. 19; *al.* Da. § 88.

22. לך התחזק] LXX, Luc., with omission of לך, Κραταιοῦ. In הִתְחַזַּק the original *pathah* of the last syllable of the *Hithpa'el* is preserved; cf. G-K. § 54 *k*.

לתשובת השנה] 'At the return of the year'; i. e. when spring comes round again after the winter, and warfare becomes practicable. So *v.* 26. Cf. 2 Sam. 11. 1 where the phrase is explained לְעֵת צֵאת הַמְּלָכִים 'at the time when kings go forth (on campaign)'; 2 Chr. 36. 10.

23. אלהי הרים וג׳] 'Gods of hills are their gods, therefore were they (the gods) too strong for us.' RV., in rendering אלהי as a sing. and making subj. of חזקו to be the Israelites themselves, is

incorrect. The Aramaeans, in accordance with their own ideas, ascribe a plurality of deities to Israel, and it is these gods, as well as their worshippers, against whom they are fighting, and whom they hope to conquer if they can decoy them from their fastnesses. LXX Θεὸς Ἰσραὴλ followed by sing. verb ἐκραταίωσεν is an intentional alteration in order to avoid the use of phraseology offensive to the unity of God. So in *v.* 28 the Israelitish prophet, in quoting the words of the Aramaeans, naturally substitutes a singular:—אלהי הרים יהוה '*A God* of hills is *Yahwe*.'

אלהיהם] LXX, Luc. add καὶ οὐ Θεὸς κοιλάδος (Luc. κοιλάδων), a gloss made for the sake of strict conformity with *v.* 28. In *v.* 23, however, the words are certainly out of place, וְאוּלָם *but however*, introducing the idea that the gods may not be gods of the plain as a suggestion not previously mentioned except by implied antithesis in אלהי הרים.

אם לא וג׳] '*Surely* we shall be stronger than they.' So *v.* 25. The same form of asseveration is found in Josh. 14. 9; Isa. 5. 9; 14. 24; Job 1. 11, and with perf. II. 9. 26; Jer. 15. 11; Job 22. 20; Ps. 131. 2. Cf. *note* on *ch.* 2. 23.

24. ממקומו] 'From his place'; i.e. his appointed position in the line of battle. LXX, Luc. εἰς τὸν τόπον αὐτῶν (Luc. αὐτοῦ), and so Jos. (*Ant.* viii. 14, § 3) ἀπολῦσαι πρὸς τὰ οἰκεῖα, is inferior, and probably arose from the common confusion of מ with ב. But neither במקומו (Th.) nor למקומו (Klo.) could correctly stand with this signification, אֶל־מ׳ being the required phrase.

פחות] 'Commanders' or 'vicegerents.' These appear to be the same as the שרי הרכב שלשים ושנים *ch.* 22. 31; cf. 20. 1. Giesebrecht, taking the term פחה as Persian in origin, is obliged to regard this verse as an interpolation, and considers that it breaks the connexion, ואתה of *v.* 25 forming the right continuation to *v.* 23, and ויעש כן, *v.* 25 *end*, being satisfied by *v.* 26 (a doubtful contention). But cf. *note* on *ch.* 10. 15.

25. מֵאוֹתָךְ . . . אוֹתָם] This form of the particle for the usual מֵאִתָּךְ, אִתָּם, occurs repeatedly in these N. Pal. narratives up to II. *ch.* 8;—*ch.* 22. 7, 8, 24; II. 1. 15; 3. 11, 12, 26; 6. 16; 8. 8;

but can scarcely be counted dialectical, depending as it does upon vocalization and *scriptio plena*, and standing also beside the more ordinary form; cf. *ch.* 20. 23; 22. 4, 24; II. 3. 7; 6. 16, 32. The form אוֹת is found several times in Jer. and Ezek., but appears elsewhere only rarely.

26. אפקה] Several cities of this name are mentioned in O. T.; but this one, which occurs again in II. 13. 17, is doubtless the same as is mentioned in Josh. 12. 18; 1 Sam. 29. 1, in the neighbourhood of Jezreel. Assyr. *Ap-ku*; *COT.* i. 194.

27. הָתְפָּקְדוּ] The same form occurs Num. 1. 47; 2. 33; 26. 62, and is intended as passive of הִתְפָּקְדוּ Judg. 20. 15, 17; 21. 9. Both forms, however, have precisely the same reflexive sense, 'set themselves for muster,' 'were mustered,' and probably Wright (*Compar. Gramm.* 208 *n.*) is correct in thinking the pronunciation as a passive הָתְפָּקְדוּ to be due to a misunderstanding of the Massoretes. הִתְפָּקֵד, without doubling of the 2nd rad., stands alone in Heb., and appears to be a relic of the reflexive of the simple stem פָּקַד, corresponding to Aram. אִתְקְטֵל, ܐܬܩܛܠ, Aeth. *taqatla*, Ar. VIII with transposition of 1st rad. and preform. إِقْتَتَلَ *'iqtatala* for *'ithqatala*, and so on the Moabite stone, *ll.* 11, 15, 19, 32 הלתחם from root לחם. Cf. Wright, *loc. cit.*; G-K. § 54 *l*; Sta. § 162; and, for other views as to the form, König, *Lehrg.* I. i. p. 198.

וכלכלו] 'And were provisioned'; passive of the Pilpel which is found in *ch.* 17. 4, 9; 18. 13; *al.* So Vulg. *et acceptis cibariis*, LXX, Luc. omit. ו *simplex* co-ordinates the two facts. Dri. *Tenses*, § 132.

כשני חשפי עזים] The subs. חשיף is elsewhere quite unknown. LXX, Luc., Vulg., Pesh., Targ. give the meaning 'like two *small flocks* of goats,' and this is generally adopted. חשף = 'strip off,' and thus חשיף 'that which is stripped off' may possibly denote *segregatum* (*Heb. Lex. Oxf.*), but the inference is precarious. Klo. emends בִּשְׁפִי מִשְׁפַּט עִזִּים 'upon the bare height, after the manner of goats.'

28. ויאמר אל מלך י׳ ויאמר] The repetition of ויאמר is certainly superfluous. Pesh. omits the first occurrence, thus making the

passage to agree with *vv.* 13, 22; while LXX, Luc., Vulg. are without the second. This latter omission is correct, the addition in MT. being probably due, as is suggested by Pesh., to an attempt to gain agreement with the preceding passages.

וידעתם] LXX καὶ γνώσῃ, Luc. γνώσει, as in *v.* 13.

30. עשרים ושבעה אלף] Pesh. ܥܣܪܝܢ ܘܫܒܥܐ ܐܠܦܝܢ, 25,000.

חדר בחדר] 'A chamber within a chamber,' i. e. 'an *innermost* chamber'; here, as in *ch.* 22. 25 (‖ 2 Chr. 18. 24); II. 9. 2†, selected as most remote and private. Jos. (*Ant.* viii. 14, § 4) explains as an *underground house;*—εἰς ὑπόγειον οἶκον ἐκρύβη.

31. ויאמרו וג׳] LXX puts the suggestion into the mouth of Ben-hadad, reading καὶ εἶπεν τοῖς παισὶν αὐτοῦ Οἶδα κ.τ.λ. τὰς ψυχὰς ἡμῶν. So Luc., with the different Οἴδατε. That this, however, is incorrect is shown by *vv.* 32, 33, where the servants *without the king* form the embassy.

כי מלכי . . . כי וג׳] For the second כי resumptive of the first, cf. *ch.* 1. 30 *note.*

בְּרֹאשֵׁנוּ] LXX, Luc., Vulg., Pesh., pl. בְּרָאשֵׁינוּ as in *v.* 32.

נפשך] Vulg., Pesh., though agreeing with MT. in placing the speech in the mouth of the servants, yet like LXX, Luc., presuppose pl. נַפְשׁוֹתֵינוּ. This is an easy alteration induced by the preceding pls. נשימה וג׳, but inferior to MT. in which the saving of the *king's life* is rightly made the object of the proposed plan.

33. והאנשים ינחשו] Vulg. excellently, *quod acceperunt viri pro omine;* i.e. they *divined* the successful issue of their mission from the favourable response אחי הוא. Cf. Sta. *Ges.* i. 445*f.* For this use of the verb cf. Gen. 30. 27 נִחַשְׁתִּי וַיְבָרְכֵנִי י׳ בִּגְלָלֶךָ 'I have observed the omens, and Yahwe hath blessed me for thy sake.' The only explanation that can be placed upon the imperf. is that it emphasizes pictorially *the coming into being* of their consciousness of the king's mood;—'and the men *began to* divine'; cf. Dri. *Tenses*, § 27 γ. The emendation of Grä. וַיְחִישׁוּ joined with וימהרו, as in Isa. 5. 19, is unnecessary.

ויחלטו הממנו] The verb occurs nowhere else, and הֲמִמֶּנּוּ is untranslateable, RV. 'whether it were his mind' (*marg.* Heb. 'from him') being indefensible. The Verss.—LXX καὶ ἀνέλεξαν τὸν λόγον ἀπὸ (Luc. καὶ ἀνελέξαντο τὸν λόγον αὐτοῦ ἐκ) τοῦ στόματος αὐτοῦ, Vulg. *rapuerunt verbum ex ore ejus,* Pesh. ܘܚܛܦܘܗܝ ܡܢܗ, Targ. וחטפוהא מיניה—are unanimous both in presupposing a different division of the words וַיַּחְלְטוּהָ מִמֶּנּוּ, and in supplying a plausible meaning for the verb;—'*and they caught it from him,*' i.e. they at once took up and repeated the title of *brother* which he had conferred upon Ben-hadad. ויחלטו being isolated, and its meaning purely conjectural, it is futile to dogmatize as to its being Qal (Sta. § 529[a]) or shortened Hiph'il form like וַיַּדְבִּקוּ, וַיַּדְרְכוּ (G-K. § 53 *n;* Kö., *Lehrg.* I. i. p. 251).

וַיַּעֲלֵהוּ] LXX, Luc. καὶ ἀναβιβάζουσιν αὐτὸν πρὸς αὐτόν. Here the subj. of the verb being wrongly conceived as pl. ויעלהו (הָאֲנָשִׁים 33[a]), πρὸς αὐτόν appears to be the translator's explan. addit. 'unto him' (Aḥab) which is thus rendered desirable to complete the sense. The view that LXX presupposes an orig. וַיַּעֲלֵהוּ אֵלָיו (Th., Kamp.) is therefore improbable.

34. חצות] 'Streets,' i.e. doubtless, as explained by Ke., Th., Ges., *Heb. Lex. Oxf.*, &c., *bazaars* where trade might be freely carried on. Ew. 'fortified quarters' is strangely alien to the term employed.

ואני וג'] The change of speaker is regarded as sufficiently marked by the content of his speech as a response to the preceding: cf. II. 10. 15.

בברית] RV. '*with* this covenant,' i.e. *at the price of* it; ב *pretii;* cf. *ch.* 2. 23 *note* on בנפשו. The fact of this alliance between Aḥab and Hadadezer is strikingly confirmed by the monolith of Shalmaneser II, where the two kings are mentioned as leagued against the Assyrian at the battle of Qarqar: cf. *Append.* 3.

וישלחהו] Luc. adds ἐκ τῆς οἰκίας αὐτοῦ καὶ ἀπῆλθεν ἀπ' αὐτοῦ.

35. איש אחד] Cf. p. 209. The identification by Jos. (*Ant.* viii. 14, § 5) of this prophet with Micaiah of *ch.* 22 is by no means improbable: cf. *vv.* 42, 43 with *ch.* 22. 8.

מבני הנביאים] 'Sons of the prophets' was the title of members of the prophetic guilds or schools which existed at Bethel, II. 2. 3;

Jericho, *vv.* 5, 15; Gilgal, 4. 38, and probably elsewhere, and were in some sense presided over by Elijah and Elisha; cf. II. 2. 15–18; 4. 1, 38 *ff.*; 6. 1 *ff.*; 9. 1. Such guilds seem to have flourished under Samuel, 1 Sam. 19. 20 (Naioth), cf. 10. 5, 10 (Gibeah), and may, perhaps, have been founded by him; cf. 7. 15–17 where *Bethel* and *Gilgal* are included with Mizpah among the cities visited by Samuel in his yearly round from his centre, Ramah. The force of the term בן נביא is well illustrated by Am. 7. 14, where Amos tells Amaziah of Bethel, לא נביא אנכי ולא בן נביא אנכי 'I was no prophet, neither was I *a prophet's son*,' i. e. I had not the advantage of any special training for the calling.

בדבר י׳] Cf. *ch.* 13. 1 *note.*

36. האריה] '*The* lion,' singled out for the part which he is to play, and already conjured up before the speaker's prophetic vision. Cf. especially *ch.* 22. 21 הָרוּחַ, and see *note* on *ch.* 13. 14.

37. ויכהו . . . ופצע] 'And the man smote him, *so as to wound him.*' Here the act denoted by פָּצֹעַ sharply limits the duration of that described by ויכהו הכה, as forming its *end* or *result*. So exactly Jer. 12. 17 ונתשתי את הגוי ההוא נתוש ואבד 'I will pluck up that nation, *so as to destroy it*.' The case cannot be classed, as by Da. (§ 86c; Jer. 12. 17 is made to fall under § 87), among cases where 'the inf. abs. after its verb suggests an indefinitely prolonged state of the action, and therefore expresses continuance, prevalence, &c.'; this being precisely what in the present instance it does not do. Cases where the second infin. expresses *concomitance of indefinite duration*, Judg. 14. 9; II. 2. 11, or simple addition of an event *in due sequence* (but *not* as the result aimed at by the previous action), Isa. 19. 22, are different in character.

38. למלך] LXX, Luc. τῷ βασιλεῖ Ἰσραήλ.

באפר] The word אפר occurs only here and in *v.* 41, but the meaning '*covering*' or '*bandage*,' given by LXX, Luc. τελαμῶνι, Targ. במעפרא, has the support of Assyr. in which *apâru* = 'to attire,' especially with a head-covering; *êpartu* = 'garment.' See Friedr. Delitzsch, *Assyr. Handwörterbuch*, *s. v.* I. אפר, and *Prolegomena*, 54; Zimmern, *Babylonische Busspsalmen*, 95; Barth,

Etym. Studien, 19. Vulg., Pesh. 'A., Σ. vocalize אֵפֶר 'ashes.' For use of art. בָּאפר cf. *ch.* 1. 1 *note* on בַּבְּגדים.

40. עבדך עֹשֶׂה הנה והנה] 'Thy servant was *a doer of hither and thither*' (הנה והנה as in II. 2. 8, 14; Josh. 8. 20†), an impossibly harsh construction. Vocalization עֹשֶׂה *st. abs.* gives the rendering '*was busy hither and thither*'; but that a man posing as having been set to guard a captive should represent himself as deliberately engaged in other matters seems scarcely probable. LXX περιεβλέψατο, Luc. περιεβλέπετο, Vulg. *me verterem*, Pesh. ܡܬܦܢܐ ܗܘܝܬ, Targ. מתפני, point to an orig. פֹּנֶה '*was turning* (looking) hither and thither,' and are followed by Th., Klo., *Heb. Lex. Oxf.* Cf. Ex. 2. 12 וַיִּפֶן כֹּה וָכֹה.

כן משפטך וג'] 'Such (*lit.* so) is thy verdict; thou thyself hast decided.' For sense of verb חרצת cf. esp. Niph. participle in the phrase כָּלָה וְנֶחֱרָצָה 'a consumption and *a strict decision*,' i.e. a consumption finally decided; Isa. 10. 23; 28. 22; Dan. 9. 27.

42. איש חרמי] 'The man of my ban'; i.e. the man devoted by me to destruction. Cf. Isa. 34. 5 עַם חֶרְמִי referring to Edom.

מיד] LXX, Luc., Vulg. suggest מִיָּדֶךָ, and so Th., Klo., Kamp., Benz., Kit.; but MT. is supported by 1 Sam. 19. 9; 26. 23; 2 Chr. 25. 20; Isa. 28. 2; Ezek. 12. 7, where בְּיָד occurs without specific suffix[1]. An expression first used, as in Prov. 6. 5 הִנָּצֵל כִּצְבִי מִיָּד, with vague and general reference, may then come to be employed where closer specification might be expected. Cf. colloquial Eng. *in hand*, *out of hand*.

43. על ביתו] Cf. *ch.* 1. 38 *note* on על גחון.

סר וזעף] So *ch.* 21. 4. '*Chafing and sullen*.' סַר, used again in fem. *ch.* 21. 5 מה זה רוחך סרה, is connected with סרר 'be refractory.' The meaning of the adj. זָעֵף is well illustrated by the use of the participle זֹעֲפִים which in Gen. 40. 6 denotes an appearance *dejected* and *gloomy* as produced by perplexing thoughts (cf. Joseph's

[1] Cf. the renderings of LXX, Vulg. in 1 Sam. 19. 9 ταῖς χερσὶν αὐτοῦ, *manu sua*; 26. 23 εἰς χεῖράς μου, *in manum meam*; 2 Chr. 25. 20 Luc. εἰς χεῖρας Ἰωάς, *in manus hostium*; where, as in our passage, the translators are at pains to make the reference precise, but presuppose no different original to MT.

question in *v.* 7 מדוע פניכם רעים היום), in Dan. 1. 10 a countenance *haggard* through spare and coarse diet. The phrase is further elucidated by the description of the king's conduct in *ch.* 21. 4ᵇ.

21. *Aḥab covets the vineyard of Naboth the Jezreelite, and obtains it by the judicial murder of the owner, planned and executed by Jezebel. The prophet Elijah announces Yahwe's sentence upon Aḥab and his house because of the deed.*

1ᵃ. LXX καὶ ἀμπελὼν εἷς ἦν τῷ Ναβουθαὶ τῷ Ἰσραηλείτῃ, i. e. וְכֶרֶם אֶחָד היה לנבות היזרעאלי: probably original. The introductory formula of MT., copied from *ch.* 17. 17 but here somewhat ill-fitting, was probably added by the scribe who interposed this *ch.* between *chh.* 20 and 22; cf. p. 210. The words are found in Luc., but that they are there a later addition is shown by the presence also of καί before ἀμπελών, as in LXX. On כרם אחד cf. p. 209.

1ᵇ. אצל היכל א׳] LXX παρὰ τῇ ἅλῳ Ἀχαάβ, i. e. אצל גֹּרֶן א׳. MT. is to some extent favoured by *v.* 2 אצל ביתי.

2. כסף מחיר זה] 'The money-value of this one'; lit. 'the money of the price of this.' כסף is *st. constr.* before מחיר as in Job 28. 15 כסף מחירה, and is not, with RV., to be taken as an accus. of limitation, 'the worth of it *in money*.' LXX, Luc., expanding זה into (Luc. τοῦ) ἀμπελῶνός σου τούτου, then repeat καὶ ἔσται μοι εἰς κῆπον λαχάνων.

3. חלילה לי מיהוה] So 1 Sam. 24. 7; 26. 11; and 2 Sam. 23. 17 Luc., Pesh., Targ. (cf. ‖ 1 Chr. 11. 19 חלילה לי מאלהי). מיהוה LXX παρὰ θεοῦ μου. Luc. παρὰ κυρίου θεοῦ μου a combination of MT. and LXX.

4. ויבא . . . וזעף] LXX καὶ ἐγένετο τὸ πνεῦμα Ἀχαὰβ τεταραγμένον, probably an alteration for exact agreement with *v.* 5. Luc. embodies the two readings, following MT. in *v.* 4ᵃ, and placing LXX reading at the beginning of *v.* 4ᵇ. On סר וזעף cf. *ch.* 20. 43 *note.*

ויסב את פניו] Cf. II. 20. 2ᵃ. Vulg., as in this passage, makes the addition *ad parietem*. LXX, Luc. *καὶ συνεκάλυψεν* seem to have read וַיְכַס for ויסב.

5. מה זה] *Ch.* 14. 6 *note*.

6. כי אדבר] Not, as RV. '*Because* I spake,' but simply 'I spake,' כי introducing the direct narration. Cf. *ch.* 1. 13 *note*. The use of the imperf. is here somewhat strange, but may perhaps be explained as laying pictorial stress upon the *commencement* of the king's overtures, a usage resembling the Eng. *historical present;* 'I *speak*' or '*begin to speak*,' when immediately negotiations are cut short by a definite refusal. Cf. Dri. *Tenses*, § 27 γ; Da. § 45, *Rem.* 2, quoting Hitzig. The suggestion of a *frequentative* force for the imperf. (Dri. *loc. cit.*) is less probable, there being no hint of this in the preceding narrative.

את כרמי] LXX, Luc. *κληρονομίαν πατέρων μου*, an alteration after *v.* 3.

7. אתה עתה] 'Dost *thou* now govern Israel?' On the interrogative force of the sentence cf. *ch.* 1. 24 *note*.

ויטב לבך] 'And let thy heart be cheerful.' Cf. *note* on טובי לב *ch.* 8. 66.

8. הספרים] Kt. הַסְּפָרִים is correct; '*the* letters' already mentioned, *v.* 8ª.

החרים] 'The nobles,' lit. '*freeborn*'; Ar. حُرّ, Aram. בר חורין, ܒܪ ܚܐܪܐ. The word doubtless belongs to the N. Pal. dialect (cf. p. 209), other occurrences in O. T. being late;—seven times in Neh. of the magnates of Judah, and so in Jer. 27. 20; 39. 6 (both passages omitted in LXX, and probably later interpolations; cf. Dri. *Introd.* pp. 248, 254 *f.*), of Edomite nobles Isa. 34. 12 (exilic); בן חורים as in Aram., Eccl. 10. 17†.

אשר בעירו וג'] 'Who were in his city, who *presided* with Naboth.' So *v.* 11 אשר הישבים בעירו 'who were *those who presided* in his city.' Naboth himself was one of the elders and nobles in whose hands the civil government of the city lay. That ישב here has the sense of *presiding*, especially as judges, is rightly recognized by Th., and by Klo. who renders 'Beisitzer.' For this use of the verb, cf. Isa. 28. 6 לַיּוֹשֵׁב עַל־הַמִּשְׁפָּט 'for him who *sits* (presides) over the judgement'; Am. 6. 3 שֶׁבֶת חָמָס 'the *seat* of violence (i. e.

of unjust judgement)'; and of Yahwe Ps. 9. 8 where the clause answering to יֹשֵׁב used absolutely is כּוֹנֵן לַמִּשְׁפָּט כִּסְאוֹ; cf. Ps. 29. 10; Joel 4. 12. RV. '*and* that dwelt with Naboth' makes the sentence simply a repetition of the statement אשר בעירו. LXX, Luc. wrongly omit this former clause, while Pesh. combines with the following: ܕܝܬܒܝܢ ܗܘܘ ܒܡܕܝܢܬܐ ܥܡ ܢܒܘܬ 'who dwelt in the city with Naboth.'

9. קראו צום] An extraordinary day of humiliation to avert the wrath of Yahwe which for some cause (supposed to be as yet unascertained) was assumed to be threatening the community. Such a special fast is mentioned as proclaimed by Jehoshaphat, 2 Chr. 20. 1–4. Cf. Th., Sta. *Ges.* i. 527.

והשיבו וג׳] Not as the suspected culprit, but as a man of marked position and piety who would naturally take the lead upon such an occasion; so Jos. (*Ant.* viii. 13, § 8) καὶ ποιησαμένους ἐκκλησίαν προκαθίσαι μὲν αὐτῶν Νάβωθον, εἶναι γὰρ αὐτὸν γένους ἐπιφανοῦς. The prominence of his position would thus the more excite the popular indignation (Th.), when the crime had been fastened upon him.

10. שנים אנשים] '*Two* men,' as at least necessary to secure a conviction; cf. Deut. 17. 6; 19. 15; Num. 35. 30; S. Matt. 26. 60 *f.*

בני בליעל] 'Villains.' The derivation and exact meaning of בליעל are highly obscure. There are two rival explanations, both of which regard the word, according to its Massoretic vocalization, as a compound. (i) בְּלִי *not* + יַעַל which is supposed to mean *worth* or *use* (cf. Hiph'il הועיל). Thus בְּלִיַּעַל = 'worthlessness,' בְּנֵי בְלִיַּעַל 'base fellows' (cf. *Heb. Lex. Oxf.*, *s. v.*). (ii) בְּלִי *not* + יַעַל for יַעֲלֶה *that which comes up*;—'not coming up,' and so 'unsuccessful' or 'ne'er-do-well' (Kimḥi בַּל יַעֲלֶה וּבַל יַצְלִיחַ, followed by Hupfeld among moderns). It is no objection to either of these explanations that the use of the term proves the conception to be not negative but positive—*malignity* or *dangerous wickedness* (Cheyne, as cited below), since instances can be quoted from all languages in which terms originally negative have gained later a very definite positive significance; cf. e.g. ἀσεβής, Germ. 'Unheil,' Old Eng. 'naughty.'

But a real difficulty in the way of the acceptance of either is the fact that the use of such a compound term in ordinary phraseology is without a parallel; expressions such as בְּלִימָה 'nothingness,' Job 26. 7; בְּנֵי בְלִי־שֵׁם 30. 8; מִלִּין בְּלִי דָעַת 38. 2 being late poetical creations, and therefore not to the point. בְּלִיַּעַל, then, is probably to be classed with צַלְמָוֶת (for צַלְמוּת) as exhibiting merely a fancy vocalization based upon relatively late tradition.

The view of Cheyne is that בליעל is to be identified with the Babylono-Assyrian goddess *Belili*, as representing the underworld, and that in later times the word may have been popularly associated with the derivation בַּל יַעֲלֶה in the sense 'the depth which lets no man return.' The chief passage cited in favour of this explanation is Ps. 18. 5[b] נַחֲלֵי בְלִיַּעַל, rendered 'streams of the underworld,' in juxtaposition to חֶבְלֵי מָוֶת *v.* 5[a], חֶבְלֵי שְׁאוֹל *v.* 6[a] (*Expositor*, June 1895, pp. 435–439; *Expository Times*, June 1897, pp. 423 *f.*; Nov. 1897, pp. 91 *ff.*; Apr. 1898, p. 332). The identification of בליעל with *Belili* is, however, denied by Baudissin and Jensen, on the grounds that there is no evidence to show that the *earth*-goddess *Belili* was ever regarded as a deity ruling the underworld; that there is no O. T. passage in which the meaning 'underworld' for בליעל is clearly present; and that there is no analogous O. T. expression in which men are brought into connexion with the underworld in order to mark them out as destructive or wicked (*Expository Times*, Oct. 1897, pp. 40–45; March 1898, pp. 283 *f.*).

If בליעל be *not* a compound term, it is natural to refer it to the root בלע 'swallow up, engulf,' and to regard the ל as ל formative, cases of which are seen in גִּבְעֹל, קַרְסֹל, כַּרְמֶל, and perhaps עֲרָפֶל. The י may then conceivably mark the word as a diminutive, according to the common Ar. usage (Wright, *Ar. Gramm.* i. § 269), to be traced also in Syr. in the words ܟܠܒܘܢܐ, ܥܠܝܡܐ, ܫܡܫܐ (Duval, *Gramm. Syr.* § 235), and in Heb. זְעֵיר, and perhaps also in שְׁפִיפוֹן and אֲמִינוֹן 2 Sam. 13. 20 (cf. Dri. *ad loc.*). Thus an original *bulai'āl* might become בְּלִיעַל, a form resembling שְׁפִיפוֹן, אֲמִינוֹן, which may be thought to stand for *shufaifān*, *'umainān*, upon the analogy of vulgar Ar. *k'fīfah*, 'little basket,' for *kufaifah*

(Wright, *Compar. Gramm.* p. 89). בליעל will then denote '*engulfing ruin*' or '*perdition*,' the diminutive marking the word as used in contempt and antipathy. Such a significance attached to the root בלע may be seen in Ps. 52. 6 כָּל־דִּבְרֵי־בָלַע, and the phrase בן בליעל may be paralleled by ὁ υἱὸς τῆς ἀπωλείας S. John 17. 12; 2 Thess. 2. 3.

After בני בליעל LXX omits all that follows in MT. down to בני בליעל of *v.* 13, apparently through homoioteleuton.

ברכת] 'Thou hast *cursed*'; lit. '*blessed*,' and so *v.* 13; Job 1. 5, 11; 2. 5, 9; Ps. 10. 3†. A sense so strangely opposed to the usual meaning of the verb is scarcely to be regarded as obtained from the idea 'greet at departing' (*ch.* 8. 66; Gen. 47. 10), so 'say farewell,' and then 'renounce' (Ges. *Thes.*, Ke., Dillmann on Job, &c., and so RV. *marg.*), there being no particle of evidence for such a transition in meaning; nor does it seem probable that the notion is that of 'a blessing overdone and so really a curse as in vulgar English as well as in the Shemitic cognates' (*Heb. Lex. Oxf.*). Rather, the word is an euphemism deliberately substituted for its direct antithesis, viz. the most fearful form of curse such as it were a sin even to mention in direct terms. Cf. among the Greeks the title Εὐμενίδες, 'the gracious goddesses,' applied euphemistically to the Ἐρινύες or Furies, and the name ὁ Εὔξεινος given to the Black sea as being ἄξεινος *in*hospitable;—'*Dictus ab antiquis Axenus ille fuit*,' Ovid, *Trist.* 4. 4, 56.

אלהים ומלך] The cursing of *God and the king* is prohibited in the Book of the Covenant, Ex. 22. 27 אלהים לא תקלל ונשיא בעמך לא תאר.

וסקלהו] The same penalty (verb רגם) is imposed for blasphemy in Lev. 24. 10–16 (H).

11^b. כאשר כתוב וג'] Luc. omits. The words are redundant after the statement immediately preceding, and may therefore be a gloss.

12. והשיבו] Not to be explained as a perf. with ו *consec.*, nor can any reason be assigned for the use of ו *simplex*. The form is an unintentional lapse into the imperat. form used in *v.* 9, and

we may correct וַיּוֹשִׁיבוּ. That the passage is not a mere gloss (Klo.) appears from the suffix of נגדו v. 13, which points back to the name נבות of this verse.

13. LXX, Luc. omit אנשי הבליעל את נבות נגד העם. But the last two words at least give a touch to the narrative not to be dispensed with.

ויעדהו . . . את נבות] Cf. *ch.* 19. 21 *note* on בשלם הבשר.

15. ויהי וג׳] LXX *καὶ ἐγένετο ὡς ἤκουσεν Ἰεζάβελ, καὶ εἶπεν πρὸς Ἀ.*, i. e. וַיְהִי כִּשְׁמֹעַ אִיזֶבֶל וַתֹּאמֶר אֶל־א׳. This less burdened sentence has to some extent the support of Luc., where the words of MT., though present, are marked as a gloss by the strange Κέχωσται for סקל; and of Pesh. which varies from MT., abbreviating ܕܡܝܬ ܢܒܘܬ, i. e. כִּי מֵת נ׳.

16. After *v.* 16[a] LXX adds *καὶ διέρρηξεν τὰ ἱμάτια ἑαυτοῦ καὶ περιεβάλετο σάκκον· καὶ ἐγένετο μετὰ ταῦτα, κ.τ.λ.* So Luc. This, however, is scarcely consistent with *v.* 27 MT.; since it is improbable that Aḥab first made a show of mourning at Naboth's death, then proceeded to take possession of his estate, and finally, upon Elijah's rebuke, secured a remand of the threatened vengeance through a repetition of the same tokens of remorse, this time, it must be supposed, sincere. Hence LXX varies from MT. in *v.* 27, making this statement to refer back to the former show of repentance narrated by the Version in *v.* 16:—*καὶ ὑπὲρ τοῦ λόγου ὡς κατενύγη Ἀ. ἀπὸ προσώπου τοῦ κυρίου, καὶ ἐπορεύετο κλαίων καὶ διέρρηξεν τὸν χιτῶνα αὐτοῦ καὶ ἐζώσατο σάκκον ἐπὶ τὸ σῶμα αὐτοῦ καὶ ἐνήστευσεν· καὶ περιεβάλετο σάκκον ἐν τῇ ἡμέρᾳ ᾗ ἐπάταξεν Ν. τὸν Ἰσραηλείτην, καὶ ἐπορεύθη. καὶ ἐγένετο ῥῆμα Κυρίου κ.τ.λ.* So substantially Luc. But all this stands self-condemned. It is impossible that Aḥab's remand should have been granted as an afterthought on account of his *first exhibition of repentance* (*v.* 16 LXX), which was clearly insincere and had not in the first place served in any way to qualify the penalty pronounced by Elijah. MT., therefore, in making the king display no sign of remorse, real or assumed, until after the prophet's threatenings, is certainly correct; and the fact that LXX text is here spurious and late is recognized by Th., who points out that

Jos. (*Ant.* viii. 13, § 8) was acquainted with a narrative in no way different from MT.

18. הנה וג׳] On omission of subj. with הנה cf. II. 6. 13 *note*.

19 *ff*. The account of this interview has been amplified by R^D. Cf. Abijah's prophecy against Jeroboam, *ch*. 14. 7–16 *notes*, and, beside the phrases there enumerated as characteristic, notice *vv*. 20, 25 התמכרך (התמכר) לעשות הרע בעיני י׳, cf. II. 17. 17 R^D†; *v*. 26 הגלולים, cf. *ch*. 15. 12 *note*; אשר הוריש וג׳, cf. *ch*. 14. 24 *note*. The original elements of the narrative, so far as they can be distinguished, are to be found in *v*. 19^a, *v*. 20 to מצאתי, *vv*. 27–29, and probably also *v*. 19^b. Less certain is the somewhat awkwardly placed statement as to Jezebel *v*. 23, which would follow more easily *after* *v*. 24, since *v*. 24 clearly forms the direct continuation to *v*. 22.

19. הכלבים] In the first place LXX, Luc. read αἱ ὕες καὶ οἱ κύνες (so *ch*. 22. 38), but that the addition is of the nature of a gloss is rendered most probable by its omission in the second place: οἱ κύνες simply, as in MT.

את דמך גם אתה] 'Thy blood, even *thine*,' or '*thy* blood also.' For this re-enforcement of the suff. by the pers. pron., cf. the exactly similar case 2 Sam. 17. 5 ונשמעה מה בפיו גם הוא 'and let us hear what is in *his* mouth also.' Cf. *ch*. 1. 26 *note* with references. At the end of the verse LXX, Luc. add καὶ αἱ πόρναι λούσονται ἐν τῷ αἵματί σου, adopted by Th. as presupposing וְהַזֹּנוֹת תִּרְחַצְנָה בְּדָמֶךָ. The reference, however, implies not the vineyard of Jezreel but the pool *of Samaria*, and is therefore doubtless a gloss derived from *ch*. 22. 38.

20. יען התמכרך] Luc. δι' ὅτι πέπρασαι μάτην, LXX διότι μάτην πέπρασαι, i. e. יען התמכרך לַשָּׁוְא 'because thou hast sold thyself *to no purpose*'; a pointed addition in view of what follows. For לשוא cf. Jer. 2. 30; 4. 30; 46. 11. The suggestion of Th., חִנָּם, is less probable, since this would rather signify '*for nought*,' i. e. without *expecting* a return.

לעשות . . . י׳] LXX, Luc. add (Luc. τοῦ) παροργίσαι αὐτόν, i. e. לְהַכְעִיסוֹ, correctly. Cf. II. 17. 17; 2 Chr. 33. 6; Deut. 4. 25; 9. 18.

21. ועצור ועזוב] Cf. *ch.* 14. 10 *note.*

23. הכלבים וג׳] Cf. II. 9. 10, 36.

בחל] RV. 'by the rampart,' and so LXX, Luc. ἐν τῷ προτειχίσματι. Vulg., Pesh., Targ., however, presuppose בְּחֵלֶק '*in the district*' of Jezreel, according to II. 9. 10, 36, 37, and this ought certainly to be adopted. The prediction was not fulfilled 'by the rampart,' but outside the palace *within* the city. חלק is only here in this connexion used of the tract of land surrounding or appertaining to *a town*, being elsewhere employed of the territory or estate of a tribe or family.

25. אשר הסתה וג׳] Possibly with reminiscence of Deut. 13. 7 כי יסיתך . . . אשת חיקך . . . לאמר נלכה ונעבדה אלהים אחרים וג׳. הֵסַתָּה as though from verb ע doubled, in place of הֵסִיתָה.

27. On the variations of LXX, Luc. in this verse, cf. *v.* 16 *note.*

ויהלך אט] 'And went about *quietly*,' i.e. in the manner of one in penitence and grief. Pesh. ܚܦܝ, Targ. יחף explain 'barefoot'; cf. 2 Sam. 15. 30; Vulg. *demisso capite:* LXX, Luc. omit. אט is a subs., *quietness* or *gentleness*, used adverbially. Elsewhere always with ל expressing condition;—Isa. 8. 6; 2 Sam. 18. 5; Job 15. 11; with suff. לְאִטִּי Gen. 33. 14. Ar. أطّ means *to creak* (of a saddle), or *to make a low moaning or plaintive sound* (of a camel). So Isa. 19. 3† אִטִּים are *whisperers*, i.e. wizards of some description.

28. אל אליהו התשבי] LXX, Luc. ἐν χειρὶ (Luc. τοῦ) δούλου αὐτοῦ Ἠλειού.

29. על ביתו] LXX, Luc. omit.

22. 1–38. *Continuation of ch.* 20. *After seven years of peace between Israel and Aram, Ahab, with the help of Jehoshaphat of Judah, determines to recover Rama of Gilead from the Aramaeans. He falls in the battle which takes place.*

Ch. 22. 2–37[a] = 2 Chr. 18. 2–34.

1. שלש שנים] After the 'covenant' described as concluded *ch.* 20. 34. The disastrous issue to which this led at Qarqar, where the confederate kings were defeated with great loss by

Shalmaneser (*Append.* 3), must have weakened the bonds of alliance, and led to a *rapprochement* between Israel and Judah. This new alliance made feasible the scheme to recover by force from the Aramaeans one of the most important cities which Ben-hadad had failed to cede according to compact. Cf. *COT.* i. 189*f.*

3. רָמֹת גלעד] Always with *script. defect.* except 2 Chr. 22. 5 רמות ג׳. Luc. in all occurrences transliterates Ῥαμὰθ Γ., while LXX varies between Ῥεμμὰθ Γ. and Ῥεμμὼθ Γ. Thus there is some presumption in favour of a vocalization רָמַת גִּלְעָד 'Rama of Gilead,' the city being so called in distinction from other places of the same name west of Jordan; and in II. 8. 29 (|| 2 Chr. 22. 6) רָמָה actually occurs. So Sta., Wellh. The form *Ramoth*, however, is substantiated as an existing form by the occurrence of the *st. absol.* רָמֹת בַּגִּלְעָד Josh. 21. 36; רָאמוֹת (רָאמֹת) בַּגִּלְעָד Deut. 4. 43; Josh. 20. 8; 1 Chr. 6. 65. The site of this Rama is doubtful. By most identification is sought with the modern *Es-Salṭ*, which would have formed a convenient point of vantage for an advance upon Samaria from an E.S.E. position. Dillmann (after Hitzig, Langer) on Gen. 31. 54 prefers the site *El-Jal'ûd*, six miles north of *Es-Salṭ*.

6. האלך על ר׳] Chr. הנלך אל ר׳. Cf. *ch.* 1. 38 *note.*

ויתן] LXX, Luc. καὶ (Luc. ὅτε) διδοὺς δώσει, i.e. וְנָתֹן יִתֵּן. Cf. Num. 21. 2; Judg. 11. 30; 2 Sam. 5. 19.

אדני] || 2 Chr. 18. 5 הָאֱלֹהִים. According to Th. many Codd. read יהוה, and this probably represents the original text, as in *vv.* 11, 12. The alteration probably arose (Th.) from the supposition suggested by Jehoshaphat's question *v.* 7, that the 400 were prophets of *Ba'al.*

7. האין פה וג׳] Render with AV. 'Is there not here a prophet of the Lord *besides?*' i.e. yet one more prophet of Yahwe in addition to these His (professed) prophets. The reason for Jehoshaphat's distrust of the 400 prophets can only be inferred. Jos. (*Ant.* viii. 15, § 4) συνεὶς ἐκ τῶν λόγων Ἰωσάφατος, ὅτι ψευδοπροφῆται τυγχάνουσιν, and similarly Ber., 'He shrewdly conjectured that Aḥab had only interrogated the prophets who were prepared to

give him a favourable answer.' RV. 'Is there not here *besides* a prophet of the Lord?' is an unwarrantable dislocation of עוֹד, intended apparently to imply that the speaker regarded the 400 not as prophets of Yahwe but of a strange god. This sense, not to be obtained from MT., is, *with omission of* עוֹד, given by LXX, Luc., Vulg., Pesh., 'Is there not here a prophet of Yahwe?' But against this is Aḥab's reply (*v.* 8) which presupposes that the 400 prophesied in the name of Yahwe, as is stated in *vv.* 11, 12.

This passage again points the inference (already drawn *ch.* 18. 31[a] *note*) that there were *two forms of Yahwe-worship* existent in the northern kingdom—that represented by the cult of the calves, and that of which such prophets as Elijah, Elisha, and Micaiah were the exponents; and that the view that the former was a perversion of the true religion was not merely the opinion of later (Deuteronomic) times, but was shared by the *contemporary* adherents of the purer form of religion. The 400 prophets cannot be thought to have belonged to the class which Jezebel used rigorous measures to extirpate (*ch.* 18. 4; 19. 10, 14; II. 9. 7), but must have been representatives of a form of Yahwe-religion which for some reason escaped attack during her persecution; and the reason for this escape may be assumed to have been that this professed Yahwe-worship could tolerate[1] the existence side by side with it of a definitely extraneous cult, even if it had not itself assimilated certain Canaanite elements[2].

On the other hand, the reason for Jezebel's vindictiveness against a certain section of Yahwe-worshippers must have been that these, by emphasis of *Yahwe's exclusive claim* (Ex. 20. 3), came into sharp collision with the form of religion which she desired to

---

[1] Cf. the indifferent attitude of the populace gathered at Mt. Carmel to the two diverse cults; *ch.* 18. 21.

[2] It may accordingly be conjectured that in II. 3. 13 Elisha's words to Joram לך אל נביאי אביך ואל נביאי אמך form not a pleonastic reference to the Ba'al prophets only, but couple together the perverted Yahwe prophets, described as the prophets of Aḥab, and the prophets of the Phoenician Ba'al who were under the special patronage of Jezebel; the former, as the latter, being really opposed to the pure religion of Yahwe.

naturalize. Such were those mentioned in *ch.* 19. 18—not merely an isolated prophet here and there, but a considerable body of the people whose number is reckoned as 7,000.

8. ימלה] Chr. יִמְלָא; 'probably more correct etymologically'; Th.

10. מלבשים בגדים] 'Clad *in robes,*' i.e. in robes of *state*. Cf. *v.* 30 לבש בגדיך 'put thou on *thy robes,*' in contrast to the preceding התחפש.

בגרן] 'In a *threshing-floor.*' Chr. ויושבים בגרן with explan. ref. of previous ישבים. Scarcely possible. RV. paraph. 'in an *open place*' is impermissible, there being no ground for assigning this general signification to גרן; and the same remark applies to the renderings of Vulg. *in area;* Luc. ἐν ὁδῷ[1]; LXX, Luc. in Chr. ἐν εὐροχώρῳ. In LXX (Kgs.) ἔνοπλοι answers to the whole מלבשים בגדים בגרן, i.e. בגרן is unrepresented, and may thus be regarded as mere dittography of בגדים. The emendations of Ew. בְּנֶשֶׁק '*in armour,*' Th., Ber. בְּרֻדִים '*embroidered*' (?) have nothing to recommend them.

11. קרני ברזל] An emblem of offensive power; cf. Deut. 33. 17; Am. 6. 13; Jer. 48. 25; Dan. 8. 3 *f.*

12. ונתן וג׳] 'Yahwe shall give (it),' with obj. understood as in *vv.* 6, 15. LXX, Luc. wrongly supply as obj. καὶ τὸν βασιλέα Συρίας.

13. דברי הנביאים] LXX, Luc. λαλοῦσι πάντες οἱ προφῆται, in Chr. ἐλάλησαν κ.τ.λ., i.e. דִּבְּרוּ הנ׳ 'the prophets have, with one consent, spoken good &c.'; superior to the somewhat harsh MT. 'the words of the prophets &c. *are* good.' So Th., Kamp., Benz., Kit. Klo. מְדַבְּרִים, less simple.

פה אחד] So Josh. 9. 2. An accus. defining the *manner* of דִּבְּרוּ.

אַחַד מהם] Cf. *ch.* 19. 2 *note.*

17. ויאמר ראיתי] After ויאמר LXX inserts οὐχ οὕτως, Luc. Οὕτως, i.e. לָכֵן as in *v.* 19; 'I saw *then* all Israel &c.'; *then,* i.e. in case you wish really to hear the truth. Adopted by Klo.

---

[1] But perhaps this is a corruption of ἐν ἅλῳ. In Pesh. (Kgs. and Chr.) ܒܐܘܪܚܐ is clearly an error for ܒܐܕܪܐ, which answers to MT.

לא אדנים וג׳] Luc. in place of לא reads Εἰ, i.e. לוּ or לֻא, and this is followed by Klo., 'If these had any master, they would return, &c.,' a reading incomparably poor by the side of MT. LXX Οὐ Κύριος τούτοις Θεός; presupposes a false repetition of לאלה as לֵאלֹהִים.

19. לכן שמע וג׳] The strange rendering of LXX, Luc. Οὐχ οὕτως, οὐκ ἐγώ· ἄκουε ῥῆμα Κυρίου· οὐχ οὕτως· εἶδον κ.τ.λ. represents at the beginning a doublet of לָכֵן, first read as לֹא כֵן, and then explained by the gloss οὐκ ἐγώ, 'Not I' (am responsible, but Yahwe). The second οὐχ οὕτως, which should not be followed by a stop, is an imitation of לכן ראיתי, *v.* 17.

שמע] Chr. שִׁמְעוּ, and so here 7 Codd. Kenn.

צבא השמים] 'The host of heaven'; an expression not used elsewhere in pre-exilic writings in the special sense of spiritual beings or angels. Cf., however, Josh. 5. 13 *ff.* (JE) where the 'man' who appears to Joshua describes himself as שַׂר צְבָא יהוה. In Isa. 34. 4 (prob. exilic) the phrase seems to describe the angels corresponding to or acting as guardians of 'all the nations' (*v.* 2), this being clearly the case in 24. 21 with the expression צבא המרום[1].

Elsewhere generally צבא הש׳ denotes the *stars*;—II. 17. 16; 21. 3, 5 (|| 2 Chr. 33. 3, 5); 23. 4, 5; Deut. 4. 19; 17. 3; Jer. 8. 2; 19. 13; Zeph. 1. 5; cf. Gen. 2. 1; Ps. 33. 6; Isa. 40. 26; 45. 12. It is a late usage in which the term is used indefinitely to denote visible heavenly bodies and invisible agencies; Neh. 9. 6; Dan. 8. 10; cf. Ps. 103. 21; 148. 2.

20. מי יפתה וג׳] For the doctrine that Yahwe, in His displeasure, incites men to their own ruin or injury, cf. Ex. 4. 21b; 10. 1, 20, 27; 11. 9, 10 (J, E, or JE); 7. 3; 9. 12 (P); Deut. 2. 30 hardening of the heart ascribed to Yahwe (cf. Isa. 6. 10); Judg. 9. 23 Yahwe sends an evil spirit between Abimelech and the men of Shechem; 2 Sam. 24. 1 incites David to a pernicious action; Isa. 19. 2, 14 stirs up Egypt against Egypt and mingles a spirit of perverseness

[1] Cf. for this doctrine Dan. 10. 13, 20, 21; 12. 1; Ecclus. 17. 17; and Deut. 32. 8 LXX (reading אֵל for ישראל).

in the midst of her; Ezek. 14. 9 deceives the false prophet to his own ruin (the same verb as in our passage פִּתֵּיתִי).

אחאב] LXX, Luc., Vulg. presuppose אחאב מלך ישראל, and so Chr.

ויאמר זה וג׳] On the contrasted order cf. *ch.* 5. 25 *note.*

21. הרוח] '*The* spirit,' vividly pictured in the speaker's imagination through the part which he fulfilled. Cf. *ch.* 20. 36 *note.*

22. The variation of Luc. after *v.* 22ª καὶ ἀπατήσω αὐτόν. Καὶ εἶπεν Δυνήσει is probably due merely to the dislocation of εἶπεν in the Greek text. LXX as MT. καὶ εἶπεν Ἀπατήσεις καί γε δυνήσει.

24. אי זה עבר] The interrog. אי זה is never elsewhere used with a verb, and Chr., in supplying הַדֶּרֶךְ before עבר, conforms to the usual constr. So Th., Klo., Kamp., Benz., Kit. On אי זה הדרך cf. *ch.* 13. 12 *note.* LXX Ποῖον πνεῦμα Κυρίου τὸ λαλῆσαν ἐν σοί suggests אֵי־זֶה רוּחַ יהוה הַמְדַבֵּר בָּךְ, i.e. not as rendered, 'What kind of spirit &c.[1]?' but '*where is the spirit of Yahwe that speaketh in thee?*' a direct challenge to Micaiah to avenge the insult, implying that, if he fails to do so, the spirit by which *he* speaks is a רוּחַ שֶׁקֶר. To this Micaiah replies, '*Behold thou shalt see* (*where it is;* i.e. the challenge shall be accepted; *not now, but*) *in that day &c.*' This is superior to the obscure sentence of MT., and probably represents the original text. Luc. exhibits a combination of LXX and MT.

26. קח את מ׳ והשיבֻהו] LXX, Luc., Pesh., Vulg. support pl. קחו את מ׳ והשיבֻהו, the reading of Chr. So Th., Klo. Sta., however, points out that in *v.* 27 LXX εἶπον, Luc. εἶπε, like MT. וְאָמַרְתָּ, favour an original sing. in *v.* 26. The substitution of pl. for sing. may be explained as due to the influence of pl. imperat. *v.* 27 שימו . . . והאכלֻהו. These refer to two persons אמון and יואש, but the address of *v.* 26 is probably to the סרים אחד of *vv.* 9 *ff.* *ZATW.* V. 173 *ff.*

אל אמון] LXX πρὸς Σεμήρ, Luc. πρὸς Σεμμήρ. Chr. LXX πρὸς Ἐμήρ, Cod. A, Luc. πρὸς Σεμμήρ. The forms with Σ probably

---

[1] Adopted by Sta. *Ges.* i. 532: 'Was für ein Geist Jahwes hat denn aus *dir* gesprochen?'

exhibit a repetition of the last letter of πρός, and LXX Chr. represents the original form in the Greek. Accordingly Sta. favours the reading אֶל־אִמֵּר, Ἐμμήρ being the LXX form for MT. אִמֵּר in Jer. 20. 1; Ezr. 2. 37, 59; 10. 20; Neh. 3. 29; 7. 40; 11. 13; 1 Chr. 9. 12; 24. 14.

27. כה אמר המלך] LXX, Luc. omit.

את זה] With great contempt:—'*This fellow*.' So exactly, with את, 1 Sam. 21. 16; 2 Sam. 13. 17 (את זאת); cf. *ch.* 20. 7; II. 5. 7; 1 Sam. 10. 27; 25. 21; Ex. 10. 7.

לחם לחץ וג׳] 'Bread in scant measure and water in scant measure'; lit. 'bread—affliction and water—affliction,' a case of apposition. So Isa. 30. 20. Cf. Dri. *Tenses*, § 189. 1.

28. ויאמר שמעו וג׳] LXX, Luc. omit. The words are clearly a gloss derived from Mic. 1. 2, and inserted for the purpose of identifying Micaiah with Micah the Morashtite. The names מִיכָיְהוּ and מִיכָה are really identical, and the prophet of the later century bears the longer name מִיכָיָה in Jer. 26. 18 Kt. The pl. עמים occurs many scores of times with the signification of *foreign nations*, seldom or never of Israel[1].

30. התחפש ובא במלחמה] 'Let me *disguise myself and enter* the battle!' The infin. absol. presents the bare idea of the verb in exclamatory and excited speech. Cf. II. 4. 43 כֹּה אָמַר י׳ אָכוֹל וְהוֹתֵר 'Thus saith Yahwe, Ye shall *eat and leave over!*' II. 3. 16; Hos. 4. 2; *al.;* Da. § 88b; Ew. § 328c.

בגדיך] LXX, Luc. τὸν ἱματισμόν μου, an easy (but false) correction deduced from the fact that Aḥab himself was disguised.

31. ומלך ארם צוה] 'Now the king of Aram *had commanded*.' On order of sentence cf. *ch.* 14. 5 *note*.

את שרי הרכב וג׳] The military commanders who filled the place previously occupied by the thirty-two vassal princes. Cf. *ch.* 20. 24 *note*.

32. ויסרו עליו] 'They turned aside against him'; somewhat

[1] Supposed cases are Deut. 33. 3 where the better reading seems to be עַמּוֹ LXX; Gen. 28. 3; 48. 4 the promise to Jacob. With suffix Judg. 5. 14; Hos. 10. 14. Cf. Dri. on *Deut. loc. cit.*

harsh. LXX, Luc. *καὶ ἐκύκλωσαν αὐτόν* agree with Chr. וַיָּסֹבּוּ עָלָיו '*they surrounded him*,' a reading certainly to be preferred. So Th., Klo. סבב על as in Job 16. 13.

34. לתמו] Lit. '*in his simplicity*' (ל of norm), i. e. without being able to assign a reason for the selection of his mark. So AV., RV. suitably 'at a venture'; Luc. *ἀφελῶς*, 'artlessly.' That this is the meaning of the phrase is rendered clear by the context of its only other occurrence, 2 Sam. 15. 11 וְאֶת־אַבְשָׁלוֹם הָלְכוּ מָאתַיִם אִישׁ מִירוּשָׁלַםִ קְרֻאִים וְהֹלְכִים לְתֻמָּם וְלֹא יָדְעוּ כָּל־דָּבָר 'And with Absalom there went 200 men from Jerusalem, summoned and going in their simplicity, *and they knew not anything*' (of the projected conspiracy). Cf. also Gen. 20. 5, 6 בְּתָם־לְבָבִי. Vulg. *in incertum sagittam dirigens*, Pesh. ܠܡܟܘܢܘ (with doublet ܠܐܘܟܡܢܐ *id.* MT.), and so Targ. לקיבליה 'straight in front of him,' seem to have imagined that the phrase denoted the letting fly of an *aimless* shaft. LXX, guessing, *εὐστόχως*.

בין הדבקים וג'] 'Between the attachments and between the coat of mail.' The subs. דֶּבֶק only elsewhere occurs in Isa. 41. 7, where it means *joining* or soldering. So *Heb. Lex. Oxf.*, following Th., Ber. *al.*, explains הדבקים 'the jointed *attachment* or *appendage* to the rigid breast-armour, which covered the abdomen.' Other explanations have merely the nature of guesses:—LXX, Luc. *ἀνὰ μέσον τοῦ πνεύμονος καὶ ἀνὰ μέσον τοῦ θώρακος*: Vulg. *inter pulmonem et stomachum;* Ew. the soft parts which *connect* the chest with the bottom of the back, so, 'between the *groin* and breastbone'; Ges. *Thes.* '*arm-pits*,' lit. joints of shoulder; Klo. '*helmet-appendages*.'

הפך ידיך] So II. 9. 23 with pl. ידיו as Kt.

המחנה] 'The army' *in action*, as in Judg. 4. 15, 16.

כי החליתי] RV. 'For I am sore wounded.' So 2 Chr. 35. 23.

35. ותעלה המלחמה] 'And the battle *waxed hotter*'; lit. *went up* or *increased*, the figure being perhaps drawn from a river which gathers force as it *rises* (Ke., Th., Ber.); cf. Isa. 8. 7; Jer. 46. 7, 8.

היה מָעֳמָד] 'Was propped up.' The participle with subs. verb expresses the *duration* of the action; Dri. *Tenses*, § 135. 5. Chr. act. היה מַעֲמִיד 'kept himself standing.'

After *v.* 35[a] LXX, Luc. add ἀπὸ πρωὶ ἕως ἑσπέρας, i.e. מִן־הַבֹּקֶר עַד־הָעָרֶב, and this is partially supported by Chr. עד הערב. In *v.* 35[b] LXX, Luc., which place וימת בערב *after* ויצק . . . הרכב, are superior.

וימת בערב] Chr. וַיָּמָת לְעֵת בּוֹא הַשָּׁמֶשׁ, either a summary conclusion formed by combining Kgs. *v.* 36[a] כבא השמש, or else the writer's eye passed to וימת of *v.* 37, and לעת וג׳ represents a corrupt reading of ויבוא שמרון.

וַיִּצֶק] '*And* the blood of the wound *flowed* &c.' This intrans. sense occurs only once besides, Job 38. 38 בְּצֶקֶת עָפָר לַמּוּצָק 'when dust *floweth* into the mass.' Imperf. Qal always elsewhere takes the form יִצֹק.

36. ויעבר הרנה] 'And there passed the cry.' The verb, if not an error for ותעבר, is masc. as coming first in the sentence; cf. *ch.* 11. 3 *note* on ויהי לו נשים. LXX, Luc., Vulg., Pesh., Targ. interpret הרנה as *the herald.*

37. וימת המלך] LXX, Luc. ὅτι τέθνηκεν ὁ βασιλεύς, i.e. כִּי מֵת הַמֶּלֶךְ '*for the king is* dead'; certainly correct. The words are part of the רִנָּה, and assign a reason for *v.* 36[b]. So Th., Klo., Kamp., Benz., Kit. On the confusion of כ and ו, cf. *ch.* 12. 30 *note.*

ויבוא] LXX, Luc. καὶ ἦλθον, i.e. וַיָּבֹאוּ, subj. being the same as the following ויקברו; correctly. So Th., Klo., Kamp., Benz., Kit. Targ., feeling the difficulty of sing. ויבוא, paraphrases ואתיוהי 'and they brought him.'

38. וישטף] Impers. '*one* washed,' and so 'the chariot *was washed.*'

והזנות רחצו] 'And the harlots washed themselves (there),' sc. in the pool into which the blood had drained. LXX, Luc. add ἐν τῷ αἵματι (Luc. αὐτοῦ). This is the only meaning of which the sentence is capable. The other Verss., probably for the sake of avoiding an objectionable statement, give to הזנות another interpretation and make it the obj. of רחצו;—Vulg. *et habenas laverunt*, Pesh. ܘܫܝܓܘ ܐܣܘܪܝܗ (transposed with וילקו וג׳), and so Targ. ומני

וזינא שטפו 'and they washed the (Pesh. his) armour.' But זַיִן *weapon* or *military equipment* of Rabb. Heb. and Aram. never occurs in Bib. Heb.; and verb רחץ is used exclusively of washing the body, whether *one's own person* (without obj.) or *some part of it* (obj. כַּפַּיִם, בָּשָׂר, *al.*) or *some one else* (Ex. 29. 4; 40. 12; Lev. 8. 6 P; Ezek. 16. 9†), or of washing the *flesh portions* of a sacrifice (Ex. 29. 17; Lev. 1. 9, 13; 8. 21; 9. 14 P†), never of washing any kind of inanimate object.

כדבר וג'] Cf. *ch.* 13. 26 *note.*

22. 39, 40. *Summary of Aḥab's reign.*

39. בית השן] 'The house of ivory.' The בתי השן of Am. 3. 15 perhaps contains an allusion to this. Cf. Ps. 45. 9 הֵיכְלֵי שֵׁן 'palaces of ivory.' Jer. 22. 15 speaks of Aḥab's fame as a builder, upon the reading of Cod. A 'Αχαάβ for ארז:—הֲתִמְלֹךְ כִּי אַתָּה מְתַחֲרֶה בְאַחְאָב 'Shalt thou reign because thou competest with Aḥab?' (in magnificence of palace architecture; cf. *vv.* 13, 14).

22. 41-51. *Jehoshaphat, king of Judah.*

Ch. 22. 41-51 forms part of the material of 2 Chr. 20. 31-37. R^D frames a collection of short notices from the Annals.

44. אך הבמות וג'] Cf. *ch.* 3. 2, 3 *note.*

47. הקדש] Cf. *ch.* 14. 24 *note.*

48, 49. ומלך וג'] Highly obscure as the text stands. RV. 'And there was no king in Edom: a deputy was king,' agrees with Targ.[1], and so Ke., Th., Kamp. But that a mere deputy, ostensibly appointed by Jehoshaphat, should be dignified with the title of *king* is incredible. Vulg. *nec erat tunc rex constitutus in Edom*, Pesh. ܘܡܠܟܐ ܠܝܬ ܒܐܕܘܡ ܕܡܩܝܡ give an intelligible sense: 'And there was no king in Edom appointed as king,' i. e. regularly constituted as such; but against this it may be urged (Sta.) that נצב

[1] Strictly speaking, Targ. ומלכא לית באדום ממנא אילהין איסטרטיגא מלכא 'And there was no king in Edom *appointed*, but *a general* was king,' exhibits a double rendering of נצב, the former '*appointed*' agreeing with Vulg., Pesh.

of the appointment of a king is unparalleled. LXX, Luc. simply transliterate נצב, and fail to afford any elucidation.

Probably, therefore, the text has suffered some corruption; and this inference is confirmed by the condition of *v.* 49[a], where עשר must be corrected עָשָׂה upon the authority of Q're, several Codd., and all Verss., and the reference of ולא הלך is, at best, highly obscure.

Sta. (*ZATW.* 1885, p. 178) by clever emendation obtains for the two verses a text which is at once lucid and but little divergent from MT. Connecting *v.* 48 with *v.* 49 he reads: וּמֶלֶךְ אֵין בֶּאֱדוֹם וּנְצִיב· הַמֶּלֶךְ יְהוֹשָׁפָט עָשָׂה אֳנִיַּת תַּרְשִׁישׁ לָלֶכֶת אוֹפִירָה לַזָּהָב וְלֹא הָלָכָה כִּי נִשְׁבְּרָה הָאֳנִיָּה (or אֳנִיָּתוֹ) בְּעֶצְיוֹן גָּבֶר׃ 'Now there was no king in Edom. And the deputy of king Jehoshaphat made a ship of Tarshish to go to Ophir for gold; but it went not, for the ship (his ship) was wrecked at Ezion-geber.' For the constr. נציב המלך יהו' cf. 2 Sam. 16. 6; 19. 17; *ch.* 1. 38; 5. 7; 10. 13; II. 19. 5, and so נציב פלשתים 1 Sam. 13. 3. So Benz., Kit. Klo. agrees with Sta. as far as regards *v.* 48 and its connexion with *v.* 49, while in this latter verse he combines Q're and Kt. 'made *ten* ships,' and finds the reference of הלך to be to the projector of the expedition.

Upon אניות תרשיש cf. *ch.* 10. 22 *note.*

22. 52–54. *Aḥaziah, king of Israel.*

54. הבעל] LXX, Luc. pl. τοῖς Βααλείμ.

ככל וג'] Luc. παρὰ πάντας τοὺς γενομένους ἔμπροσθεν αὐτοῦ is a correction in imitation of *ch.* 14. 9; 16. 25, 30, 33, but here inappropriate, since the editor would scarcely represent this king as *exceeding* his father in wickedness: cf. *ch.* 16. 30, 31; 21. 25, 26; R[D]. LXX κατὰ πάντα τὰ γενόμενα ἔμπροσθεν αὐτοῦ, i. e. doubtless כְּכֹל אֲשֶׁר הָיוּ לְפָנָיו is as good as, but not superior to MT., and may be a correction in view of the fact that the sins of Jeroboam as well as those of Aḥab are mentioned *v.* 53.

II. 1. 1. This verse clearly belongs to the series of short notices referring to the reign of Aḥaziah immediately preceding, I. 22. 52–54. The division of the Hebrew text of Kings into two books is not found in the MSS. nor in the early printed editions. It first occurs in the great Rabbinic Bible of Daniel Bomberg, published at Venice 1516–17, where an asterisk between I. 22. 54 and II. 1. 1 calls attention to a marginal note:—כאן מתחילים הלועזים ספר מלכי׳ רביעי: 'Here the non-Jews (i.e. Christians) begin the fourth book of Kings.' A similar note is found between 1 and 2 Sam. Cf. Ginsburg, *Introd. to the Massoretico-critical edit. of the Heb. Bible*, pp. 45, 930 *f.* Thus the division in MT. appears to have been an innovation from LXX, Vulg. While in LXX no known MS. presents an undivided text of 1, 2 Kgs.; 3, 4 Kgs.; Chr.; it is noticeable that in Cod. B the first verse of each second book appears also at the close of each first book, a fact which shows that the divider of the books was desirous of indicating the inner connexion existing between the first and second divisions in each case. Cf. the manner in which in MT. Ezr. 1. 1–3[a] (to ויעל) repeats 2 Chr. 36. 22, 23, of which it originally formed the unbroken continuation.

ויפשע מואב וג׳] Cf. *ch.* 3. 4 *ff.* According to the inscription of Mesha' king of Moab (*Append.* 1) the rebellion took place *during* the reign of Omri's son. Aḥab is, however, nowhere mentioned by name in the inscription.

1. 2–18. *Aḥaziah, after an accidental fall through a lattice, appeals to the oracle of Ba'al-zebub, the god of Ekron, in order to learn whether he will recover. Elijah predicts his death, on account of his unfaithfulness to Yahwe.*

2. בעד השבכה] 'Out through (*lit.* away from) the lattice.' So LXX διὰ τοῦ δικτυωτοῦ, 'A. περὶ τὸν κιγχλιδωτόν, Vulg. *per cancellos*, Targ. מן סריגתא. For the other uses of שבכה cf. I. 7. 17 *note.* Luc. presents a slightly different form of *v.* 2[a]: καὶ ἀνέβη 'Οχ. εἰς τὸ δικτυωτὸν ὑπερῷον αὐτοῦ τὸ ἐν Σαμαρείᾳ καὶ ἔπεσε καὶ ἠρρώστησε—inferior to MT.

אם אחיה וג׳] Cf. *ch.* 8. 8, 9.

מחלי זה] The constr. חֳלִי זֶה (for the normal הַחֳלִי הַזֶּה) is regular in Rabbinic Heb., but extremely uncommon in Bib. Heb. Other occurrences, cited by Kö. *Syntax*, § 334 β, are יוֹם הוּא Mic. 7. 12[a] (text doubtful), גֶּפֶן זֹאת Ps. 80. 15. LXX, Luc., Vulg., Pesh., Targ. presuppose a reading חָלְיִי זֶה 'this *my* sickness,' both here and in *ch.* 8. 8, 9. This constr., in which the demonstr. pronoun without the article follows a subs. with possessive suffix, is perfectly regular; cf. *v.* 13 עֲבָדֶיךָ אֵלֶּה; I. 8. 59; 10. 8; 22. 23; *al.;* Da. § 32 (2), *Rem.* 3; Ew. § 293; G-K. § 126*y*.

At the end of the verse LXX, Luc. add καὶ ἐπορεύθησαν ἐπερωτῆσαι (LXX δι' αὐτοῦ), i.e. וַיֵּלְכוּ לִדְרשׁ מֵאִתּוֹ, an addition which forms a suitable introduction to *v.* 3[a], and which may be compared with *v.* 4[b].

3. דִּבֶּר] LXX ἐκάλεσεν . . . λέγων, Luc. ἐλάλησε . . . λέγων. Probably LXX is a corruption of Luc. The latter presupposes the reading of MT., λέγων being merely the translator's addition: cf. I. 13. 12 *note*.

מלך שמרון] So I. 21. 1†. Luc. Ὀχοζίου βασιλέως Ἰσραὴλ ἐν Σαμαρείᾳ.

המבלי אין] For the double negative, cf. *note* on I. 10. 21.

5. מה זה] Upon the enclitic זה, cf. I. 14. 6 *note*.

6. אתה שלח] LXX, Luc. presuppose אַתָּה הֹלֵךְ; cf. *v.* 3. MT., as the easier reading, appears to be a correction. A correction in the Greek would probably have run ὑμεῖς πορεύεσθε, i.e. אַתֶּם הֹלְכִים, in strict agreement with *v.* 3.

6[b]. לכן] LXX, Luc. add τάδε λέγει Κύριος as in *v.* 4. At the end of the verse Luc. has a gloss, derived, in the main, from I. 21. (20) 21.

7. משפט] 'Description,' i.e. the summary of *distinctive characteristics*. Cf. Judg. 13. 12 מַה־יִּהְיֶה מִשְׁפַּט הַנַּעַר 'What shall be the description of the child?'

9[b]. ויעל . . . וידבר אליו] The text is somewhat expanded in Luc.: καὶ ἐπορεύθησαν πρὸς αὐτόν. αὐτὸς δὲ ἐκάθητο ἐπὶ τῆς κορυφῆς τοῦ ὄρους. καὶ ἀνέβη ὁ ἡγούμενος καὶ οἱ πεντήκοντα αὐτοῦ καὶ ἦλθον ἕως τοῦ ἀνθρώπου τοῦ θεοῦ. καὶ ἐλάλησε πρὸς αὐτὸν ὁ πεντηκόνταρχος καὶ εἶπεν κ.τ.λ.

והנה ישֵׁב] Omission of the pronominal subject of the participle is not infrequent after הִנֵּה, which calls pointed attention to a subject closely preceding. Cf. Gen. 24. 30; 37. 15; *al.;* Dri. *Tenses,* § 135 (6); Da. § 100[a]. Such a use of הִנֵּה without expression of suffix of reference is idiomatic in other cases also; cf. e. g. *ch.* 6. 13; I. 2. 29; 21. 18.

דִּבֶּר] LXX ἐκάλεσέν σε, probably an alteration of ἐλάλησε; cf. *v.* 3 *note.* Luc. τάδε λέγει, in accordance with *v.* 11 כֹּה אָמַר.

10. ואם] *'And if.'* The ו, by emphasis of *'if,'* imparts a grim sarcasm to the prophet's words; the implication being, 'You glibly term me "man of God," while overlooking my power to withstand the king's command.' Cf. I. 2. 22 *note.* In *v.* 12 ו is omitted.

11. ויען] Luc., Cod. A are correct in reading καὶ ἀνέβη, i. e. וַיַּעַל as in *vv.* 9, 13. So Th., Kamp., Benz., Kit.

12. אליהם] LXX, Luc., Pesh., 3 Codd. read אֵלָיו. So Th., Kamp., Benz., Kit.

13. שלשים] Luc., Vulg., Targ. שְׁלִישִׁי, the reference being (as in clause *b*) to the captain; cf. אַחֵר 'another' (second) *v.* 11. So Th., Klo., Kamp., Benz., Kit. MT. שְׁלִשִׁים has arisen by attraction to חמשים— 'a third fifty'; pl. as in 1 Sam. 19. 21 מַלְאָכִים שְׁלִשִׁים 'a third set of messengers.' LXX omits; Pesh. ܕܬܠܬ ܙܒܢܝܢ 'for the third time.'

ויעל ויבא] LXX, Luc. καὶ ἦλθεν, Vulg. *qui cum venisset,* omit the former verb, while Pesh. ܘܣܠܩ is without the latter. The subj. שר וג׳, following upon the second verb, occupies an awkward though not impossible position (cf. I. 10. 29[a]), and is omitted by Vulg. So Klo., Kamp., Benz.

עבדיך אלה חמשים] LXX, Vulg. omit the somewhat redundant חמשים.

14. ואת חמשיהם] LXX omits.

16. יען אשר] 'Forasmuch as' is answered by לכן 'therefore,' and the interjected question המבלי . . . בדברו destroys the construction of the sentence, and is rightly lacking in LXX, Luc. So Klo., Kamp., Benz., Kit. The words are a gloss from *vv.* 3, 6.

17. וימלך יהורם] Add אָחִיו with Luc., Θ. ὁ ἀδελφὸς αὐτοῦ, a specification presupposed by the statement of clause *b*. So Klo., Kamp., Kit.

בשנת . . . יהודה] This synchronism breaks the connexion between the statements preceding and following, and also conflicts with the synchronism of *ch.* 3. 1[a], which occupies the regular position in R[D]'s framework. As standing in MT. it is an erroneous insertion, and forms part of a distinct synchronistic system, which appears in Luc., but of which this notice and that of I. 16. 23 are the only traces in MT. See *Introduction.*

2. 1–18. *The translation of Elijah to heaven, and the gift of a double portion of his spirit to Elisha, his disciple and successor.*

1. בְּסְעָרָה] The *ḥatef-qameç* facilitates the pronunciation of the emphatic sibilant ס. Cf. Kö. *Lehrg.* I. i. 262; and *notes* on I. 13. 7; 19. 20.

הגלגל] It is the merit of Th. to have first noticed that this Gilgal, from which Elijah and Elisha *went down* (וַיֵּרְדוּ *v.* 2) to Bethel, cannot have been the Gilgal between Jericho and the Jordan, Josh. 4. 19; *al.;* and to have identified the place with *Jiljilia,* south-west of *Seilûn,* and 'near the high road between Bethel and Shechem'; cf. Smith, *Hist. Geogr.* 494. Rob. (*BR.* ii. 265 *f.*) describes the locality of *Jiljilia,* but fails to perceive the Biblical identification.

2. וחי נפשך] The vocalization חֵי is adopted by the punctuators for the sake of drawing artificial distinction between the sacred oath חַי יהוה and the non-sacred. Cf. *vv.* 4, 6; 4. 30; 1 Sam. 20. 3; 25. 26; 1. 26; 17. 55; 2 Sam. 11. 11; 14. 19; חֵי פַרְעֹה Gen. 42. 15, 16; חֵי אֲדֹנִי הַמֶּלֶךְ 2 Sam. 15. 21; חֵי אֱלֹהֶיךָ דָּן וְחֵי דֶּרֶךְ בְּאֵר־שָׁבַע Am. 8. 14.

3. אשר בית אל] 'Who were *at* Bethel.' The accusative of place, in answer to the question *where?* can thus be used in the case of proper names compounded with בֵּית; so exactly 2 Sam. 2. 32 אשר בית לחם; cf. Hos. 12. 5; Da. § 69[a]. In contrast we have ביריחו 'in Jericho,' *v.* 5.

הֶחֱשׁוּ] According to norm we should expect הַחֲשׁוּ. Another instance of the imperat. of a verb פ gutt. vocalized after the analogy of the perf. is found in Jer. 49. 8, 30 הֶעֱמִקוּ, הֶעְמִיקוּ; so infin. constr. הֶחֱזִיקִי Jer. 31. 31.

8. ויגלם] 'And rolled (it) up.' The verb, which only occurs here in Bibl. Heb., is found in Rabbinic Heb. with the same significance. Other occurrences of the root in Bibl. Heb. are found in Ezek. 27. 24 גְּלוֹמֵי תְּכֵלֶת '*wrappings* of blue' (so Aram. גְּלִימָא, ܓܠܝܡܐ); Ps. 139. 16 גָּלְמִי 'my *unformed substance*' (*embryo*; so New Heb. id.; Aram. גּוֹלְמָא).

9. יהי נא וג׳] 'Let there be now a share of two in thy spirit upon me!' Elisha claims the right of a firstborn son among the disciples of Elijah. פי שנים, as in Deut. 21. 17, lit. 'mouth (mouthful) of two,' is a share twice as large as that which is given to any one of the later-born sons. The explanation of Ew. 'two-thirds' is quite unwarranted[1]. In Zech. 13. 8 the expression has this meaning only through being brought into relationship with הַשְּׁלִשִׁית 'the third part.'

10. לֻקָּח] With dropping of מ preformative, for מְלֻקָּח. So אֻכָּל Ex. 3. 2; יוּלָּד Judg. 13. 8; מוֹרָט Isa. 18. 2, 7; הֻלָּלָה Ezek. 26. 17 (accent הֻלָּלָה). Ew. § 617[b]; G-K. § 52 *s*.

11. ויהי המה הלכים וג׳] Cf. I. 13. 20 *note*.

12. אבי וג׳] So *ch.* 13. 14, the words of king Joash to Elisha upon his death-bed. The expression seems to mean that Elijah, as after him Elisha, stands for Yahwe's invisible forces which should be Israel's true safeguard (cf. *ch.* 6. 16 *f.*), and to convey the apprehension lest this safeguard should be lost to the nation with the removal of the prophet. In the present case the use of the words naturally connects itself with the vision.

14. After the statement ויכה את המים in the first half-verse, Luc. inserts καὶ οὐ διῃρέθη, Vulg. *et non sunt divisae*—regarded by Hoo. as part of the original text, but more probably a gloss to explain

---

[1] Ew.'s words are (*Hist.* iv. p. 81), 'But although he had inherited Elijah's mantle, and many might esteem him equally great, yet it was always an essential feature of the representation of him that he had only received two-thirds of Elijah's spirit, and had indeed with difficulty obtained even that. In fact, in this sharp expression tradition expressed the most correct and striking judgement of his value, taken as a whole.' In contrast to this depreciatory estimate, cf. the words and action of the prophets, *v.* 15.

the repeated mention of the striking of the water which follows in clause *b*. Such a repeated reference to a single event, after an intervening clause or clauses, וַיַּכֶּה . . . וַיֹּאמַר . . . וַיַּכֶּה, may be paralleled by Gen. 27. 23b–27a וַיְבָרְכֵהוּ . . . וַיֹּאמֶר . . . וַיְבָרְכֵהוּ.

איה יהוה] LXX, Luc., Vulg. omit יהוה.

אף הוא] The accentuation connects אף הוא closely with ויכה וג׳, after the principal break in the verse, thus implying that the words mean 'and *he also* (like Elijah in *v.* 8) smote the waters, &c.' Had this meaning, however, been intended, we should certainly have read either וַיַּכֶּה אַף־הוּא (cf. Deut. 2. 11, 20; Lev. 26. 24, 28), or אַף־הוּא הִכָּה (cf. Lev. 26. 16, 41). As the text stands we must therefore (with Ke.) alter the accentuation, and, placing the principal break after הוא, render, 'Where is Yahwe, the God of Elijah, *even he?*' But this explanation is, as Th. notices, open to the objections that such an emphasis appears to be superfluous, and that אף (denoting properly *addition*) cannot be shown to have simply the force of a strengthened גַּם. While Pesh., Targ. support MT., Vulg. *etiam nunc*, Σ. καὶ νῦν, and perhaps LXX translit. ἀφφώ (cf. *ch.* 10. 10), suggest אֵפוֹא, connecting with the preceding interrogation, 'Where is Yahwe, the God of Israel, *now?*' This reading is followed by Th., Kamp., Benz., Kit., and some older commentators. It is true that אֵפוֹא, when used elsewhere with the interrog. אַיֵּה (Judg. 9. 38; Isa. 19. 12; Job 17. 15), immediately follows this particle, but cases can be cited in which the word, when used after other interrog. particles, occurs further on in the sentence; cf. Ex. 33. 16 וּבַמֶּה יִוָּדַע אֵפוֹא וג׳; Hos. 13. 10 אֱהִי מַלְכְּךָ אֵפוֹא.

If this emendation be not accepted, the only alternative seems to be to omit אף הוא with Luc., regarding the letters as an erroneous repetition of the preceding אליהו.

ויעבר אלישע] Luc. καὶ διῆλθε διὰ ξηρᾶς, as in *v.* 8.

15. Klo., followed by Kamp., Benz., Kit., omits ביריחו as an erroneous insertion after the pattern of *vv.* 3, 5. מִנֶּגֶד implies that the prophets were not *in Jericho*, but were standing near at hand as spectators of the scene—a fact which is clear from this verse and *v.* 7.

16. וישלכהו וג׳] After וישלכהו LXX adds ἐν τῷ Ἰορδάνῃ ἤ, i.e. בַּיַּרְדֵּן אוֹ 'and hath cast him *into the Jordan, or* upon one of the mountains, &c.' So Th., Klo. In view of the scene of Elijah's disappearance, the suggestion is very natural, and appropriately comes first.

הגיאות] Kt. הַגֵּיאוֹת as in Ezek. 6. 3, and in suff. form גֵּיאֹתֶיךָ Ezek. 35. 8. Q're הַגֵּאָיוֹת as in Ezek. 7. 16; 32. 5; 36. 4, 6. LXX, Luc. τῶν βουνῶν, i. e. הַגְּבָעוֹת, inferior to MT.

2. 19–25. *Elisha 'heals' the unwholesome water of Jericho* (19–22), *and vindicates his prophetic authority against the insults of children at Bethel* (23–25).

19. והארץ משכלת] 'And the land casts her young.' So Th., RV. הארץ is used of the *inhabitants* of the district, as in Lev. 19. 29; 1 Sam. 14. 29; 17. 46; 2 Sam. 15. 23; *al.* שִׁכֵּל as in Ex. 23. 26; Job 21. 10; Gen. 31. 38. Ges., Ke., Klo., Kamp., Benz., Kit. render, 'and the land causes untimely births'; but against this explanation it is to be noticed, with Th., that the misfortune is referred in *v.* 21 directly (מִשָּׁם) to the water.

21. רִפִּאתִי] Vocalized after the analogy of a verb ל״ה as in Jer. 51. 9 רִפִּאנוּ. Cf. *note* on I. 17. 14. An actual ל״ה form occurs in *v.* 22 וַיֵּרָפוּ. So נִרְפָּתָה Jer. 51. 9, and Pi'el וַיְרַפּוּ 8. 11 for וַיְרַפְּאוּ 6. 14.

ומשכלת] 'Nor any that casts her young.' It is more natural to take משכלת as a participle (as in *v.* 19) than to regard it, with Ges., Ke., Klo., Kamp., RV., as a subs. 'miscarriage.'

23. והוא עלה וג׳] On the constr. cf. I. 1. 14 *note.*

ויתקלסו בו] 'And reviled him.' The incident perhaps illustrates the unpopularity of Yahwe's true prophets in the chief centre of the calf-worship; cf. Am. 7. 10 *ff.* Luc. καὶ ἐλίθαζον αὐτόν, i. e. וַיְסַקְּלוּהוּ.

24. ותבקענה] 'And rent'; lit. '*cleft*' or '*tore open*,' as in *ch.* 8. 12; 15. 16.

3. *Jehoram, king of Israel. His campaign against Moab in alliance with the kings of Judah and Edom.*

2. מַצְּבַת] LXX, Luc. τὰς στήλας, Vulg. *statuas* understand as pl. מַצְּבֹת, and so Klo., Kamp., Benz., Kit. In the passage with reference to Jehoram (|| *vv.* 1–3) which follows in LXX, Luc. after *ch.* 1. 18 there is the addition καὶ συνέτριψεν αὐτάς, i.e. וַיְשַׁבְּרֵם. As Th. notices, the pillar (sing.) of MT. is probably intended to be brought into connexion with the statement of I. 16. 32. From the narrative of *ch.* 10. 18 *ff.* it is clear that Jehoram made no organized attempt to root out the worship of Ba'al-Melqart, such as is suggested by the reading of the pl. מַצְּבֹת, nor is such an attempt to be thought probable while Jezebel was still living and in possession of power.

3. בחטאות] Read sing. בְּחַטַּאת, in agreement with the suffix of מִמֶּנָּה following. So in *ch.* 13. 2, 6, 11; 17. 22. So Klo.

דבק] Cf. I. 11. 2 *note.*

לא סר ממנה] So, with reference to the sins of Jeroboam, *ch.* 13. 2, 6, 11; 14. 24; 15. 9, 24, 28; 17. 22: with מֵאַחֲרֵי 10. 29; with מֵעַל 10. 31; 15. 18. The phrase occurs in a favourable reference I. 15. 5; 22. 43 (מן); *ch.* 18. 6 (מאחרי).

4. נקד] 'A sheep-master,' or breeder of the kind of sheep called in Ar. نَقَد, a breed of small size and ugly appearance[1], but highly esteemed on account of its wool. Amos, before his prophetic call, was one of the נֹקְדִים at Teḳoa'.

והשיב] 'And he used to render'; frequentative. So Targ. adds an explanatory שנא בשנא 'year by year.' LXX adds the gloss ἐν τῇ ἐπαναστάσει, regarding the tribute as the *single* payment of an indemnity after the rebellion.

צמר] An accusative more closely defining the manner in which Mesha' paid the rams, viz. '*in wool*,' i.e. the fleeces of 100,000 rams. Cf. Dri. *Tenses*, § 194.

5. ויהי כמות וג׳] Cf. *ch.* 1. 1, with *note.*

---

[1] Lane (Lex. 2836) quotes the saying أَذَلُّ مِنَ النَّقَدِ 'more abject than the sheep called *naqad.*'

7. יהושפט] Luc., here and in *v.* 9 Ὀχοζίας, i. e. אֲחַזְיָהוּ, in accordance with the different system of synchronism which appears in this Version. See *Introd.* In *vv.* 11, 12 *bis*, 14, the title ὁ βασιλεὺς Ἰούδα takes the place of the proper name.

8. אי זה הדרך] Cf. I. 13. 12 *note.*

9. אשר ברגליהם] For the idiom cf. I. 20. 10.

12b. ויהושפט] Add מֶלֶךְ יְהוּדָה with LXX, Luc., Vulg., Pesh., 2 Codd.

13. מה לי ולך] Cf. I. 17. 18 *note.*

לך וג׳] Cf. I. 22. 7 *footnote.* LXX wrongly omits ואל נביאי אמך.

אל] 'Nay!' אל is thus used absolutely in deprecation, *ch.* 4. 16; Judg. 19. 23; Gen. 19. 18; Ruth 1. 13; 2 Sam. 13. 16 (following Luc. μή, ἀδελφέ, i. e. אַל אָחִי; cf. Dri. *ad loc.*).

14. אשר עמדתי לפניו] Cf. I. 17. 1 *note.*

15. והיה] As the text stands, והיה introduces the statement of a single event in the past, and cannot be explained as a perf. with ו *consec.* On the other hand, the occurrence in our narrative of the perf. with weak ו, in place of the normal וַיְהִי, is inconceivable. Thus Klo. is probably correct in conjecturing that והיה 'and it shall come to pass' is the continuation of Elisha's speech, and that all that originally followed has fallen out through the scribe's eye confusing וְהָיָה with וַיְהִי, which introduced the statement כְּנַגֵּן הַמְנַגֵּן of clause *b*. The view that an omission has taken place is favoured (apart from the difficulty of והיה) by the fact that in MT. there is no mention of the bringing of a minstrel—an almost indispensable detail which is found in Luc. after clause *a*;—καὶ ἔλαβον αὐτῷ ψάλλοντα. Klo. suggests the following restoration: '"And it shall come to pass, when the hand of Yahwe comes upon me, that I will declare unto thee that which Yahwe saith." And they brought him a minstrel; and it came to pass, &c.'; i. e. וְהָיָה בִּהְיוֹת עָלַי יַד י׳ וְהִגַּדְתִּי אֵלֶיךָ אֶת־אֲשֶׁר יְדַבֵּר י׳ וַיִּקְחוּ־לוֹ מְנַגֵּן וַיְהִי וג׳.

16. עשה וג׳] 'I will make this torrent-bed nothing but cisterns!' Every depression, deep or shallow, in the dry bed of the *Wady* is to suddenly become a receptacle for water. The infin. absol. עָשֹׂה takes the place of the finite verb (הִנְנִי עֹשֶׂה) in the sudden

rush of the oracle upon the prophet, 'when the speaker is too full of his subject to mention the action in any other than an ejaculatory manner, and as briefly as possible' (Ew. § 328[a]). So exactly, in another oracle by Elisha, *ch.* 4. 43 'Thus saith Yahwe, Eating and leaving over!' i. e. '*There shall be* eating &c.,' or '*Ye shall* eat &c.'; cf. I. 22. 30 *note*. This explanation of the infin. abs. עָשֹׂה is implied by Pesh. ܢܬܥܒܕ ܢܚܠܐ ܗܢܐ, Targ. יתעבד נחלא הדין 'This torrent bed *shall be made* &c.'; so Ew. § 328[c] *end; Hist.* iv. p. 88.

On the other hand, LXX, Luc. Ποιήσατε, Vulg. *Facite* regard עָשֹׂה as equivalent to an *imperative*: 'Make this torrent-bed full of cisterns!' So RV., and most moderns. This explanation is, however, less in accord with *v.* 17[a], which seems to preclude the necessity of human intervention; and is also opposed by *vv.* 22, 23, where the phenomenon described must have been produced by the sun shining upon *natural* and so irregular and wide-spreading *pools of water*, and not upon *artificial* and so (presumably) symmetrically shaped *trenches*. For the repetition גבים גבים cf. Gen. 14. 10; G-K. § 123 *e;* Ew. 313[a].

17. ומקניכם] Luc. καὶ αἱ παρεμβολαὶ ὑμῶν, i. e. וּמַחֲנֵיכֶם, is certainly correct; cf. *v.* 9[b]. So Klo., Kamp., Benz., Kit.

18. ונקל ... ונתן] 'And this shall be a light thing, &c., and he shall give &c.,' i. e. 'And this being a light thing, &c., he shall (further) give &c.' Cf. Isa. 49. 6.

19. וכל עיר מבחור] LXX, Luc. omit, and the words are regarded by Klo., Kamp., Benz., Kit. as a variant of the preceding כל עיר מבצר.

תכאבו] LXX ἀχρειώσετε, and so RV. '*ye shall mar.*' כאב, however, has always elsewhere the meaning *to be in pain*, Hiph'il *to pain*, and the use of the verb in this passage is unparalleled. Klo. emends תְּאַבְּדוּ 'ye shall destroy.'

20. כעלות המנחה] Cf. I. 18. 29 *note*.

21. וכל מואב שמעו] 'Now all Moab *had heard*.' So *v.* 22 והשמש זרחה 'and the sun *had risen*.' For the order, expressing the pluperfect, cf. *note* of I. 14. 5.

23. החרב נחרבו המלכים] Render, with RV. marg., 'The kings have surely fought together.' So Verss. הָחֳרֵב infin. abs. Pu'al

should probably be vocalized as Niph'al הֶחָרֵב. The verb חרב *slay*, occurs again in Qal, Jer. 50. 21, 27†, and is frequent in Syr. (in Pesh. generally as a rendering of הִכָּה; so e.g. *v.* 24 *bis*). Ar. حرب III. Klo. regards Targ. איתגראה איתגריאו and Luc. ἐρίσαντες γὰρ ἤρισαν (cf. *ch.* 14. 10) as presupposing an original הִתְגָּרֹה הִתְגָּרוּ; but this emendation, though adopted by Kamp., Benz., is scarcely necessary.

24. ויבו בה והכות] In place of the impossible MT., LXX, Luc. read καὶ εἰσῆλθον εἰσπορευόμενοι καὶ τύπτοντες, i.e. וַיָּבֹאוּ בֹא וְהַכּוֹת 'and they went forward smiting Moab as they went,' an emendation certainly to be adopted with Th., Klo., Kamp., Benz., Kit. הַכּוֹת appears to be a rare case of the infin. absol. with the termination ת as in the infin. constr.; so שָׁתוֹת Isa. 22. 13; אָלוֹת Hos. 10. 4; עָרוֹת Hab. 3. 13; and perhaps נִגְלוֹת 2 Sam. 6. 20. Cf. Kö. *Lehrg.* I. i. p. 536. Cases of the infin. constr. used *in place of* the infin. absol. are quoted by Da. § 86, *Rem.* 3.

25. יהרסו] 'They kept on overthrowing,' i. e. one after another. The imperfects are frequentative; cf. Dri. *Tenses*, § 113 β: 'a graphic picture of the way in which the people occupied themselves during their sojourn in Moab.'

עד השאיר וג׳] RV. 'until in Ḳir-ḥareseth (only) they left the stones thereof.' Had this meaning, however, been intended, the indispensable *only* (רַק) must have preceded בקיר חרשת, and the statement would naturally have followed immediately after the first clause of the verse, והערים יהרסו, to which it must be referred. LXX, Vulg., Pesh. presuppose the same text as MT., while in Luc., Targ. the addition of a negative before השאיר 'until there was not left, &c.,' is clearly an attempt at emendation, and limits to *one* city the thorough demolition which the context suggests to have been carried out in the case of *all*. Luc., however, has an additional statement preceding עד השאיר וג׳, viz. καὶ ἐξέσεισαν τὸν Μωάβ, i. e. probably, as Klo. suggests, וַיָּנִידוּ אֶת־מוֹאָב[1]. This seems

[1] The Hithpa'el of נוד, והתנודדה, is rendered by LXX σεισθήσεται in Isa. 24. 20. For the use of וַיָּנִידוּ in our passage, cf. Qal *wander about* or *flee away*, Gen. 4. 12, 14; Jer. 49. 30; 50. 3, 8; Hiph'il *drive about* or *scare*, *ch.* 21. 8; Ps. 36. 12.

to make plain the reference of עד השאיר. That which was left in Ḳir-ḥareseth after the ruthless expulsion of the Moabites from their territory, which is expressed by the strong term ἐξέσεισαν, was not the *stones* of the city, but, as is clear from *vv.* 26 *f.*, *the king of Moab and his immediate followers.* We may thus restore: וַיְנִידוּ אֶת־מוֹאָב עַד־הִשְׁאִיר בָּנֶיהָ בַּקִּיר חֲרֶשֶׂת וגו׳ 'and they harried Moab until *her sons* were left in Ḳir-ḥareseth, and the slingers encompassed and smote it.'

עַד־הִשְׁאִיר] הִשְׁאִיר, as in *ch.* 10. 11; Num. 21. 35; Deut. 3. 3; Josh. 8. 22; 10. 33; 11. 8 after עַד־בִּלְתִּי, and in Deut. 28. 55 after מִבְּלִי, may be regarded either as an impersonal perfect (understand subj. הַמַּשְׁאִיר; cf. *note* on יָלְדָה I. 1. 6), or as an infin. constr. vocalized with *Ḥireq* in place of *Pathaḥ*. Elsewhere in Kgs. we find עַד־הִכְרִית I. 11. 16; עַד־הִשְׁמִדוֹ I. 15. 29; *ch.* 10. 17. In this latter case the suffix indicates that the Massoretes recognized an infin. constr. form with *Ḥireq* under the preformative ה; and this is substantiated by the occurrence elsewhere of such forms as עַד־הִשְׁמִדְךָ Deut. 7. 24; 28. 48; Josh. 11. 14; אַחֲרֵי הִקְצוֹת Lev. 14. 43. Dri. (*Deut.* pp. 48, 105) rejects the hypothesis of Kö. (*Lehrg.* I. i. p. 212) that such a form can have *really* existed after the analogy of the perfect, and thinks it probable that the punctuation does not represent an original and true tradition, and that הַ— should therefore be throughout restored for הִ—.

קיר חרשת] The stronghold of Moab, mentioned again under the same name, Isa. 16. 7, and called קִיר חֶרֶשׂ 16. 11; Jer. 48. 31, 36; קִיר מוֹאָב Isa. 15. 1. Targ. in Isa. and Jer. renders by כרך, כרכא, i. e. the modern *El-Kerak* ('the fortress'), which gives its name to the surrounding district south-east of the Dead Sea. Cf. Rob. *BR.* ii. 166.

27. אשר ימלך] 'Who *was to* reign.' Cf. Dri. *Tenses*, § 39 β.

ויהי קצף גדול וג׳] 'And there came great wrath against Israel.' The 'great wrath' is that of Chemosh the Moabite deity, whom the writer supposes to have been induced by means of the costly offering to succour his worshipper and repulse the foe. Cf. Sta. *Ges.* i. p. 430; Wellh. *Prolegomena*, p. 23 *note;* Montefiore, *Hibbert*

Lectures, p. 35. Cf. the inscription of the Moabite stone, *ll.* 5 *ff.*, where Mesha' traces the affliction of Moab at the hand of Israel to the fact that 'Chemosh was angry with his land,' while so soon as the god overcomes his inertia the fortunes of his country change, and Moab is successful against Israel (*Append.* 1).

לארץ] Luc., Vulg., Pesh. presuppose לְאַרְצָם, correctly. So Klo., Kamp., Benz., Kit., Oort.

4. 1–7. *Elisha makes miraculous provision for the wife of one of the sons of the prophets.*

1. עבדך וג׳] Targ. expands the verse for the purpose of identifying the woman's husband with Obadiah of I. 18. 3 *ff.*, the ground of connexion probably being the resemblance of the statement ועבדך היה ירא את י׳ to I. 18. 3b, 12b.

2. לכי] On the form of suff. 2 fem. sing. here and in *vv.* 3, 7, cf. p. 208.

כי אם אסוך שמן] The ἅπαξ λεγ. אָסוּךְ is rendered by Pesh. ܡܫܚܘܬܐ, Targ. מנא, and so RV. 'pot.' Th.'s explanation, '*unctio*, i.e. *quantum ad unctionem sufficit*,' is more probably correct, as אָסוּךְ may thus, in accordance with its vocalization, be regarded as *stat. absol.* in apposition to שמן, 'an anointing measure—oil,' i.e. 'enough oil for an anointing.' Cf. Dri. *Tenses*, § 194.

LXX ἀλλ' ἢ ὃ ἀλείψομαι ἔλαιον, and probably Vulg. *parum olei, quo ungar*, regard אָסוּךְ as 1st sing. imperf. Qal of סוך, as though the sentence could be equivalent to כִּי־אִם הַשֶּׁמֶן אֲשֶׁר אָסוּךְ (בּוֹ). Luc. ἀλλ' ἢ ἀγγεῖον ἐλαίου . . . ὃ ἀλείψομαι exhibits a double rendering.

4. ויצקת על] 'And shalt pour *into*.' For this use of על (lit. *upon*, from above) cf. Nah. 3. 12 ונפלו על פי אוכל 'shall fall *into* the mouth of the eater.'

After *v.* 4a Luc. adds καὶ αὐτὸ οὐκ ἀποστήσεται, i.e. 'and it (the oil) shall not stay.' Cf. *v.* 6b ויעמד השמן 'and the oil stayed,' only when the vessels were exhausted.

תסיעי] So, of removing heavy objects, I. 5. 31; Eccles. 10. 9 (stones).

5. ותלך מאתו] Luc. adds καὶ ἐποίησεν οὕτως, i. e. וַתַּעַשׂ כֵּן, adopted by Klo., Kamp., Benz.

הם מגישים וג׳] On the constr. cf. I. 1. 14 *note*.

מיצקת] Kt. should probably be vocalized מֵיצֶקֶת Hiph'il, there being no occurrence of a Pi'el מְיַצֶּקֶת.

6. אל בנה] LXX, Luc. pl. πρὸς τοὺς υἱοὺς αὐτῆς, Ἐγγίσατε κ.τ.λ., probably a correction after *v.* 5.

7. ואת בניכי תחיי] All Verss. supply the needful copula before בניכי. Instances of the verb, when *following* a compound subj., agreeing with the principal member of the subj. are collected by Ew. § 340[c]. Cf. e. g. Ex. 21. 4[b]. As Klo. notices, the consonants of MT. can be vocalized וְאֶת־בָּנַיִכִי תְּחַיִּי 'and do thou keep thy sons alive &c.'

4. 8–37. *Elisha restores to life the son of the Shunammite woman.*

8. ויהי היום וג׳] 'And there came a day when Elisha passed over &c.' Lit. 'and *the* day was,' *day* being defined on account of the events which happened upon it, according to the idiom noticed, I. 13. 14 *note*. The phrase occurs elsewhere, *vv*. 11, 18; 1 Sam. 1. 4; 14. 1; Job 1. 6, 13; 2. 1.

The other explanation, which regards היום as used *adverbially*, 'and it came to pass, *on a day*, that &c.,' is less probably correct. Cf. Dri. on 1 Sam. 1. 4.

שונם] Cf. I. 1. 3 *note*.

מדי עברו] For the idiom cf. I. 14. 28 *note*.

13. מה לעשות לך] 'What (is one) to do for thee?' and so, 'What is to be done for thee?' The idiom occurs again Isa. 5. 4; 2 Chr. 25. 9; Est. 1. 15; 6. 6.

היש לדבר וג׳] Cf. Dri. *Tenses*, § 202 (1).

ותאמר וג׳] An assertion of independence. She has no need of patronage, being 'a great woman' (*v*. 8) within her own clan.

14. אבל] Cf. I. 1. 43 *note*.

15. ויאמר קרא לה] LXX omits.

16. למועד וג׳] 'At this season, next spring.' כעת חיה means

lit. 'about the time (when it is) reviving.' The phrase occurs again Gen. 18. 10, 14 (J), in the latter verse in conjunction with לַמּוֹעֵד. Cf. Gen. 17. 21 (P) לַמּוֹעֵד הַזֶּה בַּשָּׁנָה הָאַחֶרֶת 'at this time, *next year*.'

אתי] Cf. p. 208.

17. אשר] Read כַּאֲשֶׁר with LXX, Luc. ὡς, Pesh. ܐܝܟ ܕ, So Klo., Kamp., Benz., Kit.

19. שאהו] Vulg. *Tolle, et duc eum*, Pesh. ܫܩܘܠܝܗܝ ܘܐܘܒܠܝܗܝ, Targ. סבהי ואובלהי seem to presuppose the addition וַהֲבִיאֵהוּ. Cf. *v.* 20[a].

20. וישב] LXX καὶ ἐκοιμήθη, i.e. וַיִּשְׁכַּב.

23. אתי הלכתי] Cf. p. 208.

לא חדש ולא שבת] 'Not a new moon nor a Sabbath,' i.e. not a festive day. Cf. Am. 8. 5 and 1 Sam. 20. 5 with Dri.'s *note*. The universality of the festival of the new moon is illustrated by Dillmann on Lev. 23 (p. 578).

25. ותלך ותבוא] LXX δεῦρο καὶ πορεύσῃ καὶ ἐλεύσῃ, inferior to MT. Luc. exhibits a combination of the two readings.

הלז] Identical in form with Ar. *relative* أَلَّذْ, just as the fuller form הַלָּזֶה answers to Ar. اَلَّذِى. הַלָּז is equivalent to הַזֶּה or הַזּאת, with the additional demonstrative element *la*. The form is used only here with a fem. subs., but occurs elsewhere with a masc. subs. *ch.* 23. 17; Judg. 6. 20; 1 Sam. 14. 1; 17. 26; Zech. 2. 8. It should doubtless be restored with LXX הָאַרְגָּב הַלָּז in 1 Sam. 20. 19 (cf. Dri. *ad loc.*). Without a subs. Dan. 8. 16.

26. After *v.* 26[a] Luc. adds καὶ ἔδραμεν εἰς ἀπάντησιν αὐτῆς καὶ εἶπεν Εἰρήνη σοι· εἰρήνη τῷ ἀνδρί σου· εἰρήνη τῷ παιδαρίῳ.

27. ויגש וג'] Klo. compares the action of our Lord's disciples, S. Matt. 19. 13, 14.

ממני] LXX after ἀπ' ἐμοῦ makes the worthless addition καὶ σοῦ.

28. תשלה] 'Deceive' (lit. 'mislead'). שלה is frequent in Aram. in the sense 'go astray' or 'act in error,' occurring in Targ. as the equivalent of Heb. שָׁגַג or שָׁגָה. Cf. Aph'el,

Ps. 119. 10 לא תשגני מפקודיך 'Cause me not to go astray from thy commandments.' The only other occurrence of the verb in Bib. Heb. is late, 2 Chr. 29. 11, and in our passage so marked an Aramaism must be regarded as dialectical (cf. pp. 208 *f.* and *note* on *ch.* 6. 11). In 2 Sam. 6. 7 a subs. שַׁל occurs, which has been explained as equivalent to Aram. שָׁלוּ 'error,' but here the text is probably at fault. Cf. Dri. *ad loc.*

29. כי תמצא וג׳] Cf. S. Luke 10. 4.

30. וחי נפשך] Cf. *ch.* 2. 2 *note.*

34. ויגהר עליו] 'And crouched upon him.' So *v.* 35; cf. I. 18. 42 †. The verb appears to describe the drawing up of the prophet's limbs that they might coincide with the short limbs of the child. Cf. I. 17. 21[a].

35. אחת הנה וג׳] 'Backwards and forwards'; lit. 'once here and once there.' For אַחַת fem. 'once' (for פַּעַם אַחַת Josh. 6. 3, 11, 14) cf. *ch.* 6. 10; Ps. 89. 36; *al.*

ויזורר] A ἅπαξ λεγ., rendered 'sneezed,' in accordance with Targ. Job 41. 10, where זרירוי represents Heb. עטישתיו 'his sneezings.' So apparently Targ. in our passage ואיתמקק (cf. Job 41. 10 *Edit. Regia* מקקוי). Vulg. *et oscitavit*, Pesh. ܘܐܬܦܩܣ give the meaning 'yawned.' LXX omits ויזורר together with the letters יו of the preceding עליו, thus reading וַיִּגְהַר עַל־הַיֶּלֶד עַד־שֶׁבַע פְּעָמִים καὶ συνέκαμψεν ἐπὶ τὸ παιδάριον ἕως ἑπτάκις. Thus Grä. is probably correct in regarding ויזורר as having arisen through dittography from ויגהר.

In the text of Luc. καὶ ἠνδρίσατο ἐπὶ τὸ παιδάριον seems to represent a marginal variant for LXX rendering of ויגהר על הילד, while καὶ ἐνέπνευσεν ἐπ' αὐτόν[1] . . . καὶ διεκινήθη τὸ παιδάριον is a second marginal reading answering to MT. ויגהר . . . הנער.

37. ותפל על רגליו] So exactly 1 Sam. 25. 24. In Est. 8. 3 the phrase is לִפְנֵי רַגְלָיו.

---

[1] Cf. the conjectural rendering of LXX, Luc. for ויתמדד in I. 17. 21 καὶ ἐνεφύσησεν. καὶ ἐνεφύσησεν εἰς (ἐπ') αὐτόν occurs also as a various rendering of ויגהר עליו in *v.* 34. Cf. Field.

4. 38–44. *Elisha makes wholesome a pot of poisoned broth* (38–41), *and miraculously increases a small supply of provisions* (42–44).

38. הגלגלה] Cf. *ch.* 2. 1 *note.*

הגדולה] LXX omits.

39. ארת] Probably 'herbs'; Vulg. *herbas agrestes*, Targ. ירקונין. So several authorities in Isa. 26. 19. There is a root ארה='pluck' which occurs Song 5. 1; Ps. 80. 13, and as Th. and Klo. notice, the translit. ἀριώθ of LXX, Luc. suggests the form אֲרִיּוֹת which might be derived from this root.

ידעו] Luc., Vulg., Pesh. sing. יָדַע, probably correctly.

41. וקחו] '*Then* take.' Cf. Ps. 4. 4.

וישלך] LXX, Luc., Pesh., Targ. וְהַשְׁלִיכוּ 'and cast.'

ויאמר] LXX, Luc. καὶ εἶπεν 'Ε. πρὸς Γιεζεὶ (LXX τὸ παιδάριον).

After ולא היה we should perhaps add עוֹד, with LXX, Luc. ἔτι (LXX doublet ἐκεῖ), Vulg. *amplius*.

42. בעל שלשה] LXX Βαιθσαρεῖσα, Luc. Βηθσαλισά, i.e. בֵּית־שָׁלִישָׁה, according to Eusebius (Βαιθσαρισάθ) fifteen Roman miles north of Diospolis (Lydda). The modern ruin *Kafr Tilt* (ثلث = שׁלשׁ) seems to correspond with this situation. Cf. Buhl, p. 214.

כרמל] Probably 'garden-fruit.' So Lev. 2. 14; 23. 14, in each case in the enumeration of firstfruits. כרמל generally means 'garden-land.' RV. 'fresh ears of corn' follows Vulg. *frumentum novum*, Pesh. ܦܪ̈ܟܐ, Targ. פירוכין.

בצקלנו] The word is a ἅπαξ λεγ. RV. 'in his *sack*' agrees with Vulg. *in pera sua* in giving a meaning demanded by the context. Pesh. ܒܡܪܘܛܗ, Targ. בלבשיה interpret 'garment.' LXX, Luc. omit, but Cod. A transliterates βακελλέθ, and hence Lagarde (*Armen. Stud.* § 333) infers that, in place of בצקלנו, we should read בקלעת, קְלַעַת = קְלָעָה being explained by Ar. قَلَعَة *sack*, used for provisions, &c. Halévy, however (*Revue des Études Juives*, xi. 68), takes βακελλέθ to have been a marginal note transcribing the Aram. term (די לה) בקילת 'in his basket':—'קולתא is a very frequent word in the Rabbinic literature; its Arabic equivalent קֻלָּה is still at the present day very popular in the sense of *jar*, a large measure of capacity, which probably takes its origin from the Greek κόλαθος.'

43. אכול והותר] Cf. *ch.* 3. 16; I. 22. 30 *notes*.

44. ויתן לפניהם] LXX, Luc. omit.

5. *Elisha heals Na'aman, the Aramaean, of his leprosy.*

It is an open question who is the nameless king of Israel to whom reference is made in *vv.* 5–8; and the same difficulty arises in connexion with the sections 6. 8–23; 6. 24—7. 20; 8. 1–6. Probably R^D, to judge by the position in which he has incorporated the narratives in Kings, assumed that the king in question was in every case Jehoram; but, since Elisha's death did not take place until the reign of Joash (*ch.* 13. 14 *ff.*), we have, after the reign of Jehoram, a period of 28 (Jehu) + 17 (Jehoaḥaz) + *x* (Joash) years during which he may be supposed to have been active.

There is not, however, any evidence sufficient to determine the question. Kue. (§ 25. 12) cites the expression בן המרצח in 6. 32 as an indication that the king thus characterized by Elisha is not Jehoram but Jehoaḥaz, the 'murderer' being Jehu, the father of the latter (cf. *chh.* 9, 10; Hos. 1. 4); but it is scarcely possible that Elisha would so stigmatize Jehu on account of a course of action of which he was himself the instigator (*ch.* 9. 1 *ff.*). Supposing בן המרצח to contain literally a reference to *the father* of the king in question, the reference is more naturally to Aḥab (cf. the use of רצח in I. 21. 19); but, as a matter of fact, the title explains itself as called forth by the hostile menace of *the king himself* against Elisha (6. 31; cf. *note* on בן המרצח 6. 32).

Thus, failing direct evidence, all that can be said is that in the single case of the narrative 6. 1–23 the friendly terms upon which Elisha stands to the king (cf. *vv.* 9, 21 *f.*) create a slight *presumption* against identification with Jehoram, to whom, in 3. 13, 14, he openly expresses his hostility, and in favour of some member of the dynasty which the prophet had been instrumental in placing upon the throne of Israel.

Upon the time-relationship of 5. 1–27 to 6. 24—7. 20; 8. 1–6, cf. *note* on 6. 25.

1. נשא פנים] So Isa. 3. 3; 9. 14; Job 22. 8.

והאיש וג׳] Luc. simply καὶ ὁ ἄνθρωπος ἦν λεπρός, omitting גבור חיל, which is probably to be regarded, with Benz., as a marginal gloss upon the preceding איש גדול.

2. יצאו גדודים] 'Had gone forth in (lit. *as*) marauding bands.' Cf. Dri. *Tenses*, § 161 (3).

3. אַחֲלֵי 'Would that!' Only again Ps. 119. 5, with vocalization אַחֲלַי. In our passage the punctuators seem to have regarded the word as a subs. plur. constr., and this view is taken by Pesh. ܛܘܒܘܗܝ ܠܡܪܝ ܐܠܘ ܐܙܠ ܠܘܬ ܢܒܝܐ, Targ. טובי ריבוני אם ייזיל קדם נבייא 'Oh, the benefits of my lord if he would go to the prophet!' Cf. the vocalization אַשְׁרֵי.

לפני הנביא] LXX ἐνώπιον τοῦ προφήτου τοῦ θεοῦ.

After *v.* 3[b] Luc. adds καὶ δεηθείη τοῦ προσώπου αὐτοῦ, i.e. וְחִלָּה אֶת־פָּנָיו. Cf. I. 13. 6 *note*.

4. ויבא וג׳] 'And he went in, &c.' The subject, as Vulg. rightly divines, is Na'aman (RV. marg.), and not some one unnamed, 'and one went in' (RV. text, Pesh.). LXX, Luc., Targ., against gender, take Na'aman's wife as subject: 'And she went in and told her lord,' and this necessitates in Luc. the addition καὶ ἀνήγγειλε τῷ βασιλεῖ, which is duplicated at the commencement of *v.* 5 in the form καὶ ἀνηγγέλη τῷ βασιλεῖ.

כזאת וכזאת] *Ch.* 9. 12; Josh. 7. 20 (JE); 2 Sam. 17. 15 (twice)†. Cf. כָּזֹה וְכָזֶה I. 14. 5 *note*.

6. ויבא . . . לאמר] On the constr. cf. *note* on I. 16. 16.

ועתה] 'And now.' The main point of the letter, to which that which precedes leads up, is all that is quoted. Cf. *note* on I. 1. 20.

7. זה] Cf. I. 22. 27 *note*.

דעו נא וג׳] Cf. I. 20. 7.

מתאנה] 'Seeks occasion against.' So Verss. Lit. 'causes himself to meet.'

8. אלישע איש האלהים] LXX omits איש האלהים, while Luc. omits אלישע.

10. וטהר] On the idiomatic use of the imperative with ו cf. *note* on I. 1. 12.

11. ועמד] LXX, Luc. omit.

והניף וג׳] Luc. καὶ ἐπιθήσει τὴν χεῖρα αὐτοῦ ἐπὶ τὸν λεπρὸν καὶ ἀποσυνάξει αὐτὸ ἀπὸ τῆς σαρκός μου.

אל המקום] אל in place of על; cf. I. 13. 29 *note*.

12. אבנה] Read אֲמָנָה with Q're, Pesh., Targ., i.e. probably 'the constant' (perennial) river. Cf. the use of the verb אמן in Isa. 33. 16.

The Amana is identified with the modern *Nahr Baradâ*, called by the Greeks Chrysorroas, which flows down from the gorges of the Anti-Libanus (cf. Song 4. 8); the Parpar is probably the *Nahr el-A'waj*, the only other important stream in the district. Cf. Rob. *B. R.* iii. 447; Baed. 183, 345.

13. אבי] Probably to be regarded, with Th., Kamp., Benz., Kit., Oort, as a corruption of אִם, which is scarcely to be dispensed with. Klo. emends הֲלֹא כִּי. LXX omits.

דבר גדול וג׳] The order—*object, subject, verb*—is very rare. Cf. *ch.* 6. 22; Dri. *Tenses*, 208 (2).

16. אשר עמדתי לפניו] Cf. I. 17. 1 *note*.

17. ולא] 'And (if) not.' So 2 Sam. 13. 26. וַיֵּשׁ *ch.* 10. 15; cf. Judg. 6. 13.

יתן נא וג׳] The request is made upon the view that Yahwe, the national God of Israel, can only be worshipped aright upon the soil of Israel's land. Cf. the writer's *Outlines of O. T. Theology*, p. 35.

18. לדבר] LXX, Luc., Pesh. presuppose וְלַדָּבָר '*But* in this matter &c.,' correctly. So Th., Klo., Kamp., Benz.

רמן] The Assyrian *Rammânu*, 'the Thunderer,' the storm- or weather-god, apparently identical with הֲדַד; cf. I. 15. 18 *note;* Schrader, *COT.* i. p. 196; Baethgen, *Semit. Relig.* p. 75.

בהשתחויתי] On the form cf. p. 208. LXX, Luc. ἐν τῷ προσκυνεῖν αὐτόν, Vulg. *adorante eo*, i. e. בְּהִשְׁתַּחֲוֹתוֹ (בְּהִשְׁתַּחֲוָיָתוֹ), ought probably to be followed, with Th., Klo., Kamp., Benz., Kit.

19. כברת ארץ] RV. 'a little way'; *marg.* 'some way.' The expression occurs again Gen. 35. 16; 48. 7†; RV. 'some way.'

The distance denoted by כִּבְרָה (or כִּבְרַת) is quite indeterminate. Pesh. in all passages ܦܪܣܐ 'a parasang'; LXX, Luc. as one rendering in Gen. 48. 7 ἱππόδρομος, an expression perhaps equivalent to the Ar. شَوْطُ ٱلْفَرَسِ, i. e. as far as a horse can gallop; Targ. כרוב, explained as a piece of land of about an acre's extent (Aram. כרב, ܟܪܒ, Ar. كرب = 'to plough'), a rendering apparently obtained by transposition of ב and ר. In Assyrian, *kibrâtu* denotes a *region* of the earth or heaven; cf. e. g. *šàr kibrat arba'-i*, 'king of the four regions' (quarters of the earth); Delitzsch, *Assyr. Handwörterbuch*, 315. כברת also occurs in a Phoenician inscription from Ma'ṣûb, apparently with the same significance as in Assyr., in the expression כברת מצא שמש 'region of the sunrise'; cf. Halévy, *Revue des Études Juives*, xii (1886), p. 109; Lidzbarski, *Nordsemit. Epigraphik*, p. 419. E. Hoffmann, however (*Abhandlungen der Göttinger Gesellschaft der Wissenschaften*, xxxvi (1890), pp. 24 *f.*), explains the word in Phoen. and Heb. as meaning the tract of country which lies between the eye and the horizon; as much as one can see, rather than the direction in which one sees (' Sehweite, nicht Sehrichtung ').

20. כי אם רצתי] '*I will surely run.*' רצתי is a perfect of certitude; cf. Jer. 51. 14 נִשְׁבַּע י׳ צְבָאוֹת בְּנַפְשׁוֹ כִּי אִם־מִלֵּאתִיךְ אָדָם וגו׳ 'Yahwe Ṣebhā'oth hath sworn by himself, *Surely I will fill thee* with men, &c.'; Judg. 15. 7 אִם־תַּעֲשׂוּן כָּזֹאת כִּי אִם־נִקַּמְתִּי בָכֶם 'If ye act thus, *I will surely be avenged* of you.' The particles כי אם are connected closely together with a strong asseverative force, as is clear from the two passages above cited, and also from 1 Sam. 26. 10; 2 Sam. 15. 21 Kt. (in both cases after the oath חי י׳); Ruth 3. 12 Kt. (after כִּי אָמְנָם); 1 Sam. 21. 6. Cf. Dri. *Tenses*, § 139, *note* 1; Ew. § 356[b]; Kö. *Syntax*, § 391 *r*. The view which takes כי separately, as introducing the terms of the oath (cf. *note* on I. 2. 23), overlooks the fact that אם following could only, in such a case, introduce a *negation*, and not an assertion (אם לא).

21. ויפל מעל המרכבה] 'And he *lighted down from* the chariot. Cf. Gen. 24. 64 וַתִּפֹּל מֵעַל הַגָּמָל.

השלום] 'Is (all) well?' Vulg. *Recte ne sunt omnia?* or, understanding באך, as in I. 2. 13, 'Is *it* well?' i.e. 'Does *thy coming* portend no evil tidings?' Cf. *ch.* 9. 11, 17, 22, 31.

22. עתה זה] On זה cf. I. 14. 6 *note* on למה זה.

23. הואל וג׳] '*Consent*, take two talents,' or, as we should say, 'Consent to take &c.' Cf. *ch.* 6. 3 הוֹאֶל נָא וְלֵךְ; Judg. 19. 6 הוֹאֶל־נָא וְלִין; 2 Sam. 7. 29. When the verb is used of an action undertaken at one's own instance, and not at the suggestion of another, '*Resolve*' is a suitable rendering: cf. Gen. 18. 27, 31; Deut. 1. 5.

ויפרץ בו] 'And he urged him.' פרץ is used in the same sense in 1 Sam. 28. 23; 13. 25, 27, but the ordinary significance of this verb is *to break out* or *spread abroad*, and it is probable that we ought, with most critics, to substitute the verb פצר which occurs commonly with the meaning *urge* or *press upon*:—*v.* 16; *ch.* 2. 17; Gen. 19. 3, 9; 33. 11; Judg. 19. 7†.

חרטים] 'Bags.' The word only occurs again in Heb. Isa. 3. 22, where it is mentioned as an article of feminine adornment. In Ar. خَرِيطَةٌ denotes a bag or pouch made of leather, rag, or other material.

24. העפל] Probably '*the citadel*.' The universal explanation, however, among modern interpreters, seems to be 'the hill' or 'mound.' The verb עפל means *to swell*, and occurs twice in Heb., once in Pu'al עֻפְּלָה 'is puffed up,' Hab. 2. 4, and once in Hiph'il וַיַּעְפִּילוּ 'and acted arrogantly' (internal Hiph'il). The subs. עֹפֶל is used to denote a *swelling*, i.e. *tumour*, 1 Sam. 5. 6; *al.* (so in Ar.). When used in a topographical sense, the inference is generally drawn that עֹפֶל denotes a natural swelling of the earth's surface, i.e. conceivably, a low conical hill. But the connexion in which the term appears points with much greater probability to an artificial 'swelling,' i.e. a *bulging*, or *rounded keep*, or *enceinte*.

An עֹפֶל is mentioned as existing in three different localities:—(i) at Jerusalem; (ii) presumably at Samaria (here only); (iii) in the territory of Mesha', king of Moab (Moabite stone, *ll.* 21 *f.*). In each case reference is made to הָעֹפֶל *the 'ophel*, well known as such, and so on a *prima facie* view *not* a hill marked out merely by its unimportant physical characteristics[1]. Accordingly, the *'ophel* at Jerusalem is a fortified place with walls, 2 Chr. 27. 3; Neh. 3. 27; is mentioned in close connexion with המגדל הגדול היוצא 'the great projecting tower,' Neh. 3. 27; and *in parallelism with* מגדל עדר 'tower of the flock,' Mic. 4. 8. In the same way Mesha' says ואנך בנתי . . . חמת העפל ואנך בנתי שעריה ואנך בנתי מגדלתה 'And I built the wall of the *'ophel*, and I built its gates, and I built its towers.'

25. ויעמד אל אדניו] 'And stood *by* his lord.' Cf. *ch.* 11. 14 וְהַשָּׂרִים וְהַחֲצֹצְרוֹת אֶל־הַמֶּלֶךְ.

מאן] Kt. אָן occurs again 1 Sam. 10. 14 and 27. 10 according to Pesh., Targ. (in place of אל), and in the expression עַד־אָן Job 8. 2.

26. לא לבי הלך] LXX, Luc. add μετὰ σοῦ, i.e. עִמָּךְ. The meaning of the expression is, 'Was not I present in spirit?' Ew.'s explanation, which makes לִבִּי an affectionate designation of Gehazi, is strangely forced.

העת וג'] 'Was it a time to take silver, &c.?' The miracle had served to emphasize before a representative of the rival nation the unique power of Israel's God (cf. *vv.* 15, 18), and the dignity of His prophet (cf. *vv.* 8^b, 10, 16); Gehazi's rapacity, representing itself as directed by Elisha, must have tended to weaken the impression. Klo., Kamp., Benz., Kit., Oort follow LXX καὶ νῦν ἔλαβες τὸ ἀργύριον, καὶ νῦν ἔλαβες τὰ ἱμάτια, κ.τ.λ., Luc. καὶ νῦν ἔλαβες τὸ ἀργύριον καὶ τὰ ἱμάτια καὶ λήψει ἐν αὐτῷ, κ.τ.λ.[2], Vulg. *nunc igitur accepisti argentum, et accepisti, &c.*, and read וְעַתָּה לָקַחְתָּ אֶת־הַכֶּסֶף וְלָקַחְתָּ בְגָדִים וג' 'And now thou hast taken the silver, and wilt take

---

[1] The kind of hill which עפל might be expected to describe, upon the supposition that the term was so used, would scarcely be outstanding and conspicuous, but rather with a low and rounded top, the less likely to attract attention as העפל if covered, wholly or partly, by buildings. And, again upon such a supposition, it is somewhat strange that the term is not more frequently employed, and that of hills not in towns but in the open country.

[2] The position of καὶ τὰ ἱμάτια has clearly been ignorantly altered in Luc. in order to agree with *vv.* 22, 23.

garments, &c.'; וְלָקַחְתָּ being a perfect with ו *consec.*, describing the use to which Geḥazi was already planning to put the money[1]. This emendation, though yielding a good sequence, is scarcely superior to MT.

6. 1–7. *Elisha causes iron to float.*

2. איש] LXX, Luc. ἀνὴρ εἷς, owing to the influence of the following קורה אחת. So Pesh. ܟܡܐ ܚܕܐ ܫܩܝܠ.

3. האחד] '*The* one' who, as a matter of fact, *did* so speak, but according to Eng. idiom simply '*one*.' Cf. *note* on I. 13. 14 with the instance 1 Sam. 9. 9 there quoted.

הואל] Cf. *ch.* 5. 23 *note.*

4. העצים] 'The timber,' in its natural condition, destined to become the קורות (prepared) 'beams' of *v.* 2.

5. ויהי . . . הקורה] As Kamp. remarks, a man cuts down tree-trunks (עֵצִים *v.* 4) and not *beams*. Klo.'s emendation הַקַּרְדֹּם, favoured by Kamp., Benz., Kit., Oort, is worthy of notice. Render, 'as one *was swinging his axe*.' This use of הִפִּיל cannot, however, be paralleled, while that implied by the reading of MT. has the support of *ch.* 3. 19.

ואת הב"זל נפל] The use of את to introduce a new subject is sporadic, most of the certified instances belonging to the later and inferior style. Cf. Jer. 36. 22 וְהַמֶּלֶךְ יוֹשֵׁב בֵּית הַחֹרֶף . . . וְאֶת־הָאָח לְפָנָיו מְבֹעָרֶת. Other cases are cited by G-K. § 117 *m*; Ew. § 277[d]. G-K., however, considers that in our passage 'the את is probably derived from a text which read the Hiph'îl instead of נפל.'

Klo. regards אֵת as a substantive 'axe-head,' a suggestion which is favoured by Kamp., Benz., Kit., Kö. *Syntax*, § 270 *a*.

6. הרם לך] Luc. Μετεώρισον καὶ λαβὲ σεαυτῷ.

6. 8–23. *Elisha blinds and captures an Aramaean army.*

8. מקום פלני אלמני] 'Place of *so and so*,' i.e. '*such and such* a place.' So exactly 1 Sam. 21. 3, and, in addressing a person

[1] וְלָקַחַת might in this sense be very idiomatically retained; 'and art for taking.' Cf. Gen. 30. 15; Dri. *Tenses*, § 204.

unnamed, Ruth 4. 1. פלני, upon comparison of Ar. فُلَانٌ, Aram. ܦܠܢ, is usually connected with the verb פלה in the sense *distinct, specific;* אלמני with אלם 'to be dumb,' as meaning *one whose name is withheld.* In Dan. 8. 13 the contraction פַּלְמֹנִי occurs, and this form appears to be presupposed by Luc. φελμουνι in our passage.

תחנתי] Apparently 'my camp.' So Targ. בית משרנא, and perhaps LXX παρεμβαλῶ. But the form is very strange (cf. Kö. *Lehrg.* I. ii. p. 192) and the context desiderates reference not to a camp but to an *ambush.* Accordingly, Luc. reads ποιήσωμεν ἔνεδρον, καὶ ἐποίησαν, Vulg. *ponamus insidias*, Pesh. ܥܒܕܘ ܘܐܬܛܫܘ 'place an ambush and conceal yourselves.' Thus Th., followed by Kamp., Benz., Kit., *Heb. Lex. Oxf.*, emends תֵּחָבְאוּ 'conceal yourselves' (cf. *ch.* 7. 12; I. 22. 25); Oort תִּתְחַבְּאוּ; Klo. נִתְחַבֵּא 'let us conceal ourselves.' This latter, as agreeing with Luc., Vulg., may be adopted[1]. Probably, with Luc., we should add וַיִּתְחַבְּאוּ, a suitable introduction to *v.* 9.

9. נִחִתִּים] An inexplicable form. RV. 'coming down,' i.e. נָחְתִין, a very pronounced Aramaism. We may safely follow Verss., and all moderns, in reading נֶחְבָּאִים or נֶחְבִּים 'concealed.'

10. והזהירה ונשמר] Perfects with ו *consec.* in a frequentative sense, after the summary statement וישלח. Cf. Dri. *Tenses*, § 114 *a.*

11. מי מִשֶּׁלָּנוּ אל מלך ישראל] 'Who of ours is for the king of Israel?' On the use of the relative שׁ cf. p. 208. The sense of אל '*towards*,' and so '*in support of*,' may be illustrated by Hos. 3. 3; Jer. 15. 1; Ezek. 36. 9; Hag. 2. 17. So Pesh., Targ. LXX, Luc., however, in place of משלנו presuppose a verb *betray*, προδίδωσίν με. Similarly, Vet. Lat. *prodet me*, Vulg. *proditor mei.* Accordingly Bö., retaining the consonants of MT., vocalizes מַשְׁלֵנוּ 'who *hath misled us*' (cf. *note* on תשלה *ch.* 4. 28). Change of one letter gives מְגַלֵּנוּ, which is adopted by Klo., Kamp., Benz. Kit. supposes that מְגַלֵּנוּ has fallen out after מִשֶּׁלָּנוּ, upon the view that the response (*v.* 12) presupposes the suggestion that there is a

[1] Possibly, if Luc. is correct in reading פלמני for פלני אלמני, the initial נ of נתחבא has been absorbed into אלמני.

traitor in the camp, 'one of ours.' But this is sufficiently implied by הלוא תגידו לי, i.e. substantially, 'One of you must know.'

12. את הדברים] LXX, Luc., Vulg. אֶת־כָּל־הַדְּבָרִים.

אשר תדבר וג'] For the expression cf. Eccles. 10. 20.

13. איכה] Kt. אֵיכָה is probably correct. Cf. p. 209.

הנה בדתן] It is idiomatic to omit expression of the subject with הִנֵּה, when it may be readily inferred from the context. Cf. *v.* 20; I. 21. 18; Dri. *Tenses*, § 135 (6), *note* 4. So, with participle, 6. 25 *note*.

דתן] LXX, Luc. Δωθάειμ, i.e. דֹּתַיִם; cf. עֶגְלַיִם by the side of עֶגְלוֹן. Dothan is the modern *Tell Dôtân*, a green hill with a few ruins about ten miles north of Samaria. Cf. Eusebius, *Onom.;* Baed. 261; Buhl, 24 *f.*, 102.

15. וישכם וג'] MT. is somewhat confused. The subj. of ויצא, in accordance with 15^b, must be Elisha, but following as it does upon what precedes, it can scarcely be different from that of וישכם, viz. in accordance with MT., משרת. Again, the servant is called משרת in 15^a, נערו in 15^b, and the expression וישכם . . . לקום 'and he got up early to arise,' is at best extremely harsh. Klo. happily restores order by emending מְמָּחֳרָת for מְשָׁרֵת (cf. Ex. 32. 6; Judg. 6. 38; 1 Sam. 5. 3), and substituting בַּבֹּקֶר for לָקוּם after Luc. τὸ πρωΐ[1], Vulg. *diluculo*:—'And the man of God arose early on the morrow in the morning, and went forth, &c.' So Kamp., Benz., and substantially Kit.[2]

17. את עיני הנער] LXX, Luc. τοὺς ὀφθαλμοὺς αὐτοῦ.

18. וירדו] Vulg. supplies the subj. *Hostes vero descenderunt*. 'They came down' from the hills surrounding the small valley in the midst of which *Tell Dôtân* lies.

סנורים] 'Blindness.' Only again Gen. 19. 11. The word is perhaps a Shaph'el formation from נור, *sanwara*, 'make blind' (lit. 'bright,' euphemistically). Cf. Kö. *Lehrg.* I. ii. 404.

19. זה] So again for זאת Ezek. 40. 45; Eccl. 2. 2, 24; 5. 15, 18;

---

[1] Luc. has also ἀναστῆναι, clearly as a gloss derived from LXX.

[2] Kit. reads וַיְהִי מִמָּחֳרָת וג', a reading which he apparently refers to Klo.

7. 23; 9. 13, and in the phrase כָּזֹה וְכָזֶה I. 14. 5; Judg. 18. 4; 2 Sam. 11. 25†. The form resembles Aram. דָּא, and may be dialectical. Cf. p. 208.

20. והנה וג׳] Cf. *v.* 13 *note.*

21. האכה אכה] Cf., for the repetition, Ezek. 14. 3[b], which should perhaps be vocalized הַאִדָּרֹשׁ אִדָּרֵשׁ לָהֶם. Most critics, however, restore an infin. absol. הִדָּרֹשׁ, and so in our passage LXX Εἰ πατάξας πατάξω, Pesh. ܡܚܡܚܐ ܐܡܚܐ ܐܢܘܢ suggest the reading הַהַכֵּה אַכֶּה.

22. האשר שבית וג׳] Klo. inserts a negative לא after Luc. οὓς οὐκ ᾐχμαλώτευσας . . . οὐ (read σύ LXX) τύπτεις; 'Wilt thou slay those whom thou hast not captured with thy sword and with thy bow?' So Benz., Kit. This is probably correct rather than MT. which is scarcely consonant with the frequent practice of the חֵרֶם, sanctioned and even enforced by members of the prophetic school; cf. e.g. I. 20. 42; 1 Sam. 15. 3, 33. Kamp. favours MT.

23. ויכרה וג׳] The context demands the meaning 'And he made them a great feast'; and so Vulg., Pesh., Targ.; but כרה with this meaning is not elsewhere found in Heb. Perhaps the root is the same as Assyr. *karû*, 'bring,' *kirêtu*, 'feast' (to which guests are *brought* or *invited*). So in the Balawat inscription, *ki-re-ti iškun*, 'he made a feast'; Delitzsch, *Assyr. Handwörterbuch*, p. 352. Klo. emends וַיַּעֲרֹךְ מַעֲרָכָה 'And he laid a spread,' after LXX, Luc. καὶ παρέθηκεν αὐτοῖς παράθεσιν, but this expression so used is unparalleled in Heb.[1] More probably the Greek represents a free guess at the unknown words.

6. 24—7. 20. *Samaria is besieged by the Aramaeans, and reduced to great straits through famine. The city is relieved through a panic which seizes the besieging army.*

24. בן הדד] Cf. *note* on I. 15. 18. If this narrative be wrongly assigned to the reign of Jehoram (cf. p. 278), the reference will be to the successor of Ḥazael (cf. *ch.* 13. 24).

[1] The regular phrase is עָרַךְ שֻׁלְחָן. Cf. Isa. 21. 5; Ps. 23. 5; 78. 19; Prov. 9. 2.

25: ויהי רעב גדול] It is not quite clear whether the writer regards the famine as simply due to the rigour of the siege, or as in a measure independent of it. The fact that the king of Israel considers Elisha as the main cause of the calamity (*v.* 31) favours the latter supposition, and the same inference is perhaps to be drawn from the reference to the opening of 'the windows of heaven,' *ch.* 7. 2. In this case the famine is probably the same as that mentioned in *ch.* 8. 1–6, which lasted seven years (*v.* 2). *Ch.* 8. 1–6 represents Geḥazi as still holding the position of Elisha's favoured servant; therefore 8. 1–6; 6. 24—7. 20 are presumably earlier than 5. 1–27 which relates the smiting of Geḥazi with leprosy.

והנה צרים] Expression of the subject is omitted in accordance with idiom. See cases cited by Dri. *Tenses*, § 135 (6), and cf. *note* on *v.* 13.

ראש חמור] Th. quotes a parallel from Plutarch, *Artaxerx.* 24: τὰ ὑποζύγια μόνον κατέκοπτεν, ὥστε ὄνου κεφαλὴν μόλις δραχμῶν ἑξήκοντα ὤνιον εἶναι.

בשמנים] LXX, Luc. πεντήκοντα.

הקב] The *kab* is only here mentioned in the OT., but occurs in New Heb. both as a dry and fluid measure. Josephus represents רֹבַע הַקַּב by ξέστης, a measure which is known to be equivalent to the Heb. לֹג. The fourth part of a *kab* was therefore about a pint. Cf. Benz. *Archäologie*, 182; Nowack, *Archäologie*, i. 202 *ff.*

חרייונים] The Verss. follow Kt., and, reading as two words חֲרֵי (חֲרֵי) יוֹנִים, render 'doves' dung.' Q're דִּבְיוֹנִים is of unknown derivation. The strangeness of such an article as used for food has aroused suspicion. Thus Ges. *Thes.* cites the view of Bochart that 'doves' dung' may have been the popular name for some vegetable product (roasted chick peas) just as in Ar. the name خرو العصافر 'sparrows' dung' is applied to the herb *kali*, and in German *assafoetida* is named *Teufelsdreck*. Klo. emends חַרְצַנִּים 'sour wine' (? Num. 6. 4), Cheyne (*Expositor*, 1899, p. 32) חֲרוּבִים 'carob pods,' a word well known in New Heb. and Syriac, and restored by the same writer also in *ch.* 18. 27 = Isa. 36. 12 (חֲרוּבֵיהֶם for חריהם), Isa. 1. 20 (חֲרוּבִים תֹּאכֵלוּ for חֶרֶב תְּאֻכְּלוּ); cf. S. Luke 15. 16.

It is, however, by no means certain that MT., Kt., in its literal acceptation, is incorrect. A parallel in Jos. *Bell. Jud.* v. 13, § 7 depicts the extremities to which men may be brought by a prolonged siege:—μετὰ ταῦτα δ' ὡς οὐδὲ ποηλογεῖν ἔθ' οἷόν τ' ἦν περιτειχισθείσης τῆς πόλεως, προελθεῖν τινας εἰς τοσοῦτον ἀνάγκης, ὥστε τὰς ἀμάρας ἐρευνῶντας καὶ παλαιὸν ὄνθον βοῶν προσφέρεσθαι τὰ ἐκ τούτων σκύβαλα, καὶ τὸ μηδ' ὄψει φορητὸν πάλαι τότε γενέσθαι τροφήν. Again, Post (in Hastings, *BD.* i. 629) quotes, on the authority of Houghton, a statement from a Spanish author that in the year 1316 so great a famine distressed the English that 'men ate their own children, dogs, mice, and *pigeons' dung*.'

26. הושיעה וג'] Cf. 2 Sam. 14. 4ᵇ. Similarly *v.* 28ᵃ is exactly paralleled by 2 Sam. 14. 5ᵃ.

27. אל יושעך וג'] Difficult. As the text stands, it is best to render, 'If Yahwe help thee not, whence shall I help thee?' lit. 'Let not Yahwe help thee, whence &c.?' a case of the jussive used in the protasis of a hypothetical sentence. So Dri. *Tenses*, § 152 (3); G-K. § 109 *h*. The alternative is to regard אל as used absolutely in deprecation: 'Nay! let Yahwe help thee.' Cf. *note* on *ch.* 3. 13.

Pesh. is noticeable as suggesting the reading לָהּ for אַל: ܘܐܡܪ ܠܗ̇ ܢܦܪܘܩܝܟܝ ܡܪܝܐ 'And he said *to her*, Let Yahwe deliver thee!' Is it, however, possible (in view of the dialectical peculiarities of these narratives; pp. 208 *f*.) that we should find in אל the Aram. אֶלָּא '*except*'?

29. ותחבא את בנה] Luc. adds καὶ οὐκ ἔδωκεν αὐτὸν ἵνα φάγωμεν καὶ αὐτόν.

30. והוא עבר] Luc. καὶ αὐτὸς εἱστήκει, i. e. וְהוּא עֹמֵד, probably correct. So Klo., Kamp., Benz., Kit.

31. כה יעשה וג'] Cf. I. 2. 23 *note*.

32. והזקנים וג'] Cf. Ezek. 8. 1; 20. 1. Luc. καὶ πάντες οἱ πρεσβύτεροι.

וישלח איש מלפניו] RV. 'And [the king] sent a man from before him.' So Luc. inserts ὁ βασιλεύς. The sentence is probably a clumsy interpolation to explain the following reference המלאך and כי שלח. Wellh. (*C.* 360) drastically removes all reference to the messenger by excision both of this sentence and of ראו כבא ... אחריו, and emendation of המלאך in its first occurrence to הַמֶּלֶךְ, as also in *v.* 33.

בטרם] Read וּבְטֶרֶם with Luc., Vulg., Pesh.

בן המרצח הזה] As is remarked by Klo., Benz., Kit., the expression does not refer literally to the king's father (Aḥab? cf. p. 278), but characterizes the king himself. 'Mördersohn' = 'Mordbube.' Cf. 1 Sam. 20. 30 (reading בֶּן־נַעֲרַת הַמַּרְדּוּת; cf. Dri. *ad loc.*); Isa. 57. 3 בְּנֵי עֹנְנָה זֶרַע מְנָאֵף וַתִּזְנֶה.

ולחצתם וג'] 'And press him with the door,' i.e., as we should say, 'Shut the door *in his face*.'

33. המלאך] Read הַמֶּלֶךְ with Ew., Wellh., Grä., Klo., Kamp., Kit., Benz., Oort. Mention of the king's arrival is presupposed by *ch.* 7. 2 (cf. *v.* 17 בְּרֶדֶת הַמֶּלֶךְ אֵלָיו), and the words of *v.* 33b are only explicable if placed in the king's mouth.

זאת הרעה] Cf. *note* on זה היום I. 14. 14.

7. 1. סאה] A *seä* contained about a peck, and was equivalent to six measures of the *kab* (*ch.* 6. 25), and twenty-four of the *log*. Cf. Benz. *Archäologie*, 181 *ff*.

וסאתים שערים בשקל] LXX omits through homoioteleuton.

2. השליש] Cf. I. 9. 22 *note*.

למלך] Read הַמֶּלֶךְ with several Codd., all Verss. and modern authorities.

נשען על ידו] Cf. *ch.* 5. 18.

ארבות בשמים] 'Windows *or* sluices (LXX, Luc. καταρράκτας) in the heavens,' through which the rain was thought to be poured down; Gen. 7. 11; 8. 2; Mal. 3. 10; cf. Isa. 24. 18. The point of the speech seems to be that, even if Yahwe were at once to send rain, it would be impossible for such a state of plenty to come about *by to-morrow*.

6. מלכי החתים] The kings of the Ḥittites are mentioned again in I. 10. 29 as providing themselves with horses from *Muṣri* (cf.

note ad loc.). The Ḥittite kingdom lay in north Syria, having its capital at Ḳadesh on the Orontes. In 2 Sam. 24. 6 David's northern boundary is said to have extended as far as 'the land of the Ḥittites to Ḳadesh[1].' The land of the Ḥittites is also mentioned in Judg. 1. 26, and in Judg. 3. 3 הַחִתִּי ought probably to be substituted for הַחִוִּי: 'the Ḥittites who inhabit the hill-country of the Lebanon' (cf. Moore, *ad loc.*). כל ארץ החתים Josh. 1. 4 is perhaps a later gloss, identifying the Ḥittites with the Canaanites. On the Ḥittites as they figure in the Egyptian and cuneiform inscriptions, cf. Sayce in Hastings, *DB.* ii. 390 *ff.*; Dri. *Authority*, 83 *ff.*

ואת מלכי מצרים] Probably we should vocalize מֻצְרִים or מֻצְרִים, and render, 'and the kings of Muṣri.' An alliance of the Ḥittites with Egypt would have been highly improbable, and could scarcely have suggested itself to the Aramaeans, while an alliance of the two north Syrian kingdoms for the purpose of turning their flank was a danger well calculated to cause a panic. On Muṣri, cf. I. 10. 28 *note.*

7. המחנה כאשר היא] RV. 'even the camp as it was.' But מחנה is always elsewhere masc. We may read בַּמַּחֲנֶה כַּאֲשֶׁר הֵמָּה with Luc. ὡς ἦσαν ἐν τῇ παρεμβολῇ: cf. *v.* 10[b]. The reading במחנה is also presupposed by LXX, Vulg., Pesh.

אל נפשם] Cf. I. 19. 3 *note.*

8[a]. ויטמנו] LXX omits.

9. לא כן אנחנו עשים] 'We are not doing *right.*' Cf. *ch.* 17. 9 דְּבָרִים אֲשֶׁר לֹא־כֵן.

עוון] 'Punishment.' So Gen. 4. 13. Cf. Num. 14. 34; Isa. 53. 11; *al.*

10. שַׁעַר] Pl. שַׁעֲרֵי is demanded by the following לָהֶם, and by הַשְּׁעָרִים *v.* 11. So Th., Kamp., Kit., Oort.

אהלים] LXX, Luc. αἱ σκηναὶ αὐτῶν, i.e. וְאָהֳלֵיהֶם, correctly. So Klo., Kamp., Benz. Kit. הָאֹהָלִים.

---

[1] Reading אֶרֶץ הַחִתִּים קָדֵשָׁה, after Luc. εἰς γῆν Χεττιεὶμ Καδῆς, for the senseless ארץ תחתים חדשי of MT. Cf. Dri. *ad loc.*

11. ויקרא] Read וַיִּקְרְאוּ with LXX, Luc., Targ. Vulg. *Ierunt ergo*, Pesh. ܘܩܪܘ also presuppose a plural.

12. בהשדה] Cases in which the ה of the article remains unsyncopated after an inseparable preposition are cited by G-K. § 35 *n*. The occurrences are 'almost exclusively in the later Books.'

13. ויקחו וג׳] The text is seriously corrupted. The general resource is to regard the first אשר נשארו בה as a doublet of הנשארים, and to reject the second אשר נשארו בה down to ישראל as an error occasioned by repetition of the former. But even so the point of the remark, 'Lo, they are as all the multitude of Israel that are consumed,' is obscure. What we should expect is some statement such as that of the lepers in *v.* 4, viz. that, whatever may be the fate of the scouts, they will be no worse off than those who remain in the beleaguered city. Possibly therefore the text may have originally run:—שִׁלְחוּ אֲנָשִׁים וְיִקְחוּ חֲמִשָּׁה מִן־הַסּוּסִים הַנִּשְׁאָרִים אִם־יִחְיוּ הִנָּם כְּכָל־הֲמוֹן יִשְׂרָאֵל אֲשֶׁר נִשְׁאֲרוּ פֹּה וְאִם־יֹאבְדוּ הִנָּם כְּכָל־הֲמוֹן יִשְׂרָאֵל אֲשֶׁר תָּמּוּ 'Send men, and let them take five of the horses which survive; if they live, lo, they are as all the multitude of Israel that survive here, and if they perish, lo, they are as all the multitude of Israel that are consumed.' The reading פֹּה for בָהּ is suggested by LXX ὧδε, while the alternative ואם יאבדו וג׳ appears in Targ. ואם ייבדון הא אינון ככל המונא ישראל דספו; cf. Pesh. ܐܢ ܐܬܠܩܚܘ 'If they be taken, &c.'

14. רכב סוסים] LXX ἐπιβάτας ἵππων, Luc. ἀναβάτας ἵππων, i.e. רֹכְבֵי סוּסִים 'mounted men'; cf. *ch.* 9. 18. Scouts would naturally be sent out on horseback rather than in chariots.

15. בהחפזם] Kt. בְּהֵחָפְזָם is correct. The Niph'al is used elsewhere, 1 Sam. 23. 26; Ps. 48. 6; 104. 7.

16. כדבר י׳] Luc. adds ὃν ἐλάλησεν Ἐλισσαῖε.

17. כאשר דבר . . . אשר דבר] Scarcely original. Probably we have a combination of two different readings—כַּאֲשֶׁר דִּבֶּר simply, and כִּדְבַר . . . אֲשֶׁר דִּבֶּר. The former has the support of Vulg., Pesh., and is probably correct.

8. 1–6. *Elisha again assists the Shunammite woman.*

1. אל האשה וג׳] *Ch.* 4. 8–37.

ונורי באשר תגורי] Dri. on Deut. 1. 46 calls the mode of expression 'the *idem per idem* idiom, often employed in the Semitic languages, when a writer is either unable or has no occasion to speak explicitly.' Cf. also Dri. on 1 Sam. 23. 13, where instances in Ar. are quoted from Lagarde, *Psalterium Hieronymi* (1874), 156*f.*; Dri. *Tenses*, § 38 β *note*.

וגם בא וג׳] 'And, moreover, it shall come &c.' בא is the participle, used as a *futurum instans*.

2. Luc. omits ותקם, and adds, after בארץ פלשתים, καθ' ὡς εἶπεν αὐτῇ ὁ ἄνθρωπος τοῦ θεοῦ.

3. מארץ פ׳] LXX adds εἰς τὴν πόλιν.

5. את המת] Luc. τὸν υἱὸν αὐτῆς τὸν τεθνηκότα, LXX υἱὸν τεθνηκότα, inferior to MT.

8. 7–15. *Elisha's interview with Ḥazael at Damascus.*

8. מחלי זה] Cf. *ch.* 1. 2 *note*.

10. לא] All Verss. agree with Q're לו, which is certainly original. Cf. *v.* 14. Probably the alteration to the negative was due to a desire to remove from Elisha the imputation of falsehood.

והראני] Perf. with ו simplex, co-ordinated with the preceding.

11. ויעמד וג׳] 'And he steadied his countenance, and set (it on him) till he was ashamed.' So RV. 'And he settled his countenance steadfastly (upon him), until he was ashamed.' The Hiph'il הֶעֱמִיד is here applied to a concentration of the gaze upon a single object to the exclusion of all extraneous distraction. After וַיָּשֶׂם we should expect אֵלָיו (cf. Ezek. 6. 2; 13. 17; *al.*) or עָלָיו (Ezek. 29. 2; 35. 2). The subject of עַד־בֹּשׁ is naturally Ḥazael. Elisha looked him out of countenance.

A variety of explanations of the passage have been suggested. LXX (vocalizing וַיַּעֲמֹד) καὶ παρέστη τῷ προσώπῳ αὐτοῦ, καὶ ἔθηκεν ἕως αἰσχύνης, expanded by Luc. καὶ ἔστη Ἀζαὴλ κατὰ πρόσωπον αὐτοῦ, καὶ παρέθηκεν ἐνώπιον αὐτοῦ τὰ δῶρα ἕως ᾐσχύνετο. Vulg. *Stetitque cum eo, et conturbatus est* (i. e. וַיִּשֹּׁם) *usque ad suffusionem vultus.* Targ.

ואסחר ית אפוהי ואוריך עד סגי 'And he turned away his face and delayed a very long time.' Pesh. omits. Benz., Kit., reading וַיִּשֹּׁם or וַיָּשָׁם (cf. Vulg.), explain, 'And he stared immoveably before him, and became horrified in the extreme,' understanding the first statement as referring to the setting in of the prophetic ecstasy, while the second depicts the effect produced upon the prophet by his vision. But the sense given to עד בש 'aufs äusserste' (*ch.* 2. 17; Judg. 3. 25) is improbable, since the naming of the subject in the following sentence ויבך איש האלהים seems to be intended to contrast with the implied different subject of בש (viz. Ḥazael), and is out of place if the subject of בש be the same as that of ויבך, וישם, ויעמד. Grä. emends וַיַּסְתֵּר for ויעמד (cf. Targ.) and וַיִּדֹּם for וישם, 'And he hid his face and was silent, &c.' Klo.'s explanation is strangely impossible.

13. כי] Cf. I. 1. 13 *note*.

מה עבדך וג'] 'What is thy servant, the dog, that he should do this great thing?' LXX, Luc. ὁ κύων ὁ τεθνηκώς, as in 2 Sam. 9. 8; cf. 1 Sam. 24. 15; 2 Sam. 16. 9. So Klo., Oort, Winckler.

15. המכבר] RV. 'coverlet.' Cf. כְּבִיר הָעִזִּים 1 Sam. 19. 13, 16, spread by Michal over the head of Teraphim in David's bed. The word is a ἅπαξ λεγ., and seems to denote something of *intertwined* or *woven* workmanship. כְּבָרָה Am. 9. 9 = 'sieve.'

וימלך חזהאל] Shalmaneser II mentions two campaigns against '*Ḫa-za-'-ilu* of Damascus'; in the eighteenth year of his reign (B.C. 842; cf. *Append.* 4), and again in the twenty-first year (B.C. 839).

8. 16–24. *Jehoram, king of Judah.*

Ch. 8. 17–23 = 2 Chr. 21. 5–10[a]. R[D] *vv.* 16–19, 23.

16[a]. ויהושפט מלך יהודה] Rightly omitted by LXX, Pesh. The words have come in through error from the latter half of the verse.

17. שמנה שנה] Q're corrects to שנים, in accordance with the almost invariable rule that numerals from 2 to 10 take the object numbered in the pl. Other exceptions, cited by G-K. § 134 *e*, are *ch.* 22. 1 (שְׁמֹנֶה שָׁנָה uncorrected); 25. 17 (Q're pl.); Ex. 16. 22; Ezek. 45. 1. LXX τεσσαράκοντα ἔτη.

19. ולא אבה י׳ להשחית] So (without prep. ל) *ch.* 13. 23; Deut. 10. 10.
ניר] Cf. I. 11. 36 *note*.

לבניו] But the lamp was not given *for* the sons, since the sons are themselves the lamp. ‖ 2 Chr. 21. 7, Luc., Vulg., Targ., feeling the difficulty, read וּלְבָנָיו; but this does not really effect any improvement. LXX omits. No doubt Klo., Kamp., Benz., Kit., Oort are right in emending לְפָנָיו; 'to give him a lamp *before Him* all the days.' Cf. I. 11. 36 לְפָנַי בִּירוּשָׁלַםִ.

20. בימיו] Cf. I. 16. 34 *note*.

21. צעירה] The place is unknown. Ew. would read צֹעֲרָה 'to Zo'ar,' but against this it is to be noticed with Buhl (*Edomiter*, p. 64 *f.*) that LXX, Luc. in our passage transliterate Σειώρ, Σιώρ, while צֹעַר is always represented by Σηγώρ, Σιγώρ; the inference being that ע in צָעִיר = ع, while in צֹעַר it = غ. Th. suggests שְׂעִירָה 'to Se'ir.' ‖ 2 Chr. עִם־שָׂרָיו.

21[b]. The half-verse seems to be seriously corrupt.

(1) The constr. ויהי הוא קם וג׳ is inexplicable. Accents connect ויהי closely with הוא קם (cf. ‖ 2 Chr. 21. 9 ויהי קם); but the idea of *duration* usually conveyed by the constr. of participle with substantive verb (Dri. *Tenses*, § 135. 5) is out of harmony with the sense of the passage. The alternative, adopted by LXX, Luc., Pesh., Targ., is to make a break after ויהי, and to treat הוא קם לילה as a circumstantial clause, קם being a perfect. Upon this view, however, the analogy of the cases cited by Dri. *Tenses*, § 165, demands a change of subject in the (presumed) principal sentence which follows:—'And it came to pass, whilst he arose by night [some one else acted in such a way].'

(2) As the text stands, the statement is made that Joram, the subject of ויכה, smote את שרי הרכב. These, however, as is clear from *v.* 21[a], belonged to his own forces. The least correction, therefore, that can be made is to follow Kit. in reading וְאִתּוֹ שָׂרֵי הָרֶכֶב 'And the captains of the chariots were with him.'

(3) Verse 22 makes it plain that Joram's attempt to re-subjugate Edom was futile. What we therefore desiderate in *v.* 21[b] is probably an account of the falling of Joram and his army into

an ambush laid by the Edomites, from which escape was only made by cutting a way through the surrounding enemy and beating a hurried retreat. As to the precise wording of such a narrative the passage in its present state affords no sufficient clue.

22. עד היום הזה] Cf. I. 8. 8 *note*.

אז] Cf. I. 3. 16 *note*.

לבנה] Cf. *ch.* 19. 8, from which it appears that the city was of strategical importance, probably lying south-west of Judah upon the way to Egypt. Eusebius places Libna among the cities in the neighbourhood of Eleutheropolis. Cf. Buhl, p. 193.

בעת ההיא] Cf. I. 14. 1 *note*.

8. 25–29. *Aḥaziah, king of Judah.*

Ch. 8. 26–29 forms the basis of 2 Chr. 22. 2–6. R^D *vv.* 25–27.

25. שתים עשרה] *Ch.* 9. 29 אחת עשרה. So in the present passage, Luc., Pesh.

26. עשרים ושתים] || 2 Chr. ארבעים ושתים.

בת עמרי] Luc. corrects θυγάτηρ 'Αχαάβ, in accordance with *v.* 18. בת, however, probably has here the more general sense of '*descendant*.' Cf. I. 15. 2.

27. כי חתן וג׳] LXX omits. || 2 Chr. כִּי אִמּוֹ הָיְתָה יוֹעַצְתּוֹ לְהַרְשִׁיעַ.

28. ברמת גלעד] Cf. II. 22. 3 *note*.

ארמים] We should naturally expect הָאֲרַמִּים. || 2 Chr. has the strange הָרַמִּים, which LXX, Luc. represent by οἱ τοξόται, i. e. הַמּוֹרִים '*the archers*'; cf. 1 Sam. 31. 3; 2 Sam. 11. 24. This reading is very probably original. So Klo.

29. יכהו] The use of the imperf. seems to be inexplicable; cf. Ew. § 346^c, *note* 2; Dri. *Tenses*, § 27 γ. || 2 Chr. הִכֻּהוּ.

ארמים] LXX and || 2 Chr. omit.

9. 1—10. 28. *Jehu, an officer of the host of Israel, is anointed king at the command of Elisha. He destroys the whole house of Aḥab, and extirpates Ba'al-worship from Israel.*

9. 2. יהוא] *Ja-u-a apal Ḫu-um-ri-i*, i. e. 'Jehu son of Omri' (cf. I. 16. 23 *note*), is twice mentioned in the cuneiform inscriptions of Shalmaneser II, as bringing tribute to the Assyrian king. The

first inscription is found upon the obelisk, above a representation of the embassy presenting the tribute before Shalmaneser. In the second inscription (*Annals*, III, Rawlinson 5, no. 6, 40–65), after an account of the conquest of Ḥazael of Damascus, Shalmaneser states that 'at that time I received the tribute of the Tyrians, Sidonians, of Jehu son of Omri.' Cf. *Append.* 4. It may be inferred, therefore, that the aid of Assyria had been solicited by Jehu to meet the encroachments of Ḥazael, to which brief reference is made in *ch.* 10. 32, 33, just as in later times it was solicited by Aḥaz of Judah against the alliance of Israel and Aram; *ch.* 16. 6 *ff.*; cf. Isa. 7. 1–9.

חדר בחדר] Cf. I. 20. 30 *note.*

3. אל ישראל] A large number of Codd. read על for אל, both here and in *v.* 12. Other examples of the confusion between אל and על are noticed on I. 13. 29 *note.*

4. הנער הנביא] הנער *st. constr.* with the article, through erroneous approximation to the preceding הנער. Cf. Kö. *Syntax*, § 303 *c.*

6–10. The hand of R^D is very apparent in *vv.* 8, 9. Cf. *notes* on I. 14. 1–18.

7. והכיתה] LXX, Luc. καὶ ἐξολοθρεύσεις, i.e. probably וְהִכְרַתָּה[1]; cf. 2 Chr. 22. 7. So Klo., Kamp., Kit., Benz.

After אדניך LXX adds ἐκ προσώπου σου, Luc. ἐκ προσώπου μου.

ונקמתי] LXX, Luc. read 2nd pers. 'and thou shalt avenge,' making the same change in *v.* 8 והכרתי. MT. is preferable.

8. ואבד] Vulg., Pesh., Targ. presuppose וְאִבַּדְתִּי 'and I will destroy.' LXX, Luc. καὶ ἐκ χειρός, i.e. וּמִיַּד, accepted by Klo., Oort.

10. בחלק יזרעאל] Cf. I. 21. 23 *note.*

11. ויאמר] All Verss. presuppose וַיֹּאמְרוּ, correctly.

השלום] Luc. adds καὶ εἶπεν αὐτοῖς Εἰρήνη. καὶ εἶπον αὐτῷ—an unnecessary redundancy.

המשגע] Cf. Hos. 9. 7; Jer. 29. 26.

שיחו] 'His conversation.' Cf. Ps. 104. 34, and the use of the verb Job 12. 8; *al.*

---

[1] Ἐξολεθρεύειν occurs only once as a rendering of הִכָּה, viz. Josh. 11. 14, whereas it is constantly employed (as in *v.* 8) to represent הִכְרִית.

12. אל ישראל] Luc. ἐπὶ τὸν λαόν μου Ἰσραήλ. Cf. *v.* 6.

13. אל גרם המעלות] The meaning is very uncertain. Ges., Ew., Ke., upon the analogy of the use of עֶצֶם, suppose that the expression may mean 'upon the steps *themselves*,' i.e. 'upon the *bare* steps.' Grä. emends עַל־מְרוֹם המ׳ 'upon the elevation of the steps.'

14[b]. ויורם] Very probably Grä. is correct in substituting יֵהוּא for יוֹרָם:—'Now Jehu was keeping Ramoth Gilead ... but Jehoram had returned to be healed &c.'

15. אם יש נפשכם] 'If it be your mind,' i.e. If ye are desirous of making me king. LXX, Luc. add μετ' ἐμοῦ, but this is unnecessary. Many Codd. read את נפשכם, as in Gen. 23. 8.

לגיד] Kt. לַגִּיד, with ה syncopated after the preposition ל. Cf. G-K. § 53 *q*.

16. שכב שמה] In place of these words LXX, Luc. present a second rendering of *v.* 15[a]—clearly a marginal gloss which has usurped the place of the true reading. Notice ἐθεραπεύετο for ἀπέστρεψεν . . . ἰατρευθῆναι—ἀπὸ τῶν τοξευμάτων ὧν κατετόξευσαν αὐτόν for ἀπὸ τῶν πληγῶν ὧν ἔπαισαν αὐτόν—οἱ Ἀραμιείν for οἱ Σύροι. LXX rounds off the gloss with ὅτι δυνατὸς καὶ ἀνὴρ δυνάμεως.

ואחזיה וג׳] On the order of sentence expressing the pluperfect cf. *note* on I. 14. 5.

17. שפעת אני ראה] שפעת is either a mistake for שפעה owing to the previous occurrence of the *st. constr.*, or else, as Klo., Kamp., Benz., Kit., Oort suggest, a genitive, *sc.* אֲנָשִׁים, has fallen out. שפעה probably denotes a *company* or *multitude*, agreeably to the use of the word in Isa. 60. 6; Ezek. 26. 10[1]. So Luc. ὄχλον, Vulg. *globum*, and most moderns. LXX, however, renders κονιορτόν[2], and so Kit.

18. השלום] Cf. *ch.* 5. 21 *note*.

מה לך וג׳] 'What hast thou (as an emissary of Aḥab's son)

---

[1] The root שפע in Aram. means *to overflow*, and accordingly the subs. שִׁפְעָה is used in Heb. of *overflowing* or *abundance* of water, Job 22. 11; 38. 34; שֶׁפַע Deut. 33. 19.

[2] Luc. in the first occurrence has a doublet τὸν κονιορτὸν τοῦ ὄχλου. The original reading must obviously have been τὸν ὄχλον.

to do with peace?'—the implication (cf. *v.* 22) being 'How can peace exist so long as the house of Aḥab exists?' Cf. the phrase מה לי ולך I. 17. 18 *note*.

עד־הֵם] We ought probably to read עֲדֵיהֶם. Cf. Job 32. 12 עֲדֵיכֶם.

20. עד אליהם] Cf. the phrase עַד לְ I. 18. 29 *note*.

בשגעון] 'Madly,' or, as RV., 'furiously.' So 'A. ἐν παραπληξίᾳ, Σ. ἀτάκτως, Vulg. *praeceps*, Pesh. ܡܫܬܪܗܒܐܝܬ, and probably LXX, Luc. ἐν παραλλαγῇ [1]. In contrast, Targ. renders בניח 'quietly,' and this interpretation is adopted by Jos. (*Ant.* ix. 6, § 3):—σχολαίτερον δὲ καὶ μετ' εὐταξίας ὥδευεν 'Ιηοῦς.

ינהג] Probably describing Jehu's habit:—'he is wont to drive.' In description of a (single) present event we should of course expect הוּא נֹהֵג.

22. מה השלום] For the sense 'What peace?' (RV.) we should expect מַה־שָּׁלוֹם, and this is adopted by Klo., Kit., who suppose that the ה before שלום has come in by dittography. Benz., following Targ., vocalizes מָה הֲשָׁלוֹם, explaining 'Jehu answers: Between us there can be no "How do you fare?" so long as &c.' But the sense assigned to הֲשָׁלוֹם is not that which it possesses in this connexion. Cf. *note* on *ch.* 5. 21.

עד זנוני וג׳] The sense of עד is 'at' or '*during*.' Cf. Judg. 3. 26 עַד הִתְמַהְמְהָם '*During* their delay'; Jon. 4. 2 עַד־הֱיוֹתִי עַל־אַדְמָתִי 'Whilst I was (*during* my being) in my country.' Grä.'s emendation עִם for עַד is unnecessary. LXX ἔτι, i.e. עֹד (so Klo.), is greatly inferior to MT.

23. ויהפך י׳ ידיו] Cf. I. 22. 34.

24. מלא ידו בקשת] '*Armed* (lit. *filled*) his hand with the bow.' Cf. 2 Sam. 23. 7 יִמָּלֵא בַרְזֶל וְעֵץ חֲנִית 'arms himself with iron and a spear's shaft'—'lit. *fills himself*, viz. in so far as the hand using the weapon is concerned' (Dri. *ad loc.*)[2].

---

[1] The subs. occurs again in 'A.'s rendering of Job 4. 13ᵃ ἐν παραλλαγαῖς ἀπὸ ὁραματισμῶν νυκτός, i.e. probably 'In trances of visions of the night.' Cf. Σ. ἐν ἐκπλήξει ἀπὸ ὁραμάτων νυκτερινῶν.

[2] It should, however, be remembered that the context of this passage is very dubious, and that יִמָּלֵא disappears under Budde's emendation.

החצי] So in 1 Sam. 20. 36, 37 (twice), and 38 Kt. for the usual הַחֵץ.

25. שלשה] Cf. I. 9. 22 *note*.

כי זכר וג׳] LXX, Luc., Vulg., Pesh. presuppose כִּי זֹכֵר אֲנִי כִּי אֲנִי וג׳ 'For I remember that I and thou &c.' This is probably correct, MT. being due to homoioteleuton.

את רכבים צמדים] The impossible את must be rejected as dittography of the preceding אתה. The use of the pl. צְמָדִים 'pairs' is inexplicable. Ges.-Buhl, making a new division of the letters צמדמאחרי, reads צֶמֶד מֵאַחֲרֵי, and Kit., while rightly rejecting מֵאַחֲרֵי, favours the sing. צֶמֶד 'as a pair,' i. e. 'together,' and thinks that the pl. may have arisen through assimilation to the preceding pl. רכבים. Possibly צמדים ought to be vocalized as a passive participle צְמֻדִים (נִצְמָדִים) 'joined,' i. e. 'in company.'

26. אם לא וג׳] Cf. I. 20. 23 *note*.

27. גם אתו הכהו] It is necessary to follow Pesh. and add וַיַּכֻּהוּ, which has fallen out through similarity to the preceding word. So most moderns. Vulg. makes the insertion *after* אל המרכבה, and LXX, Luc. supply it *in place of* הכהו.

יבלעם] A city of Manasseh west of Jordan, Josh. 17. 11; Judg. 1. 27, called בִּלְעָם in 1 Chr. 6. 55; the modern *Bel'ame*, six hours north of *Nâblus*. Baed. 262; Buhl, 102, 201 *f*.

28. עם אבתיו] LXX, Luc. omit.

29. ובשנת וג׳] A redactional notice. Cf. *ch*. 8. 25 *note*. Luc. adds καὶ ἐνιαυτὸν ἕνα ἐβασίλευσεν ἐν Ἰερουσαλήμ after 8. 26.

30. ותשם וג׳] 'And set her eyes in *stibium*.' פּוּךְ is the *koḥl* of the Arabs (cf. the verb כחל Ezek. 23. 40), i. e. sulphide of antimony reduced to a black powder which is mixed with oil and used for painting the eye-lashes and brows, in order to make the eyes appear large and dark. Cf. Jer. 4. 30 כִּי־תִקְרְעִי בַפּוּךְ עֵינַיִךְ 'though thou enlargest thine eyes with *stibium*.' Benz. *Archäologie*, 110.

31. השלום זמרי וג׳] RV. rightly, 'Is it peace, thou Zimri, thy master's murderer?' It is idiomatic in Heb. to change to the 3rd pers. after an opening vocative. Cf. cases cited by Dri. *Tenses*, § 198, *Obs*. 2, and add Isa. 51. 7 and Job 18. 4 (with inverted order).

הֲשָׁלוֹם, as Th. rightly emphasizes, must have the same sense as in *vv.* 17, 18, 19, 22. Jezebel reminds Jehu of the speedy fate of Zimri (I. 16. 9–18), and gives him the opportunity of making peace with *her*, the hitherto all-powerful mistress of the kingdom. To give to הֲשָׁלוֹם the meaning 'How fare you?' deprives the queen of her policy.

32. מי אתי מי] 'Who is *with me*, who?' i.e. *on my side.* For this use of את cf. *ch.* 6. 16; Isa. 43. 5; 63. 3; Jer. 1. 19; Ps. 12. 5. The reading of LXX, Luc. Τίς εἶ σύ; κατάβηθι μετ' ἐμοῦ (Luc. πρός με) probably has its origin in a double rendering of אתי, vocalized in the first place as אַתְּ, while κατάβηθι may answer to the second מי read as רְדִי. Klo. makes κατάβηθι the equivalent of תֵּרְדִי, a corrupt reading of תָּרִבִי, and so emends מִי אַתְּ תָּרִבִי עִמִּי 'Who art thou, that thou wouldest contend with me?'—a reading in no way comparable to MT.

שנים שלשה] 'Two *or* three.' Cf. Isa. 17. 6 . . . שְׁנַיִם שְׁלֹשָׁה גַּרְגְּרִים אַרְבָּעָה חֲמִשָּׁה 'Two *or* three berries . . . four *or* five.' LXX, Luc. omit שלשה.

33. וירמסנה] Verss. וַיִּרְמְסוּהָ, rightly making the horses the subject.

36. עבדו] LXX omits.

37. הָיְתָ] Kt. should probably be vocalized הָיָת, the older form of the 3rd fem. sing. perf. of verbs ל״ה which occurs in a few other cases:—עָשָׂת Lev. 25. 21; הִרְצָת Lev. 26. 34; הֶלְאָת Ezek. 24. 12; הָגְלָת Jer. 13. 19.

אשר לא יאמרו וג׳] Vulg., by omission of the negative, *ita ut praetereuntes dicant: Haeccine est illa Iezabel?* Luc. adds καὶ οὐκ ἔσται ὁ λέγων Οἴμοι.

10. 1. ולאחאב] According to the contents of Jehu's letter, *vv.* 2, 3, the seventy princes are sons of Jehoram rather than of Aḥab. Cf. the phrases בְּנֵי אֲדֹנֵיכֶם and עַל־כִּסֵּא אָבִיו. Thus Sta. (*ZATW.*, 1885, pp. 279 *f.*) regards *v.* 1ª as a later and erroneous gloss. It is not, however, unreasonable to suppose that בָּנִים is here used not in the strictly literal sense, but of *descendants* of Aḥab in any degree (cf. בֵּית אֲדֹנֵיכֶם *v.* 3), any one of whom might have been set up to resist the usurper. Cf. *note* following on the use of the number *seventy*. Jehu's commission (*ch.* 9. 7) is explicitly not against Jehoram but against *the house of Aḥab*, and to describe the members of this house no other term could have been chosen by the writer than בְּנֵי אַחְאָב.

שבעים בנים] It is remarkable that *seventy* is the number of the sons of Gideon-Jerubba'al, Judg. 8. 30 *ff.*, and of the relations of Bar-Çûr of Ya'di (Panammu inscription, *l.* 3: D. H. Müller, *Die altsemit. Inschr. von Sendschirli*), who, in each case as here, are massacred to secure succession to the throne. Possibly, therefore, as Müller (*op. cit.*, p. 9) suggests, seventy is a round number to denote the whole of the royal kin[1].

אל שרי יזרעאל הזקנים] Luc. πρὸς τοὺς στρατηγοὺς τῆς πόλεως καὶ πρὸς τοὺς πρεσβυτέρους[2], Vulg. *ad optimates civitatis, et ad maiores natu*, i. e. אֶל־שָׂרֵי הָעִיר וְאֶל־הַזְּקֵנִים—certainly correct: cf. *v.* 5 MT. יזרעאל of MT. has arisen from a mistaken combination of the letters העירואל. Jehu was himself at Jezreel, and would scarcely have sent a letter to the authorities of that city with regard to the royal princes who were in Samaria. So Klo., Kamp., Benz., Kit.

ואל האמנים אחאב] Luc. καὶ πρὸς τοὺς τιθηνοὺς τῶν υἱῶν 'Αχαάβ, i. e. וְאֶל־הָאֹמְנִים אֶת־בְּנֵי אַחְאָב, probably correct. So Klo., Kamp., Benz., Kit.

2. ועתה] Cf. *ch.* 5. 6 *note*.

עיר מבצר] LXX, Luc., Vulg., Pesh., Targ. עָרֵי מִבְצָר. So Jos., and Th., Klo., Kamp., Benz., Kit.

5. אשר על הבית] Cf. I. 4. 6 *note*.

עשה] LXX, Luc. ποιήσομεν.

6. שנית] Several Codd., and LXX, Luc. שֵׁנִי—'a *second* letter.'

אנשי בני אדניכם] As the text stands, the first *st. constr.* is in apposition to the second (suspended construct state)—'The men, the sons of your master.' Cf. Da. § 28, *Rem.* 6. Possibly אנשי is

[1] In Judg. 12. 13 *f.* the *descendants* of Abdon are seventy; forty sons and thirty grandsons, riding upon seventy asses.

[2] LXX agrees with Luc., except in the substitution of Σαμαρείας for τῆς πόλεως, an alteration made for the sake of precision.

merely a doublet of ראשי. Kamp., Oort omit the word. Sta. emends אַנְשֵׁי בֵּית א׳. Luc. λαβέτο ἕκαστος τὴν κεφαλὴν τοῦ υἱοῦ τοῦ κυρίου αὐτοῦ, i. e. probably קְחוּ אִישׁ אֶת־רֹאשׁ בֶּן־אֲדֹנֵיכֶם; adopted by Benz., Kit. as far as regards the use of איש.

ובאו] LXX, Luc., Pesh. וְהָבִאוּ 'and bring (them).' So Th., Sta., Klo.

7. וישחטו] LXX, Luc., Pesh. וַיִּשְׁחָטוּם, correctly:—'slew them, even seventy men.'

בַּדּוּדִים] 'In baskets': so all Verss. On the use of the article cf. I. 1. 1 *note* on בִּבְגָדִים.

8. המלאך] '*The* messenger.' Cf. I. 13. 14 *note*.

הביאו] LXX Ἤνεγκα—probably an easy alteration of MT.

9. ומי הכה וג׳] It is assumed that the populace know who were the perpetrators of the massacre, but not the fact that Jehu was the instigator of it. The inference is therefore clear to fair-minded men (צַדִּקִים אַתֶּם) that this is no case of the unscrupulous securing of his own interests by a single individual, but that circumstances are working together to bring about the destruction of the house of Aḥab (*v.* 10).

11. וכל גדליו] Luc. καὶ πάντας τοὺς ἀγχιστεύοντας αὐτοῦ, i. e. וְכָל־גֹּאֲלָיו 'even all *his kinsmen*':—probably correct; cf. I. 16. 11 *note*. So Klo.

הִשְׁאִיר] Cf. *ch.* 3. 25, *note* 2.

12. ויקם וג׳] By the side of וילך, ויבא is redundant; at least we should expect it to *follow* וילך and immediately precede שמרון, as in Pesh. LXX, Luc., Vulg. omit ויבא, probably correctly. Perhaps the word is a corruption of יֵהוּא. So Klo., Benz., Kit.

בית עקד] The rendering of RV. 'shearing house,' marg. 'house of gathering' (Targ. בית כנישת), is merely conjectural. The verb עקד, Gen. 22. 9†, means, as in New Heb., Ar., and Aram., *to bind*.

13. ויהוא] Read וְהוּא, with Dri. *Tenses*, § 169, *Obs.* 2. The events described by *v.* 12^{b} and *v.* 13^{a} are thus pointedly synchronized in accordance with the idiom of the language:—'He was at Beth-ʽeqed of the shepherds by the way, when he found &c.' Cf. 1 Sam. 9. 11; Judg. 18. 3; Gen. 38. 25. It is noticeable that

Luc., Vulg. omit the proper name, and may thus be regarded as supporting the emendation[1].

לשלום] The expression which ordinarily has the meaning 'to enquire after' is לִשְׁאֹל לְשָׁלוֹם פ׳; 2 Sam. 11. 7; 1 Sam. 10. 4; 17. 22; *al.* If this phrase in full was originally written in our passage, the omission of לשאל is earlier than the Verss., all of which agree with MT.

14. ויתפשום חיים] LXX omits; Luc., Pesh. apparently read ויתפשום simply.

אל בור בית עקד] LXX, Luc. omit בור.

15. לקראתו] Luc. ἐν τῇ ὁδῷ ἐρχόμενον εἰς ἀπάντησιν αὐτοῦ. בַּדֶּרֶךְ (if not a doublet of בֶּן־רֵכָב) may be original: ἐρχόμενον, like ܕܐܬܐ ܠܗ of Pesh., is due to the translator.

היש וג׳] Doubtless we ought to follow LXX, Luc. in reading הֲיֵשׁ לְבָבְךָ אֶת־לְבָבִי יָשָׁר, thus securing a perfect parallelism with the following clause. So Th., Klo., Benz., Oort. Kamp., Kit. adopt the less probable order הֲיֵשׁ לְבָבְךָ יָשָׁר אֶת־לְבָבִי.

ויש] '"If it be" (said he).' The writer regards it as sufficiently evident that וְיֵשׁ וג׳ is the *response* to the preceding יֵשׁ. Cf. I. 20. 34. Probably the additions of LXX, Luc. καὶ εἶπεν Εἰού, Luc. καὶ εἶπεν αὐτῷ 'Ιού, Vulg. *inquit*, Pesh. ܘܐܡܪ ܠܗ (*after* ויש, which is assigned to Jonadab as though יש ויש meant 'It is indeed!') are due in each case to the translator.

With וְיֵשׁ cf. וָלֹא *ch.* 5. 17 *note.*

16. וירכבו אתו] Read וַיַּרְכֵּב אֹתוֹ with LXX, Luc., Pesh. So Th., Oort. וַיִּרְכַּב אִתּוֹ Klo., Kamp., Benz.; וַיִּרְכְּבוּ אִתּוֹ Kit.

17. עַד־הִשְׁמִדוֹ] Cf. *note* 2 on 3. 25.

18. ויהוא יעבדנו] Luc. καὶ ἐγὼ δουλεύσω αὐτῷ, Vulg. *ego autem colam eum;*—inferior to MT.

19. כל עבדיו] Klo., Kamp., Benz., Kit. cut out the two words as an erroneous insertion from *v.* 21. Jehu summons the *prophets*

---

[1] It is certain that Vulg., reading וְהוּא מָצָא, would have left the pronoun unexpressed, and rendered, as is actually the case, *invenit*. Cf. in Vulg. the other cases of the idiom cited. That the same course may have been followed in the Greek may be inferred from the rendering of Gen. 38. 25.

and *priests* of Ba'al, who are commanded to proclaim a solemn assembly, to which the *worshippers in general* are summoned (*v.* 20 *f.*). It is noticeable that in Luc. καὶ πάντας τοὺς δούλους αὐτοῦ *follows* καὶ τοὺς ἱερεῖς αὐτοῦ, as though inserted from the margin.

20. ויקראו] LXX, Luc., Vulg. sing. וַיִּקְרָא.

21. LXX erroneously expands the verse from *v.* 19.

פה לפה] *Ch.* 21. 16†.

22. המלתחה] The context demands the meaning 'wardrobe'; cf. Vulg. *vestes*. In Eth. እልታሕ: *'eltāḥ* denotes a kind of *tunic;* cf. Dillmann, *Lexicon*, 45 *f.*

המלבוש] LXX, Luc. ὁ στολιστής, i.e. הַמַּלְבִּישׁ.

23. 'מעבדי י] Luc. adds καὶ ἐξαποστείλατε αὐτούς. καὶ εἶπον Οὐκ εἰσὶν κ.τ.λ.; adopted by Klo.

24. ויבאו] LXX sing. καὶ εἰσῆλθεν. Cf. the sing. reference to Jehu as the chief offerer in *v.* 25 כְּכַלֹּתוֹ. So Klo., Sta., Kamp., Benz., Kit. Luc. places 24ª after 24ᵇ, and adds, after εἰσῆλθον, the gloss εἰς τὸν οἶκον τοῦ προσοχθίσματος. Elsewhere in the context בעל = Βάαλ, never προσόχθισμα.

שמנים] Luc. τρισχιλίους, Pesh. ܬܠܬܡܐܐ ܘܬܡܢܝܢ, 380.

'האיש וג] As יִמָּלֵט is vocalized, the sentence is extremely difficult. Read יְמַלֵּט with Th., Klo., Kamp., Benz., Kit.:—'The man *who suffers to escape* any of the men, &c., his life shall be for his life.'

על ידיכם] 'Into (lit. *upon*) your hands.' So, after נתן, Gen. 42. 37; after הִגִּיר, Jer. 18. 21; Ezek. 35. 5; Ps. 63. 11.

25. ככלתו] Pesh. ܟܕ ܫܠܡܘ, i.e. כְּכַלֹּתָם.

לרצים] Cf. I. 1. 5 *note*.

ולשלשים] Cf. I. 9. 22 *note*.

וישלכו] The object is missing. RV., 'cast them out,' finds the reference to be to the corpses of the slain; but it is reasonable to expect this to be more precisely indicated. Klo. is right in finding the object of וישלכו to lie concealed under הרצים והשלשים, the repetition in detail of the subject of the verb in MT. being scarcely less strange than the omission of the object. He ingeniously suggests וַיַּשְׁלִכוּ אַרְצָה הָאֲשֵׁרִים 'and they cast the Asherim down to the ground.' This restoration, however, is not very likely to represent the original if the emendation adopted in *v.* 26 be correct, which thus makes reference to the (single) Ashera of the temple.

עד עיר וג׳] 'To the *city* of the house of Ba'al' can hardly be correct. Klo.'s emendation עַד־דְּבִיר וג׳ 'to the *adytum*, &c.' (cf. I. 6. 16 *note*), is very suitable to the context, though it is illegitimate to cite the rendering of Luc. ἕως τοῦ ναοῦ τοῦ Βάαλ in support of the emendation[1]. The other Verss. agree with MT.

26. מצבות] The Verss. presuppose a sing. מַצֵּבַת, in accordance with the suffix of וישרפוה. But, as Sta. (*ZATW.*, 1885, p. 278) remarks, the *stone* Maççēba cannot have been burnt, and it is therefore probable that we ought to substitute אֲשֵׁרַת 'the Ashera of the house of Ba'al,' in accordance with I. 16. 33, וַיַּעַשׂ אַחְאָב אֶת־הָאֲשֵׁרָה: cf. *ch.* 23. 6. So Kamp., Benz., Kit., Oort. On the character of the Ashera cf. I. 14. 15 *note*.

27. מצבת] Sta., Kamp., Benz., Kit. emend מִזְבַּח, the first comparing I. 16. 32, and, for the expression נתץ מזבח, Ex. 34. 13; Deut. 7. 5; 12. 3; Judg. 2. 2; 6. 28 *ff.* Mention of the destruction of the *altar* is to be expected, supposing the clause to be not merely a doublet of that which follows (Klo.), which it resembles somewhat suspiciously.

למחראות] Kt. לְמַחֲרָאוֹת.

10. 29–36. *Summary of Jehu's reign: his character and his foreign relations.*

R^D *vv.* 28–31, 34–36; *vv.* 32, 33 summarized from the Annals.

29. עגלי הזהב] '(Namely) the golden calves,' in apposition to חטאי י׳. Vulg., with a view to make the connexion more clear, inserts *nec dereliquit*, Targ. אישתעבד ל.

32. בימים ההם] The same phrase is used by R^D in *ch.* 15. 37; 20. 1. Cf. *note* on I. 3. 16.

---

[1] דְּבִיר in I. 6. 5, 16, 19, 21, 23, 31; 7. 49; 8. 8 appears as δαβείρ; and, assuming that τοῦ ναοῦ could answer to דביר, as in Ps. 28 (LXX 27). 2, בית remains unrepresented, and דְּבִיר הַבַּעַל simply is scarcely likely to have been read by the translator.

לקצות בישראל] 'To cut Israel short,' lit. 'to cut off in Israel.' The expression is strange, though Hab. 2. 10 קְצוֹת עַמִּים רַבִּים affords an instance of the use of the verb קצה in this sense. The original reading is probably preserved by Vulg. *taedere super Israel*, i.e. לָקוּץ בְּיִשְׂרָאֵל 'to loathe Israel'; cf. Gen. 27. 46 קַצְתִּי בְחַיַּי, *Taedet me vitae meae*. So Klo. Targ. למתקף רוגזיה seems to have read לִקְצוֹף 'to be angry with,' and this is adopted by Th., Kamp., Benz., Kit.

33. מן הירדן וג'] The double mention of הגלעד introduces confusion, and Grä., Buhl. (*Geogr.* 70) simplify the description by cutting out the first הגלעד, and also the ו before the second. The fact that, at the time of the fall of Omri's dynasty, Rama of Gilead appears to have been the most northern point of Israel's dominions east of Jordan causes some critics (cf. Sta. *ZATW.*, 1885, p. 279; Benz., Kit.) to regard the verse, either as a whole or in part, as a later addition.

33[b]. מערער וג'] The same description of the position of עֲרֹעֵר, with the addition of שְׂפַת before נַחַל, is found in Deut. 2. 36; 3. 12; 4. 48; Josh. 12. 2; 13. 9, 16. The site of 'Aro'er is found in a heap of ruins called *'Ar'âîr*, south of *Dîbân*, and standing on a hill on the northern side of the ravine of Arnon. Buhl, 269.

והגלעד] Luc. adds καὶ 'Ιαβόκ.

34. וכל גבורתו] LXX, Luc. add καὶ τὰς (Luc. αἱ) συνάψεις ἃς συνῆψεν, i.e. וְקִשְׁרוֹ אֲשֶׁר קָשַׁר. Cf. I. 16. 20; *ch.* 15. 15.

36. At the end of the verse Luc. adds ἐν ἔτει δευτέρῳ τῆς Γοθολίας βασιλεύει κύριος τὸν 'Ιοὺ υἱὸν Ναμεσσί, and then continues with a summary account of Aḥaziah's reign, derived in the main from *ch.* 8. 25 *ff.*, with a brief mention of the events of *ch.* 9 in so far as they concern the death of Aḥaziah.

11. *Athaliah the queen-mother usurps the throne of Judah. At the end of six years Jehoiada the priest effects a revolution, and sets Jehoash, the rightful heir, upon the throne.*

Ch. 11 forms the basis of 2 Chr. 22. 10—23. 21.

This chapter and its sequel, *ch.* 12. 5–17, form, with *chh.* 16.

10–16; 22. 3—23. 25, a series of Judaean narratives which reflect prominently the influence of the priests as conservators of the religion of Yahwe, and in which the interest centres to a great extent round the Temple at Jerusalem. Probably therefore, as Sta. suggests, the source from which the narratives were drawn may have been the Temple-archives.

Sta. (*ZATW.*, 1885, pp. 280 *ff.*) has pointed out that *ch.* 11 is probably a combination of two narratives. The first, *vv.* 4–12, 18b–20, is a continuous whole; the second, *vv.* 13–18a, merely a fragment. According to the first, Jehoiada effects the revolution by the aid of the royal bodyguard (הָרָצִים); in the second, it is the people (הָעָם) who are prominent. The insertion of הָרָצִין in *v.* 13 in apposition to הָעָם is clearly a redactional device, and traces of the redactor's hand are also to be found in *v.* 15 (see *ad loc.*).

The recognition of this composite character of the narrative explains certain difficulties which are patent if it be read as a continuous whole. Thus, it cannot be thought that the destruction of the temple of Ba'al (*v.* 18a) took place between the anointing and enthronement of Jehoash. It would naturally occur *after* the measures taken against Athaliah, and not as an episode in their course. Again, it is difficult to understand why the setting of a guard over the Temple (*v.* 18b) should have been necessary *after* the death of Athaliah (*vv.* 15, 16). The purpose of such a guard can only have been to protect the Temple against the danger of an attack by the queen and her adherents. It is strange, also, if the narrative be a whole, that there should be two accounts of the death of Athaliah; *vv.* 15, 16 and *v.* 20b.

The main difference between the two narratives seems to be that while the fragment emphasizes the *religious* importance of the revolution, the continuous narrative regards it purely as an event of civil importance. This difference does not set the two accounts at variance; the religious revolution may well have followed in the train of the civil.

The parallel narrative of 2 Chr. has been considerably expanded in parts by the editor, the priests and Levites being introduced and made to take the place which is occupied in Kings by the royal bodyguard.

11. 1. ותראה] Omit ו with Q're and ‖ 2 Chr.

ותאבד] ‖ 2 Chr. וַתְּדַבֵּר, a scribal error.

2. יהושבע] ‖ 2 Chr. יְהוֹשַׁבְעַת. She is there stated to have been אֵשֶׁת יְהוֹיָדָע הַכֹּהֵן.

בן אחזיה] LXX *υἱὸν ἀδελφοῦ αὐτῆς*, i.e. בֶּן־אָחִיהָ. Luc. combines the two readings.

אתו ואת מנקתו] ‖ 2 Chr. prefixes וַתִּתֵּן, which is indispensable. So Ew., Th., Klo., Kamp., Benz., Kit.

ויסתרו אתו] LXX, Luc., Vulg., Pesh. וַתַּסְתֵּר אֹתוֹ. So ‖ 2 Chr. וַתַּסְתִּירֵהוּ.

4. יהוידע] Luc. adds *ὁ ἱερεύς*, i.e. הַכֹּהֵן, as in *vv.* 9 *ff.* The specification is necessary unless it be supposed that the narrative originally contained an earlier reference to Jehoiada, such as that of ‖ 2 Chr. noticed on *v.* 2.

המאיות] Kt. only again *vv.* 9, 10, 15. Kö. discusses the form and concludes that the י is merely euphonic, *mēyóth* for *mē'óth*, representing the pronunciation adopted for the avoidance of hiatus, as in Aramaic. *Lehrg.* I. i. p. 217; cf. p. 481.

לכרי] So *v.* 19 and 2 Sam. 20. 23 Kt. Probably the *Carians* are denoted. Cf. R. Sm. *OTJC.*[2], p. 262 *note.*

ולרצים] Cf. I. 1. 5 *note.*

ויכרת . . . בבית י׳] LXX *καὶ διέθετο αὐτοῖς διαθήκην Κυρίου καὶ ὥρκωσεν*, i.e. וַיִּכְרֹת לָהֶם בְּרִית י׳ וַיַּשְׁבַּע אֹתָם, probably correct. בבית י׳ at the end is superfluous, while ברית י׳ may be paralleled from 1 Sam. 20. 8. So Klo.

5–7. As Wellh. (*C.* 361) points out, *v.* 6 is clearly a gloss, the שתי ידות וג׳ of *v.* 7 answering to השלשית וג׳ of *v.* 5. By removal of this insertion, and reading וְשֹׁמְרֵי (as in *v.* 5) for וְשָׁמְרוּ in *v.* 7, we obtain an intelligible text in *vv.* 5, 7, 8:—'And he commanded them, saying, This is the thing which ye shall do; the third part of you who go in on the Sabbath and keep the guard of the king's house, and the two divisions of you, even all who go forth on the Sabbath and keep the guard of the House of Yahwe about the king, ye shall compass the king round about, &c.' The point is obviously that all the bodyguard is to be concentrated at the Temple, no part of it being at Athaliah's disposal at the palace: cf. *v.* 9.

5. At the end LXX adds ἐν τῷ πυλῶνι.

6. בשער סור] ‖ 2 Chr. בְּשַׁעַר הַיְסוֹד.

הבית מסח] The unintelligible מסח is omitted by LXX, and by ‖ 2 Chr. in the free explanation, וְכָל־הָעָם בְּחַצְרוֹת בֵּית יְהוָה. Field cites a Schol. which states the existence of a reading ἀμμελέχ, i.e. הַמֶּלֶךְ, adopted by Kit.

8. אל השדרות] 'Up to the ranks,' i.e. the lines of men surrounding the king, suggested by the previous והקפתם וג'. The word is the same as New Heb. סֵדֶר, Aram. סִדְרָא, ܣܕܪܐ. Vulg., *septum templi*, misunderstands. ‖ 2 Chr. אֶל־הַבַּיִת.

10. החנית] ‖ 2 Chr. הַחֲנִיתִים. So Th., Klo., Kamp., Benz., Kit.

השלטים] RV., here as in the other occurrences of the word, '*the shields*.' This rendering seems to be demanded by Song 4. 4, where כֹּל שִׁלְטֵי הַגִּבּוֹרִים stands in explanatory apposition to אֶלֶף הַמָּגֵן. Th. on 2 Sam. 8. 7 favours the more general meaning 'armour,' and the same view is taken by W. E. Barnes, who classifies the ancient renderings of the word: *Expos. Times*, Oct. 1898, pp. 43 *f*. The fact, however, that שלטים (here and in Jer. 51. 11) occurs in connexion with other specified items of military equipment is against the view that the term is used in a general and not a special sense. According to LXX, Luc. in I. 14. 26, the שִׁלְטֵי הַזָּהָב which David took from the servants of Hadadezer, king of Zoba, were carried off by Shishak, king of Egypt, during the reign of Rehoboam. Cf. *note ad loc.*

11. למזבח ולבית] RV. 'along by the altar and the house.' The meaning seems to be that the guards formed a semicircle extending from the south to the north corner of the Temple, and surrounding the brazen altar which stood before the Temple. Thus all the space between the porch and the altar would be enclosed. It is, however, highly doubtful whether ל can bear the sense '*along by*,' and whether, granted this sense, the writer would have chosen

to convey the explanation given above in so obscure a manner. Pesh. represents סביב . . . למזבח by ܘܐܬܩܝܡܘ ܥܠ ܡܕܒܚܐ ܘܥܠ ܒܝܬ ܡܠܟܐ. If we may regard ܒܝܬ ܡܠܟܐ as due to an erroneous explanation of הבית 'the house' (i.e. the Temple) as 'the king's house,' we obtain the good sense, סָבִיב לַמִּזְבֵּחַ וְלַבָּיִת 'round about the altar and the Temple.' סָבִיב seems to have been wrongly placed in MT., and then explained by the addition עַל־הַמֶּלֶךְ, a statement which at this stage of the proceedings is incorrect.

12. העדות] RV., following Verss., 'the testimony,' i.e., apparently, a written law-book, committed to the young king as head over the theocratic state; cf. Deut. 17. 18 *ff.* There is not, however, anywhere else allusion to such a custom as the laying of a book (?) upon (sc. the head of) a king at his coronation; the term עֵדוּת is a late one; and, if it represented the law of the kingdom embodied in a concrete form, it would be natural to expect that this fact would be more precisely indicated (e.g. סֵפֶר הָעֵדוּת). Thus it is reasonable to suspect the text of corruption. Wellh. (*C.* 361) makes the happy emendation הַצְּעָדוֹת '*the bracelets*,' which formed, with הַנֵּזֶר 'the diadem,' the royal insignia. Cf. 2 Sam. 1. 10[1].

13. הרצין העם] Obviously the two terms cannot stand together *ἀσυνδέτως*. הרצין is a gloss, roughly inserted for the purpose of connecting the narrative with that which precedes. Cf. *note* on the composition of the narrative. העם is probably used in a military sense. Cf. I. 16. 15 *note.*

14. אל המלך] '*By* the king.' For this sense of אל cf. *note* on I. 6. 18.

15. פְּקֻדֵי החיל] LXX *τοῖς ἐπισκόποις*, i.e. פְּקִידֵי, adopted by Sta., Kamp., Benz., Kit., is doubtless correct. MT. can only mean 'those of the army who were *mustered.*'

את שרי המאיות is superfluous by the side of פקידי החיל, and must be regarded as a gloss from *vv.* 4, 9, 10, of the same character as

---

[1] Reading הַצְּעָדָה for אֶצְעָדָה, with Wellh., Dri., Budde, &c.

that noticed in *v.* 13. The same is probably the case with the words אל מבית לשדרת, which seem to conflict with *v.* 15[b]. The queen is to be taken *outside* the Temple, and therefore not *inside* the ranks which, according to *v.* 8, surround the king within the Temple.

16. וישמו לה ידים] 'And they laid hands on her.' So LXX, Luc., Vulg., Kamp., Benz., Kit. The rendering, 'And they made way (lit. place) for her,' Pesh., Targ., adopted among moderns by Ke., Th., Klo., AV., RV., is not to be paralleled[1].

19. וישבו] LXX, Luc. καὶ ἐκάθισαν αὐτόν. So || 2 Chr. וַיּוֹשִׁיבוּ אֶת־הַמֶּלֶךְ.

12. 1–4. *Introduction by* R[D] *to the reign of Jehoash.*

Ch. 12. 1–3 = 2 Chr. 24. 1, 2.

12. 1, 2. Luc. reads יְהוֹאָשׁ בֶּן־אֲחַזְיָהוּ in the synchronism of *v.* 2, and inserts *v.* 1, the statement of the king's age at accession, *after* the synchronism, thus conforming to the order which is constant elsewhere in the introductory formula. See *Introduction.*

3. ויעש וג'] 'And Jehoash did that which was right in the sight of Yahwe all his days, forasmuch as Jehoiada the priest instructed him.' So Ew., Th.[2], Kamp. The antecedent of אשר is found in יהואש; lit. '*he who* Jehoiada instructed.' Cf. e.g. Gen. 42. 21 אֲשֶׁר רָאִינוּ '*we who* saw' (or, '*in that* we saw'); *Heb. Lex. Oxf.*, *s.v.* אשר, 8 *c.* AV., RV., Kit., following LXX, Luc., Vulg., render 'all his days wherein Jehoiada the priest instructed him,' thus limiting the period of the king's good living to the life-time of Jehoiada, in accordance with || 2 Chr. 24. 2, כָּל־יְמֵי יְהוֹיָדָע הַכֹּהֵן, and the narrative of 2 Chr. 24. 17–22 which relates the defection of Jehoash from the religion of Yahwe and his murder of the son of Jehoiada. But the normal method of expressing such a sense

---

[1] יָדַיִם in Josh. 8. 20 does not mean *place* or *room* (Ges. *Thes.*), but *power*, as in Ps. 76. 6; singular יָד Deut. 32. 36. Cf. Dillmann, *ad loc.*; *Heb. Lex. Oxf.*

[2] Pesh., Targ. are ambiguous in meaning, and cannot be cited, as by Th., in favour of this rendering. The accentuation of MT., however, in placing the principal break upon יָמָיו, is certainly intended to convey the meaning adopted.

would have been כָּל־הַיָּמִים אֲשֶׁר וגו׳, as e.g. in 1 Sam. 1. 28. כָּל־יָמָיו is elsewhere in every occurrence used absolutely, without further definition, in the sense '*all his life long*':—I. 15. 14, ‖ 2 Chr. 15. 17; *ch.* 15. 18; 2 Chr. 18. 17; 34. 33; Deut. 22. 19, 29; Eccl. 2. 23; 5. 16†. Moreover, as Ew. points out, it seems to be clear that R[D] was unacquainted with any narrative of the king's defection, for 'had this been so, then the older historical work must have told us how Joash showed himself faithless afterwards; but so far is this from being the case, that the piety of his successor is afterwards compared with his own, and that of both regarded as inferior to David's alone, 2 Ki. 14. 3 (the Chronicles omit this passage); even Uzziah is only treated as their equal, 2 Ki. 15. 3; 2 Chr. 26. 4.'

It is, of course, possible that the statement אשר הורהו וגו׳ may be an early marginal note intended to qualify the absolute כל ימיו, in accordance with the narrative of Chr. This supposition is perhaps favoured by the reading of ‖ 2 Chr. כל ימי יהוידע, which looks like a limited explanation of כל ימיו simply.

4. רק הבמות וגו׳] Cf. I. 3. 2, 3 *note.*

12. 5–17. *Measures taken by Jehoash for the repair of the House of Yahwe.*

2 Chr. 24. 4–14 gives a different narrative of the same events.

5. כסף עובר וגו׳] Very difficult. As the text stands, כסף עובר must mean 'current money' (RV.). Cf. Gen. 23. 16. Then the four following words are rendered by RV. 'the money of the persons for whom each man is rated'; *marg.* Heb. 'each man the money of the souls of his estimation.' The construction is here similar to that of Gen. 9. 5 אִישׁ אָחִיו 'each man his brother,' i.e. 'each man's brother'; Gen. 15. 10 אִישׁ בִּתְרוֹ 'each its half,' i.e. 'the half of each.'

Luc. represents כסף עובר . . . ערכו by ἀργύριον συντιμήσεως ἀνδρός, ἀργύριον συντιμήσεως ψυχῶν, i.e. כֶּסֶף עֶרֶךְ אִישׁ וגו׳. It is certainly a great simplification of the text if we suppose, with Sta., Kamp., Benz., Kit., that these first three words, '*the money of each man's assessment*' (cf. Lev. 27. 2 *ff.*), represent the original text, and that כסף נפשות ערכו is an explanatory gloss which has come into the text as a doublet.

כל כסף] It is necessary to insert ו before כל, '*and* all the money &c.' The freewill offering of money which a man's heart prompts him to make is clearly distinct from the sum which is assessed by tariff.

6. איש מאת מכרו] Apparently, 'each from his acquaintance,' RV. The scope with which מַכָּר (only again *v.* 8) is employed is highly obscure, and the word is justly regarded with suspicion by Kamp., Benz. LXX ἀπὸ τῆς πράσεως αὐτοῦ (Luc. αὐτῶν) vocalizes מִכְרוֹ ; Vulg. *juxta ordinem suum* (?).

בדק] 'Dilapidation.' Cf. *ch.* 22. 5; Ezek. 27. 9, 27.

לכֹל] 'For everything,' i. e. '*wherever*.'

9. קְחַת] This form, in place of the ordinary קַחַת, appears here only. Kö. (*Lehrg.* II. i. 490) cites the similar segholate *st. constr.* forms חֲדַר, זְרַע, נְטַע, שְׁבַע, תְּשַׁע, בְּעַד. Cf. G-K. § 93 *h.*

10. ארון אחד] אֲרוֹן, though vocalized as *st. constr.*, can only be regarded as *st. abs.;* Kimḥi's explanation, 'the chest of (*belonging to*) some one,' being excluded by || 2 Chr. 24. 8 וַיַּעֲשׂוּ אֲרוֹן אֶחָד, and the statement of Ew., § 286[d], that 'the numeral אֶחָד *one*, though mostly used as an adjective, may nevertheless be subordinated to its noun, put in the construct state,' being in the present case inconceivable. Cf. Kö. *Syntax*, § 310 *d.* Probably the vocalization here and in Lev. 24. 22, מִשְׁפַּט אֶחָד, is merely an error of the punctuators. פַּחַת אַחַד וגו׳ II. 18. 24 (cf. *note*) is perhaps different.

אצל המזבח] The statement that the chest was placed *beside the altar* seems scarcely to accord with the fact that it was given into the charge of the keepers of the threshold, who placed in it the money which they received from persons entering the House of Yahwe. Hence Sta., following the suggestion of the LXX transliteration in Cod. A, αμμασβη, emends אֵצֶל הַמַּצֵּבָה, a suggestion favoured by Kamp., Kit., Oort. The fact that Maççēbōth existed subsequently in the Temple appears from *chh.* 18. 4; 23. 4 *ff.* Klo. emends אֵצֶל הַמְּזוּזָה '*beside the doorpost*,' and this agrees well with the following בַּיָּמִין Kt., and is favoured by Benz., who objects to the former suggestion on the ground that Maççēbōth usually stood in Semitic sanctuaries near the altar and not near the entrance.

‖ 2 Chr. 24. 8 בְּשַׁעַר בֵּית י׳ חוּצָה.

ונתנו] Frequentative, '*used to place.*' So *v.* 12. Cf. the imperfects of *vv.* 14–17. For the reversion to the imperf. with ו *consec.* in *vv.* 11, 12ᵇ cf. Dri. *Tenses*, § 114.

המובא] LXX, Luc. τὸ εὑρεθέν, as in *v.* 11.

11. ויצרו] Luc. omits, while Pesh. places after וימנו.

13. אבני מחצב] So *ch.* 22. 6.

ולכל וג׳] 'And for all for which outlay should be made upon the house.' אשר יצא, lit. 'for which it (i.e. הכסף *v.* 12ᵃ) should go forth.'

לְחָזְקָה] 'For repair.' Probably the vocalization should be לְחַזְּקָהּ 'to repair it'; cf. Luc., Pesh., Targ. So Klo., Benz.

17. כסף אשם וג׳] The reference appears to be to fines in money. Cf. Wellh. *Prolegomena*, 73.

12. 18–22. *Closing events of the reign of Jehoash, summarized by* Rᴰ.

Ch. 12. 18–22 forms the substance of 2 Chr. 24. 23–27.

18. אז יעלה] Cf. I. 3. 16 *note.*

21. בית מלא] Cf. *note* on הַמִּלּוֹא I. 9. 15.

22. ויוכר וג׳] ‖ 2 Chr. זָבָד בֶּן־שִׁמְעָת הָעַמּוֹנִית וִיהוֹזָבָד בֶּן־שִׁמְרִית הַמּוֹאָבִית.

13. 1–9. *Jehoaḥaz, king of Israel.*

Rᴰ frames short notices from the Annals.

13. 3. כל הימים] 'All the days,' viz. of Jehoaḥaz. Cf. *note* on I. 5. 15. The statement is made rather loosely if the events of *v.* 5 belong to this reign.

4. ויחל וג׳] For the expression cf. I. 13. 6 *note.*

5. ויצאו] Luc. καὶ ἐξήγαγεν αὐτούς, i. e. וַיֹּצִיאוּם.

מתחת יד ארם] Luc. adds καὶ ἀπεστράφη ὅριον Ἰσραὴλ αὐτοῖς.

באהליהם] Not strictly 'in their tents,' but '*in their homes.*' Cf. I. 8. 66; Judg. 19. 9, and the phrase of I. 12. 16; 2 Sam. 20. 1.

7. כי לא השאיר וג׳] The reference of כי is to *v.* 4^b, and the subject of השאיר is not Yahwe (Th., Kamp., Kit.) nor Ḥazael (Benz.), but is indefinite (הַמַּשְׁאִיר; cf. I. 1. 6 *note* on יִלְּדָה):—'For there was not left to Jehoaḥaz &c.' So LXX, Luc. οὐχ ὑπελείφθη, Vulg. *non sunt derelicti*, Pesh. ܠܐ ܐܫܬܒܩܘ ܗܘܐ.

לדש] 'For treading.' Klo. emends לָרֹק after Luc. ἕως τοῦ λεπτυνθῆναι, and so Kamp., Benz., Oort. The change is unnecessary.

After *v.* 7 Luc. inserts *v.* 23 of MT. Probably this is correct. The mention of Jehoash's successes against Aram would form a reason for transferring the verse from its position in Luc. to that which it occupies in MT., whilst no reason can be cited for the converse change. Again, it is clear that the position assigned by Luc. to *vv.* 12, 13 MT. is correct; and this creates a strong presumption in favour of the position of *v.* 23 in Luc.

13. 10–25. *Jehoash, king of Israel.*

R^D *vv.* 10–13; two Elisha-narratives from North Palestinian sources, *vv.* 14–19, 20, 21; short notices from the Annals framed by R^D *vv.* 22–25.

Vet. Lat. (Cod. Vind.) places 13. 14–21 between 10. 30 and 10. 31, making the narrative refer not to Jehoash but to Jehu.

10. בשנת שלשים ושבע] This synchronism disagrees with the statement of *v.* 1, that Jehoaḥaz, who reigned seventeen years, came to the throne in the twenty-third year of Jehoash. We should therefore expect the synchronism to be בשנת שלשים ותשע 'in the thirty-ninth year'; and this alteration agrees with *ch.* 14. 1, where the second year of Jehoash of Israel synchronizes with the accession of Amaziah.

שש עשרה שנה] Pesh. ܬܠܬܥܣܪܐ ܫܢܝܢ 'thirteen years.'

12, 13. These two verses appear in Luc. at the close of the chapter, a position which, in accordance with the scheme of R^D, is clearly correct. Luc. also replaces the unusual formula וירבעם ישב על כסאו in *v.* 13^a by the regular καὶ ἐβασίλευσεν 'I. υἱὸς αὐτοῦ ἀντ' αὐτοῦ at the end of *v.* 13^b.

The formula for the close of this reign is repeated in *ch.* 14. 15, 16, where it is due to the preceding account of Jehoash in relationship to Amaziah. As this narrative, however, forms part of the history of the reign of Amaziah, the introduction of *vv.* 15, 16 breaks the connexion, and is probably the work of a later hand. The repetition is not found in Luc.

14. אשר ימות בו] Not, as RV., 'whereof he died,' but, 'whereof *he was to die*.' Cf. Dri. *Tenses*, § 39 β.

ויבך על פניו] Cf. Gen. 50. 1 וַיִּפֹּל יוֹסֵף עַל־פְּנֵי אָבִיו וַיֵּבְךְּ עָלָיו.

אבי וגו'] Cf. *ch.* 2. 12 *note.*

17[b]. ויאמר . . . ויור] LXX omits through oversight.

באפק] Cf. I. 20. 26 *note.*

18. קח החצים] Luc. Λαβὲ πέντε βέλη.

19. להכות] '(It was) for smiting,' and so 'Thou shouldest have smitten.' Cf. 2 Sam. 4. 10 אֲשֶׁר לְתִתִּי לוֹ 'To whom (it was) for my giving,' i.e. 'To whom I should have given.' Dri. *Tenses*, § 204. Klo.'s emendation לוּ הִכִּתָ, after the rendering of LXX, Luc. εἰ ἐπάταξας, is unnecessary.

חמש או שש פעמים] Vulg. adds *sive septies.*

20. יבאו] Probably, 'kept on coming.'

בא שנה] The text gives no sense, but LXX, Luc. ἐλθόντος τοῦ ἐνιαυτοῦ suggest the emendation כְּבֹא הַשָּׁנָה 'when the (new) year came.' Cf. the phrase of I. 20. 22, 26 לִתְשׁוּבַת הַשָּׁנָה. Vulg. *in ipso anno*, Pesh. ܒܗ ܒܫܢܬܐ ܗܝ must have read בָּהּ שָׁנָה as though for בָּהּ בַּשָּׁנָה, an Aramaic construction. Benz. emends בַּשָּׁנָה 'yearly'(?); Kit. שָׁנָה בַּשָּׁנָה.

21. ויהי הם קברים וגו'] Cf. I. 13. 20 *note.*

23. ולא השליכם וגו'] Cf. *ch.* 17. 20 (R^D).

24. וימלך בן הדד בנו] Winckler (*Alttest. Untersuchungen*, 66) gives reasons for identifying this king with *Mari'*, king of Damascus, who was brought into subjection by the Assyrian king Rammân-nirari III in his campaign against the nations of the West, between B.C. 806–803. Cf. *KB.* i. 191; Winckler, *Keilinschrift. Textbuch*, 12 *f.*

25. את ערי ישראל] Luc. adds καὶ ὅσα ἔλαβεν.

14. 1–22. *Amaziah, king of Judah.*

Ch. 14. 1–14, 17–22 = 2 Chr. 25. 1–4, 11, 17–28; 26. 1, 2.

R^D embodies short notices from the Annals, together with a complete narrative (*vv.* 8–14; cf. p. 215) from an unknown source.

14. 2. יהועדין] ‖ 2 Chr. supports Q're יְהוֹעַדָּן. So Vulg., Pesh., Targ. LXX, Luc. Ἰωαδείμ. Cod. A. Ἰωαδείν.

3, 4. רק לא כדוד וג׳] ‖ 2 Chr. 25. 2^b sums up the limitations to the favourable verdict in the terse statement רַק לֹא בְּלֵבָב שָׁלֵם.

4. רק הבמות וג׳] Cf. I. 3. 2, 3 *note.*

5^b. המלך] LXX, Luc. omit.

6^b. ככתוב וג׳] Citation is made by R^D directly from Deut. 24. 16. For ימות Kt., יָמֻת Q're, Deut. reads יוּמָתוּ. ‖ 2 Chr. 25. 4 יָמוּתוּ.

7. הוא הכה] The emphatic הוא (almost '*It was he who* smote &c.') occurs again *vv.* 22, 25; 15. 35^b; 18. 4, 8, and may be regarded as a mark of the style of R^D in connecting together detached notices relating to one particular king.

בני המלח] Kt. is supported by ‖ 2 Chr. 25. 11; 1 Chr. 18. 12; Q're בְּנֵי מֶלַח by 2 Sam. 8. 13; Ps. 60. 2.

ותפש] Perfect with weak ו, a mark of decadence in style, due not to R^D, but to his source. So elsewhere in later extracts from the Annals, *ch.* 18. 4; 21. 4, 6. The style of R^D is always, like that of Deuteronomy his model, of the best (cf. e.g. *ch.* 17); the style of the extracts is on a level with that of the lengthy narrative *ch.* 22. 3—23. 25, and may be taken as representing the popular style (as distinct from the prophetic or literary style) of the closing years of the kingdom of Judah.

הסלע] Cf. Judg. 1. 36; Isa. 16. 1; 42. 11 (סֶלַע without article). The usual identification with *Petra* (cf. Baed. 206) is denied by Buhl, *Edomites*, 34 *ff.* ‖ 2 Chr. 25. 11 finds reference to '*the crag*' from which ten thousand captive Edomites were thrown headlong. The name יָקְתְאֵל (LXX, Luc. Καθοήλ) as an Edomite city does not appear elsewhere.

8. אז] Cf. I. 3. 16 *note.*

10. ונשאך] Probably perf. with weak ו 'and thy heart *hath lifted*

thee up.' Another occurrence is found in *v.* 14 וְלָקַח. Cf. *note* on ותפש *v.* 7.

הכבד] 'Enjoy your honour' ('let yourself be honoured').

ולמה] The force of ו is sarcastic: '*Pray*, why?' Cf. I. 2. 22 *note.*

11. בית שמש] Cf. I. 4. 9 *note.*

13. ויבאו] Luc., Vulg. presuppose וַיְבִיאֵהוּ as in ‖ 2 Chr. 25. 23, probably correctly.

בשער אפרים] Read מִשַּׁעַר א׳ with Luc., Vulg., Pesh., Targ., ‖ 2 Chr.

שער הפנה] Cf. 2 Chr. 26. 9; Jer. 31. 38. A שַׁעַר הַפִּנִּים is mentioned in Zech. 14. 10.

14. ולקח] לקח is omitted in ‖ 2 Chr. 25. 24, and it is therefore possible that the word may be a later insertion made to supply the missing verb, which may have been וַיִּקַּח, or לָקַח following after התערבות. Cf., however, ונשאך *v.* 10 *note.*

15, 16. Omitted in Luc. Cf. *note* on *ch.* 13. 12, 13.

18ª. After אמציהו, LXX adds καὶ πάντα ἃ (Luc. ὅσα) ἐποίησεν.

19. לכישה] An old Amorite city, several times named in the Tell el-Amarna inscriptions; probably the modern *Tell el-Ḥasi* some distance east of Gaza, and close to the south of *'Ajlân*, i.e. Eglon. Cf. Smith, *Geogr.* 234; Baed. 140; Buhl, 191 *f.*

21. את עזריה] Luc. adds υἱὸν αὐτοῦ. Pesh. ܥܘܙܝܐ conforms to ‖ 2 Chr. 26. 1 עֻזִּיָּהוּ.

22. הוא בנה] Cf. *note* on הוא הכה *v.* 7.

14. 23–29. *Jeroboam II, king of Israel.*

R^D frames short notices from the Annals.

23. מלך ישראל בשמרון] The usual phrase is על ישראל בשמרון, and this appears in LXX, Targ., while Luc. combines the two readings.

ארבעים ואחת שנה] Luc. καὶ τεσσαράκοντα καὶ ἓν ἔτος ἐβασίλευσεν ἐν Σαμαρείᾳ.

25. מלבוא וג׳] Cf. I. 8. 65 *note.*

גת חפר] Mentioned again in the description of the territory assigned to the tribe of Zebulun, Josh. 19. 13. Tradition, both

Christian and Mohammedan, places the tomb of Jonah at *el-Meshhed*, about three miles to the north-east of Nazareth, and this village is therefore usually regarded as the site of Gath Ḥepher. Rob. *BR*. ii. 350; Baed. 285; Buhl, 219.

26. מרה מאד] As vocalized מֹרֶה 'rebellious' gives no sense. The Verss. render 'bitter,' which is doubtless the meaning intended, but fem. מָרָה is out of agreement with masc. עֳנִי. Hence Kamp. would emend כִּי מַר הוּא, a suggestion favoured by Benz., Kit. It is simpler to transpose the ה of מרה, and to read הַמַּר 'the very bitter affliction of Israel.'

ואפס עצור וג׳] Cf. I. 14. 10 *note*.

27. למחות וג׳] So Deut. 9. 14; 29. 19.

28. ואשר השיב וג׳] Certainly corrupt. The rendering of RV., Kamp., 'How he recovered Damascus, and Ḥamath, (which had belonged) to Judah, for Israel,' cannot be obtained from the text; reference in such terms to the state of affairs *under David* is impossible, since David's kingdom is never designated as 'Judah'; and, even if such reference could be substantiated, it would be untrue, since Ḥamath never formed part of David's kingdom (cf. 2 Sam. 8. 9 *ff.*). LXX, Luc., Vulg., Targ. present the same text as MT., but Pesh. reads ܘܐܗܦܟ ܕܪܡܣܘܩ ܘܚܡܬ ܠܐܝܣܪܝܠ, i.e. by substitution of לְיִשְׂרָאֵל for לִיהוּדָה בְּיִשְׂרָאֵל 'and restored Damascus and Ḥamath to Israel.' This text is adopted by Ew., Th., Kit., Oort[1], but is directly contradictory, as regards Ḥamath, to the statement of *v.* 25ª. Winckler (*Ges.* i. 147 *f.*) takes הֵשִׁיב in the sense '*drove back*' (cf. Isa. 36. 9; השיב מלחמה Isa. 28. 6), and supposes that some words have fallen out after חמת which would have explained the connexion with יהודה; while Klo. disposes of the reference to Ḥamath, boldly emending וַאֲשֶׁר הֵשִׁיב אֶת־דַּמֶּשֶׂק מִתַּחַת לְיַד בֶּן־הֲדַד בֶּן־חֲזָאֵל.

If it might be supposed that את דמשק had been misplaced from the preceding sentence, very slight alteration would give the text וַאֲשֶׁר נִלְחַם אֶת־דַּמֶּשֶׂק וַאֲשֶׁר הֵשִׁיב אֶת־חֲמַת יְהוָֹה מִיִּשְׂרָאֵל 'and

[1] Schrader (*COT. ad loc.*) reads similarly לְמַלְכֵי יִשְׂרָאֵל.

how he fought with Damascus, and how he turned away the wrath of Yahwe from Israel.' Cf. *ch.* 10. 32.

29. Before עם מלכי ישראל the words וַיִּקָּבֵר בְּשֹׁמְרוֹן, in accordance with the usual formula, have probably fallen out. So Luc. καὶ ἐτάφη ἐν Σαμαρείᾳ, and, in part, Pesh. ܘܐܬܩܒܪ ܥܡ ܐܒܗ̈ܘܗܝ.

15. 1–7. *Azariah, king of Judah.*

Ch. 15. 2, 3, 5–7 = 2 Chr. 26. 3, 4, 21–23.

R^D frames short notices from the Annals.

15. 1. עזריה] This name appears in *ch.* 14. 21; 15. 1, 7, 17, 23, 27; and in the form עֲזַרְיָהוּ in *ch.* 15. 6, 8. עֻזִּיָּה is used in *ch.* 15. 13, 30; עֻזִּיָּהוּ in *ch.* 15. 32, 34. עֲזַרְיָה is read in place of עֻזִּיָּה in *v.* 13 by LXX, Luc., Vulg., Targ., and by LXX, Luc. in *v.* 32. In *v.* 30, LXX Ἀχάς, Luc. omits. עֻזִּיָּה is uniformly substituted for עֲזַרְיָה by Pesh. The form עֻזָּא occurs in *ch.* 21. 18; cf. *note ad loc.*

Outside Kings, with the exception of 1 Chr. 3. 12 עֲזַרְיָה, עֻזִּיָּהוּ is used in 2 Chr. 26. 1—27. 2 (13 times), and in Isa. 1. 1; 6. 1; 7. 1; עֻזִּיָּה in Hos. 1. 1; Am. 1. 1; Zech. 14. 5.

The supposed reference to this king in the Assyrian inscriptions under the name *Az-ri-ya-a-u* (*COT.* i. 208 *ff.*) is denied by Winckler (*Altorient. Forschungen*, i. 1 *ff.*): cf. also Maspero, iii. p. 150, *note* 3.

4. רק וג׳] Cf. I. 3. 2, 3 *note.*

5. בבית החפשית] The meaning is obscure. RV. 'a several house,' i.e. lit. 'a house of separateness.' So Targ. paraphrases ויתב בר מן ירושלם 'and he dwelt *outside of Jerusalem*'; Pesh. ܘܝܬܒ ܒܒܝܬܐ ܡܛܫܝܐܝܬ 'and he dwelt in a house in privacy.' חפשית, however, according to the root-meaning, should denote not *separateness* but *freedom.* Klo.'s suggestion is noteworthy:—בְּבֵיתֹה חָפְשִׁית 'in his house at freedom,' i.e. not under restraint. חפשית is thus used adverbially, like אֲחֹרַנִּית Gen. 9. 23. Stade (*ZATW.* vi. 156 *ff.*) emends בְּבֵית הַחֹרֶף 'in the winter-house.'

על הבית] Cf. I. 4. 6 *note.*

15. 8–12. *Zechariah, king of Israel.*

R^D frames short notices from the Annals.

10. קבל עם] Senseless; the rendering 'before the people,'

adopted by RV. after Pesh., Targ., Vulg., being out of the question. We should, doubtless, follow Luc. ἐν Ἰεβλαάμ, and emend בְּיִבְלְעָם 'in Ibleam.' On the situation of Ibleam cf. *ch.* 9. 27 *note*.

12. הוא דבר י׳ וג׳] Cf. *ch.* 10. 30.

15. 13–16. *Shallum, king of Israel.*

R^D frames short notices from the Annals.

16. תפסח] Clearly not the תִּפְסַח of I. 5. 4 on the Euphrates. Th. emends תַּפּוּחַ, a town which lay in the territory of Ephraim near to the border of Manasseh; Josh. 16. 8; 17. 7, 8. This suggestion, which is borne out by Luc. Ταφωέ, is adopted by Buhl (*Geogr.* 178), Klo., Kamp., Benz., Kit.

כי לא פתח וג׳] Slightly corrupt. Read, after LXX, Pesh., כִּי לֹא פָתְחוּ לוֹ וַיַּךְ אֹתָהּ וְכָל־הָרוֹתֶיהָ בִּקֵּעַ.

15. 17–22. *Menaḥem, king of Israel.*

R^D frames short notices from the Annals.

17. מנחם] Mentioned by Tiglath-Pileser III as *Mí-ni-ḫi-im-mi* of Samaria in a list of tributary kings, B.C. 738; *COT.* i. 215; Dri. *Authority*, 98.

18. מעל] LXX ἀπὸ πασῶν, i. e. מִכָּל־—correct.

18, 19. כל ימיו: בא פול] Read, with LXX, Luc., בְּיָמָיו בָּא פוּל 'In his days came up Pul &c.' So moderns. כל ימיו at the end of *v.* 18 is an unusual addition; and *v.* 19 in MT. commences abruptly, and needs the mark of connexion which is supplied by בימיו as used elsewhere by R^D (cf. I. 16. 34 *note*).

19. פול] Identical with תִּגְלַת פִּלְאֶסֶר of *v.* 29; *ch.* 16. 7, 10. *Pûlu* of the Babylonian dynastic list corresponds to *Tukul-ti-abal-i-šar-ra* of the Babylonian chronicle. Cf. *KB.* ii. 290 *f.;* Dri. *Authority*, 97.

להחזיק וג׳] LXX omits.

20. ויצא וג׳] 'And Menaḥem *imposed* (lit. *brought forth*) the money *upon* Israel'; so RV. '*exacted . . . from.*' Such a use of the Hiph'il of יצא is, however, without a parallel; and probably Klo. is correct in emending וַיְצַו מ׳ אֶת־כָּל יִשְׂרָאֵל וְאֶת־כָּל־גִּבּוֹרֵי הַחַיִל.

So Benz., Kit. הכסף may then be supposed to have been introduced in imitation of *ch.* 12. 12, 13, after the corruption of ויצו into ויצא.

15. 23–26. *Pekaḥiah, king of Israel.*

R[D] frames a short notice (*v.* 25) from the Annals.

23. שנתים] Luc. δέκα ἔτη.

25. שלישו] Cf. I. 9. 22 *note.*

בארמון בית מלך] Cf. I. 16. 18. Probably Kt. is correct. Cf. את בית מלך of I. 16. 18, and *note* on I. 12. 31.

את ארגב ואת האריה] Scarcely possible. Even supposing that the place-name ארגב and the strange האריה with the article prefixed can be used as personal names, it is reasonable to expect some precise information as to the position of the men beyond the mere mention of their names, nor is it clear (supposing את to mean 'with') whether they were conspirators with Pekaḥ or victims together with Pekaḥiah. Klo. emends אֶת־אַרְבַּע מֵאֹת גִּבֹּרָיו 'with his 400 warriors,' the allusion being to the royal bodyguard which Pekaḥ with his small band managed by a *coup* to annihilate. Probably, however, Sta. (*ZATW.* vi. 160) is nearer the truth in regarding both names as place-names (cf. Vulg. *iuxta Argob et iuxta Arie*) which have come in by mistake from *v.* 29, and should be read as אֶת־אַרְגֹּב וְאֶת־חַוּוֹת יָאִיר.

15. 27–31. *Pekaḥ, king of Israel.*

R[D] frames notices from the Annals (*vv.* 29–30[a]).

27. עשרים שנה] The Assyrian inscriptions do not admit of a reign of such a length. Tiglath-Pileser mentions Menaḥem as his tributary in B.C. 738 (cf. *note* on *v.* 17), and also refers to the dethronement and execution of Pekaḥ in B.C. 734–732 (cf. *v.* 30 *note*). Thus, even supposing B.C. 738 to have been the last year of Menaḥem, we have at most six years for the reigns of Pekaḥiah and Pekaḥ. If Pekaḥiah reigned two years (i.e. possibly a little more than one year), Pekaḥ may have reigned from four to five years.

Hommel (Hastings, *BD.* i. 186) comments on the fact that exactly the same things are related of Pekaḥiah as of Pekaḥ, and that the names are virtually the same, and deduces the inference that there really existed only one king Pekaḥ (or Pekaḥiah), who reigned two years, between Menaḥem and Hoshea.

29. בא תגלת פלאסר] The account of this campaign is contained, in a somewhat mutilated condition, in the Annals of Tiglath-Pileser. Cf. Rost, 78 *ff.;* Dri. *Authority*, 98 *f.*

את עיון ואת אבל בית מעכה] Cf. I. 15. 20 *note.*

ינוח] The site is uncertain. Conder (*Lists*, 38; and in Hastings, *BD.*, *s. v.*) cites *Yanuḥ* near Tyre, but Buhl (*Geogr.* 229) maintains that this situation is too far west of the other places named. Guérin's identification with Hunîn, west of the Upper Jordan, is mentioned by Buhl (*Geogr.* 237). The place of the same name mentioned in Josh. 16. 6, 7 on the border of Ephraim is too far south to be identical.

קדש] *Ḳades*, standing on a lofty plateau, west-north-west of the Lake of *Ḥûle*. Rob. *BR.* iii. 366 *ff.;* Baed. 297.

חצור] Cf. I. 9. 15 *note.*

הגלילה] Cf. I. 9. 11 *note.*

30. ויקשר וג׳] The statement of Tiglath-Pileser (cf. Rost, 80 *f.*), '*Pa-ḳa-ḫa* (Pekaḥ) their king they slew, *A-u-si-'* (Hoshea) to reign over them I appointed,' makes it clear that the revolution was effected under the auspices of Assyria.

בשנת עשרים ליותם] Clearly an erroneous statement. Pekaḥ's operations against Judah, in alliance with Rezin, which appear to have been begun during Jotham's reign (*v.* 37), were carried on into the reign of Aḥaz; *ch.* 16. 5 *ff.;* Isa. 7. 1 *ff.*

15. 32–38. *Jotham, king of Judah.*

Ch. 15. 33, 34, 35[b], 36, 38 = 2 Chr. 27. 1–3[a], 7–9.

The whole account is cast by R[D].

32. At the end of the verse Luc. adds ἐπὶ Ἱερουσαλήμ.

35. רק וג׳] Cf. I. 3. 2, 3 *note.*

הוא בנה] Cf. *note* on הוא הכה *ch.* 14. 7.

37. בימים ההם] Cf. *ch.* 10. 32 *note.*

רצין] Frequently mentioned by Tiglath-Pileser as *Ra-ṣun-nu.*

Cf. *COT.* i. 252 *f.* His predecessor upon the throne of Damascus was perhaps טַבְאַל, or more correctly טָבְאֵל, to whom allusion is made in Isa. 7. 6[1]. Cf. Winckler, *Alttest. Untersuchungen*, 74.

16. *Aḥaz, king of Judah.*

Ch. 16. 2–4, 19, 20 = 2 Chr. 28. 1–4, 26, 27.

Verses 1–9, 17–20 contain notices from the Annals, framed by R^D. Verses 10–16 form a continuous narrative, probably derived from the same source as *ch.* 11; 12. 5–17. See p. 307.

16. 1. אחז] Tiglath-Pileser mentions, in a list of tributaries, *Ya-u-ḫa-zi* of Judah, i. e. יְהוֹאָחָז, the full form of the name אָחָז. The date is B.C. 728, the last year but one of Tiglath-Pileser. *KB.* ii. 20 *f.*; Rost, 72 *f.*; *COT.* i. 225; Dri. *Authority*, 100.

2. There is clearly some discrepancy between the statements of this verse and *ch.* 18. 2. If Aḥaz died at the age of thirty-six (20 + 16), and Ḥezekiah was twenty-five years old at his accession, then Aḥaz must have become a father at the age of eleven!

3. כתעבות וג׳] Cf. I. 14. 24 *note.*

4. ועל הגבעות וג׳] Cf. I. 14. 23 *note.*

5. אז יעלה] Cf. I. 3. 16 *note.*

6. בעת ההיא] Cf. I. 14. 1 *note.*

השיב רצין וג׳] It is quite clear that the Massoretes are correct in reading וַאֲדוֹמִים, and that this correction carries with it the correction of the preceding לַאֲרָם into לֶאֱדֹם (cf. I. 9. 26; 22. 48 *ff.*; II. 14. 7, 22). So Th., Sta., Kamp., Oort. Probability is also in favour of Klo.'s emendation מֶלֶךְ אֱדֹם in place of רְצִין מֶלֶךְ אֲרָם. So Benz., Kit. It is far more likely that the king of Edom should have seized the opportunity of Aḥaz's engagement with the northern confederacy in order to once more gain possession of his seaport town, than that the king of Aram should have despatched a purposeless expedition against the remote eastern point of Aḥaz's dominions.

עד היום הזה] Cf. I. 8. 8 *note.*

---

[1] The reference of 'the son of Ṭab'el' is most naturally to Rezin. The name Ṭab'el ('El is wise') is Aramaic, and identical in form with Ṭabrimmon, I. 15. 18.

7. הקומים] A rare form of participle act. Qal of the verb ע״ו. Cf. לוֹט Isa. 25. 7, בּוֹסִים Zech. 10. 5, and perhaps גֹּחִי Ps. 22. 10. See Wright, *Compar. Gramm.* 250; G-K. § 72 *p*.

8. שחר] So in I. 15. 19.

9. קירה] LXX omits; Luc. τὴν πόλιν (? קִרְיָה). Benz., Kit., Oort, on the ground of the omission, suppose that the name is a later insertion derived from Am. 1. 5. The situation of קיר is unknown. According to Am. 9. 7 the district was the original home of the Aramaeans.

10. דומשק] Probably an error for the form דַּרְמֶשֶׂק, which appears in Chr., and is regular in Syriac, and in the Targum of Pseudo-Jonathan.

אוריה הכהן] Cf. Isa. 8. 2.

11. LXX omits from כן עשה down to מדמשק in *v.* 12, probably through homoioteleuton, though the narrative runs quite smoothly without the words omitted. Luc. agrees with MT. except for the omission of the first מדמשק before כן עשה וג׳.

12. ויקרב . . . המזבח] LXX omits.

על המזבח] על for אל. Cf. I. 1. 38 *note* on על גחון.

ויעל עליו] 'And went up upon it.' Cf. I. 1. 53 *note* on מעל המזבח.

14. ואת המזבח . . . ויקרב] On constr. cf. I. 9. 21 *note*.

המזבח הנחשת] The original text must have read הַמִּזְבֵּחַ simply, and הנחשת is a gloss from *v.* 15b, correctly distinguishing the old altar from the new. LXX omits ואת המזבח, thus causing it to appear that the ritual described in *v.* 13 was still carried on upon the old (brazen) altar. This is adopted by R. Sm. (*Relig. Sem.*[2], *note L*), who further reads וַיִּקְרַב, as in *v.* 12, for וַיַּקְרֵב, thus making the verse from that point to be 'an elaborate description of the new ritual introduced by the king.' The context, however, desiderates the precise statement of MT. as to the new position of the brazen altar, which was clearly supplanted by the new altar (*v.* 15a), and devoted only to a special purpose (*v.* 15b). The LXX omission may thus be regarded as merely due to homoioteleuton.

15. ויצוהו וג׳] Kt. with pronoun-suffix anticipating the object, as in Syriac. Cf. I. 19. 21 *note*. Possibly, however, the words את אוריה הכהן may be a later explanatory insertion.

את עלת הבקר ואת מנחת הערב] The distinction appears to coincide with the ritual of Ezek. 46. 13–15, where there is only mention of a morning עולה. In *ch.* 3. 20 the term מנחה is applied to the morning sacrifice, and in I. 18. 29, 36 to the evening sacrifice. In the time of P the עולה has become both a morning and evening institution; Num. 28. 1 *ff.* Jer. 14. 12 draws a distinction, as in our passage, between עולה and מנחה; but it is by no means to be hence inferred (RV.) that מנחה therefore possesses the restricted sense of 'meal-offering,' as in P. Cf. *note* on מנחה I. 18. 29; Wellh. *Prolegomena*, 79, *note* 1.

כל עם הארץ] LXX, Luc., παντὸς τοῦ λαοῦ, omit הארץ. For the phrase of MT., *the people in general*, cf. *ch.* 11. 14, 18, 19, 20; 15. 5; 21. 24; 23. 30.

יהיה לי לבקר] The significance is obscure. בִּקֵּר means *to examine* (lit. *divide*, and so presumably *look at in detail;* cf. Ar. بَقَرَ *cleave, slit*). This meaning is clear for most of the occurrences in Bib. Heb.:—Lev. 13. 36 'The priest shall not *examine* (the suspected leper) for the yellow hair'; Lev. 27. 33 'he shall not *examine* (the tithe of the herd and flock) whether it be good or bad'; Ezek. 34. 11, 12 'will *look after* (or *look for*, i.e. *search out*) my flock'; Prov. 20. 25, probably 'after vowing, he begins *to make inquiry*,' i.e. *to examine* his financial position (cf. Toy *ad loc.*). Ps. 27. 4 לְבַקֵּר בְּהֵיכָלוֹ is involved in the same ambiguity as our passage; '*to look at* his Temple,' or '*to make inquiry in* his Temple.' In Rabb. Heb. בִּיקֵּר is used of *examining* sacrificial animals for blemishes.

Accordingly, the explanation of our passage least open to objection is that of AV., RV., R. Sm. (*Relig. Sem.*[2], *note L*), 'and the brazen altar shall be for me *to inquire by*'; i.e. lit. *to investigate*, sc. the oracle, perhaps by examination of portions of the sacrifice. Cf. the action ascribed to the king of Babylon, Ezek. 21. 26 רָאָה בַּכָּבֵד. So approximately Pesh. ܢܗܘܐ ܠܝ ܠܡܫܐܠܘ 'shall be for me to make request by.' Less probable is the explanation of Klo., 'for me *to look at*'; the idea of close scrutiny which is implied in the verb being inconsistent as applied to the altar, which must have been long familiar to the king, and which was (on this explanation) about to undergo degradation. Least probable, and without support from usage elsewhere, is the explanation of Kamp., Benz., Kit., 'shall be for me *to think of*,' i.e. 'I must decide at my leisure what is to become of it.' Cf. Vulg. *erit paratum ad voluntatem meam.*

17. המסגרות המכנות] The construction is impossible. Probably we should read מִסְגְּרוֹת הַמְּכֹנוֹת with Verss., or else emend הַמִּסְגְּרוֹת מֵהַמְּכֹנוֹת. Cf. Kamp. Klo., Benz. suppose that את המסגרות ought to follow מעליהם. On הַמִּסְגְּרוֹת cf. I. 7. 28 *note*.

הכיר] We should expect הַכִּיֹּרִים. Cf. I. 7. 38 *ff.*

הבקר הנחשת] הנחשת is probably, as in *v.* 14, a later addition.

מרצפת] 'A pediment.' Cf. the use of רִצְפָּה 'pavement,' 2 Chr. 7. 3; *al.*; and the participle רָצוּף Song 3. 10.

18. מיסך השבת] Highly obscure. Q're מוּסַךְ, if correct, should denote something *covered in*; hence RV. 'the covered way (*marg.* covered place) for the Sabbath.' LXX, however, reads τὸν θεμέλιον τῆς καθέδρας, i.e. מוּסַד הַשֶּׁבֶת; cf. I. 10. 19. Pesh. explains ܒܝܬ ܡܘܬܒܐ; Targ. שבתא (τεῖχος) טיכום.

17. 1–6. *Hoshea, king of Israel. Fall of the kingdom.*

Winckler (*Alttest. Untersuchungen*, 15 *ff.*) argues with much cogency that in *vv.* 3–6 we have a combination of two narratives. Supposing the narrative to be single, the course of events can only have been as follows. Hoshea comes to the throne as the vassal of Tiglath-Pileser (*ch.* 15. 30 *note*); he revolts against Shalmaneser, and is again reduced to vassalage (*ch.* 17. 3); he again revolts, and is deposed and made prisoner (*ch.* 17. 4); the king of Assyria (Shalmaneser) besieges Samaria for three years (*ch.* 17. 5); at the end of three years (in the first year of Sargon; *v.* 6 *note*) Samaria falls, and the population is deported to Assyria. It is, however, highly improbable that Israel remained for three years without a king, after the deposition of Hoshea, and, as a matter of fact, *v.* 6 states that the fall of the capital took place 'in the ninth year of Hoshea,' i.e. in his ninth reigning year. *Ch.* 18. 9^b–11 describes only one campaign of Assyria against Israel and the fall of Samaria after a three years' siege, and it is noticeable that this account is nearly verbally identical with *ch.* 17. 5, 6. Probably therefore *ch.* 17. 3, 4 represents another and independent account drawn from a different source to *ch.* 17. 5, 6=18. 9^{b}–11 (Annals). The form of the statements of *v.* 3 suggests that the writer was ignorant of the true state of affairs, viz. that Hoshea was from the first a vassal of Assyria, and supposed that his dependence was the direct result of a campaign (עליו עלה וג׳) distinct from that in which he lost his throne (*v.* 4). Winckler meets the difficulty by the supposition that R^{D} read in his source והיה (frequentative?) in place of ויהי—'inasmuch as Hoshea was (already) his vassal, &c.'; but such a construction is impossible.

17. 1. בשנת וג׳] The synchronism is inconsistent with the preceding synchronisms of *chh.* 16, 17, but agrees, as Benz. notices, with the statement of Luc. in *ch.* 16. 23 as to the length of the reign of Pekaḥiah.

2. רק לא וג׳] Luc. παρὰ πάντας τοὺς γενομένους ἔμπροσθεν αὐτοῦ, i. e. מִכֹּל־אֲשֶׁר וג׳; cf. I. 14. 9; 16. 25, 30, 33. The reason why R^{D} should make exception in favour of Hoshea is not apparent from his narrative; while, on the other hand, it is eminently suitable to his scheme that the last king of Israel should be painted in the blackest colours of all. Cf. *vv.* 7 *ff*.

4. קשר] LXX ἀδικίαν, i.e. שֶׁקֶר, adopted by Th., Kamp., Benz., Kit.

סוא] Generally identified with *Šabaku*, who founded the twenty-fifth (Ethiopian) dynasty. Cf. *COT. ad loc.*; Dri. *Authority*, 100. Sargon (*KB*. ii. 54 *f*.) mentions *Sib'u* general (*turtan*) of Egypt as defeated by him, together with *Ḫanunu*, king of Gaza, at Raphiaḥ (B.C. 720), but he expressly distinguishes him from Pharaoh (*Pir'u*), *king* of Egypt. If, therefore, with Schrader, we vocalize סֶוֶא and identify with *Sib'u*, it is clear that the title מלך מצרים is at any rate inapplicable at the time when Hoshea's overtures were made. See, however, Winckler's note, *Keilschrift. Sargons*, p. 101.

Luc., in place of אל סוא וג׳, reads πρὸς Ἀδραμέλεχ τὸν Αἰθίοπα τὸν κατοικοῦντα ἐν Αἰγύπτῳ. Καὶ ἦν Ὡσῆε φέρων δῶρα τῷ βασιλεῖ Ἀσσυρίων ἐνιαυτὸν κατ' ἐνιαυτόν, ἐν δὲ τῷ ἐνιαυτῷ ἐκείνῳ οὐκ ἤνεγκεν αὐτῷ μαναά. καὶ ὕβρισε τὸν Ὡσῆε ὁ βασιλεὺς Ἀσσυρίων καὶ ἐπολιόρκησεν αὐτὸν κ.τ.λ.

6. לכד מלך אשור וג׳] Not Shalmaneser, as in *v.* 3, but *Sargon;* cf. the great triumphal inscription *ll.* 23 *ff.*:—'Samaria I besieged and conquered; 27,290 of its inhabitants I carried into captivity, fifty chariots I seized from them; the rest of them I allowed to retain their possessions (?); I set my officers over them; the tribute of the former king I laid upon them.' *KB.* ii. 54 *f.*; Dri. *Authority,* 101. Schrader (*COT. ad loc.*) quotes evidence to show that the conquest of Samaria must have taken place in the year of Sargon's accession, i.e. B.C. 722.

וישב וג׳] חבור is mentioned in the inscriptions as the *Ḥa-bur,* a tributary of the Euphrates; גוזן is *Gu-za-na,* which is assigned to the district of Mesopotamia. חלח is doubtful, but may be *Ḥalaḫḫu* in Mesopotamia. Cf. *COT. ad loc.*

17. 7–23. *Commentary by* R[D] *upon the causes which brought about the downfall of the Northern Kingdom.*

The phraseology of R[D] is very marked throughout the section. Notice אֱלֹהִים אֲחֵרִים *v.* 7 (I. 9. 6 *note*); הוֹרִישׁ *v.* 8 (I. 14. 24 *note*); עַל כָּל־גִּבְעָה וג׳ *v.* 10 (I. 14. 23 *note*); לְהַכְעִיס *vv.* 11, 17 (I. 14. 9 *note*); הַגִּלֻּלִים *v.* 12 (I. 15. 12 *note*); שֻׁבוּ מִדַּרְכֵיכֶם הָרָעִים *v.* 13 (I. 13. 33 *note*); שִׁמְרוּ מִצְוֹתַי וג׳ *vv.* 13, 19 (I. 2. 3 *note*); עֲבָדַי הַנְּבִיאִים *vv.* 13, 23 (as in I. 9. 7; 21. 10; 24. 2); וַיַּקְשׁוּ אֶת־עָרְפָּם *v.* 14 *note;* וַיֵּלְכוּ אַחֲרֵי *v.* 15 (I. 11. 5 *note*); הַהֶבֶל *v.* 15 (I. 16. 2 *note*); וַיִּתְמַכְּרוּ וג׳ *v.* 17 (I. 21. 20, 25); לַעֲשׂוֹת הָרַע וג׳ *v.* 17 (I. 11. 6 *note*); וַיִּתְאַנַּף *v.* 18 (I. 11. 9 *note*); לֹא סָרוּ מִמֶּנָּה *v.* 22 (*ch.* 3. 3 *note*).

Verses 19, 20 are certainly a later insertion, subsequent to the commencement of the Judaean exile, and due to R[D2]. The opening of *v.* 21, כי קרע וג׳ '*For* he rent &c.,' clearly refers immediately to the statement of *v.* 18, ויתאנף . . . ויסרם 'was very angry . . . and removed them'; but the sequence is destroyed by the interpolation, כי *v.* 21 being deprived of all point. The whole reference of the section is to the causes which brought about the rejection of the kingdom of *Israel*, no reference being elsewhere made to Judah except in *v.* 13, where וביהודה is probably by the same hand as *vv.* 19, 20.

Stade (*ZATW.* vi. 163 *f.*) regards *vv.* 7–17 as an exilic addition, later than R^D, upon the grounds that the writer of these verses ascribes Molech-worship (*v.* 17^a) and Assyrian star-worship (*v.* 16^b) to the Northern Kingdom—the abuses which later on were rife in the Southern Kingdom under Manasseh (*ch.* 21. 3, 6), and also because certain phrases appear to exhibit the influence of Jeremiah; cf. *v.* 13 שבו מדרכיכם הרעים with Jer. 18. 11; 25. 5; 35. 15; 36. 3, 7; ויעד י׳ וג׳ with Jer. 7. 25 *ff.*; 11. 7 *ff.*; *v.* 15^b וילכו אחרי ההבל ויהבלו with Jer. 2. 5. The reflections embodied in these verses are, however, in strict accordance with R^D's plan which runs throughout his work, as the number of phrases above cited as characteristic of his hand sufficiently show, nor is it at all unnatural that the editor, who worked not many years after Josiah had removed from Judah the foreign abuses of Manasseh's reign, should ascribe the same kind of religious abuses to the kingdom of Israel, side by side with the worship of Yahwe under the form of a calf. Nor, again, need the phrases above mentioned imply dependence upon the written prophecies of Jeremiah, any more than need other phrases used by R^D elsewhere, in common with Jeremiah[1], go to prove that R^D and Jeremiah were one and the same person. All that clearly emerges from the fact of such resemblances is that the two writers were members of one prophetic school of thought, i.e. the Deuteronomic. Cf. Dri. *LOT.*[6] p. 203 at end.

7. ויהי כי חטאו] 'Now it (viz. the foregoing) came to pass because &c.' Luc. καὶ ἐγένετο ὀργὴ κυρίου ἐπὶ τὸν Ἰσραήλ, δι' ὅτι ἥμαρτον κ.τ.λ., i.e. וַיְהִי אַף י׳ בְּיִשְׂרָאֵל כִּי חָטְאוּ—superior to MT.

[1] Cf. כי שמך נקרא וג׳ I. 8. 43 *note;* אשלח מעל פני I. 9. 7 *note;* כל עבר וג׳ I. 9. 8 *note;* לא שב מדרכו הרעה I. 13. 33 *note;* הנני מביא רעה אל (על) I. 14. 10 *note;* עבדי (עבדיו) הנביאים *ch.* 9. 7; 17. 13, 23; 21. 10; 24. 2; Jer. 7. 25; 25. 4; 26. 5; 29. 19; 35. 15; 44. 4. Other resemblances, from the later *chh.* of 2 Kings, are cited by Dri. *LOT.*[6] p. 203.

8. וילכו בחקות הגוים] Cf. Lev. 18. 3; 20. 23 (H).

ומלכי ישראל וג׳] Senseless. Cf. RV.'s attempt at a rendering. No doubt ומלכי ישראל is a corruption of מִלִּפְנֵי יִשְׂרָאֵל, a doublet of the preceding three words; and אשר עשו 'who performed (them,' sc. the statutes of the nations) is probably a marginal gloss made subsequently to the corruption to explain the occurrence of 'the kings of Israel' in this connexion.

9. ויחפאו] The rendering of RV. 'did secretly' can scarcely be maintained, and LXX ἠμφιέσαντο, 'clad themselves in,' in accordance with the use of חִפָּה 'overlay' in 2 Chr., is preferable, if the text be genuine. Pesh., Targ. render vaguely ܐܡܪܘ, אמרו; and Vulg. *offenderunt* seems only to be guessing. Klo. emends וַיְבַדְּאוּ 'devised'; cf. Job 13. 4 רֹפְאֵי אֱלִיל probably 'contrivers of nought' (|| טֹפְלֵי שֶׁקֶר). So Benz., Kit.

לא כן] Cf. *ch.* 7. 9.

ממגדל וג׳] So *ch.* 18. 8. The expression, as here used, describes the smallest and largest of communities.

10. מצבות ואשרים] Cf. *notes* on I. 14. 15, 23.

13. כל נביאו כל חזה] Vulg. *omnium prophetarum et videntium*, Targ. כל ספר וכל מליף suggest כָּל־נָבִיא וְכָל־חֹזֶה. This is preferable to the supposition that the text originally read כָּל־נְבִיאָיו simply, and כָּל־חֹזֶה came in later as a gloss.

14. ויקשו את ערפם] So Deut. 10. 16; Jer. 7. 26; 17. 23; 19. 15; Neh. 9. 16, 17, 29; 2 Chr. 30. 8†. Cf. the expressions עָרְפְּךָ הַקָּשֶׁה Deut. 31. 27; קְשֵׁה עֹרֶף Deut. 9. 6, 13; Ex. 32. 9; 33. 3, 5; 34. 9 (JE).

כערף] LXX, Luc. ὑπὲρ τὸν νῶτον, Person. ܡܢ ܩܕܠ read מֵעֹרֶף.

17. ויקסמו וג׳] On the meaning of the terms used in Hebrew to describe various kinds of divination cf. Dri. on Deut. 18. 10. נחש is uncertain (probably applied in the case of Joseph's cup, Gen. 44. 5, 15, to *hydromancy*, but also used more generally): קסם=Ar. قَسَمَ *to divide*, x. إِسْتَقْسَمَ *to get a part allotted to oneself, to draw lots*, especially with headless arrows, as is described, in the case of the king of Babylon, in Ezek. 21. 26*f*. After *v*. 17[b] Luc. adds καὶ ἐποίησαν ἐφοὺδ καὶ θεραφείμ.

18. לא נשאר רק] For the construction of רק with the negative,

'*not . . . except*,' cf. I. 8. 9 אֵין בָּאָרוֹן רַק שְׁנֵי לֻחוֹת הָאֲבָנִים. The negative is really redundant. Cf., with the same verb, Ex. 8. 5, 7; Deut. 3. 11; 1 Sam. 5. 4.

20. וימאס] Luc. presupposes וַיִּמְאֲסוּ בַּיהוָֹה כָּל־זֶרַע יִשְׂרָאֵל וַיִּתְאַנַּף י׳ בָּם וַיְעַנֵּם וג׳.

21. וידא] Q're וַיַּדַּח is probably correct.

והחטיאם] Perf. with weak ו, unusual in R^D's own composition. Cf. *note* on ותפש *ch.* 14. 7.

23. עד היום הזה] Cf. I. 8. 8 *note*.

17. 24–41. *The foreign settlers in the district of Samaria.*

The narrative is certainly composite. Verses 32, 33, 41, in speaking of the races which were settled by the king of Assyria in the cities of Samaria, say that they 'feared Yahwe,' while retaining the worship of their own national deities. In *v*. 34, on the contrary, it is stated with great emphasis that they 'feared not Yahwe.' Again, while *vv*. 24–34^a refer exclusively to the *foreign* settlers, and only mention the introduction into their midst of a single priest of Israelitish nationality (*v*. 28 אֶחָד מֵהַכֹּהֲנִים), to whom was due their instruction in the worship of Yahwe, *vv*. 34^b–40 are couched in such terms as can only refer to *Israelites as such*, of however mixed and renegade a strain. Notice especially *vv*. 35, 38, the reference to the Deuteronomic covenant; *v*. 36 'Yahwe, who brought you up out of the land of Egypt.'

Thus this latter section must be regarded as a later addition to the narrative of Kings[1], referring probably to the Samaritans of post-exilic times. Verse 40^b rounds off the interpolation by the repetition of *v*. 34^a—the statement of the older narrative to which the later writer attaches his addition. Verses 24–34^a, 41, on the other hand, form, in part at least, an ancient narrative embodied by R^D. Stade (*ZATW*. vi. 167 *ff*.) regards *vv*. 24–28, 41 as the original kernel which has received the later extension, *vv*. 29–34^a. Possibly

[1] R^{D2}; cf. וְאֶת־הַחֻקִּים וג׳ תִּשְׁמְרוּן *v*. 37 (I. 2. 3 *note*); בִּזְרוֹעַ נְטוּיָה *v*. 36 (I. 8. 42 *note*); כָּל־הַיָּמִים *v*. 37 (I. 9. 3 *note*); אֱלֹהִים אֲחֵרִים *vv*. 35, 37 (I. 9. 6 *note*).

this latter may be assigned to R^D himself:—*v.* 32[b] resembles I. 12. 31, and in *v.* 34[a] עַד הַיּוֹם הַזֶּה is an expression commonly employed by R^D (cf. I. 8. 8 *note*).

24. ויבא וג׳] The fact that Sargon imported foreign prisoners of war into Samaria is attested by his inscriptions, though the peoples mentioned are not those of our passage. A mutilated passage, however, in his annals refers to a campaign in his first year (subsequent to the conquest of Samaria) which (as read by Winckler, *Alttest. Untersuchungen*, 105) was directed against the tribe of Tu'muna, which had apparently allied itself 'with Merodach-Baladan, king of Kaldu, who against the will of the gods had usurped the sovereignty of Babylon.' This was followed by a deportation of prisoners into 'the land Ḫatti,' a term which may include Samaria. In another passage he states that he settled in Samaria 'men of Tamud, Ibâdid, Marsîman, Ḫayâpâ, the remote Arbâi inhabiting the desert.' This took place in his seventh year, i.e. B.C. 715. Cf. Delitzsch, *Paradies*, 304; *COT.* i. *ad loc.*; Winckler, *Keilschrifttexte Sargons*, i. 20 *f.*; *KB.* ii. 42 *f.*

כּוּתָה is *Kûtû* of the inscriptions, the modern *Tell-Ibrâhîm*, north-east of Babylon. סְפַרְוַיִם probably denotes the two Sippars, *Sippar son of Šamaš* (the sun-god), and *Sippar of Anunitu(m)*, between Bagdad and Babylon. For this identification a form סְפָרַיִם might have been expected, and this is perhaps to be found in *v.* 31[b] Kt. Some critics, however, have been led by the reference to Sepharvaim in *ch.* 18. 34=Isa. 36. 19, in close connexion with Ḥamath, Arpad, and Samaria, to infer that its situation is to be sought in the west; and סִבְרַיִם Ezek. 47. 16 is cited as possibly identical. Cf. Dillmann on Isaiah *ad loc.* The unknown עַוָּה is doubtless the same as עִוָּה of *ch.* 18. 34—by inference a western state.

Winckler (*Alttest. Untersuchungen*, 95–107) conjectures that confusion has been introduced into the text between Sargon's importation and that of Assurbanipal, to which allusion is made in Ezra 4. 8–10. Sargon makes no mention of the capture of prisoners of war from Babylon and Kutha. Babylon was not besieged by him until B.C. 710, and then he came not as enemy to the Babylonians, but as deliverer from the Chaldean yoke of Merodach-Baladan. His successor, Sennacherib, cannot have formed such a settlement of Babylonian captives, and the same is the case with Esarhaddon, the reference to this king in Ezra 4. 2 being clearly an error for Assurbanipal (אסנפר as in Ezra 4. 10). Assurbanipal, however, carried out a successful campaign against Sippar, Kutha, and Babylon, all of which are mentioned in *ch.* 17. 24, supposing ספרוים to be an erroneous alteration of an original ספר. Winckler regards the inclusion of Ḥamath and Awwa as of a piece with this alteration, the reason being that the two names stand together with Sepharvaim (the *Syrian* city) in the speech of the Rabshakeh, *ch.* 18. 34. For 'no Assyrian king would have introduced settlers from Ḥamath into Samaria, since such a measure would have failed of its object, viz. the placing of unruly elements at a distance from their native soil. Ḥamathites would not have remained long in Samaria, but would soon have made their escape back to their home which lay so near.' Thus, according to Winckler, the narrative of Kings affords us no authentic account as to the nationality of the peoples introduced into Samaria by Sargon. These arguments are accepted by Benz. It may be doubted, however, whether there is evidence sufficient to substantiate Winckler's theory. For example, in default of precise information as to the reasons which may have influenced Sargon in the disposal of his prisoners of war, the argument by which Winckler rejects the mention of Ḥamath and Awwa appears to be highly arbitrary. Again, Assurbanipal, so far from mentioning any transportation of the people of Sippar, Kutha, and Babylon, definitely states that he allowed the remnant of them to remain in Babylonia (*KB.* ii. 192 *f.*).

Kit. accepts Winckler's argument with regard to Ḥamath and Awwa, but demurs to his main theory as without basis, either in the Old Testament or in the inscriptions.

25. האריות] On the use of the article cf. *note* on I. 13. 14.

26. ויאמרו] Impersonal; 'And it was told.'

27. הִגְלִיתֶם] Luc. ὧν ἀπῴκισα, i.e. הִגְלִיתִם—certainly correct.

וילכו וישבו] Luc., Vulg., Pesh. וְיֵלֵךְ וְיֵשֵׁב, correctly.

30. סכות בנות] Uncertain. The interpretation of Delitzsch (*Paradies*, 215) *Sakkut-binûtu*, 'supreme judge of the Universe,' is rejected by Schrader (*COT. ad loc.*), who suggests identification with *Zîr-bânit* or *Zar-pa-ni-tuv*, the consort of *Marduk*. Jensen (*ZA*. iv. 352) regards בְּנוֹת as equivalent to *banîtu*, an epithet of *Ištar*. Cheyne (*Expos. Times*, x. 429) proposes to emend סַכּוּת כֵּיוָן, the two names which denote the Babylonian Saturn. Cf. Am. 5. 26.

נרגל] Nergal appears in the inscriptions as the god of Kutha. He is the lord of hell, and the god of war and pestilence. As a destructive agency his symbol is the lion. Jensen (*Kosmologie*, 476 *ff.*) explains the name as compounded of *Ni*+*uru*+*gal*= *Ni*+*unu*+*gal*='Lord of the great city,' or rather 'dwelling,' i.e. the Underworld. Cf. also *COT. ad loc.*

31. אדרמלך] Probably 'Adar is king' (*or* 'counsellor'). Adar appears as a west Semitic god in the name יתנאדר 'Adar has given' (Baethgen, *Semit. Religionsgeschichte*, 54), but is best known as an Assyrian god, the name, according to Schrader, being Akkadian in origin, and originally pronounced *A-tar*, 'father of decision.' אדרמלך occurs as the name of a son of Sennacherib in *ch.* 19. 37, a fact which favours the view that we have here the name of an *Assyrian* deity, and so lends weight to the view (above noticed) that ספרוים denotes Sippar rather than a western city.

ענמלך] Perhaps equivalent to ענומלך, i.e. 'Anu is king' (*or* 'counsellor'). Anu is the god of heaven, supreme among the deities of Assyria and Babylon.

אלה ספרים] Kt. (according to Ginsburg, אֵל הספרים) seems to make reference to one deity only, and similarly Luc. omits ענמלך, and reads τῷ 'Αδραμέλεχ Θεῷ Σεπφαρείμ.

32. מקצותם] 'From among the whole of them.' Cf. I. 12. 31 *note*. LXX, Luc. offer a double version of this verse, the second

corresponding to MT., while the first runs *καὶ ἦσαν φοβούμενοι τὸν κύριον, καὶ κατῴκισαν τὰ βδελύγματα αὐτῶν ἐν τοῖς οἴκοις τῶν ὑψηλῶν ἃ ἐποίησαν ἐν Σαμαρείᾳ, ἔθνος ἔθνος ἐν πόλει ἐν ᾗ κατῴκουν ἐν αὐτῇ*, i. e. probably וַיִּהְיוּ יְרֵאִים אֶת־י׳ וַיַּעֲשׂוּ לָהֶם (or וַיּוֹשִׁיבוּ) שִׁקֻּצֵיהֶם בְּבָתֵּי הַבָּמוֹת אֲשֶׁר עָשׂוּ בְשֹׁמְרוֹן גּוֹי גּוֹי בָּעִיר אֲשֶׁר יָשְׁבוּ (הֵמָּה יֹשְׁבִים or) שָׁם. This reading bears the stamp of superiority, MT. probably representing the restoration of an imperfect text upon the lines of I. 12. 31.

18—20. *Ḥezekiah, king of Judah.*

Ch. 18. 1–8 is mainly the work of R^D, based upon the notices of *vv.* 4, 7^b, 8. The substance of *vv.* 7^b, 8 is probably drawn from the Annals. With regard to *v.* 4 this is not so clear. The verse shows marks of a late style (perfect with weak ו, as in 21. 4, 6; 23. 4 *ff.*), and sketches the outline of a religious reformation which appears in all essentials to have resembled and anticipated the reformation of Josiah. Hence some critics regard the notice as a late and unhistorical interpolation (cf. Stade, *Ges.* i. 607 *f.*; *ZATW.* iii. 8 *ff.*; vi. 170 *ff.*; Wellh., *C.* 291).

The occurrence of a reformation under Ḥezekiah is supported by 18. 22 (which must, with the rejection of 18. 4, be likewise branded as a later misconception), and perhaps also by the statement of Jer. 26. $17–19^a$, which speaks of the influence exercised upon Ḥezekiah and all Judah by the preaching of Micah the Morashtite. Mic. 1. 5^b MT. mentions the בָּמוֹת of Jerusalem for reprobation; but this passage must not be pressed, because LXX, Pesh., Targ. presuppose a different reading[1]. Certainly Isaiah does not seem to have had in view any centralization of Yahwe's cultus, such as was prominent in Josiah's reformation; but his attacks upon the idol-worship (Isa. 2. 8, 18, 20; 31. 7; cf. 10. 10, 11), tree-worship (1. 29), and necromancy (8. 19), which seem to have been rife in the kingdom of Judah, are in agreement with

[1] חַטַּאת 'sin,' parallel to פֶּשַׁע 'transgression,' as in *v.* 4^a. The reading of MT. is, however, accepted by Kit. (*Hist.* ii. 357), who regards the rendering of the Versions as merely a simplification.

such a movement in the direction of the pure worship of Yahwe. Probably, therefore, as is allowed by Sta. (*Ges., loc. cit.*), the statement of *v.* 4ᵇ is based upon authentic information as to such a reform, and this has been later on expanded in *v.* 4ᵃ, under the influence of the accomplished fact of Josiah's reformation.

18. 2. אבי] Shortened form of אֲבִיָּה 2 Chr. 29. 1.

4. הוא הסיר] On the use of הוא cf. *ch.* 14. 7 *note*.

נחשתן] Vocalization connects the name with נְחֹשֶׁת, with a formative termination 'brazen one.' It seems certain, however, that the word is connected with נָחָשׁ; and, unless there is intended a play upon the similarity in name of the thing 'serpent,' *and* its material 'brass,' it is possible that the vocalization is incorrect. Cf. Luc. Νεεσθάν. For conjectures as to the form and its meaning cf. *Heb. Lex. Oxf.*, *s. v.*

5. ואחריו וג'] Scarcely original. The clumsily connected sentence ואשר היו לפניו introduces a statement which we should have expected to occupy the first place (cf. I. 3. 12); and the statement ואחריו וג' is in direct contradiction to *ch.* 23. 25, where Josiah is regarded, from the standpoint of R^D, as the ideal of a religious king. Probably therefore we should omit אחריו and the ו before ואשר, and read וְלֹא הָיָה כָמֹהוּ בְּכָל־מַלְכֵי יְהוּדָה אֲשֶׁר הָיוּ לְפָנָיו.

6. וידבק ביהוה] On the use of דבק by R^D cf. *note* on I. 11. 2.

לא סר מאחריו] Cf. *ch.* 3. 3 *note*.

את משה] Luc. τῷ Μωσῇ παιδὶ αὐτοῦ.

7. והיה] Probably frequentative, in reference to the repeated occasions depicted by יֵצֵא.

9–12. A notice from the Annals, introduced by the synchronism of R^D, *v.* 9ᵃ, and closed by his comment *v.* 12. The notice is identical with *ch.* 17. 5, 6.

18. 13—**20.** 19. *Sennacherib's campaign against Judah* (18. 13—19. 37): *sickness and recovery of Ḥezekiah* (20. 1–11): *embassy of Merodach-Baladan* (20. 12–19).

Chh. 18. 13, 17—20. 19 = Isa. 36. 1—38. 8; 38. 21—39. 8. The section *vv.* 14–16, which is not found in Isaiah, is distinguished from 18. 13, 17 *ff.* by the form of the name חִזְקִיָּה (instead of חִזְקִיָּהוּ) which occurs also in *vv.* 1, 10 (Annals). The notice appears to be in strict agreement with the Assyrian record (cf. *Append.* 5, col. iii. ll. 11 *ff.*), and is probably a genuine excerpt from the Annals.

It is generally agreed that the narrative of Isa. 36. 1—39. 8 cannot be traced to Isaiah himself, but must be of a considerably later date. Notice the mention of Sennacherib's death (Isa. 37. 38 ‖ *ch.* 19. 37), which did not happen until B.C. 681, twenty years after the campaign against Jerusalem, and certainly later than the death of Isaiah. Again, it seems to be clear that the Isaiah section (except 38. 9–20, from another source) must have been extracted from our Book of Kings by the editor of Isa. 1—39. For certain phrases which are due to R^D in the Kings-narrative appear also in Isaiah:—cf. למען דוד עבדי *ch.* 19. 34 ‖ Isa. 37. 35; את אשר התהלכתי . . . בעיניך *ch.* 20. 3 ‖ Isa. 38. 3; and the redactional phrases בימים ההם *ch.* 20. 1 ‖ Isa. 38. 1; בעת ההיא *ch.* 20. 12 ‖ Isa. 39. 1. Kings is also superior to Isaiah in the account of Ḥezekiah's sickness. Isa. 38. 4–8 has been abbreviated; 38. 21, 22 is misplaced.

The Kings-narrative 18. 13, 17—20. 19 seems to represent a combination of three sources. Sta. (*ZATW.* vi. 174) notices that Isaiah's threat against Sennacherib occurs three times in similar terms: 19. 7; 19. 28^b; 19. 33. The contents of Sennacherib's letter (19. 10–13) merely repeat in brief that which has already been said by the Rabshakeh (18. 28–35). Again, it is highly improbable that Sennacherib, after hearing the news with regard to Tirhaḳah (19. 9^a), should have imagined that the mere dispatch of a letter would be likely to compel Ḥezekiah's submission, after the failure of previous verbal negotiations. The true sequel to 19. 9^a seems to be 19. 36 *f.*; upon receiving information of Tirhaḳah's hostile movement, Sennacherib raises the siege of Jerusalem and returns to Assyria. We have, then, two separate accounts of the Assyrian campaign, 18. 13, 17—19. 9^a, 36 *f.*, and 19. 9^b–35; 19. 9^b having probably been slightly modified by the redactor. Further, the section 19. 9^b–35 itself appears to be composite in character. The taunt-song *vv.* 21–28, with its accompanying sign *vv.* 29–31, stands apart from the prosaic statement *vv.* 32–34. לכן 'therefore' of *v.* 32 answers, not to anything in the prophecy preceding, but to *v.* 20^b β, אשר התפללת ... שמעתי 'Whereas thou hast prayed ... I have heard'; and, as has been noticed above, *vv.* 28^b, 33 are duplicates of the same statement. Thus *vv.* 21–31, generally regarded by critics as an authentic prophecy of Isaiah, appear to have been inserted into the midst of the prophetical history 19. 9^b–20, 32–34, *v.* 21^a representing the redactor's link.

The narrative of 20. 1–19 probably belongs to the author of one of the two preceding narrative sections. Cheyne, following Duhm, selects the second narrative, 19. 9^b *ff.* Notice, as a point of connexion, the occurrence of a prayer of Ḥezekiah in each section, 19. 15 *ff.*; 20. 2 *f.* Very possibly the chronological notice at the beginning of 18. 13, 'In the fourteenth year of king Ḥezekiah,' properly refers to the events of 20. 1–19, and occupies its present position upon the false assumption that Sennacherib's invasion took place in the same year as Ḥezekiah's sickness and recovery. This arrangement is probably due to R^D, who removed the note of time from its true position at the head of the narrative of 20. 1 *ff.*, replacing it by his synchronistic phrase, 'In those days[1].' Notice the reference to Assyria in 20. 6. The whole verse, from וּמִכַּף 'and from the hand &c.,' must be due to the author of the mistaken synchronism. Cf. the latter half with 19. 34.

13. ובארבע עשרה שנה] The sixth year of Ḥezekiah for the fall of Samaria, B.C. 722 (*v.* 10), cannot be reconciled with the fourteenth year for Sennacherib's campaign, B.C. 701, and it seems the best course to regard this latter date as true for the sickness of Ḥezekiah and the embassy of Merodach-Baladan (*ch.* 20), which will then fall cir. B.C. 714. Thus Ḥezekiah's reign may

[1] Cf. *note* on *ch.* 18. 13.

be supposed to have closed B.C. 699, i.e. some fifteen years after B.C. 714 (*ch.* 20. 6[a]).

על כל ערי וג׳] According to the inscription of the Taylor cylinder, col. iii. l. 13 (cf. *Append.* 5), Sennacherib captured forty-six fortified towns, besides innumerable fortresses and small places.

14. וישלח וג׳] LXX, Luc., Vulg. supply an object מַלְאָכִים.

לכישה] Cf. *ch.* 14. 19 *note.*

שלש מאות וג׳] The sum is given in the inscription (col. iii. l. 34) as thirty talents of gold and 800 talents of silver. Schrader quotes Brandis for the view that the difference in the statement of the amount of the silver is due to the difference in weight between the Babylonian *light* and the Palestinian *heavy* talent.

16. בעת ההיא] Cf. I. 14. 1 *note.*

17. תרתן] Assyr. *tartânu* or *turtânu*, title of the commander-in-chief of the Assyrian army. || Isa. 36. 2 omits this official and the one following.

רב סרים] Probably the Hebrew perversion ('chief of the eunuchs') of an Assyrian title which is unknown to us.

רב שקה] Probably in Assyr. *râb-šaḳê*, i.e. 'high officer.' Cf. *šud-šaḳû* or *šud-šaḳê*, 'high-lord, chieftain.' Delitzsch, *Assyr. HWB.* 685.

ויעלו ויבאו] Rightly omitted in the second place by LXX, Luc., Vulg., Pesh.

בתעלת וג׳] Cf. Isa. 7. 3. The site is unknown. For the conjectures which have been offered cf. Dillmann on Isa. 7. 3.

18. על הבית] Cf. I. 4. 6 *note.*

19. אשר בטחת] Luc. ἣν πέποιθας σὺ καὶ πᾶς Ἰούδα. Possibly the addition may be due to corruption of Σὺ εἶπας, i.e. אָמַרְתָּ, which is missing in Luc., at the beginning of the following verse. LXX εἶπας.

22. בירושלם] || Isa. 36. 7 omits.

24. פחת אחד וג׳] 'One satrap of the least of my lord's servants.' פַּחַת must be regarded as attracted into the construct state of its adjective אַחַד, as is the case in the expression אֵשֶׁת יְפַת תֹּאַר Deut.

21. 11. The general verdict is for the excision of פחת as a corrupt insertion, but the construction, though harsh, can scarcely be asserted to be impossible, in view of our limited knowledge of the possibilities of Hebrew syntax. Cf. Kö. *Syntax*, §§ 277 *o*, 337 *o*. On the meaning and use of פֶּחָה cf. *note* on I. 10. 15.

25. עליתי] LXX, Luc. ἀνέβημεν.

27. העל וג׳] Notice the confusion between על and אל:—על אדניך ואליך ... על האנשים. || Isa. 36. 12 reads האל אדניך. On this confusion between the prepositions cf. *note* on על נחון I. 1. 38, and the full list of instances given in *Heb. Lex. Oxf.*, *s. v.* על § 7 *c*.

29. מידו] Luc., Vulg., Pesh., Targ. rightly presuppose מִיָּדִי. || Isa. 36. 14 omits.

31. עשו אתי ברכה] RV., following Targ., 'Make *your peace* with me.' This use of ברכה 'blessing,' in the sense of *a mutual well wishing* taking the form of a *treaty*, is unique.

32. וחיו] On the idiomatic use of the imperative in place of the cohortative cf. I. 1. 12 *note*.

34. איה וג׳] The allusion is perhaps to Sargon's defeat of *Ya'u-bi'di* king of Ḥamath, who had induced the Assyrian provinces of Arpad, Ṣimirra, Damascus, and Samaria to join with him in revolt. This coalition was crushed at Qarqar in B.C. 720. Cf. *KB.* ii. 56 *f.* אַרְפָּד the modern *Tell-Erfâd*, to the north of Aleppo, had been conquered by Tiglath-Pileser III, in B.C. 743–740. *KB.* i. 212 *f.* Upon סְפַרְוַיִם cf. *ch.* 17. 24 *note*. הֵנַע and עִוָּה (omitted in || Isa. 36. 19) are unknown[1]. The latter is doubtless the same as עַוָּה of *ch.* 17. 24.

The second half of the verse runs in Luc. καὶ ποῦ εἰσὶν οἱ θεοὶ τῆς χώρας Σαμαρείας; μὴ ἐξείλαντο τὴν Σαμάρειαν ἐκ χειρός μου; וְאַיֵּה אֱלֹהֵי אֶרֶץ שֹׁמְרוֹן הֲכִי הִצִּילוּ וג׳. The insertion is indispensable, the subject presupposed by הצילו being obviously 'the gods of Samaria.' So Klo., Kamp., Benz., Kit., Oort.

---

[1] Targ. הלא טלטילינון ואגליאינון 'Has he not dispersed them and carried them captive?' takes the forms as verbs, Hiph'il of נוע and Pi'el of עוה. Similarly Σ. in Isa. 37. 13 ἀνεστάτωσε καὶ ἐταπείνωσε.

36. והחרישו] ‖ Isa. 36. 21 וַיַּחֲרִישׁוּ, correctly.

העם] LXX, Luc. omit.

37. קרועי בגדים] Lit. 'rent as to garment.' Cf. *note* on I. 15. 23.

19. 2. After καὶ Σομναν τὸν γραμματέα Luc. has the curious insertion καὶ τὸν Σαιτην καὶ τὸν Σουμαιησουμαι καὶ τὸν Μακραπην τὸν γέροντα. Possibly Σαιτην and Σουμ. represent marginal notes of three various spellings of the name שבנא; the second perhaps Σουμα ἢ Σουμα by transposition of the letters of Σομνα.

3. ללדה] LXX, Luc., Vulg., Pesh. presuppose לַיֹּלֵדָה 'to her who is in travail,' probably correctly. So Klo. Cf. Mic. 4. 9, 10; Hos. 13. 13; Jer. 49. 24. The form לֵדָה as infin. constr. for the normal לֶדֶת occurs elsewhere Hos. 9. 11; Jer. 13. 21.

4. והוכיח] RV. 'And will rebuke the words which Yahwe thy God hath heard.' So Pesh., Targ. והוכיח is thus perf. with ו consec. in continuation of ישמע. LXX, Luc., Vulg. treat והוכיח as infin. constr., equivalent to וּלְהוֹכִיחַ, thus regarding מֶלֶךְ־אַשּׁוּר as the subject.

8. לבנה] Cf. *ch.* 8. 22 *note*.

9. וישמע אל וג׳] ‖ Isa. 37. 9 reads על for אל.

תרהקה] Mentioned by Sennacherib not by name but as 'the king of *Miluḫḫi*,' Taylor cylinder, col. ii. ll. 69 *ff.* (cf. *Append.* 5). The name is given by Assurbanipal as *Tar-ḳu-u*, Egyptian *T-h-r-ḳ*.

וישב וישלח] ‖ Isa. 37. 9 וישמע וישלח 'and when he had heard, he sent.' וישב was doubtless written by the hand which connected the following narrative with the preceding, i.e. presumably the hand of R[D] (cf. p. 339): hence וישמע may be judged to be a corruption of וישב. LXX in Isaiah combines the two readings: καὶ ἀκούσας ἀπέστρεψεν καὶ ἀπέστειλεν.

10. LXX omits the introductory sentence down to the first לאמר, probably through homoioteleuton with the end of *v.* 9.

11. להחרימם] '*As regards* devoting them to destruction.'

12. אשר שחתו אבותי] Luc. οὓς διέφθειραν οἱ πατέρες μου αὐτοὺς καὶ τὰς χώρας αὐτῶν. The reading of LXX has arisen through corruption of οὓς into οὐ.

את גוזן וג׳] On גוזן cf. *ch.* 17. 6. חרן is *Ḥarran* of the inscriptions, Charrae of the Romans, in north-west Mesopotamia, situated on the Belias, a tributary of the Euphrates. רצף, mentioned in the inscriptions as *Ra-ṣa-ap-pa* or *Ra-ṣap-pa*, is the Ῥησάφα of Ptolemaeus (v. 15), and the modern *Ruṣâfa*, on the route from Sura to Palmyra in the Euphrates valley *Ez-Zôr* (cf. Delitzsch, *Paradies*, 297). The בני עדן belonged to the Aramaean state *Bît-Adini*, situated between the Euphrates and the Belias, which offered stubborn resistance to Assur-naẓir-pal, and was conquered by his successor Shalmaneser II in B.C. 856 (Hommel, *Assyria* in Hastings, *BD.* i. 183b, 184b; Maspero, iii. 30 *f.*, 66). The site of תלאשר (‖ Isa. 37. 12 תְּלַשָּׂר) must naturally be sought for in the same neighbourhood, and is probably to be identified with *Til-ašurri* in the land of the Ḥittites (cf. Winckler, *Geschichte Babyloniens*, 269, 335 *f.*).

Luc. separates תלאשר from necessary connexion with בני עדן by the insertion of *καί*, i.e. וַאֲשֶׁר בִּתְלַאשָּׂר.

13. איו וג׳] 'Where is *he*, (viz.) the king of Ḥamath?' So Isa. 19. 12 אַיָּם אֵפוֹא חֲכָמֶיךָ; Mic. 7. 10 אַיּוֹ י׳ אֱלֹהָיִךְ. ‖ Isa. 37. 13 reads אַיֵּה.

מלך חמת וג׳] Cf. *ch.* 18. 34 *note*.

15. ויתפלל ח׳ לפני י׳] LXX omits.

י׳ אלהי ישראל] Luc. Κύριε παντοκράτωρ, ὁ Θεὸς Ἰσραήλ, Pesh. ܡܪܝܐ ܚܝܠܬܢܐ: ܐܠܗܗ ܕܐܝܣܪܝܠ presuppose the insertion of צְבָאוֹת after י׳, as in ‖ Isa. 37. 16.

ישב הכרבים] Cf. 1 Sam. 4. 4; 2 Sam. 6. 2. ‖ 1 Chr. 13. 6; Ps. 80. 2; 99. 1. The reference is primarily to the presence of the שְׁכִינָה above the כַּפֹּרֶת in the innermost sanctuary of the Temple.

אתה הוא האלהים] So 2 Sam. 7. 28. Probably '*Thou* (with emphasis; lit. 'Thou-He') art the God'; or else 'Thou art He, (namely) the God.' Cf. Dri. *Tenses*, § 200.

16a. וּשְׁמָע] *Ḥatef-pathaḥ* frequently occurs under initial sibilants after ו copulative. Cf. I. 14. 21 וּשֲׁבַע; *ch.* 9. 17 וּשֲׁלַח; and other instances cited in G-K. § 10 *g*. Cf. *note* on I. 13. 7.

אשר שלחו] Read אֲשֶׁר שָׁלַח with LXX, Luc., Vulg., Pesh., and

‖ Isa. 37. 17; i.e. probably 'which he hath sent' (LXX, Luc.), or possibly 'who hath sent' (Vulg.).

17. החריבו] Probably we should read הֶחֱרִימוּ, in agreement with *v.* 11. So Benz., Kit., and (on Isa.) Duhm, Cheyne, Marti, and doubtfully Dillmann.

את הגוים] ‖ Isa. 37. 18 erroneously אֶת־כָּל־הָאֲרָצוֹת.

ואת ארצם] LXX omits. Luc. *καὶ πᾶσαν τὴν γῆν αὐτῶν.* Vulg. *et terras omnium.*

18. ונתנו] Irregular usage of the perfect with weak ו. ‖ Isa. 37. 19 is correct in reading infin. abs. וְנָתֹן, in accordance with idiom. Da. § 88[a].

19. כי אתה וג׳] ‖ Isa. 37. 20 omits אלהים erroneously.

20. י׳ אלהי ישראל] LXX, Luc. Κύριος (LXX adds ὁ Θεὸς) τῶν δυνάμεων Θεὸς Ἰσραήλ.

21. בתולת בת ציון] Suspended construct state. Cf. *note* on אַנְשֵׁי בְּנֵי־אֱלֹנֵיכֶם *ch.* 10. 6.

ראש הניעה] A gesture of mockery. Cf. Ps. 22. 8; 109. 25; Lam. 2. 15; Job 16. 4.

22. חרפת וגדפת] Weak ו *co-ordinates* two synonymous ideas. Cf. Dri. *Tenses*, § 132.

23. ברכב] Q're בְּרֹב in agreement with the text of many Codd., all Verss. and ‖ Isa. 37. 24.

וָאֶכְרֹת] LXX, Luc., Vulg. are probably correct in reading וָאֶכְרֹת, and similarly וָאָבוֹא, and *v.* 24 וָאַחֲרִב, *v.* 25 (except Vulg.) וַתְּהִי. So most moderns.

מלון קצה] 'His farthest lodging-place'; lit. 'the lodging-place of his end.' מלון as in Isa. 10. 29. LXX *μέσον*, Cod. A, Luc. *μέρος* are doubtless emendations of a transliteration *μέλων*. Q're קִצּוֹ appears in the text of many Codd.

‖ Isa. 37. 24 offers the inferior reading מְרוֹם קִצּוֹ.

24. ואחרב] In reference to 'all the Nile-streams of Egypt,' וָאחרב must be regarded as a perfect of certitude; and this is quite consistent with the known intentions of Sennacherib, and the boastful tenour of the words which are put into his mouth.

מצור] Winckler (*Alttest. Untersuchungen*, 170) supposes that the original vocalization was מִיצוֹר or מִצּוֹר, on the ground that the form *Mi-iç-ça-ri* occurs twice on the Amarna tablets. The Massoretic vocalization will then be due to identification of the name with the Hebrew word meaning 'fortification.'

25. הלא וג׳] Render as in RV., with the alteration וַתְּהִי 'that thou becamest,' in place of וּתְהִי, rendered 'that thou shouldest be,' and the addition of 'and' before 'now.' The thought of the verse is that of Isa. 10. 5 *ff*.

The first part of the verse down to למימי קדם is omitted by LXX.

ויצרתיה] Omit ו with LXX, Luc., Vulg., Pesh. So Marti.

עתה] Read וְעַתָּה with LXX, Luc., Vulg., Pesh.

לַהְשׁוֹת] Standing for לְהַשְׁאוֹת (|| Isa. 37. 26) with syncope of ו. Cf. G-K. §§ 23 *f.*, 75 *qq*.

נִצִּים] Participle Niph'al of נצה. The only other occurrence of the verb is in Jer. 4. 7, where תִּנָּצֶינָה should probably be restored for Qal תִּצֶּינָה.

26. קצרי יד] 'Short of hand,' i. e. unequal to the task of saving themselves. So, with the verb, Isa. 50. 2 הֲקָצוֹר קָצְרָה יָדִי מִפְּדוּת; 59. 1; Num. 11. 23.

ויבשו] || Isa. 37. 27 וָבֹשׁוּ, perfect with ו co-ordinate.

ושדפה לפני קמה] RV., 'and as corn blasted before it be grown up,' follows the rendering of Vulg. *quae arefacta est antequam veniret ad maturitatem*; cf. Targ. דישלוק עד לא מטא למיהוי שובלין. Such a sense, however, cannot be extracted from the original as it stands; and, if we are to retain it, the least alteration will be הַשָּׁדוּף לִפְנֵי קָמוֹ, referring back to חֲצִיר גַּגּוֹת. But there can be no doubt that Wellh. (*C.* 360) is right in finding in לפני קמה a corruption of לְפָנַי קֻמְךָ which connects with וְשִׁבְתְּךָ of the following verse: 'Before me is thy rising up and thy lying down.' This supersedes the emendation of Th. לִפְנֵי קָדִים 'before the east wind.' Possibly, then, שְׁדֵפָה may stand by itself in the sense 'blasted' (sc. corn); and this is preferable to || Isa. 37. 27 שְׁדֵמָה, which seems to give no sense in this connexion. Klo.'s emendation וּשְׁפָיִים is worthy of notice: 'grass of the house tops *and of the downs*.' So Cheyne. For שפיים as barren uplands, cf. Isa. 41. 18; Jer. 12. 12.

28. שאננך] RV. text, 'thine arrogance,' in agreement with LXX, Luc. τὸ στρῆνός σου, Vulg. *superbia tua*, a rendering perhaps to be justified by Ps. 123. 4. RV. marg., 'thy careless ease,' is the more usual meaning. This latter rendering, however, is unsuitable to the context and parallelism; and the same remark applies, in a less degree, to the former rendering. Probably the emendation שְׁאוֹנְךָ 'thy tumult,' adopted by Benz., Kit., Budde, Grätz, Cheyne, is correct.

ושמתי וג׳] The figure is that of a savage beast led captive by a ring in its nose. Cf. Ezek. 19. 4, and the similar figure of Ezek. 29. 4; 38. 4.

29. ספיח] 'That which groweth of itself'; from unused root equivalent to Ar. سَفَحَ *pour out*, and so, the produce of grain *spilled* or *self-sown*. סָחִישׁ (|| Isa. 37. 30 שָׁחִים) is by inference the self-sown produce of this natural crop in the second year. So Verss.

31. Q're צְבָאוֹת is supported by the text of many Codd., all Verss., and || Isa. 37. 32.

33. יבא] Read בָּא with || Isa. 37. 34.

34. להושיעה] LXX omits. In Luc. the whole of *v.* 34[a] has fallen out.

ולמען דוד עבדי] Cf. I. 11. 12 *note*.

35. The catastrophe, as might have been expected, is passed over in silence in the Assyrian inscriptions; but the fact that Sennacherib does not make claim to have captured Jerusalem is in agreement with our narrative. Herodotus (ii. 141) records an Egyptian tradition, according to which Sennacherib's army was easily routed at Pelusium because innumerable field-mice had during the night gnawed through its bow-strings and the thongs of its shields.

36. וילך וישב] Luc. omits.

37. נסרך] No such god is known in the Assyrian inscriptions.

Halévy (*Mélanges de crit.* 177) plausibly conjectures that the name should be נסוך, i.e. *Nusku*, a solar deity.

ויהי הוא משתחוה וג׳] On the construction cf. I. 13. 20 *note*.

אדרמלך] Cf. *note* on *ch.* 17. 31.

שׂראצר] According to Schrader (*COT. ad loc.*) the name is shortened from *Nergal-šar-uṣur* (cf. Jer. 39. 3, 13). He refers to Abydenus, as quoted by Eusebius, who states that Sennacherib was assassinated by *Adramelus*, and succeeded by *Nergilus*, and that this latter was put to death by *Axerdis*. If, as seems obvious, Adramelus corresponds to אדרמלך and Axerdis to אסרחדן, then Nergilus may be thought to answer to שׂראצר.

בניו] Q're has the support of many Codd., all Verss., and || Isa. 37. 38.

אררט] Assyr. *Urarṭu*, the land of Armenia.

20. 1. בימים ההם] Cf. *ch.* 10. 32 *note*.

צו לביתך] Cf. I. 2. 1 *note*.

כי מת אתה] 'For thou art *about to die*'; the participle denoting the *futurum instans*. The same idiomatic expression occurs Gen. 20. 3; 48. 21; 50. 5, 24; Deut. 4. 22; Jer. 28. 16. Cf. also Deut. 17. 6 הַמֵּת 'the doomed man.'

2. וַיַּסֵּב] On the Aramaizing form cf. G-K. § 67 *y*.

4. ויהי וג׳] On the construction cf. Dri. *Tenses*, § 165. || Isa. 38. 4 is much abbreviated.

העיר] Read חָצֵר with the text of several Codd., and all Verss. On חָצֵר used definitely without the article cf. I. 7. 8 *note*. The middle court was the courtyard of the palace, called חָצֵר הָאַחֶרֶת I. 7. 8 in contrast to the Temple (innermost) court. Cf. *note* on I. 6. 36.

5. נגיד] Cf. I. 1. 35 *note*.

6. למעני וג׳] || Isa. 38. 6 omits.

7. קחו וג׳] LXX, Luc., Pesh. presuppose the reading יִקְחוּ . . . וְיָשִׂימוּ . . . וְיֶחִי 'Let them take . . . and place . . . that he may recover.' This is probably original, Ḥezekiah's request for the sign in *v.* 8 naturally presupposing that recovery is only as yet promised and not accomplished. וַיִּקְחוּ *v.* 7^b must have been

inserted after 'וישימו וג had been taken as describing a completed sequence of events.

|| Isa. 38. 21 (which, with *v.* 22, is misplaced) reads . . . יִשְׂאוּ וְיִמְרְחוּ . . . וְיֶחִי. The verb מרח, a ἅπαξ λεγ. in Heb., is explained from the Ar. مَرَخَ *anoint, smear.*

8. 'מה אות וג] || Isa. 38. 22 'מה אות כי אעלה בית י.

9. 'הלך וג] The only possible rendering is that of RV. marg. 'The shadow is gone forward &c.' But it is evident from Ḥezekiah's reply, *v.* 10, that an alternative is offered to him. We must therefore emend הֲיֵלֵךְ, which is expressed by Targ. היהך, and presupposed by the other Verss. So Th. (doubtfully), Klo., Kamp., Benz., Kit., Oort.

11^b. As the text stands, יָרְדָה can only refer to the *masc.* הַצֵּל. The true subj. of the verb is, however, preserved by Pesh., Targ., viz. הַשֶּׁמֶשׁ, which should be inserted after יָרְדָה, or after אָחָז as in Isaiah (see below). The statement then runs:—'And he brought back the shadow on the steps by which the sun had gone down on the step-clock of Aḥaz, ten steps.' This slight correction (Th., Oort) is more obvious than the supposition that במעלות אשר ירדה is an erroneous insertion from || Isa. 38. 8.

The Isaianic account omits the offer of an alternative sign; *v.* 8 with the emendations הַצֵּל for צֵל, הַשֶּׁמֶשׁ for בַּשֶּׁמֶשׁ (Kautzsch and others) reading as follows:—הִנְנִי מֵשִׁיב אֶת־הַצֵּל הַמַּעֲלוֹת אֲשֶׁר יָרְדָה בְּמַעֲלוֹת אָחָז הַשֶּׁמֶשׁ אֲחֹרַנִּית עֶשֶׂר מַעֲלוֹת וַתָּשָׁב הַשֶּׁמֶשׁ עֶשֶׂר מַעֲלוֹת בַּמַּעֲלוֹת אֲשֶׁר יָרָדָה׃ 'Behold I will bring back the shadow so many steps as the sun has gone down upon the step-clock of Aḥaz, even ten steps. And the sun returned ten steps upon the steps by which it had gone down.'

The character of the sun-clock called מעלות can only be conjectured. Most probably it was 'a pointed pillar (obelisk) upon a (round or square) plinth, to which a flight of steps led up. This pillar cast the shadow of its point at midday upon the highest, and at morning and evening upon the lowest step (west or east), and thus indicated the time of day.' Cf. Dillmann on Isaiah *ad loc.* The clock may have been introduced by Aḥaz from Assyria (cf. *ch.* 16. 10 *ff.*). According to Herodotus (ii. 109) the Babylonians were the inventors of the πόλος or concave sun-dial upon which the shadow was cast by the γνώμων, and of the division of the day into twelve hours.

12. בעת ההיא] Cf. I. 14. 1 *note.*

בראדך בלאדן] Read מראדך בלאדן with several Codd., LXX, Luc., Pesh., Targ., and ‖ Isa. 39. 1. The Assyrian form is *Marduk-abal-idinna.* Merodach-Baladan appears at first as king of the *Kaldu.* His kingdom is called *Bît-Yakin*, 'by the salt waters,' i. e. the Persian Gulf. He paid homage and tribute to Tiglath-Pileser in B.C. 729 (Rost, 60 *f.*), but seems to have seized the opportunity of the death of Shalmaneser and the accession of Sargon to constitute himself king of Babylon. His principal ally was *Ḫumbanigaš* king of Elam. Sargon directed an expedition against the allies (B.C. 721); but little is known about it, and it seems to have met with ill success. *Ḫumbanigaš* of Elam died in B.C. 717, and was succeeded by his less able son *Šutur-naḫundi.* Merodach-Baladan retained the sovereignty of Babylon for twelve years, until Sargon, having settled his affairs in the west and north, was able to direct his arms against him. After a campaign which occupied B.C. 710–709, Sargon entered Babylon in triumph. He claims to have taken Merodach-Baladan prisoner (Winckler, *Sargon*, 84 *f.*, 122 *f.*, 150 *f.*), but elsewhere (Winckler, *Sargon*, 58 *f.*) seems to state that he fled away and could not be found. The latter alternative seems to be the more probable, since a Merodach-Baladan appears some years later as king of Babylon for nine months, until conquered and driven out by Sennacherib (B.C. 704: cf. Tiele, *Bab. Gesch.* i. 246). Cf. Winckler, *Sargon*, pp. xv *f.*, xvii, xxxi–xxxix; Maspero, iii. 222 *ff.*, 254 *ff.*

There can be no doubt that Merodach-Baladan's embassy to Ḥezekiah took place some time prior to B.C. 710, whilst he was forming alliances in order to meet the advance of Sargon, which he must have foreseen as inevitable so soon as the latter should find himself free to operate against him. According to the chronology of Kings, Ḥezekiah's sickness happened in B.C. 714

(cf. *ch.* 18. 13 *note*), and the embassy arrived shortly afterwards, i.e. probably any time between the end of B.C. 714 and the beginning of B.C. 712.

בן בלאדן] In the inscriptions he appears as 'son of *Yakin*,' doubtless a dynastic title. Cf. the title 'son of Omri,' applied by Shalmaneser II to Jehu, as king of the land which was known to Assyria as *Bît-Ḫu-um-ri-a*. Cf. *notes* on *ch.* 9. 2; I. 16. 23.

ספרים] Duhm, Cheyne, Marti emend סָרִיסִים 'eunuchs,' a correction which is suitable to the suffix objects in *v.* 13 וישמע עליהם וג׳.

כי שמע] || Isa. 39. 1 incorrectly וַיִּשְׁמַע, through confusion of כ and ו. Cf. *note* on I. 12. 30.

13. וישמע] Read וַיִּשְׂמַח 'And Ḥezekiah *was glad* because of them,' with several Codd., LXX, Luc., Vulg., Pesh.[1], and || Isa. 39. 2. So moderns.

את כל בית נכתה] כל is omitted by many Codd., Vulg., Pesh., and || Isaiah. The meaning of בית נכתה can only be guessed from the context; so Luc. τὸν οἶκον τῆς ὑπάρξεως αὐτοῦ, Pesh. ܒܝܬ ܓܙܗ, Targ. בית גנזוהי, '*his treasure-house*'; Vulg. *domum aromatum*, and so 'A., Σ. in || Isa. τὸν οἶκον τῶν ἀρωμάτων. In Assyr. *bît nakanti* denotes 'treasure-house,' *nakantu* or *nakamtu*, plural *nakamâti*, meaning 'treasure,' and *nakâmu*, 'to heap up.' Cf. Delitzsch, *Assyr. HWB.* 462. Hence some authorities (cf. *Heb. Lex. Oxf.*) propose to read בֵּית נְכֹתָיו, making the word equivalent to *nakavâti* for *nakamâti*.

ובכל ממשלתו] Luc. καὶ ἐν παντὶ θησαυρῷ αὐτοῦ.

14. ומאין יבאו] 'And from whence *may they come?*' A more polite form of question than the categorical מֵאַיִן בָּאוּ. Cf. Dri. *Tenses*, § 39 γ.

15. לא היה דבר] LXX, Luc., Pesh. add בְּבֵיתִי.

באצרתי] LXX, Luc. וּבְאֹצְרֹתָי.

16–18. No kind of allusion is found elsewhere in the known prophecies of Isaiah to a Babylonian captivity, the prophet's

[1] Also Targ., according to de Rossi, in one MS. and in *Edit. Venet.*

political horizon being bounded by the great powers of his times, Assyria and Egypt. Thus it is probable that these verses have been worked over by R^{D2} in exilic or post-exilic times.

16. יהוה] Luc. Κυρίου παντοκράτορος.

17. הנה ימים באים] Luc. adds φησὶ Κύριος, i. e. נְאֻם י׳; cf. e. g. *ch.* 19. 33; 22. 19 in Luc.

18. ממך] Sta. emends מִמֵּעֶיךָ 'from thy bowels,' after Gen. 15. 4; 2 Sam. 7. 12, and regards the following אשר תוליד as a gloss which owes its origin to the corruption ממך.

19ᵇ. הלוא וג׳] LXX omits. Pesh. ܢܗܘܐ ... ܕܝܢ ܐܘܠܐ, Luc. γενέσθω, Vulg. *sit*, agree with ‖ Isa. 39. 8 כי יהיה וג׳, properly 'There shall be &c.'

20. ואשר עשה וג׳] 2 Chr. 32. 30 describes the method adopted by Ḥezekiah in order to provide a water-supply for Jerusalem: וְהוּא יְחִזְקִיָּהוּ סָתַם אֶת־מוֹצָא מֵימֵי גִיחוֹן הָעֶלְיוֹן וַיַּיְשְּׁרֵם לְמַטָּה מַעֲרָבָה לְעִיר דָּוִיד. There exists an ancient tunnel which was cut in order to supply the pool of Siloam from the spring now called the Virgin's Fountain (cf. *note* on עין רגל I. 1. 9). 'The distance in a straight line is 368 yards, but by the rocky channel 586 yards.' In the mouth of this tunnel, where it opens into Siloam, there was discovered in 1880 an inscription which records the manner in which two parties of workmen quarried at either end, and met in the middle (cf. *Append.* 2; Baed. 97 *f.*). Both tunnel and inscription may reasonably be supposed to be due to Ḥezekiah. Sta., however (*Ges.* i. 592 *ff.*), thinks that the tunnel was already in existence in the time of Aḥaz, and quotes Isa. 8. 6 in support of his contention.

21. After *v.* 21ᵇ Luc. adds καὶ ἐτάφη μετὰ τῶν πατέρων αὐτοῦ ἐν πόλει Δαυίδ.

21. 1–18. *Manasseh, king of Judah.*

Ch. 21. 1–9, 18 = 2 Chr. 33. 1–9, 20.

The narrative throughout is the work of R^D, based upon very brief notices (*vv.* 3, 4ᵃ, 5, 6ᵃ, 7ᵃ, 16ᵃ), derived, presumably, from the Annals. The section *vv.* 10–15 appears to presuppose the captivity of Judah, and must therefore, in its present form, be assigned to R[D2]. The following phrases of R[D] have in most cases already been noticed:—

2. כתועבת הגוים וג׳] I. 14. 24 *note.*

4, 7. אשים את שמי] I. 9. 3 *note.*

7. ובירושלם אשר בחרתי] I. 8. 16 *note.*

8. אשר נתתי לאבותם] I. 8. 34 *note.*

אם ישמרו לעשות] So I. 11. 10 (*note*); *ch.* 17. 37; 2 Chr. 33. 8; 1 Chr. 22. 12; Deut. 5. 1, 29; 6. 3, 25; 7. 11; 8. 1; 11. 22, 32; 12. 1; 13. 1; 15. 5; 17. 10; 19. 9; 24. 8; 28. 1, 15, 58; 31. 12; 32. 46; Josh. 1. 7, 8; 22. 5 (D[2]).

10. עבדיו הנביאים] Cf. *ch.* 9. 7; 17. 13, 23; 24. 2; Jer. 7. 25; 25. 4; 26. 5; 29. 19; 35. 15; 44. 4. Elsewhere Am. 3. 7; Zech. 1. 6; Ezra 9. 11; Dan. 9. 10.

11. הרע וג׳] I. 14. 9 *note.*

11, 21. גלולים; בגלוליו] I. 15. 12 *note.*

12. הנני מביא רעה על] I. 14. 10 *note.*

21. 1. מנשה] Both Esar-haddon and Assurbanipal refer to this king as *Mí-na-si-í* or *Mi-in-si-í*, king of Judah, in a list of twenty-two kings of the land of Ḫatti. Cf. *COT. ad loc.*

2. כתועבת] Luc. *καὶ ἐπορεύθη κατὰ πάντα τὰ βδελύγματα κ.τ.λ.*

3. צבא השמים] The stars; cf. *note* on I. 22. 19. The worship of the heavenly bodies was indigenous in Babylon in the earliest times, and was no doubt introduced into Judah through intercourse with Assyria. Whether this Babylonian cult was known and practised in the Northern Kingdom also before its fall, as is affirmed in *ch.* 17. 16[b], has been questioned. Cf. p. 331.

4. ובנה] The use of perfect with weak ו, here and in *v.* 6, must be ascribed to the decadent style of the Annalist. Cf. *note* on ותפש *ch.* 14. 7.

מזבחת] LXX, Luc. sing. *θυσιαστήριον.* So LXX in *v.* 5.

5. בשתי חצרות וג׳] The House of Yahwe seems to have had only one courtyard; cf. I. 6. 36 *note; ch.* 20. 4. Possibly the reference may include the חָצֵר הָאַחֶרֶת or חָצֵר הַתִּיכֹנָה, properly

the Palace-courtyard, which, as Kit. remarks, passed over in the time of the second Temple into a wider Temple-courtyard.

6. ועשה] 'Appointed,' or 'instituted.' Cf. I. 1. 5 *note.*

אוב וידענים] 'Necromancers and wizards.' אוֹב seems to denote, in the first place, the ghost itself, which was said to dwell *in* the medium (Lev. 20. 27). Similarly, the witch of Endor is a בַּעֲלַת אוֹב 'possessor of a ghost' (1 Sam. 28. 7), and Saul's request to her is קָסֳמִי־נָא לִי בָּאוֹב 'Divine for me, I pray thee, through the ghost' (*v.* 8). In Deut. 18. 11 the diviner is called שֹׁאֵל אוֹב 'one who consults a ghost.' The voice of the אוֹב is low and thin, and appears to come from the ground (Isa. 29. 4).

The transference of the term from the ghost to the medium, as in our passage, ‖ 2 Chr. 33. 6; 1 Sam. 28. 3, 9, appears to be a secondary usage. According to Schwally, the reverse process took place in the case of יִדְּעֹנִי, the prime meaning being 'wizard,' and hence, as with Aram. זַכּוּרָא, a secondary application being made to the ghost. Cf. *Das Leben nach dem Tode,* 69 *f.* If, however, the meaning of יִדְּעֹנִי be either 'knowing one' or 'familiar,' it is more natural to find first reference to the ghost, as in the case of אוֹב. Cf. *Heb. Lex. Oxf., s. v.* The root-meaning of אוֹב can only be remotely conjectured, and the distinction between אוב and ידעני is unknown.

7. את פסל האשרה] Cf. I. 14. 15 *note.*

אשר עשה] LXX, Luc. omit.

בבית הזה . . . אשר בחרתי . . . אשים] LXX, Luc. ἐν τῷ οἴκῳ τούτῳ . . . ἐξελεξάμην . . . καὶ θήσω (Luc. θεῖναι), omitting אֲשֶׁר before בָּחַרְתִּי, and reading וְאָשִׂימָה or לָשׂוּם for אָשִׂים.

8. ישמרו] Luc. ἀκούσωσι, i. e. יִשְׁמְעוּ.

9. את הרע] LXX adds ἐν ὀφθαλμοῖς Κυρίου, Luc. ἐνώπιον Κυρίου.

11. הרע] LXX, Luc., Vulg. omit.

מכל] Luc. κατὰ πάντα, i. e. כְּכֹל.

12. אשר כל שמעיו וג׳] Cf. 1 Sam. 3. 11; Jer. 19. 3.

13. ונטיתי וג׳] For the figure cf. Isa. 34. 11; Lam. 2. 8.

כאשר ימחה וג׳] Pesh., in place of this simile, reads ܘܐܣܚܘܦ

ܘܢܚܒܠܝܗ̇ ܟܠܗ̇ ܒܝܫܬܐ ܕܥܒܕ ܡܢܫܐ ܒܝܗܘܕܐ 'and will destroy it, on account of all the evil which Manasseh wrought in Judah.'

מחה והפך] Read, with most moderns, מָחֹה וְהָפֹךְ 'wiping and turning (it).' The second infin. stands in simple sequence to the first, as e.g. in Isa. 19. 22, noticed under I. 20. 37 *note*.

18. עזא] Sta. (*Ges.* i. 569) quotes Wellh. for the suggestion that עֻזָּא (cf. 2 Sam. 6. 3) is a contracted form of עֲזַרְיָה, which was in later times confused with the name עֻזִּיָּה, so that this latter was written in place of the contraction. Cf. *ch.* 15. 1, *note* on עזריה.

On the narrative of 2 Chr. 33. 11–13, which relates the captivity, repentance, and restoration of Manasseh, cf. Dri. *Authority*, 114 *ff.*

21. 19–26. *Amon, king of Judah.*

Ch. 21. 19–24 = 2 Chr. 33. 21–25.

R^D frames brief notices from the Annals.

24. עם הארץ] Cf. *ch.* 16. 15 *note*.

26. בקברתו] Luc. ἐν τῷ τάφῳ τοῦ πατρὸς αὐτοῦ.

22. 1—**23.** 30. *Josiah, king of Judah. The finding of the Book of the Law, and the religious reformation to which it gave rise.*

Ch. 22. 1—23. 3 = 2 Chr. 34. 1, 2, 8–32.

Ch. 23. 4–20 is the probable source of the summary 2 Chr. 34. 3–7.

Ch. 23. 30^b = 2 Chr. 36. 1.

The lengthy narratives of the Chronicler which relate the keeping of the passover, 2 Chr. 35. 1–19 (cf. *ch.* 23. 21–23), and Josiah's defeat and death at the hands of Necho, king of Egypt, 2 Chr. 35. 20–27 (cf. *ch.* 23. 29, 30), appear to be based upon extraneous sources.

Ch. 22. 3—23. 25 is a continuous narrative, probably drawn from the Temple-archives (cf. *note* on *ch.* 11, pp. 307 *f.*). Deuteronomic phrases are found in 23. 3, 19, 25[1], and in the speech of Ḥuldah,

[1] לשמר ... נפש *v.* 3 (I. 2. 3, 4 *note*); להכעים *v.* 19 (I. 14. 9 *note*); וכמהו וג' *v.* 25 (I. 3. 12 *note*; I. 8. 48 *note*).

22. 15–20[1], which seems to show signs of revision by R^D[2] in exilic times. Certainly this later editor is responsible for the addition 23. 26, 27[2], at the close of the narrative, which strikes a note strangely alien to the enthusiasm of the pre-exilic author in view of Josiah's reformation (cf. especially 23. 22, 25).

Ch. 23. 29, 30 is probably drawn from the Annals.

22. 3. בשמנה . . . יאשיהו] LXX, Luc. add *ἐν τῷ μηνὶ τῷ ὀγδόῳ.*

4. ויתם] RV. 'that *he may sum* the money'; lit. 'may bring to an end,' and so, by inference, 'return the full amount of.' No parallel, however, can be cited for such a use of the verb. Comparison of *v.* 9, הִתִּיכוּ, suggests the emendation וְיַתֵּךְ, 'that he may pour out,' a reading which seems to be presupposed by Luc. *καὶ χωνεύσατε*, Vulg. *ut confletur*, and which is adopted by Ginsburg, Grä., Kit., Oort. LXX *καὶ σφράγισον*, i.e. וַחֲתֹם, is favoured by Th., Kamp., Benz., but appears less suitable. Klo. וְיִתַּכֵּן 'that he may weigh'; cf. הַמְתֻכָּן *ch.* 12. 12. || 2 Chr. 34. 9 וַיִּתְּנוּ.

5. ויתנה על יד] Lit. 'And let them place it *upon the hand* &c.' So exactly Gen. 42. 37 תְּנָה אֹתוֹ עַל־יָדִי. Cf. also the expression הִגִּיר עַל־יַד Jer. 18. 21; Ezek. 35. 5; Ps. 63. 11.

ויתנו אתו] Luc. *καὶ ἔδωκαν αὐτὸ κατὰ τὸ ῥῆμα τοῦ βασιλέως.*

בבית] Q're בית, in agreement with *v.* 9. Cf. *ch.* 12. 12.

7. לא יחשב] Frequentative; 'there was not (from time to time) made audit of.' Cf. *ch.* 12. 16.

10. Before לאמר Luc. adds *περὶ τοῦ βιβλίου.*

12. עבד המלך] Apparently a special title, 'the servant of the king' *par excellence.* The title has been found in ancient Heb. character upon a seal. Cf. Benz. *Archäologie*, 310*f.*

13. עלינו] Luc. *ἐν αὐτῷ*, i.e. עָלָיו, the reading of two Codd., is probably correct. Cf. || 2 Chr. 34. 21 עַל־הַסֵּפֶר הַזֶּה. So Th., Klo., Kamp., Benz., Kit., Oort.

---

[1] הנני מביא רעה וג׳ *v.* 16 (I. 14. 10 *note*); אלהים אחרים *v.* 17 (I. 9. 6 *note*); למען הכעסני *v.* 17 (I. 14. 9 *note*).

[2] הכעיסו *v.* 26 (I. 14. 9 *note*); אסיר מעל פני *v.* 27, cf. *ch.* 17. 18, 23; 24. 3; Jer. 32. 31; so with שִׁלַּח I. 9. 7; Jer. 15. 1; with הִשְׁלִיךְ *ch.* 13. 23; 17. 20 (מִן in place of מֵעַל); אשר בחרתי *v.* 27 (I. 8. 16 *note*).

14. אשת] LXX μητέρα.

במשנה] 'In the second (district).' Cf. Zeph. 1. 10, and, according to the probable interpretation, הָעִיר מִשְׁנֶה Neh. 11. 9. The precise significance with which the term is employed is unknown. According to Neh. 3. 9, 12 we find Jerusalem divided into two districts in post-exilic times for administrative purposes. Possibly the משנה may have been the new as distinct from the old city. So Ges.-Buhl.

18. הדברים וג׳] '(As regards) the words which thou hast heard.' Luc., however, offers the reading Ἀνθ' ὧν ἤκουσας τοὺς λόγους μου, καὶ ἠπαλύνθη ἡ καρδία σου, Vulg. *Pro eo quod audisti verba voluminis, et* &c., i. e. (יַעַן) אֲשֶׁר שָׁמַעְתָּ הַדְּבָרִים וַיֵּרַךְ לְבָבְךָ.

19. ולקללה] Luc. omits.

20. על המקום הזה] Add וְעַל־יֹשְׁבָיו with Luc., and || 2 Chr. 34. 28. So Klo. Oort וְיֹשְׁבָיו.

23. 1. ויאספו] LXX, Luc. presuppose sing. וַיֶּאֱסֹף, as in || 2 Chr. 34. 29.

2. והנביאים] Six Codd. agree with || 2 Chr. 34. 30 in reading וְהַלְוִיִּם. The mention of הַנְּבִיאִים is somewhat unexpected, in view of the fact that no mention is made of prophets in *ch.* 22, but only of Ḥuldah the prophetess. On the other hand, the fact that הלויים is the more obvious reading creates the suspicion that it is a correction, since no reason can be assigned for the substitution of הנביאים for הלויים.

4. כהני המשנה] RV. 'the priests of the second order.' In *ch.* 25. 18 a single כֹּהֵן מִשְׁנֶה, 'second (i. e. vice) priest,' is mentioned, in contrast to כֹּהֵן הָרֹאשׁ, and Targ. סגן כהניא is probably correct in making reference in the present passage also to a single individual.

ולאשרה] Cf. I. 14. 15 *note*.

בשדמות קדרון] RV. 'in the fields of Kidron.' Elsewhere שדמה is peculiar to poetry. Luc. ἐν τῷ ἐμπυρισμῷ, i. e. בְּמִשְׂרְפוֹת, adopted by Klo., Kamp., Benz., Kit., and interpreted as (*lime-*)*kilns*. Cf. Isa. 33. 12.

ונשא] Here and elsewhere in the narrative the use of the perfect with weak ו is a mark of decadence in style. Cf. *note* on ותפש *ch.* 14. 7.

5. ויקטר] Emend וַיְקַטְּרוּ with LXX, Targ. Luc., Vulg., Pesh. suggest לְקַטֵּר, but may equally be supposed to be reproducing in their renderings the idea of purpose implied in וַיְקַטְּרוּ.

ולמזלות] 'And for the heavenly mansions.' In Ar. مَنْزِل *manzil* denotes a *lodging-place* or *mansion;* and the pl. اَلْمَنَازِل is used of the twenty-eight *mansions* of the moon. In Assyr. (Delitzsch, *Assyr. Handwörterbuch*) *manzazu* denotes 'a place of standing,' from the root *nazâzu*, 'to stand.' This word occurs on the fifth table of the Babylonian Creation series, which begins, 'He made the mansions (*manzazi*) of the great gods' (Jensen, *Kosmologie*, 288 *ff.;* Schrader, *COT.* i. 15). Further, there is a fem. form of *manzazu*, viz. *manzaltu* (= *manzaztu*), *mazaltu*. For this Delitzsch quotes III Rawlinson, 59, 35[a]: 'The gods in heaven in their mansions (*man-zal-ti-šu-nu*) set me.' Jensen (*Kosmologie*, 347 *f.*) mentions the same facts. While, however, Delitzsch identifies these *manzalti* with the zodiacal stations (*Prolegomena*, 54), Jensen thinks that they were perhaps fifty in number[1], corresponding to the number of the great gods, and thus can scarcely denote merely the signs of the zodiac, but rather certain fixed stars and planets, lists of which are to be found in the inscriptions, but of which the identification seems to be possible in a few cases only (*Kosmologie*, 146 *ff.*)[2].

In Rabbinic Heb. מזלות is used to denote the twelve zodiacal signs (*Berachoth*, 32[b]; *Shabbath*, 75[a]), but also the planets, regarded as stars of good or ill fortune (*Bereshith rabba*, 10, 10[c]; *al.*). In agreement with this latter signification, we have, according to the restoration of de Vogüé, the dedication למזל נעם,

[1] The number of the *manzazi* appears to have originally existed on the Creation tablet.

[2] Jensen finds allusion to the zodiacal signs in the *maši* stars of l. 2 of the Creation tablet above cited. The word *miṣrâta* (not *mizrâta*) or *iṣrâta*, which occurs in l. 3, cannot, with Sayce (*Religion of Bab.*, 389), be identified with מַזָּרוֹת.

answering to the Greek Ἀγαθῇ τύχῃ in a Phoenician inscription from Larnaka of about the fourth century B.C. (*CIS.* 95).

It is doubtful whether מַזָּרוֹת of Job 38. 32 is identical with מַזָּלוֹת. LXX in both passages transliterates μαζουρώθ, while Targ., in accordance with Kings, uses in Job the rendering שטרי מזליא.

6. קבר בני העם] The common burial-place of those who were without name and memorial. Cf. Jer. 26. 23.

7. הקדשים] Cf. I. 14. 24 *note*.

בתים] Scarcely explicable in connexion with ארגים. RV. 'hangings' is unjustifiable; and 'tent-shrines' might have been called מִשְׁכָּנוֹת, but scarcely בָּתִּים. The transliteration of LXX χεττιείν suggests to Klo. an original כתנים for כֻּתֳּנוֹת 'tunics,' a reading which is supported by Luc. στολάς, and may well be original. So Benz.

8. גבע] Cf. I. 15. 22 *note*.

את במות השערים] Emend, with most moderns after Hoffmann, *ZATW*. ii. 175, אֶת־בָּמוֹת (LXX, Luc. בֵּית) הַשְּׂעִירִים 'The high-places (*or* house) of the Satyrs.' Cf. 2 Chr. 11. 15; Lev. 17. 7.

בשער העיר] Luc. adds πύλην ἐκκεκεντημένων, and according to Field, Quinta τὴν πύλην τῶν τετρωμένων (or τετραυματισμένων), i. e. perhaps שַׁעַר הַדָּגִים 'the fish-gate'; cf. the rendering of LXX in Zeph. 1. 10, ἀπὸ πύλης ἀποκεντούντων.

9. לא יעלו] 'Did not go up'; frequentative. The regulation of Deut. 18. 6 *ff.* seems to have been intended to place the provincial priesthood upon a level with the priesthood of the central sanctuary, as regards service as well as maintenance. This regulation, so far as it concerned equality of service, appears from our passage to have remained a dead letter, doubtless owing to the exclusiveness of the Jerusalem priesthood. The provincial appears to have sunk at once into the subordinate position of the 'Levite,' as defined in the Priestly Code (I. 8. 4 *note*). Cf. also Ezek. 44. 10–16.

10. התפת] R. Sm. (*Rel. Sem.*[2], 377) conjectures that תפת is properly the Aram. name for a *fireplace*, upon the assumption of a variant ܬܦܬܐ, תְּפַת, for the Syr. ܐܬܦܝܐ. Cf. the use made of the

name in Isa. 30. 33. The vocalization תֹּפֶת, like that of מֹלֶךְ, עַשְׁתֹּרֶת, probably points to a later approximation to the vocalization of בֹּשֶׁת 'shameful thing.' Cf. the substitution of בֹּשֶׁת for בַּעַל in the text of Hos. 9. 10; Jer. 3. 24; 11. 13.

גי בני הנם] Elsewhere always גֵּי בֶן־הִנֹּם, or abbreviated גֵּי הִנֹּם. Q're is supported by many Codd., and by LXX, Luc., Vulg., Pesh., Targ.

לבלתי להעביר] לְבִלְתִּי לְ occurs only here. Cod. 304 de Rossi, LXX, Pesh. omit לבלתי, taking להעביר to express the purpose of the existence of the תפת :—'that a man might offer &c.' Thus it is possible that לבלתי is a later insertion, made by a scribe who understood the clause as explaining the purpose of וטמא.

11. בפרורים] RV. 'in the precincts.' הַפַּרְבָּר 1 Chr. 26. 18, doubtless the same, is stated to have been on the west of the Temple. New Heb. פַּרְוָר, Aram. פַּרְוָרָא denote a *suburb*. Ges. *Thes.* 1123 finds the origin of the term in Persian فَرْوَار, a *summer-house*, or *open kiosk* (lit. *light-possessing*). Dri. (*s.v. Parbar*, Hastings, *BD.* iii) remarks that, if the term is to be traced to the Persian, its occurrence in Kings must be regarded as a mark of post-exilic revision.

שרף באש] Luc. adds ἐν τῷ οἴκῳ ᾧ ᾠκοδόμησαν βασιλεῖς Ἰσραὴλ ὑψηλὸν τῷ Βάαλ καὶ πάσῃ τῇ στρατιᾷ τοῦ οὐρανοῦ.

12. הגג עלית אחז] הַגָּג clearly refers to the roof of the Temple, and עֲלִיַּת אָחָז, in apposition, must have come into the text as a gloss. Benz., Kit. conjecture that Aḥaz may have erected a shelter for the altars upon the Temple roof; cf. the עֲלִיַּת־קִיר of *ch.* 4. 10.

אשר עשו מלכי י׳] Luc. ἃ ἐποίησεν Ἀχάζ.

וַיָּרָץ] As the text stands, RV. 'and beat them down,' making the verb Imperf. Qal of רצץ, must be adopted. So Luc. καὶ συνέτριψε—apparently a third rendering of the word. Th., Oort follow Kimḥi in vocalizing וַיָּרֶץ (Imperf. Hiph'il of רוץ), 'and banished them,' in agreement with Targ. וארחק מתמן. Klo. cites the second rendering of Luc., καὶ ἐξήνεγκεν αὐτά, for the emendation וַיֹּצִאֵם, a suggestion favoured by Benz., Kit.

13. הר המשחית] 'The hill of the destroyer.' Only mentioned here. Klo. suggests that the name, if genuine, may have reference to 2 Sam. 24. 16. Targ. טור זיתיא 'mount of olives' suggests הַר הַמִּשְׁחָה 'mount of oil,' as occasionally in the Talmuds according to Neubauer, *Geographie du Talmud*, 147. So Hoffmann, *ZATW*. ii. 175; Perles, *Analekten*, 31 *f.*

15. וישרף את הבמה] Impossible. The במה itself, i. e. the *situation* of the altar, could not be burnt; nor can it be supposed that the term is used vaguely in place of בֵּית הַבָּמָה. LXX, Luc. read καὶ συνέτριψεν τοὺς λίθους αὐτοῦ, i. e. וַיְשַׁבֵּר אֶת־אֲבָנָיו—doubtless the original text. So Klo., Benz., Kit., Oort.

הדק וג׳] 'Crushing (them) to dust'; lit. 'he crushed &c.,' perf. used *asyndetos* in a circumstantial clause. Cf. Dri. *Tenses*, § 163.

אשרה] We ought probably to read הָאֲשֵׁרָה, or אֲשֵׁרָתָהּ.

16ᵇ. כדבר וג׳] After איש האלהים LXX, Luc. add ἐν τῷ ἑστάναι Ἰεροβοὰμ ἐν τῇ ἑορτῇ ἐπὶ τὸ θυσιαστήριον. καὶ ἐπιστρέψας (Luc. Ἰωσίας) ἦρεν τοὺς ὀφθαλμοὺς αὐτοῦ ἐπὶ τὸν τάφον τοῦ ἀνθρώπου τοῦ θεοῦ, i. e. בַּעֲמֹד יָרָבְעָם בֶּחָג עַל־הַמִּזְבֵּחַ וַיִּפֶן וַיִּשָּׂא אֶת־עֵינָיו עַל־קֶבֶר אִישׁ הָאֱלֹהִים. These words must have fallen out of the text through homoioteleuton. As MT. stands, the repeated אשר קרא וג׳ is awkward and redundant, while the details supplied by the missing words are felt to be wanting to the narrative. So Th. (וַיָּשָׁב for καὶ ἐπιστρέψας), Klo., Benz., Oort.

17. הציון הלז] 'Yonder tomb-stone.' ציון occurs again in Ezek. 39. 15 to denote a stone set up to mark the locality of an unburied body, and in pl. in Jer. 31. 21 of stones placed as way-marks. The word is used in the same sense in New Heb., together with a verb צִיֵּן *to mark*, e. g. the site of sepulchres as being unclean.

On הלז cf. *ch.* 4. 25 *note*.

הקבר איש האלהים] If the text be correct, הקבר can only be taken as an instance of the article with the *st. constr.* Benz., Kit. emend זֶה קֶבֶר 'This is the grave &c.' for הַקֶּבֶר; Klo., Da. (§ 20, *Rem.* b) הוּא קֶבֶר—a suggestion which is open to the objection that הוא would more naturally fall after איש האלהים.

הַמִּזְבַּח בית אל] The vocalization of MT., with the rendering of RV. 'the altar of Bethel,' is to be rejected. The correct vocalization is הַמִּזְבֵּחַ *st. absol.*, and בית אל is to be regarded as an accusative (cf. *ch.* 2. 3; 10. 29) defining the place of the event described by ויקרא וג׳:—'and proclaimed these things which thou hast done against the altar at Bethel.' Cf. Dri. *Tenses*, § 191, *Obs.* 2.

18. וימלטו עצמתיו] Luc. καὶ διεσώθη τὰ ὀστᾶ τοῦ προφήτου τοῦ πρεσβυτέρου τοῦ κατοικοῦντος ἐν Βαιθὴλ μετὰ κ.τ.λ., i.e. וַיִּמַּלְטוּ עַצְמוֹת הַנָּבִיא הַזָּקֵן הַיֹּשֵׁב בְּבֵית־אֵל וג׳—probably original. Cf. I. 13. 31*f.*

19. להכעים] LXX, Luc., Vulg., Pesh. add את יהוה.

20. אשר שם וג׳] Pesh., ܘܣܡܘ ܒܣܡܐ ܥܠ ܡܕܒܚܐ, 'who placed sweet savours upon the altars,' appears to have read שָׂמוּ for שָׂם, a use of the verb which is justified by Deut. 33. 10^{b}.

21. At the end of the *v.* Luc. adds καὶ ἐποίησαν οὕτως.

22. כי לא נעשה] RV. '*Surely* there was not kept &c.' It seems, however, preferable, in view of כי אם וג׳ of *v.* 23, to render 'For there had not been kept &c.'

כפסח הזה] 'Such a passover as this,' referring to ככתוב וג׳ of *v.* 21. LXX τὸ πάσχα τοῦτο, i.e. הַפֶּסַח הַזֶּה, seems to state that the passover was not kept at all during the period named.

24. את האבות וג׳] Cf. *ch.* 21. 6 *note.*

התרפים] A kind of idol, as is proved by the designation אלהים, Gen. 31. 30, 32; apparently of human form and size (1 Sam. 19. 13*ff.*), though sometimes much smaller (Gen. 31. 34). Like אלהים, the plural תרפים may denote one image (cf. Sam. *l.c.*), or more than one (Gen. *l.c.; al.*). תרפים are found as household gods in the possession of the Aramaean Laban (Gen. 31. 19*ff.*), the Ephraimite Micah (Judg. 17*f.*), and Michal, David's wife (1 Sam. 19. 13*ff.*). Ezekiel pictures them as consulted by the king of Babylon (21. 26). It is clear that תרפים were employed as oracle-givers. In Judg. 17*f.*; Hos. 3. 4 they are mentioned in connexion with the oracular אֵפוֹד; in 1 Sam. 15. 23; Zech. 10. 2; Ezek. 21. 26, 27 with the form of divination called קֶסֶם (cf. *ch.* 17. 17 *note*). Their association in our passage with אֶת־הָאֹבוֹת וְאֶת־הַיִּדְּעֹנִים (cf. *ch.* 21. 6 *note*) appears to connect them with the practice of necromancy. The wide-spread character of the תרפים cult among the Semitic races (as attested by the Biblical references above cited) has led Schwally (*Das Leben nach dem Tode*, 36) to identify it with ancestor-worship; cf. also Sta. *Ges.* i. 467; Nowack, *Archäologie*, ii. 23. A strange Jewish tradition explains תרפים as the pickled head of a first-born son, which was fastened on the wall of a house, and worshipped as an oracle; cf. *Pirqê de R. Eliezer*, *ch.* 36 (eighth century A.D.); Jerus. Targ. on Gen. 31. 19; cited by Buxtorf, *s.v.* תרפים.

הגללים] Cf. I. 15. 12 *note.*

29. בימיו] Cf. I. 16. 34 *note.*

נכה] Necho II, son of Psammeticus I, was second king of the twenty-sixth dynasty, and reigned B.C. 610–595. Cf. Hastings, *BD.* iii. 504. The strange rendering of Pesh. ܚܓܝܪܐ, Targ. פרעה חגירא 'Pharaoh the lame,' connects נְכֹה with נְכֵה רַגְלַיִם.

במגדו] Cf. I. 4. 12 *note.* Herodotus (ii. 159) places the encounter at Μάγδωλος, i.e. מִגְדֹּל, probably the place of that name on the N.E. border of Egypt; Ex. 14. 2; Num. 33. 7; Jer. 44. 1; *al.*

After לקראתו Pesh. adds ܠܡܬܟܬܫܘ ܥܡܗ. ܘܐܡܪ ܠܗ ܦܪܥܘܢ. ܠܐ ܗܘܐ ܥܠܝܟ ܐܢܐ ܐܬܝܬ. ܗܦܘܟ ܡܢܝ. ܘܠܐ ܫܡܥܗ ܠܦܪܥܘܢ. ܘܡܚܝܗܝ ܦܪܥܘܢ. 'to fight with him; and Pharaoh said to him, I am not come against thee; turn aside from me. And he hearkened not unto Pharaoh, and Pharaoh smote him.' This is probably a reminiscence of 2 Chr. 35. 21 *ff.*

כראתו אתו] 'When he saw him,' i.e. when they joined battle. On the analogy of the use of the Hithpa'el in *ch.* 14. 8, Benz., following Winckler, proposes to read the Niph'al כְּהֵרָאֹת אִתּוֹ—scarcely a necessary emendation.

30. עם הארץ] Cf. *ch.* 16. 15 *note.*

23. 31–35. *Jehoaḥaz, king of Judah.*

Ch. 23. 31–34 forms the source of 2 Chr. 36. 2–4. Short notices, probably from the Annals, are framed by R^D (R^{D2}).

31. חמוטל] In *ch.* 24. 18; Jer. 52. 1 †Kt. חֲמִיטַל. This form of

the name is given in our passage also by LXX Ἀμειταί, Cod. A, Luc. Ἀμιτάλ, Vulg. *Amital.*

לבנה] Cf. *ch.* 8. 22 *note.*

33. ויאסרהו . . . במלך] LXX, Luc. καὶ μετέστησεν αὐτὸν . . . τοῦ μὴ βασιλεύειν (Luc. αὐτόν), i.e. וַיְסִרֵהוּ . . . מִמְּלֹךְ. Cf. ‖ 2 Chr. 36. 3. So Oort. It is, however, scarcely possible to suppose that ברבלה וג׳ originally followed וַיְסִרֵהוּ, and does not properly belong to MT. וַיַּאַסְרֵהוּ. Thus the passage seems to be involved by the combination of two readings:—'bound him in Ribla in the land of Ḥamath,' and, 'removed him from reigning in Jerusalem.' Klo., Kamp., Benz., Kit. retain MT. ויאסרהו, and regard ממלך בירושלם as a gloss introduced from 2 Chr. 36. 3.

וככר זהב] Luc., Pesh. presuppose עֶשֶׂר כִּכְּרֵי זָהָב 'ten talents of gold.'

34. וַיָּבֹא] LXX, Luc., Vulg. וַיָּבֵא.

35. את עם הארץ] The sentence is awkward in the extreme if these words be regarded as in apposition to איש כערכו; and the alternative suggested by Benz., '*With* (i.e. by the help of) the people of the land' (cf. LXX, Luc. μετὰ τοῦ λαοῦ τῆς γῆς), is out of the question. Doubtless Klo. is right in regarding את עם הארץ as a gloss explanatory of את הארץ of the first half of the verse.

23. 36—**24.** 7. *Jehoiakim, king of Judah.*

Chh. 23. 36—24. 6 are summarized in 2 Chr. 36. 5–8. R^D (R^{D2}) frames short notices, probably drawn from the Annals.

24. 1. בימיו] Cf. I. 16. 34 *note.*

After נבכדנאצר Luc. adds ἐπὶ τὴν γῆν, while Pesh. adds ܥܠ ܐܘܪܫܠܡ 'against Jerusalem' after מלך בבל.

Nebuchadnezzar's campaign against Egypt (cf. *v.* 7) took place, according to Berossus, in the last year of his father Nabopolassar, i.e. B.C. 605. The news of Nabopolassar's death caused him to hasten back to Babylon, after he had brought his campaign to a successful issue. According to Jer. 46. 2 the defeat of the Egyptian army at Carchemish took place in Jehoiakim's fourth year (B.C. 604), and Jer. 25. 1 co-ordinates the fourth year of Jehoiakim with the first year of Nebuchadnezzar.

That Jehoiakim became 'servant' to Nebuchadnezzar through this campaign seems to follow both from the fragmentary account of Kings and also from the fact that Berossus speaks of τοὺς αἰχμαλώτους τῶν Ἰουδαίων among other prisoners of war. Thus, if the 'three years' of *ch.* 24. 1[b] be correct, and if the length of Jehoiakim's reign extended to eleven years (*ch.* 23. 36), Jehoiakim must have remained in rebellion against Nebuchadnezzar for four years.

The reference to Egypt's loss of Syria in *v.* 7 demands that in the original narrative an account of Nebuchadnezzar's victory at Carchemish must have followed *v.* 1[a]. Cf. Winckler, *Alttest. Untersuchungen*, 81 *f.*

2. ואת גדודי ארם] אֱדֹם rather than אֲרָם is to be expected in connexion with מוֹאָב and בְּנֵי עַמּוֹן, and this emendation is favoured by Grä., Klo., Benz.

After בני עמון Luc. adds καὶ ἐκ τῆς Σαμαρείας, i.e. וּמִשֹּׁמְרוֹן— possibly original, though not (with Klo.) to be substituted for וישלחם.

3. על פי י׳] LXX, Luc., Pesh., Targ. seem to have read עַל־אַף י׳ 'on account of the anger of Yahwe,' as in *v.* 20. The introductory אַךְ appears to be characteristic of this editor; cf. *ch.* 23. 26; 35.

4. וגם דם הנקי וג׳] 'And also (because of) the innocent blood which he shed.' If the text is correct, the force of the ב of בחטאת (*v.* 3) must be carried over into this clause.

6. וישכב וג׳] These words are omitted in 2 Chr. 36. 8 MT., but appear in the LXX text, with the addition καὶ ἐτάφη ἐν γανοζαὴ μετὰ τῶν πατέρων αὐτοῦ, i.e. וַיִּקָּבֵר בְּגַן עֻזָּא עִם־אֲבֹתָיו (cf. *ch.* 21. 26). Sta. *Ges.* i. 679 *note* conjectures that this reference to the burial-place originally stood in Kings, and was derived thence by the Chronicler, but that the notice was subsequently struck out in view of the prediction of Jer. 22. 19. So Wellh. (*C.* 359), Benz.

7. מנחל מצרים] Cf. *note* on נבול מצרים I. 5. 1.

24. 8–17. *Jehoiachin, king of Judah.*

Ch. 24. 8–17 is briefly summarized in 2 Chr. 36. 9, 10. No reference is made to the Annals, and it is possible that R^{D2} may be writing from personal knowledge of events, independently of a written source. Sta. (*ZATW.* iv. 271 *ff.*) regards *vv.* 13, 14 as a later insertion, properly referring to the events of 586 B.C. It is difficult to reconcile the 10,000 of *v.* 14 with the numbers given in *v.* 16; מִשָּׁם in *v.* 13 has no antecedent to which to refer back[1], whilst וַיֶּגֶל in *v.* 15 refers directly to *v.* 12. The chief objection, however, to the reference of these verses to 597 B.C. is to be found in their contents. Verse 13 speaks of *all* the treasures of the City and Temple as carried off by Nebuchadnezzar, and the golden vessels as melted down. But from *ch.* 25 (‖ Jer. 52) and Jer. 27. 18–20, 28. 2 *f.* the inference is that only a part of the City and Temple treasures were carried off on this occasion, and that the greater part was seized by the Chaldeans in 586 B.C. Thus the contents of *v.* 13 are suitable as a description of the events of 586 B.C., but not of those of 597 B.C. The same inference is to be drawn from the contents of *v.* 14. *All* Jerusalem was first deported in 586, and a characteristic of this deportation was that only the דלת הארץ remained (25. 12). On the other hand, as appears from Jer., the deportation at the close of Jehoiachin's reign consisted only of the higher classes (cf. e.g. Jer. 27. 20 את יכניה . . . ואת כל חרי יהודה וירושלם) and the men who bore arms, i.e. practically the same category as is named in *v.* 16.

8. ושלשה חדשים] 2 Chr. 36. 9 adds וַעֲשֶׂרֶת יָמִים.

10. בעת ההיא] Cf. I. 14. 1 *note.*

12. על מלך בבל] על for אל. Cf. *note* on על גחון I. 1. 38.

בשנת שמנה למלכו] B.C. 597. Jer. 52. 28 places the event in the seventh year of Nebuchadnezzar.

13. Luc. prefixes the statement καὶ εἰσῆλθε βασιλεὺς Βαβυλῶνος εἰς τὴν πόλιν, i.e. וַיָּבֹא מֶלֶךְ בָּבֶל אֶל־הָעִיר—an addition desiderated by מִשָּׁם of the following sentence.

[1] But cf. *note* on *v.* 13.

14. גּוֹלָה] The participle singular is used of *a single exile* 2 Sam. 15. 19; fem. Isa. 49. 21. It is clear, however, from *vv.* 15, 16 that we should vocalize גּוֹלָה a collective, 'captives.'

הַמַּסְגֵּר] Probably 'the lock-smiths.' So *v.* 16; Jer. 24. 1; 29. 2; in each case collective sing., and in connexion with הֶחָרָשׁ, by inference 'the workers in *wood*.' Elsewhere (Isa. 24. 22; 42. 7; Ps. 142. 8 *f.*) מַסְגֵּר denotes '*place* of locking,' i. e. 'dungeon.'

דלת עם הארץ] 'The poorest of the people of the land.' Cf. Jer. 39. 10 וּמִן־הָעָם הַדַּלִּים אֲשֶׁר אֵין־לָהֶם מְאוּמָה. On the fem. collective cf. Da. § 14. 2.

15. ואת אולי הארץ] RV. 'and the *chief men* of the land.' Q're אֵילֵי, as in Ezek. 17. 13. The word is perhaps from a root אול 'to be foremost'; but it is possible that the insertion of the ו or י is an intentional alteration to distinguish from the divine title אֵל. Cf. *Heb. Lex. Oxf.*, *s. v.* אֵל § 1.

24. 18—**25.** 7. *Zedekiah, king of Judah.*

Ch. 24. 18—25. 7 = Jer. 52. 1–11.

18. חמיטל וג׳] Cf. *ch.* 23. 31 *note.*

20. עַד־הִשְׁלִכוֹ] Cf. *note* on עַד־הִשְׁאִיר *ch.* 3. 25.

25. 1. בעשור לחדש] LXX, Luc. omit.

3. בתשעה לחדש] It is impossible that mention should be made of the day of the month when the month itself has not been specified. Pesh. ܘܒܚܕܥܣܪܐ ܫܢܝܢ ܠܡܠܟܘܬܐ ܕܨܕܩܝܐ. ܒܝܪܚܐ ܚܡܝܫܝܐ. ܒܬܫܥܬܐ ܒܗ ܒܝܪܚܐ:, i. e. וּבְעַשְׁתֵּי עֶשְׂרֵה שָׁנָה לַמֶּלֶךְ צ׳ בַּחֹדֶשׁ הַחֲמִשִׁי בְּתִשְׁעָה לַחֹדֶשׁ. This, however, conflicts with the earlier date given in *v.* 8 for a subsequent event. Th., Klo., Kamp., Benz., Kit., Oort supply בַּחֹדֶשׁ הָרְבִיעִי after Jer. 39. 2; 52. 6.

4. וכל אנשי המלחמה וג׳] The missing verb is supplied by ‖ Jer. 52. 7 יִבְרְחוּ וַיֵּצְאוּ מֵהָעִיר; cf. Jer. 39. 4. So exactly Pesh. ܥܪܩܘ ܘܢܦܩܘ ܡܢ ܡܕܝܢܬܐ; while LXX, ἐξῆλθον, supplies the latter verb, Vulg., *fugerunt*, the former. We are still, however, confronted by the difficulty of the sing. וַיֵּלֶךְ in *v.* 4ᵇ, without specified subj. This appears as plur. וַיֵּלְכוּ in ‖ Jer. 52. 7, and Pesh. in our passage is again in agreement. This is scarcely satisfactory, because the

king is only mentioned for the first time in *v.* 5 as having left the city with the men of war. The solution of the difficulty is probably to be found in Luc., which supplies in *v.* 4[a] before וכל אנשי וג׳ καὶ ἐξῆλθεν ὁ βασιλεύς. We may thus read in *v.* 4[a] וַיֵּצֵא הַמֶּלֶךְ וְכָל־אַנְשֵׁי הַמִּלְחָמָה, retaining sing. וַיֵּלֶךְ in *v.* 4[b] as referring to the principal actor. The plur. of Luc. καὶ ἐπορεύθησαν is probably the translator's alteration.

6. רבלתה] ‖ Jer. adds בְּאֶרֶץ חֲמָת, as in *ch.* 23. 33.

וידברו] Many Codd., all Verss., and ‖ Jer. 52. 9 read sing. וַיְדַבֵּר. The phrase דבר משפטים את פ׳ occurs again in Jer. 1. 16; 4. 12; 12. 1; 39. 5, and pl. משפטים (as in ‖ Jer. 52. 9) is the reading of several Codd. in our passage.

7. שחטו] Emend שָׁחַט, after LXX, Luc., Vulg., Pesh. Cf. ‖ Jer. 52. 10 וַיִּשְׁחַט.

ויביאהו בבל] ‖ Jer. 52. 11 adds וַיִּתְּנֵהוּ בְבֵית־הַפְּקֻדֹּת עַד־יוֹם מוֹתוֹ.

25. 8–26. *Destruction of the Temple and City of Jerusalem. Gedaliah, governor of Judah.*

Ch. 25. 8–21 = Jer. 52. 12–27.

Ch. 25. 22–26 is a much abbreviated account of the events described in Jer. 40. 7—43. 6, to which source R[D 2] clearly owes his information. Jer. 52, on the other hand, seems to be a later addition to the prophet's book excerpted from Kings[1], naturally with omission of 25. 22–26, as having been already related in fuller detail.

8. בשבעה לחדש] Three Codd., Luc., Pesh. בְּתִשְׁעָה לַחֹדֶשׁ; ‖ Jer. 52. 12 בֶּעָשׂוֹר לַחֹדֶשׁ. Klo., Benz. make the erroneous statement that Luc. agrees with ‖ Jer.

היא שנת וג׳] B.C. 586.

9. ואת כל בית גדול] 'And every house of a great one.' So Pesh., Targ. The statement is superfluous after the preceding ואת כל בתי ירושלם, and is regarded by Benz., Kit. as an explanatory gloss.

---

[1] Notice the closing words of Jer. 51, 'Thus far are the words of Jeremiah.'

10. אשר רב טבחים] Read אֲשֶׁר אֶת־רַב־טַבָּחִים, with ‖ Jer. 52. 14. Luc. omits אשר וג׳, while the whole *v.* is wanting in LXX.

11. ההמון] 'The remnant of *the multitude*' is indistinguishable from 'the remnant of the people' mentioned just previously. ‖ Jer. is doubtless correct in reading הָאָמוֹן '*the artificers*,' or '*master-workmen*.' Cf. *ch.* 24. 14.

At the end of the *v.* Pesh. adds ܘܐܘܒܠ ܐܢܘܢ ܠܒܒܠ 'and brought them to Babylon.'

12. ולגבים] Q're יֹגְבִים, as in ‖ Jer. 52. 16, is supposed to mean 'husbandmen.' Kt. גָּבִים 'ploughmen' (lit. 'diggers') is preferred by Kö., *Lehrg.* I. ii. 105. Q're is to some extent supported by Jer. 39. 10[b] וַיִּתֵּן לָהֶם כְּרָמִים וִיגֵבִים; though here also it is possible that יְגֵבִים, of uncertain meaning (RV. 'fields'), is an alteration of גֵּבִים 'cisterns' (*ch.* 3. 16; Jer. 14. 3).

13–17. Cf. *notes* on I. 7. 15 *ff.*

15. אשר זהב וג׳] 'That which was of gold he took in gold, and that which was of silver in silver'; i.e. all the vessels &c. of these precious metals, as so much gold and silver.

18. כהן משנה] Cf. *ch.* 23. 4 *note.*

19. אשר הוא פקיד] ‖ Jer. 52. 25 reads הָיָה for הוּא.

מראי פני המלך] So Est. 1. 14. Cf. 2 Sam. 14. 24, 28. The expression denotes a privileged position of intimate attendance upon the king.

ואת הספר וג׳] Read *st. constr.* סֹפֵר, with ‖ Jer. 52. 25. Luc., καὶ τὸν Σαφάν, takes the word as a proper name סָפָן (or שָׁפָן), and this is adopted by Klo. But the statement המצבא וג׳, 'who *mustered* the people of the land,' makes it clear that the reference is not to the שר הצבא himself, but to an official who had charge of the *conscription*, and so appropriately a סֹפֵר.

23. והאנשים] Read וְאַנְשֵׁיהֶם, with LXX, Pesh., Targ., as in *vv.* 23[b], 24. So ‖ Jer. 40. 7.

המצפה] Cf. I. 15. 22 *note.*

25. 27–30. *Kindness shown to the captive Jehoiachin by Evil-Merodach, king of Babylon.*

Ch. 25. 27–30 = Jer. 52. 31–34.

27. בשנת מלכו] B.C. 561.

מבית כלא] LXX, Luc., Pesh. are probably correct in reading וַיֹּצֵא אתו מִבֵּית כֶּלֶא, as in ‖ Jer.

28. מעל כסא] ‖ Jer. מִמַּעַל לְכִסֵּא is preferable.

30. ארחתו] 'His allowance' (&c. of food). So Jer. 40. 5; cf. Prov. 15. 17. In Assyr. *iaraḫtu* denotes a portion of corn.

דבר יום ביומו] Cf. I. 8. 59 *note*.

APPENDIX

1.

Inscription of Mesha', king of Moab[1].

1 אנך . משע . בן . כמשכן . מלך . מאב . הד

2 יבני | אבי . מלך . על . מאב . שלשן . שת . ואנך . מלכ

3 תי . אחר . אבי | ואעש . הבמת . זאת . לכמש . בקרחה | בנסך

4 שע . כי . השעני . מכל . השלכן . וכי . הראני . בכל . שנאי | עמר

5 י . מלך . ישראל . ויענו . את . מאב . ימן . רבן . כי . יאנף . כמש . באר

6 צה | ויחלפה . בנה . ויאמר . גם . הא . אענו . את . מאב | בימי . אמר . כדבר

7 וארא . בה . ובבתה | וישראל . אבד . אבד . עלם . וירש . עמרי . את[אר]

8 ץ . מהדבא | וישב . בה . ימה . וחצי . ימי . בנה . ארבען . שת . ויש

9 בה . כמש . בימי | ואבן . את . בעלמען . ואעש . בה . האשוח . ואב[ן]

10 את . קריתן | ואש . גד . ישב . בארץ . עטרת . מעלם . ויבן . לה . מלך . י

11 שראל . את . עטרת | ואלתחם . בקר . ואחזה | ואהרג . את . כלה[עם]

12 הקר . רית . לכמש . ולמאב | ואשב . משם . את . אראל . דודה . וא[ס]

13 חבה . לפני . כמש . בקרית | ואשב . בה . את . אש . שרן . ואת . אש

14 מחרת | ויאמר . לי . כמש . לך . אחז . את . נבה . על . ישראל | וא

15 הלך . בללה . ואלתחם . בה . מבקע . השחרת . עד . הצהרם | ואח

16 זה . ואהרג . כלה . שבעת . אלפן . גברן . וגרן | וגברת . ו[גר]

17 ת . ורחמת | כי . לעשתר . כמש . החרמתה | ואקח . משם . א[ת . כ]

18 לי . יהוה . ואסחב . הם . לפני . כמש | ומלך . ישראל . בנה . את

19 יהץ . וישב . בה . בהלתחמה . בי | ויגרשה . כמש . מפני ו

20 אקח . ממאב . מאתן . אש . כל . רשה | ואשאה . ביהץ . ואחזה .

---

[1] The readings adopted in doubtful places are those of Lidzbarski, *Ephemeris für Semit. Epigr.* I. i. Upon the language of the inscription cf. Dri. *Notes on the Hebrew Text of Samuel*, pp. lxxxv *ff.*; *Encyc. Bibl.* iii. *s.v.* Mesha.

21 לספת . על . דיבן | אנך . בנתי . קרחה . חמת . היערן . וחמת

22 העפל | ואנך . בנתי . שעריה . ואנך . בנתי . מגדלתה | וא

23 נך . בנתי . בת . מלך . ואנך . עשתי . כלאי . האשו[ח . למ]ין . בקרב

24 הקר | ובר . אן . בקרב . הקר . בקרחה . ואמר . לכל . העם . עשו . ל

25 כם . אש . בר . בביתה | ואנך . כרתי . המכרתת . לקרחה . באסר

26 י . ישראל | אנך . בנתי . ערער . ואנך . עשתי . המסלת . בארנן . [ו]

27 אנך . בנתי . בת . במת . כי . הרס . הא | אנך . בנתי . בצר . כי . עין .

28 ש . דיבן . חמשן . כי . כל . דיבן . משמעת | ואנך . מלכ

29 ת[י] מאת . בקרן . אשר . יספתי . על . הארץ | ואנך . בנת

30 י . [את .] מהדבא . ובת . דבלתן | ובת . בעלמען . ואשא . שם . את . נקד

31 צאן . הארץ | וחורנן . ישב . בה . בת וק . אש

32 ויאמר . לי . כמש . רד . הלתחם . בחורנן | וארד

33 [ויש]בה . כמש . בימי . ועל דה . משם . עש

34 שת . שדק | ואנ

1. I am Mesha', son of Chemosh[kān ?], king of Moab, the Daibonite.
2. My father reigned over Moab for thirty years, and I reigned
3. after my father, and I made this high-place to Chemosh in QR[Ḥ]H, . . .
4. . . . because he had saved me from all the . . . , and because he had caused me to see my desire upon all my haters. Omri
5. king of Israel afflicted Moab many days, because Chemosh was angry with his
6. land; and his son succeeded him, and he also said, I will afflict Moab. In my days said he [thus ?];
7. but I saw (my desire) upon him and upon his house, and Israel perished with an everlasting destruction. And Omri had taken possession of the [land ?]
8. of Mĕhēdĕba, and one (i.e. Israel) dwelt therein during his days and half his son's days, even forty years; but
9. Chemosh restored it in my days. And I built Ba'al-Me'on, and I made therein the reservoir (?), and I built

10. Qiryathên. And the men of Gad had dwelt in the land of 'Aṭaroth from of old; and the king of Israel had built for himself
11. 'Aṭaroth. And I fought against the city and took it, and I slew the whole of it, [the people of ??]
12. the city, a gazingstock (?) to Chemosh, and to Moab. And I took captive thence the altar-hearth of Dawdoh (?), and I dragged
13. it before Chemosh in Qeriyyoth. And I settled therein the men of SRN and the men of
14. MḤRT. And Chemosh said to me, Go, take Nebo against Israel, and I
15. went by night and fought against it from break of dawn until noon, and I took
16. it, and I slew the whole of it, 7,000 men, and male strangers, and [female strangers],
17. and female slaves; for to 'Ashtor-Chemosh had I devoted it, and I took thence the
18. vessels of Yahwe, and I dragged them before Chemosh. Now the king of Israel had built
19. Yahaṣ, and he abode therein when he fought with me. But Chemosh drove him out from before me; and
20. I took from Moab 200 men, even all its chiefs, and I took them up against Yahaṣ, and took it,
21. to add (it) unto Daibon. I built QRḤH, the wall of Ye'ārin, and the wall of
22. the keep. And I built its gates, and I built its towers, and
23. I built the king's house, and I made the sluices of the reservoir for water in the midst of
24. the city. Now there was no cistern in the midst of the city in QRḤH. And I said to all the people, Make
25. yourselves every man a cistern in his house; and I cut out the cutting for QRḤH by means of the
26. prisoners of Israel. I built 'Aro'er, and I made the highway by the Arnon.

27. I built Beth-Bamoth; for it was pulled down. I built Beṣer, for ruins

28\. . . . . of Daibon (were) fifty, for all Daibon was obedient. And I ruled

29. over . . . 100 in the cities which I had added to the land. And I built

30. Mĕhēdĕba, and Beth-Diblathên, and Beth-Ba'al-Me'on, and I took thither the *naqad*-keepers,

31\. . . . . sheep of the land. And as for Ḥoronên, there dwelt therein . . . . . .

32\. . . . . . . and Chemosh said to me, Go down, fight against Ḥoronên. So I went down . . .

33\. . . . . and Chemosh restored it in my days, and . . . thence . . .

34\. . . . . And I . . . . .

2.

The Siloam Inscription[1].

1 . . . הנקבה . וזה . היה . דבר . הנקבה . בעוד . . . .

2 הגרזן . אש . אל . רעו . ובעוד . שלש . אמת . להכ̄[ת נשמ]ע . קל . אש . ק̄

3 רא . אל . רעו . כי . הית . זדה . בצר . מימן . . . . . . ובים . ה

4 נקבה . הכו . החצבם . אש . לקרת . רעו . גרזן . על [. ג]רזן . וילכו .

5 המים . מן . המוצא . אל . הברכה . במאתים . ואלף . אמה . ומא̄

6 ת . אמה . היה . גבה . הצר . על . ראש . החצב̄ם̄ .

1. [Behold] the piercing through! And this was the manner of the piercing through. Whilst yet [the miners were lifting up]
2. the pick each towards his fellow, and whilst yet there were three cubits to be [cut through, there was heard] the voice of each call-

---

[1] Text as in Lidzbarski, *Nordsemit. Epigr.* p. 439. Translation, with conjectural supplement, from Dri. *Notes on the Hebrew Text of Samuel*, p. xvi.

3. ing to his fellow, for there was a fissure (?) in the rock on the right-hand . . . . And on the day of the
4. piercing through, the miners (lit. hewers) smote each so as to meet his fellow, pick against pick; and there flowed
5. the water from the source to the pool, 1,200 cubits; and one hun-
6. dred cubits was the height of the rock over the head of the miners.

3.

Inscription of the Monolith of Shalmaneser II, ll. 78–102[1].

[78] In the Eponym-year of Daian-Asshur (B. C. 854), in the month Airu, on the 14th day, I left Nineveh, crossed the Tigris, advanced against the cities [79] of Giammu on the Baliḥ. Before the terror of my lordship, the panic of my mighty weapons, they were afraid, and with their own weapons Giammu their lord [80] they slew. Into Kitlala and Til-ša-apli-aḥi I advanced, my gods in his palaces I set up, revelling in his palaces I instituted. [81] His treasure-house I opened, his treasure I found, of his goods (and) possessions I made spoil, to my city Asshur I brought (them). From Kitlala I departed; to Kar-Šulman-ašarid [82] I drew nigh; on boats of sheep-skin for the second time the Euphrates at high water I crossed. The tribute of the kings on that side of the Euphrates, (namely) of Sangar of [83] Gargamiš (Carchemish), of Kundašpi of Qummuḥ, of Arami son of Gûši, of Lalli of Milida, of Ḥaiâni son of Gabar, [84] of Kalparuda of Patin, of Kalparuda of Gurgum, silver, gold, lead, copper, copper vessels,—[85] at Asshur-utir-aṣbat on that side of the Euphrates, which is above (the river) Sagur, (and) which the Ḥittites Pitru (Pethor ?) [86] name, (even) there I received. From the Euphrates I departed; to Ḥalman (Aleppo) I drew nigh. Battle with me they dreaded; my feet they embraced. [87] Silver

[1] Nos. 3, 4, and 5 are based upon the text and translation of *KB.*, and Winckler, *Keilschrift. Textbuch,* and upon Delitzsch, *Assyrisches Handwörterbuch.*

(and) gold as their tribute I received; offerings before Rammân of Ḥalman I brought.

From Ḥalman I departed; to the two cities [88] of Irḥulini of Ḥamath I drew nigh. Adinnu, Mašgâ, Arganâ, the city of his kingship, I conquered. His spoil, his goods, [89] the possessions of his palaces I brought forth; to his palaces I set fire. From Arganâ I departed; to Qarqar I drew nigh; [90] Qarqar, the city of his kingship, I laid waste, I destroyed, with fire I burned. 1,200 chariots, 1,200 horsemen, 20,000 men of Hadadezer [91] of Damascus; 700 chariots, 700 horsemen, 10,000 men of Irḥulini of Ḥamath; 2,000 chariots, 10,000 men of Aḥab [92] of Israel; 500 men of Guai (Coa); 1,000 men of (the land) Muṣri; 10 chariots, 10,000 men of (the land) Irqanat; [93] 200 men of Matinu-ba'li (Mattan-ba'al) of Armada (Arvad); 200 men of (the land) Usanata; 30 chariots, 10,000 men [94] of Adunu-ba'li (Adoni-ba'al) of Šiana; 1,000 camels of Gindibu' of Arba . . . . . . 1,000 men [95] of Ba'sa, son of Ruḥubi (Reḥob), of Ammon;—these twelve kings to his assistance he took; for [96] battle and combat against me they advanced. With the exalted succour which Asshur, the lord, rendered, with the mighty power which Nergal, who marched before me, [97] bestowed, with them I fought; from Qarqar unto Gilzân their defeat I accomplished; 14,000 [98] of their troops with weapons I laid low; like Rammân upon them a flood I rained down; I scattered their corpses; [99] the surface of the wilderness (?) I filled with their numerous troops; with weapons I caused their blood to flow . . . [100] . . . . . . [101] the river Orontes . . . I dammed (?). In the midst of that battle their chariots, their horsemen, [102] their horses, their teams I captured.

4.

Fragment of the Annals of Shalmaneser II.

[1] In the eighteenth year of my reign for the sixteenth time the Euphrates [2] I crossed. Ḥazael of Damascus [3] in the multitude of his troops [4] placed confidence, and his troops [5] without number assembled. [6] Senir, a mountain-peak [7] in the neighbourhood of

Lebanon, his stronghold [8] he made. With him I fought, [9] his siege I conducted. 6,000 [10] of his men of war with weapons [11] I laid low; 1,121 of his chariots, [12] 470 of his war-horses, together with his baggage, [13] I took from him. For the saving [14] of his life he betook himself off. [15] In Damascus, the city of his kingship, I besieged him; [16] his plantations I cut down. To the mountains [17] of Ḥauran I went; cities [18] without number I destroyed, I laid waste, [19] with fire I burned; their prisoners [20] without number I carried off. [21] Unto the mountains of the range Ba'li-ra'si, [22] a promontory, I went; the image of my kingship [23] there did I set up. At that time [24] the tribute of the Tyrians, [25] of the Zidonians, of Ja-u-a (Jehu) [26] the son of Omri I received.

Descriptive Inscription from the Obelisk of Shalmaneser.

Tribute of Ja-u'-a (Jehu) son of Omri; silver, gold, a bowl (? *šaplu* [1]) of gold, goblets (? *zuqût*) of gold, a ladle (? *qabuâti* [2]) of gold, pitchers (? *dalâni* [3]) of gold, bars of lead, a staff (? *ḥuṭartu* [4]) for the hand of the king, spear-shafts (? *budilḥâti*) I received of him.

5.

Narrative of Sennacherib's Third Campaign (B.C. 701), *from the Taylor Cylinder*, Col. II. l. 34–Col. III. l. 41.

[34] In my third campaign to the land Ḥatti (Ḥittite land) I went. [35] Lulî (Elulaeus), king of Zidon—the dread of the majesty [36] of my lordship overwhelmed him, and to a far-off spot [37] in the midst of the sea he fled, and his land I reduced to subjection. [38] Great Zidon, Little Zidon, [39] Beth-Zitti, Zarepta, Maḥalliba, [40] Ušû, Akzib, Akko, [41] his strong cities, the fortresses, the spots for pasture (?) [42] and for watering, his intrenchments (?), were overwhelmed by the might of the arms [43] of Asshur, my lord, and submitted themselves [44] under my feet. Tuba'lu (Ittoba'al) upon the royal throne [45] over them I seated, and the payment of the tribute of my lordship, [46] yearly without intermission, I laid upon him. [47] Minḥimmu

---

[1] Heb. סֵפֶל. [2] Heb. קֻבַּעַת. [3] Heb. דְּלִי. [4] Heb. חֹטֶר.

(Menaḥem) of Samsimuruna, [48] Tuba'lu of Zidon, [49] Abdili'ti of Arvad (Arados), [50] Urumilki of Gebal (Byblos), [51] Mitinti of Ashdod, [52] Buduilu of Beth-Ammon, [53] Kammušunadbi (Chemosh-nadab) of Moab, [54] Malikrammu (Malkiram) of Edom, [55] all the kings of the West country (Martu), [56] rich presents, weighty tribute, moveable (?) possessions [57] before me brought, and kissed my feet. [58] But Zidqâ, king of Ashqelon, [59] who had not bowed himself under my yoke—the gods of his father's house, himself, [60] his wife, his sons, his daughters, his brothers, the seed of his father's house [61] I dragged forth, and to Assyria I conveyed them.

[62] Šarruludâri, son of Rukibti, their former king, [63] over the people of Ashqelon I placed, and the tribute-offering [64] of subjection to my lordship I imposed upon him, and he became subject (?) to me. [65] In the course of my campaign Beth-Dagon, [66] Joppa, Bene-baraq, Azuru, [67] the cities of Zidqâ, which under my feet [68] had not speedily submitted, I besieged, conquered, carried off their spoil. [69] The leaders, nobles, and people of Amqarruna (Eqron), [70] who had cast Padî (their king by virtue of a sworn covenant [71] with Assyria) into fetters of iron, and to Ḥazaqiyau (Ḥezekiah) [72] of Judah had delivered him with hostile intent, (he shut him up in darkness;)—[73] their heart trembled. The kings of Egypt—[74] the archers, the chariots, the horses of the king of Miluḥḥi, [75] forces innumerable they summoned together, and came [76] to their aid. Before Altaqu (Elteqeh) [77] the battle-array was set against me; they lifted up (?) [78] their weapons. In reliance upon Asshur, my lord, I fought [79] with them, and effected their defeat; [80] the commander of the chariots and the sons of the king of Egypt, [81] together with the commander of the chariots of the king of Miluḥḥi, alive [82] in the midst of the battle my hand took prisoners. Altaqu [83] (and) Tamnâ (Timnath) I attacked, conquered, and carried forth their booty.

Col. III. [1] Against Amqarruna (Eqron) I advanced, and the chief officers, [2] the magnates who had offended, I slew; [3] and on stakes around the city I impaled their corpses. [4] The inhabitants of the town, who had practised wickedness and mischief, [5] as prisoners

I counted; the rest of them, [6] who had not practised wickedness and misdeed, who in their transgression [7] had not shared, their amnesty I proclaimed. Padî, [8] their king, from Jerusalem [9] I brought, and on the throne of lordship over them [10] I installed him, and the tribute of my lordship [11] I imposed upon him. But Ḥezekiah [12] of Judah, who had not bowed himself under my yoke, [13] 46 of his fortified towns, fortresses, and small cities [14] in their neighbourhood innumerable, [15] with casting down of battering-rams and assault of siege-engines, [16] with attack of infantry, of mines, ... , [17] I besieged, I captured. 200,150 souls, young, old, male, and female, [18] horses, mules, asses, camels, oxen, [19] and sheep, without number, from the midst of them I brought forth, and [20] as spoil I counted them. Himself, like a bird in a cage, in the midst of Jerusalem, [21] the city of his kingship, I shut up. Fortifications against him [22] I erected, and those coming forth from the gates of his city [23] I turned back. His cities, which I had plundered, from his territory [24] I severed, and to Mitinti king of Ashdod, [25] Padî king of Amqarruna (Eqron), and Zilbel [26] king of Ḥaziti (Gaza) I gave them, and diminished his territory. [27] To the former payment—their yearly tribute—[28] the tribute of subjection to my lordship I added, and [29] I laid it upon them. Himself, Ḥezekiah, [30] terror of the glory of my lordship overwhelmed him; and [31] the *Urbi* and his trusty soldiers, [32] which for the defence of Jerusalem, the city of his kingship, [33] he had introduced, laid down their arms (?). [34] Together with 30 talents of gold (and) 800 talents of silver, precious stones (?), [35] sparkling . . . -stones, great lapislazuli-stones (?), [36] couches of ivory, thrones of state of elephant-skins (and) [37] ivory, . . . -wood, . . . -wood, everything available, an enormous treasure, [38] and his daughters, the women of his palace, his male [39] and female servants (?), to Nineveh, the city of my lordship, [40] after me I caused to be brought; and for the payment of tribute [41] and the rendering of homage he despatched his envoy.

ADDITIONS

I. 1. 9. עין רגל] In favour of the view as to the site taken in the *note ad loc.*, and against the rival identification with *Bîr Eyûb*, cf. J. F. Stenning, art. *En-Rogel* in Hastings, *BD.* i. 711.

2. 10. עיר דוד] For further authorities for finding the site upon the south-east hill, cf. G. A. Smith, art. *Jerusalem* in *Encyc. Bibl.* ii. 2417 *f.*

10. 28. ומוצא וגו׳] Further arguments for the view that Solomon's supply of horses was drawn, not from Egypt, but from the North-Syrian Muṣri are given by T. K. Cheyne, *Encyc. Bibl.* iii. 3162.

II. 3. 20. מדרך אדום] Luc. ἐξ ὁδοῦ τῆς ἐρήμου Σοὺδ ἐξ Ἐδώμ. So Vet. Lat. with *Sur* (שׁוּר Ex. 15. 22) for Σούδ.

13. 17. וחץ תשועה בארם] Luc. καὶ βέλος σωτηρίας ἐν Ἰσραήλ, Vet. Lat. *et sagitta salutis in israel*—superior to M.T.

באפק] Vet. Lat. *in aseroth quae est contra faciem samariae.* At the end of the verse Vet. Lat. continues *et aperuit fenestram secundam. Et dixit sagittare et sagittavit sagittam salutis dm̄i et sagittam salutis israel. Et dixit helisseus percuties syriā totam.* This looks like a doublet, introduced into the text with the gloss *et aperuit fenestram secundam.* That this is the case cannot, however, be affirmed with certainty, in view of the repetition of the second symbolic action which is desiderated by Elisha in *v.* 19. If the addition be genuine, we must suppose ויאמר [אלישע] to have fallen out after ויור.

INDEX

Abstract subs. for adj., page 18, 144.
Accusative of limitation, 48, 56, 199, 230, 253, 264, 268.
Adverbial use of subs., 250.
Agreement of subj. and adj., 231.
— of subj. and predicate, 53, 156, 219, 220, 258, 274.
Apposition, 2, 45, 56, 65, 97, 200, 256.
Article, idiomatic use of, 1, 81, 181, 241, 255.
— as relative, 156.
— omitted with demonstr. pronoun, 262.
— omitted with subs. when used with adj., 81.

Casus pendens, 69.
Circumscription of genitive, 5, 8, 26.
Circumstantial clause, 6, 11, 12, 70, 102, 126, 182, 189, 199, 295.
Construct state, suspended, 302.
Co-ordination in time, 6.

Dialect of North Palestine, 208.
Diminutives, 246.

Geographical sites:—
Abel-beth-ma'achah, 198.
Amana, 280.
Anathoth, 22.
Aphek, 238.
Argob, 45.
Aro'er, 307.
Arpad, 342.
Avva, 334.

Ba'alath, 138.
Ba'al-shalishah, 277.
Bethel, 177.
Beth-Ḥanan, 41.
Beth-Ḥoron, 137.
Beth-Shan, 44.
Beth-Shemesh, 41.

Cabul, 135.
Cinnereth, 198.
Coa, 151.
Cuthah, 334.

David, city of, 17, 380.
Dothan, 286.

Eden, 344.
En-Rogel, 5.

Gath-Ḥepher, 319.
Geba, 199.
Gezer, 137.
Giḥon, 8.
Gilgal, 264.
Gozan, 330.

Ḥabor, 330.

Ḥalaḥ, 330.
Ḥaran, 343.
Ḥazor, 136.

Ible'am, 300.
Ijjon, 198.

Januaḥ, 324.
Jarmuth, 42.
Joḳme'am, 44.
Jordan, circuit of, 102.

Ḳir-ḥareseth, 272.

Lachish, 319.
Libnah, 296.

Megiddo, 43.
Millo, the, 136.
Mizpah, 199.
Muṣri, 151, 291.

Pharpar, 280.

Ramah, 197.
Ramoth-Gilead, 251.
Reshef, 344.

Sela, 318.
Sepharvaim, 334.
Shechem, 173.
Shephelah, the, 151.
Shiloh, 188.
Shunem, 3.
Socoh, 42.
Succoth, 102.

Tappuaḥ, 322.
Telasshur, 344.
Tishbeh, 217.

Zarephath, 218.
Zarethan, 44.
Zeredah, 169.
Zion, 17.

Ḥatef-shewa with a sibilant, 180, 231, 264, 344.

Hebrew words and phrases :—
אֲבָל, 11.
אוֹב, 354.
אוֹת־ for אֶת־, 237.
אָז, 35.
אֶחָד as indefinite article, 209.
אֵי־זֶה, 255.
אַל used absolutely, 289.
אֶל, peculiar use of, 72, 182, 311.
אֶל for עַל, 72, 184, 201, 228, 297.
אִם in single direct questions, 7.
אָמְנָם, 116.
אָמַר = *assign*, 161.
אָמַר לְ, 54.
אַף־כִּי, 117.
אֲרוֹן בְּרִית י׳, 31.
אֲשֵׁרָה, 190.
אֲשֶׁר לְ, 5, 8.
אֵת, sign of accusative, before indef. obj., 178.
— sign of accusative, marking new subj., 284.
אֵת = *with*, 142.

ב pretii, 22, 207, 240.
בְּלִיַּעַל, 245.
בֶּן־הַיְמִינִי, 16.
בְּנֵי־קֶדֶם, 50.
בִּקֵּר, 327.
בֵּרֵךְ = *curse*, 247.

גֹּאֵל, 201.

גְּבִירָה, 161.
הַלָּז, 275.
הֵשִׁיב פָּנִים, 19.

ו consecutive epexegetical, 15.
— consecutive introducing predicate, 169.

זָבַל, 110.
זֶה enclitic, 189.
זָחַל, 5.

יִדְּעֹנִי, 354.

כִּבְרַת אֶרֶץ, 280.
כִּי introducing direct narration, 6, 244.
— introducing oath, 21.
כִּי . . . כִּי, resumptive, 8.
כָּרָה, 287.

ל formative, 246.
ל = *at*, 142.
ל of norm, 257.
לֹא used absolutely, 162.
— with jussive, 16.
לֵאמֹר, subject of, 201.

מ preformative in substantives, signification of, 143.
מַזָּלוֹת, 358.
מִן־, idiomatic uses of, 3, 12, 177. מֵאֵת, 8, 52. מֵעַל, 13, 15, 24. מֵעִם, 24. מִקְצֵה, 178.
מִנְחָה, 48, 225, 327.
מַצֵּבָה, 192.

סֹכֵן, 2.

עֵבֶר, 49. מֵעֵבֶר, 44.
עַל for אֶל, 10, 131, 220, 221, 242.
עַל = *incumbent upon*, 40.
עִם, idiomatic uses of, 5, 33, 35, 115, 157.
עֹפֶל, 282.
עָצַב, 3.
עָצוּר וְעָזוּב, 186.
עָשָׂה used absolutely, 118.

פֶּחָה, 147, 237.
פַּרְוָרִים, 360.

קָסַם, 332.

שׁ relative, 208.
שָׁלָה, 275.
שְׁלָטִים, 310.
שָׁלִישׁ, 139.

תְּרָפִים, 362.

'Idem per idem' idiom, 293.
Imperative with ו in place of cohortative, 6.
Imperfect, with frequentative force, 1, 32, 194, 268, 338, 359.
— pictorial, 239.
Impersonal construction, 4, 20, 48, 180, 187.
Infinitive absol., use of, 241, 256, 269.
— in ־וֹת, 271.
Infinitive constr., use of, 317.
— Hiph'il with Ḥireq under preformative ה, 272.

Negative duplicated, 148.
Nomen unitatis, 12.

Oath, 12, 21, 281.
Omission of pronom. subject of participle, 262.
Order of sentence, 4, 18, 55, 120, 280.

Participle, agreement of, with suffix of antecedent subject, 189.
— force of, 3, 47, 218, 257.
Perfect with article prefixed, 156.
— with ו consecutive as imperative, 13.
Perfect with weak ו, 77, 124, 157, 236, 238, 293, 318, 345, 353, 357. Cf. 194, 247, 269.
Personal pronoun reinforcing suffix pronoun, 7, 249.
Pluperfect, 188, 270.

Question indicated by tone of voice, 7.

Relative omitted, 33.
Resumption, 8, 14, 118, 239.

Termination תַ in proper names, 42.

Vocative continued by third person, 300.